RECONCEPTUALISING GLOBAL FINANCE AND ITS REGULATION

The current global financial system may not withstand the next global financial crisis. In order to promote the resilience and stability of our global financial system against future shocks and crises, a fundamental reconceptualisation of financial regulation is necessary. This reconceptualisation must begin with a deep understanding of how today's financial markets, regulatory initiatives and laws operate and interact at the global level. This book undertakes a comprehensive analysis of such diverse areas as regulation of financial stability, modes of supply of financial services, market infrastructure, fractional reserve banking, modes of production of global regulatory standards and of the pressing need to reform financial sector ethics and culture. Based on this analysis, *Reconceptualising Global Finance and Its Regulation* proposes realistic reform initiatives, which will be of primary interest to regulatory and banking legal practitioners, policy makers, scholars, research students and think tanks.

ROSS P. BUCKLEY is the CIFR King & Wood Mallesons Professor of International Finance Law at UNSW Australia. He has led three major Australian Research Council projects and published nine books and more than 100 book chapters and articles in all leading jurisdictions. In 2012, Buckley received the only Discovery Outstanding Researcher Award awarded in law by the Australian Research Council.

EMILIOS AVGOULEAS holds the International Banking Law and Finance Chair at the University of Edinburgh and is the Head of the Commercial Law Group. He is also a member of the Stakeholder Group of the European Banking Authority (EBA) in the 'Top-Ranking Academics' section. An acknowledged expert on financial market regulation, banking law and finance and global economic governance, he has published extensively and advised numerous governments, development organisations and central banks.

DOUGLAS W. ARNER is a professor, Co-Director of the Duke-HKU Asia America Institute in Transnational Law, and a Member of the Board of Management of the Asian Institute of International Financial Law at the University of Hong Kong, as well as a Senior Fellow at the University of Melbourne. One of the world's leading experts on international financial regulation, he has published fifteen books and more than 100 articles on international financial law and regulation.

Reconceptualising Global Finance and Its Regulation

Edited by

ROSS P. BUCKLEY

UNSW Australia

EMILIOS AVGOULEAS

University of Edinburgh

DOUGLAS W. ARNER

University of Hong Kong

CAMBRIDGE
UNIVERSITY PRESS

CAMBRIDGE
UNIVERSITY PRESS

University Printing House, Cambridge CB2 8BS, United Kingdom

One Liberty Plaza, 20th Floor, New York, NY 10006, USA

477 Williamstown Road, Port Melbourne, VIC 3207, Australia

4843/24, 2nd Floor, Ansari Road, Daryaganj, Delhi - 110002, India

79 Anson Road, #06-04/06, Singapore 079906

Cambridge University Press is part of the University of Cambridge.

It furthers the University's mission by disseminating knowledge in the pursuit of education, learning and research at the highest international levels of excellence.

www.cambridge.org
Information on this title: www.cambridge.org/9781107498389

© Cambridge University Press 2016

First published 2016
First paperback edition 2017

A catalogue record for this publication is available from the British Library

Library of Congress Cataloging in Publication data
Reconceptualising global finance and its regulation / Ross P. Buckley, University of New South Wales; Emilios Avgouleas, University of Edinburgh; Douglas Arner, University of Hong Kong.
pages cm
Includes index.
ISBN 978-1-107-10093-0 (Hardback)
1. Financial institutions, International–Law and legislation. 2. International finance–Law and legislation. 3. Financial institutions–Law and legislation. I. Buckley, Ross P., editor. II. Avgouleas, Emilios, editor. III. Arner, Douglas A., editor.
K4450.5.R43 2015
332ʹ.042–dc23 2015022561

ISBN 978-1-107-10093-0 Hardback
ISBN 978-1-107-49838-9 Paperback

This volume is dedicated to Professor Joseph Jude Norton:
wise teacher, mentor and friend to each of its editors

Contents

Contributors

Kern Alexander holds the Professorial Chair in Law and Finance at the University of Zurich. He is the author of many research articles in academic journals and several books. He was the Specialist Adviser to the British Parliament's Joint Select Committee on the Financial Services Act 2012 and a member of the Expert Panel on Financial Services of the European Parliament (2009–14).

Douglas W. Arner is a professor, Co-Director of the Duke-HKU Asia America Institute in Transnational Law, and a Member of the Board of Management of the Asian Institute of International Financial Law at the University of Hong Kong, as well as a Senior Fellow at the University of Melbourne. One of the world's leading experts on international financial regulation, he has published fifteen books and more than 100 articles on international financial law and regulation.

Emilios Avgouleas holds the Chair in International Banking Law and Finance at the University of Edinburgh and is the Head of the Commercial Law Group. He is a member of the Stakeholder Group of the European Banking Authority (EBA) in the 'Top-Ranking Academics' section. He is also an acknowledged expert on financial market regulation, banking law and finance and global economic governance. He has published extensively in the wider fields of finance law and economics and behavioural finance, including two acclaimed research monographs.

Lawrence G. Baxter is the William B. McGuire Professor of the Practice of Law at Duke Law School. He teaches courses in financial regulation. He has taught and published widely in various countries. He was also a business executive in a major US banking organisation for many years.

Sir William Blair practised at the English bar in banking and finance law, becoming a Queen's Counsel in 1994 and a High Court judge in 2008. He serves on the Board of

Trustees of the British Institute of International and Comparative Law and of London's Financial Markets Law Committee, and he chairs the Monetary Law Committee of the International Law Association. He became President of the Board of Appeal of European Supervisory Authorities in 2012. He chairs the Law and Ethics in Finance Project, an informal group concerned with standards in the financial sector.

Ross P. Buckley is the CIFR King & Wood Mallesons Professor of International Finance Law, Scientia Professor and Member, Centre for Law, Markets & Regulation at UNSW Australia. He has consulted to government departments in Australia, Indonesia, Vietnam and the United States, and he has twice been a Fulbright Scholar and many times a half-bright scholar.

David C. Donald is a professor in The Chinese University of Hong Kong's Law Faculty. He previously taught at the University of Frankfurt's Institute for Law and Finance and worked as a commercial lawyer in the United States and Europe. His research focuses on comparative corporate and securities law.

Anna Gelpern is a law professor at Georgetown and a non-resident senior Fellow at the Peterson Institute for International Economics. She has published articles and co-authored a law textbook on international finance, served in legal and policy positions at the US Treasury and practiced in New York and London.

Erik F. Gerding is a professor at the University of Colorado Law School. He is the author of *Law, Bubbles, and Financial Regulation* (Routledge 2014).

James Hodges is a research assistant and part-time lecturer on the LLM at Warwick University, focusing on the regulation of mergers and acquisitions and other forms of corporate transaction, in particular, in the context of the financial services sector. He is also general counsel of Hydrodec Group plc.

Robin Hui Huang is Professor of Law in the Faculty of Law, The Chinese University of Hong Kong, currently serving as Executive Director of the Centre for Financial Regulation and Economic Development. He previously taught in the Faculty of Law, University of New South Wales, where he now holds a position of Adjunct Professor. His recent publications include *Securities and Capital Markets Law in China* (Oxford University Press, 2014) and *Institutional Structure of Financial Regulation: Theories and International Experiences* (co-editor: Professor Dirk Schoenmaker) (Routledge, 2015).

Amir N. Licht is Professor of Law at Radzyner School of Law at the Interdisciplinary Center Herzliya, where he was also dean of the law school. He earned his LL.M. and S.J.D. from Harvard Law School and undergraduate degrees in law and economics from the Tel Aviv University.

Donato Masciandaro is Professor of Economics and holds the Chair in Economics of Financial Regulation at Bocconi University, Milan. He is Head of the Department of Economics and Director of the Paolo Baffi Centre on Central Banking and Financial Regulation. He served as Visiting Scholar at the IMF Institute, as well as Consultant at the Inter-American Development Bank and at the United Nations.

Ruth Plato-Shinar, a law professor, is the Director of the Center for Banking Law at the Netanya Academic College, Israel. Her fields of research are banking law, financial regulation, finance and ethics and financial consumer protection. Her book *The Bank's Fiduciary Duty* has been quoted by the Israeli Supreme Court in various cases. She is also a member of the Advisory Board of the Israeli Supervisor of Capital Markets.

Steven L. Schwarcz is the Stanley A. Star Professor of Law & Business at Duke University and Senior Fellow of the Centre for International Governance Innovation. His areas of research and scholarship include insolvency and bankruptcy law, international finance, capital markets, systemic risk and commercial law. He holds a Juris Doctor from Columbia Law School and a bachelor of science degree in aerospace engineering (summa cum laude).

Wei Shen is KoGuan Chair Professor of Law at Shanghai Jiao Tong University Law School. He received his PhD from London School of Economics and Political Science. His main research interests include financial regulation, corporate governance and international investment law. He is an arbitrator with Hong Kong International Arbitration Centre, Shanghai International Arbitration Center and Shanghai Arbitration Commission.

Dalvinder Singh is Professor of Law, University of Warwick; Director of the LLM International Economic Law and LLM International Corporate Governance and Financial Regulation, managing editor of the *Journal of Banking Regulation*, and member of the Research and Guidance Committee of the International Association of Deposit Insurers, Basel, Switzerland.

Brian W. Tang is Managing Director and founder of Asia Capital Markets Institute (www.asiacmi.com) and Honorary Fellow of the Asian Institute of International Financial Law. He was formerly Asia-Pacific Investment Banking Division counsel at Credit Suisse, Hong Kong, and Senior Associate at Sullivan & Cromwell, New York.

Yingmao Tang is an associate professor at Peking University Law School. He was previously a lawyer at Sullivan & Cromwell. His research areas include finance regulation, the Chinese judicial system and nuclear law. He received his LLB from Peking University Law School and his J.S.D. from Yale Law School.

Dr. Michael W. Taylor has had careers in both academia and finance, including several leading central banks and international financial institutions. Among his extensive publications are the seminal paper 'Twin Peaks: A regulatory structure for the new century', published in 1995, and the textbook *Global Bank Regulation* (2010).

Dr. Rolf H. Weber is ordinary Professor for Civil, Commercial and European Law at the University of Zurich, Switzerland; Visiting Professor at the University of Hong Kong and Attorney-at-Law in Zurich. His main fields of research are international business law, competition law and international financial market law. His publication list can be viewed at www.rwi.uzh.ch/lehreforschung/alphabetisch/weberr/person.html.

Chao Xi is Professor at the Faculty of Law, The Chinese University of Hong Kong, where he concurrently serves as assistant dean (graduate studies) and director of LLM Programmes. His research has received significant funding support from the HKSAR Research Grants Council, the PRC Ministry of Education and the Sumitomo Foundation.

David Zaring is Associate Professor at the Wharton School. He writes at the intersection of financial regulation, international law and domestic administration. He has written more than thirty articles, including publications in the Cornell, Michigan, NYU, UCLA and Virginia law reviews and a number of international law journals.

Dr. Dirk Zetzsche is Professor of Banking and Securities Law and Propter Homines Chair at the University of Liechtenstein, as well as one of the directors of the Center for Business & Corporate Law at the University of Duesseldorf (Germany).

Acknowledgements

We would like to thank King & Wood Mallesons and the Centre for International Finance and Regulation (CIFR) (Project E135), funding from which supported this project and the editing of this book. CIFR is a Centre of Excellence for research and education in the financial sector, which is funded by the Commonwealth and NSW governments and supported by other consortium members (see www.cifr.edu.au).

We would also like to thank the Hong Kong Research Grants Council Theme-based Research Scheme project 'Enhancing Hong Kong's Future as a Leading International Finanical Centre', which provided financial support for the event as well as significant amounts of the underlying research.

In addition, we would like to thank the Faculties of Law of the University of Hong Kong, UNSW Australia and the University of Edinburgh as well as the Hong Kong Financial Services Development Council for their support of the project.

Finally, we would also like to acknowledge and thank Flora Leung of the Asian Institute of International Financial Law of the Faculty of Law of the University of Hong Kong for her efficient and tireless efforts in organising the workshop that brought together most of the authors in Hong Kong in December 2013; and Ross Willing and especially Nicole Mazurek for their important assistance in Sydney with compiling this volume.

Introduction and Context

1

Introduction

Douglas W. Arner, Ross P. Buckley and Emilios Avgouleas

The Global Financial Crisis (GFC) of 2008 should have caused a deep and profound rethinking of how financial markets work and are regulated, and of financial law more generally. The great depression of the early 1930s certainly did so, and resulted in a complete rethinking of banking and financial law in the United States with the enactment of the Securities Act of 1933[1] and the Securities Exchange Act of 1934[2] and the separation of commercial and investment banking by the Glass-Steagall Act of 1933,[3] as well as the establishment of the Bretton Woods system in the wake of World War II.[4]

The United Kingdom has had the Vickers Report[5] and the Kay Report.[6] The United States has had Dodd-Frank.[7] The European Union has had a plethora of directives and regulations.[8] But none of these reviews, reforms, or legislative

---

[1] Pub L No 73–22, 48 Stat 74 (1933), codified at 15 USC § 77a.

[2] Pub L No 73–291, 48 Stat 881 (1934), codified at 15 USC § 78a.

[3] The Glass–Steagall Act comprises ss 16, 20, 21, and 32 of the Banking Act Pub L No 73–66, 48 Stat 162 (1933).

[4] See Douglas Arner and Ross Buckley, 'Redesigning the Architecture of the Global Financial System' (2010) 11:2 *Melbourne Journal of International Law* 185.

[5] Independent Commission on Banking (ICB), *Final Report Recommendations* (12 September 2011) <http://webarchive.nationalarchives.gov.uk/20131003105424/https:/hmt-sanctions.s3.ama zonaws.com/ICB%20final%20report/ICB%2520Final%2520Report%5B1%5D.pdf>. This report is often referred to as the 'Vickers Report' after Sir John Vickers, chair of the ICB.

[6] John Kay, *The Kay Review of UK equity markets and long-term decision making* (July 2012) <www.bis.gov.uk/assets/biscore/business-law/docs/k/12–917-kay-review-of-equity-markets-final-report.pdf>.

[7] *Dodd-Frank Wall Street Reform and Consumer Protection Act*, Pub L No 111–203, § 2, 124 Stat 1376 (2010); G North and RP Buckley, 'The Dodd-Frank Wall Street Reform and Consumer Protection Act: Unresolved Issues of Regulatory Culture and Mindset' (2012) 35(2) *Melbourne University Law Review* 479.

[8] In the past 4 years, almost thirty legislative files relating to financial services have been passed by the European Parliament: Alex Barker and Martin Arnold, 'Super Tuesday for EU Bank Regulation', *Financial Times* (online) (15 April 2014) <www.ft.com/intl/cms/s/0/93dc374e-c4ba-11e3–9aeb-00144feabdco.html#axzz2zrkNK9fV>. Examples include: Regulation (EC)

measures has implemented changes that are truly fundamental, as was done in the 1930s, with the possible exception of the creation of the European Banking Union and the Single Supervisory Mechanism (SSM) in the EU. Australia had a substantial review of its financial sector underway in 2014 but the Financial Systems Inquiry[9] in no sense sought to reconceptualise Australia's regulatory regime. Likewise, the crisis has resulted in a series of pronouncements and regulatory reforms from the Group of 20 (G20) and the Financial Stability Board (FSB), both of which have been strengthened in the wake of the crisis.[10]

Yet, in our view, no jurisdiction has undertaken the sort of fundamental rethinking that the largest crisis since 1929 should have provoked, and that the crisis of 1929 did provoke. The reasons for this are many, but owe much to the political power of the financial sector generally, for the sector's extraordinary profitability of the past 20 years has brought with it extraordinary influence and power.[11] Likewise, compared to the establishment of the Bretton Woods system, the post-crisis international developments (namely strengthening of the G20 and FSB) have been very modest to say the least, once again with the possible exception of the SSM in the EU.

No 1060/2009 of the European Parliament and of the Council of 16 September 2009 on Credit Rating Agencies [2009] OJ L 302/1 ('EU CRA Regulation'); Regulation (EU) No 1092/2010 of the European Parliament and of the Council of 24/11/2010 on European Union macroprudential oversight of the financial system and establishing a European Systemic Risk Board (the 'ESRB Regulation'); Regulation (EU) No 575/2013 of the European Parliament and of the Council of 26 June 2013 on prudential requirements for credit institutions and investment firms ('EU Capital Requirements Regulation'); Committee of European Banking Supervisors, Guidelines on Remuneration Policies and Practices (10 December 2010) 60, 65 <www.eba.europa.eu/documents/10180/106961/Guidelines.pdf>.

9   The Commonwealth government released the terms of reference of the Financial Systems Inquiry in December 2013 and initial submissions on the issues within these terms of reference closed on 31 March 2014: Australian Prime Minister and Treasurer, *Financial System Inquiry* (20 November 2013) <www.pm.gov.au/media/2013-11-20/financial-system-inquiry> and *Financial System Inquiry* (2014) <http://fsi.gov.au>.

10   See Douglas Arner and Michael Taylor, 'The Global Credit Crisis and the Financial Stability Board: Hardening the Soft Law of International Financial Regulation?' (2009) 32 *University of New South Wales Law Journal* 488; Emilios Avgouleas, *Governance of Global Financial Markets: The Law, the Economics, the Politics* (Cambridge University Press, 2012), chapters 6 and 7.

11   In the fourth quarter of 1990 the profits of the US bank industry were $1.39 billion, in the second quarter of 2013 they were $42.2 billion, even allowing for the time value of money that remains a dramatic increase: Emily Stephenson, 'U.S. Bank Industry Profits Hit Record $42.2 Billion In Second Quarter', *Reuters* (online), 29 August 2013 <www.reuters.com/article/2013/08/29/us-financial-regulation-earnings-idUSBRE97S0O520130829>; and 'Bank Profits Fell 31% During Last Quarter of 1990', *The New York Times* (online), 14 March 1991 <www.nytimes.com/1991/03/14/business/bank-profits-fell-31-during-last-quarter-of-1990.html>. See also Luigi Zingales, 'How Political Clout Made Banks Too Big to Fail', *Bloomberg* (online), 30 May 2012 <www.bloomberg.com/news/2012-05-29/how-political-clout-made-banks-too-big-to-fail.html> and Simon Johnson and James Kwak, 13 *Bankers* (Vintage, 2011), excerpt available at <http://13bankers.com/excerpt/>.

The world of finance has changed profoundly in the past 40 years, but because the changes have been incremental, few people appreciate their scope and scale. We have selected 40 years as the time frame. In 1971 the United States went off the gold standard, the system put in place at Bretton Woods to keep finance national began to unravel, international financial markets began to globalise, and the initial moves to establish a single financial market and single currency in Europe began..

The massive changes in the past 40 years in what banks do, and who works within them, are two factors that lie at the heart of the GFC. Banking is a different industry than it was.[12] We need to assess how the international financial system has changed fundamentally in the past 40 years, and respond to these changes. So let us start with an overview of recent internationally mandated reforms. These comprise principally:

(i)   Revising capital adequacy rules, with the introduction of Basel III
(ii)   Seeking to end 'too-big-to-fail'
(iii)   Monitoring and regulating the shadow banking system
(iv)   Regulation of over-the-counter (OTC) derivatives
(v)   Strengthening and converging accounting standards
(vi)   Building a common Legal Entity Identifier system
(vii)   Reducing reliance on credit ratings and improving oversight of credit rating agencies
(viii)   Reforming compensation practices

These are eight significant initiatives, with which we largely agree.[13] Our issue with the response to the GFC has not been that it is wrong-headed, but simply that it has not gone far enough to respond to the profound changes in banking and capital markets of the past 40 years.

The reforms listed earlier, in the main, respond directly to the causes of the GFC and it is entirely understandable that a political process responds in this way to a crisis, that is, try to identify what caused the last crisis and work to preventing it from re-occurring. However, this is precisely what defence planners are derided for: preparing to fight the last war.

There will be another major financial crisis in the next decade or two; the history of the last 40 years (let alone of the last 400 years) assures us of this, and it almost certainly will not be like the GFC. We can be certain another major crisis is coming as we now have a globalised international financial system without a global financial regulator, a global lender of last resort or a global sovereign bankruptcy regime, and to be stable all national systems require a financial regulator, lender of

---

[12]   See Chapter 2, Buckley, 'The Changing Nature of Banking and Why It Matters'.
[13]   See, Ross P Buckley, 'The G20's Performance in Global Financial Regulation', (2014) 37 (1) *University of New South Wales Law Journal* 63–93; Douglas Arner, 'Adaptation and Resilience in Global Financial Regulation' (2011) 89 (5) *North Carolina Law Review* 1579.

last resort, and bankruptcy regime.[14] These regulatory lacuna are unsurprising as Keynes and White in 1943 designed the postwar financial architecture to promote international trade but keep finance essentially national. In fact, as the financial market turmoil of mid-2015 indicates, we in fact may be quite close to the onset of the next crisis. So once we moved to a truly international financial system we needed new regulatory institutions which were missing, and while we have sought to provide such a regulatory superstructure through the Bank for International Settlements (BIS), FSB and other such bodies. But these are in no way an adequate replacement for the very great powers, formal and informal, of the financial regulator that all national financial systems need to be stable.

So if we are not to fall into the trap of engineering the global financial system to prevent the latest crisis, we must reconceptualise the system's regulation so that its regulation is truly responsive to the system as it is today. This is a much more difficult task than merely attempting to respond to the latest crisis, but given the latest crisis will not be the last, it is also absolutely necessary. It is the task we, and the other contributors, have set ourselves in this volume.

Funded by the Hong Kong Research Grants Council Theme-based Research Scheme project 'Enhancing Hong Kong's Future as a Leading International Financial Centre', the Centre for International Finance and Regulation, Sydney, as well as the University of Edinburgh, the University of Hong Kong, and UNSW Australia, this volume seeks to turn from analysis of the last crisis and the response thereto toward thinking forward to the needs of the international financial system and building legal and regulatory systems that will seek to reduce the likelihood and severity of future crises. It brings together the lion's share of the world's leading academics working in the area of financial law and regulation and seeks to identify issues and approaches for further attention going forward.

Reflecting this background and objective, the volume is divided into six sections. This first section seeks to provide analysis and context based on the ideas presented briefly in this introduction, namely considering the reality of today's

---

[14] RP Buckley, 'How the International Financial System, to Its Detriment, Differs from National Systems, and What We Can We Do About It', (2004) 34 *University of Hong Kong Law Journal* 321–338. Many commentators assume the IMF is the international lender of last resort, but the four elements of Walter Bagehot's classic prescription for a lender of last resort are that it is able to make available large amounts of capital, quickly, at high interest rates and on good security: Walter Bagehot, *Lombard Street: A Description of the Money Market* (Scribner, Armstrong & Co., 1873). However, the IMF lacks the resources to make available sufficiently large volumes of capital to quell market fears, often struggles to act quickly, does not for political reasons charge interest rates high enough to limit moral hazard, and sovereign borrowers typically lack the capacity to give good security over sufficient assets beyond their borders. So while much has changed since Bagehot wrote 'Lombard Street', if the IMF is truly to serve as a lender of last resort, we probably need to put in place some very extensive swap lines between national central banks that can be triggered quickly purely by the IMF, and even then, we are left with some very difficult to solve moral hazard problems with the IMF as initiator of those credit lines.

global financial system and its regulatory context. Following this introduction, in Chapter 2, Ross Buckley of UNSW Australia considers first the evolution of banking and the implications of its new nature for regulatory design. In the third chapter, Lawrence Baxter of Duke University analyzes the real challenges of seeking to regulate globally active financial markets and institutions in a fragmented world of domestic legal systems.

The second section of the volume addresses the global financial architecture: the systems put in place at an international level to deal with the problems inherent in global finance. In the first chapter of this section (Chapter 4), Douglas Arner of the University of Hong Kong and Michael Taylor of Moody's discuss the evolution of the FSB and its role in the post-GFC regulatory environment. In Chapter 5, David Zaring of the University of Pennsylvania analyzes the development of the various financial networks that underlie the soft law approach to global finance embodied in the FSB. In Chapter 6, Chao Xi of the Chinese University of Hong Kong considers the specific context of China and the role of domestic influences in driving China's implementation of international standards in the context of Basel III.

The third section of the volume considers the changing role of central banks and the new challenges they are facing. In the first chapter of this section (Chapter 7), Donato Masciandaro of Bocconi University seeks to reconceptualise central banking in the wake of the GFC. Following this, Kern Alexander of the University of Zurich and Steven Schwarcz of Duke University discuss the new international focus on macroprudential supervision and its difficulties. In Chapter 9, Anna Gelpern of Georgetown University and Erik Gerding of the University of Colorado consider the problem of safe assets underlying many aspects of finance and regulation and find the current framework wanting in light of real-world issues.

The volume's fourth section turns to aspects of global finance requiring reconceptualisation. In Chapter 10, Wei Shen of Shanghai Jiao Tong University discusses the new environment of the internationalisation of China's currency, the RMB, and the challenges this poses to international financial centres. In Chapter 11, David Donald of the Chinese University of Hong Kong evaluates the central issues of market quality and moral hazard in financial market design. In Chapter 12, Ruth Plato-Shinar of Netanya Academic College analyzes the changing nature of bank secrecy and its role in post-GFC global finance. In Chapter 13, Amir Licht of the Interdisciplinary Centre Herzliya focuses on the challenges of quantitative analysis in global regulatory evaluation in considering the specific case of transnational securities fraud.

In the fifth section, the authors consider the specific challenges of too-big-to-fail / too-big-to-save financial institutions and shadow banking. Setting the stage, in Chapter 14, Emilios Avgouleas of the University Edinburgh discusses the inherent problems in large banks and their regulation. In Chapter 15, Dalvinder Singh and James Hodges of Warwick University consider the attempts to deal with regulatory enforcement in the regional context of the EU. In Chapter 16, Yingmao Tang of Peking University considers the emergence of shadow banking and the particular challenges in addressing it in a developing economy such as that of China. In Chapter 17, Robin Hui of the Chinese University of Hong Kong follows on from this with an in-depth analysis of the specific issues in China.

The final section of the volume seeks to consider the role of culture and ethics, perhaps in addition to regulation, soft or hard. In Chapter 18, Brian Tang of the Asian Capital Market Institute discusses the challenges and mechanisms mooted in the context of building professionalism in financial markets, including arguing for major efforts in this respect in Asia. In Chapter 19, Dirk Zetzsche of the University of Liechtenstein writes of the role of ethics in financial center competition in an environment of increasing regulatory harmonisation. In Chapter 20, Rolf Weber of the University of Zurich considers the specific challenges of addressing human rights in financial institutions policies and procedures. Finally, in Chapter 21, Sir William Blair of the High Court of England and Wales argues for reconceptualising the roles of professional standards in supporting regulation.

Looking forward, there remain significant opportunities to properly reconceptualise global finance and its regulation. Unfortunately, it may well require another crisis to truly do this.

2

The Changing Nature of Banking and Why It Matters

Ross P. Buckley

INTRODUCTION

Banks have been a ubiquitous feature of almost all successful civilisations. Organisations discharging early banking functions operated in ancient Babylon,[1] and gained much greater sophistication in ancient Greece and Rome.[2]

When asked what they understand a bank to be, most people describe an institution that accepts deposits and makes loans – what we generally understand as a 'retail' bank.

However, the banks at the centre of our global financial system are utterly different. Entities such as JP Morgan Chase, UBS or Deutsche Bank do a great deal more than take deposits and grant loans.

Prior to the 1970s bankers were prudent, deeply cautious people who gave advice predicated on a good knowledge of the needs and interests of the customer.[3] Bank managers tended to have real authority as banks were quite decentralised

Sincere thanks to the Centre for International Finance and Regulation in Sydney, whose funding (project no. E135) supported the workshop in Hong Kong at which this was first presented, the research that underpins it, and the editing of this volume. CIFR is a Centre of Excellence for research and education in the financial sector funded by the Commonwealth and NSW Governments and supported by other consortium members (see www.cifr.edu.au). Thanks also for the enlightening feedback from participants at the Hong Kong workshop and to Rebecca Stanley and Ross Willing for their very helpful research assistance. All responsibility is mine.

[1] Richard Grossman, *Unsettled Account: The Evolution of Banking in the Industrialized World since 1800* (Princeton University Press, 2010), 30.
[2] See generally: W. V. Harris, *The Monetary Systems of the Greeks and Romans* (Oxford University Press, 2008); Paul Millet, *Lending and Borrowing in Ancient Athens* (Cambridge University Press, 2002); and Glyn Davies, *A History of Money: From Ancient Times to the Present Day* (University of Wales Press, 2002), chapter 3.
[3] Ismael Erturk and Stefano Solari, 'Banks as Continuous Reinvention' (2007) 12(3) *New Political Economy* 369.

organisations, and thus bank managers tended to be highly respected members of their local communities.

These days are long gone. Most branches in my country, Australia, no longer have a full-time manager. Most Australians, at least the more sophisticated ones, understand that when a bank employee recommends a certain investment, they are typically incentivised by a commission to do so. Banks have changed from a relatively local institution working in the client's interests, to a far more complex organisation that is intent on maximising profits and the number of products it can sell to customers.

This change has been so dramatic that many of the world's largest and best-known banks are barely recognisable from the organisations they were in the 1970s, let alone their ancient forebears. The implications of those changes are profound, especially if we think of the economic consequences of the allocation of much of our most talented human capital away from high value-added roles in the real economy to the banking sector.

This chapter will seek to explore the full dimensions of this transformation and analyse why it matters for how we think about banks today, and the regulations we pass to govern them.

The chapter is in four further parts. First, it identifies the major changes that have occurred in banking over the past 40 years. Second, it analyses why banks exist – their core purposes. Third, it explores the implications of these major changes, in particular, as to how we should think about banks. And, finally, it concludes by suggesting that drawing a sharper distinction between a traditional bank and the new type of super-bank may be really useful for policy and public discussion.

CHANGES IN BANKING

Much of what occurs at international financial institutions would not be recognised as banking by the modern layperson. Indeed, even a banker from 40 years ago would hardly recognise what they would see today. If a lawyer from 1970 was brought forward in time and put in a modern day courtroom, most things would be familiar: the solemnity, the architecture of the court room, the mode of dress, the procedure, the objections being made by counsel. Since 1970 the manner of lawyers, the way they carry themselves, the way they are trained, the way they think and look backwards to find authority for what they propose doing, has all changed very little. Indeed, a lawyer transported forward in time from 17th century England would likewise see much in a contemporary courtroom they would recognise. Yet if a banker from as recently as 1970 was brought forward in time to 2015 and placed in a modern investment bank, or in the investment banking arm of a commercial bank, much would seem profoundly different.

Personnel

The first and major difference would be in the people. The manner of bankers, the way they carry themselves, the way they are trained, the way they see the world, has all changed profoundly. Bankers in 1970 had basic arithmetic. You needed some math to run a bank, but it was mostly primary school math, not the calculus of high school.

Bankers in 1970 were as prudent, cautious and dull as lawyers, perhaps more so.[4] If we consider a sophisticated market like London, the traditional degree to have taken to go into a bank was in Classics (Greek and Latin) or History.[5] This remained the case in the United Kingdom (UK) until well into the 1980s. Having studied classics or been an officer in a good regiment were considered good training for banking as banking was perceived to be about prudence and judgment, and the study of history or military officer training were seen to promote careful deliberation and sound judgment.[6]

Today younger bankers are typically highly trained in mathematics and quantitative skills – degrees in finance, quantitative economics or perhaps even physics are considered good training for a job. Although some may come from more diverse backgrounds, such as law, training in the humanities is rare. As a consequence most bankers today see the world through a quantitative analytical lens rather than the more qualitative lens associated with studies of the classics, history or politics.

Attitude

In the 1980s UK banking went from being an industry that sought to help its customers make money, to being an industry that looked for people from whom they could make money.[7] Much the same could be said of the United

---

4   Susan Strange, *Casino Capitalism* (Manchester University Press, 2nd ed, 1997), 2.
5   Paul Thompson, 'The Pyrrhic Victory of Gentlemanly Capitalism: The Financial Elite of the City of London, 1945–90' (1997) 32(3) *Journal of Contemporary History* 283, 301.
6   These thoughts are not new. Susan Strange in 1986 described how '[b]ankers used to be thought of as staid and sober men, grave-faced and dressed in conservative black pinstripe suits, jealous of their reputation for caution and for the careful guardianship of their customers' money,' but warned that the international financial system had already become a 'gambling hall' and would soon resemble 'nothing as much as a vast casino': Susan Strange, earlier n 4, 1–2. She was prescient in the extreme.
7   Sue Jaffer, Nicholas Morris, Edward Sawbridge and David Vines, 'How Changes to the Financial Services Industry Eroded Trust' in Nicholas Morris and David Vines (eds), *Capital Failure* (Oxford University Press, 2014), 54. See also: Greg Smith, 'Why I Am Leaving Goldman Sachs', *The New York Times* (online), 14 March 2012 <www.nytimes.com/2012/03/14/opinion/why-i-am-leaving-goldman-sachs.html?pagewanted=all&_r=0>; Frank Partnoy, *F.I.A.S.C.O: Blood in the Water on Wall Street* (W.W. Norton & Company, 2009); and Frank Partnoy, *Infectious Greed: How Deceit and Risk Corrupted the Financial Markets* (Public Affairs, 2010).

States, and of Australia, though change in Australia probably occurred a tad later, in perhaps the 1990s.

When contemporary bankers consider the societal impact of their work they would be likely to defer to Smith's dictum that '[b]y pursuing his own interest, he frequently promotes that of the society more effectually than when he really intends to promote it',[8] or as Gordon Gecko would put it: 'greed is good'. The popularity of Smith's 'invisible hand', mentioned only once in *The Wealth of Nations*[9] yet cited so often in modern business and economic life, has had a profound influence. Today's ultra-numerate bankers with little knowledge of history or the humanities are more inclined to accept the world-view that markets and corporations exist only to produce profits and nothing more.

This attitude is reflected in the behaviour of banks. The recent LIBOR scandal involving major banks is clear evidence of an attitude that prioritises the profits of the bank over all else.[10] The attempts to conceal trading losses on derivative bets by JP Morgan Chase employees[11] is equally an example that reflects this attitude, as was the bank turning a blind eye to the operations of its client Bernard Madoff, the man behind the largest Ponzi scheme in history.[12] Goldman Sachs' omission of key facts regarding the synthetic collaterialized debt obligation (CDO) known as ABACUS 2007-A[13] and Barclays' circumvention of sanctions against Iran, Cuba and Libya are yet further examples.[14]

---

[8] Adam Smith, *The Wealth of Nations* (Penguin, 1986), 364.

[9] Ibid.

[10] See generally: Eric Talley and Samantha Strimling, 'The World's Most Important Number: How a Web of Skewed Incentives, Broken Hierarchies, and Compliance Cultures Conspired to Undermine Libor', in Justin O'Brien and George Gilligan (eds), *Integrity, Risk and Accountability in Capital Markets: Regulating Culture* (Hart Publishing, 2013). For a better way forward on LIBOR see Justin O'Brien, 'Singapore Sling: How Coercion May Cure the Hangover in Financial Benchmark Governance' (Working Paper No 29, Harvard University Edmond J. Safra Center for Ethics, 5 November 2013).
'Ex-Barclays Staff Charged Over Libor Scandal', *Sky News* (online), 17 February 2014 <http://news.sky.com/story/1212954/ex-barclays-staff-charged-over-libor-scandal>.

[11] 'Timeline: Libor-Fixing Scandal', *BBC News* (online), 6 February 2013 <www.bbc.com/news/business-18671255>; Patricia Hurtado et al., 'Ex-JP Morgan Traders First Charged in $6.2 Billion Loss', *Bloomberg* (online), 15 August 2013 <www.bloomberg.com/news/2013–08–14/ex-jpmorgan-bankers-charged-by-u-s-in-6–2-billion-loss.html>.

[12] Jessica Silver-Greenberg and Ben Protess, 'JP Morgan Chase Nears a $2 Billion Deal in a Case Tied to Madoff', *The New York Times* (online), 5 January 2014 <http://dealbook.nytimes.com/2014/01/05/jpmorgan-chase-nears-a-2-billion-deal-in-a-case-tied-to-madoff/?_php=true&_type=blogs&hp&_r=2>; Jonathan Stempel, 'Madoff Said JP Morgan Executives Knew of His Fraud: Lawsuit', *Reuters* (online), 20 February 2014 <www.reuters.com/article/2014/02/20/us-jpmorgan-madoff-idUSBREA1J21W20140220>.

[13] Dan Wilchens and Karen Brettell, 'Factbox: How Goldman's ABACUS Deal Worked', *Reuters* (online), 16 April 2010 <www.reuters.com/article/2010/04/16/us-goldmansachs-abacus-factbox-idUSTRE63F5CZ20100416>; SEC, 'Goldman Sachs to Pay Record $550 Million to Settle SEC Charges Related to Subprime Mortgage CDO' (Press Release no 123, SEC, 2010) <www.sec.gov/news/press/2010/2010–123.htm>.

[14] Michael Rothfeld, David Enrich and Jay Solomon, 'Barclays in Sanctions Bust', *The Wall Street Journal* (online), 17 August 2010 <http://online.wsj.com/news/articles/

In Smith's earlier work, *The Theory of Moral Sentiments*, he argues that people are motivated by desires to be respected and regarded as honourable.[15] Such an understanding would have resonated with the sober and dull bankers in the decades before 1970. It no longer does. Bankers today are remunerated as if they are primarily motivated by money.

The shift in the values and attitudes of bankers has without question had a profound effect on the industry and the way in which it behaves. The fundamental purpose of a bank has shifted from providing a social good – by intermediating capital, providing services to its customers and employment to its workers – to earning profits for its employees and itself.

Remuneration

A further significant change in banking has been in the way in which bankers are remunerated. Prior to the 1970s, the salaries on offer were comparable to other areas of professional practice in the economy. As identified by Philipon and Reschef:

> the relative skill intensity and relative wages of the financial sector exhibit a U-shaped pattern from 1909 to 2006. From 1909 to 1933 the financial sector was a high skill, high wage industry. A dramatic shift occurred during the 1930s: the financial sector rapidly lost its ... wage premium relative to the rest of the private sector. The decline continued at a more moderate pace from 1950 to 1980. By that time, wages in the financial sector were similar, on average, to wages in the rest of the economy. From 1980 onward, another dramatic shift occurred. The financial sector became once again a high skill, high wage industry. Strikingly, by the end of the sample relative wages and relative education levels went back almost exactly to their pre-1930s levels.[16]

Not only has the amount of compensation increased dramatically in recent times, the structure of remuneration has also changed. Whereas in the past bankers were principally remunerated by salary, with little performance-based pay,[17]

SB10001424052748703908704575433781894978828>; Dominic Kennedy, 'Lloyds, Barclays Helped Iran Evade Anti-Terrorism Sanctions', *The Australian* (online), 15 October 2010 <www.theaustralian.com.au/archive/business-old/lloyds-barclays-helped-iran-evade-anti-terrorism-sanctions/story-e6frg96f-1225939097490>.

[15] Adam Smith, *The Theory of Moral Sentiments* (Cambridge University Press, 2002), 72. Complementing such a perspective is the recent work of Avner Offer arguing that poor ethics often lead to inefficient economic outcomes: Avner Offer, 'A Warrant for Pain: Caveat Emptor vs. the Duty of Care in American Medicine, c. 1970–2010', chapter 15 in Morris and Vines (eds), in the work cited, n 7.

[16] Thomas Philippon and Ariell Reshef, 'Wages and Human Capital in the U.S. Financial Industry: 1909–2006' (Working Paper 14644, National Bureau of Economic Research, 2009) <www.nber.org/papers/w14644.pdf>, 3.

[17] Sue Jaffer, Nicholas Morris, Edward Sawbridge and David Vines, 'How Changes to the Financial Services Industry Eroded Trust', earlier n 7, 35.

today banks have a clear preference to pay their staff in bonuses rather than fixed wages.[18]

Remuneration plays a key role in the motivation and culture of firms, not to mention in terms of who they attract as employees.[19] As will be outlined below, these changes in the personal remuneration of bankers has interacted powerfully with other changes to misalign profoundly interests in the banking sector.

Complexity and Opacity of Products

This change in the purpose of banking, and in the type of people joining the industry, has coincided with a rapid ramp up in the sophistication and complexity of financial products.

Contracts for the future delivery of goods have an ancient past,[20] but western civilization has existed for centuries without complex derivative trading. The modern derivatives market began in Chicago in the 1970s with the Chicago Board Options Exchange, which would ultimately revolutionise the world of investment.[21] During the 1980s and 1990s, a vast array of increasingly more complex and opaque financial instruments was developed.[22]

The complexity of modern financial products means customers often lack the capacity to compare different products and determine if they are buying a good investment or not.

Legalisation of Gambling

What a bank does has changed profoundly. Banks in 1970 essentially intermediated money. They received deposits and made loans. Banks today, at least the investment banks and investment banking arms of major commercial banks, derive less of their income from financial intermediation than from speculating on markets, underwriting stock and bond issuances, giving sophisticated advice on mergers and acquisitions and selling financial products to customers, amongst other activities.

[18] John Thanassoulis, 'The Case for Intervening in Bankers' Pay' (2012) 67(3) *Journal of Finance* 849, 849 and Lucian A. Bebchuk and Holger Spamann, 'Regulating Bankers Pay' (2009) 98(2) *Georgetown Law Journal* 247, 247.

[19] See, Deborah Gregory, *Unmasking Financial Psycopaths: Inside the Minds of Investors in the Twenty-First Century* (Palgrave MacMillian, 2014); Clive R. Boddy, 'The Corporate Psychopaths Theory of the Global Financial Crisis' (2011) 102 *Journal of Business Ethics* 255.

[20] Ernst Juerg Weber, 'A Short History of Derivative Security Markets' (Discussion Paper 08.10, University of Western Australia Business School, 2008), 5.

[21] Emily Lambert, 'The Man Who Gave Us Derivatives', *Forbes* (online), 17 January 2011 <www.forbes.com/sites/emilylambert/2011/01/17/the-man-who-gave-us-derivatives/>. See also Emily Lambert, *The Futures: the Rise of the Speculator and the Origins of the World's Biggest Markets* (Basic Books, 2011) and Don M. Chance, *Essays in Derivatives* (Wiley, 1998).

[22] Steven L. Schwarcz, 'Regulating Complexity in Financial Markets' (2009) 87(2) *Washington University Law Review* 211.

A banker travelling forward in time even 40 years would not recognise most of what a bank does today as being 'banking' business. Indeed, much of the business of a contemporary bank would have been unenforceable in 1973. A banker travelling forward in time would look with horror upon speculative financial derivatives contracts as transactions that could bring a bank undone.

I was practising law in Hong Kong 30 years ago when we were asked for an opinion from a major U.S. investment bank on its proposal to start offering futures contracts on currency. Our legal advice was to the effect that the Gambling Ordinance meant that such contracts entered into by clients for the genuine hedging of risks were valid and enforceable but the same contracts entered into to speculate on a currency's future value were unenforceable. Hong Kong law restricted gambling at the time to race tracks and mah-jong houses. Our client thanked us for the advice, said it intended to do the business anyway and take the risk, and filed our advice in the smallish round filing cabinet that lives on the floors of most offices.

Historically, purely speculative contracts were unenforceable because gambling was perceived to be a social ill. The *Gaming Act 1845* (8 & 9 Vict.c.109) in the UK made gaming houses illegal and gaming or wagering agreements unenforceable. It was enacted on the recommendation of a House of Commons' Select Committee Report on Gaming in 1844. U.S. law was to the same effect,[23] as was Australia's.[24]

For over a century, courts in all these countries took the view that derivatives contracts (as they came later to be known) entered into by at least one party for hedging purposes were valid under these enactments, but derivatives entered merely to place a bet on the price of something were invalid and unenforceable.[25] Accordingly, a contract by which a farmer locks in a price for their wheat crop when it is harvested, or by which an airline guarantees a future price for jet fuel, were both valid, but a contract by which a speculator places a bet on future wheat or fuel prices was not.[26]

Over time, legislatures began to exempt derivatives contracts from the application of these laws. In the words of Philip Wood, 'many states have introduced exceptions to gaming laws in order to facilitate markets ... and to remove the threat of nullity. The rationale is either there is a satisfactory alternative system of

---

[23] Section 5–401 of the General Obligations Law of the State of New York provided that '[a]ll wagers, bets or stakes, made to depend upon any...unknown or contingent event whatever shall be unlawful' and Section 5–411 provided that '[a]ll contracts for or on account of any money or property, wagered, bet or staked, as provided in Section 5–401, shall be void'.

[24] For instance, *Gaming and Betting Act 1912* (NSW).

[25] Lynn Stout, 'Derivatives and the Legal Origin of the 2008 Credit Crisis' (2011) 1 *Harvard Business Law Review* 1, 4; see also *Earl Ellesmere v Wallace* [1929] 2 chapter 1; *Lipkin Gorman v Karpnale* [1992] 4 All ER 512.

[26] See *See v Cohen* (1923) 33 CLR 174 and note the opposite result by the time of *Morgan Grenfell and Co Ltd v Welwyn Hatfield DC* [1995] 1 All ER 1, 2.

protection or the contracts are entered into between sophisticated institutions, which do not need the protection of gaming legislation'.[27]

In the UK, Section 63 of the *Financial Services Act 1986* (UK) exempted 'investments', broadly defined, from the application of the *Gaming Act 1845*.[28]

New York courts carved out an exception to the State gambling laws for certain financial contracts. The remaining, and restraining, uncertainty in the United States was removed by the *Commodity Futures Modernization Act of 2000* (CFMA),[29] which excluded the application of any state or local laws in respect of gaming, with the aim of giving legal certainty to derivatives trading.[30]

The U.S. Financial Crisis Inquiry Commission concluded in its Final Report that OTC derivatives contributed significantly to the crisis, and that the enactment of the CFMA legislation 'to ban the regulation by both the federal and state governments of over-the-counter (OTC) derivatives was a key turning point in the march toward the financial crisis'.[31] In the words of Lynn Stout, the CFMA was a 'sudden and wholesale removal of centuries-old legal restraints on speculative trading in over-the-counter (OTC) derivatives',[32] that played a large role in the 2008 crisis.[33] In hindsight, the removal of derivatives from the purview of gaming laws went largely unremarked at the time, but was to contribute substantially to the global financial crisis (GFC).

Our time travelling banker would be very surprised to discover a bank engaging in transactions he would view as unenforceable. He would be even more surprised by the scale of these transactions within the operations of a super-bank.

Derivatives as a proportion of bank assets are difficult to calculate because of differing accounting treatment on either side of the Atlantic. In the UK, derivatives currently represent about 27% of the total assets of Barclays and RBS.[34] In Australia,

---

[27] Philip Wood, *Set-Off and Netting, Derivatives, Clearing Systems* (Thompson, 2nd ed, 2007) [13–009].

[28] This exemption was maintained by Section 412 of the *Financial Services and Markets Act 2000*, and Section 334 of *The Gaming Act 2005 (UK)*.

[29] 7 USC §§ 1–27f (2013). See also Cravath, Swaine and Moore, *Commodity Futures Modernization Act of 2000* (Memorandum for ISDA members, 5 January 2001) <www.isda.org/speeches/pdf/analysis_of_commodity-exchange-act-legislation.pdf>.

[30] In Australia, New South Wales first enacted a carve out to facilitate the establishment of the Sydney Futures Exchange in 1979: *Futures Market Act 1979* (NSW) s 7; and this was followed in 1989 by a general validation of exchange-traded futures contracts in the *Corporations Act 1989* (Cth) Section 1141. Later, Section 1101I of the *Corporations Act 2001* excluded all financial products, broadly defined, including derivative products, from gaming and wagering laws.

[31] FCIC, 'The Financial Crisis Inquiry Report' (Final Report of the National Commission on the Causes of the Financial and Economic Crisis in the United States, January 2011) xxiv.

[32] Lynn Stout, earlier n 25, 21.

[33] For a full history of the CFMA, its origins and recent attempts to restore regulatory limits on speculative derivatives via the Dodd-Frank Act see Lynn Stout, earlier n 25.

[34] Derivate Financial Instruments accounted for 324,335 million (26%) of the 1,231,388 million pounds of total assets held by Barclays at 31 December 2013: Barclays PLC, *Annual Report 2013* <http://reports.barclays.com/ar13/>, 160. Derivatives accounted for 288,039 million (28%) of the 1,027,878 million pounds of total assets held by RBS at 31 December 2013: Royal Bank of

derivatives represent between 4% and 6.5% of assets of the four major banks, calculated much as for the British banks.[35] In the United States, the published ratios are tiny, in the order of 2.7% for JP Morgan Chase and 0.08% for Bank of America.[36] However, U.S. accounting rules permit most derivatives to be kept off balance sheet. U.S. rules allow banks to 'net' their derivatives and show net positions with trading partners on an assumption of simultaneous settlement. JP Morgan Chase, the largest U.S. institution, had $2.4 trillion in assets on its balance sheet at the end of 2013 but derivatives with a market value of an additional $1.5 trillion that were not shown, so in total derivatives represented over 40% of its assets.[37]

Scotland, *Annual Report* 2013 <www.investors.rbs.com/results-centre/annual-report-subsidiary-results/2013.aspx>, 164.

[35] Derivatives accounted for 45,340 million (6%) of the 753,876 million Australian dollars of total assets held by the CBA in 2013: Commonwealth Bank of Australia (CBA), *Annual Report* 2013 <www.commbank.com.au/content/dam/commbank/about-us/shareholders/pdfs/annual-reports/2013_CBA_Annual_Report_19_August_2013.pdf> 72 and 136. Derivative financial instruments accounted for 45.9 billion (6.5%) of the 703 billion Australian dollars of total assets held by ANZ in 2013: ANZ, 2013 *Annual Report* <www.shareholder.anz.com/sites/default/files/event_files/2013%20Annual%20Report%20Final.pdf>, 19. Derivative financial instruments accounted for 28,358 million (4%) of the 696,603 million Australian dollars of total assets held by Westpac on 30 September 2013: Westpac Banking Corporation, 2013 *Annual Report* <www.westpac.com.au/docs/pdf/aw/ic/2013_WBC_Annual_Report.pdf>, 88. Trading derivatives accounted for 39,214 million (4.8%) of the 808,427 million Australian dollars of total assets held by NAB on 30 September 2013: National Australia Bank (NAB), 2013 *Annual Financial Report* <www.nab.com.au/content/dam/nab/about-us/shareholder-centre/annual-reports/pdf-reports/afr-financial-report.pdf>, 69.

[36] Derivative receivables accounted for 65,759 million (2.7%) of the 2,415,689 million American dollars of total assets held by JP Morgan Chase on 31 December 2012: JP Morgan Chase & Co, *Annual Report* 2012 <http://files.shareholder.com/downloads/ONE/2974511299x0x652147/a734543b-03fa-468d-89b0-fa5a9b1d9e5f/JPMC_2012_AR.pdf>, 106. Derivative financial instruments accounted for 8,251,000 (0.08%) of 10,789,225,000 American dollars of total assets held by BAML on 31 December 2013: Bank of America Merrill Lynch International Limited, *Director's Report and Financial Statements for the year ended 31 December 2013* <http://investor.bankofamerica.com/phoenix.zhtml?c=71595&p=subsidiaries#fbid=OntvNgkDWAQ>, 25.

[37] James R. Barth and Apanard Prabha, *Breaking (Banks) Up Is Hard to Do: New Perspective on 'Too Big to Fail'* (Milken Institute, February 2013) <www.milkeninstitute.org/pdf/Breaking Banks.pdf>; Yalman Onaran, 'U.S. Bank Balance Sheets May Hide Risk', *Bloomberg* (online), 21 February 2013 <www.businessweek.com/articles/2013-02-21/u-dot-s-dot-bank-balance-sheets-may-hide-risk>; Steve Denning, 'Why JP Morgan Chase is Unsafe at Any Scale', *Forbes* (online), 4 December 2013 <www.forbes.com/sites/stevedenning/2013/04/12/why-jpmorgan-chase-is-unsafe-at-any-scale/>. Admati and Hellwig explain the netting of derivatives assets in relation to JP Morgan: Anat Admati and Martin Hellwig, *The Banker's New Clothes: What's Wrong With Banking and What to Do About It* (Princeton University Press, 2013), 84–86. The discrepancy between U.S. regulations (GAAP) and the Europeans (IFRS) accounting rules for JP Morgan Chase =~1.8trillion. U.S. regulations effectively allow derivative assets to be 'netted' on the assumption of simultaneous settlement. Admati and Hellwig point out that this substantially reduces a bank's overall equity and therefore stability. For a full account, see Antonio Corbi, 'Netting and Offsetting: Reporting Derivatives under US GAAP and under IFRS' (ISDA Report, 23 May 2012) <www2.isda.org/functional-areas/accounting-and-tax/gaap-us/>.

JP Morgan Chase had a notional amount of $71.8 trillion in derivatives contracts, according to September 2013 data from the Office of the Comptroller of the Currency.[38] Second and third on the list are Citibank, with $58.5 trillion, and Bank of America, with $44.5 trillion.[39]

Derivatives therefore represent between 30% and 40% of the assets of some of the largest U.S. and UK banks. Some of these will be for genuine hedging purposes. Most will be purely speculative.[40]

I put forward the idea in Australia that we need a different word to describe two institutions, one of which primarily earns its income intermediating funds, and has perhaps 5% of its assets in derivatives, and another which primarily earns its income trading assets and selling complex opaque new financial products, and which has perhaps 40% of its assets in derivatives. I thought if 'bank' were the correct word for the former institution it was not for the latter and a new word was required.[41] A leading Australian banking regulator interjected at that point and said, 'We have a word for that sort of institution already – it is called a casino'.[42]

Of course, these firms with a high percentage of assets in speculative derivatives have a substantial cross-over with a new term introduced into the post-GFC lexicon, a globally systemically important financial institution, a G-SIFI.[43]

---

[38] Michael Rapoport, 'Funding Value Adjustment Proves Costly to J. P. Morgan's 4Q Results', *The Wall Street Journal* (online), 14 January 2014 <http://blogs.wsj.com/moneybeat/2014/01/14/funding-value-adjustment-proves-costly-to-j-p-morgan-4q-results/>.

[39] Ibid.

[40] Wayne Guay and S.P. Kothan, 'How Much Do Firms Hedge with Derivatives?' (2003) 70 *Journal of Financial Economics* 423. The empirical evidence on the actual use of derivatives by corporations for speculative purposes is mixed and inconclusive: Raffaele Scalcione, *The Derivatives Revolution: A Trapped Innovation and a Blueprint for Regulatory Reform* (Kluwer Law International, 2011), 43; and other studies confirm the difficulty of tracking what derivatives are actually used for. See, George Aragon and Spencer Martin, 'A Unique View of Hedge Fund Derivatives Usage: Safeguard or Speculation?' (2012) 25 *Journal of Financial Economics* 436. See also generally Timothy Lynch, 'Gambling by Another Name; The Challenge of Purely Speculative Derivatives' (2012) 17 *Stanford Law, Business, and Finance* 67.

[41] Along the same lines, see, John A. Kay, 'Should We Have Narrow Banking?' (*The Future of Finance: The LSE Reports*. London: School of Economics and Political Science, 2010); John A. Kay, 'Narrow Banking and All That', (Hume Occasional Paper no 84, David Hume Institute, 2010); John A. Kay, 'Narrow Banking', (Centre for the Study of Financial Innovation, 2009); The Independent Commission on Banking, 'Final Report Recommendations', Independent Commission on Banking (September 2011).

[42] According to Admati and Hellwig, 'gambling in derivatives may have more favourable odds than gambling in casinos. The principle, however, is the same: if compensation allows bankers to benefit from large gains while not suffering much from losses, taking risks may be attractive': Anat Admati and Martin Hellwig, *The Banker's New Clothes*, earlier n 37, 123. For a devastating critique of the contemporary use of derivatives: see 'Interview: Joseph Stiglitz', *Frontline* <www.pbs.org/wgbh/pages/frontline/warning/interviews/stiglitz.html>.

[43] Basel Committee on Banking Supervision, *Global Systemically Important Banks: Assessment Methodology and the Additional Loss Absorbency Requirement* (November 2011) <www.bis.org/publ/bcbs207.htm>, 1.

G-SIFIs are defined as any firm, as designated by the Financial Stability Board (FSB), whose collapse would pose a risk to the global economy or, in popular parlance, any firm that is 'too big to fail'.[44] These institutions, which by definition, have a great deal of their risk externalised purely because of their size and importance, are in fact one and the same as the super-banks, whose assets are tied up in speculative derivatives.

The current global financial landscape has at its core this very new type of institution. It is a far cry from what we would traditionally consider to be a bank.

PURPOSES OF BANKING

So why do banks exist, and prosper?

Banks can fulfill at least four key functions. First, banks can enable people to save money safely. Second, banks can intermediate capital, that is supply it to those who can productively use it.[45] This matters just as much as other utilities, such as water and electricity.[46] Third, banks can allocate risk in the economy to those who are willing to bear it.[47] Fourth, banks can serve as a source of objective financial advice that benefits their customers and allows the better ordering of their affairs. Indeed, banking is arguably almost as important to society as the legal or health care systems.[48]

However, given the changes of the past 40 years, many of these purposes are no longer being well met. Much modern trading has nothing to do with allocating capital to the most productive areas of the economy.[49] Most traders care little for the underlying value of an asset and are primarily only concerned with its price in the next second, minute or hour (i.e. whether a quick profit can be made).[50] Second, the remuneration on offer, and scale of modern banking, represents a misallocation of our most valuable form of capital: human capital. Drawing talent

---

[44] Ibid; see also Andrew G Haldane, 'On Being the Right Size' (speech delivered at the Institute of Economic Affairs' 22nd Annual Series, 25 October 2012), www.bankofengland.co.uk/publications/Documents/speeches/2012/speech615.pdf.

[45] Shelagh Heffernan, *Modern Banking in Theory and Practice* (Wiley, 1996).

[46] Charles A.E. Goodhart, 'If Banks Should Act as Utilities, Why Not Treat Them as Such?', *Vox*, 30 August 2011 <www.voxeu.org/article/if-banks-should-act-utilities-why-not-treat-them-such>.

[47] Paul Beaudry and Amartya Lahiri, 'Risk Allocation, Debt Fueled Expansion and Financial Crisis' (Working paper no. 15110, National Bureau of Economic Research, 2009), 2.

[48] Sanderson Abel, 'Role of Banks in the Economy', *The Herald* (online), 10 October 2013 <www.herald.co.zw/role-of-banks-in-the-economy/>.

[49] Paul Krugman, 'Three Expensive Milliseconds', *The New York Times* (online), 13 April 2014 <www.nytimes.com/2014/04/14/opinion/krugman-three-expensive-milliseconds.html?_r=0>.

[50] Harman Gill, 'Have Financial Markets Just Become Elaborate Casinos?', *Nottingham Economic Review* (online), 19 June 2012 <http://neronline.co.uk/2012/06/19/have-financial-markets-just-become-elaborate-casinos/>; Australian Risk Policy Institute (ARPI), 'High Frequency Trading: More Than Two Rights Make a Wrong' (White paper, ARPI, 2 March 2014), 4.

away from productive areas of the economy to construct increasingly complex financial products, which do not assist in facilitating saving or allocating capital can, as recent research has shown, serve as a drag on economic growth.[51]

Banks, and trading, can provide a valuable service in allocating risk, but increasingly of late the net effect of the means of doing so is higher total levels of risk in the financial system.

Further, the provision of objective financial advice is no longer a priority for many banks, especially the larger ones more removed from their communities. The attitude and incentives of a large modern bank are aligned with the profitability of the bank and away from the diligent provision of objective advice in the best interests of the client. Indeed, in the system I know the best – the Australian system – banks tend to recommend clients obtain financial advice (for a substantial fee) from 'independent' financial planners before choosing between the financial products on offer by the bank.

So if many banks now serve very different purposes to those which they historically served, should we be thinking differently about these institutions?

IMPLICATIONS OF THE FUNDAMENTAL CHANGES IN BANKING

Misaligned Interests

Banks and bankers seem to no longer be sufficiently incentivised to provide their best professional advice to clients. Instead banks and their employees pursue profit above all else. This is particularly seen in products with 'fat tail risks'.

Fat tail risks are risks that are potentially large (hence fat) and are perceived as being highly unlikely to eventuate (hence tail).

New financial products with embedded fat tail risks make it beguilingly attractive for bankers to enhance their performance by buying such products.[52] The derivative built into these products pays a regular fee in exchange for insurance of an unlikely but very large risk. So these products out-perform others in good times but may decline precipitately in value in bad times. This is not such a problem for the banker as the only skin they have in the game in the bad times is their annual bonus, and they will have collected and banked higher bonuses in all the preceding good years. It is much more of a problem for the bank itself or for the customer whose funds the banker is investing, as in the bad times the fat tail risk may well wipe out much or all of the investment's value. In the words of Noe and Young,

> The key problem that compensation contracts in the financial industry must tackle is tail risk. This term refers to small probability events that have large adverse

---

[51] Stephen G Cecchetti and Enisse Kharroubi, 'Reassessing the Impact of Finance on Growth' (Working Paper No 381, Bank for International Settlement, July 2012).

[52] Sue Jaffer, Nicholas Morris, Edward Sawbridge and David Vines, 'How Changes to the Financial Services Industry Eroded Trust', earlier n 7, 21.

consequences. Such events are popularly known as 'black swans' ... The term suggests that such events occur naturally and they are extremely unlikely. We claim, however, that standard compensation contracts in the financial sector often encourage people to *engineer* the swans; that is, they undertake investment strategies that have a certain probability of blowing up. Furthermore the probability of a blow-up can be quite sizable and still be rational from the standpoint of the agent (though not from the standpoint of the shareholders).[53]

For most bankers these choices are probably not made cynically. Human nature being what it is, the typical banker is not going to be clear-eyed about the size of the tail risks. They are far more likely to convince themselves that the tail risks, if they even fully understand them, are small and represent an entirely acceptable trade-off for the higher current returns on offer.

Nonetheless, the advent of complex, relatively opaque products with tail risks has resulted in a profound misalignment of the motivations and interests of banker and customer, and of employee and employer. Indeed, viewed in this light, the popularity of CDOs and other products with large tail risks in the lead up to the GFC were about more than the ever present search for yield;[54] they were popular because their opacity allowed sellers and buyers alike to believe what they wanted to believe, which was that one really could earn higher returns without taking on higher risks.[55]

Prior to the GFC, many CDOs were a credit default swap (CDS) attached to a securitisation structure and the CDS provided an extra income stream in addition to that from the asset securitisation. But too often the essential risk underpinning the securitisation and the CDS was the same – the U.S. residential property market. So the purchaser of a CDO saw a financial product offering higher returns than a regular securitised portfolio of mortgages, and what could not be seen without many hours of careful analysis, was one big fat tail risk.

Human Capital

Our modern world is characterised by ever-increasing complexity.[56] Intelligence is the ability to deal with complexity.[57] Intelligence is a highly controversial topic and beyond the purview of this paper. What should not be controversial however, is that

[53] Thomas Noe and H. Peyton Young, 'The Limits to Compensation in the Financial Sector' in Nicholas Morris and David Vines (eds), *Capital Failure* (Oxford University Press, 2014), 2.

[54] Mark Zandi, *Financial Shock* (FT Press, 2008), 118; Anna Katherine Barnett-Hart, 'The Story of the CDO Market Meltdown: An Empirical Analysis' (Honours thesis, Department of Economics, Harvard College, 19 March 2009), 94.

[55] Rodrigo Catril, 'The Trouble with CDOs', NAB *Insights*, 20 August 2010 <http://private wealth.nab.com.au/nabprivate/insights/people/rodrigo_catril/the_trouble_with_cdos.html>.

[56] My gas hot water system stopped working recently. The repairman brought a computer, plugged it in, and the hot water system told his computer the causes of its recent failures. This small gas hot water system has in it a computer chip that stores details of its faults.

[57] Linda S. Gottfredson, 'Why g Matters: The Complexity of Everyday Life' (1997) 24(1) *Intelligence* 79, 93.

however one measures intelligence, and whatever one believes about the ability of education and training to enhance the productivity or capacities of the individual, we live in a world of increasing complexity in which highly capable people are therefore in increasingly short supply. Indeed, in the modern world, intelligence may be the most precious commodity there is and there is not a lot of it. Only 5% of a population has an IQ over 125.[58]

In the old days banking as an industry did not absorb a high number of highly intelligent people. It was dull, risk-averse, prudent and not particularly well remunerated by professional standards.[59] In Paul Krugman's words, 'only the least ambitious of my classmates sought careers in the financial world. Even then, investment banks paid more than teaching or public service – but not that much more, and anyway, everyone knew that banking was, well, boring'.[60]

Contrast this to a former student of mine, who was studying pre-med at Duke in the late 1990s when Goldman Sachs made a presentation on campus contrasting the earnings of New York's leading surgeons with New York's leading financial traders. Until that day my student had always assumed he would be a surgeon like his father. After that day, he was headed to Goldman Sachs. Eventually his enthusiasm foundered on his inability to find meaning in finance, and he was a student of mine in law, before eventually leading a company providing specialist products to the mining industry in Australia. His story is not atypical. Joseph Stiglitz has argued that this amounts to a misallocation of a scarce human capital:

> ...as some of America's most talented young succumbed to the allure of easy money – brilliant minds that, in another era might have made real discoveries that enhanced our knowledge or real innovations that would have enhanced societal wellbeing. In earlier decades, our best students went into a variety of areas – some into medicine, many into research, still others into public service and some into business. Each found fulfillment of their potential at the same time they served their communities in one way or another. ... In this modern era of a finance-dominated economy, unfortunately, a disproportionate share of our most talented youth went into finance, lured by the outsized compensation. The costs to our society of this misallocation are incalculable.[61]

No one would want to live in a society that legislated against bright people working for banks. That would be nonsensical. But if a sector is drawing in too many scarce resources because it offers disproportional returns, there may be a case for making

---

[58] Ibid, 120; Earl Hunt, *Human Intelligence* (Cambridge University Press, 2010), 5.

[59] Sue Jaffer, Nicholas Morris, Edward Sawbridge and David Vines, 'How Changes to the Financial Services Industry Eroded Trust', earlier n 7, 35.

[60] Paul Krugman, 'Making Banking Boring', *The New York Times* (online), 9 April 2009 <www.nytimes.com/2009/04/10/opinion/10krugman.html>.

[61] Joseph E. Stiglitz, 'Incentives and the Performance of America's Financial Sector' (Testimony at the Hearing on Compensation in the Financial Industry, House Committee on Financial Services, 22 January 2010), 8 <www.astrid-online.it/rassegna/Rassegna-I/26–01–2010/stiglitz_22_01_10.pdf>.

that sector less profitable and less attractive as an employment destination. In an important recent study, Cecchetti and Kharroubi examined the impact of finance on growth and development at the aggregate level and found that mature sophisticated economies get to a point where greater size and sophistication in banking and financial markets become associated with lower economic growth. They found that because the finance sector competes with other sectors for scarce resources, in contrast to the common misconception, rapid growth of finance can have an adverse impact on aggregate real growth. In essence, rapid growth of a financial sector can serve as a drag on an economy and shift resource allocation and distribution in sub-optimal ways.[62]

Former Chairman of the UK's Financial Services Authority, Adair Turner, regards this as a 'key insight'. He argues that '[t]here clearly are bits of the financial system, and particularly the bits that relate to fixed income securities, trading, derivatives, hedging, but possibly also aspects of the asset management industry and equity trading, which have grown beyond a socially reasonable size'.[63] Recent research by Christiane Kneer confirms this hypothesis that the absorption of talent into the banking sector hurts the real sectors of the economy and may be a factor behind the marginal cost to economic growth in expanding financial services.[64]

This reveals a key problem caused by the changes in banking over the past 40 years: the growth in our financial system comes at a cost to other areas of society and the economy.

Regulatory Implications

We think in words; so the words we use have tremendous implications. At present we use the word 'bank' to describe globally systemically important financial institutions, the so-called G-SIFIs, and local community banks that do little more than accept savings and make loans.

Much of the regulation flowing from the Bank of International Settlements (BIS), the FSB, the Financial Action Task Force (FATF) and other soft law, standard setting, regulatory bodies is designed primarily to address the problems of G-SIFIs in the European Union and United States. The desirability of some of these new regulatory initiatives for most banks in East Asia or Australia – or small Midwestern banks in the United States for that matter – is highly questionable.[65]

---

[62] Stephen G Cecchetti and Enisse Kharroubi, earlier n 51.

[63] Adair Turner, 'How to Tame Global Finance', *Prospect* (online), 27 August 2009 <www.prospectmagazine.co.uk/magazine/how-to-tame-global-finance/#.UqBaP5RrYVk>.

[64] Christine Kneer, 'The Absorption of Talent into Finance: Evidence from U.S. Banking Deregulation' (Working Paper No 391, De Nederlandsche Bank, September 2013), 21 <www.dnb.nl/en/binaries/Working%20Paper%20391_tcm47-296165.pdf>.

[65] 3Indeed, some authors argue that administrative regulation does not work for G-SIFIs. See, Noel Whiteside, 'Creating Public Value: The Theory of the Convention', in John

Certainly many people in Australia, and not only those working for banks, view some of the new regulations emerging from the BIS and FSB as quite unsuited to Australian conditions. The process has been described to me as a 'new colonialism'. If this is the case for Australia, how much more must it be the case for many developing countries? One area in which I have some expertise is mobile financial services in developing countries and it is a good example of the problem. The pressing need in so many countries is to promote financial inclusion. Well over a billion adults have a mobile phone and no bank account in poorer nations. The FATF promoted strict know-your-customer rules to guard against money laundering and the financing of terrorism – which are primarily problems for rich nations. The FATF rules required identification standards beyond the reach of most poor people in poor nations and so served as a roadblock to achieving the priority for most poorer nations – the provision of financial services to their poor. This impacted the ability of people in poor nations to safely save money, remit it back to their villages and receive government payments safely without large losses due to corruption. In July 2013, FATF revised its standards and promoted a more risk-based application of them to address this unintended consequence. Nevertheless, the entire episode serves as a potent example of how rules promulgated in Washington, Brussels and Basel, may not suit much of the rest of the world.[66]

The G-SIFI distinction was made, of course, so as to target certain regulation at only these institutions, but it nonetheless seems that when international regulators say 'bank' for non-G-SIFI regulations, their conception of a bank remains primarily that of a high-risk-taking financial speculator, whereas when most Australians say 'bank' their conception is of something that is home grown and relatively basic. The language of the elite and the language of the layperson do not mesh. Technical language that stretches the meaning of words beyond their ordinary meaning is common in any profession (with medicine and law to the fore) but we need to be clear as to what we are thinking about when we use the word 'bank'.

By making a much clearer and stronger distinction between old style banks and the new super-banks, we would be better able to target regulation that could allow for both institutions to achieve their legitimate purposes while mitigating the excesses that currently pervade the system. Perhaps as importantly, a clearer intellectual distinction between traditional style banks and the new super-banks would promote clearer thinking through the issues by all involved in finance.

Benington and Mark H. Moore, *Creating Public Value: Theory and Practice* (Palgrave Macmillan 2011).

[66] Louise Malady, Ross P. Buckley and Douglas W. Arner, 'Developing and Implementing AML/CFT Measures Using a Risk-Based Approach for New Payments Products and Services' (Paper No. 28, Centre for International Finance and Regulation, June 2014).

Societal Consent

Another issue to consider in relation to the growth of the new super-banks is whether we, as citizens, ever agreed to this type of financial architecture?[67]

The changes that facilitated much of the growth were seemingly minor when made: small provisions that exempted financial derivatives from the application of the gaming laws. It is highly unlikely when legislatures voted on these changes that anyone could have foreseen the longer-term consequences.

Moreover, most of the changes that have occurred – the attitudes of bankers, from where they are recruited, and how they are remunerated – have never been an issue for legislatures; and the complexity and the opacity of what banks actually do today is beyond the understanding of most intelligent laypeople. Frankly, much of what a super-bank does today is beyond the understanding of most of its employees. It is apparent from multiple discussions with bankers that while each may well understand their own role well, very few bankers, and only those at the very highest levels of the bank, actually understand the bank's entire business.

The analysis of the changes in banking shows that the current architecture of international finance was never planned nor foreseen. The consequence of a series of seemingly innocuous changes has been the creation of vast, complex financial speculators at the very core of the international economy.

Something as fundamental as the way in which money is intermediated and for what purposes is rightly of concern to any democratic society. It has a profound effect on the lives of all citizens – yet we live in a system to which virtually no-one assented. If we take democratic ideals seriously, this should be a point of serious concern.

It is important that the public understand the changes that have taken place. Those of us who analyse the regulation of the global financial system have a responsibility to communicate these changes broadly and clearly.[68] Otherwise we risk thwarting the efforts of educated citizens to understand, and possibly insist upon the reform of, the system upon which we all, directly and indirectly, rely.

CONCLUSION

Banking was once a highly prudent, relatively boring industry that operated to serve its clients' interests. Today, much of the behaviour in the financial industry would frighten bankers of the past. Banks have become large, complex organisations

---

[67] For further discussion of this issue see Sylvia Walby, 'Finance Versus Democracy? Theorizing Finance in Society' (2013) 27(3) *Work Employment and Society* 489.

[68] A good example of a book which does just this very well is Anat Admati and Martin Hellwig, *The Banker's New Clothes*, earlier n 37.

intent on maximizing profits. The dramatic changes that have occurred in the banking industry since the 1970s have revolutionised the concept of a 'bank' – and it was largely the characteristics of this modern style 'bank' that triggered the global financial crisis.

The GFC was caused by a range of factors: (i) a belief in efficient capital markets that are welfare enhancing with very little regulation, (ii) a raft of consequential deregulating initiatives, (iii) the attempt to align employee and bank interests through most remuneration being by way of bonuses, (iv) the incentive for employees to seek out (or create) products with fat tail risks that offer higher short-term returns and thus higher bonuses and (v) the incentive for banks to merge and grow larger and thereby secure more of the benefits of lower wholesale funding costs that accrue from the implicit government guarantee of solvency for 'too-big-to-fail' banks.[69]

The final three factors that contributed to the GFC remain largely in place today. It is clear, from a regulatory standpoint, that there is a great deal of work to do in order to create a financial system that fulfills its essential role in the economy, without subjecting the rest of society to an unacceptable risk of wholesale economic collapse and accompanying mass human misery.

The aim of this chapter has been to illuminate the extraordinary changes that have occurred in the banking industry over the past 40 years. In this relatively short period of time we have seen an enormous shift in the type of people working in the industry, the attitudes of banks, the remuneration of their workers, the complexity of the products and services they offer and the legalization of gambling. While identifying a series of problems arising from these changes, it is beyond the scope of this chapter to prescribe solutions to many of the problems raised – that is the role of many of the chapters that follow.

Nevertheless, the starting point for any discussion of banking reform must be to understand accurately the current landscape. The banks of old continue to exist, but a new type of institution has emerged over the past 40 years to become the central piece of the architecture of the new globalised economic system: the G-SIFI. This chapter has argued that these institutions are characterised by: substantial asset holdings in 'speculative derivatives' or, as many regard it, gambling; a tendency to offer such high rewards as to attract a disproportionate amount of human capital; a perspective on their institutional purpose that is utterly at odds with historical conceptions of banking; and systemic importance to the extent that their failure cannot be countenanced.

Banks, as traditionally understood, are institutions with social utility: they mediate capital, allocate risk, provide liquidity to the economy and sound financial

---

[69] Jeffrey M. Lacker, 'Testimony on Bankruptcy and Financial Institution Insolvency' (Statement to Subcommittee on Regulatory Reform, Commercial and Antitrust Law of the Committee on the Judiciary, Washington, December 2013), 1.

advice to their customers. Indeed, it is difficult to imagine a functional economy without them. The new breed of super-bank is a different question. The social utility of the G-SIFI must be considered in the context of the Damoclean sword they have created to hang above us all. Some may still regard this as a bank, but it is not the type of bank that has ever been known to the world before – history has shown that we can survive without them; only time will tell if we can survive with them.

3

Understanding the *Global* in Global Finance and Regulation

Lawrence G. Baxter

"Global" is an evocative adjective that generates, alternately, excitement and despair.[1] It comes into vogue every few decades, the recent past being no exception. The latest cycle of "globalization" reached its apogee in 2008, evolving through the three-decade period from about 1980 to 2010 and roughly tracking the great trade breakthroughs of the World Trade Organization (WTO),[2] North American Free Trade Agreement (NAFTA),[3] and so on, until the near collapse of the eurozone in the wake of the Global Financial Crisis (GFC).[4] As Niall Ferguson warned presciently in 2005, we have seen such eras of optimism before.[5] Yet, the cyclical nature of globalization notwithstanding, in many ways the "global" dimension is more real and present than ever, as manufacturing, technology, transportation and the digital integration of economies have made the fortunes of formerly distant places very proximate to all of us.[6]

In certain respects, financial systems have encountered "the end of geography."[7] From the perspective of many large financial firms, globalization has indeed

---

[1] ECONOMIST, *When did globalisation start?*, September 23, 2013, at www.economist.com/blogs/freeexchange/2013/09/economic-history-1/.

[2] See www.wto.org/index.htm.

[3] See www.nafta-sec-alena.org/Default.aspx?tabid=97&language=en-US.

[4] Histories and analyses of the GFC already abound. See, e.g., Johan A. Lybeck, A Global History of the Financial Crash of 2007–10 (2011).

[5] Niall Ferguson's *Sinking globalization*, For. Affairs (March/April 2005), available at www.foreignaffairs.com/articles/60622/niall-ferguson/sinking-globalization.

[6] The view expressed here regarding cycles of globalization is possibly too Western-centric. A widely disseminated report by Standard Chartered Bank's Global Research Group would disagree with the opinion expressed earlier that we have reached the end of another cycle of globalization. STANDARD CHARTERED BANK GLOBAL RESEARCH, THE SUPERCYCLE REPORT (2010), available at https://research.standardchartered.com/configuration/ROW%20Documents/The%20Super-Cycle%20Report_14_11_10_16_32.pdf. The report views the new "super-cycle" of globalization as really having begun in 2000 and likely to last until 2030, and it anticipates a huge financial deepening in Asia and other emerging economies.

[7] RICHARD O'BRIEN, GLOBAL FINANCIAL INTEGRATION: THE END OF GEOGRAPHY (1991).

become a phenomenon distinct, in important ways, from other terms that are frequently used interchangeably with "global," such as "international," "multi-national" and "transborder."

Unsurprisingly, "global finance," the subject of this book, has become a perfectly comfortable and appropriate term. Too comfortable – because we seldom pause to dwell on what "global" really means to finance and what some of its more far-reaching implications are. This chapter explores the "global" view of modern financial firms and how such a view drives the need for global governance and regulation while at the same time undermining the realization of adequate structures to meet this demand. At first glance, it might appear that our global regulatory institutions are indeed keeping up with the emergence of truly global finance. Deeper consideration, however, reveals a much more problematic panorama.

The development of global business and finance promoted the creation of transnational governance organizations such as the G20,[8] the Bank for International Settlements (BIS),[9] the Basel Committee on Banking Supervision (BCBS)[10] and the Financial Stability Board (FSB)[11] and has extended into financial supervision the activities of international financial institutions (IFIs) such as the World Bank for Reconstruction and Development (World Bank)[12] and the International Monetary Fund (IMF).[13] Yet at the same time, the rising power of global financial institutions has fostered national reactions against both globalization and global governance, a Balkanization that perpetuates, perhaps even accentuates, rather than diminishes the "global paradox" once thought resolved by liberal international relations theorists.[14] In an era when a "global" solution to modern finance is most needed, it seems further away than ever. The primary reason, it will be argued, lies in the nature of modern global finance itself.

These developments have progressed amid, have influenced, and have been influenced by a much larger change in the nature of global relationships. Having evolved from a system of custom and natural law–based norms into the Westphalian regime characterized by the mutual interactions of sovereign states,[15] international ("global") financial regulation is now reforming around a world ordered

---

[8] www.g20.org.
[9] www.bis.org/index.htm.
[10] www.bis.org/bcbs/index.htm.
[11] www.financialstabilityboard.org.
[12] www.worldbank.org.
[13] www.imf.org/external/index.htm.
[14] See further the discussion *infra* text accompanying notes 35–7.
[15] On the rise and fall of the Westphalian regime of state sovereignty and controversies surrounding whether the state system is in decline, e.g., HEDLEY BULL, THE ANARCHICAL SOCIETY (4th ed. 2012); PHILIP BOBBITT, THE SHIELD OF ACHILLES: WAR, PEACE, AND THE COURSE OF HISTORY (2002) chapter 7; David Held, *The Changing Structure of International Law*, THE GLOBAL TRANSFORMATIONS WEBSITE, available at www.polity.co.uk/global/pdf/GTReader2e Held.pdf (last visited November 5, 2012); William Twining, *A Post-Westphalian Conception of Law*, 37 L. & SOC. REV. 199 (2003).

by what Philip Bobbitt has called a "society of market states."[16] In this global
society, globalized financial institutions have come to occupy a central role in
public ordering, and the emerging regime of financial regulation is assuming very
different forms from those familiar in traditional international law. This is a world
in which treaties are no longer as dominant as perhaps they used to be, and non-
governmental organizations, individuals and groups have significant standing. It is
a world in which, along with business[17] and state competition,[18] we are seeing a mix
of multipolar market power, collaboration among states and financial firms, competition and conflict. This complex ordering (and disordering) is likely to shape the
possibilities that lie ahead for global financial activity and its regulation.

FROM "INTERNATIONAL" TO "GLOBAL"

Banking activities have always tended to follow the patterns of trade across large
geographies, whether such patterns crossed political boundaries or not. The
Knights Templar, perhaps the first great bankers to the world, were able to provide
finance without borders in a world before sovereign nations. The Medicis and other
great Italian dynasties did the same. To such bankers the term "global" might have
been puzzling for its irrelevance as a restriction to their business: their world simply
was global, at least to the extent that the known world was all that mattered.

Enter the Sovereign

The rise of the nation state, of sovereignty and sovereigns (the bankers' biggest
clients), introduced new dimensions to bank activities and their regulation: in
particular the concepts of "international," "multinational" and "transnational."
Different laws and restrictions mattered as one crossed sovereign boundaries; these
constraints *really mattered* to the extent that money and banking lie so close to the
breasts of sovereigns.

In turn, it became important to know whether a financial transaction was
"domestic" or crossed jurisdictional boundaries. For financial companies, corporate structure and accountability became important because the legal forms of their

---

[16] Bobbitt, *supra* note 15, chapter 10.
[17] One recent business mantra, related to game theoretic applications, is the concept of
"co-opetition," a strategy by which businesses can learn to compete and cooperate with other
businesses in order to extract maximum potential value from the marketplace. See, e.g., Adam
M. Brandenburger & Barry J. Nalebuff, Co-opetition (1996).
[18] A particularly insightful recent analysis of the adversarial/cooperative relations between the
United States and China is Noah Feldman, Cool War: The Future of Global Competition (2013). One can see such "conflicted" and strained relationships in many areas of
financial regulation. See, e.g., the sanctions applied by US regulators to foreign banking
organizations and the reactions by governments to the United States, discussed further, *infra* at
notes 81–6.

operating entities were the product of the laws and regulations of the distinct, sovereign nations within which they operated.

For centuries in the era of the sovereign states, banks and other finance companies simply accommodated the jurisdictional boundaries by observing national law (where they were allowed by host countries to enter from abroad), taking advantage where this was useful of differences in the content of domestic laws (regulatory arbitrage), or interacting at arm's length with correspondents where this was necessary to overcome jurisdictional restrictions. Unlike the systems governing shipping, war and international relations, there was no significant *lex mercatoria* for banking regulation, no customary international law and no significant international treaties. International banking law was best analogized to a system of "bumper cars" in which the legal impact and constraints upon cross-border financial transactions depended largely on mutual and ad hoc agreements between pairs or groups of countries.[19]

Interconnectedness and Liberalization

Two major developments in globalization precipitated the evolution beyond *international* finance and toward *global* finance. The first flowed from the demise of Bretton Woods and the end of fixed exchange rates.[20] This introduced a substantial new element of *risk* into cross-border banking, the fluctuation and volatility of exchange rates that, because of the *interconnectedness* of currency counterparties, quickly demonstrated the dependency of financial institutions across borders. *Bankhaus Herstatt* triggered a new awareness of the limitations of the bumper cars framework.[21]

The second was the facilitation of much greater cross-border financial activity, precipitated by various rounds of *financial liberalization*, ranging from the negotiation of the Financial Services Annex of the WTO,[22] to the financial sections of

---

[19] Michael Malloy, *Bumper Cars: Themes of Convergence in International Regulation*, 60 FORDHAM L. REV 23 (1992).

[20] See, e.g., *Nixon and the End of the Bretton Woods System, 1971–1973* (US Dept. of State, Office of the Historian), http://history.state.gov/milestones/1969–1976/nixon-shock.

[21] The failure of *Bankhaus Herstatt*, following almost immediately upon the breakdown of the Bretton Woods system and the world's new exposure to floating exchange rates, led directly to the creation of the Basel Committee on Banking Supervision. See www.bis.org/bcbs/history.htm. On the failure and its impact, see, e.g., *The long, dark shadow of Herstatt*, ECONOMIST, April 12, 2001, www.economist.com/node/574236; Gergana Koleva, *'Icon of Systemic Risk' Haunts Industry Decades After Demise*, AM. BANKER, June 23, 2011, www.american banker.com/bankthink/bankhaus-herstatt-icon-of-systemic-risk-1039312-1.html. (The AMERICAN BANKER also republished its historic front page reporting the failure. See www.american banker.com/175/cologne-bank-shut-exchange-losses-cited-1039304-1.html.)

[22] See the Financial Services Annex to the General Agreement on Trade in Services, www.wto .org/english/tratop_e/serv_e/10-anfin_e.htm.

regional treaties such as NAFTA.[23] Banks, mainly Western and well endowed with capital, searched for the richer returns offered by new development. They were able, in many cases for the first time, and were encouraged, to enter underdeveloped markets. The great enterprise of global "financial deepening" had begun in earnest.[24] Finance had become truly global, rushing to meet the vacuums presented by new markets wherever they were, facilitated through new techniques of debt and equity exchange financing,[25] and operating irrespective of national boundaries.[26]

GLOBAL FINANCIAL REGULATION: FROM COORDINATION TO HARMONIZATION TO UNIFICATION?

The Basel Committee

The failure of *Bankhaus Herstatt* in 1974[27] highlighted for central bankers across the world the perils of interconnectivity. Regulators seized the small German bank at the end of the workday in Germany; yet because of the time difference, New York counterparty banks were caught in the middle of the East Coast workday by the default. The Bank for International Settlements was prompted to create the primary international fulcrum for international banking regulation, namely the Basel Committee on Bank Supervision (BCBS).[28] From the BCBS has since flowed a long series of increasingly detailed supervisory principles, culminating in the Basel III capital regime,[29] that are designed to develop and maintain as close coordination among national financial regulators as possible.

G20 and Financial Stability Board

Associated with the work of the BCBS has been that of a number of other committees and forums to develop standards and a certain degree of consensus on the principles of bank supervision, treatment of offshore financial centers,

---

[23] See NAFTA chapter 14 "Financial Services," at www.nafta-sec-alena.org/Default.aspx?tabid=97&ctl=SectionView&mid=1588&sid=827a9405-deb8-4285-bf07-790c6550c6f5&language=en-US.

[24] On which, see, e.g., Nobuhiro Kiyotake & John Moore, *Financial Deepening*, 3(2–3) J. Eur. Econ. Ass'n 701 (2005).

[25] See Ross P. Buckley, Debt-for-Development Exchanges: History and New Applications (2011).

[26] For general reviews of this process of global banking growth and its relationship to financial liberalization, see, e.g., Alfred Slager, The Internationalization of Banks chapter 1 (2006); Douglas W. Arner, Financial Stability, Economic Growth and the Role of Law (2007).

[27] See text *supra* at note 21.

[28] www.bis.org/bcbs/index.htm.

[29] For the details and Basel III texts, see www.bis.org/bcbs/basel3.htm.

international money laundering, accounting standards and the like. The World Bank and IMF have established a peer-review system to try to lift the standards observed by all nations.[30] Perhaps the most far-reaching efforts beyond those of the BCBS itself have been those driven by the Group of Twenty (G20)[31] in reaction to the GFC, and the Financial Stability Board[32] (upgraded by the G20 from the former Financial Stability Forum) to address the dangers posed by so-called systemically important financial institutions and banks. The FSB has become, in effect, the key coordinator for implementation of the G20 policy agenda and development of what has been called the "New International Financial Architecture."[33]

Transnational Regulatory Networks and "Soft Law"

Various attempts have been made to provide an underlying theory concerning the legal status and legitimacy of these largely committee-driven and, mostly, non-treaty-based developments.[34] One explanation is that promoted by liberal international relations authorities such as Robert Keohane and Anne-Marie Slaughter, namely the theory of "transnational regulatory networks" (TRNs). Anne-Marie Slaughter, for example, developed the concept of TRNs to describe this mechanism as a hallmark of a "new world order."[35] TRNs are celebrated as a means of resolving the "global paradox," in terms of which "[w]e need more government on

---

[30] On the IMF/World Bank Financial Sector Assessment Program (FSAP), see www.imf.org/external/np/fsap/fssa.aspx (IMF); and http://web.worldbank.org/WBSITE/EXTERNAL/TOPICS/EXTFINANCIALSECTOR/0,,contentMDK:22142161~menuPK:6459396~pagePK:210058~piPK:210062~theSitePK:282885,00.html. Other organizations such as the BCBS and FSB have also instituted peer assessment programs.

[31] See the description of the G20 and its mission by the G20 Information Center, www.g20.utoronto.ca/g20whatisit.html.

[32] www.financialstabilityboard.org.

[33] See Joseph J. Norton, *Banking Law Reform and Users-Consumers in Developing Economies: Creating an Accessible and Equitable from the "Excluded,"* 42 Tex. Int'l L. J. 789 at 792 n. 7 (and the sources there cited).

[34] The work of the World Bank, IMF and the European Union is of course treaty based.

[35] Anne-Marie Slaughter, A New World Order (2004). See also Kal Raustiala, *The architecture of international cooperation: trans-governmental networks and the future of international law,* (2002) 43 Virginia Journal of International Law 1; David Zaring, *International law by other means: the twilight existence of international financial regulatory organizations,* (1998) 33 Texas International Law Journal 281; Pierre-Hugues Verdier, *Transnational regulatory networks and their limits,* (2009) 34 Yale Journal International Law 113. TRNs have been long in their evolution: see Alan Boyle and Christine Chinkin, The making of international law (2007) at 51. See also Lawrence G. Baxter, *The Internationalisation of law – the 'complex' case of bank regulation,* in The Internationalisation of Law: Legislating, Decision-Making, Practice and Education 3 at 18–19 (Mary Hiscock & William van Caenegem eds. 2010); Diane Stone, *Transfer agents and global networks in the 'transnationalization' of policy,* 11:3 J. Eur. Pub. Pol'y 545 (2004).

a global or regional scale, but we don't want the centralization of decision-making power and coercive authority so far from the people actually to be governed."[36]

TRNs reconcile these conflicting demands by enabling national regulatory representatives (who are theoretically accountable to more directly elected domestic superiors) to collaborate in the development of a moderately consistent set of global principles upon which modern finance can be based. With each nation applying its own enforcement mechanisms, international financial regulation acquires a kind of transnational reality. Of course, whether these explanations satisfy the basic demands of democracy or, as Ross Buckley puts it elsewhere in this volume, "societal consent," is another matter.[37]

The emergence of international financial regulatory standards is also accommodated within more orthodox public international law doctrine under the epithet of "soft law."[38] In common with many other areas of international principle not buttressed by formal treaties, such international regulation has a very real presence in the formal enforcement mechanisms of domestic jurisdictions. Indeed, David Zaring has plausibly argued that global financial regulation is as real as many more traditional and better-recognized areas of public international law.[39]

Trade Liberalization and the Free Flow of Finance

Treaties promoting financial liberalization and access by foreign banks to new markets have also assumed and encouraged graduated reciprocity between signatories. While the underlying principle of reciprocity has been implicit to some extent in the financial annexes to regional trade treaties and common application of the most favored nation (MFN) principle,[40] the most prominent and far-reaching examples being embraced within the EU single banking passport and, more recently, the European Banking Union.[41] This trend has tended to encourage the adoption of the principle of "mutual recognition" between host jurisdictions of the supervisory primacy by "headquarters" regulators.

---

[36] Slaughter, *supra* note 35, at 8.

[37] Ross Buckley, *The Changing Nature of Banking and Why it Matters*, chapter 2 *supra*.

[38] Emilios Avgouleas, Governance of Global Financial Markets: The Law, the Economics, the Politics chapter 5 (2012); Chris Brummer, Soft Law and the Global Financial System: Rule Making in the 21st Century (2012); Jean Galbraith & David Zaring, *Soft Law as Foreign Relations Law*, 99 Corn. L. Rev. 735 (2014). And see further Douglas Arner & Michael Taylor, *The Financial Stability Board and the Future of International Financial Regulation*, *infra* chapter 4.

[39] David Zaring, *Legal Obligation in International Law and International Finance*, 47 Cornell J. Int'l L. 175 (2015). Professor Zaring elaborates more fully in this volume on the network of networks that now comprise the international financial regulatory regime. See David Zaring, *Financial regulation's overlooked networks*, *infra* chapter 5.

[40] See generally, e.g., Brummer, *supra* note 388, at 52–7; David Zaring, *Finding Legal Principle in Global Financial Regulation*, 52 Va. J. Int'l L. 683, at 706–07 (2012).

[41] http://ec.europa.eu/internal_market/finances/banking-union/index_en.htm.

In the view of some, these developments seemed to presage the real possibility that the financial regulatory regimes of various nations might actually be harmonized, if not actually rendered uniform. Such aspirations matched reasonably the emerging reality of modern banking, namely that it was being conducted with less and less regard to geographic boundaries.[42]

With such rapid progress occurring within the span of only three or four decades, it is no surprise that some might have believed that this TRN or soft law would harden into something close to a more formal and meaningful regime of global financial regulation. Such a view might even have found support in academic analyses of trends in international relations, among which was the declaration by one such expert that a "World State" was "inevitable."[43] Indeed, a progression from coordination to harmonization and even to actual unification seemed not only possible but, as the following section will argue, actually essential if modern finance is to be subject to any efficient and reliable regulation at all.

BUSINESS GLOBALIZATION: ENTERPRISES
THAT WILL NOT BE EASILY GOVERNED

Globalization has, however, proved to be a multi-faceted concept, at least as it is manifested in finance. One of the most problematic features of true globalization has become starkly apparent. Perhaps more than in any other industry, financial services run along nearly instantaneous digital tracks. The impact of events in one-quarter of the globe will be nearly instantly felt everywhere, never more dramatically illustrated than with the GFC. The reverberations from the collapse of Lehman Brothers affected every major financial center.[44] The interconnectedness – even the *perceived* interconnectedness – of Lehman counterparties and their counterparties froze the global economy and precipitated an already teetering financial system into full-blown crisis.[45]

These events drove the G20 nations resolve in declaring a commitment to concerted action in order to recover from the GFC and prevent future systemic meltdowns.[46] Major reforms were also initiated in the United States, United

---

[42] This latter trend will be explored further in the next section.

[43] Alexander Wendt, *Why a World State is Inevitable*, 9 EUR. J. INT'L REL. 491 (2003).

[44] AVGOULEAS, *supra* note 38, 76. For the full story on Lehman's collapse, see LAWRENCE G. MCDONALD & PATRICK ROBINSON, A COLOSSAL FAILURE OF COMMON SENSE" THE INSIDE STORY OF THE COLLAPSE OF LEHMAN BROTHERS (2009).

[45] One need not enter into the (largely pointless) debate whether the failure of Lehman Brothers on September 15, 2008, was the real or even the proximate *cause* of the Crisis. The point is that the markets were shocked upon realizing that there would be no government bailout of Lehman, and this triggered a global credit freeze which, in turn, contributed to a worldwide financial crisis.

[46] The G20's direct involvement in attempts to stabilize the global economy began with the group's DECLARATION SUMMIT ON FINANCIAL MARKETS AND THE WORLD ECONOMY (Washington, DC November 15, 2008), www.g20.org/sites/default/files/g20_resources/library/

Kingdom, Europe and elsewhere. Given this impetus, one might have expected far far-reaching and collaborative actions by all the world's leading economies, even leading ultimately to a much more coherent and perhaps even uniform regime of international financial regulation. Banking *operations* have themselves become more global than ever.

Global Operational Integration

So the need for global governance has become greater than ever, just as global governance itself has been weakening.

Let us consider why this is happening. Two closely related developments seem dominant, the subtle nuances of which are sometimes missed even where their verbiage has become commonplace. First, the technological revolution, particularly in communications, has facilitated seamless business activity across the globe. Second, there has been a massive and corresponding surge in global *corporate* (and not merely *economic*) activity that has become possible as a result of technology and that has transformed global business from the "*inter*-national" to the seamlessly *global*.

Accompanying this business transformation has been the emergence – also facilitated by the technology revolution – of truly global finance. As has often times perversely been the case, the flag has followed business, instead of the other way around. Because business is now really global, the "flag" has itself had to be everywhere simultaneously, and the only way sovereigns can meet this demand is through the process of coordination, contestation and reliance upon multi-leveled domestic implementation that Professor Zaring describes in his defense of soft law as public international law.[47]

Global Technology

The world has experienced numerous technological revolutions.[48] So there is nothing historically unique about the one we have been experiencing for the past fifty to sixty years. The current revolution, however, has had a dramatic impact on the nature of modern business and, particularly, on its conduct and operations. The logistics of "big box" stores, such as those operated by Walmart and the airlines, as examples, can be managed more centrally than ever before because of real-time connectivity enabled by communications technology. Even more so has this been

---

Washington_Declaration.pdf. This declaration has been followed by a series of communiqués based on the work of the FSB and BCBS.

[47] See Zaring, *supra* note 39.

[48] CARLOTA PEREZ, TECHNOLOGICAL REVOLUTIONS AND FINANCIAL CAPITAL: THE DYNAMICS OF BUBBLES AND GOLDEN AGES (2002).

the case with the accompanying finance necessary to fund such businesses.[49] Finance flows freely and almost instantaneously across vast global networks without the need to stop or even pause at national borders. Furthermore, large-scale financiers have made no secret of their belief that the Walmart global model is one that will be followed by large financial institutions as well.[50]

This technological integration is itself not an unmitigated good. With connectivity comes also contagion, with technologically-based business comes technological dependency, and with technological dependency comes technologically-driven vulnerability. These dependencies can sometimes have dangerous consequences, not only for banks and their customers, but even for international relations between states.[51] Yet it is a world in which we now find ourselves, and it is one to which public international law must itself adjust.

Global Business and Finance

The nature of the change is subtle but important. By "global" I do not merely mean that cross-border activities require intense multi-state or "international" cooperation; it goes far deeper than this. Until relatively recently international trade and finance was largely a bilateral and modular affair between separate organizations exporting to each other or providing correspondent services as agents of each other, and operating through separate and locally incorporated subsidiaries, businesses. Now financial institutions are able to operate *as if there were no borders or corporate segments at all.*

This development has had a profound impact on business operations. It has enabled businesses and financial institutions to become truly "global" and not just "international" in their operations. Banks are able to institute seamless corporate operations through the medium of branches instead of subsidiaries, and they have indeed lobbied for and secured the right to do so in many if not most jurisdictions.

---

[49] See, e.g., Jane K. Winn, *Catalytic Impact of Information Technology on the New International Financial Architecture*, 34 INT'L LAWYER 137 (2000).

[50] Mr. Dimon, Chairman and CEO of JP Morgan Chase & Co., for example, has been quite clear on this point. See, e.g., Gabriel Sherman, *The End of Wall Street As They Knew It*, N.Y. MAG. (February 5, 2012), http://nymag.com/news/features/wall-street-2012-2/ (quoting Mr. Dimon as saying that "companies big and small will still need underwriting, credit, capital management, and advice. McKinsey did a report that showed that the credit needs of multinationals are going to double in the next ten years, ... The net worth of the world is going to double in the next decade. Institutional funding will double in the next ten years. We're a store, you can buy bonds, FX, advice – we provide great products at a great price. That store is not going to go away. If you're a big, smart investor and we can give you the best price and the best service, you'll still be coming here, just like Wal-Mart and Costco". Mr. Dimon has asserted this position on other occasions as well, and many top financiers share his views.

[51] Consequences currently reflected in "flash crashes" on trading exchanges, international concerns about the fairness and safety of high frequency trading, major systems outages for large banks, and the vulnerability of banking networks to international, sometimes state-sponsored, cyberattacks.

The result is that when JP Morgan Chase & Co. (JPM), for example, operates a branch in London, this branch is a direct and undifferentiated presence of JPM's bank in New York.[52]

There are obvious advantages for the efficiency of business operations, yet these advantages are often accepted without an understanding of the disadvantageous implications. For example, one of the most visible consequences of seamless globalization has been the tight interconnectedness, particularly in finance, of business operations. Because there are fewer "firewalls" in the form of corporate legal entity separations, the contagion triggered by one company as it finds itself in difficulties can quickly spread across borders and, in the case of finance, across to other firms.[53]

Because of these factors, large financial firms do not think in terms of national jurisdictions at all, except when obliged to by the law. They organize their lines of business along functional and market lines, and these lines do not follow national boundaries. They are explicit about this, commonly using the term "global" as part of the title of the particular business division concerned and organizing that way,[54] and acknowledging their "global citizenship."[55] The consulting firms, which have a major influence on corporate strategy, urge large financial firms to address the issues from a global perspective, and analyze the challenges associated with global business from that perspective.[56] In the rhetoric of one of the leading proponents of

---

[52] Global banks tend to prefer using branches instead of subsidiaries if so allowed by host state law. This enables them to deploy capital across the whole branch network instead of having to meet capital requirements on a subsidiary-by-subsidiary basis, and it greatly facilitates and reduces the cost of operations because branch structures permit platforms to be used on a seamless basis across the branch network. Multiple legal entities subject to a variety of host state laws also require much more complex coding for shared platforms that might be deployed to support them. The bank structure is even more attractive to many British and European banks, where the *bank* (as opposed to holding company) tends to be the primary corporate unit in the overall conglomerate structure.

[53] Ironically, this form of globalization has brought us full circle to an earlier age of globalization, one in which merchant ships sailed the seven seas. While the connectivity such merchant shipping presented was much slower than that provided by the near-real-time networks of today, the effect of global shipping was to create forerunners for modern international financial regulation and public international law in the form of then-novel concepts such as flags of state and flags of convenience – in turn fragments of state sovereignty entering each other's spheres of jurisdiction with the necessity of mutual compromise and the development of the law of admiralty.

[54] See, e.g., Deutsche Bank: www.gtb.db.com ("Global Transaction Services"). Deutsche Bank, in common with its peers, also emphasizes its "global network": www.db.com/en/content/company/Global-Network.htm.

[55] See, e.g., Citigroup: www.citigroup.com/citi/about/global_citizenship.html ("global citizenship").

[56] Analyses by the major consulting forms are replete with references to the overwhelming dominance of globalization as an organizing principle. See the many reports produced by McKinsey's Global Institute, at www.mckinsey.com/insights/mgi; IBM Global, at www-935.ibm.com/services/us/gbs/consulting/; McKinsey refers to the "global grid," which it says must be built into every company because "every company is now a global company":

these developments, multinational enterprises are giving way to *globally integrated organizations* (GIEs).[57] Bank thought leaders share this perspective.[58] And we have yet to figure out the relationship between these developments and the responsibilities of vast global organizations that might profess "global citizenship" yet not really fit within any established legal framework.[59]

Less noticed but equally important is a subtle difference between global capital markets and global banking markets that intensifies the "global" perspective even when national or domestic markets remain important. Because of the availability of seamless communications and the great increase in capital mobility resulting from financial liberalization across many of the world's economies, the ability to raise capital across borders is increasingly enticing. In theory, it seems that global capital markets *optimize globally*, meaning that the most efficient allocation of capital will come from a seamless global framework. It is therefore not surprising that the policy direction of capital markets organizations such as the International Organization of Securities Companies (IOSCO) is strongly toward further liberalization across borders and towards a truly global capital market and a global institutional framework.[60]

CONSEQUENCES FOR GLOBAL GOVERNANCE

National Concerns – An Added Dimension of Complexity

On the other hand, however, it is not at all clear that *banking markets* and their *supervision* optimize globally. Precisely because of the quasi-governmental

---

www.mckinsey.com/insights/innovation/the_global_grid. See also EY, TRANSFORMING BANKS, REDEFINING BANKING: GLOBAL BANKING OUTLOOK 2014–15 (2014), downloadable at www.ey .com/GL/en/Industries/Financial-Services/Banking–Capital-Markets/Transforming-banks– redefining-banking (last visited July 13, 2014).

[57] SAMUEL J. PALMISANO, RE-THINK: A PATH TO THE FUTURE (2014). Mr. Palmisano is the former CEO of IBM and Director of the Center for Global Enterprise (http://thecge.net). See also, e.g., Sam Palmisano, *A New Model for Going Global*, CNBC COMMENTARY April 1, 2014, available at www.cnbc.com/id/101544248; Samuel Palmisano, *How Multinationals Have Been Superseded*, FIN. TIMES June 11, 2006, www.ft.com/intl/cms/s/1/c9fad85e-f96a-11da-8ced-0000779e2340.html#axzz2yU8psmw5

[58] See, e.g., Allan D. Grody & Peter J. Hughes, *Modern Banking Is a Global Enterprise*, AM. BANKER, *April 7, 2014, available at www.americanbanker.com/bankthink/modern-banking-is-a-global-enterprise-1066717-1.html.*

[59] The literature on this subject is growing rapidly. For an extended discussion, see, e.g., GRAHAME F. THOMPSON, THE CONSTITUTIONALIZATION OF THE GLOBAL CORPORATE SPHERE? (2012).

[60] This is a theme expressed by many global financiers and it has been nicely summed up in a speech by the Secretary General of IOSCO. See Remarks by David Wright, Secretary General of IOSCO, to The Atlantic Council, Washington, DC 10 December 2012, available at www.iosco.org/library/speeches/pdf/20121210-Wright-David.pdf.

functions performed by banks and the local sources of their funding and political support,[61] it might well be that global banking *regulation*, as distinct from banking *operations* and concomitant *political action*, *optimizes locally*. If this is correct, it is likely that the process described by Professor Zaring will become more complicated and intense than ever. The "soft law" architecture and processes of the New Financial Architecture might even, paradoxically, become a model for twenty-first century public international law itself. Certainly, the pressure for continuing negotiation toward a legal and regulatory regime that facilitates the growth of global business and finance is unlikely to stop, as is the demand for systems for resolving transnational business failures.

Balkanization

Progress toward coherent global reform has been faltering. In some respects, national reactions to global efforts have actually produced greater Balkanization. In the United States, egged on by the banks themselves, prominent legislators have even attempted to prevent the implementation of Basel III-based reforms.[62] At the same time, US regulators have imposed even more severe constraints on foreign banking organizations (FBOs), leading to complaints in other countries, particularly within the European Union. The European Banking Union – one of the signature efforts to address the implications of widespread systemic risk across borders – has been met with considerable hostility in the United Kingdom, including threats to withdraw. More broadly, the European Union and the United States have found that they might have to exclude financial services from what would otherwise become the broadest regional trade treaty ever developed.[63] Other nations have also baulked at efforts to impose global standards, what has even been described as a "new colonialism,"[64] indicating broad resistance to any trend toward global harmonization.

---

[61] Lawrence G. Baxter, *Betting Big: Value, Caution and Accountability in an Era of Large Banks and Complex Finance*, 31 Rev. Banking & Fin. L. 765 (2011–12), at 818–25.

[62] See, e.g., the bill introduced by Senators Sherrod Brown (D-Ohio) and David Vitter (R-LA) that would prohibit any further implementation of Basel III: Terminating Bailouts for Taxpayer Fairness Act of 2013, S. 798, § 3(e). The Bill was introduced as an amendment (Vitter Amdt. No. 689) and voted up overwhelmingly in a protest vote on www.senate.gov/legislative/LIS/roll_call_lists/roll_call_vote_cfm.cfm?congress=113&session=1&vote=00070, then quietly dropped by the Senate leadership. See Shahlen Nasiripour and Michael McAuliff, *With the Lights On, 99 Senators Voted Against Wall Street. The Lights Went Off and They All Fled*, Huff. Post December 17, 2013, www.huffingtonpost.com/2013/12/17/budget-deal-2013-megabanks_n_4462305.html (updated January 23, 2014).

[63] Shawn Donnan, *EU threatens to cut financial services from trade deal*, Fin. Times, June 13, 2014 (reporting on the Transatlantic Trade and Investment Partnership currently being negotiated between the EU and United States).

[64] Ross Buckley, *The Changing Nature of Banking and Why it Matters*, chapter 2 *supra*.

The Atlantic Council has addressed the tendency toward Balkanization and divergence in a pair of reports published in 2010,[65] and 2013.[66] These reports, focusing on developments primarily in Europe and the United States following what was, to some extent, a "North Atlantic Crisis,"[67] noted not only the obstacles to US and European harmonization but also the fact that Asian interests are themselves quite different.[68] As the CEO of the Hong Kong Securities and Futures Commission noted at a follow up conference, "transatlantic … preferences differ considerably from that of the Asian market, which continues to focus on its underdeveloped capital market, problems with SME funding, a general lending gap and infrastructure."[69]

Feeding the Global Maw

Fears once expressed about global corporations becoming larger, more powerful, and more relevant to people's lives are now a truly awesome reality – "awesome" in the strictest sense of the word. What Hong Kong Shanghai Bank (HSBC) does in London is tightly connected, and often an integral element of, what HSBC is doing in New York or Hong Kong or Shanghai. We have seen some of the consequences recently in the fines imposed on global banks headquartered in other countries for violating New York and US wire transfer laws.[70] So it seems likely that various aspects of public international law will be drawn into areas of controversy and misfeasance driven by the presence of global business operations.

The impact on the methodology and processes of public international law is likely equally profound: in following business, the flag (i.e., sovereign states) have had no choice but to "negotiate" mutually acceptable standards and deference to

---

[65] Douglas Elliott (rapporteur), The Danger of Divergence: Transatlantic Cooperation on Financial Reform (2010), www.atlanticcouncil.org/publications/reports/the-danger-of-divergence-transatlantic-cooperation-on-financial-reform.

[66] Chris Brummer (rapporteur), The Danger of Divergence: Transatlantic Financial Reform & the G20 Agenda (2013), www.atlanticcouncil.org/publications/reports/the-danger-of-divergence-transatlantic-financial-reform-the-g20-agenda.

[67] A possibility raised in its summary of the 2010 report, Atlantic Council, *The Danger of Divergence: Transatlantic Cooperation on Financial Reform*, October 6, 2010, at www.atlantic council.org/publications/reports/the-danger-of-divergence-transatlantic-cooperation-on-finan cial-reform.

[68] See further Chao Xi, *Why Has Basel III Become Hard Law for China? The Domestic Political Economy of International Financial Law*, *infra* chapter. 6.

[69] Quoted in a summary of the conference, Atlantic Council, *The Danger of Divergence: Discussion of Brussels, EU Reforms at the European Parliament*, February 12, 2014, available at www.atlanticcouncil.org/events/past-events/the-danger-of-divergence-ttip-and-the-import ance-of-a-global-perspective.

[70] Well-publicized examples in the financial world are the settlements by British, French and Swiss banks for violations of US wire transfer laws aimed at enforcing sanctions against Iran, combating drug laundering and tax evasion. The most recent examples are the fines levied by the United States against HSBC and BNP Paribas.

each other, while acknowledging the power of "home state" rules within their "host state" jurisdictions.[71] The entire BCBS/FSB processes, described in other chapters in this book,[72] as well as the history of European integration, are illustrations of this change. Chris Brummer has described the emergence of a new form of "mini-lateralism," in which a conglomeration of discreet bilateral alliances, together with the veneer of "soft law, sometimes concerted central bank actions[73] and other forms of 'financial engineering' are supplanting the vision of multilateralism and global harmony."[74]

Global Autonomy

Let us examine some of these developments as they proceed directly from financial globalization. First, the sheer power of global banks has enabled them to create a partially autonomous, "self-governing" world of financialization, most particularly in the world of derivatives. While recent reform efforts in the United States and Europe have attempted to move swaps derivatives to regulated exchanges, earlier deregulation enabled the growth of a vast industry of over-the-counter (OTC) derivatives that still comprise the vast proportion of derivatives transactions and risk exposures in the global economy.[75] OTC business is largely conducted according to the rules of the International Swaps and Derivatives Association (ISDA),[76] an entirely industry-based, non-governmental organization that tends to favor the progressive global unification of derivatives rules under industry governance.[77] This preference, opaque and accessible only to members of ISDA – the world's largest financial firms – is promoted by ISDA members and shows little prospect of becoming incorporated into recognizable government forms of regulation.[78]

---

[71] These assumptions were the basis for the first major agreement on principles of global bank supervision, namely the Basel Concordat.

[72] See, e.g., chapters 4, 5, and 6.

[73] For an extended discussion of the extensive powers of central bankers, see, e.g., Neil Irwin, The Alchemists: Three Central Bankers and a World on Fire (2013); Liaquat Ahamed, The Bankers Who Broke the World (2009).

[74] Chris Brummer, MiniLateralism: How Trade Alliances, Soft Law, And Financial Engineering Are Redefining Economic Statecraft (2014).

[75] While the risk exposure has reduced somewhat, perhaps because of reforms requiring the use of exchanges for swaps, the notional amounts of OTC derivatives contracts, including credit default swaps, is running in the $600 to over $700 trillion range. See Bank for International Settlements, Quarterly Review (March 2014) at A10, available at www.bis.org/publ/qtrpdf/r_qs1403.pdf.

[76] www2.isda.org.

[77] See, e.g., ISDA derivitiViews, Jan. 29, 2014, *http://isda.derivativiews.org/2014/01/29/market-fragmentation-is-becoming-a-reality/*.

[78] See also, Tim Büthe & Walter Mattli, The New Global Rulers: The Privatization of Regulation in the World Economy 32 (2011).

Financial Center Competition

Secondly, the world's largest financial centers display a continuing interest in attracting and keeping as much financial business as possible.[79] Specific market centers actively collaborate with global firms to achieve this ambition, and this market-based collaboration, like the earlier offshore financial centers and unlike traditional sovereign action that was at least politically accountable in some sense, serves to promote further opportunities for regulatory arbitrage that run counter to the aspirations of the G20 for a more coordinated world of financial governance.[80]

New Tentacles of Sovereign Power

Running in a different direction, yet just as much the product of financial global-ization, certain sovereigns have acquired enormous – some would say dispropor-tionate – power as a result of the globalization of financial networks. In the United States, for example, the US Treasury, and even the State of New York have been able to use the criticality of the payments system to impose very substantial sanctions on banks around the world when such firms have not complied with US anti-money-laundering (AML) and tax evasion laws, even in situations in which these firms have not conducted the offending transactions within the United States itself.[81] Such power has led other major banking nations to force changes to their own, long-standing banking laws.[82] Whether the objectives and results are good or bad is beside the point: the fact is that certain financial markets now provide a fulcrum for some sovereigns to exercise substantial "extra-territorial" power,[83] a development almost certain to invite retaliation by other centers and further Balkanization of global governance. French and European officials, for example, like their British counterparts earlier,[84] have expressed outrage at the huge US fines

---

[79] One of the classic expressions of this market ambition is the recent speech by Mark Carney, Governor of the Bank of England, declaring that "we [meaning London] are open for business." Mark Carney, *The UK at the heart of a renewed globalisation* (speech given at an event to celebrate the 125th anniversary of the FINANCIAL TIMES, London October 24, 2013), www.bankofengland.co.uk/publications/Documents/speeches/2013/speech690.pdf.

[80] See Dirk Zetzsche, *Competitiveness of Financial Centers in Light of Financial and Tax Law Equivalence Requirements*, *infra* chapter. 19.

[81] See JUAN C. ZARATE, TREASURY'S WAR: THE UNLEASHING OF A NEW ERA OF FINANCIAL WARFARE (2013).

[82] Under pressure from the United States, Switzerland has substantially amended its bank secrecy laws. The Swiss Foreign Account Tax Compliance Act was brought into force by the Swiss Federal Council on June 30, 2014.

[83] European derivatives regulation is also likely to have extensive extraterritorial effect. See the review by Alexandria Carr, *The Extraterritorial Effect of the EU Regulation of OTC Deriva-tives*, HARV. L. SCH. FOR. CORP. GOV. & FIN. REG., June 14, 2014, http://blogs.law.harvard.edu/corpgov/2014/06/14/the-extraterritorial-effect-of-the-eu-regulation-of-otc-derivatives-2/.

[84] Fines imposed by US regulators on the London-headquartered Barclays, HSBC and Standard Chartered Bank, for violations of US anti-money-laundering regulations led to angry reactions

($8–$10 billion or more) that were sought and ultimately applied against BNP Paribas,[85] as well as the continuing possibility of further huge fines relating to rate-setting impropriety.[86]

Banks Versus the State

Against this backdrop, the chase for yield that is driving global financial firms is also leading to global/domestic conflict. Just as the delays or failures in global financial reform have generated domestic pressures for national solutions, so too has the urgency to maintain financial yield within the big banks led such banks to consider, and in some cases even implement, evasive action to avoid national restrictions. Deutsche Bank and Barclays both attempted, with partial success, to restructure in order to avoid the new requirements of the US Dodd-Frank Act.[87] More recently, the Royal Bank of Scotland has restructured its US operations in order to avoid the new US Intermediate Holding Company requirements for foreign banking organizations. Such actions will create advantages and disadvantages across the global

and charges of ulterior motives in Britain and tensions between US and British regulators. See, e.g., Standard Chartered: *Boris accuses US regulators of being "motivated by jealousy,"* TELEGRAPH, August 9, 2012, www.telegraph.co.uk/finance/newsbysector/banksandfinance/ 9462...ered-Boris-accuses-US-regulators-of-being-motivated-by-jealousy.html; Walter Ellis, *America is turning on British banks in order to protect Wall Street*, TELEGRAPH BLOGS, August 8, 2012, http://blogs.telegraph.co.uk/news/walterellis/100175525/america-is-turning-on-british-banks-in-order-to-protect-wall-street/; Jim Pickard, *British MPs accuse US of anti-City agenda*, FIN. TIMES, August 7, 2012, www.ft.com/intl/cms/s/0/4425bcea-e0b2–11e1–8d0f-00144feab49a .html?; Tom Burgis & Patrick Jenkins, *King questions StanChart probe*, FIN. TIMES, August 8, 2012, www.ft.com/intl/cms/s/0/2ce700dc-e145–11e1–839a-00144feab49a.html; Dana Cimilluca & Victoria McGrane, *Trans-Atlantic Tensions Increase*, WALL ST. J., August 13, 2012, http://professional.wsj.com/article/SB10000872396390444042704577...992700.html?. One British banker was quoted in documents as saying, "Who are you tell us, the rest of the world, that we're not going to deal with Iranians."

[85] BNP Paribas was ultimately fined $8.9 billion and subjected to a number of other restrictions and sanctions. For a recap, see, e.g., Jessica Silver Greenberg & Ben Protess, *Grieving Father Pulls a Thread That Unravels BNP's Illegal Deals*, N.Y. Times Dealb%k, June 30, 2014, at http://dealbook.nytimes.com/2014/06/30/a-grieving-father-pulls-a-thread-that-unravels-illegal-bank-deals/.

[86] See, e.g., Noémie Bisserbe & David Enrich, *ECB Officials Anxious About Impact of U.S. Fines on E.U. Banks*, WALL ST. J. June 3, 2014, http://online.wsj.com/articles/ecb-officials-anxious-about-impact-of-u-s-fines-on-eu-banks-1401798968; Michael Stothard, *France slams US over possible $10bn-plus fine against BNP Paribas*, FIN. TIMES, June 3, 2014, www.ft.com/ intl/cms/s/0/9a8e516c-eafd-11e3–9c8b-00144feabdc0.html?#axzz33atKaZwS; Ben Protess and Jessica Silver-Greenberg, *French Officials Twist U.S. Arms in Bank Inquiry*, N.Y. TIMES DEALB%K June 2, 2014, http://dealbook.nytimes.com/2014/06/02/french-officials-twist-u-s-arms-in-bank-inquiry/.

[87] See David Enrich & Laura Stevens, *Deutsche Avoids Dodd-Frank Rule*, WALL ST. J., March 22, 2012, http://online.wsj.com/news/articles/SB10001424052702303812904577295614224666918; Tom Braithwaite & Shahien Nasiripour, *Deutsche Bank avoids US capital rules*, FIN. TIMES, March 21, 2012, www.ft.com/intl/cms/s/0/f2d96462-738e-11e1-94ba-00144feab49a.html.

competitive stage rather than an "even playing field"; and will thus possibly lead to retaliatory actions by other national jurisdictions, thereby further distancing the vision of global governance.

Nor has the reaction been confined to countries other than the United States. In the United States there has been a significant element of hostility toward international efforts at coordination. One bill introduced into Congress by a liberal Democrat and a conservative Republican would actually prohibit the further implementation of Basel III in the United States.[88] No doubt some of this hostility has been encouraged by US banks that are opposed to standards thought to be unnecessary or unfair.[89] That global banks, for which one might imagine a set of uniform or harmonized global rules would actually be convenient, would oppose such a development demonstrates the enormous domestic political and even cultural obstacles to further global coordination.

These, and many other factors, not least the use by states of financial networks as a means of implementing their policies on matters such as sanctions and tax evasion, suggest that bank/state configurations are making prognostication on the impact of globalization on financial markets murkier than ever.[90]

International Solutions?

One example where traditional public international law techniques are manifestly inadequate for the modern global economy is the use of treaties to address global financial instability. Observers steeped in the orthodoxy of PIL have proposed that we should create a World Financial Organization (WFO) along the lines of the WTO,[91] yet this suggestion seems quaintly out of touch with modern political reality.[92] So too, must it be said of the very thoughtful, treaty-based solution of a global banking regulator recently developed and refined most prominently by

---

[88] See *supra* note 62.

[89] Some US bank executives have railed against the complexity and severity of Basel III, even though, ironically, even stricter rules have ultimately been implemented within the United States. This in turn has led to protests by foreign banks and their supporting governments.

[90] I have developed some of the more recent themes in a working paper, tentatively titled *Extraterritorial Impacts of Recent Financial Regulation Reforms: A Complex World of Global Finance* (2014), available at http://scholarship.law.duke.edu/faculty_scholarship/3355/.

[91] See, e.g., Barry Eichengreen, *Not a New Bretton Woods But a New Bretton Woods Process*, in WHAT G20 LEADERS MUST DO TO STABILIZE OUR ECONOMY AND FIX THE FINANCIAL SYSTEM (Barry Eichengreen & Richard Baldwin eds. 2008) 25, available at www.voxeu. Org/reports/G20_summit.pdf; Peter Boone and Simon Johnson, *Will the Politics of Global Moral Hazard Sink Us Again?*, in THE FUTURE OF FINANCE (Adair Turner et al 2010) 247 at 269. For some historical context see, e.g., HEIDI MANDANIS SCHOONER AND MICHAEL W. TAYLOR, GLOBAL BANKING REGULATION: PRINCIPLES AND POLICIES (2010) at 292–94.

[92] See further, e.g., Lawrence G. Baxter, *Exploring the WFO Option for Global Banking Regulation*, in GLOBALIZATION AND GOVERNANCE (Laurence Boulle ed. 2011) 113–24; BRUMMER, *supra* note 38, at 269–71.

Emilios Avgouleas,[93] a cumbersome and laborious model unlikely to meet the needs of politically responsive regulation in a rapidly moving global marketplace.[94]

CONCLUSION

International financial regulation in a multipolar, multilateral world was difficult enough. Yet in that framework, nations could at least coordinate the regulation of their financial institutions on a reciprocal basis, and financial firms were not so globally encompassing as to find cross-border restrictions a serious impediment to their operations and profitability. These circumstances have all changed. "International" has morphed into "global," and global finance implies omnipresence, with borders being irrelevant to business operations, strategy, deployment of capital and management. Global firms are competing head-to-head with each other, irrespective of their "national" origins. To use Professor Schweller's imagery, we have entered an "age of entropy."[95]

At the same time, the plight of any one of these firms can have a simultaneous impact on many, if not all of the others. When any one of these behemoths is larger, in terms of global assets, than the entire annual GDP of many large individual nations, the collapse of one firm can constitute a severe threat to the financial system of any or all nations. Global financial firms have joined their global industrial counterparts to wield extraordinary power over economies and political frameworks.[96]

We demand that such systemic, even existential, risk be contained through regulation. But can we say that we are closer to meaningful global regulation than we were before 2008? Until the bankruptcy of a global firm can be credibly resolved across borders, it seems fatuous to claim that we are. Notwithstanding assurances from some national regulators, the global orderly resolution framework remains little more than a theoretical regime.[97] With the renewal of domestic reactions

---

[93] See AVGOULEAS, *supra* note 38, chapter 8.

[94] This inability to move very quickly is perhaps a basic problem of the Banking Union in Europe.

[95] Randall L. Schweller, *The Age of Entropy: Why the New World Order Won't be Orderly*, FOR. AFFAIRS, June 16, 2014, www.foreignaffairs.com/articles/141568/randall-l-schweller/the-age-of-entropy?.

[96] Professor Wilks aptly describes how corporations acquire greatly enhanced political power by virtue of their global operations. STEPHEN WILKS, THE POLITICAL POWER OF THE BUSINESS CORPORATION, esp. chapter 3 (2013). See also the discussions in THOMPSON, *supra note* 59; TIM BÜTHE AND WALTER MATTLI, THE NEW GLOBAL RULERS, *supra* note 78.

[97] As one leading expert has put it, notwithstanding all the work already done by United States, British and European regulators, "cross-border resolution without government intervention [i.e. some kind of bailout] is still at best uncertain for banks and wholly unaddressed for nonbanks." *What It Takes for the FDIC SPOE Resolution Proposal to Work*, HARV. L. SCH. FOR. CORP. GOV. & FIN. REG., April 5, 2014, http://blogs.law.harvard.edu/corpgov/2014/04/05/what-it-takes-for-the-fdic-spoe-resolution-proposal-to-work/. *Compare*, Daniel Indiviglio, *A Hurdle to Winding Down a Failing Global Bank*, N.Y. TIMES DEALB%K, November 18, 2013, http://dealbook.nytimes.com/2013/11/18/a-hurdle-to-winding-down-a-failing-global-bank/?_php=true&_type=blogs&_r=0.

against foreign measures, it would appear that we are indeed further away from a meaningful global regulatory system than ever.

To the extent that the purveyors of global finance are unlikely to withdraw to their national bases, to the extent that financialization has taken such deep root that it is unimaginable that it might shrink to more manageable levels, and to the extent that the thirst of developing economies for ever-greater inflows of capital will probably not diminish, it is likely that the hiatus between global finance and matching global regulation will remain, if not grow deeper.

Where does this leave us? Will we be driven out of desperation to muster the collective resolve to create a World Finance Organization through a global treaty? Will we instead see deeper national trenches that restrict global finance and trigger thunder flashes of extraterritorial retaliation? Will we see more efforts at financial freedom like those to which some sponsors of Bitcoin aspire?[98] These are the challenges forming the agenda for reconceptualizing global finance, challenges that will not lessen but only grow more intense while we await the next financial crisis.

---

[98] Bitcoin as a means of securing freedom from government-controlled money is a dream among many Bitcoin supporters. See, e.g., Blog, *Crypto-Anarchy and Libertarian Entrepreneurship – chapter 3: The Killer App of Liberty*, THE MISES CIRCLE, http://themisescircle.org/blog/2013/05/29/crypto-anarchy-and-libertarian-entrepreneurship-chapter-iii/.

I

Global Financial Architecture: Evolution, Shortcomings, Interdependence

4

The Financial Stability Board and the Future of International Financial Regulation

Douglas W. Arner and Michael W. Taylor

BACKGROUND

At the April 2009 London Summit, the Group of Twenty (G20) leading industrialized and emerging economies placed the Financial Stability Board (FSB) at the center of intensified international regulatory cooperation in the wake of the Global Financial Crisis of 2008 (GFC). The FSB was established as the successor to the Financial Stability Forum (FSF), which had in turn been a response to the 1997–98 Asian Financial Crisis. Since its creation by the G7 finance ministers and central bank governors in 1999, the FSF had aimed to promote international financial stability through enhanced information exchange and international cooperation in financial market supervision and surveillance. To this end, it brought together national authorities responsible for financial stability in significant international financial centers, international financial institutions, sector specific international groupings of regulators and supervisors, and committees of central bank experts. However, this coordination mechanism not only failed in building a system of regulation sufficient to prevent the GFC but also wilted in the heat of the GFC. When the cracks in the global financial system began to appear in the first part of 2007, the FSF was, in the words of Paul Blustein, "slow... at discerning the financial system's fragility, and at directing preventive and preparatory action."[1] Later during the crisis, a key meeting had to be abandoned as officials attended to more pressing domestic concerns.[2]

The G20 leaders who reconstituted the FSF as the FSB made a series of changes that were intended to enhance its effectiveness, both from the point of view of

---

[1] Paul Blustein, "How Global Watchdogs Missed A World of Trouble," CIGI Papers, No.5, July 2012, p.8. Blustein stresses that his findings are the result of interviews with "scores of policy makers who worked on the FSF in various capacities, and on thousands of pages of previously undisclosed documents, mostly notes, minutes and confidential summaries of the FSF's meetings," p.6.

[2] Blustein, op. cit., p.21 ("Fiasco in Amsterdam.").

coordinating the policy response to the GFC and identifying financial system fragility in the future. The first was to expand its membership to encompass, in addition to its original members, all G20 nations: Spain, Singapore, Hong Kong, Switzerland, and the European Union (EU). The result was a body which included representatives of economies that accounted for approximately eighty-five percent of global economic output and regulators of the main international financial centers, as well as the international standard setting bodies, such as the Basel Committee on Banking Supervision (BCBS), and relevant international financial institutions, among them the International Monetary Fund (IMF), the World Bank, and the Organisation for Economic Co-operation and Development (OECD).

Secondly, the expanded Financial Stability Board was also granted a significantly enhanced mandate. Although the mandate grew into an extensive list of functions and activities, they can be broadly grouped into three main areas:

1. to assess vulnerabilities affecting the financial system and identify and oversee actions needed to address them;
2. to develop policy, either directly or through coordinating the activities of the international standard setting bodies; and
3. to ensure the effective implementation of international standards.

Most of the specific functions assigned to the FSB related to one or other of these overarching responsibilities, for example, conducting Early Warning Exercises in collaboration with the IMF (responsibility 1); undertaking joint strategic reviews of the policy development work of the international standard setting bodies to ensure their work is timely, coordinated, focused on priorities, and addresses gaps (responsibility 2); and managing contingency planning for cross-border financial firms (responsibility 3).

Despite this extensive range of responsibilities, the FSB, like the various international networks of supervisors that it exists to coordinate, is not a creation of international law. Rather than being the product of a new treaty, the FSB was founded by a Charter[3] which explicitly gave rise to no binding obligations under international law, and is governed by Articles of Association (under Swiss domestic law) that provide a wide-ranging opt-out for its members. Thus the system that was established in 2009 continued to exhibit many of the same features of a soft law international regime that prevailed prior to the GFC. The primary mechanism for ensuring that FSB members would meet the obligations to which they had committed were moral suasion exerted through peer pressure behind closed doors and, in exceptional circumstances, through the public 'naming and shaming' of non-compliant jurisdictions.

---

[3] The Charter was adopted on September 25, 2009, and revised in June 2012. All references are to the 2012 Charter unless otherwise stated. The Charter can be found at www.financialstabil ityboard.org/publications/r_120809.pdf.

On reviewing the initial outlines of the FSB structure, we previously argued that greater institutional backing for the FSB was unlikely to be achievable without moving to a fully treaty-based, hard law solution.[4] While the soft law arrangements had the potential to enhance the ongoing supervision of cross-border financial groups and would lead to generally higher supervisory standards throughout the world, we argued that this type of structure would be unlikely to deliver improvements to one of the major issues for which enhanced coordination was being sought, namely improved crisis-management arrangements and agreements on burden sharing. In the latter case, only a hard law solution, perhaps imposing binding arbitration on the relevant parties, is likely to be effective, but the political will to develop such an approach was not evident at the 2009 G20 London Summit and has not been evident since, despite the advent of the most significant global financial crisis since the 1930s.

With the FSB now having reached its fifth anniversary, and its mode of operation having become clearer in the interim, it is timely to take stock of its achievements to date and to consider the extent to which our initial scepticism about its structure has been justified. In the next section, we examine the FSB in practice, including its decision-making processes and internal structures, as well as the achievements of its work programme to date. The third section of this chapter examines a number of unresolved issues in the composition and functioning of the FSB, and also examines the progress made in finalizing its core policy agenda. We also consider the extent to which its role involves duplication and overlap with other international agencies. In the fourth section, we consider options for the future development of the FSB as well as the potential alternatives, based on a hard law framework, that we considered in our initial review when the FSB was established. Section five concludes.

THE FSB IN PRACTICE

Membership

Like other international coordinating bodies, the FSB has to strike a balance between an inclusive membership and effective decision-making. As an extreme example of inclusiveness trumping effective decision-making is the European Systemic Risk Board (ESRB) that was established to monitor emerging financial stability risks in the European Union following the 2009 Larosiere report. The ESRB has approximately 100 members drawn from the 28 EU member states and relevant EU institutions, although only a minority are able to vote at its meetings.[5]

---

[4] Douglas W. Arner and Michael W. Taylor, "The Global Financial Crisis and the Financial Stability Board: Hardening the Soft Law of International Financial Regulation?" (2009) 32(2) *UNSW Law Journal* 488.

[5] www.esrb.europa.eu/pub/pdf/other/Perm_memb_GB_2014.pdf?73f38b2e5b5af36054001226b9 ba6a8f.

Although the FSB's expanded membership includes ministries of finance, central banks, and regulatory agencies, an unequal allocation of seats among the member countries has helped to keep its size to more manageable limits, thus balancing inclusiveness with effective decision-making more effectively than the ESRB. Nonetheless, the expansion in the membership potentially raised the number of people around the table from about forty-two, in the days of the FSF, to its current seventy, leading to fears that the body might be too large for effective decision-making. The FSB's first chairman, Mario Draghi, attempted to address this concern by establishing a Steering Committee in the spring of 2009 which provided a mechanism for a smaller *Directoire* of members, mainly drawn from the former FSF membership, to set the FSB's agenda and monitor progress. This move was not, however, uncontroversial, resulting in the G20 leaders intervening in 2011 in their Cannes Summit Declaration to request that the "FSB steering committee should include the executive branch of governments of the G20 Chair and the larger financial systems as well as the geographic regions and financial centers not currently represented, in a balanced manner consistent with the FSB Charter." In other words, it would appear that both the finance ministries and the emerging economies newly represented on the FSB were feeling excluded from its decision-making process, and the Steering Committee's membership was expanded to accommodate these concerns. The recomposition has led to an increase of eleven seats on the Steering Committee.[6]

The tension between ensuring that the FSB's membership is sufficiently broadly based to be representative of the global financial system while at the same time being sufficiently small to facilitate effective decision-making is compounded by the unequal representation of member countries noted previously. According to the FSB's website, for example, the United States is represented by the Federal Reserve Board, the Treasury Department, and the Securities and Exchange Commission. China, Japan, France, Germany, Italy, India, and the UK also have three representatives each. Some middle-sized economies, such as the Netherlands and Korea have two members, while most emerging economies (such as South Africa, Saudi Arabia, and Indonesia) were assigned only one representative. According to the FSB's Charter, the "number of seats in the Plenary assigned to Member jurisdictions reflects the size of the national economy, financial market activity and national financial stability arrangements of the corresponding Member jurisdiction."[7] In practice, however, there appears to be a bias in favor of the major economies.

---

[6] FSB "Report to the G20 Los Cabos Summit on Strengthening FSB Capacity, Resources and Governance 18–19 June 2012," p.4. www.financialstabilityboard.org/publications/r_120619c .pdf.

[7] FSB Articles of Association, Article 11 available at www.financialstabilityboard.org/publica tions/r_130128aoa.pdf.

In response to criticisms from some emerging economies that they were disadvantaged by its membership structure, the FSB undertook a review of its representation and presented its recommendations to the G20 heads of government at their November 2014 summit in Brisbane. An April 2014 progress report to the G20 finance ministers and central bank governors had indicated that this review was unlikely to result in fundamental changes in representation, given that the FSB regards its current membership of seventy as "the upper limit" consistent with representativeness and effectiveness, and it declared that there was no appetite either for moving toward a "constituency-based" form of representation or for reducing the countries represented on the FSB.[8] The final report reflected these interim findings and concluded that five emerging markets – Argentina, Indonesia, Saudi Arabia, South Africa, and Turkey – should be assigned a second seat on the Plenary. To ensure no expansion in the overall size of the Plenary, the IMF, World Bank, and three standard setting bodies – the International Organization of Securities Commissions (IOSCO), BCBS, and International Association of Insurance Supervisors (IAIS) – agreed to give up their second seat.[9] The extent to which this move may make the FSB a less effective coordinator of standard setting activities remains to be seen.

However, the review did not address an arguably more serious issue of membership bias, the overrepresentation of EU member states at the expense of the rest of the world. Not only do the larger EU economies (Germany, France, UK, and Italy) each have three seats on the FSB, but European institutions – namely the European Commission and the European Central Bank (ECB) – also have their own seats. With the eurozone member countries having now agreed to hand over the supervision of the largest, most systemically important banks to the ECB, and with regulations increasingly written at the EU level by the European Commission and its specialist agencies (the European Banking Authority, European Insurance and Occupational Pensions Authority, and the European Securities and Markets Authority), there would seem to be a strong case for scaling down the representation of a number of EU member states. However, in the monetary policy field similar arguments have existed since the introduction of the euro in 1999 without it, however, resulting in diminished representation of the relevant states in bodies such as the IMF's Executive Board.

One clear benefit from the membership review was the agreement to "enable non-Member authorities (either from or beyond the Member jurisdictions) to be involved in the work of the FSB's Committees and working groups, either through membership of these bodies or attendance at individual meetings." This agreement

---

[8] Chairman's letter to the G20 finance ministers and central bank governors, April 2014, available at www.financialstabilityboard.org/publications/r_140411.pdf.

[9] Report to the G20 Brisbane Summit on the FSB's review of the structure of its representation, November 2014, available at www.financialstabilityboard.org/wp-content/uploads/Report-to-the-G20-Brisbane-Summit-on-the-FSB's-Review-of-the-Structure-of-its-Representation.pdf.

permits the FSB to offer greater flexibility for institutions other than those that formally represent their countries to take part in standing committees and working groups. An example is allowing agencies which are not formally represented, such as the US Commodity Futures Trading Commission (US CFTC) or the Securities and Futures Commission of Hong Kong (HK SFC), to take part in some working groups that are relevant.

DECISION-MAKING

The effectiveness of decision-making in international forums is in part a function of the level of representation of the member institutions: ideally, the representatives on a body like the FSB should be empowered to give binding commitments on behalf of their institutions without the need to refer back to head office, a practice that would result in substantial delays in achieving agreement on key policy initiatives. The need for its members to be sufficiently empowered to commit their respective institutions is reflected in the FSB's Articles of Association which state that "Representation at the Plenary shall be at the level of central bank governor or immediate deputy; head or immediate deputy of the main supervisory/regulatory agency; and deputy finance minister or deputy head of finance ministry." The Bank of England, for example, was formerly represented by a deputy governor (though now the governor, as chair), and a similar level of representation appears to be the case for several central banks from the larger economies. The level of representation among the emerging economies appears to be higher (e.g., a number of emerging market central bank governors sit on the FSB).[10] It remains unclear, though, whether this arrangement will continue into the future should the imbalance in representation noted previously persist. In addition, as the urgency of reform begins to wane in the post-crisis period, the temptation for most members will be to downgrade their representation given the substantial time commitment involved in attending FSB meetings.

The Articles of Association further state that the FSB's Plenary, its chief decision-making body, operates by "consensus."[11] This implies that agreement of all members is required for major policy decisions, with the result that the FSB is obliged to find common ground among its members before it is able to adopt new policy initiatives. This contrasts with the majority or qualified majority voting processes of other, treaty-based international bodies.[12] Moreover, as Article 3(3) of the Articles of Association makes clear, a member's domestic legal and policy framework has precedence over any decisions or obligations arising from FSB

---

[10] www.financialstabilityboard.org/about/plenary.pdf.
[11] FSB Articles of Association, Article 6.
[12] For example, decisions in the EU's council of ministers are taken by qualified majority, as are decisions in the IMF's Executive Board.

membership, while Article 10 provides an all-encompassing opt-out should any member choose to utilize it:

> The policy making and related activities of the [FSB] shall be governed by the FSB Charter. These activities, including any decisions reached in their context, shall not be binding or give rise to any legal rights or obligations under the present Articles. Members can recuse themselves at any time from these activities or decision-making where such activities or decision-making are not consistent with their legal or policy frameworks.[13]

Thus it would appear that the FSB has no ability to impose binding obligations on its members should it seek to adopt any policies without reaching full consensus (an approach that is sometimes described as "practical consensus" as it avoids the need for complete unanimity and thus prevents any one member from preventing a decision from being reached) and should a dissenting member choose to ignore its decisions. This represents a major limitation on the FSB's ability to discharge the responsibilities placed on it by the G20 leaders, especially when dealing with potentially highly politically sensitive issues such as the distribution of losses in a cross-border bank resolution.

INTERNAL STRUCTURE

The FSB's internal structure largely mirrors the threefold set of responsibilities that we outlined earlier. In addition to the Plenary and the Steering Committee, the FSB has established three Standing Committees that are responsible for conducting vulnerabilities assessments, supervisory and regulatory cooperation, and implementation monitoring, respectively. In addition, one change resulting from the 2012 revision to the Charter was the creation of a standing committee on budget and resources that reflected the growing institutionalization of the FSB (discussed in the next section).

The functions of each of the Standing Committees are set out in the FSB Charter. Article 14 provides that the Standing Committee on Assessment of Vulnerabilities (SCAV) shall have the following functions:

(1) monitor and assess vulnerabilities affecting the global financial system and propose to the Plenary actions needed to address them;

(2) monitor and advise on market and systemic developments, and their implications for regulatory policy; and

(3) provide input for the Early Warning Exercise conducted in collaboration with the IMF.

---

[13] FSB Articles of Association, Article 10.

Article 15 details the functions of the Standing Committee on Supervisory and Regulatory Cooperation (SCSRC) as being to:

(1) address key financial stability issues relating to the development of supervisory and regulatory policy, identify relative priorities, and seek to ensure that the different policy initiatives fit together into a coherent whole;

(2) assist in managing the coordination issues that arise among supervisors and regulators on issues that have cross-sector implications and raise any need for policy development required to close regulatory gaps that pose risk to financial stability;

(3) set guidelines for and oversee the establishment and effective functioning of supervisory colleges; and

(4) advise on and monitor best practice in meeting regulatory standards with a view to ensure consistency, cooperation, and a level playing field across jurisdictions.

Finally Article 16 sets out the functions of the Standing Committee on Standards Implementation (SCSI):

(1) ensure comprehensive and rigorous implementation monitoring of international financial standards, agreed G20 and FSB commitments, recommendations and other initiatives in consultation and coordination with other relevant bodies, through mechanisms such as the Coordination Framework for Implementation Monitoring (CFIM);

(2) undertake peer reviews amongst its members;

(3) report to the Plenary on members' commitments and progress in implementing international financial standards, agreed G20 and FSB commitments, recommendations and other initiatives; and

(4) encourage global adherence to prudential regulatory and supervisory standards, such as through the FSB's Framework for Strengthening Adherence to International Standards.

In addition to these three Standing Committees, the 2013 revision to the FSB's Charter resulted in the creation of a Budget and Resources Committee which is responsible for assessing the resource needs of the FSB Secretariat and developing a medium term budget and resource framework as well as approving an annual budget. This Committee is also empowered to make recommendations to the Plenary for ways of enhancing the sources of the FSB's revenue.[14]

A final tier of FSB committees are the Regional Consultative Groups that bring together FSB and non-FSB members around six geographical regions (the Americas, Asia, Europe, Middle East, Africa, and the Confederation of Independent

---

[14] FSB Charter, Article 17.

States). The function of these Groups, as revealed through the relatively terse press releases issued by the FSB after each meeting, seem to be mainly an opportunity for the FSB to explain its policies and initiatives to non-member countries. It is unclear to what extent these bodies facilitate a genuine dialogue between members and non-members.

GROWING INSTITUTIONALIZATION

The decision to reconstitute the FSF as the FSB left open the question of the body's future status as part of the international financial architecture. Should the FSB be regarded primarily as a crisis-management body that is brought to life only when needed for the purposes of crisis management and coordination or is it intended to become a permanent part of the global financial architecture, the counterpart of the IMF in the field of financial stability and regulation? In the former scenario, the FSB might be mothballed between financial crises, only to be reactivated when the need arises for a more coordinated international effort at crisis management and planning. It would be managed in the interim by a small Secretariat on a care and maintenance basis, although there would need to be clear criteria for determining when the body should be activated. The alternative would be to put the FSB on a permanent footing as an international agency, in which case it would have a large permanent staff, a dedicated funding source, and separate legal personality.

At the G20 Cannes Summit in November 2011, the G20 leaders called for "the establishment of the FSB on an enduring organizational footing." Noting that they had given the FSB a strong political mandate, the leaders recognized the need "to give it a corresponding institutional standing, with legal personality and greater financial autonomy, while preserving the existing and well-functioning strong links with the BIS [Bank for International Settlements]."[15] This commitment pointed in the direction of the second of the two possible models, although it should be noted that a formal treaty would normally be needed to establish a body with these characteristics and the G20 leaders displayed no appetite for engaging on a round of treaty negotiations on financial stability and regulation. The reference to maintaining the existing strong links with the BIS was another indication that the leaders did not – at least at that juncture – envisage making it a full-fledged part of the international financial architecture. The BIS has provided the venue for many of the FSB's meetings, while also providing facilities for the Secretariat, and paying the salaries of most of the Secretariat staff.

Perhaps not surprisingly, therefore, the promised enhancements to the FSB's institutional standing turned out to be relatively modest. Although the G20

---

[15] G20 Cannes Summit Declaration, November 2011, para. 38, available at www.g20.org/sites/default/files/g20_resources/library/Declaration_eng_Cannes.pdf.

St Petersburg summit in September 2013 welcomed "the establishment this year of the FSB as a legal entity with greater financial autonomy and enhanced capacity to coordinate the development and implementation of financial regulatory policies,"[16] in practice very little had appeared to have changed. The FSB itself informed the G20 leaders that it "considers a treaty-based intergovernmental organisation not to be an appropriate legal form at this juncture"[17] although without offering any explanation of its reasons for having drawn this conclusion. A lack of consensus among the members about the role that the FSB should play in the international financial architecture is the most likely explanation for the FSB having invoked that trusty standby of all bureaucrats – "the doctrine of the unripe time."[18]

The FSB's legal personality arises from having been established as an "association by the name of 'Financial Stability Board' ('FSB') (hereinafter 'the Association') ... pursuant to Article 60 of the Swiss Civil Code."[19] Article 60 provides that "Associations with a political, religious, scientific, cultural, charitable, social or other noncommercial purpose acquire legal personality as soon as their intention to exist as a corporate body is apparent from their articles of association." The FSB thus joins bodies such as the International Committee of the Red Cross (ICRC), the International Federation of Football Associations (FIFA), and other nonprofit bodies as being governed under this provision of the Swiss Civil Code. Although many such bodies have an international membership, they are rarely involved in the development and formulation of public policy. The FSB may be – as its current chairman claimed in a speech while still governor of the Bank of Canada – a "post-modern" international financial organization, but it is also *sui generis* in terms of its legal status and standing.

A similar compromise appears to have been at work in determining the FSB's funding. Unlike the IMF, for example, the FSB has no independent source of revenue with which to fund its operations. The option of introducing a membership fee was considered but rejected as the FSB informed the G20 leaders: "The FSB should not introduce a membership fee at this stage for augmenting the resource pool of the FSB."[20] As with the recommendation concerning a treaty-based institution, the rationale for the FSB having taken this position was not explained. Instead, as Article 7 of the Articles of Association makes clear:

[16] G20 St Petersburg Summit Declaration, September 2013, para. 64, available at www.g20 .utoronto.ca/2013/2013–0906-declaration.html#finreg.

[17] FSB "Report to the G20 Los Cabos Summit on Strengthening FSB Capacity, Resources and Governance," para. 11.

[18] So named by F M Cornford in his MICROCOSMOGRAPHIA ACADEMICA (Cambridge: Bowes & Bowes, 1908).

[19] FSB Articles of Association, Article 1 available at www.financialstabilityboard.org/publica tions/r_130128a0a.pdf.

[20] FSB "Report to the G20 Los Cabos Summit on Strengthening FSB Capacity, Resources and Governance," para.14.

"The Association will be funded by the Bank for International Settlements (BIS) on the basis of and in accordance with the terms of a renewable 'Multi-Year Funding Agreement' and by voluntary contributions from Members."[21] One clear implication of this arrangement is that the members could not agree on an alternative funding source, such as a membership fee, which would have provided the FSB with independent funds of its own. Instead, it is directly dependent on one of its member institutions – the BIS – for most of its financial and logistical needs, a unique position for any international body to be in.

As an Association under Swiss law, the FSB is not entitled to the same privileges and immunities normally granted to international organizations by their founding treaties, and to obtain them it would need to enter into a separate agreement with the Swiss authorities. In consequence, the FSB remains beholden to the BIS to obtain the needed immunities by operating as an association under the BIS Headquarters Agreement. The FSB submission to the G20 leaders at their Los Cabos meeting did, however, propose that this arrangement should be revisited after the elapse of five years, holding out the possibility of the FSB negotiating a separate Headquarters Agreement of its own.

FSB WORK PROGRAMME

During the relatively short period of its existence, the FSB has pursued an ambitious policy agenda, first under the chairmanship of Mario Draghi (at the time the governor of the Banca d'Italia, the Italian central bank) and currently under Mark Carney (who was, when appointed, the governor of the Bank of Canada but who became governor of the Bank of England part way through his first term). To a substantial degree the agenda followed by the FSB during this period has reflected the priorities established under the Draghi chairmanship, with Carney aiming to bring these initiatives to a conclusion. Relatively few new initiatives have been commenced under the latter's chairmanship.

The FSB's work programme over the past five years was neatly encapsulated in the Communique issued by the G20 leaders following their summit in St Petersburg in September 2013:

> In the past 5 years, we have made substantial progress in implementing internationally consistent reforms to our financial systems. All major jurisdictions, in part or in full, have:
>
> - implemented new global capital standards (Basel 3);
> - completed the necessary frameworks for OTC derivatives to be traded on exchanges or electronic trading platforms, centrally cleared, and reported;

---

[21] FSB Articles of Association, Article 7, available at www.financialstabilityboard.org/publica tions/r_130128aoa.pdf.

- identified global systemically important banks and insurers, and agreed to subject them to heightened prudential standards to mitigate the risks they pose;
- implemented agreed tools and procedures for the orderly resolution of large, complex financial institutions without taxpayer loss; and
- progressed in addressing potential systemic risks to financial stability emanating from the shadow-banking system.[22]

With the exception of the first of these bullet points, all have been initiatives in which the FSB has taken the lead, either directly or through the coordination of other standard setting bodies. Even with respect to the first of these, the FSB has played a prominent role in ensuring the implementation of Basel III through its implementation monitoring efforts, specifically the Coordination Framework for Implementation Monitoring (CFIM) and its peer reviews of individual members.

It would be beyond the scope of this chapter to assess whether the measures that have been pursued by the FSB are an adequate response to the scale of the GFC, or even if they adequately address some of its principal causes. The fact is that these measures were identified early on in the crisis response as requiring international coordination and the FSB has set out to provide this. The fundamental issue in assessing the FSB's effectiveness as a coordinating body is the extent to which progress has been made in giving effect to the financial system reforms.

In this respect, progress appears to have been patchy. For example, although many jurisdictions have adopted the framework for the central clearing of over-the-counter (OTC) derivatives, there remain a number of unresolved jurisdictional conflicts, despite the FSB's best endeavors. The fundamental issue concerns whether derivatives rules for clearing houses in other jurisdictions are equivalent to those in the host jurisdiction and therefore can be substituted for those of either the EU or the United States, avoiding the need for parties to a derivatives transaction to comply with two overlapping, but not necessarily mutually consistent, sets of rules. At the FSB's behest, the EC and US CFTC agreed to a "path forward" in June 2013, but a year later, as Reuters reported, differences in margining rules were still inhibiting the EC from finding US rules equivalent to its own.[23] While it would be unfair to blame the FSB for this on-going jurisdictional dispute, the fact that it lacks the power to impose a solution on its members to ensure that the international financial system does not become fragmented by conflicting regulations indicates a fundamental weakness in the soft law framework.

Agreeing to a framework for the resolution of cross-border banking groups points to a similar shortcoming in the FSB's ability to make decisions that bind its members. The FSB can point to progress in encouraging member countries to

---

[22] G20 Declaration, St Petersburg, September 2013, para. 61, www.g20.utoronto.ca/2013/2013–0906-declaration.html#finreg.

[23] www.reuters.com/article/2014/06/27/eu-regulations-clearing-idUSL6N0P83L720140627.

adopt the Key Attributes, its set of international standards for bank resolution regimes. Nonetheless, adoption of the Key Attributes in their entirety remains patchy, as the FSB's own peer review revealed. Moreover, the degree of commitment of some members – especially those in Asia – to the new bank resolution framework remains in question.

The patchy adoption of the Key Attributes does not bode well for another major component of the FSB's cross-border resolution regime: the willingness of the authorities in multiple countries to defer to the resolution approach adopted by the authorities in a globally systemically important financial institution's (G-SIFI) home country. This so-called 'Single Point of Entry' approach has been promoted by the Federal Deposit Insurance Corporation (FDIC) and Bank of England, but notwithstanding their in-principle agreement on this resolution approach, considerable doubts remain about how it will be used in practice. Meanwhile, authorities in other countries have fewer incentives to cooperate than the authorities in Britain and the United States, thus bringing into question how widely this resolution approach will be adopted. But without agreeing to binding rules in advance, the temptation will be for authorities to adopt the same *sauve qui peut* strategies that prevailed during the GFC and which the FSB was established, in part, to address.

WHERE NEXT?

Unresolved issues

There are a number of unresolved issues in respect of the FSB's current work as well as in terms of its structure.

In respect of membership, there are certainly concerns regarding whether or not it has the right composition, given the diversity of developed and emerging economies involved. At the same time, while it may (and perhaps should) be possible to add (e.g., as a commitment/demonstration of compliance) or remove members (e.g., for non-compliance), politically it is unlikely that the basic structure can be changed in the short term. Nonetheless, the balance of members remains a concern, given the variance in numbers of seats across members. The seats however are an expression of the institutions which are most directly involved in issues of concern, particularly important given the organization's current soft law nature and therefore necessary to ensure implementation within the context of individual domestic legal mandates and scopes of authority. The likely result is an increase in the numbers of institutions involved (e.g., the US CFTC and HK SFC examples mentioned previously). This brings with it the risk of making the body too large and unwieldy (cf. ESRB), particularly given a consensus-based system.

A related issue concerns in particular the emerging market economy (EME) members. Historically under the FSF, these members were largely seen (and behaved as) standard-takers rather than being involved in setting and directing the agenda and development of technical approaches. In the wake of the GFC, emerging markets aspire to take a larger role given the shifts in the global economy and the relative robustness of their regulatory regimes. At the same time, many developing countries are still largely observers on many issues (such as OTC derivatives) where they feel they have little direct interest or expertise, given the development level of their markets. In this context, some of the regional groups (e.g., Asia) are beginning to become more effective opinion forming mechanisms to reflect EME member interests into the FSB itself. Outside of Asia, however, the regional groups have yet to begin to take a more active approach in seeking to promote regional interests.

In respect of policy issues, there remain real concerns about effectiveness in addressing core post-crisis agenda issues. In the context of addressing G-SIFIs/TBTF (too-big-to-fail), despite substantial progress on the regulatory side (through Basel III in particular), there remain serious issues regarding the effectiveness of crisis-management and resolution mechanisms in the event of any future cross-border financial crisis. In addition, experiences arising in the OTC derivatives context involving extraterritoriality and conflicting domestic approaches to implementation of internationally agreed approaches, significantly weaken effectiveness. Likewise, the combination of divergent approaches to implementation of international standards combined with divergent policy choices in member jurisdictions beyond international agreements (e.g., Volcker, ring-fencing) are raising real issues of market fragmentation and potentially deglobalization (although to date this has not been the explicit objective).

Finally, these policy issues illustrate the challenges in one of the FSB's core mandates: implementation and monitoring. While monitoring (through the FSB itself, the G20, the various standard setting organizations, and the IMF's Financial Sector Assessment Program (FSAP) process) appears to be functioning remarkably well in terms of both participation and identification of issues, without enforcement mechanisms there are limits to the effectiveness of peer pressure and transparency. In addition, the various review processes are constant taxes on the resources of both the FSB and its members (of all sorts).

POSSIBLE APPROACHES

It is thus clear that even without major structural changes, there are issues which must be addressed for the FSB in its current guise. Certainly, the question of whether the FSB should be a crisis-management task force only or a permanent body now appears to be firmly answered: it is a permanent body addressing both crisis prevention as well as crisis management. Nonetheless, this is a major agenda for a soft law body, even a "hardened" one such as the FSB which remains far from an embryo international organization. Likewise, the FSB must balance coordination and policy experimentation: how much regulatory competition or experimentation is necessary or beneficial versus potentially harmful (through regulatory arbitrage, insufficient regulation, or excessive restriction). Finally, there remain legitimacy issues, particularly in Asia, with some viewing the organization as largely US and EU dominated and reflecting their interests (when in agreement) or divisions (when not), to the detriment of the very different needs and objectives (in many cases, though certainly not in respect of basic agreement regarding the importance of financial stability) in Asia and perhaps in EMEs generally.

ALTERNATIVES

In our previous analysis, we reviewed a range of options for strengthening the system of international regulation post-GFC. To date, probably the most appealing mechanisms outside of treaty reform would focus on hardening the FSB's soft law framework through the development of a comprehensive multilateral memorandum of understanding, comparable to that to which IOSCO members subscribe, which would involve the signatories accepting a number of demanding obligations with respect to regulatory information sharing and cooperation. This could cover the full scope of the FSB charter and would thus provide a mechanism to add in new members (as they demonstrate the necessary legal powers and authorizations to meet all obligations) and also to remove members for non-compliance. A further option would be to expand the BIS's mandate and powers to subsume the FSB's functions. The advantage would be that the BIS structure could be applied to the FSB, hardening it into a formal international organization albeit one between nonstate entities. However, given the membership (both government agencies – such as ministries of finance – and treaty-based international and regional organizations), such a structure would be technically challenging within the BIS's existing legal framework. Indeed, as it would require the BIS membership to expand beyond central banks, to include ministries of finance as well as regulatory agencies, this means the option is a likely nonstarter for political reasons, even if the technical challenges could be overcome. Moreover, given the lack of resources of regulatory agencies outside of central banks and ministries of finance, this is not likely to address some of the core issues addressed previously.

Remaining options probably all require a treaty-based approach, with all of the challenges which this entails and which are in fact the central reason why soft law approaches have proliferated in recent decades. Given that a treaty-based approach (whether for a new organization or to address specific issues such as resolution) has not proven possible in the wake of the GFC (although it has in the context of the EU in the wake of the eurozone debt crisis of 2010), it seems unlikely to be any more viable today, as interests increasingly fragment between G20 members. However, an eventual move to a treaty-based framework may be inevitable, as has been the experience in the EU in moving to the Single Supervisory Mechanism and Single Resolution Mechanism when soft law approaches based around informal groups of regulators failed to address fundamental issues of coordination.

CONCLUSION

Overall, despite some achievements, especially in the immediate aftermath of the crisis, we feel that in its present guise the FSB still falls some way short of addressing the policy issues identified by the crisis. Although the FSB will continue to evolve, like the FSF before it, the early promise and expectations seem unlikely to be realized. Without a sense of common crisis, the effectiveness of a consensus-based body is likely to decrease over time. With the impetus provided by the crisis having now dissipated, there seems little prospect of moving toward a hard law structure in the short- to medium-term, but it may be that only such a structure can ultimately provide the secure foundations needed by a global financial system, as has been the case in the regional context as demonstrated by the EU experience. As a result, it may well take yet another crisis in order to move to the next stage, as in fact was the case in the EU. In the regional context, other regions are now grappling with the lessons of the EU experience and seeking to build arrangements that – while not like those of the EU – are able to address the conflict between open financial markets and financial stability. These over time may yield additional experiences to inform the global level. At the same time, given the now clear direction to move forward with alternatives to the IMF in the wake of both China's continuing rise and also in the wake of the continued US failure to ratify agreed changes to the organization, there may yet be scope for the development of hard law alternatives.

5

Financial Regulation's Overlooked Networks

David Zaring

INTRODUCTION

In international financial regulation, some of the organizations that make financial regulatory policy have been celebrated more than others. Reams of scholarship have been produced about the Basel Committee on Banking Supervision, for example, and IOSCO has enjoyed plenty of press as well. David Singer's well-received book on the development of international financial regulation has focused on those two regulatory networks, along with IAIS, the international organization of insurance supervisors.[1] Ethan Kapstein has also focused on the Basel Committee in his own book-length work.[2] And Tony Porter has also concentrated on those organizations as well.[3] Tim Buthe and Walter Mattli have also written on the IAIS as well as the International Organization for Standardization and the International Electrotechnical Commission.[4] These examples, of course, constitute a limited sample; they are book-length treatments written by international relations scholars. My own work has focused on the same regulatory networks, although not entirely (but certainly largely), with only passing mention of the others that contribute to the regulatory enterprise. A similar focus may be attributed to other network scholarship in law reviews.[5]

---

[1] DAVID ANDREW SINGER, REGULATING CAPITAL: SETTING STANDARDS FOR THE INTERNATIONAL FINANCIAL SYSTEM (Cornell University Press, Cornell Studies in Money Ser., 2010).

[2] ETHAN B. KAPSTEIN, SUPERVISING INTERNATIONAL BANKS: ORIGINS AND IMPLICATIONS OF THE BASLE ACCORD (Princeton Univ. Int'l Econ., Essays in Int'l Fin. Ser., 1991).

[3] TONY PORTER, STATES, MARKETS AND REGIMES IN GLOBAL FINANCE (St. Martin's Press 1993).

[4] TIM BÜTHE AND WALTER MATTLI, THE NEW GLOBAL RULERS: THE PRIVATIZATION OF REGULATION IN THE WORLD ECONOMY (Princeton University Press 2011).

[5] See Douglas W. Arner and Michael W. Taylor, The Global Financial Crisis and the Financial Stability Board: Hardening the Soft Law of International Financial Regulations, 32(2) U. NEW S. WALES 488 (2009) (focusing on the role and effectiveness of the FSB), Emiliio Avgouleas, Rationales and Designs to Implement an Institutional Big Bang in the Governance of Global Finance, 36 SEATTLE U. L. REV. 321 (2013) (discussing Basel, IOSCO and the IMF with

But this attention, while largely warranted, can miss other important contributions to the networked form of financial regulation. This paper reviews the accomplishments of the networks that form the periphery, rather than the core, of financial regulation, and sites them into the larger context of international financial regulation. It organizes their role around their role in the signature post-crisis regulatory institution. The new Financial Stability Board (FSB) has created a "Compendium of Standards" that looks to the core principles from networks other than the Basel Commission, IOSCO, and IAIS that it views as fundamental for a well-working system of financial oversight.[6] It has offered membership to other networks as well.[7] These networks have played important roles in the regulation of money laundering, deposit insurance, and other subjects. In light of the incorporation of these institutions into the architecture of financial administration, it is perhaps worth focusing on what it is they do and how they do it.

The existence of so many financial regulatory institutions, even if some are quite small and may amount to little more than task forces within the ambit of the Basel Committee, suggests that financial regulation still remains a task-specific, disaggregated enterprise. Consider, for example, deposit insurance. It is conceivable that the Basel Committee or IAIS could develop principles for effective deposit insurance; it contributes to financial stability, which is the raison d'être of the Basel Committee, and it is also, of course, an insurance product which insurance supervisors, one would imagine, understand. The fact that they have not done so is a testament to, even in the most organized of jurisdictions, the regulatory fragmentation of financial oversight.[8]

---

reference to the financial crisis), Chris Brummer, *How International Financial Law Works (And How it Doesn't)*, 99 GEO. L.J. 257 (2011), Ross Buckley, *Reforming the International Monetary Fund*, 3 GLOBAL POLICY 102 (2012), Eric J. Pan, *Challenge of International Cooperation and Institutional Design in Financial Supervision: Beyond Transgovernmental Networks*, 11 CHI. J. INT'L L. 243 (2010), Pierre-Hugues Verdier, *The Political Economy of International Financial Regulation*, 88 IND. L. J. 1405 (2013), David Zaring, *Best Practices*, 81 N.Y.U. L. REV. 294 (2006); Maximillian L. Feldman, Note, *The Domestic Implementation of International Regulations*, 88 N.Y.U. L. REV. 401 (2013).

[6] *See About the Compendium of Standards*, FIN. STABILITY BD., www.financialstabilityboard .org/cos/index.htm (last visited Nov. 21, 2013) (describing the Compendium of Standards as a "list[of] the various economic and financial standards – by both subject area and issuing body – that are internationally accepted as important for sound, stable and well-functioning financial systems"); *Compendium of Standards – Issuing Body – Last 5 Years*, FIN. STABILITY BD., www.financialstabilityboard.org/list/fsb_cos_issuing_body/index.htm (last visited Nov. 21, 2013) (listing the various standards that comprise the Compendium of Standards by issuing body).

[7] *See, e.g., Links to FSB Members*, FIN. STABILITY BD., www.financialstabilityboard.org/ members/links.htm (last visited Nov. 21, 2013) (listing as members of the FSB "[i]nternational standard-setting bodies" including the Committee on the Global Financial System (CGFS), the Committee on Payment and Settlement Systems (CPSS), and the International Accounting Standards Board (IASB), among others).

[8] Instead, Basel has worked with the deposit insurance network, instead of supplanting it. The Basel Committee and the International Association of Deposit Insurers (IADI) have released Core Principles for Effective Deposit Insurance Systems. *Core Principles for Effective Deposit*

We also see some evidence that financial regulatory networks remain lean, with tiny budgets and little capacity to add new functions to their extant roles.[9] Instead, new networks are spun off from the old ones, beginning perhaps as task forces and developing into their own low-key cross-border enterprises.

The networks themselves form more ground-level supervision and are consistent with my view of the increasing development of the financial regulatory space into something that looks like a transnational disaggregated agency. They fill in the gaps of the new regulatory regime, offering briefer, and issue-specific, sets of principles and opportunities for meetings meant to foster the exchange of ideas, and the transnational development of regulatory expertise. They also underscore the increasing elaboration of the transnational financial regulatory regime.

In what follows, I begin with an overview of my perspective on increasing legalization and the agency-like nature of international financial regulation. I posit that its architecture, featuring increasing regularity and understandability, is a legal effort. I then review six networks, all of which play a role in the FSB's new standard-setting enterprise, and three of which are members of the board itself. For each, I discuss their principal standard-setting accomplishment and investigate their organization. The goal is to provide a factual basis for the claim that financial regulatory networks often look almost identical. They are leanly staffed, rely on their members for personnel, have small budgets, and serve as conduits for the exchange of information, and often, as an initial matter, the development of core principles. Identifying these common developments in the organization and accomplishments of each network runs the risk of repetition. Nonetheless, little attention is being paid to for the networks discussed here as part of the architecture of financial regulation, and collecting their organization and accomplishments in the space of one chapter may serve as its own contribution.

BACKGROUND

Above all, these networks contribute to an emerging architecture that I have defined and explained in other work.[10] The old efforts to deal with the cross-border externalities of finance, which were limited in their ambition and breadth,

---

Insurance Systems – Final Paper, BANK FOR INT'L SETTLEMENTS, www.bis.org/publ/bcbs156 .htm (last visited Dec. 3, 2013).

[9] The International Association of Deposit Insurers, for example, had a total operating revenue of less than $1.3 million USD for the fiscal year ended March 31, 2012 – one-third of which constituted a contribution from BIS. IADI, 2011/2012 ANNUAL REPORT 32, *available at* www.iadi.org/annual_reports/IADI_AnnualReport_2011-low.pdf (reported in Swiss Francs; converted using December 3, 2013 Bloomberg conversion ratio of 1:1057). BIS, on the other hand, had about $1.35 billion in operating income for the same time period. BANK FOR INT'L SETTLEMENTS, 83RD ANNUAL REPORT 2012/2013 127 (June 23, 2013), *available at* www.bis.org/ publ/arpdf/ar2013e.pdf (reported in Special Drawing Rights currency; converted using December 3, 2013 International Monetary Fund conversion ratio of 1:53439).

[10] *See, e.g.*, David Zaring, *Rulemaking and Adjudication in International Law*, 46 COLUM. J. TRANS. L. 563 (2008).

have been reformed in the wake of the financial crisis. Instead, a new order that is hierarchical, procedurally regular, and politically supervised has emerged. This new order pervades the Basel Committee, IOSCO, and IAIS in particular, but also very much applies to the more interstitial outfits that have won less fame in the scholarly literature.

Those values, of course, are the values of the administrative state. Elsewhere, I have argued that the political supervision, increasingly regularized output, and bureaucratic order make international financial regulation look increasingly like an administrative agency stretched into a global multilateral context.[11]

This "agencification" creates a two-step process toward legal obligation. The international context of financial regulation, where the policy is made, is the first step of the process – it is the policy formulation step, and it imposes no binding obligations on anyone. Those obligations come, if at all, after the international process has ended, and financial regulators have returned to their countries to go through the processes that make domestic administrative rules binding law, the second step.

But this hardly makes the international part of international financial regulation superfluous. In fact, the first step in international financial regulation is the particularly interesting one. It is the source of the principles of international financial regulation and the starting point for any significant effort. It has added hierarchy, structure, and distributional consequence to regulatory efforts since the financial crisis.

Post-crisis financial regulation has resulted in institutionalization along hierarchical lines, with a political overseer, a regulatory supervisor, and a group of task-specific but increasingly coordinated regulatory networks making the rules for banks, capital markets participants, insurers, and other financial intermediaries. What those regulators do, moreover, is both procedurally regular and increasingly explicable with resort to organizing principles that mimic the fundamental principles espoused by hard law international organizations like the World Trade Organization and the European Union.

The transformation of international financial regulation has not only been a matter of the imposition of procedural regularity, bureaucratization, and a degree of political oversight, but the added legal dimension has also helped to define the enterprise. As part of this post-crisis reform, there is an identifiable commitment to a variety of legal principles that undergird the particular regulatory decisions made in international financial regulation. At least six such principles can be identified in the organization and institutionalization of the post-crisis financial

---

[11] *See, e.g.,* David Zaring, *Finding Legal Principle in Global Financial Regulation,* 52 VA. J. INT'L L. 685 (2012) (arguing that, international regulatory cooperation in the financial industry is developing along parallel lines to domestic agencies and that this development can be described in terms of six fundamental legal principles).

regulatory settlement.[12] Although many of these principles are rooted in the cooperation extant before the financial crisis, it is with the flurry of activity after the crisis that has brought them to the fore.[13]

The legal principles include a commitment to *national treatment*, meaning that domestic and foreign financial intermediaries should be subject to roughly similar rules within a single jurisdiction, and a *most favored nation* principle identifiable through the consensus practices of the organizations. These principles are institutionalized through *rulemaking*, rather than adjudication – international financial regulation sets its standards in advance and without the assistance of a tribunal. Those standards are then administered through adherence to a principle of *subsidiarity*, whereby each agency engaged in the global financial regulatory architecture is charged with implementing the rules and standards agreed to internationally in its own domestic jurisdiction without direct international supervision. That subsidiarity is paired with a *peer review* process meant to check the implementation decisions of member agencies in lieu of a third-party dispute resolution such as that offered by the international tribunal. Finally, international financial regulation has organized itself according to the *network* form, as demonstrated by each of the less-well known networks.

THE OVERLOOKED NETWORKS

There are two important ways that the overlooked regulatory networks have been integrated into this new order of international financial regulation. First, some of them have been integrated into that order through membership in the FSB.[14] The Committee on the Global Financial System, and the less esoteric and more practical Committee on Payment and Settlement Systems, are examples of these sorts of networks. They have been joined on the FSB by the International Accounting Standards Board, an important network that includes private participants as

---

[12] Elsewhere, I have similarly argued that financial regulatory reform can be described in terms of these six principles. *See, e.g., id.*

[13] *Id.* at 686 (noting that the inadequate response of existing networks to the financial crisis set the stage for the future reform of the network model); *cf.* Elizabeth F. Brown, *The Development of International Norms for Insurance Regulation*, 34 BROOK. J. INT'L L. 953, 956 (2009) (discussing international regulation of insurance markets and citing as one of the sources of regulation network-created principles or guidelines); Pierre-Hugues Verdier, *Mutual Recognition in International Finance*, 52 HARV. INT'L L.J. 55 (2011) (examining one of the principles epitomizing international financial regulation in the wake of the financial crisis, mutual recognition, and exploring its benefits and drawbacks and applications to other contexts); Yesha Yadav, *The Specter of Sisyphus: Re-Making International Financial Regulation After the Global Financial Crisis*, 24 EMORY INT'L L. REV. 83 (2010) (analyzing international financial regulatory mechanisms during the global financial crisis and proposing considerations for reform).

[14] *See Links to FSB Members*, FIN. STABILITY BD., www.financialstabilityboard.org/members/links.htm (last visited Dec. 8, 2013).

well as public overseers, which is attempting to devise a global set of standards for accounting returns. These less well-known networks are also joined by the Basel committee, IOSCO, and IAIS on the Board, along with various G 20 member agencies, and the European Commission, the International Monetary Fund, the OECD, and the World Bank.[15]

The other way that networks play a role in the new financial architecture is by providing a set of standards that is endorsed by the FSB and, in turn, the G 20 as appropriate minimum metrics of effective financial supervision.

The Committee on the Global Financial System, the Committee on Payment and Settlement Systems, the Financial Action Task Force, the International Association of Deposit Insurers, and the International Auditing Insurance Standards Board, are examples of these kinds of networks.

Like all networks, these networks offer basic principles to which all of their members are supposed to commit themselves. Such principles are generally broad, and are one of the first accomplishments of most regulatory networks.

By being taken up by the FSB, the overlooked networks have demonstrated their attractiveness to regulators concerned with the systemic stability of the financial system. It is accordingly useful to spend some time discerning how these networks do their job.

The Quiet Standard Setters

Many overlooked networks that now participate in the project of international financial regulation draw their strength from two kinds of endorsements by the FSB. Some provide standards that have been endorsed by the board, while others have been invited to join it.

The Board has created a so-called "Compendium of Standards" that it characterizes as "internationally accepted as important for sound, stable, and well-functioning financial systems."[16] The standards are meant to "strengthen domestic financial systems by encouraging sound regulation" and improve "international financial stability by facilitating better informed lending and investment decisions, improving market integrity, and reducing the risks of financial distress and contagion."[17] The board identified twelve policy areas that it views as "key for sound financial systems and deserving of priority implementation."[18] Some of these principles are provided by networks that do little else – the International Auditing

---

[15] *Id.*

[16] *About the Compendium of Standards*, Fin. Stability Board, www.financialstabilityboard.org/cos/ (last visited Dec. 4, 2013).

[17] *Why Are Standards Important?*, Fin. Stability Board, www.financialstabilityboard.org/cos/wasi.htm (last visited Dec. 4, 2013).

[18] *Key Standards for Sound Financial Systems*, Fin. Stability Board, www.financialstabilityboard.org/cos/key_standards.htm (last visited Dec. 4, 2013).

and Assurance Standards Board and International Association of Deposit Insurers are examples of those sorts of networks.

We see in both the telltale models of network organization, devised for the purpose of coordinating regulatory approaches and developing best practices for more obscure parts of the financial regulatory system.

International Association of Deposit Insurers

The International Association of Deposit Insurers has become the principle forum for deposit insurers across the globe.[19] Like most networks, it facilitates the gathering of knowledge and the sharing of expertise, in its case, on the subject of deposit insurance – a component of financial stability that was, for many years, by no means widespread, and even today, is much less central to many countries than it is to the United States. The IADI is accordingly not a large network, featuring agencies from only those countries that offer deposit insurance to their citizens, or, less actively, those that are considering doing so.[20]

The number of jurisdictions considering deposit insurance has increased in the wake of the financial crisis. One of the principal functions of deposit insurance is to prevent customer panics that destabilize the financial system. Deposit insurance gives depositors comfort that their funds are not at risk, even if the economy is insalubrious or there are more particular concerns over the continued viability of any particular bank. By the network's calculations, over 100 countries have some form of deposit insurance – a number dramatically in excess of the fewer than a dozen that had deposit insurance in 1974 (and a claim that appears to come perilously close to overstatement).[21] Europe, via the European Union, had adopted deposit insurance requirements that were meant to apply to all member countries in its 1994 directive by the European Parliament and the council.[22] Nonetheless, during the financial crisis, the quality and extent of deposit insurance was thought to be one of the regrettable features of the financial systems of a variety of jurisdictions.

Deposit insurance works, at least usually, through dues paid by insured financial institutions to a government-run deposit insurer.[23] The insurer, in turn, tries to

---

[19] Wally Suphap, *Toward Effective Risk-Adjusted Bank Deposit Insurance: A Transnational Strategy*, 42 COLUM. J. TRANSNAT'L L. 829, 855 (2004) (noting that, while there is not global deposit insurance oversight organization, the IADI is the largest, and seemingly most active, of its type).

[20] *See How to Join IADI*, INT'L ASS'N OF DEPOSIT INSURERS, www.iadi.org/aboutIADI.aspx?id=49 (last visited Dec. 9, 2013).

[21] *Deposit Insurance Systems Worldwide*, INT'L ASS'N OF DEPOSIT INSURERS, www.iadi.org/iadi_members.html (last visited Dec. 12, 2013).

[22] Council Directive 94/19/EC 1994 O.J. (L 135) 5–14 (EC).

[23] Edward J. Kane and Asli Demirguc-Kunt, *Deposit Insurance Around the Globe: Where Does it Work?* 7 (Nat'l Bureau of Econ. Research, Working Paper No. 8493, 2001), *available at* www.nber.org/papers/w8493.

make sure that financial institutions are operated relatively safely and soundly. In the United States, the FDIC plays this regulatory role – it scrutinizes the stability of the banks that it insures, but it also plays the role of a balance sheet-obsessed corporation, in that it collects dues, marshals a fund, and pays out upon insolvencies.[24] The FDIC, unlike every deposit insurer, also plays a role in taking insolvent financial institutions through bankruptcy. The fund guarantees the deposits of consumers, and quickly marshals the assets of the bank to sell them off to an acquirer or wind up operations as quickly as possible.

IADI was founded on May 6, 2002,[25] and is based, like the Basel Committee, IAIS, the Committee on Payment Systems, and others, at the Bank for International Settlements in Basel, Switzerland.[26] With the assistance of the Basel Committee on Banking Supervision, IADI has developed joint core principles for effective deposit insurance systems – principles to which all seventy-one of its member organizations[27] are supposed to commit. Those principles were promulgated on June 18, 2009.[28]

The IADI, like many networks, is governed by an executive council.[29] It has a tiny secretariat and does much of its work, as do other networks, through standing committees. While only deposit insurance organizations can become IADI "members," the association also invites other organizations in countries that are considering developing deposit insurance systems to participate as "associates"[30]; the goal is one of proselytization, as well as the exchange of information. The association also allows other not-for-profit entities that have a direct interest in the effectiveness of deposit insurance system to be involved as "observers"[31]; this may be a function not only of stakeholder participation, but also of fundraising. IADI, like other low-key networks, have little access to funding; membership fees and registration fees to the annual meeting are part of the fundraising effort.[32] Other

---

[24] *Deposit Insurance Summary*, Fed. Deposit ins. Corp., www.fdic.gov/deposit/deposits/dis/ (last visited Dec. 12, 2013).

[25] *History*, Int'l Ass'n of Deposit Insurers, www.iadi.org/aboutIADI.aspx?id=45 (last visited Dec. 3, 2013).

[26] Int'l Ass'n of Deposit Insurers, www.iadi.org/ (last visited Dec. 3, 2013).

[27] *Overview of the Association*, Int'l Ass'n of Deposit Insurers, www.iadi.org/aboutIADI.aspx?id=48 (last visited Dec. 12, 2013).

[28] Press Release, Bank for Int'l Settlements, Core Principles for Effective Deposit Insurance Systems: Paper Issued by Basel Committee and IADI (June 18, 2009), *available at* www.bis.org/press/p090618.htm.

[29] Statutes of the International Association of Deposit Insurers 7 (Revised Oct. 25, 2012) [hereinafter IADI Statutes], *available at* www.iadi.org/aboutiadi.aspx?id=71; *see also* Int'l Ass'n of Deposit Insurers, 2011–2012 Annual Report 18, *available at* www.iadi.org/annual_reports/IADI_AnnualReport_2011-low.pdf.

[30] *How to Join IADI*, *supra* note 20.

[31] *Id.*

[32] Article 5 of the IAID statutes lists among as its "financial resources" the initial fund contribution by its members, the annual fee collected from participants; and donations, grants or other sources of revenue. IADI Statutes, *supra* note 29, at 5. Beginning in the 2009–2010 fiscal year,

organizations that have cooperative arrangements with IADI are considered "partners" – they work with IADI to further the association's objectives.[33]

Unlike other regulatory networks, the IADI does not maintain a monopoly on issuing guiding principles. It has endorsed guidance developed by IADI members and third parties like APEC and the Financial Stability Forum, making clear that at least part of what it does is to serve as an information clearinghouse.[34]

Although IADI is not a member of the FSB, its published principles and guidance papers have been designated by the FSB as standards that help to stabilize national and international financial systems. In fact, the Core Principles for Effective Deposit Insurance Systems is listed by the FSB as part of its CoS.[35]

The deposit insurance core principles were developed with the assistance of the Basel Committee and reflect a commitment to a series of preconditions for deposit insurance, and some principles for their use. As the network has said, "[a] deposit insurance system will be most effective if a number of external elements or preconditions are in place."[36] These preconditions are aspirational, and include incontestable values like macroeconomic stability, strong prudential regulation, and sound governmental agencies. No one is against those sorts of policies, and so it is difficult to know how constraining they are meant to be.

Once in place, however, the network has developed some principles that are meant to be assessed by outsiders, and understandable by jurisdictions hoping to implement deposit insurance. These principles are broad in their own right, but include some requirements and checklists that do in fact constrain agencies. For example, in its enhanced guidance papers, the network outlines specific procedures that deposit insurers must take in setting coverage levels and primary methods for

---

dues were payable in Swiss Francs (CHF). *How to Join the IADI, supra* note 20. Members pay an initial fund contribution of CHF 11,390 (approximately $12,732 USD as of December 2013) and an annual fee of the same amount; Associates and Observers pay an initial fund contribution of CHF 5,695 (approximately $6,366 USD) and an annual fee of CHF 8,542.50 (approximately $9,549 USD) and partners pay no fees. *Id.* The 2011–2012 IADI annual report indicated that the organization had collected CHF 784,487 ($876,914 USD) as of fiscal year end March 31, 2012. INT'L ASS'N OF DEPOSIT INSURERS, 2011–2012 ANNUAL REPORT, *supra* note 29, at 28. The annual fee for the 2013 IADI annual conference, held in November 2013 in Buenos Aires, Argentina, was $850 USD per delegate. Letter from Int'l Ass'n of Deposit Insurers to IAIDI Members, Support Staff, and Colleagues, *available at* www.iadi.org/docs/Dear%20IADI%20Members%20and%20Support%20staff_AGM%20Notice.pdf (last visited December 18, 2013).

[33] *Overview of the Association*, INT'L ASS'N OF DEPOSIT INSURERS, www.iadi.org/aboutIADI.aspx?id=48 (last visited Dec. 5, 2013).

[34] *IADI Research and Guidance Papers*, INT'L ASS'N OF DEPOSIT INSURERS, www.iadi.org/Research.aspx?id=55 (last visited Dec. 5, 2013).

[35] *Key Standards for Sound Financial Systems, supra* note 18.

[36] BASEL COMM. ON BANKING SUPERVISION AND INT'L ASS'N OF DEPOSIT INSURERS, CORE PRINCIPLES FOR EFFECTIVE DEPOSIT INSURANCE SYSTEMS: A METHODOLOGY FOR COMPLIANCE ASSESSMENT 5 (Dec. 2010) [hereinafter BASEL AND IADI, CORE PRINCIPLES], *available at* www.bis.org/publ/bcbs192.pdf.

reducing moral hazards in the deposit insurance context.[37] For example, the principles start out as broad proclamations of deposit insurance objectives like "the stability of the financial system and [the protection of] depositors" as well as the importance of "appropriate design features and ... other elements of the financial system safety net" in mitigating moral hazards.[38] The deposit insurer is required to "be operationally independent, transparent, accountable and insulated from undue political and industry influence."[39] The principles also address more specific procedures like mandatory membership for "all financial institutions accepting deposits from those deemed most in need of protection (e.g. [sic] retail and small business depositors) to avoid adverse selection" and primary role of banks in paying for deposit insurance "since they and their clients directly benefit from having an effective deposit insurance system."[40]

In addition, the principles also speak in more specific terms of characteristics of an effective deposit insurance system. For one, they discuss the drawbacks of a "blanket guarantee" of deposits and the desirability of a quick transition within countries from blanket guarantee to limit guarantee systems.[41] They also advise regulators to ensure the necessary funding is in place to support a deposit insurance system, and counsel that "[p]rimary responsibility for funding the deposit insurance system [should be] borne by member banks and [ideally] is enforceable by the deposit insurer."[42] Finally, the principles recommend that legal protection against lawsuits should be afforded to "[t]he deposit insurer and individuals working for the deposit insurer ... for their decisions and actions taken in 'good faith' while discharging their mandates," but that those individuals should also be required to adhere to applicable conflict-of-interest rules and codes of conduct.[43]

IADI looks like a lot of other networks, only with a relatively narrow issue area. It shows the prevalence of the network form in the financial regulatory space, and the consistency that characterizes the evolution of that form.

International Auditing and Assurance Standards Board

If IADI represents a relatively small network of financial insurers with quasigovernmental roles, the IAASB is an ethics regulator. As an ethics regulator, the board

---

[37] *See, e.g.*, INT'L ASS'N OF DEPOSIT INSURERS, ENHANCED GUIDANCE FOR EFFECTIVE DEPOSIT INSURANCE SYSTEMS: MITIGATING MORAL HAZARD (May 2013), *available at* www.iadi.org/docs/ IADI_Mitigating_Moral_Hazard_Enhanced_Guidance_2013–05.pdf. For more enhanced guidance papers providing guidance on a variety of areas relating to developing sound deposit insurance systems, see *IADI Research and Guidance Papers*, www.iadi.org/Research.aspx? id=55 (last visited Dec. 18, 2013).

[38] BASEL AND IADI, CORE PRINCIPLES, *supra* note 36, at 10.

[39] *Id.* at 12.

[40] BASEL AND IADI, CORE PRINCIPLES, *supra* note 36, at 15, 18.

[41] *Id.* at 17.

[42] *Id.* at 18.

[43] *Id.* at 20.

validates the profession-like status of the accounting industry. Ethics regulators of the professions define and police malpractice, the sine qua non of professional status – MBA programs and consultancies often regret the lack of a malpractice sanction; they worry that it is a sign that business management and consultancy is not a profession.

The predecessor to the IAASB, the International Auditing Practices Committee (IAPC) was founded in March, 1978.[44] It published the International Standards on Auditing (ISAs) in 1991.[45] Today, the IAASB attempts to set "high quality" international standards for auditing and quality control, and, accordingly, that auditing practices (rather than accounting standards, which are the province of the very important IASB discussed *infra*) are followed in a generally similar manner.[46] To facilitate this process, the IAASB began what it calls the Clarity Project in 2004 with the goal to update and clarify the ISAs – integrating new drafting conventions, eliminating possible ambiguities, and "improving the overall readability and understandability of the ISAs."[47]

It reports to a group of auditing practice supervisors, themselves grouped as a network known as the Public Interest Oversight Board (PIOB).[48] The PIOB is meant to ensure that the IAASB to follow some degree of due process and to act in ways consistent to the public interest.[49] And so standards of conduct for accountants are the product of the IAASB (and, for that matter, the PIOB, which is more explicitly comprised of government supervisors of accountants). As such, the IAASB publishes an annual handbook that summarizes new standards and pronouncements pertaining to international audits and quality control.[50] Additionally, the organization also develops specialized standards for specific auditor functions. The IAASB has developed, for example, the ISAE 3000 assurance standards to provide for how an engagement of assurance may be carried out[51] and ISAE 3420 that

---

[44] *About IAASB*, Int'l Fed'n of Accountants, www.ifac.org/auditing-assurance/about-iaasb (last visited Dec. 18, 2013).

[45] *Id.*

[46] *Id.*

[47] *Clarity Center*, Int'l Fed'n of Accountants, www.ifac.org/auditing-assurance/clarity-center (last visited Dec. 5, 2013).

[48] Int'l Auditing and Assurance Standards Bd., 2012 Annual Report 3 [hereinafter IAASB, 2012 Report], *available at* www.ifac.org/sites/default/files/publications/files/IAASB%20ANNUAL-2012-V10-SPREADS.pdf.

[49] *Id.*

[50] *See, e.g.,* Int'l Auditing and Assurance Standards Bd., 2013 Handbook of International Quality Control, Auditing, Review, Other Assurance, and Related Services Pronouncements (Sept. 19, 2013) [hereinafter IAASB, 2013 Handbook], *available at* www.ifac.org/publications-resources/2013-handbook-international-quality-control-auditing-review-other-assurance-a.

[51] Int'l Auditing and Assurance Standards Bd., International Standard On Assurance Engagements 3000, *available at* www.google.com/url?sa=tandrct=jandq=andesrc=sand source=webandcd=1andcad=rjaandved=0CDEQFjAAandurl=http%3A%2F%2Fwww.ifac.org %2Fsites%2Fdefault%2Ffiles%2Fpublications%2Ffiles%2FB005%25202013%2520IAASB%2520

prescribes how report on the compilation of pro forma financials included in a prospectus.[52] The IAASB in this sense is a global professional organization for accountants. Its principal achievement has been defining the objectives and scope of the audit of financial statements, an ongoing process with multiple rounds of comments and drafts.[53] Again, all countries interested in passing IMF FSAP scrutiny has to adopt these principles.

In adopting new standards, the IAASB follows a traditional notice and comment process in developing and adopting new standards.[54] It tends to begin with a consultation process involving stakeholders. Then the draft of a pronouncement is posted on the organization website and comments are invited.[55] Eventually, final pronouncements are published, along with a summary of comments received.[56] In addition to this "rigorous due process," the IAASB aspires toward transparency.[57] All meetings are open to the public and all relevant papers, along with audio recordings of those meetings, are published on the website.

The auditing standards are meant to be professional standards that would apply to auditors. They are meant to be "high-quality international standards for auditing, quality control, review, other assurance, and related services."[58] For example, the ISA regarding audit documentation requires the auditor to perform very specific record keeping and verification measures.[59] "The auditor shall document discussions of significant matters with management" and "[i]f the auditor identified information that is inconsistent with the auditor's final conclusion regarding a

Handbook%2520ISAE%25203000_0.pdfandei=XBGzUsiDG5KzsATK4oG4DQandusg=AFQj
CNFBh_JjB8lLolEi-2CJhWTy9-2fiwandsig2=fd-LkiZ1hCpJF1r7ZY7J5Qandbvm=bv.58187178,
d.cWc (last visited Dec. 18, 2013).

[52] Int'l Auditing and Assurance Standards Bd., International Standard On Assurance Engagements 3420, *available at* www.google.com/url?sa=tandrct=jandq=andesrc=sandsource= webandcd=1andved=0CC4QFjAAandurl=http%3A%2F%2Fwww.ifac.org%2Fsites%2Fdefault %2Ffiles%2Fpublications%2Ffiles%2FB011%25202012%2520IAASB%2520Handbook%2520ISAE %25203420-final.pdfandei=-xGzUpnsDoPesAS_-4CoDwandusg=AFQjCNFchKoHWHQlah wnoDkhFkj6QJ2j2Aandsig2=C7stLOv1VYWwh48YiNUYegandbvm=bv.58187178,d.cWcand cad=rja (last visited December 18, 2013).

[53] *Audit Quality*, Int'l Fed'n of Accts., www.ifac.org/auditing-assurance/projects/audit-quality (last visited Dec. 5, 2013).

[54] *About IASB*, Int'l Fed'n of Accts., www.ifac.org/auditing-assurance/about-iaasb (last visited Dec. 5, 2013).

[55] *See, e.g., IAASB Consults on Five-Year Strategic Objectives and Work Priorities*, Int'l Auditing and Assurance Standards Bd., www.ifac.org/news-events/2013–12/iaasb-consults-five-year-strategic-objectives-and-work-priorities (last visited Dec. 18, 2013).

[56] *See, e.g.,* IAASB Reports on Findings From Post-Implementation Review of the Clarified ISAs, Int'l Auditing and Assurance Standards Bd., www.ifac.org/news-events/2013–07/iaasb-reports-findings-post-implementation-review-clarified-isas (last visited Dec. 18, 2013).

[57] International Auditing And Assurance Standards Board Fact Sheet 1 (Dec. 2013), *available at* www.ifac.org/sites/default/files/uploads/IAASB/IAASB%20FactSheet.pdf

[58] *Id.*

[59] Int'l Fed'n of Accts., International Standard On Auditing 230: Audit Documentation 145–46 (Dec. 15, 2009), *available at* www.ifac.org/sites/default/files/publications/files/A012% 202012%20IAASB%20Handbook%20ISA%20230.pdf.

significant matter, the auditor shall document how [he] addressed the inconsistency."[60] However, substantial leeway is given to the individual auditor as they are free to "design and perform tests of controls to obtain sufficient appropriate audit evidence."[61]

As is often the case with auditing requirements, standards are many, encompassing guidance documents, principles, and white papers aplenty. As part of the Clarity Project, the board staff has supplemented the clarified standards with questions and answers publications as well as nonauthoritative videos and slideshows to flesh out the details. Every year, the IAASB also publishes a handbook summarizing all amendments and pronouncements as well as an annual report that covers newly issued standards and reports on the status of ongoing projects.[62] Additionally, the board also publishes implementation guides meant to aid practitioners in understanding and applying the international standards in their work.[63]

This IAASB looks like other networks, but it also suggests that, along with the IASB, the critical gatekeeper profession in the view of financial regulators is the profession of accounting. Subject to oversight by two regulatory networks, albeit networks composed of privately employed accountants in addition to government officials, accounting offers an example of an expansion from standard setting for regulators, to standard setting for private watchdogs who assist regulators – an expansion of the reach of the form, if a modest one.

Financial Action Task Force on Money Laundering

Established in 1989 by the G-7 Summit, the Financial Action Task Force (FATF) is an intergovernmental body that sets standards and promotes "measures for combating money laundering, terrorist financing, and other related threats to the integrity of the international financial system."[64] Unlike other regulatory networks, FATF operates under "a fixed life span," meaning that the task force will dissolve at the set end date without a decision to continue by its ministers.[65] Under the most recent mandate, approved in April of 2012, the FATF is scheduled to operate until 2020.[66] The task force currently has a membership of thirty-four countries and two regional

---

[60] *Id.* at 146.
[61] Int'l Fed'n of Accts., International Standard On Auditing 330: The Auditor's Responses To Assessed Risks 326 (Dec. 15, 2009), www.ifac.org/sites/default/files/publica tions/files/A020%202012%20IAASB%20Handbook%20ISA%20330.pdf.
[62] *See* IAASB, 2013 Handbook, *supra* note 50; IAASB, 2012 Report, *supra* note 48.
[63] *See, e.g., Guidance and Support Tools*, Int'l Auditing and Assurance Standards Bd., www.ifac.org/publications-resources/clarified-international-standards-auditing-clarity-resources-brochure (last visited Dec. 18, 2013).
[64] *Who We Are*, FATF, www.fatf-gafi.org/pages/aboutus/ (last visited Nov. 17, 2013).
[65] *What We Do*, FATF, www.fatf-gafi.org/pages/aboutus/whatwedo/ (last visited Dec. 5, 2013).
[66] Financial Action Task Force Mandate 2012–2020, 8 (Apr. 20, 2012), *available at* www.fatf-gafi.org/media/fatf/documents/FINAL%20FATF%20MANDATE%202012-2020.pdf.

organizations – the European Commission and the Gulf Co-Operation Council.[67] The FATF relies heavily on its eight associates, "a global network of FATF-Style Regional Bodies," to promote compliance and adoption of the FATF recommendations within their regions.[68] The FATF also has a number of observer organizations that are interested in antimoney landing measures, like the African Development Bank and Interpol.[69]

The FATF's mission is to develop a set of standards to fight against money laundering and terrorist financing. The 40+9 recommendations were completed in October of 2004 – the original forty recommendations, issued in 1990, were structured as an action plan to combat money laundering and the nine special recommendations were developed later after fighting terrorist financing was added to FATF's mission in 2001. The recommendations were thoroughly reviewed and updated in 2012 to reflect the new threats and technologies. For example, one recommendation "requires that the laws and regulations that govern non-profit organizations be reviewed so that these organizations cannot be abused for the financing of terrorism."[70] In keeping with the times, the FATF also recently issued guidance regarding the role of "prepaid cards, mobile payments and internet-based payment services" in terrorist financing.[71] Though the technology discussed may be relatively novel, the recommendations are hardly groundbreaking – the report calls for "effective recordkeeping" and "customer due diligence" as well as conventional licensing arrangements and basic international cooperation.[72] In addition to frequent meetings, the FATF has also held meetings of experts to evaluating existing recommendations and identify areas for improvement.

In addition to developing standards, the FATF also functions like a third-party inspector of its members' money laundering and terrorist financing countermeasures and their progress in adopting FATF recommendations. The task force also monitors nonmember jurisdictions through its International Co-operation Review Group to identify countries where antimoney laundering and countering financing of terrorism measures are lacking or insufficient. It has a shaming mechanism similar to the one implemented by IOSCO – FATF publicly identifies "high-risk and noncooperative" jurisdictions and "call[s] upon its members and urge[s] all

---

[67] *Id.* at 9.

[68] Press Release, FATF, *FATF Steps Up the Fight Against Money Laundering and Terrorist Financing* (Feb. 16, 2012), *available at* www.fatf-gafi.org/topics/fatfrecommendations/documents/fatfstepsupthefightagainstmoneylaunderingandterroristfinancing.html.

[69] *FATF Members and Observers*, FATF, www.fatf-gafi.org/pages/aboutus/membersandobservers/ (last visited Dec. 5, 2013).

[70] *Best Practices: Combating the Abuse of Non-Profit Organizations (Recommendation 8)*, FATF, www.fatf-gafi.org/documents/guidance/bpp-npo-2013.html (last visited Dec. 5, 2013).

[71] FATF, GUIDANCE FOR A RISK-BASED APPROACH: PREPAID CARDS, MOBILE PAYMENTS AND INTERNET-BASED PAYMENT SERVICES 3 (June 2013), *available at* www.fatf-gafi.org/media/fatf/documents/recommendations/Guidance-RBA-NPPS.pdf.

[72] *Id.* at 12.

jurisdictions to strength preventive measures and apply effective counter-measures against" those problematic jurisdictions.[73]

Antimoney laundering is not particularly a threat to the stability of the financial system, though it can destabilize it as termites to a house. With the exception of BCCI, a large, interconnected bank is unlikely to find itself insolvent because of exposure to criminality and tax fraud.

The Standard Setters Tapped For Membership in the FSB

Three other networks play more elaborate roles in the international financial regulatory architecture. One of these networks is quite important in their own right, while two others look rather like the networks that are not members of the board but have been asked to provide it with standards.

The IASB has enjoyed a rather high profile, even if it has not often been placed in the center of the financial regulation revolution. In short periods, it has transformed the practice of accounting and been the central, if not the sole, driver in working regulatory sea changes. The IASB has overseen the transformation of accounting standards the world over and in all countries, with one exception: the United States. Those countries have signed onto the IASB's signature product, the International Financial Reporting Standards (IFRS).

The other two networks that have joined the board are much more low-profile. The Committee on Payment and Settlement Systems plays an interstitial role in reforming settlement processing. It promulgates principles meant to govern how these processes work. The Committee on the Global Financial System has done not much more than to promulgate a particularly gauzy set of principles; it seems like an offshoot of the Basel committee. It is meant to look at macroprudential safety and stability.

These networks, like the others, offer the core principles that are standard fare for such institutions. They also seek to build capacity on behalf of member agencies or chartered accountants across the world. But with regard to financial stability, the IASB fits into financial regulations only orthogonally.

Accounting standards are critically important for publicly traded companies and, accordingly do make a big difference for banks listed on stock exchanges. But they are not designed, in and of themselves, to ensure financial system stability. Rather, they serve as the mechanism that can make sense of whether a bank is in fact stable, with reference to its profit and loss statement.

The more obscure members of the board do have fundamental roles to play in systemic stability. Payment systems are often ignored by financial regulators, but have often proved to be critical components of the spread of financial panic and

---

[73] *High-Risk and Non-Cooperative Jurisdictions* FATF, www.fatf-gafi.org/topics/high-riskandnon-cooperativejurisdictions/ (last visited Dec. 5, 2013).

contagion. And, of course, a committee concerned with macroeconomic stability is almost by definition engaged in this sort of project that has animated Basel, IOSCO, and IAIS.

Nonetheless these two networks are engaged in it differently. Technical concerns rooted in efficiency, as well as systemic stability, or forward-thinking predictions about early warnings simply do not contribute to the whole picture of financial regulation, or even much of it. In this sense they too, are orthogonal to the network project, which has left them more likely to be in the shadows than some of the prominent other groupings of financial regulators.

International Accounting Standards Board

IASB is the network that does in accounting what IOSCO has not been willing to do in securities regulation. That task entails the development of International Financial Reporting Standards, or global rules for bookkeeping that would apply regardless of the market or entity.

The attractiveness of common accounting standards is straightforward in a global context. Common standards allow investors to evaluate the returns of publicly traded companies the world over.[74] For that matter, companies would be able to prepare one set of returns that would satisfy the regulators in any market in which their stock is listed, and "[g]iven the increasingly global nature of investment and finance ... such a language [as embodied in common standards] would help communications between investors and issuers in capital markets, improving transparency and understanding of the financial position and performance of the issuers."[75]

Despite these incentives, the SEC essentially opted out of the informal effort to create common standards that would work for any company and any exchange.[76] It presumably assumed that it had no need for foreign standards. It announced

---

[74] David Tweedie and Thomas R. Seidenstein, *Setting A Global Standard: The Case for Accounting Convergence*, 25 Nw. J. Int'l L. and Bus. 589, 591 (2005) ("[A] common financial language, applied consistently, will enable investors to compare the financial results of companies operating in different jurisdictions more easily."); *see also International Financial Reporting Standards Questions and Answers*, AICPA IFRS Resources, www.ifrs.com/updates/aicpa/ifrs_faq.html#q5 (last visited Nov. 25, 2013).

[75] Comments on Concept Release On Allowing U.S. Issuers To Prepare Financial Statements In Accordance With International Financial Reporting Standards, Exchange Act Release No. 33–831, 2007 WL 4985355, at 1 (Nov. 12, 2007) (comments of Richard Martin, Head of Financial Reporting, Association of Chartered Certified Accountants).

[76] *See* Harold S. Bloomenthal and Samuel Wolff, 3F Federal Securities and Corporate Law § 27:82.52 (2nd ed. 2013) (describing the SEC's evaluation of the viability of adopting IFRSs and explaining that the last formal efforts came on July 13, 2012 with the publication of a Final Staff Report on a Work Plan for incorporating IFRSs, a document that left the question of whether and how adoption might take place unanswered).

"concerns with respect to the IASB governance structure," among other things.[77] These sorts of strategies capsized IOSCO's 1980s efforts to develop such a standard; the SEC has also failed to seriously participate in the informal network that succeeded IOSCO in trying – the IASB, though it did participate in the arm's-length IOSCO committee that monitored IASB's progress.[78] But while during the twentieth century, American regulators could insist on unique American standards, in the twenty-first century, the preeminent place of those standards has become much more tenuous, because of the global acceptance of a European rooted principles-based system.[79]

Like IOSCO, IASB began as an informally constituted committee; it was formed in 1973 by the (primarily private) standard setters of Australia, Canada, France, Germany, Ireland, Japan, Mexico, the Netherlands, the United Kingdom, and, indeed, it included the United States.[80] Like IOSCO, IASB looks like a network – it is informal as well, only partially public, and not subject to the ordinary requirements and limitations of international law. These are differences the SEC has noted: "IOSCO is a committee of securities regulatory agencies, [while] the IASC is an independent, private sector organization,"[81] but the organization has moved increasingly to publicize its deliberations, in an effort, some commentators believe, to win acceptance of IFRS by the United States.[82]

The organization tried to develop the sort of accounting standards that could stand in for the diverse standards available around the world. It did so one painful standard at a time, with regular meetings around the world, and the ready cycling in of representatives from various jurisdictions in the standard

---

[77] John W. White, Div. of Corp. Fin. U.S. Sec. and Exch. Comm'n, 35th Annual Securities Regulation Institute, San Diego, California (Jan. 23, 2008), *available at* www.sec.gov/news/speech/2008/spch012308jww.htm.

[78] James D. Cox, *Regulatory Duopoly in U.S. Securities Markets*, 99 COLUM. L. REV. 1200, 1208 (1999) (describing this event in some detail, and noting that the stature of IASC during the mid-1990s presented the SEC with a difficult decision concerning whether to recognize its accounting standards for SEC filings and how the SEC therefore engaged with IASC, directly and through the International Organization of Securities Commissions (IOSCO), laying out basic criteria it would have to meet and providing a "stream of comment letters" on IASC proposals).

[79] Roberta S. Karmel, *The EU Challenge To The SEC*, 31 FORDHAM INT'L L.J. 1692 (2008) (discussing the mutual recognition principle in financial regulation, its origins in the European Union (EU) and the pressure by the EU and various other players on the U.S. to engage in mutual recognition efforts).

[80] George Mundstock, *The Trouble With FASB* 28 N.C. J. INT'L L. AND COM. REG. 813, 842 (2005) (noting that the forerunner to the IASB, the IASC, was created in 1973).

[81] *Pursuant to Section 509(5) of the National Securities Markets Improvement Act of 1996: Report on Promoting Global Preeminence of American Securities Markets*, U.S. SEC. AND EXCH. COMM'N (Oct. 1997), www.sec.gov/news/studies/acctgsp.htm.

[82] The restructuring "include[s] changes in the IASC's objectives and strategy, due process, standards implementation and enforcement, and funding mechanisms." Maureen Peyton King, Note, *The SEC's (Changing?) Stance on IAS*, 27 BROOK. J INTL L 315, 332 (2001).

development process.[83] In this neither the SEC nor American accountants played a particularly important role.

During the late 1980s, the United States abandoned accounting standardization, and killed IOSCO's initial efforts along these lines. The result drove IOSCO's headquarters from North America to Europe and recentered the global effort on accounting in the competing network represented by IASB. As former SEC Commissioner Roberta Karmel has said,

> "[a]t this time, the SEC also determined not to adopt a process-oriented approach to IASB standards ... Rather, it intended to assess each IASB standard after its completion, and then recognize acceptable standards ...... [It only] decided instead to consider all IASB standards after the IASB completed its core standards work program."[84]

None of this stopped IFRS, however. The adoption of the standard throughout the European Union in 2005, and similar decisions by Australia, Hong Kong, and South Africa, tipped over a process that means that over one hundred countries are now requiring or permitting IFRS.[85] As John White, a former director of the agency's division of corporate finance, has noted, the European accounting system that IASB adopted is the one that seems to have caught on better with the world markets than has the arguably more rigorous US GAAP.[86]

A part of the International Financial Reporting Standards (IFRS) Foundation, the IASB is an independent standard-setting body that is responsible for the development of the IFRSs. The board currently composes of sixteen members – all accounting and auditing professionals – and all meetings are open to the public and available via webcast. Some meetings, or particular sessions of the meetings, are held jointly with the Financial Accounting Standards Board (FASB). After every monthly meeting, tentative decision reached by the IASB is published in the monthly IASB update. Public engagement and stakeholder involvement play prominent roles in IASB standard setting as all IASB publications are published for public comment.[87] As part of the development of IFRSs, the board publishes all proposed rules and amendments as well as guidances on rules in specific areas.

---

[83] In this it benefitted from the support of the International Federation of Accountants (IFAC), another network, though one entirely private, and not one with its own designs on accounting standardization – it was happy to delegate that process to IASB.

[84] Roberta S. Karmel, *The EU Challenge To The SEC*, 31 Fordham Int'l L.J. 1692, 1701 (2008).

[85] Christopher Cox, Chairman, U.S. Sec. and Exch. Comm'n, "International Business – An SEC Perspective" Address To The American Institute Of Certified Public Accountants' International Issues Conference, Washington, D.C. (Jan. 10, 2008), *available at* www.sec .gov/news/speech/2008/spch011008cc.htm.

[86] White, *supra* note 77 ("[T]he rest of the world is already heading in this direction and their endpoint is IFRS — not U.S. GAAP.").

[87] *About the IFRS Foundation and the IASB*, IFRS, www.ifrs.org/The-organisation/Pages/IFRS-Foundation-and-the-IASB.aspx (last visited Nov. 29, 2013).

The IASB is supported in its functions by the IFRS Interpretations Committee. Consisting of fourteen members with a variety of professional backgrounds, the committee reviews current issues in the accounting profession and provides guidance on the resolution of those issues within the IFRSs. Committee meetings are also available to the public and broadcast on the web.

In order to guarantee the organization's independence, the foundation is funded by a number of national economies. While each country pays a different amount, the sums are based on the country's GDP. IASB's trustees continue to work on a funding regime that would guarantee independence while allowing the IASB some operational flexibility and stability in the long run. As such, the IASB recently rejected EU's attempt at imposing funding conditions.[88]

Though independent, the IASB is held accountable through its unique governance structure and transparent procedures. The organization operates under a constitution and is overseen by the Monitoring Board. The trustees are primarily responsible for appointing members to and establishing the operating procedures and due process for the IASB, the Interpretations Committee, and the Advisory Council. The work of the trustees is overseen by the Trustees' Due Process Oversight Committee and the trustees are accountable to the Monitoring Board.

Even without the support of the United States, international convergence on accounting standards happened anyway. A December 2002 survey of fifty-nine countries' accounting standard setters revealed that ninety percent of the standard setters intend to converge to IFRS.[89] "Most countries are moving towards IFRSs," one observer has said, as these countries found the standards to be congenial and reputable.[90]

The SEC in the end was left with little choice on accounting standards – it decided that it had to defer to the successful global network, though it has been slow to embrace it. In 2006, it established a "database on application of IFRS," where "[IOSCO] members can exchange information about problems and non-compliance with [the standard]."[91] IOSCO "assesses the data[,] and where it reveals varying interpretations, [] refers the[m] to the [IASB]," the organization responsible for developing IFRS standards[92] IOSCO has a long-standing relationship with the

---

[88] The European Parliament wanted to condition funding upon the serious consideration of prudence-based accounting by the IASB. Huw Jones, *IASB Accounting Body Rejects EU Parliament's Funding Conditions*, REUTERS (Oct. 14, 2013, 3:01 PM), www.reuters.com/art icle/2013/10/14/us-accounting-iasb-idUSBRE99D0KU20131014.

[89] Donna L. Street, *GAAP Convergence 2002: A Survey of National Efforts to Promote and Achieve Convergence with International Financial Reporting Standards* 2, available at www.ifad.net/ content/ie/ie_f_gaap_frameset.htm.

[90] Stuart H. Deming, *International Accounting Standards*, 40 INT'L LAW. 363, 366 (2006).

[91] *Review of Financial Reporting by Issuers – Cycle 5*, FIN. MKTS. AUTH. N.Z., http://seccom2 .test.netco.co.nz/publications/documents/cycle-5/11.shtml?print=true (last visited Nov. 18, 2013).

[92] *Id.*

IASB,[93] and it claims continues to "contribut[e] actively to the work of the IASB, through participation in various expert committees and responses to consultation,"[94] and "continue[s] to monitor the work of the IASB[]."[95] But the SEC has been unwilling to join IFRS, at least until recently, and is only now making its presence felt, after those standards were devised, and after the SEC has declared its intention to adopt them.[96]

In the end, the SEC had to bow to the power of this network. As former SEC Chair Cox would admit, "our recent decision to accept IFRS financial statements in SEC filings was crafted in such a way as to support the efforts of the IASB, and many other nations, to establish IFRS as a single, global set of standards, and not so many national flavors."[97]

In my view, the story of this network is a story of a move from enforcement cooperation through IOSCO, which permits countries to opt in and opt out as they wish, and to retain their regulatory standards, to something in which the costs of exit – and, in the SEC's case, nonparticipation – are too high to bear, because the advantages of standardization – a major advantage of network effects – were realized by IASB, but not by IOSCO. This was because IASB created a standard that tipped, making it impossible to resist. It is a network that moved from club goods to high exit costs.

The IASB is a creature of the new millennium, during which its IFRS process was completed, while the United States agreed to take those standards seriously. After the implosion of Enron and WorldCom, and during the increasingly widespread adoption of IFRS, the IASB has received more attention from outsiders than has IOSCO, and increasing appearances in the Federal Register as well. Its two spikes have coincided with two occasions during which the SEC has considered adopting IFRS.

Committee on Payment and Settlement Systems

The CPSS is an example of a network organized to assist the Basel Committee on a critical issue of systemic stability. Intriguingly, the network exists independently of

---

[93] In 1996, "IOSCO join[ed the IASB] as observer," and in 1999, IASB formed an "agreement with IOSCO to complete core standards by 1999," where "on successful completion IOSCO [would] consider endorsing IASs for cross-border offerings." "IOSCO review[ed the]...IASC core standards," and in 2000, "IOSCO recommend[ed] that its members allow multinational issuers to use 30 IASC standards in cross-border offerings and listings." See INTRODUCTION TO INTERNATIONAL ACCOUNTING: WHY Accounting DIFFERS FROM PLACE TO PLACE.

[94] IOSCO, 2005 ANNUAL REPORT 6, *available at* www.iosco.org/annual_reports/annual_report_2005/.

[95] IOSCO, 2006 ANNUAL REPORT 6, *available at* www.iosco.org/annual_reports/annual_report_2006/annual_report_2006.html.

[96] 72 Fed. Reg. 37962-01, 2007 WL 1985828.

[97] Bradley Cox, Chairman, U.S. Sec. and Exch. Comm'n, Address to the American Institute of Certified Public Accountants' International Issues Conference (Jan. 10, 2008), *available at* www.sec.gov/news/speech/2008/spch011008cc.htm.

the committee, marking a preference among financial regulators for a degree of fragmentation and specialization in their efforts. In other respects, of course, it looks very much like the other networks that concern themselves with banking.

Founded in 1990 as a continuation of the group of experts on payments systems and the ad hoc Committee on Interbank Netting Schemes, the CPSS is one of the permanent committees of the Bank of International Settlements that, until 2009, reported to the G10 governors. Since then, the committee has expanded to include twenty-five central banks and, as such, the committee now reports to the Governors of the Global Economy Meeting. The committee "addresses general concerns regarding the efficiency and stability of payment, clearing, settlement and related arrangements" as well as "issues related to these systems or arrangements" and their impact on major financial markets and monetary policy.[98] The CPSS periodically publishes reviews of payment systems in various countries –generally called "Red Books." The Red Book, on the other hand, is a report on the payment and settlement systems in the selected countries. The most recent edition of the Red Book was published in 2003 but the included statistics are updated annually and published separately.

In order to pursue its work, the committee cooperates with other international organizations – including IOSCO, Basel, and the FSB – and other global payment system institutions to address common concerns. For example, the CPSS and IOSCO have been working together to monitor the implementation of the Principles for Financial Market Infrastructures (PFMIs), which the two organizations issued jointly in 2012.[99] In late 2013, CPSS and IOSCO released the PFMIs for public comment, noting that the principles were developed with the fundamental notion that "financial market infrastructures (FMIs) should provide relevant information to participants, relevant authorities and the broader public."[100] In conjunction with publication of the PFMIs, the CPSS has also developed guidance for FMIs to cultivate disaster preparedness plans in the face of financial threats,[101] an important goal given that the absence of such "comprehensive and effective recovery plans [could cause] the disorderly failure of such FMIs [and] could lead to severe systemic disruptions."[102] Due to the international nature of its work, the

---

[98] CPSS: *History, Organisation, Cooperation*, BANK FOR INT'L SETTLEMENTS, www.bis.org/cpss/cpssinfoo1.htm (last visited Nov. 20, 2013).

[99] Press Release, Bank for International Settlements, Implementation of PFMIs Monitored by CPSS and IOSCO (Apr. 17, 2013), *available at* www.bis.org/press/p130417.htm.

[100] *Cover Note, Publication of a Consultative Document on Public Quantitative Disclosure Standards for Central Counterparties*, BANK FOR INT'L SETTLEMENTS (October 15, 2013), www.bis.org/publ/cpss114covernote.pdf.

[101] *Recovery Of Financial Market Infrastructures – Consultative Report*, BANK FOR INT'L SETTLEMENTS (Oct. 2013), www.bis.org/publ/cpss109.htm.

[102] COMMITTEE ON PAYMENT AND SETTLEMENT SYS. BOARD OF THE INT'L ORGANIZATION OF SEC. COMMISSIONS, CONSULTATIVE REPORT – RECOVERY OF FINANCIAL MARKET INFRASTRUCTURES 1 (Aug. 2013), *available at* www.bis.org/publ/cpss109.pdf.

CPSS also maintains relationships with non-CPSS central banks and publishes reviews of payment system developments in those countries.

The CPSS may also be a vote that redoubles the votes of the Basel Committee on the board; it may also be a gesture of take the technical world of payment systems seriously in reforming global finance. But in my view, its independence is intriguing. For example, while the CPSS does accept requests to complete specific studies from the governors of the Global Economy Meeting, it also undertakes various investigations at its own discretion, setting up working groups as it deems necessary.[103]

Committee on Global Financial System

Found in 1999, the CGFS's existence as the deep-thinking network in the financial regulatory arsenal again suggests a taste for task-specificity among our financial regulators. The CGFS focuses on helping its members recognize, analyze, and respond to threats that imperil the stability of the financial markets and the global financial system.[104] The CGFS is designed to monitor financial stability and, as the Basel Committee puts it, "serve central banks in their pursuit of monetary and financial stability."[105] The committee has thirty-one member institutions and has been overseen by the president the Federal Reserve Bank of New York.[106] Indeed, one New York Fed president previously led the CPSS from 2009 through 2012.[107]

Unlike the CPSS, the CGFS covers a broad policy area. As the name implies, the committee is conceived as a "forum for the monitoring and examination of broad issues relating to financial markets and systems."[108] The committee is to focus on monetary and financial stability and work to increase the transparency of the financial markets. As part of its work analyzing the stability of the global financial system, the committee has published numerous reports and papers on the subject, two of which have been included by the FSB in the Compendium of

---

[103] CPSS: *History, Organisation, Cooperation*, BANK FOR INT'L SETTLEMENTS, www.bis.org/cpss/cpssinfo1.htm (last visited Nov. 29, 2013).

[104] For background on the Committee for Payment and Settlement Systems, see BANK FOR INT'L SETTLEMENTS, www.bis.org/cpss/index.htm (last visited Nov, 2013). For a scholarly discussion, see Carl Felsenfeld and Genci Bilai, *The Role of the Bank for International Settlements in Shaping the World Financial System*, 25 U. PA. J. INT'L ECON. L. 945, 989–990 (2004).

[105] BANK FOR INT'L SETTLEMENTS, 81ST ANNUAL REPORT 2010/11 101 (June 26, 2011), *available at* www.bis.org/publ/arpdf/ar2011e.htm.

[106] *Committee on the Global Financial System*, BANK FOR INT'L SETTLEMENTS, www.bis.org/cgfs/ (last visited Nov. 20, 2013).

[107] *William C. Dudley*, FED. RESERVE BANK OF N.Y., www.newyorkfed.org/aboutthefed/orgchart/dudley.html (last visited Nov. 29, 2013).

[108] *Fact sheet: Committee on the Global Financial System*, BANK FOR INT'L SETTLEMENTS, www.bis.org/about/factcgfs.htm (last visited Nov. 20, 2013).

Standards.[109] The Committee's 2013 publication on asset encumbrance, financial reform, and the demand for collateral assets notes a global increase in requiring collateral in financial transactions in the wake of the financial crisis.[110] In keeping with the committee's focus on working toward improved transparency in the financial system, the report urges that banks be required "to provide regular, standardised public disclosures on asset encumbrance" and "should be asked to perform regular stress tests that evaluate encumbrance levels under adverse market conditions."[111]

CONCLUSION

The story presented in this overview of other regulatory networks is one of rational organization, albeit rational organization that evolves along path dependent lines. The network form is not clearly institutionally superior to all other kinds of cross-border organization, impressive although its accomplishments in financial regulation have often been. Some networks, like the network on payment systems, represents organizational distinctions that simply do not exist among domestic regulators, none of whom have payment system agencies.

But the story told here is a taste for the network form, and a willingness to endure disparate networks connected through the centralized mechanism of the FSB. Although all networks are different in their remit, they are organized in pretty much the same way, and take on similar kinds of tasks, particularly as they begin their work. To be sure, the Basel Committee and the IASB have organized their fields in ways that the other networks have not. But over the development of the six networks considered here, whose contributions to financial stability are not always recognized, clear patterns emerge.

These patterns are consistent with my view that the network form is preferred in international financial regulation; that rulemaking is the ordinary output of these networks, which each promulgate principles to start; that the process of peer review is meant to organize and regulate the networks; and that there may be some agreements among the basic principles that each of the disparate networks developed – a taste for consensus, for example, and a general belief in national treatment.

Of course, there may be other reasons for the precise architecture of the networks we see. The FATF would surely not be so prominent were it not for the war on

---

[109] *Compendium of Standards – Issuing Body – Committee on the Global Financial System (CGFS)*, Fin. Stability Board, www.financialstabilityboard.org/list/fsb_cos_issuing_body/tid_85/index.htm (last visited Nov. 20, 2013).

[110] *Asset Encumbrance, Financial Reform and the Demand for Collateral Assets* (Committee on the Global Fin. Sys., CGFS Papers No. 49, May 2013), *available at* www.bis.org/publ/cgfs49.pdf.

[111] *Id.* at 2–3.

terror. The payment systems network maybe a gesture, rather than a commitment. And the accounting networks integration into the whole may be a sign of the political importance of the accounting profession. By the same token, the number of banking-related networks may be a reflection of turf expansion by banking regulators.

None of this means that the network form is ordained by reason, and forged in inevitability. But it does mean that bureaucratic organization is increasingly reaching disaggregated international financial regulatory space.

6

Why Has Basel III Become Hard Law for China? The Domestic Political Economy of International Financial Law

Chao Xi

BASEL III AS HARD LAW FOR CHINA: A PUZZLE

For a substantial period of time after the Basel Committee on Banking Supervision ("Basel Committee") released Basel III in 2011, front pages in financial media were filled with coverage on the "uneven", or delayed, implementation of Basel III in some major jurisdictions, most notably, the European Union and the United States.[1] In sharp contrast is China's enthusiastic embracing of Basel III. As early as 2011, the China Banking Regulatory Commission (CBRC), China's banking regulatory authority, instigated a campaign to fast-track Basel III implementation in China.[2] It mandated, in general, a significantly advanced implementation time-table than that Basel III requires of its member countries. To be more specific, *all* Chinese banks were instructed to start to implement Basel III capital rules from January 1, 2012, one year earlier than was required under Basel III. Systemically important banks (SIBs) were required to meet Basel III capital requirements by the end of 2013, and non-SIBs by the end of 2016. In both cases the Basel III implementation was scheduled substantially ahead of Basel III targets. In a similar vein, the implementation of Basel III liquidity rules would start on January 1, 2012, and Chinese banks were given until the end of 2013 and the end of 2016, respectively, to meet the Basel III liquidity coverage ratio and the Basel III net stable funding ratio.

The author wishes to thank Douglas Arner and Ross Buckley for their excellent comments, and Dini Sejko for his helpful research assistance. The usual disclaimer applies. This research has been supported by a General Research Fund grant (CUHK-457611) and a Theme-based Research Scheme grant (T31–717–12R) from the Research Grants Council of the Hong Kong SAR.

[1] See, e.g., Alberto Sisto and John O'Donnell, "Regulators Say EU to Delay Basel Bank Capital Rules", Reuters, December 11, 2012; Svenja O'Donnell, "Lagarde Says Basel III Delays Worry IMF as Standards Threatened", Bloomberg, March 19, 2013.

[2] The campaign was launched by way of a policy document entitled the *Guidelines on Implementing New Regulatory Standards in China's Banking Sector* [中国银行业实施新监管标准的指导意见], issued by the CBRC on April 27, 2011.

Had this campaign been implemented, China would have been well advanced in implementing Basel III liquidity rules. The CBRC's campaign met, however, with stiff opposition from the regulated banking industry. In the face of opposition, the CBRC postponed its initial implementation timetable, bringing it more in line with the Basel III implementation agenda.[3]

Notwithstanding, China has remained an active player, if not one of the forerunners, in the implementation of Basel III. This is exemplified by China's initiative in the Basel Committee's Regulatory Consistency Assessment Programme (RCAP), a detailed assessment of the content and substance of the final regulations implementing the Basel III package in individual Basel member states. Published in September 2013, the RCAP report on China's domestic implementation of the Basel III capital framework graded the overall framework of China's capital regulation as "compliant", suggesting that China's implementation of Basel III was closely aligned with Basel III global standards.[4] This placed China amongst the first Basel member countries to secure the "compliant" grade in the RCAP assessment.[5] In other words, Basel III has already become hard law for China.

China's enthusiasm for domestic implementation of Basel III presents an intriguing case for the comparative literature on financial regulation, in particular, the "soft" nature of international financial law.[6] A strand of scholarship in this ongoing discourse highlights the role of domestic politics in shaping international financial institutions and legal order. Basel I, according to Oatley and Nabors, is a creation of the U.S. politicians to resolve domestic political dilemmas.[7] When it comes to the implementation of Basel I, empirical research has established that there is a strong correlation between a country's decision on whether to voluntarily adopt Basel I and its domestic political system.[8] The case of China emerging as a leader in the global implementation of Basel III promises new insights. Not long ago,

---

[3] See *infra* Parts II and III.

[4] Basel Committee, *Regulatory Consistency Assessment Programme (RCAP): Assessment of Basel III Regulations – China* (2013).

[5] At the time of publication of the China RCAP report, only Singapore and Switzerland had been graded as "compliant". The European Union, Japan, and the United States had already undergone the RCAP assessment, but they yet have to obtain the "compliant" grade. See "Report on China's implementation of Basel III published by the Basel Committee", www.bis.org/press/p130927.htm, and individual country RCAP reports.

[6] See, e.g., Chris Brummer, "Why Soft Law Dominates International Finance – And Not Trade" (2011) 13 Journal of International Economic Law 623; Douglas W. Arner and Michael Taylor, "The Global Financial Crisis and the Financial Stability Board: Hardening the Soft Law of International Financial Regulation?" (2009) 32(2) *University of New South Wales Law Journal* 488.

[7] Thomas Oatley and Robert Nabors, "Redistributive Cooperation: Market Failure, Wealth Transfers, and the Basle Accord" (1998) 52 *International Organization* 35.

[8] Daniel E. Ho, "Compliance and International Soft Law: Why Do Countries Implement the Basle Accord?" (2002) 5 Compliance and International Soft Law: Why Do Countries Implement the Basle Accord? 647.

Liu Mingkang, then CBRC Chairman, when responding in 2003 to the Basel Committee's third consultative paper on Basel II, stated emphatically in his letter to the Basel Committee that "... [China] will remain on Basel I, at least for a few more years after the G10 implementation date of 2006".[9] Why has China taken active steps to comply with Basel III, when many other major jurisdictions were delaying its implementation?

This chapter approaches this question from a political economy perspective. It argues that China's adoption of Basel III has been driven, in part, the "private" institutional interests of the CBRC. It demonstrates that the CBRC's regulatory mandates necessitate efforts to put in place and enforce strict capital standards and rules that ran counter to the powerful domestic vested interests, inter alia, the regulated Chinese banks, and the all-mighty central and local government agencies, as well as state-owned enterprises, that own and control these banks. As an adaptive strategy, the CBRC has relentlessly pushed for the adoption of capital standards and rules it favors in the Basel III decision-making process, so as to lend itself the authority and legitimacy necessary to enact and enforce its favored rules against regulated Chinese banks in the name of complying with China's international commitments under Basel III.

The rest of the chapter is structured as follows. Part 2 evaluates the CBRC's authority, both formal and *de facto*, over the regulated banking institutions. It shows that the CBRC has considerable leverage and power over the banking sector it is tasked with regulating. Part 3 discusses Chinese banks' deep political embeddedness in the Party-state, of which the CBRC is part. Using the CBRC's ill-fated campaign to fast track the implementation of Basel III, this part further demonstrates how Chinese banks' political connectedness empowers them to the extent of pushing back the CBRC's regulatory agenda. Part 4 proceeds to approach China's adoption of Basel III in light of the dynamic interplay between the CBRC and the regulated banking institutions. It argues that the implementation of Basel III was the CBRC's strategic adaptation to the political economy of financial regulation in China. Part 5 concludes.

THE CBRC: A STRONG REGULATOR?

The CRBC is China's primary banking regulatory authority, and it is a ministerial-level regulatory agency answerable directly to the State Council, China's cabinet. The CBRC emerged on China's banking regulatory landscape relatively late (in April 2003). Its creation is attributable to a major debate amongst Chinese policy makers in the early 2000s on whether the central banking role and the bank

---

[9] Letter to the Basel Committee on Banking Supervision from Liu Mingkang, then Chairman of the China Banking Regulatory Commission (July 31, 2003), available at www.cbrc.gov.cn/EngdocView.do?docID=466.

supervisory role should be separated and given to separate agencies.[10] More concretely, the policy question then was as to whether the People's Bank of China (PBOC), China's central bank, should be stripped of its banking regulatory function, and whether the responsibilities for banking supervision and regulations should be assigned to a separate regulatory body.[11] Without going into further details, suffice it to say that the Chinese leadership eventually resolved in favor of separating the central banking role and the bank supervisory role. The function of banking supervision was carved out from the PBOC, and has since been vested in the CBRC. Thus, the CBRC has the statutory mandate to supervise and regulate all banking institutions in China and their business operation.[12]

For any newly created regulatory agency, an immediate question that arises is to what extent it has been empowered to achieve its statutory objectives, which in the case of the CBRC are to "promote lawful and prudent operation of the banking sector, and to maintain public confidence in the banking sector".[13] In other words, how strong is the regulator? The question is both formal and empirical.

On a formal level, a broad range of powers have been conferred on the CBRC.[14] Firstly, the CBRC has been given the agency rule-making authority to set rules, regulations, and standards that bind the banking institutions falling into its regulatory jurisdiction. It also exercises discretion to grant or deny entry into China's tightly controlled, and highly lucrative, banking sector. The regulated bank's offering of products and services is subject to the CRBC's *ex ante* scrutiny and approval, and the appointment of bank senior executives requires, *de facto*, the CBRC's vetting and endorsement. Like its Western counterparts, the CBRC is also authorized to conduct on-site examination and off-site surveillance. Secondly, the CBRC has also been authorized to take regulatory and enforcement actions against violations of banking laws, and against noncompliance with the standards and guidelines it sets. The CBRC's regulatory interventions can take a variety of forms. It can take the informal form of a private conversation with the bank's directors and senior executives, warning them of the identified weaknesses. More formal regulatory measures can also be taken against the noncompliant banking institutions and their senior executives. These include (a) suspending part of the bank's existing business operations, or withholding the approval of any new business activities;

---

[10] See Dali Yang, *Remaking the Chinese Leviathan: Market Transition and the Politics of Governance in China* (Stanford University Press, 2004), pp. 81–91.

[11] For a comparative study, see, e.g., Heidi Mandanis Schooner, "The Role of Central Banks in Bank Supervision in the United States and the United Kingdom" (2003) 28 *Brooklyn Journal of International Law* 411.

[12] Art 2, 2003 PRC Law on Banking Regulation and Supervision [zhonghua renmin gongheguo yinhangye jiandu guanlifa], promulgated by the National People's Congress Standing Committee on December 27, 2003.

[13] Art 3, 2003 Banking Supervision Law.

[14] Chapters III and IV, 2003 Banking Supervision Law. See, in general, Zhongfei Zhou, *Banking Laws in China* (Kluwer Law International, 2007); SHEN Wei, *The Anatomy of China's Banking Sector and Regulation* (Wolters Kluwer, 2014).

(b) restricting the distribution of dividends and other entitlements; (c) restricting the bank's assets transfer transactions; (d) ordering the bank's controlling shareholder to sell its control; (e) ordering the removal of directors and senior executives; and (f) withholding the approval of branching applications. The CBRC has also been empowered to wind up banking institutions under certain circumstances.

It is not safe, however, to assume that the CBRC's seemingly wide range of formal authority can necessarily be translated into substantive leverage and influence over its regulated banking institutions.[15] To be sure, it is beyond the scope of this research to empirically assess in any comprehensive manner the CBRC's actual authority over its regulated banking institutions. A useful proxy is the regulatory and enforcement actions that the CBRC has taken against banking law violations.[16] Here, our focus is on the regulatory *output*, as little information is publicly available on the regulatory input (inter alia, staffing and budget resources of the CBRC).[17] Three variables on the regulatory output have been identified. The first variable is the size of illegal transactions, measured by the total amount of funds involved in those transactions. It usefully indicates in monetary terms the scale and impact of the CBRC's regulatory actions. The second variable looks at the number of banking institutions against which the CBRC has taken regulatory and enforcement actions, and the third variable focuses on the number of bank senior executives whom the CBRC has disqualified. Together, these two variables offer a useful glimpse into the intensity of the CBRC's regulatory measures against both culpable institutions and culpable individuals.[18]

The previous table offers a broad-brush portrait of the regulatory and enforcement actions that the CBRC has taken in the eleven years since its creation in 2003. It is perhaps worth noting what appears to be a counterintuitive observation: Whereas the size of illegal transactions exposed by the CBRC has demonstrated a clear upward trend (from RMB177 billion in 2003 to RMB2300 billion in 2013), the number of senior bank executives disqualified by the CBRC has kept on declining from 257 in 2003 to 38 in 2013. Why this is so is beyond the scope of the current

---

[15] Chung-min Tsai, "Regulating China's Power Sector: Creating an Independent Regulator without Autonomy" (2014) 218 *The China Quarterly* 452.

[16] There is a large and growing literature on the public enforcement of *securities* laws. See, e.g., Howell E. Jackson and Mark J. Roe, "Public and Private Enforcement of Securities Laws: Resource-Based Evidence" (2009) 93 *Journal of Financial Economics* 207; John Armour, "Enforcement Strategies in UK Corporate Governance: A Roadmap and Empirical Assessment" in Alessio M. Pacces (ed), *The Law and Economics of Corporate Governance: Changing Perspectives* (Edward Elgar, 2010).

[17] See, in general, John C. Coffee, "Law and the Market: The Impact of Enforcement" (2007) 156 University of Pennsylvania Law Review 229.

[18] The impact of enforcement on the regulated firms has, it has been argued, only limited deterrence because the costs fall largely on the firm (and its innocent shareholders) rather than the culpable executives. See, e.g., John C. Coffee, "Reforming the Securities Class Action: An Essay on Deterrence and Its Implementation" (2006) 106 Columbia Law Review 1534.

TABLE 1 *The CBRC's Regulatory and Enforcement Actions, 2003–2013*

Year	Size of Illegal Transactions (in Billion RMB)	Number of Sanctioned Banking Institutions	Number of Disqualified Senior Executives
2003	177	1,512	257
2004	584	2,202	244
2005	767	1,205	325
2006	1,015	1,104	243
2007	856	1,360	177
2008	1,288	873	78
2009	1,151	4,212	86
2010	1,537	2,312	49
2011	1,263	1,977	66
2012	1,160	1,553	55
2013	2,300	1,341	38
Total	12,098	19,651	1,618

Source: CBRC Annual Reports, various years.

research. We concern ourselves primarily with what the statistics tell us about the impact that the CBRC's regulatory measures are likely to have on its regulated banking sector. There are two ways by which this can be measured. First, we benchmark the regulatory outcomes against the Chinese banking sector that the CBRC is tasked with supervision and regulation. Take the 2013 statistics for example. The illegal transactions unveiled by the CBRC in 2013 involved an aggregate amount of RMB2300 billion, accounting for 1.5 percent of the total assets of China's banking sector. The number of banking institutions against which the CBRC took regulatory actions in 2013 amounted to a much more significant 33.9 percent of all banking institutions, both domestic and foreign, operating in China. Second, we compare the quantity of the CBRC's regulatory actions with those of its Western counterparts. The difficulty of this exercise is certainly with comparability, and our comparison is admittedly crude and, at best, indicative. On average, the annual number of Chinese banking institutions sanctioned by the CBRC during the period between 2003 through 2013 is 1786. This compares rather favorably to 63 enforcement actions taken by the U.S. Federal Reserve in 2013,[19] and to, on average, 131 formal capital enforcement actions taken annually by the U.S. Federal Reserve, FDIC, OCC, and OTC during the period between 1993 and 2010.[20]

To be sure, the measurements mentioned earlier are not without flaws and limitations. They, however, seem to provide support for the view that the CBRC has indeed taken, not infrequently, regulatory and enforcement actions against

[19] www.federalreserve.gov/newsevents/press/enforcement/2013enforcement.htm.
[20] Julie A. Hill, "Bank Capital Regulation by Enforcement: An Empirical Study" (2012) 87 Indiana Law Journal 645.

violations and noncompliance, and that the CBRC is likely to wield considerable leverage and influence over how its regulated banking institutions conduct their affairs. Put it in other words, the CBRC is a strong regulator.

THE CBRC: A WEAK REGULATOR?

In the preceding part, we have made a case for the argument that the CBRC plays a significant and meaningful role in the oversight of the Chinese banking sector; it has teeth and does bite. One must, however, resist the temptation of hastily coming to conclusion that the regulator–regulated relationship in China is one of absolute dominance. In this part, we will demonstrate that the regulated Chinese banks are deeply embedded in China's politics and governance, and that can, and they do, wield considerable power and influence in China's financial policymaking process.

Chinese banks' embeddedness in China's formal governance manifests itself in a number of significant ways. An important source of Chinese banks' political connectedness is the ownership arrangement. Chinese banks, with few exceptions, are owned and controlled by mighty central and local government agencies, as well as giant and powerful state-owned enterprises. The following table lists fifteen Chinese largest banking institutions and their respective largest/controlling share-holder. The Big-Four state-owned commercial banks all have the Central Huijin Investment Ltd., the investment arm of the China Investment Corporation, China's sovereign wealth fund, as its largest shareholder. The second largest shareholder of the Industrial and Commercial Bank of China, the world's largest bank by market capitalization, is the Ministry of Finance, which also controls the Bank of Communications, China's fifth largest bank. Most other banks in this league table are controlled either by the investment arms of local governments (for example, Industrial Bank, Evergrowing Bank, China Zheshang Bank, and China Bohai Bank), or by central government-controlled state-owned enterprises, or their subsidiaries (for instance, Hua Xia Bank, China Merchant Bank, Shanghai Pudong Development Bank, and China CITIC Bank).

Chinese banks' political influence also derives from the rank of their top executives in the Chinese Communist Party hierarchy. Many top executives of the major Chinese banks are themselves political heavyweights. They rank in the Party-state system on an equal footing with top regulators of the CBRC. Chair-persons of some of the Big-Four state-owned banks, as with the Chairman of the CBRC, sit on the Central Committee of the Chinese Communist Party. While the CBRC Chairman is a full member of the Central Committee, some Chair-men of the Big-Four state-owned banks serve as alternate members. The revolving door also exists; and it is not unusual that top executives of the largest Chinese banking institutions become candidates for top posts in regulatory agencies. A number of chairmen of the Big Four state-owned banks have been appointed as Chairmen of the CBRC, the China Securities Regulatory Commission, and

TABLE 2 *The Largest/Controlling Shareholder of China's Largest Banking Institutions Measured by Market Capitalization*

Bank	Largest/Controlling Shareholder
Industrial and Commercial Bank of China	Central Huijin Investment Ltd.
China Construction Bank	Central Huijin Investment Ltd.
Agricultural Bank of China	Central Huijin Investment Ltd.
Bank of China	Central Huijin Investment Ltd.
Bank of Communications	Ministry of Finance
Industrial Bank	Finance Bureau of Fujian Province
Hua Xia Bank	Shougang Group
China Merchant Bank	China Merchants Steam Navigation Co. Ltd.
Ping An Bank	China Ping An Insurance (Group)
Shanghai Pudong Development Bank	China Mobile Guangdong
China CITIC Bank	China CITIC Group
China Everbright Bank	Central Huijin Investment Ltd.
Evergrowing Bank	Yantai Blue Sky Investment Holding
China Zheshang Bank	Financial Development Company, Zhejiang Province
China Bohai Bank	TEDA Investment Holding

Source: 2013 annual reports of the banks.

the China Insurance Regulatory Commission. Indeed, Liu Mingkang, the foundation Chairman of the CBRC, was Chairman of the Bank of China (BOC) before he was put at the helm of the CBRC.

Thus, leveraging on the banks' strong political ties with the central and local governments, as well as the political clout of top bank executives, Chinese banks have at their disposal both political power and resources that give them an important role in China's financial policymaking. For the purposes of our discussion, a vivid illustration of the enormous ability that Chinese banks possess to sway the balance in financial policy setting is the CBRC's ill-fated attempt to fast track implementation of Basel III.

As mentioned in passing in Part 1, the CBRC in 2011 attempt to roll out an unusually ambitious implementation scheme of Basel III. The scheme was arguably both more rapid and more stringent than Basel III.[21] It met with stiff opposition from the regulated banking industry. Senior executives of state-owned banks openly voiced concerns about implementing Basel III at its full force within a shortened phase-in period. Liu Jun, Vice Chairman of China Everbright Bank, one of the largest nationwide commercial banks, contended that Basel III was tailored-made with primarily the interests of Western banks in mind, and that a "rushed"

---

[21] He Jianqing, "Impact of China's Version of Basel III on its Banking Sector" ["中国版巴塞尔协议III"对银行业的影响分析], *Financial Forum* [金融论坛], Issue 8 2011, 25–32.

implementation might be ill-suited for China's economic structure and growth pattern, and would put at risk Chinese banks' growth and competitiveness.[22] Ba Shusong, Chief Economist of the China Banking Association, and also senior economist at the official think-tank affiliated to the State Council, echoed these views. Ba cautioned that banks might have to rely on the already weak Chinese capital markets to raise the necessary equity as required by Basel III. Given the development stage of China's banking sector, full implementation of Basel II should be prioritized over the Basel III adoption, Ba suggested.[23]

In the face of opposition, the CBRC caved in and returned to its traditional gradualist approach to Basel implementation. Most notable is the revised implementation timetable publicized in December 2012.[24] Abandoning the initial schedule to start implementation of Basel III capital rules in January 2012, the CBRC postponed the implementation until January 2013, bringing it in line with the Basel III implementation agenda. The requirement for a 2.5 percent countercyclical buffer, which SIBs were initially required to meet by the end of 2013, needs only be met in steps, increasing by 0.5 percent in 2013 and then adding an extra 0.4 percent over each of the next five years until the end of 2018. Overall, Chinese banks have been given a six-year grace period until the end of 2018 to meet the Basel II capital requirements, two years later than the initial target of the end of 2016. The CBRC had hoped that this delayed timetable would "reduce the implementation pressure on banks".[25]

STRATEGIC ADAPTATION: BASEL III HELPS MAKE THE CBRC A STRONGER REGULATOR

Our discussions so far have helped unveil the dynamics between the CBRC and the regulated Chinese banking institutions. While the CBRC wields considerable leverage and authority over the banking institutions under its jurisdiction, these institutions derive significant power and influence from its political embeddedness in the Chinese Party–state, of which the CBRC is part. Their strong connectedness with the powerful state actors enables them to lobby against, and resist, the CBRC's regulatory impositions. The question is how this interplay between the regulator and the regulatees informs China's active adoption of Basel III.

---

[22] Liu Jun, "Basel III : China Must Avoid a Dilemma of Being 'Trapped'" [巴塞尔协议III:中国要避免"双套牢"困局], *Economic Herald* [经济导报], September/October 2012, 46–47.

[23] Ba Shusong, "Basel III : Adoption and Implementation in China" [巴塞尔资本协议III在中国的落地与实施], *First Financial Daily* [第一财经日报], October 10, 2012.

[24] *Circular on Relevant Matters on the Transitional Period for the Implementation of the Administrative Measures on the Capital of Commercial Banks (On Trial Implementation)* [关于实施《商业银行资本管理办法(试行)》过渡期安排相关事项的通知], issued by the CBRC on December 7, 2012.

[25] Simon Rabinovitch, "China Gives Banks Basel III Timetable", *Financial Times*, December 7, 2012.

We shall argue that the CBRC's regulatory mandates necessitate efforts to put in place and enforce strict capital standards and rules that ran afoul of powerful domestic vested interests, inter alia, the regulated Chinese banks, and the all-mighty central and local government agencies, as well as state-owned enterprises, that own and control these banks. As an adaptive strategy, the CBRC has relentlessly pushed for the adoption of capital standards and rules it favors in the Basel III decision-making process, so as to lend itself the authority and legitimacy necessary to enact and enforce domestically its favored rules against regulated banks in the name of complying with China's international commitments under Basel III. This argument is laid out in greater detail in the rest of this part.[26]

In 2008, the weighted average CAR of the Chinese banking sector increased sharply by 3.6 percent to a historical high of 12 percent, far exceeding the statutory minimum 8 percent.[27] This sector-wide weighted average CAR dropped, however, in 2009 to 11.4 percent.[28] This decline was attributed in large part to the rapid growth of the banks' assets as banks were placed under great pressure to help finance the Chinese government's huge stimulus program aimed at neutralizing the impact of the GFC on the Chinese economy. New loans extended in the first four months of 2009, alone, exceeded the total of 2008.[29] A CBRC document reportedly stated that the sector-wide average CAR slid by more than one percent to less than 11 percent at the end of June 2009 from 12 percent at the end of 2008.[30] At the Bank of China (BOC), China's fourth largest bank, where lending rose the most in 2009 amongst the big four (Big-Four) state-owned giant banks, capital adequacy fell to 11.63 percent at the end of September 2009 from 13.43 percent at the start of 2009, representing a sharp fall of more than one and half percents in merely nine months.[31]

This excessive credit expansion and resulting sharp decline in the CARs were apparently of great concern to the CBRC, which has seen the regulation of capital adequacy levels one of its top priorities. The CBRC soon took bold steps to tighten capital adequacy regulation right at the time Chinese banks saw their own balance sheets sharply expanding. In November 2009, without formally changing the overall regulatory framework for capital adequacy, the CBRC officially announced its embracement of the regulatory tool of a countercyclical

---

[26] The analysis in this part has drawn substantially from Chao Xi, "Domestic Politics as International Norms: China's Changing Roles in International Banking Regulation" (2014) 30 Banking and Finance Law Review 479.

[27] CBRC 2008 Annual Report, p. 33.

[28] CBRC 2009 Annual Report, p. 10.

[29] Andrew Batson and Jason Leow, "Chinese Banks Lend Now, May Pay Later", *Wall Street Journal*, 29 May 2009.

[30] Wang Ming and Rose Yu, "China's Banks Face Challenge to Loan Growth", *Wall Street Journal*, August 4, 2009.

[31] Andrew Peaple, "Cracks Appearing Among China's Banks", *Wall Street Journal*, November 3, 2009.

capital buffer. On top of the 8 percent capital requirement, an additional countercyclical capital buffer of 3 percent was imposed on SIBs and 2 percent on small and medium-sized banks, respectively.[32] Thus, the required minimum capital adequacy ratio was hiked to 11 percent for SIBs, and 10 percent for small and medium-sized banks. This was a bold and decisive move. It is noteworthy that it was only in September 2009 that the GHOS announced its commitment to introducing a framework for countercyclical capital buffers above the minimum requirement. And it was not until July 2010 that the Basel Committee held a consultation on a proposal for a countercyclical capital buffer regime.[33] The CBRC's decision to impose countercyclical capital buffers on Chinese banks placed China amongst the first countries to do so.

Moreover, the enforcement of these heightened capital requirements was high on the CBRC's regulatory agenda. The CBRC had taken enforcement actions against those banks that reported a sharp decline in capital adequacy as a consequence of excessive credit expansion. These actions ranged from private regulatory meetings with senior executives of the banks concerned to the issuance of regulatory "risk alert" letters. In more serious circumstances, the CBRC could order the suspension of certain business activities of the banks concerned.[34] This, of course, put Chinese banks under considerable pressure to meet the stricter capital requirements.

One way for Chinese banks to reverse their deteriorated capital adequacy ratios was, of course, fund-raising so as to strengthen their capital bases. This explains the wave of major fund-raising activities carried out by Chinese banks in the immediate aftermath of the 2009 credit spree. In 2010, the majority of China's sixteen listed – and larger – banks implemented or unveiled their capital replenishment plans to raise funds from the domestic bond market and the stock markets in Shanghai and Hong Kong.[35] In particular, ICBC, CCB, and BOC, ranked as the first, second and fourth largest commercial banks in China, raised capital of USD 6.6 billion, USD 9.1 billion and RMB 6.6 billion in 2010 respectively, through right issues in Shanghai and Hong Kong's stock markets. Moreover, the medium-sized China CITIC bank also raised USD 6.3 billion to boost its capital, including USD 2.4 billion through subordinated debt issuance in domestic bond market and USD 3.9 billion through right issues in Shanghai and Hong Kong's stock markets.[36]

Large-scale capital raising from the stock markets was not, however, without limitations. Firstly, the massive influx of new bank shares and bonds put

[32] Wang Huaqing, "Speech on Lujiazui Forum", CBRC, June 26, 2010. Available at www.cbrc .gov.cn/chinese/home/docView/20100626338BC7648D2D8AADFF190E28CAED5100.html

[33] See Basel Committee, "Countercyclical Capital Buffer Proposal – Consultative Document", available at www.bis.org/publ/bcbs172.htm.

[34] CBRC 2009 Annual Report, p. 64.

[35] Rose Yu, "Chinese Banks to Seek $11 Billion", *Wall Street Journal*, January 8, 2011.

[36] Alicia Garcia Herrero, Le Xia, Stephen Schwartz and Serena Zhou, "Success in Capital-raising Contains Risks", *China Banking Watch*, November 19, 2010.

significant downward pressure on the already feeble Chinese stock markets. China's benchmarking Shanghai Composite Index was amongst of the worst performers globally in the post-GFC area. The scale and intensity at which banks tapped the stock markets created significantly more demand for funds that investors could supply, and that could further push down share prices.[37] Secondly, and relatedly, the banks' ability to raise funds through subordinated bond issuance was severely curtailed by the CRBC's rules introduced in late 2010, restricting the use of subordinated bonds as a source of capital.[38] Subordinated bond issuing was a primary way for Chinese banks to raise capital. In the first seven months in 2009, alone, Chinese banks issued USD30.97 billion of subordinated bonds, representing a lion share of the banks' overall fund-raising.[39] More than half (51 percent) of the subordinated bonds issued by Chinese banks were actually cross-held by other Chinese banks, according to a CRBC document, raising concerns that no real fresh capital was channeled into the banking system to help shield banks against systemic risks.[40] The CBRC rules limited subordinated bonds to up to 25 percent of the bank's core capital, and banned in general cross-holding of subordinated bonds by banks.[41]

With these market and regulatory impediments to the banks' ability to strengthen their capital bases, Chinese banks could hardly count on fund-raising alone to meet the CBRC's tightened capital adequacy requirements. An alternative is to control the growth of their assets. To do this, banks could rein in lending. Although that might have seemed a plausible and sound approach, reining in lending was, nonetheless, out of the question. For one thing, Chinese banks, virtually all state-controlled, were under overwhelming influence by the central and local governments to continue lending so as to keep the investment-driven Chinese economy going.[42] For another, Chinese banks have enjoyed legally protected interest margins, and asset growth indeed helps boost their profitability, creating strong financial incentives for banks themselves to keep on lending.[43]

The tightening of capital adequacy regulation by the CBRC, on the one hand, and the banks' difficulties to meet the heightened capital adequacy requirements, on the other have resulted in considerable tensions between the CBRC and the regulated banks. The regulator–regulated relationship is by no means one of

---

[37] Dinny McMahon, "Chinese Regulator Approves Big Fund Raisings", *Wall Street Journal*, May 28, 2010.

[38] *Circular on Improving the Capital Replenishment Mechanisms for Commercial Banks* [关于完善商业银行资本补充机制的通知], issued by the CBRC on October 18, 2009. Hereinafter, Capital Circular.

[39] Wang Ming and Rose Yu, "China's Banks Face Challenge to Loan Growth", *Wall Street Journal*, August 4, 2009.

[40] *Ibid.*

[41] Capital Circular, *supra* note 38.

[42] Javed Hamid and Stoyan Tenev, "Transforming China's Banks: The IFC's Experience", *Journal of Contemporary China* (2008) 449.

[43] *Ibid.*

dominance. Chinese banks can, and they do, wield considerable power and influence in China's financial policymaking process. For one thing, Chinese banks, with few exceptions, are owned and controlled by mighty central and local government agencies, as well as giant and powerful state-owned enterprises. For instance, all Big-Four state-owned commercial banks have the Central Huijin Investment Ltd., the investment arm of the China Investment Corporation, China's sovereign wealth fund, as its dominant shareholder. The largest shareholder of ICBC, the world largest bank by market capitalization, is the Ministry of Finance, which also controls the Bank of Communications, China's fifth largest bank. For another, top executives of the major Chinese banks are themselves political heavyweights. They rank in the Party-state system on an equal footing with the Chairman of the CBRC. Chairpersons of the Big-Four state-owned banks, as with the Chairman of the CBRC, all sit on the Central Committee of the Chinese Communist Party. The CBRC Chairman is a full member of the Central Committee, and Chairmen of the Big-Four state-owned banks serve as alternate members. Thus, leveraging on the banks' strong political ties with the central and local governments, as well as the political clout of top bank executives, Chinese banks have at their disposal both political power and resources that give them an important role in China's financial policymaking.

As noted earlier, the CBRC's efforts to tighten capital regulation have considerably limited the regulated banks' abilities to expand credit funding the post-GFC stimulus program steered by the Chinese central and local governments. Also eroded was the banks' enviable profitability. The banks, in concert with the powerful government agencies that own and control them, would presumably have strong interests in resisting the more stringent capital standards imposed by the CBRC. The banking industry's opposition to the CBRC's initial, ambitious blueprint to accelerate the implementation of Basel III, as demonstrated in the preceding part, is a vivid demonstration of banks mobilizing and "revolting" against the CBRC's financial decision-making that they disfavored. Their strategy was one of discrediting Basel III, more precisely an accelerated implementation of Basel III, as posing serious risks to the well-being of China's banking sector and, more generally, China's credit-driven growth in the aftermath of the GFC.

Against this backdrop, Basel III, portrayed as international best practices in banking regulation and an international agreement that binds China, would lend to the CBRC the authority and legitimacy necessary for it to fulfill its regulatory mandates. But for Basel III, the CBRC would find it very difficult to put in place and enforce capital rules that apparently are not in line with powerful, organized vested interests. This would have motivated the CBRC to engage actively in the making of Basel III: Capital standards favored by the CBRC would presumably face a lesser degree of domestic resistance should they be endorsed and adopted by Basel III and become "international banking standards". The same could be said about the CBRC's proactive stance toward the RCAP assessment, as noted in the preceding part. The CBRC would find it easier to push for the adoption of tighter capital regulation in the name of meeting China's commitments to the Basel Committee.

CONCLUDING REMARKS

Why do nations invest the resources to comply with international financial law that is not legally binding? This Chapter presents a case study on China, which has adopted and implemented Basel III, without delay. It argues that China's choice has been driven by, in part, the institutional interests of its banking regulatory agency. Basel III importantly lends the CBRC the authority and legitimacy necessary to enact and enforce its favored capital rules against the powerful vested interests, that is, the regulated Chinese banks, and the all-mighty central and local government agencies, as well as state-owned enterprises, which own and control these banks. The adoption and implementation of Basel III is, in this sense, the CBRC's strategic adaptation to China's unique domestic political economy. More broadly, this research highlights the need for one to look beyond the general rhetoric of the state actor's interests and preferences, and to identify the underlying interests and incentives of domestic-level players that play an important role in shaping the higher, and more visible, interests and preferences of the national states.

II

The Changing Face of Central Banking

7

Reconceptualizing Central Banking: From the Great Inflation to the Great Recession and Beyond

Donato Masciandaro

INTRODUCTION

The history of central banks is rich in modifications to their role and functions. In the last thirty years – before the 2008 crisis – the mandate of central banks has been progressively narrowed. In a large number of countries, the central bank mandate has been focused on the area of monetary policy with a particular focus on the goal of price stability. This narrowing of the mandate has been accompanied by changes in their governance arrangements. These arrangements emphasize the importance of central bank independence from the political process.

The crisis posed new challenges for modern central banking where monetary policy is conducted by an independent central bank following an interest rate rule approach to stabilize inflation and output gaps while being less involved in pursuing banking stability. A significant number of reforms are taking place, which concern in particular the central bank's role in the structure of supervision.

In 2010, the U.S. legislature passed the Dodd Frank Act, rethinking the role of the FED in the reshaping of the structure of financial supervision. Even if during the discussion of the bill U.S. lawmakers debated the possibility of restricting some of the FED's regulatory powers, as well as increasing political control over the central bank, the Dodd Frank Act actually ended up increasing the responsibilities of the FED as prudential supervisor. In Malaysia, the 2009 Central Bank Law provided an opportunity for more involvement in supervision for the central bank. In the current evolution of the Basel Capital Accord, the activation of counter-cyclical prudential measures has been put in the hands of central banks.

In Europe, policymakers are moving to finalize reforms concerning the involvement of central banks in supervision both at the regional and national levels. In 2010, the European Systemic Risk Board (ESRB) was established to provide macro-prudential supervision and this new institution is dominated by the European Central Bank (ECB). On June 2012, the heads of state and government of the Euro zone revealed a proposal to establish the Single Supervisory Mechanism, which will be headquartered in the ECB.

Concerning individual EU members, in 2011, with the new banking act, the German government dismantled its unified financial supervisor (BAFIN) in favor of the Bundesbank, which is now the main banking supervisor. In 2010, the UK government put the key prudential functions of the Financial Services Authority (FSA) within the purview of the Bank of England. In 2010, the Irish Financial Services Regulatory Authority was legally merged with the central bank. Further, an analysis of the reforms undertaken in Bulgaria, the Czech Republic, Estonia, Hungary, Latvia, Poland, and Slovakia reveals that the trend towards supervisory consolidation has not resulted in smaller central bank involvement.

In this respect, it is interesting to note that before the crisis the central bank was the main prudential supervisor in less than half of EU countries (thirteen out of twenty-seven). After the Crisis, with the establishment of new supervisory regimes in Belgium, France, Germany, and the United Kingdom, the main prudential supervisor is now the central bank in more than half of them (eighteen out of twenty-eight).

These episodes provide signals of a sort of back to the future in central banking governance, given that before the crisis the direction of the changes in the supervisory structure had been characterized by the separation of central banking from supervision. How should the concept of central banking be reconceptualized while taking into account these ongoing reforms?

This study offers three contributions. Section 2 discussed the economics of the key feature of the modern central bank governance, its independence, focusing on what could be its determinants. The results are used to build up in Section 3 a simple political economy reasoning, which highlights the drivers that can explain the central bank governance when the policymakers are delegated by the citizens to design the optimal central bank setting. The framework is used in Section 4 to evaluate the evolution of the central bank governance before and after the crisis in the light of the recent reforms. Section 5 concludes.

DESIGNING CENTRAL BANK GOVERNANCE AND THE ROLE OF
INDEPENDENCE: INSIGHTS FROM ECONOMIC LITERATURE

Up to thirty years ago economic theory did not attribute importance to the concept of central bank governance. The institutional setting became important when economic theory started to stress its role in determining macroeconomic performances, namely during the New Classical Revolution. The essential role of the central bank was further confirmed in the New Keynesian analysis of the monetary policy.[1]

---

[1] For well-done reviews, see Eijffinger S. and De Haan J., *The Political Economy of Central Bank Independence*, Special Papers in International Economics, Stanford University, n.19 (1996); Cukierman A., "The Economics of Central Bank Independence", in W. Holger (ed.),

The theoretical bottom line can be summarized as follows: policymakers tend to use monetary tools with a short sight perspective, using the inflation tax to smooth different kind of macroeconomic shocks, trying to exploit the trade-off between real gains and nominal (inflationary) costs. The intuition is simple. The modern economies are based on nominal contracts, including wages and financial contracts. Other things being equal, the contracts are based on inflation expectations, which are calibrated on the monetary policy stance. If the policymakers are politicians – that is, they are career concerned agents – they wish to solve every problem in a short-term horizon, in order to maximize the probability to be elected. Therefore they have strong incentives to cheat the markets, announcing ex ante low inflation policies and implementing ex post high inflation policies. Inflation surprises cut real wages and real interest rates, stimulating the economy and reducing the real burden of the public debt. The inflation tax finances the stabilization policies.

But the more the markets are efficient, the greater the risk that short-sighted monetary policies will merely produce inflation. In fact the rational private agents fully anticipate the political incentives to use the inflation tax, fully adjusting the nominal variables. In this framework, the Friedman-Lucas[2] proposition on monetary policy neutrality holds: more money growth produces just more inflation, without any effect on growth.

Furthermore, the political inflation bias can dynamically generate greater uncertainty and negative externalities, such as moral hazard risks. The inflation tax is inefficiently used in a systematic way, becoming basically high and volatile thereby producing only macroeconomic distortions.

The inefficient use of inflation tax was empirically confirmed by the fact that the optimal taxation theory did not find any support in the data.[3] The optimal taxation theory claims that the benevolent policymaker chooses the rate of any taxation, including the inflation tax, to minimize the present value of the social cost; consequently inflation and tax rates have a positive relationship. If the optimal taxation theory empirically fails, it is natural to conclude that the government is not benevolent, being affected by inflation biases.

Macroeconomic Policy and Financial Systems, The McMillan Press (1996); Cukierman A., "Central Bank Independence and Monetary Policymaking Institutions: Past, Present and Future", *European Journal of Political Economy*, Vol. 24, 722–36 (2008); and Walsh, C., "Central Bank Independence", in S.N. Durlauf and L.E. Blume (eds.), *The New Palgrave Dictionary of Economics*, Palgrave MacMillan (2008); Eijffinger S. and Masciandaro D. (eds.), "Modern Monetary Policy and Central Bank Governance", Edward Elgar, Cheltenham (2014).

[2] Friedman M., "The Role of Monetary Policy", *American Economic Review*, 58, 1–17 (1968); Lucas R. E., "Some International Evidence on Output Inflation Tradeoffs", *American Economic Review*, 63, 326–35 (1973).

[3] For a survey, see Nolivos R. D. and Vuletin G. (2011), "The Role of Central Bank Independence on Optimal Taxation and Seignorage", *Working Paper Series*, Paolo Baffi Centre, Bocconi University, n.103.

Therefore banning the use of the monetary policy for inflation tax purposes becomes the social goal. The institutional setting gains momentum; the relationships, namely governance, between the policymaker, who designs the overall economic policy, and the central bank, which is responsible for the monetary policy, become crucial in avoiding the inflation bias. The more the markets are rational, the more the rules of the game between policymakers and central bankers gain momentum.[4] The optimal central bank governance has to be essentially a medal with two sides.

On the one side, the central banker has to be independent, meaning that the central bank enjoys the ability to implement the noninflationary monetary policy without any external (political) short-sighted interference.

We already noted that the politicians would like to use the monetary expansion to fix macroeconomic problems, as unemployment or sovereign debt financing. The independent central bank is not obliged to please the politicians, including their preferences towards fiscal deficit monetization.

The central banker becomes a veto player against inflationary monetary policies. On the other side, the central banker has to be conservative, where conservativeness refers to the importance that he or she assigns to price stability in its relation to other macroeconomic objectives. The conservativeness is a necessary step for preventing the central banker himself or herself from becoming a source of inflation bias. Independence and conservativeness become the conditions that facilitate the implementation of credible noninflationary monetary policies.[5] Independence can be considered a device for implementing conservative monetary policies.[6]

But the private agents trust the central banker only if effective rules on accountability and transparency hold. In other words, a conservative central bank is credible if it works in an institutional setting, which guarantees independence

---

[4] Barro R. and Gordon D. B., "Rules, Discretion and Reputation in a Model of Monetary Policy", *Journal of Monetary Economics*, 12, 101–21(1983); Backus D. and Driffil J., "Inflation and Reputation", *American Economic Review*, 75, 530–38 (1985); Rogoff, K. S., "The Optimal Degree of Commitment to an Intermediate Monetary Target", *Quarterly Journal of Economics*, 100, 1169–90 (1985); and Lohmann S. (1997).

[5] On the relationship between CBI and central banker conservativeness, see also Eijffinger S. C. W. and Hoeberichts M., "The Trade Off between Central Bank Independence and Conservativeness", *Oxford Economic Papers*, 50, 397–411 (1998); Fisher S., "Central Bank Independence Revised", *American Economic Review*, Papers and Proceedings, 85, 201–6 (1995); and McCallum B. T., "Two Fallacies Concerning Central Bank Independence", *American Economic Review*, 85, 207–11(1995). On monetary conservativeness and fiscal policy, see Niemann (2011).

[6] Eijffinger and Hoeberichts and Eijffinger S. C. W. and Hoeberichts M., "The Trade Off between Central Bank Independence and Conservatism in a New Keynesian Framework", *European Journal of Political Economy*, 24 (1998), 742–7 (2008) shed light on the tradeoff between conservativeness and independence: downgrading in central bank independence can increase the central banker conservativeness. The first article used the neoclassic framework, while the second one applied a new Keynesian model to obtain the same result.

and accountability, acting in a transparent way[7] and implementing an effective communication policy.[8]

The relationship between independence and accountability represents the core of so-called central bank governance.[9] Central bank governance has become the institutional setting for implementing day to day monetary policy[10]: given the long-run goal to avoid the risk of inflation, the modern central banker can also smooth the real business cycles,[11] using monetary policy rules.[12] Monetary policy is the product of a complex interaction between three main components: monetary institutions, central banker preferences, and policy rules.

---

[7] On transparency, see Eijffinger S. and Geraarts P. , "How Transparent are Central Banks?", *European Journal of Political Economy*, 22, 1–21 (2006) and Hughes H. A. and Libich J., "Central Bank Independence, Accountability and Transparency: Complements or Strategic Substitutes?", *CEPR Discussion Papers*, n.5470 (2006).

[8] On communication, see Cukierman A. and Meltzer A., "A Theory of Ambiguity, Credibility and Inflation under Discretion and Asymmetric Information", *Econometrica*, 54, 1099–128 (1986); Goodfriend M., "Monetary Mistique: Secrecy and Central Banking", *Journal of Monetary Economics*, 17, 63–92 (1986); Issing O., "Communication, Transparency, Accountability: Monetary Policy in the Twenty-First Century", *Quarterly Review*, Federal Reserve Bank of Saint Louis, 87, 65–83 (2005a); and Blinder A., Ehrmann M., Fratzscher M., De Haan J., and Jansen D. J., "Central Bank Communication and Monetary Policy: A Survey of Theory and Evidence", *Journal of Economic Literature*, 46, 910–45 (2008).

[9] Briault C. B., Haldane A. G., and King M. A., "Central Bank Independence and Accountability: Theory and Evidence", *Working Paper Series*, Bank of England, n.49 (1996); Lybek T. and Morris J. A., "Central Bank Governance: a Survey of Boards and Management", *IMF Working Papers*, International Monetary Fund, n.236 (2004); Crowe C. and Meade E., "The Evolution of Central Bank Governance around the World", *Journal of Economic Perspectives*, 21, 69–90 (2007); Frisell L., Roszbach K., and Spagnolo G., "Governing the Governors: a Clinical Study of Central Banks", *Sveriges Riksbank Working Paper Series*, n. 221 (2008); and Hasan I. and Mester L., "Corporate Governance and Effective Central Banking: Cross-Country Empirical Evidence" (2010), in P. Syklos, M. Bohl and M. Wohart (eds.), *Frontiers in Central Banking*, Elsevier, Amsterdam.

[10] Taylor J., "The Effectiveness of Central Bank Independence Versus Policy Rule", *Business Economics*, 48, 155–62 (2013) casted doubts on the role of the CBI in generating rules based monetary policies.

[11] Bernanke B. and Gertler M., Inside the Black Box: The Credit Channel of Monetary Policy Transmission, *Journal of Economic Perspectives*, 9, 27–48 (1995); Clarida R., Gali J., and Gertler, M., The Science of Monetary Policy: A New Keynesian Perspective, *Journal of Economic Literature*, 37, 1661–707 (1999); Woodford M., Optimal Interest Rate Smoothing, *Review of Economic Studies*, 70, 861–86 (2003); and Gali J. and Monacelli T., Monetary Policy and Exchange Rate Volatility in a Small Open Economy, *Review of Economic Studies*, 72, 707–34 (2005).

[12] Taylor, J., Discretion versus Policy Rules in Practice, *Carnegie – Rochester Series on Public Policy*, 39, 195–214 (1993); Henderson D. W. and McKibbin W., A Comparison of Some Basis Monetary Policy Regimes for Open Economies: Implications of Different Degrees of Instrument Adjustment and Wage Persistence, *Carnegie – Rochester Series on Public Policy*, 39, 221–317 (1993); Persson T. and Tabellini G., Designing Institutions for Monetary Stability, *Carnegie – Rochester Series on Public Policy*, 39, 53–84 (1993); Svensson L., Optimal Inflation Targets, "Conservative" Central Banks, and Linear Inflation Contracts, *American Economic Review*, 87, 98–114 (1995); and Walsh, C., Optimal Contracts for Central Bankers, *American Economic Review*, 85, 150–76 (1995).

In this article, our variable of interest is the optimal degree of central bank independence (CBI), other things being equal, including the rules on accountability and transparency.

For our purposes, the huge[13] CBI literature can be described as a two-stage process. Initially, scholars involved in the field sought to verify theoretical conjectures with comparative, institutional, and empirical analyses. After constructing indices of independence of the central banks[14] and having historical alternative models of independent and dependent monetary authorities,[15] scholars had attempted to determine whether the degree of independence could be considered

---

[13] Vuletin G. and Zhu L., Replacing a Disobedient Central Bank Governor with a Docile One: A Novel Measure of Central Bank Independence and its Effect on Inflation, *Journal of Money, Credit and Banking*, 43, 1185–215 (2011) claimed that up to 2011 around 9,000 articles have been devoted to the role of CBI on inflation.

[14] After the seminal central bank independence indices published by Bade R. and Parkin M., "Central Bank Laws and Monetary Policy: A Preliminary Investigation," *University of Western Ontario*, Ontario (1977) and by Grilli V., Masciandaro D., and Tabellini G., "Political and Monetary Institutions and Public Financial Policies in the Industrial Countries", *Economic Policy*, 13, 341–92 (1991) different indicators were proposed; for a discussion, see Berger H., De Haan J., and Eijffinger S., "Central Bank Independence: an Update of Theory and Evidence", *CESifo Working Papers*, n. 255 (2000). Cukierman A., *Central Bank Strategy, Credibility, and Autonomy*, MIT Press, Cambridge, Massachusetts (1992) was the first to distinguish legal and de facto indicators of independence. Updates of these indices were proposed in Cukierman A., Webb S. B., and Neyapti B., "Measuring the Independence of Central Banks and its Effects on Policy Outcomes", *World Bank Economic Review*, 6, 353–98 (1992); Cukierman A., Miller G., and Neyapti B., "Central Bank Reform, Liberalization, and Inflation in Transition Economies. An International Perspective", *Journal of Monetary Economics*, 49, 237–64 (2002); and Jacome L. and Vasquez F., "Any Link between Legal Central Bank Independence and Inflation? Evidence from the Latin American and the Caribbean", *IMF Working Paper Series*, International Monetary Fund, n.75 (2005) for the Cukierman index, and in Arnone M., Laurens B.J., Segalotto J., and Sommer M., "Central Bank Autonomy: Lessons from Global Trends", *IMF Working Papers*, International Monetary Fund, n.88 (2007) for the Grilli, Masciandaro, and Tabellini index. Crowe and Meade (2007) developed measures of central bank independence and transparency. Vuletin and Zhu (2011) proposed a new de facto index of independence, identifying two different mechanisms embedded in the measure of the turnover rate of central bank governor.

[15] Toniolo, G. (ed.), "Central Bank Independence in Historical Perspective, de Gruyter", Berlin-New York (1988); and Wood J., "The Meanings and Historical Background of Central Bank Independence", *Working Paper Series*, Paolo Baffi Centre, Bocconi University, n.5 (2008). On the FED, see Waller C., "Independence + Accountability: Why the FED is a Well Designed Central Bank", *Quarterly Review*, Federal Reserve Bank of St. Louis, 93, 239–301 (2011); Bernanke B., "A Century of US Central Banking: Goals, Frameworks, Accountability", *Journal of Economic Perspectives*, 27, 3–16 (2013a); and Gorton and Metrick (2013); on the FED and the Bank of England, see Goodfriend (2012); on the Bundesbank, see Issing O., "Why Did the Great Inflation not Happen in Germany?", *Quarterly Review*, Federal Reserve Bank of Saint Louis, 87, 329–35 (2005b) and Beyer A., Gaspar V., Gerberding C., and Issing O., "Opting out of the Great Inflation", *NBER Working Paper Series*, National Bureau of Economic Research, n.1496 (2008); on the Bank of Italy, see Gaiotti E. and Secchi A., "Monetary Policy and Fiscal Dominance in Italy from the Early 1970s to the Adoption of the Euro: a Review", *Occasional Papers*, Banca d'Italia, n.141 (2012).

a driver in explaining the most important macroeconomic phenomena: inflation, public debt, interest rates, income, and growth.

The overarching hypothesis turned on whether the existence of the monetary veto player reduced the intended and unintended effects of the misuse of the inflation tax and produced positive spillover on other macrovariables. In the first wave of studies, central bank independence was essentially considered an exogenous (independent) variable that could be useful for explaining macroeconomic trends.

The step forward in the research was to consider the degree of CBI as an endogenous (dependent) variable; the effect of which had yet to be demonstrated. This enquiry gave rise to a number of questions: Which are the drivers that can motivate the decision of one or more countries to maintain or reform their monetary regimes, namely the degree of independence of their central banks? Why and how the policymakers are forced to implement monetary reforms that reduce their powers in using the inflation tax, increasing the degree of independence of the central bank?

Various interpretative hypotheses have been advanced to explain the genesis of the political process that leads a monetary regime to assume given characteristics. Development in endogenizing central bank independence, namely its effectiveness, has been the subject of analysis in both economics and political science.

One group of scholars has sustained the possibility that the degree of CBI depends on the level to which constituencies strongly averse to the use of the inflation tax are present, which drives policymakers to bolster the status of the central bank (*the constituency view*). A second group of scholars has stressed that the aversion to use the inflation tax is structurally written in the features of the overall legislative and/or political system, which influence the policymakers to decide whether to have a setting of monetary powers with an independent central bank (*the institutional view*). A third group of scholars has stressed the role of culture and tradition of monetary stability in a country in influencing policymakers' choices (*the culture view*). The three views have in common a preference for the citizen to determine the degree of CBI. In the constituency view the present preferences against the use of the inflation tax are relevant; in the institutional and culture views the past anti-inflationary preferences influence the present policymakers' decisions.

Furthermore, it is worth noting that the three views can be intertwined for the purpose of determining under which economic, institutional, and cultural conditions it is that reforms of the CBI will or will not take place. It is also evident that these studies acquire greater importance in periods, as the present one, during which there is a tendency to reform, or at least to question, the design of central bank governance.

All in all, the review of the literature shows that whatever is the adopted view in explaining the CBI evolution we have to focus our research attention on two crucial elements: on the one side, the social preferences; on the other side, the incentives and constraints that shape the behavior of the agent responsible for the monetary setting design, namely the incumbent policymaker.

CITIZENS, POLITICIANS, AND THE DESIGN OF
CENTRAL BANK GOVERNANCE

This section examines the design of central bank governance using a delegation model[16] that offers, in a unique framework, all the insights offered in the abundant, consolidated, and still growing literature on the topic that we have presented in the previous section.

In doing so we adopt a political economy approach[17] that argues that policy-makers' actual choices related to central bank governance are conditional on the economic and institutional environment existing at a given time. This in turn determines the political weights put on the costs and benefits associated with CBI.

Our framework is based on two hypotheses. First of all, gains and losses of a given central bank setting are variables computed by the incumbent policymaker, who maintains or reforms the central bank regime following his or her own preferences. Secondly, policymakers are politicians, and as such, they are held accountable at elections for how they have managed to please voters. All politicians are career-oriented agents, motivated by the goal of pleasing voters in order to win elections. The main difference among various types of politicians concerns which kinds of voters they wish to please in the first place. Therefore the CBI is likely to change over time following the political preferences, which are not automatically coincident with the social ones.

Consider an economy with rational expectations and uncertainty. We suppose that citizens dislike monetary settings where the incumbent governments can manage directly and discretionally the monetary policy. Citizens know that politicians may have an incentive to inflate the economy in order to address different kind of macroeconomic shocks. In other words, politicians have an incentive to systematically use inflation tax.

---

[16] The model has been introduced in Romelli D. and Masciandaro D., "Ups and Downs." Central Bank Independence from the Great Inflation to the Great Recession: Theory, Institutions and Empirics, Financial History Review, (2015), forthcoming.; the model modified the theoretical framework proposed in Masciandaro D., "Politicians and Financial Supervision outside the Central Bank: Why Do They Do it?", *Journal of Financial Stability*, 5, 124–47 (2009).

[17] Masciandaro D., "E Pluribus Unum? Authorities Design in Financial Supervision: Trends and Determinants", *Open Economies Review*, 17, 73–102 (2006), Masciandaro D., "Divide et Impera: Financial Supervision Unification and the Central Bank Fragmentation Effect", *European Journal of Political Economy*, 23, 285–315 (2007), Masciandaro D. and Quintyn, M., "Helping Hand or Grabbing Hand? Politicians, Supervisory Regime, Financial Structure and Market View", *North American Journal of Economics and Finance*, 19, 153–74 (2008), and Masciandaro (2009).

Rational citizens fully anticipate the political inflation bias and therefore monetary policies risk economic costs of high inflation without providing any real gains. All citizens, or at least the majority of the voters, dislike the use of inflation tax and like monetary stability, which means that the government cannot systematically use inflation to change the income and wealth distribution. In other words, we are studying a democracy where citizens dislike political inflationary biases.

The inflation bias arises in all the macroeconomic cases where the government gives a higher expected value to the short-run benefits relative to the long-run costs of the inflation tax. But citizens understand the political bias and rationally adjust their expectations: in equilibrium there is inflation above the social optimal level and no real effects. Therefore if the government is the monetary policy authority, monetary policy is likely to be time inconsistent: every preannounced monetary path is not credible.

Here CBI comes in. CBI becomes a possible institutional device for addressing political bias: monetary policy is delegated to an unelected bureaucracy, the central bank, which is committed to pursuing the goal of monetary stability and does so in a conservative fashion. In other words, it is able to avoid any inflationary bias as it is independent from the government while at the same accountable to the parliament. The citizens acknowledge that the definition of the optimal level of CBI means to exploit the trade-off between avoiding the inflationary bias in normal times and having a stabilization device in extraordinary times.

Citizens care about the effectiveness of the central bank regime according to a classic well-behaved concave function u = U (y): social welfare increases with the optimal level of CBI. Linear preferences are used:

$$U(y) = y \qquad (1)$$

In a democracy, citizens assign to the elected policymaker the task of designing the optimal level of CBI, which is the setting that guarantees the monetary policy effectiveness. For the sake of simplicity, we suppose that the elected policymaker represents both the legislative and the executive powers. Put another way, the interests of the majority of the parliament and of the government in charge are perfectly aligned.

The incumbent policymaker is delegated by society to define and implement the optimal level of CBI. The policymaker reward is based on how he or she (hereafter she) carries out her job, namely defining and implementing the level of CBI.

Our policymaker is a politician. Here we assume that the policymaker wishes to please the citizens; one more assumption could be that the policymaker's aim is to please specific constituencies, namely the lobbies.[18] We adopt the *helping hand view* of the policymaker's type: she wishes to please citizens rather than a particular

---

[18] See Masciandaro (2009).

constituency or lobby (*grabbing hand view*). It will be interesting to demonstrate that notwithstanding the policymaker wishes to please the citizens the final outcome, which is the actual CBI, can be different from the social optimal one.

The level y of CBI is determined by the policymaker's ability Ω and by her effort a.

$$y = a + \Omega \qquad (2)$$

Let us describe the delegation framework. The sequence of events is as follows:

1) Society chooses to delegate to the policymaker the task of designing the optimal level of CBI.
2) Next, the policymaker chooses effort a, before knowing her ability Ω in implementing this particular task (developing a CBI regime is not a usual nor a day to day operation).
3) The policymaker implements the CBI regime, revealing her ability Ω.
4) Citizens observe the CBI level, not the relationship between effort and ability, given that they cannot distinguish innate talent from contingent effort, and reward the policymaker for this task.

Coming back to the policymaker, her utility function Z_{HH} is defined as:

$$Z_{HH} = R(U) - C(a) \qquad (3)$$

Where $R(U)$ is the reward function and $C(a)$ is the cost function. The political reward is a function of the social utility while the political costs are a function of the effort in implementing the task. The policymaker evaluates every task assignment while taking into account the political rewards and costs in doing so. Let us describe the three crucial features of the policymaker:

A) Ability: the ability of the policymaker is a random variable with the usual normal distribution (where Ω_{AV} is the mean).

B) Political reward: The incumbent policymaker wishes to be reelected. The government needs to provide enough utility to the majority of voters; then her utility function is the social welfare function U.

In general, the policymaker wishes to please voters and her goal is the alignment of interest between her and citizens. But then each delegated task, or each specific alignment, can be more or less convenient from the policymaker's point of view in terms of political gains. We denote the political value she assigns to fulfil the specific task on CBI with β, where $0 \leq \beta \leq 1$. Therefore

$$R(U) = \beta U \qquad (4)$$

The incentives alignment between the policymaker and citizens is a necessary and sufficient condition to define the optimal behaviour of the policymaker. One more step is necessary to find out the effective political reward. The reward will be useful if the citizens' utility exceeds the minimum threshold of utility that they expect from an incumbent government. For the sake of simplicity, we assume that the threshold is satisfied.

C) Political costs: The policymaker knows that, if monetary policy is delegated to an independent bureaucracy committed to a monetary stability goal, rigidities in implementing accommodative policies (conservative veto player event) may arise: the inflation tax cannot be used to finance stabilization policies;

In other words, we assume that from the policymaker's point of view the political costs of implementing a CBI regime will depend on her expectations of facing a macroeconomic situation calling for a lax monetary policy during her office, which cannot be implemented given the existence of a nonaccommodative central banker.

From the citizen's point of view, the government can be a natural scapegoat in each crisis situation, but she is not able to control monetary policy tools to implement the right short-sighted policy. In each case the government is likely to be blamed; nonlinear political costs will arise, given that the reputation losses will hit the overall credibility of the government, not just its effectiveness in designing the monetary setting.

Therefore the policymaker's cost function can assume the following simple specification:

$$C(a) = ca^2 \qquad (5)$$

With $c = c_0 + c_1(probME)$ and where *probME* is the probability that macroeconomic shocks that the government would like to address using an accommodative monetary policy will occur.

The political cost of the effort in establishing CBI depends on how the incumbent government is blamed when the shocks occur, namely the size of reputation losses.

When a shock occurs, citizens can be more or less sensitive to the use of accommodative policies. From the government's point of view, the crisis likelihood per se is not relevant, but its political cost affects her reputation. The reputation factor is represented by the parameter c_1.

We will see that the size of the reputational costs can determine the difference between the optimal CBI and the actual one. In conclusion, for the incumbent policymaker the political cost in developing a CBI regime is represented by the likelihood of facing a macroeconomic crisis without the possibility of implementing the desired ad hoc short sighted monetary policy.

THE CENTRAL BANK INDEPENDENCE BEFORE AND AFTER THE CRISIS: UPS AND DOWNS

Now we can use the theoretical skeleton to mimic the evolution of the central bank governance in the advanced countries before and after the crisis.

Establishing a CBI regime is a two-step process: defining the policymaker effort and then evaluating the CBI level. In defining her optimal effort a_1 the policymaker maximizes her objective function. Then her ability Ω_{HH} becomes evident, the level of CBI can be evaluated using the CBI equation (2) and her final political reward can be calculated. It follows that the policymaker maximizes social welfare net of costs of executing the task:

$$\max Z_{HH} = \max[R(U)-c(a_1)]$$

$$R(U)-c(a_1) = \beta(U)-c(a_1)$$

Given that the level of social utility is equal to the level of CBI, which is a function of the policymaker effort, it is evident that both the rewards and the costs depend on the effort:

$$\beta(a_1 + \Omega)-ca_1^2$$

From the first order condition the optimal effort will be

$$\frac{\delta Z_{HH}}{\delta a_1} = \beta-2c_1 a = 0$$

$$a_1 = \frac{\beta}{2c_1} \tag{6}$$

Figure 1 shows that the optimal effort of the policymaker depends on both the political gains and the political costs in designing an independent central bank. In the Figure line PC represents the political costs in establishing an independent central bank, which are increasing in the parameter c, while line PG depicts the political gains, which depend on the parameter β. Higher gains will produce higher effort and consequently higher level of CBI, and the same is true when the costs for the policymaker in facing a monetary veto player are decreasing.

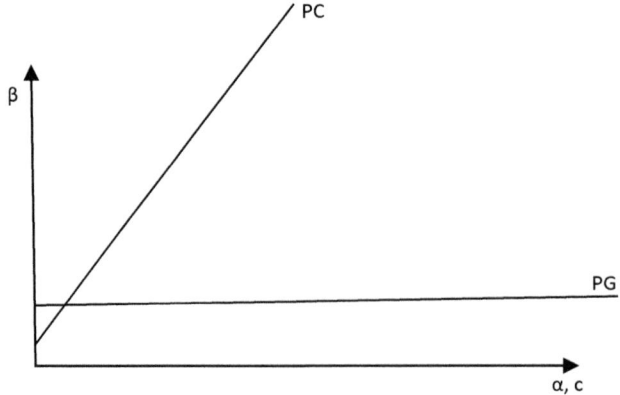

FIGURE 1 Central bank independence: political gains vs political costs.

The equilibrium level y of the CBI will be determined by the policymaker's ability Ω_{HH} and by her effort a_1:

$$y_{HH} = a_1 + \Omega_{HH} = \frac{\beta}{2c_1} + \Omega_{HH} \tag{7}$$

Given the exogenous policymaker ability, on one hand the level of CBI depends on how politically relevant it is for the government to develop a central bank regime pleasing the majority of voters, which dislikes the inflation tax as economic policy tool. In other words, the policymaker's perception of the relevance of the central bank setting matters. On the other hand, the government takes into account the expected costs of facing a conservative veto player in monetary affairs when macroeconomic shocks have to be addressed.

The parameter c_1 can be easily used to show under which conditions the actual level of CBI is different from the social optimal one (Figure 2). In fact, we can suppose that the citizens acknowledge the need in extraordinary times to address shocks using the inflation tax, which is perfectly consistent with the aim to avoid in normal times the inflationary bias. The social optimal value of the reaction parameter c_1^{soc} is different from zero. For the sake of simplicity, we can assume that

$$c_1^{soc} = 1$$

Line SC represents the social costs in designing an independent central bank.

Now, if the reputational costs for the government in facing macroeconomic shocks is particularly high, it is likely that $c_1 > c_1^{soc}$; the political costs, Line PC, are higher than the social one and consequently the optimal political effort αp will be lower than the optimal social effort αs. Therefore the actual level of CBI designed by the policymaker will be lower than the social optimal one.

Which was the situation before the crisis? In the three decades before the 2008 financial meltdown, safeguarding the monetary stability became a primary goal in several advanced, emerging, and less developed countries, and the CBI was

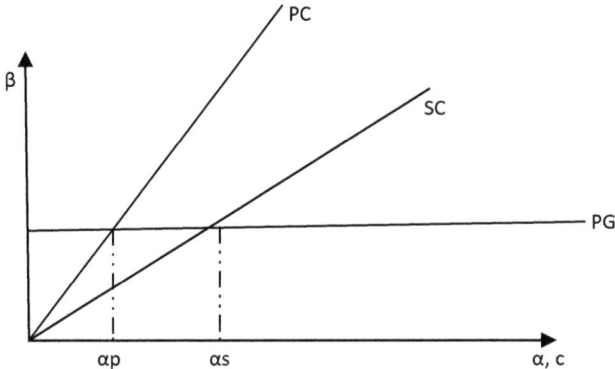

FIGURE 2 Central bank independence: government vs social planner.

the selected institutional device to raise the commitment in avoiding the use of the inflation tax.[19] The expected high political gains pushed several governments all around the world[20] to enhance the degree of CBI in their countries, agreeing to restrict their future freedom in using the inflation tax through the presence of a veto player. The monetary policy action was associated with less variance of both inflation and output.[21]

Then the crisis came. Is it possible to identify the possible drivers of a CBI reform after the 2008 financial meltdown? In general, we assume that gains and losses of a CBI regime are variables computed by the incumbent policymaker, who maintains or reforms the central bank regime, following her preferences. Therefore any situation that influences the policymaker's gains and losses in changing the monetary regime can produce incentives to modify the CBI level.

If the incumbent governments feel that society's aversion to inflation is increasing, a central bank reform is likely to produce higher political gains. In our model, the value of the parameter β increases as well as the level of CBI. Nowadays in the advanced countries both inflation and inflation expectations seem to be stable at low but positive levels[22] and the same is true for inflation volatility[23]; a demand by the citizens for increasing the CBI level is unlikely to be evident. Furthermore, if deflation becomes a concrete macroeconomic problem political pressures can arise in order to reduce the central bank conservativeness and/or the CBI.

It is worth mentioning the recent case in Japan. As soon as he was appointed in 2013, Prime Minister Shinzo Abe promised to appoint a new governor of the Bank of Japan and redefine the monetary stability goal. The new Bank of Japan goal was to increase the inflation rate objective above 2 percent – it was fixed to 1 percent – in order to boost economic growth.[24]

At the same time, any situation that changes the policymaker's political costs c_i in reforming the monetary regime can produce incentives to modify the CBI. The policymaker's incentives to decrease the CBI in order to be able to implement monetary accommodation are likely to increase if the incumbent governments are facing macroeconomic shocks such as the following: 1) recession busts; 2) public deficit financing; and 3) bailout needs.

---

[19] Cukierman (1996) and Eijffinger and De Haan (1996).

[20] The increase in the central bank independence all around the world during the eighties and the nineties is documented in Arnone et al. (2007).

[21] Bernanke B., *The Great Moderation*, "Remarks at Eastern Economic Association, Annual Meeting, Washington D.C.", February (2004) , and Taylor (2013).

[22] Among others, see Fleckenstein M., Longstaff F. A., and Lusting H., "Deflation Risk", *NBER Working Paper Series*, National Bureau of Economic Research, Washington D.C. (2013), n. 19238 and IMF (2013), "The Dog That Didn't Bark; Has Inflation Been Muzzled or Was Just Sleeping", *World Economic Outlook*, International Monetary Fund, Chapter 3.

[23] Taylor (2013).

[24] On Japan, see Neely C. J., "Political Pressures on the Bank of Japan: Interference or Accountability?" *Economic Synopses*, Federal Reserve of Saint Louis, 7, 1–2 (2013).

Today all three drivers can be in action. Therefore if the crisis can increase the political costs, the politicians can have an incentive to decrease the CBI; the situation depicted in Figure 2, namely the political effort is smaller than the social effort, is more likely to occur.

THE CENTRAL BANK INVOLVEMENT IN SUPERVISION AND ITS INDEPENDENCE

So far the reforms of the central bank settings after the crisis were exclusively focused on the central bank involvement in supervision. Are these changes relevant in modifying the CBI?

In general, the likelihood of increases to CBI levels will be greater when the impact on the central banks' effectiveness as a veto player against the political inflationary biases is higher. In this respect, the intended and unintended consequences on independence of a change to central banks' involvement in supervision are far from obvious and predictable.

Let us consider the two dimensions that are usually considered in evaluating the level of CBI[25]: political independence and economic independence. Political independence refers to the discretion given to the central bank in the design and implementation of the policy consistent with the monetary stability goal. Economic independence is related to the freedom of the central bank in choosing the set of instruments consistent with the design of the monetary policy. Therefore the more the central banks' involvement in supervision weakens the priority of the monetary stability in defining and implementing the goals and instruments of monetary policy action, the lower the CBI will be.

To the best of our knowledge, the only comparative analysis of the levels of independence, which takes into account where the supervision is located,[26] shows that the location matters. An analysis of the status quo before the crisis demonstrated that supervisors who were located inside a central bank were granted the highest degree of independence in supervision. In other words, the fact that the central banks enjoy high level of independence, moving supervision within the central bank perimeter is likely to automatically increase the autonomy of that policy.[27] Furthermore, unified supervisors located outside a central bank were

[25] Grilli et al. (1991), Debell G. and Fischer S., "How independent should a central bank be?" *Working Papers in Applied Economic Theory*, Federal Reserve Bank of San Francisco, n.5 (1994), and Fisher (1995).

[26] Masciandaro D., Quintyn M., and Taylor M., "Inside and outside the central bank: Independence and Accountability in Financial Supervision: Trends and Determinants", *European Journal of Political Economy*, 24, 833–48 (2008).

[27] Cukierman A., "Regulatory Reforms and the Independence of Central Banks and Financial Supervisors" (2013b), in M. Balling, E. Gnan, and P. Jackson (eds.), *States, Banks and the Financing of the Economy: Monetary Policy and Regulation*, SUERF Studies, n.3, Larcier, Bruxelles.

granted the lowest degree of the same kind of independence. However, the relevance of these results is limited by the fact that concepts and definitions of independence are different in the two fields of monetary policy and supervision[28]; in general, the question of the central bank involvement can be evaluated from two symmetric points of views: on the one side, the effectiveness of the supervision; on the other side, the efficacy of the monetary policy. This article is focused on the monetary policy side of the story.[29]

What happens when this moves in the opposite direction, namely central banks that are specialized in monetary policy coming back to supervision? Is the independence as monetary authority affected when the central bank is responsible for financial stability? It is a matter of fact that in the recent reforms of the central bank settings in the United States and Europe the financial stability goal has been elevated.[30] The implications of the CBI are far from consolidated.

Some scholars[31] have claimed that the central bank involvement in supervision can reduce the CBI, given that being in charge as banking supervisor can weaken the central bank commitment, as well as its credibility, as veto player against inflation. The first argument against the involvement is the possibility of conflict of interest in managing the two policies that can reduce the effectiveness in pursuing the monetary stability goal. Furthermore, the probability of conflict of interest can be endogenous, if the probability of financial instability increases when the central bank combines monetary and financial stability, this may increase the moral hazard and contribute to the failure of banking firms. Consequently, the second argument is the reputational risks that arise when a central bank is also a supervisor. Failures in supervision can reduce the central bank reputation, which is a necessary asset that gives rise to the credibility of a monetary agent.

Other scholars[32] however have noted that the effect of involvement in supervision on the capacity of the central bank to be an effective monetary authority does not allow for clear-cut conclusions, given that arguments for involvement can be found in the literature. Basically, the central bank involvement in supervision is supported by argument related to the information advantages and economies of

---

[28] Masciandaro et al. (2008). On analogies and differences between the roles of independence with respect to the conduct of monetary policy and with respect to supervision, see Arnone M. and Gambini A., "Architecture of Supervisory Authorities and Banking Supervision" (2007), in D. Masciandaro and M. Quintyn (eds.), *Designing Financial Supervision Institutions: Independence, Accountability and Governance*, Edward Elgar, Cheltenham, 262–308 and Cukierman (2013b). On the empirics of the central bank independence as supervisor, see Gaganis C. and Pasiouras F., "Financial Supervision Regimes and Bank Efficiency: International Evidence", *Journal of Banking and Finance*, 37, 5463–75 (2013).

[29] Masciandaro (2012b) addresses the supervisory policy side.

[30] Cukierman (2013a) and (2013b), Masciandaro D. and Nieto M. (2013), Governance of the Single Supervisory Mechanism: Some Reflections, *Revue d'Economie Financière*, 112, 51–70.

[31] Grilli et al. (1991), Issing (2012) and Orphanides A. (2013), Is Monetary Policy Overburdened? *BIS Papers*, n.435.

[32] Eijffinger and De Haan (1996).

scale that derive from monetary policy conduct and from having the supervisory functions under the central bank umbrella. Both policies take gains in having the same authority in charge: it has been argued that the financial stability supervisors need to fully control the monetary base for managing the liquidity of the financial system.[33]

Taking the middle ground, some scholars[34] have concluded that the consistency between the central bank involvement in addressing financial stability and the effectiveness of the monetary policy action in controlling the inflation risk cannot be excluded a priori. Therefore the existing literature on the relationship between the effectiveness of the monetary veto player and its involvement in supervision thus far provides no uniform and definitive conclusions.

Additionally, we can elaborate on one more perspective: other things being equal, the citizens' vote on CBI accepting other risks in order to avoid suffering the consequences of the inflation rate. If it is this the case, the question of the redistributive effects linked to the monetary policy action can become relevant.[35] For the sake of simplicity, consider a population whose preferences against inflation are homogenous, but pros and cons of the banking bailouts are heterogeneously distributed among the citizens. If banking instability occurs, banking

---

[33] Charles Goodhart, "The Changing Role of Central Banks", BIS Discussion Paper 326 (2010).

[34] Fisher (1995) claimed that the role of the central banker as supervisor was not of much importance. See also Goodhart, C. and Schoenmaker D., "Should the functions of monetary policy and banking supervision be separated?", *Oxford Economic Papers*, 47, 539–60 (1995), Cukierman (1996), Franck R. and Krausz M., "Why Separate Monetary Policy from Banking Supervision?", *Journal of Comparative Economics*, 36, 388–411 (2008), Crockett A., "Central Bank Governance under New Mandates", *BIS Papers*, Bank for International Settlements, n.55 (2010), Papademos L., Central Bank Mandates and Governance Arrangements, *BIS Papers*, n.55 (2010), Svensson L., "Inflation Targeting after the Financial Crisis, Challenges to Central Banking", *Reserve Bank of India* Conference, mimeo (2010), Aydin and Volkan (2011), Woodford (2012), Cukierman (2013a) and (2013b), Reichlin L. and Baldwin R., *Is Inflation Targeting Dead? Central Banking After the Crisis*, CEPR book, London (2013), Reis R., "Central Bank Design", *NBER Working Paper Series*, National Bureau of Economic Research, n.19187 (2013), and Borio C., "Monetary Policy and Financial Stability: What Role in Prevention and Recovery?", *BIS Papers*, n.440 (2014). On the empirical relationship between CBI and involvement in supervision, see Dalla Pellegrina L., Masciandaro, and Pansini R. V., "The Central Banker as Prudential Supervisor: Does Independence Matter?", *Journal of Financial Stability*, 9, 415–27 (2013).

[35] On the relationship between monetary policy, inflation, and redistributive effects, see Posen (1995), Bullard J. and Waller C. J., "Central Bank Design in General Equilibrium", *Journal of Money, Credit and Banking*, 36, 95–113 (2004), Doepke M. and Schneider M., "Inflation and the Redistribution of Nominal Wealth", *Journal of Political Economy*, 114, 1069–97 (2006), Alesina A. and Tabellini G., "Bureaucrats or Politicians? Part I: A Single Policy Task", *American Economic Review*, 97, 169–79 (2007), Berriel T., "Nominal Portfolio Choice and the Redistribution Effects of Inflation Surprises", *Working Paper Series*, Princeton University, mimeo, (2009). Coibion O., Gorodnichenko Y., Kueng L. and Silvia J., "Innocent Bystanders? Monetary Policy and Inequality in the U.S.", *NBER Working Paper Series*, National Bureau of Economic Research, n.18710 (2012), and Hau H. and Lai S., "Asset Allocation and Monetary Policy: Evidence from the Eurozone", *CEPR Discussion Paper Series*, Centre for Economic Policy Research, n.9581 (2013).

bailout will likely have wealth distributional effects. If banking bailout is linked to the central bank independence, the citizens can change their preferences on CBI depending on the potential financial effects.[36] In this respect, it is interesting to note that the crisis likely implies a negative shock to the reputation of the central banks,[37] which are linked to the financial instability problems per se. The concerns over financial stability can have implications for the status of independence through the distributional effects on the financial portfolios.

The implications for the analysis of the impact on CBI on concrete reforms of the central bank involvement in supervision are straightforward: it is necessary to evaluate the consequences of reforming central bank involvement in supervision, if any, on the capacity of the central bank to maintain its effectiveness as monetary veto player. In this respect, let us comment on a significant example in the case of the European Central Bank (ECB), which can be considered the benchmark of the modern specialized central bank that now will be more involved in supervision.

It has been claimed[38] that today the ECB enjoys a sufficient level of independence as bank supervisor seemingly "piggy backing" on the arrangements that ensure monetary policy independence. However, such independence would be further enhanced by i) the exercise of self-restraint by the European parliament in its responsibilities of appointment and dismissal of the chair and vice chair of the supervisory board so that political considerations derived of their supervisory decisions do not interfere with their European mandate; ii) the necessary addition of supervisors' legal immunity when exercising their job in good faith. In other words, the effects on the independence of the ECB in hosting the single supervisory mechanism are far from being definitively settled.

CONCLUSION

Before the great crisis, changes in the central bank landscape were characterized by two intertwined features: independent monetary specialization and supervisory neglect. These characteristics are two sides of the same coin: the modern central banker was essentially an independent monetary policy agent, focused on monetary goals, which were pursued by maneuvering interest rates.

These trends become evident upon observing the route that the major central banks have followed. The central banks with full responsibility for monetary stability, the Federal Reserve System (FED), the European Central Bank (ECB), the Bank of England, the Bank of Japan, and the Swiss National Bank, did not have full responsibility for banking supervision. This does not mean that these central

---

[36] Masciandaro and Passarelli (2013).
[37] Issing (2012).
[38] Masciandaro and Nieto (2013).

banks were not concerned with banking stability, but they generally dealt with it from a macroeconomic perspective and only in line with their primary mission of pursuing monetary action.

The modern central bank mainstream can be summarized using the principal-agent terminology.[39] The citizens, which represent the principal, realized that on average the politicians in charge tend to use monetary policy tools to obtain short term macroeconomic goals. The reason is that the politicians are naturally short-sighted agents, given that they try to maximize their probability of remaining in charge. Therefore politicians tend to use monetization to address urgent problems in terms of unemployment, fiscal unbalances, and banking bailouts. But the more the markets are rational and efficient, the more it is likely that monetization policies simply produce more inflation and uncertainty, without any real gains.

The citizens realize the politicians' biases in using monetary policy powers and find it optimal to change the rules of the game: the monetary policy has to be delegated to an independent and unelected bureaucracy, namely the central bank.

Consequently for monetary policy effectiveness, it is crucial that the mission of the central bank is well defined and established, using three criteria. First of all, the main goal of the central bank has to be monetary stability; this can serve to avoid the employment bias that is the temptation to use monetary tools to elude labor market inefficiency problems. Secondly, the central bank cannot finance public deficits and debts; this restriction may help to avoid the fiscal bias that is the temptation of fiscal monetization. Thirdly, central bank involvement in supervision and regulation has to be minimized; this step may assist in avoiding the banking bias that is the temptation of bailout monetization.

Furthermore, the mission of the central bank has to be protected from risks of political capture, emphasizing both its independence from executive power and its accountability with respect to legislative power. Before the crisis, the independence of central banks was the benchmark for evaluating the effectiveness of monetary institutions, and was supported by empirical analyses, which stressed the association between central bank independence and inflation performance.

But now, after the crisis, the scenario is changing. The desire to avoid new cases of systemic banking instability and, at the same time, to address the deep economic crisis, has focused new attention on the architecture of the central bank regimes.

Policymakers in all countries continue to contemplate whether or not to reshape their central bank settings. New proposals to reform these systems have been enacted or are under discussion, at least in Europe and in the United States. In both cases the common trend seems to be an increasing involvement of the central banks in the supervisory field, also taking into account the new distinction between macrosupervision and microsupervision.

---

[39] Masciandaro, D., "Central Banking 2.0: Fitting the Mainstream", *Journal of Financial Stability*, 9, 371–72 (2013a).

It is evident that central banking pillars of monetary specialization and supervisory neglect must be reconsidered. But how? Is it possible to maintain the benefits of the central bank mainstream while at the same time taking into account the importance of financial stability? Consequently, is it possible to reintroduce banking responsibilities into the central bank domain in a way consistent with the present institutional setting, namely without introducing risks of political capture and/or banking capture?

In consideration of these questions, the overall suggestion of this article is that reconsidering the central banking benchmark implies a relevant risk assumption, which so far has been underestimated. How to hedge this risk is a fundamental issue that must be considered to understand not only the economics, if any, of the present demand for central bank reforms, but also which political economy drivers are motivating this demand.

8

The Macroprudential Quandary: Unsystematic Efforts to Reform Financial Regulation

Kern Alexander and Steven L. Schwarcz

INTRODUCTION

The financial crisis of 2007–2009 exposed serious failings in financial regulation. Prior to the crisis, prudential financial regulation was based on a "microprudential" approach in which the main objective was to remove market imperfections at the firm level with the belief that efficient risk management by firms would minimize risk for the system as a whole.[1] As the crisis intensified, however, the Financial Stability Forum concluded in April 2008 that "[a] striking aspect of the turmoil has been the extent of risk management weaknesses and failings at regulated and sophisticated firms."[2] Indeed, weaknesses and failings in financial risk management at the firm level have led academics and policymakers to distinguish between "microprudential regulation," which operates to correct "market failures" by increasing the efficiency of financial firms and markets, and "macroprudential regulation,"[3] which operates to protect the financial system's integrity as a "system" (i.e., a network)[4]. An important

I thank Alexandra Balmer and Philippe Hovaguimian for their research assistance.
I thank Martin L. Horowitz and Bill Warren for excellent research assistance. Portions of this chapter are based in part on Prof. Schwarcz's forthcoming article, *Regulating Financial Change: A Functional Approach*, forthcoming 100 Minnesota Law Review, Issue No. 4.

[1] *See* K. Alexander, J. Eatwell and J. B. Gosse, "Financial Markets and International Regulation," in J. Eatwell, T. McKinley and P. Petit (eds), *Challenges for Europe in the World, 2030* (Ashgate 2014) 106.

[2] Financial Stability Forum, Report of the Financial Stability Forum on Enhancing Market and Institutional Resilience (April, 2008) 10 <www.financialstabilityboard.org/publications/r_0804.pdf> accessed 22 July 2014.

[3] C. Borio, *Towards a Macroprudential Framework for Financial Supervision and Regulation?* in Economic Studies (2013), 183f.

[4] See European Systemic Risk Board, 'The ESRB Handbook on Operationalising Macroprudential Policy in the Banking Sector' September, 2015) pp. 23–27 (stating that '[t]he ultimate objective of macro-prudential policy is to contribute to the safeguarding of the stability of the financial system as a whole'.) also see the path-breaking definition and analysis of macroprudential regulation in: M. Brunnermeier, A. Crockett, C. Goodhart, A. Persaud, and

aspect of macroprudential regulation addresses how "the nature of regulation applied to an individual institution depends crucially on how 'systemic' its activities are," and is "related ... to its size, degree of leverage and inter-connectedness."[5]

This chapter analyzes macroprudential regulation[6] from this perspective and how it is being implemented in the United States, the European Union, and the United Kingdom. Part I traces the general evolution of financial regulation from a microprudential focus on individual firms to a broader approach emphasizing the linkages between firms and investors across financial markets and the infrastructure and operation of those markets. Part II discusses the problem of ad hoc macroprudential regulation and how this can lead to suboptimal regulatory outcomes. Parts III–VII consider in greater detail the macroprudential reforms and frameworks being developed by international "soft law" organizations like the Financial Stability Board (FSB) and Basel Committee on Banking Supervision as well as governments in North America and Europe. Part VIII considers practical examples of "unsystematic" macroprudential regulation and the regulatory challenges posed, while part IX addresses the need for coherence and consistency in the design of a macroprudential regulatory regime.

LINKING MICROPRUDENTIAL AND MACROPRUDENTIAL REGULATION

Many commentators have concluded that a major weakness in prudential bank regulation before the 2007–2009 crisis was that banking supervision and regulation was disproportionately focused on bank balance sheets and less concerned with financial institutions spreading risk throughout the broader financial system in order to evade stricter regulatory requirements. There was also a conventional view that the spreading of risk through the use of credit default swaps and securitization structures reduced banking sector instability because other market participants (i.e., long-term institutional investors) were willing to invest in bank credit and absorb the related risk. The spreading of risk throughout the wholesale debt markets was viewed to be beneficial for financial stability and thought to lead to a more resilient financial system.[7]

The off-balance-sheet spreading of bank risk, however, failed to take into account structural risks and linkages in the financial system that could create systemic risks. There were inadequate macroprudential regulatory and supervisory

---

H. Shin, "The Fundamental Principles of Financial Regulation" (2009) Geneva Reports on the World Economy 11 (International Centre for Banking and Monetary Studies) 18.

[5] *See* Brunnermeier et al., op. cit. 4, p. 11.

[6] Unless the context indicates otherwise, references in this chapter to "financial regulation" mean macroprudential financial regulation.

[7] Brunnemeister et al., *supra* note 4, p. 18.

controls in place, resulting in massive amounts of leverage building up across the financial system and an over-reliance by banks on short-term wholesale funding.[8] Moreover, central bankers failed to understand the linkages between monetary policy and prudential financial regulation and in particular how accommodative interest rate policies can cause asset price bubbles and high levels of leverage in the financial system. The prevailing approach to prudential regulation was essentially microprudential; that is, it was concerned mainly with the stability of individual financial institutions and the response of individual banks to exogenous risks, while ignoring the correlation of risks across asset classes and counterparty credit and liquidity risks in wholesale securities and derivatives markets.[9] The crisis has led to a restructuring of regulation along a macroprudential dimension that aims to identify and control risks both at the level of individual financial institutions and across the financial system. This means that the concept of prudential regulation has expanded to include not only the refinement of microprudential regulatory and supervisory measures for individual banks and financial firms, but also to include linking the regulation of individual firms to developments in the broader financial system and macroeconomy as well as regulating the financial infrastructure (such as clearing and settlement systems).

Although financial regulation is beginning to respond to systemic threats, the subsequent section demonstrates that responses are often driven more by political and emotional reactions to the global finance crisis than by logic. As a result, such "macroprudential" regulation is being promulgated and applied in an ad hoc (and thus unsystematic) way, rather than in a way that ensures regulatory consistency and completeness. The consequence is that such regulation almost certainly will not optimally reduce, and might even increase, systemic risk. Moreover, such regulation might unnecessarily impair microprudential regulation's goal of increasing economic efficiency.

THE PROBLEM OF AD HOC APPROACHES IN MACROPRUDENTIAL REGULATION

In redesigning financial regulation along macroprudential lines, policymakers and regulators tend to focus on the past, what economists have called "the powerful role of historical perception as a framing device."[10] The opinions of European policymakers designing the European Union's monetary union, for example, were "heavily informed by past risks," notably the possibility that excessive budget deficits

---

[8] Ibid. pp. 26–27.
[9] Ibid.
[10] *See, e.g.,* B. Eichengreen, *Euro Area Risk (Mis)management,* in "Recalibrating Risk: Crises, Perceptions, and Regulatory Change" (Edward Balleisen et al., eds., 2014).

could spark high inflation (such as the German hyperinflation of the 1920s).[11] As a result, EU policymakers ignored emerging problems, like the fact that euro area banks were even more highly leveraged than U.S. banks.[12]

Policymakers and regulators also respond to the media, which can create distortions by emphasizing what journalists find accessible, and even sophisticated journalists are sometimes imprecise and biased. Furthermore, after a financial crisis, people naturally want to prevent the next crisis. Regulators, who are themselves usually subject to political short-termism,[13] typically respond by focusing on ex ante preventative regulation, or at least regulation aimed at preventing the next financial meltdown. But that focus is insufficient because it is impossible to always predict the cause of the next financial crisis. Indeed, although panics are often the triggers that commence a chain of systemic failures, it is impossible even to identify all the causes of panics.

For these and other reasons, policymakers and regulators often take an ad hoc (and thus unsystematic) approach to regulation, viewing financial regulation as a collection of ideas. Each of the ideas might make sense in some context; collectively, however, the ideas might not yield a coordinated regulatory framework. Thus, as shown in the following section, regulators and policymakers generally view macroprudential regulatory measures as a loose assortment of "tools" in their "toolkit." Even the theoretical scholarship on law and finance takes a somewhat similar ad hoc approach, yielding "propositions [that] can serve as a tool kit" for regulatory scrutiny.[14]

Examples from Regulatory Theory

This ad hoc approach results in either overly specific regulatory proposals without realistic guidance as to their application or use, or overly broad propositions that provide no concrete regulatory guidance at all. As an example of overly specific regulatory proposals, the "emergent macroprudential 'toolkit' as currently constituted" is said to comprise cross-sectoral leverage ceilings, credit and credit-growth ceilings, reserve and capital buffer requirements, minimum liquidity requirements, limits on maturity mismatches, dynamic countercyclical provisioning, and surveillance and data collection. Although this litany represents a range of diverse approaches, it provides no guidance as to which "tools" should be used in which circumstances, or as to how they should be calibrated. The misapplication of these tools – such as

---

[11] Ibid.
[12] Ibid.
[13] Politicians have short-term reelection goals whereas good regulatory solutions are often long-term.
[14] D. Awrey, C. Baker and K. Pistor, "An Overview of the Legal Theory of Finance", 2 (unpublished manuscript on file with author, 2014).

imposing excessively restrictive leverage or credit and credit-growth ceilings[15] – may be as likely to cause financial problems, however, as to solve them.[16]

Moreover, the very justification for certain of these tools may be questionable. Consider credit and credit-growth ceilings, for example. The justification for these tools is said to be the "compelling evidence that credit booms tend to precede particularly severe and prolonged downturns," which is resulting in "growing support for the view that policymakers should use a variety of tools to minimize ... excessive credit growth" that could fuel asset bubbles.[17] Even though evidence of the mere tendency for credit booms to precede severe economic downturns does not prove a causal relationship, at least some economists conclude from this evidence that the "primary purpose" of macroprudential tools should be "controlling credit growth."[18] And even if the causal relationship were proved, the evidence does not yet appear to provide a clear basis for quantifying a limitation on credit growth. Too strict a limitation could be counterproductive because it might unnecessarily limit economic growth.[19]

As an example of overly broad regulatory propositions, scholars argue that "four interwoven propositions" underlie the legal theory of finance: that financial markets are made up of private contracts and public rules; that the public rules (and associated legal institutions) support these contracts and their enforcement; that the financial system is inherently hierarchical in that the only true lenders of last resort are sovereign states that control their own currency and are able to issue debt in that currency, and that rights and obligations under contracts, private rules, and public laws to which market participants are subject may not be strictly enforced if, in a crisis, nonenforcement is needed to protect the financial system; and that while these rules and laws are necessary to support the development of financial markets, they are also a potentially significant source of financial instability.[20] These propositions ring true, but they are too general to inform the making of actual financial regulation.

This dilemma – that guidelines for macroprudential regulation tend to be either too narrow or too broad – is not limited to financial market regulation. Even in the relatively narrow context of banking regulation, for example, senior officials

---

[15] The imposition of excessively restrictive leverage or credit ceilings, for example, would restrict optimal economic growth. *See infra* note 19 and accompanying text.

[16] *Cf.* Awrey et al., *supra* note 14, 2 (observing that although legal "rules are necessary to support the development of financial markets, they are also a potentially significant source of financial instability") (emphasis in original).

[17] D. J. Elliott, G. Feldberg and A. Lehnert, *The History of Cyclical Macroprudential Policy in the United States* (2013) 2 (Fed. Reserve Bd., Finance and Economics Discussion Series No. 2013–29).

[18] Ibid.

[19] George Cooper, "The Origin of Financial Crises: Central Banks, Credit Bubbles, and the Efficient Market" 121 (2008) (noting that economic growth is strongly tied to the availability of credit and that when credit contracts, so will the economy.)

[20] Elliott et al. *supra* note 17, at 2–5.

propose diverse "policy instruments" without clarity or definition as to how or when to deploy them.[21] The following sections will discuss in greater detail the ad hoc nature of many reforms. However, they will also reveal that progress is being made in some areas toward a more systematic approach to macroprudential regulation.

INTERNATIONAL DEVELOPMENTS IN MACROPRUDENTIAL REGULATION

This section considers the recommendations and proposals of the Basel Committee on Banking Supervision and the FSB and whether they are examples of ad hoc macroprudential regulation. The Basel Committee on Banking Supervision ("Basel Committee") serves as the primary international body responsible for setting banking standards and guidelines.[22] The Basel Committee emerged after the collapse of the Bretton Woods system and published the first Basel Concordat in 1975 and the first Basel Capital Accord in 1988 to address respectively concerns about cross-border banking supervision and bank capital adequacy.[23] The FSB[24] is a similar intergovernmental body set up by the G20 – a group of finance ministers and central bank governors from twenty major national economies – to promote financial stability through better coordination on the international level as well as more effective regulatory policies.[25] Since the financial crisis both international bodies have cooperated in developing proposals for macroprudential reforms – the Basel Committee focusing exclusively on banking supervision and the FSB on the financial services sector at-large.

Since the financial crisis, the FSB's work on macroprudential policy has focused on tracking the general progress made in designing and implementing macropru-dential standards,[26] and reviewing the effectiveness of macroprudential reforms in

---

[21] European Systemic Risk Board, Flagship Report On Macroprudential Policy In The Banking Sector (2014) 8f <www.esrb.europa.eu/pub/pdf/other/140303_flagship_report.pdf?dof12e526e9b00e7c4a137f97776b96c> accessed 22 July 2014.

[22] Bank for International Standards, About the Basel Committee, www.bis.org/bcbs/about.htm (last visited Jul. 28, 2014). The Basel Committee on Banking Standards is housed at the Bank for International Settlements in Basel. Ibid.

[23] *See* Bank for International Settlements, A Brief History of the Committee 1–2 (July 2013) www.bis.org/bcbs/history.pdf. *See* also Kern Alexander, "Global Financial Standard Setting, the G10 Committees, and International Economic Law", 34 *Brooklyn Journal of International Law*, 861-(2009).

[24] The Financial Stability Forum was reconstituted as the Financial Stability Board in 2009 with a clearer mandate and broader membership. *See* L. C. Baker, "Private Actors and Public Governance Beyond the State: The Multinational Corporation, the Financial Stability Board, and the Global Governance Order" (2011) 18 Ind. J. Global Legal Studies 751, 785.

[25] *See* Financial Stability Board, History <www.financial stabilityboard.org/about/history.htm> accessed 18 June 2014.

[26] *See* generally: Financial Stability Board, Macroprudential Policy Tools and Frameworks: Progress Report to G20 (27 October 2011) <www.financialstabilityboard.org/publications/r_111027b.htm> accessed 22 July 2014.

individual member states.[27] The FSB has not yet identified a comprehensive substantive macroprudential regulatory framework.[28] Indeed, its primary current focus is on centralizing macroprudential regulatory supervision, not on designing substantive macroprudential rules.[29] It thus has been recommending that nations adopt a "prudential policy framework [to] explicitly address systemic risk, adopt a systemwide analytical perspective, and target tools at systemic risk" by creating a single regulator with a clear mandate and broad powers.[30]

To the extent it has engaged in substantive macroprudential regulation, the FSB has been cautious, recognizing that there is still "no widely agreed upon and comprehensive theoretical framework."[31] It appears to be taking somewhat of an experimental approach, hoping that countries' use of and experience with different macroprudential tools will "help shed some light" on the effectiveness of those tools.[32] To that end, the FSB is tracking countries' progress in macroprudential reforms,[33] including "intensive monitoring and detailed reporting" that include member states' implementation of the Basel III capital and liquidity standards, over-the-counter (OTC) derivative markets reforms, compensation practices, resolution regimes, prudential standards for SIFIs, and enhanced standards for shadow banking.[34] The FSB has also been attempting to collect data needed to identify systemic risk, which "remains very much a work in progress."[35]

To the extent the FSB has been considering how to design a substantive macroprudential regulatory framework, its guidance has been mostly generic and applicable to any financial regulation: that the regulation be fair, simple, transparent, easy

---

[27] *See, e.g.,* Financial Stability Board, Peer Review of Germany (9 April 2014) <www.financialst abilityboard.org/publications/r_140409.htm> accessed 22 July 2014.

[28] Cf. Progress Report to the G20, *supra* note 26, 9.

[29] The FSB's focus on producing strong supervisory regimes for macroprudential regulations is intended to help macroprudential regulators produce more coherent regulations and foster more effective international cooperation. *See* Ibid. at 18–19. Strong supervisory regimes will also help regulators to resist political pressures associated with regulating tail-end risks. *See* Financial Stability Board, Macroprudential Policy Tools and Frameworks: Update to the G20 Finance Ministers and Central Bank Governors (14 February 2011) 11 <www.imf.org/external/ np/g20/pdf/021411.pdf> accessed 22 July 2014.

[30] Ibid. 4. In its 2013 survey of member states, the FSB found that seventeen countries have "establish[ed] [a] regulatory framework for macroprudential oversight"; thirteen countries have "enhance[ed] systemwide monitoring and the use of macroprudential instruments"; and seventeen countries have generally "[i]mproved cooperation between supervisors and central banks." *See* Financial Stability Board, Table: Status of implementation of G20/FSB recommendations based on self-reported progress by member jurisdictions in IMN 2013 Survey, <www.financialstabilityboard.org/implementation_monitoring/other.htm> (accessed 18 June 2014).

[31] *See* PROGRESS REPORT TO G20, *supra* note 26, 9.

[32] *See* Ibid. 12.

[33] *See* Ibid. 3.

[34] *See* Financial Stability Board, Priority Areas, <www.financialstabilityboard.org/implementa tion_monitoring/reform.htm> (accessed 18 June 2014).

[35] *See* Progress Report to the G20, *supra* note 26, 9.

to apply, and have low implementation costs.[36] Although some of the FSB's substantive regulatory guidance appears more specific – for example, that macroprudential regulation should address the accumulation of risks both over time and across sectors[37] – its application of that guidance is unresolved. For example, the FSB proposes a macroprudential countercyclical capital buffer aimed at addressing "excess aggregate credit growth" as a tool to address the accumulation of risk over time.[38] However, it concedes that "the exercise of discretion will remain critical" in determining when to activate that buffer.[39] And although it recommends five "[o]verarching principles" for regulation of the shadow-banking sector, the FSB leaves it up to individual countries to "select the appropriate tool(s) from the policy toolkit."[40] As discussed earlier, a regulatory toolbox that provides no guidance as to which tools should be used in which circumstances, or as to how they should be calibrated, invites misapplication of the tools.[41]

This fragmented and disjointed approach to the rationale and implementation of macroprudential regulation at the international level suggests the potential for a wide array of national approaches that are based on principles and operational guidelines that are not always coherent or consistent.

For its part, the Basel Committee has taken a broader macroprudential supervisory approach that involves, among other things, devising banking standards to measure and limit leverage levels in the financial system as a whole, requiring financial institutions to have enhanced liquidity reserves against short-term wholesale funding exposures, and, more generally, countercyclical capital regulation – requiring banks to hold more regulatory capital during good times and permitting them to hold less than the normal minimum amount during bad times. Under Basel III,[42] countercyclical capital requirements would link capital charges to

---

[36] *See* Financial Stability Forum, Working Group on Market and Institutional Resilience, Addressing Financial System Procyclicality: A Possible Framework 5 (1 September 2008).

[37] *See* Financial Stability Board et al., Macroprudential Policy Tools and Frameworks: Update to the G20 Finance Ministers and Central Bank Governors (2011) 2 <www.financialstability board.org/publications/r_1103.pdf> accessed 18 June 2014.

[38] *See* Ibid. 5f. This proposal is in accord with the Basel III recommendations made by the Basel Committee on Banking Supervision. *See* Basel Committee on Banking Supervision, Basel III: A Global Regulatory Framework for More Resilient Banks and Banking Systems 57 (rev. 2011).

[39] Ibid. 5.

[40] *See* Financial Stability Board, Strengthening Oversight and Regulation of Shadow Banking: Policy Framework for Strengthening Oversight and Regulation of Shadow Banking Entities (2013) 12 <www.financialstabilityboard.org/publications/r_121118.htm> accessed 18 June 2014.

[41] See ESRB, *supra* note 4.

[42] Basel III requires an increased level of Tier One regulatory capital to 7.0 percent (including a capital conservation buffer), a tighter definition of tier one capital to include only ordinary common shares, an additional 2.5 percent countercyclical capital ratio (yet to be determined for implementation); and liquidity requirements that include a ratio for stable wholesale funding, liquidity coverage ratios, and an overall leverage ratio. Recent the Basel Committee has agreed on an additional capital charge of up to 2.5 percent regulatory capital for large and inter-connected systemically important financial institutions (SIFIs).

points in the macroeconomic and business cycle. For example, the bank supervisor would be empowered to apply stricter requirements at predetermined times when the economy is growing strongly above its normal trend growth rate, and to lower the required amount if the economy was performing below trend or if in a recession. The Basel Committee has also adopted an "internationally harmonized" leverage ratio[43] and a global minimum standard for funding liquidity and liquidity ratios that are deemed to be necessary to promote consistency in macroprudential regulatory frameworks.

To support its work the Basel Committee has introduced a framework for national authorities to consider how to implement countercyclical capital buffers. In doing so, it is reviewing the appropriate set of macroeconomic indicators (e.g., credit variables) and micro-indicators (banks' earnings) to determine how and when countercyclical regulatory charges and buffers should be imposed. This will necessarily involve banks using more forward-looking provisions based on expected losses over the economic cycle.

The Basel Committee has emphasized that a more effective macroprudential capital regime requires enhanced quality and transparency of tier one capital that allows shareholders to absorb losses more readily and that imposes losses on certain creditors and bondholders as part of a resolution framework. While the Basel III framework represents a step toward a more comprehensive supervisory framework for banks, it reflects the fact that, thus far, macroprudential regulation focuses too much on "risks arising from the leverage on the balance sheet of banks."[44] This narrow focus, however, may miss how unleveraged financial institutions such as asset managers contribute to risk in the financial system.[45]

U.S. FINANCIAL REGULATION

The history of macroprudential regulation in the United States reflects a reliance on "policies [that] remain somewhat poorly defined."[46] Moreover, there is "ambiguity about when (if ever) such [macroprudential regulatory] tools should be used to promote financial stability" as opposed to promoting microprudential goals such as "safety and soundness or consumer protection."[47] That ambiguity is compounded

---

[43] The leverage ratio is necessary to address gaps in the regulatory capital regime involving banks classifying a high proportion of their assets as nonrisk weighted and thereby not subject to capital requirements. Basel III provides a leverage ratio of 3 percent defined as total tier one equity capital divided by total assets (risk-weighted and nonrisk weighted) to absorb more losses in a situation where there is a sharp and sudden deterioration of bank assets.

[44] Andrew G. Haldane, Executive Director, Financial Stability, Bank of England, Speech at the London Business School: The Age of Asset Management 13 (4 April 2014).

[45] *See* ibid.

[46] *See* Elliott et al, *supra* note 17, 6.

[47] Ibid.

by fragmented supervisory authority, in which the power to use macroprudential tools is sometimes given to regulators who lack an explicit mandate to promote financial stability.[48]

The post-financial-crisis discussions on macroprudential regulatory reform identify various regulatory tools, often focusing on a countercyclical and flexible approach to capital requirements.[49] Capital requirements are intended to protect financial institutions against unexpected losses. As illustrated later here, however, a poorly executed countercyclical and flexible approach to capital requirements can backfire, actually triggering a crisis.

Capital requirements in their modern form – based on ratios rather than fixed dollar amounts – were introduced into banking regulation in the 1980s.[50] Savings and loan institutions ("S&Ls") "were [similarly] subject to minimum capital ratios that were mandated by statute."[51] Some time thereafter, however, the banking industry, and especially S&Ls, faced a period in which rising interest rates made lending less attractive to borrowers.[52] To avoid having to commit government funds to bail out financially stressed S&Ls, regulators relieved part of the stress by engaging in a type of countercyclicality: they eased the capital ratios in order to "help banks muddle through [that] difficult period."[53] However, the result of that forbearance, in conjunction with other regulatory-relief steps, was to rapidly expand the size of the savings-and-loan industry – from $686 billion in 1982 to $1.1 trillion 1985.[54] When the savings-and-loan industry eventually collapsed, its increased size led to the largest federal bailout in history up to that time.[55]

---

[48] Ibid. 7.

[49] *See* K. N. Johnson, "Macroprudential Regulation: A Sustainable Approach to Regulating Financial Markets" (2013) U. Ill. L. Rev. 881, 916 (discussing flexible capital requirements as a macroprudential tool); Richard Berner, Director of Office of Financial Research, Remarks at the Joint Conference of the Federal Reserve Bank of Cleveland and Office of Financial Research, Financial Stability Analysis: "Using the Tools, Finding the Data" (May 30, 2013) (identifying countercyclical capital requirements as a tool to reduce or neutralize "threats to financial stability").

[50] Elliot et al., *supra* note 17, 34 (discussing how bank regulators switched from using capital requirements based on fixed dollar amounts to capital requirements based on the ratio of capital to total assets, and how the Basel I Accord spread that latter regulatory approach internationally).

[51] Ibid.

[52] Ibid.

[53] Ibid. (Observing that this countercyclicality was imprecisely implemented).

[54] Ibid. The eased capital ratios enabled rapid growth. For example, a $2 million dollar investment in a new S&L could be leveraged into $1.3 billion in assets. *See* 1 Division Of Research And Statistics, Federal Deposit Insurance Corporation, History Of The 80s –Lessons For The Future (1997) 172f <www.fdic.gov/bank/historical/history/index.html>.

[55] *See* L. A. Cunningham and D. Zaring, "Three or Four Approaches to Financial Regulation: A Cautionary Analysis Against Exuberance in Crisis Response" (2009) 78 Geo. Wash. L. Rev. 39, 51.

After the 2008 financial crisis, the United States recognized that its financial regulation focused too heavily on microprudential regulation.[56] The response was the Dodd-Frank Act,[57] the preface of which states it is "[a]n Act to promote the financial stability of the United States by improving accountability and transparency in the financial system, to end 'too big to fail,' to protect the American taxpayer by ending bailouts, to protect consumers from abusive financial services practices, and for other purposes."[58] But while many of Dodd-Frank's regulatory tools purport to focus, at least nominally, on systemic risk,[59] the act lacks a comprehensive framework that integrates those tools.[60] Furthermore, its approach to systemic risk relies heavily on firm-centric solutions,[61] largely ignoring financial markets.

In time, however, Title I of the Dodd-Frank Act may set the groundwork for a more comprehensive future macroprudential framework[62] by creating the Financial Stability Oversight Council (FSOC), which brings together top regulators from across the government in order to identify and address systemic risk.[63] A new Office of Financial Research will support FSOC's mission by collecting data across

[56] *See* C. D. Block, "A Continuum Approach to Systemic Risk and Too-Big-To-Fail" (2012) 6 Brook. J. Corp. Fin. and Com. L. 289, 317

[57] *See* Johnson, *supra* note 49, 917.

[58] Dodd Frank Wall Street Reform and Consumer Protection Act, PL 111–203, 124 Stat 1376 (2010) (the "Dodd-Frank Act").

[59] *See, e.g.*, Dodd-Frank Act § 502 (establishing a Federal Insurance Office to "identifying issues or gaps in the regulation of insurers that could contribute to a systemic crisis in the insurance industry").

[60] *See* Smith, Muñiz-Fraticelli, *infra* note 144, 618; *Cf.* D. Kohn, Institutions for Macroprudential Regulation: The UK and U.S. (Brookings Institution, 17 April 2014) <www.brookings.edu/research/speeches/2014/04/17-institutions-macroprudential-regulation-kohn> accessed 22 July 2014 (observing that the Dodd-Frank Act "grafted the macroprudential regulator" on top of the existing fragmented regulatory structure).

[61] Examples of Dodd-Frank's firm-centric approach include the SIFI designation, which triggers enhanced prudential standards for firms (*see* Dodd-Frank Act § 113), and the requirement for large bank holding companies and SIFIs to have living wills (*see id.* § 165(d)). The SIFI-designation process is ultimately based on government discretion, involving broad guidelines such as size and interconnectedness that prevents firms from predicting whether they will be subjected to heightened regulatory scrutiny. *See id.* § 113(a); *also* § 165(a). That also poses a risk that regulators will be under-inclusive in subjecting firms to that scrutiny. *See, e.g.*, Smith, Muñiz-Fraticelli, *infra* note 144144, at 624 (noting generally that "[i]dentifying set individual and groups will always raise questions of underinclusiveness in financial regulation"). Dodd-Frank also enables the so-called Volcker Rule, which prohibits banks from proprietary trading and entering into certain relationships with hedge fund and private equity funds. Dodd-Frank Act § 619. Differentiating proprietary trading from permissible hedging will involve complex determinations. *See* A. E. Wilmarth Jr., "The Dodd-Frank Act: A Flawed and Inadequate Response to the Too-Big-To-Fail Problem" (2011) 89 Or. L. Rev. 951, 1028. As noted later, it also may decrease the efficiency of firms. *See infra* note 174. Moreover, by applying the prohibition on proprietary trading only to banks, the regulation risks incentivizing banks to move proprietary trading to less regulated areas. Wilmarth, *supra* at 1028.

[62] Johnson, *supra* note 49, 917.

[63] Dodd-Frank Act §§ 111–112.

regulators in order to identify potential macroprudential risks.[64] In addition to its general oversight and advisory role, FSOC can make recommendations on a "comply or explain" basis to other government agencies.[65]

U.S. regulators recognize there is still much to be done in order to design macroprudential regulation to address systemic risk.[66] It is unlikely that the United States will develop a truly comprehensive macroprudential framework anytime soon.[67]

THE U.K.'S MACROPRUDENTIAL FOCUS

Post-financial-crisis macroprudential regulation in the United Kingdom partly reflects an ad hoc approach, though UK macroprudential regulation appears to be striving more toward a systematic and comprehensive framework than its U.S. counterpart. The governing laws are the Financial Services Act of 2012 (the "UK Financial Services Act"),[68] which creates the "independent" Financial Policy Committee (FPC) at the Bank of England as the primary macroprudential regulatory coordinator,[69] and the Financial Services Act of 2013 (the "UK Banking Reform Act"), which ring-fences the banking system among other reforms.[70] These two laws serve as the cornerstone of the more systematic macroprudential reforms taking place in the UK.

In analyzing British regulatory failures before the crisis, the Turner Review found that a lack of macroprudential regulation was more directly relevant to causing the financial crisis than any specific failure relating to an individual firm.[71] *The Review* suggested that had there been a better understanding of the link between financial stability and macroeconomic stability there could have been more effective measures formulated to address specific risks of individual banks and firms.[72] *The Review* cited the liquidity risks manifest in the maturity transformation function of banks, the level of asset prices in property, equity and securitized credit

---

[64] Ibid. § 153.

[65] Ibid. § 120.

[66] Benjamin S. Bernanke, Competition Implementing a Macroprudential Approach to Supervision and Regulation, Speech at the 47th Annual Conference on Bank Structure and (Chicago Illinois 5 May 2011).

[67] Indeed, uncertain regulatory guidelines might be politically intentional. *See, e.g.,* e-mail from Charles Klingman, Critical Infrastructure and Compliance Policy Department of U.S. Treasury, U.S. Financial Stability Oversight Council, to the author (12 May 2014): "If a regulator is too specific or clear in how to use tools, then there will be those stating that such usage would be deeply unfair and improper. So, the tools are rarely well targeted because such targeting would be the subject of deep controversy, and if the likely targeting of a tool is readily discernable from the tool itself then it is also subject to withering attack."

[68] Financial Services Act, 2012 (UK) c. 21.

[69] Ibid, c. 21, § 4.

[70] Financial Services (Banking Reform) Act, 2013, c. 33, § 4 (UK).

[71] The Financial Services Authority, The Turner Review (HMSO 2009) 83.

[72] Ibid. 85.

as well as the level of leverage in the financial system as areas where regulators and supervisors could develop a better understanding of how systemic risk can arise. The Bank of England comes under specific criticism in *the Review* for not formulating policy to offset the risks identified in the Bank's Financial Stability Reviews conducted in the years before the crisis.

While the supervision of individual financial institutions was a great concern to the FSA (a chiefly microprudential perspective), there was not enough investigation into sectoral or systemic risks present in the structure of the system.[73] To remedy this, the Financial Services Act 2012 created a new institutional framework for financial regulation consisting of a "twin peaks" approach to microprudential supervision, consisting of a Prudential Regulation Authority, responsible for supervising individual banks and insurance firms, and a Financial Conduct Authority, responsible for investor protection and market abuse. The act also created the FPC to serve as the UK's primary macroprudential overseer.[74] The FPC is tasked with coordinating and directing macroprudential reforms through making recommendations and issuing directives regarding the use of macroprudential measures and instruments and assessing macroprudential conditions in the financial sector.[75] The FPC is expected to conduct research on macroprudential risks and to challenge conventional wisdom in microprudential regulatory practices to ensure that generally accepted principles are continually tested. For instance, by challenging conventional wisdom, the FPC is also expected to challenge the judgments of other supervisors and international organizations, such as the International Monetary Fund that issued a report a year before the crisis began in 2006 claiming that "the dispersion of credit risk by banks to a broader... group of investors... helped make the... financial system more resilient."[76]

In addition, a more effective macroprudential supervisory regime may lead the UK's principles-based approach to regulation and supervision to become more rules-based at the level of the financial system. The Financial Services Act 2012 has authorized the FPC to implement a "macroprudential" regulatory model to control systemic risks in the financial system. Macroprudential regulation can be divided into three main areas: 1) the regulation of individual firms must take into account both firm level practices and broader macroeconomic developments in determining how regulatory requirements will be imposed (i.e., growth of asset prices and contracyclical bank provisioning), 2) controls on the levels of risk-taking and leverage at the level of the financial system, and 3) the regulation of the

---

[73] Ibid. 85.

[74] Financial Services Act, 2012, c. 21, § 4 (UK)

[75] Both the PRA and FCA are subject to directions and recommendations on a comply-or-explain basis by the FPC in regards to macroprudential measures to the entities or activities they oversee. *See* Financial Services Act, 2012, c. 21, §§ 4–6 (UK).

[76] International Monetary Fund, Financial Stability Report (April 2006) <www.imf.org/external/pubs/ft/GFSR/2006/01/> accessed 23 July 2014.

infrastructure of the financial system – clearing, settlement, and payment systems – along with requirements that OTC derivative contracts are centrally cleared and that securities and currency settlement networks are robust and resilient. Another lesson for the UK is that the new focus on macroprudential controls at the level of the financial system will require the PRA and FPC to play a greater role in monitoring systemic risk and imposing controls at the level of the financial system. In other words, the FPC with support from the PRA and FCA will become the key player in the regulation of systemic risk. The FPC would exercise primary regulatory authority to address the market failures that arise from interconnected financial markets and the shifting of risk off-balance sheet to 'shadow' sectors of financial markets. As a result, the UK's new regulatory regime, based on macro and micro rule-based controls, will change the nature of financial regulation dramatically and possibly lead to new regulatory risks that will arise because of the responses of market participants who will undoubtedly seek to avoid these regulatory controls by adopting innovative financial instruments and structures.

This is not to say that the UK's new regulatory regime completely avoids ad hoc or unsystematic regulation. That act fails to designate or describe which tools the FPC may use to fulfill its statutory objective of identifying, monitoring, and taking action to remove or reduce systemic risk.[77] Although the FPC is working with UK and European prudential regulators to consider and implement macroprudential tools – that include stress testing, tighter mortgage-loan underwriting requirements, and capital requirements[78] – that work does not appear to be systematic. Each tool, for example, is considered in isolation, rather than as part of a larger, comprehensive framework for managing systemic risk. The FPC's Financial Stability Report thus reviews its progress in designing and implementing macroprudential tools but does not explain how or when these tools should be used in relation to one another.[79] This ad hoc exploratory approach may well reflect the limited historical data on the effect of macroprudential tools, which leaves the FPC in uncharted territory.[80] To that extent, an ad hoc approach indeed makes sense insofar as it can, as the FPC appears to be attempting to, consider the costs, benefits, and functions of each tool.[81]

UK macroprudential regulation thus has both ad hoc and systematic aspects. From a supervisory standpoint, however, the United Kingdom may administratively be heading toward a more systematic and comprehensive framework, in part because it now has a primary macroprudential coordinator, the FPC, which can

---

[77] *See* Financial Services Act, 2012, cl. 21, § 4 (UK).
[78] *See* FINANCIAL POLICY COMMITTEE, FINANCIAL STABILITY REPORT at 49–54 (November 2013).
[79] FINANCIAL STABILITY REPORT, *supra* note 78, at 49–68.
[80] *See* Bank of England and Financial Services Authority, Instruments of Macroprudential Policy 18 (Discussion Paper) (December 2011), *available at* www.bankofengland.co.uk/publi cations/Documents/other/financialstability/discussionpaper111220.pdf.
[81] *See id.* at 18–26.

make recommendations, and sometimes even issue directions, to other UK financial regulators.[82] This degree of coordination should allow the United Kingdom to avoid some of the dangers that can arise, including in the United States, when macroprudential regulation is left up to a fragmented set of regulators.[83] Indeed, the FPC is better situated than its closest U.S. counterpart – the Financial Services Oversight Council (FSOC), which is limited to identifying SIFIs and making recommendations on a comply-or-explain basis[84] – to create a systematic and comprehensive framework for macroprudential regulation.[85]

EUROPEAN UNION MACROPRUDENTIAL REGULATION AND SUPERVISION[86]

Similarly to the UK, the European Union has embarked on a major institutional restructuring of financial regulation by creating a European System of Financial Supervision ("ESFS") consisting of three microprudential supervisory authorities – the European Banking Authority, the European Securities and Markets Authority and the European Insurance and Occupational and Pension Authority – and a European Systemic Risk Board (ESRB) to conduct macroprudential oversight of the European financial system. And the ongoing euro area sovereign debt crisis has led to further legislative proposals granting the European Central Bank bank-supervisory powers and the creation of a single resolution mechanism in the eurozone that will be administered by a single resolution board and supported by a single resolution fund that will be financed by bank levies and supported by national resolution funds that

---

[82] Awrey et al., *supra* note 14; Cooper, *supra* note 19 and accompanying text. Prior to the UK Financial Services Act, the United Kingdom – like most countries – lacked a macroprudential regulator. Rawlings, *All Change: The Fall of the FSA and the Further Rise of the Bank of England*, 30 No. 4 Banking and Fin. Services Pol'y Rep. 16, 20 (2011).

[83] *Cf.* Elliott et al., *supra* note 17, 7 (observing "the inherently fragmented authority governing the use" of macroprudential tools in the United States).

[84] *See* 12 U.S.C. § 5322 (2010) (listing FSOC's duties and powers). FSOC lacks the power to issue directions and force action by any other regulatory agencies. *See* Ibid. FSOC's recent experience, in which it recommended that the U.S. Securities and Exchange Commission (SEC) issue money-market mutual fund regulations, also shows the limitations of its comply-or-explain recommendation powers. The SEC simply rejected FSOC's recommendation. *See* Kohn, *supra* note 60.

[85] *Cf.* Kohn, *supra* note 60.

[86] The ESFS was adopted based on proposals by the De Larosiere Committee in February 2008 in the wake of the financial crisis that was aimed at further institutional consolidation of the previous Lamfalussy framework that had sought enhanced supervisory coordination and harmonised implementation of EU financial legislation. The Lamfalussy institutional framework, however, had failed to produce more harmonized standards of financial regulation across member states because it was not able to overcome different sets of national standards, responsibilities and powers of member-state supervisors that had hampered the European financial integration process and had resulted in disjointed supervisory practices and a failure to identify and monitor risks building up in the financial system. *See* IMF (2007).

would together finance the resolution of weak eurozone banks. The section will address the ESFS with respect to how it coordinates macro and microprudential supervision and regulation, and also address the new supervisory powers of the European Central Banks and its related macroprudential mandate.

The European System of Financial Supervision attempts to link in a coherent way the European Systemic Risk Board's (ESRB) macroprudential supervision and oversight function with the three European Supervisory Authorities (ESAs) function for coordinating the harmonized implementation of microprudential supervisory powers.[87] Indeed, the linkage is essential for building an efficient EU supervisory regime that allows member states to exercise more effective supervisory oversight over individual firms and investors, while monitoring, measuring and issuing recommendations and warnings about systemic risk in the broader European financial system and across global financial markets. Moreover, the ESFS and the three ESAs will ensure that member-state regulatory and supervisory authorities can work more effectively together at the microprudential level to control and manage systemic risk and develop a harmonized regulatory code and implementation across all EU states.[88]

European Systemic Risk Board's Macroprudential Function

The European parliament and council of ministers approved Regulation 1092/2010 in 2010 creating a European Systemic Risk Board (ESRB).[89] The ESRB is chaired by the president of the European Central Bank and serves as the EU's principal macroprudential oversight council.[90] Much of the ESRB's work focuses on monitoring systemic risk and providing guidance on possible macroprudential tools.[91] The ESRB may also make recommendations to particular EU macroprudential

---

[87] *See* K. Alexander, Which supervisory model for Europe (2010) Report to the Committee on the Financial Crisis <www.europarl.europa.eu/document/activities/cont/201103/20110324 ATT16356/20110324ATT16356EN.pdf> accessed 23 July 2014.

[88] *See* K. Alexander, "Reforming EU Financial Supervision: Adapting EU Institutions to Market Structures" (2011) Journal of the European Law Academy 12(2) 229, 240–43; K. Alexander, Note on EU Bank Resolution and the ECB (9 October 2012) written evidence before the House of Lords Europe Committee, Appendix 2, 103ff (on file with author).

[89] *See* Regulation 1092/2010 on European Union macroprudential oversight of the financial system and establishing a European Systemic Risk Board, O.J. 2010 L33/1. The ESRB's became operational on 16 December 2010. The impetus for the creation of the ESRB was the proposal for a European Systemic Risk Committee by the De Laroisere Committee in 2009. *See generally* Report of the High-Level Group on Financial Supervision in the EU (Brussels 25 February 2009) (hereinafter *De Larosiere Report*) (also calling for enhanced capital buffers offered by Basel III, new leverage requirements, greater financial transparency, and structural reforms in the banking sector). *See* P. J. Green, J. C. Jennings-Mares, Regulatory Reform In Europe: What To Expect in 2014 (Februray 2014), Thompson Reuters Tax and Accounting No. 6,1–3.

[90] *See De Larosiere Report, supra* note 89, 46.

[91] *See* European Systemic Risk Board, The ESRB Handbook on Operationalizing Macroprudential Policy in the Banking Sector 18–20 (2014).

regulators and member states on an "act or explain" basis in order to address risk emerging across Europe or in individual countries.[92]

Thus far, the ESRB's recommendations have targeted specific types of institutions or activities such as banks, money-market funds, and foreign-currency lending, although a few of its recommendations deal with macroprudential goals more generally.[93] The ESRB's primary progress toward developing a comprehensive macroprudential framework has been limited to the banking sector. To that end, it has designated four intermediate objectives that drive its macroprudential reforms: controlling excessive credit growth and leverage, mitigating excessive maturity mismatch, limiting exposure concentrations among individual institutions, and correcting misaligned incentives.[94] It also has recommended regulatory tools to address each of these objectives, including countercyclical capital buffers and leverage ratios to control excessive credit growth and leverage.[95] Although the ESRB provides detailed and thorough guidance on these regulatory tools,[96] it envisions each tool to be chosen from the toolkit at the regulator's discretion.[97] To that extent, its approach is still unsystematic.

The ESRB nonetheless comes closer than most other macroprudential regulators to achieving a comprehensive regulatory framework. For example, it recommends prioritizing and limiting the use of certain tools, such as systemic risk buffers and national flexibility measures, only where the other tools have failed to sufficiently mitigate risks.[98] Furthermore, it provides some guidance on the order in which EU countries should activate categories of macroprudential tools.[99]

In addition to the work of the ESRB, the European Commission is also proposing structural reforms to the banking system recommended by the so-called Liikanen Report.[100] The Liikanen Report proposes, for most banks,[101] the separation, or

---

[92] Ibid. *See* Commission Regulation 1092/2010, 2010 O.J. (L 331) 3. Those regulators who receive recommendations must "provide an adequate justification in the case of inaction.

[93] *See* European Systemic Risk Board, Recommendations <www.esrb.europa.eu/pub/recommendations/html/index.en.html> accessed 24 June 2014.

[94] *See* The ESRB Handbook, *supra* note 91, 7.

[95] *See* Ibid. 8–10. The ESRB provides a "nonexhaustive list of suitable instruments" to address the Board's intermediate objectives. Ibid. The use of these instruments relies on the ESRB's macroprudential strategy that involves "instrument selection and calibration" based on "risk identification and assessment." *See* Ibid. at 14.

[96] *See, e.g.,* Ibid. 26–47 (discussing the use and calibration of countercyclical capital buffers).

[97] *Cf.* Ibid. 17. The ESRB speaks about "the selection and calibration of macroprudential instruments" in order to address particular types of risk.

[98] *See* Ibid. 18–19.

[99] *See* Ibid. 171.

[100] Final Report of the High-Level Expert Group on Reforming the Structure of the EU Banking Sector (2012) i (hereinafter Liikanen Report). Erkki Liikanen was the chair of this Expert Group.

[101] *See* Liikanen Report, *supra* note 100 (proposing ring-fencing for any bank or credit institution whose proprietary trading consists of at least 15–20% of its activity or whose assets pass a certain dollar threshold).

ring-fencing,[102] of proprietary trading and other risky activities from the bank's deposit-taking activities.[103] The Report's rationale is that other regulatory reforms did "not fully correct incentives for excessive risk taking, complexity, and intragroup subsidies."[104] The Liikanen Report's proposed ring-fencing has been criticized, though, because it will be difficult to define and identify proprietary trading[105] and also because some fear that the ring-fencing would drive proprietary trading to the less regulated shadow-banking sector.[106]

Banking Union and Macroprudential Supervision

In late June 2012, the European Council of Ministers issued a decision to create a euro area banking union designed to build a more effective banking supervision regime in the euro area and across the European Union by empowering the European Central Bank to be the bank supervisor for euro area and other partici- pating member states. The banking union proposal consisted of three main pillars: a unified eurozone banking supervisory regime, a recovery and resolution frame- work (a single resolution mechanism), and a deposit guarantee system.[107] The three elements of banking union were considered necessary to stabilize the eurozone financial system by proposing to allow the European Stability Mechanism to recapitalize ailing euro area banks on the condition that these banks are subject to strict ECB supervision and conditionality and by justifying the ECB's use of extraordinary monetary policy measures ("outright monetary transactions") to increase liquidity support for eurozone sovereigns and banks. The council's decision was followed by the European Commission's proposed regulation[108] in September 2012 conferring bank supervisory powers on the European Central Bank, and another regulation amending the European Banking Authority's powers regarding its interaction with the ECB in respect of the supervision of credit

---

[102] For a comprehensive discussion and analysis of ring-fencing, *see* S L Schwarcz, Ring-Fencing (2013) 87 Southern California Law Review 69.

[103] *See* Liikanen Report, *supra* note 100, 100. Those deposit-taking activities would take place in a separately capitalized subsidiary. *See* Ibid. at 101.

[104] *See* Ibid. 94. Cf. ICB Final Report, *supra* note 127 and accompanying text (discussing the Vickers Report, which also recommended bank ring-fencing).

[105] *See* The Liikanen Review: Into the Ring (6 October 2012) The Economist <www.economist .com/node/21564233>. This same criticism is made of the Volcker Rule, which purports to ban proprietary trading in banks and SIFIs. *See infra* Part III.B.2 (discussing the Volcker Rule). *See* also Chair of E.U. Expert Group Calls Volcker Rule The Most Narrow and Radical Approach (17 May 2013) 7 Hedge Funds and Private Equity: Regulation and Risk Mgmt. Update No. 3.

[106] *See* J. Brunsden, *Liikanen's Bank-Separation Proposal Sparks Opposition, EU Says* <www.bloomberg.com/news/2012-12-20/liikanen-s-bank-separation-proposal-sparks-oppos ition-eu-says.html> (last visited 25 June 2014).

[107] Council, Conclusions, 29 June 2012, EUCO 76/12., p. 3.

[108] Commission, Proposal for a Council Regulation conferring specific tasks on the European Central Bank concerning policies relating to the prudential supervision of credit institutions, COM(2012) 511 final (Brussels 12 September 2012).

institutions.[109] Both regulations were eventually adopted by the EU parliament and council in October 2013.[110]

The ECB's supervisory powers will be exercised through a Single Supervisory Mechanism (SSM) consisting in the cooperation of national competent authorities (NCAs) with an executive board within the ECB – a Single Supervisory Board (SSB). The ECB will be primarily responsible for the licensing of all banks in the eurozone or participating member states, as well as for the monitoring and enforcing of various prudential regulations, such as capital adequacy requirements, liquidity buffers and leverage limits, against certain *significant* eurozone/participating banks under its direct supervision.[111] Among those tasks, the ECB will be empowered to approve bank recovery plans[112] or make use of the CRD IV supervisory measures aiming to address systemic risks at the level of individual banks.[113] For banks not significant enough to fall under the direct supervision of the ECB, these tasks will be exercised by the NCAs, nonetheless following the regulations, guidelines, and general instructions issued by the ECB to that effect.[114]

Final amendments to the SSM regulation also included additional powers for the ECB to exercise certain macroprudential powers in limited situations. The SSM's macroprudential tasks are set forth in article 5, entitled "Macroprudential tasks and tools," which include the discretion to impose stricter prudential requirements under CRD IV, including higher capital buffers, on individual banks based on macroprudential factors in the country where the bank is based.[115] Although the exercise of these macroprudential tools rests primarily with the national competent authorities (NCAs);[116] the ECB may intervene and utilize these tools "if deemed necessary,"[117] and in adopting a particular measure is then required to take the specific circumstances of the member state's financial and economic situation into account[118] as well as "duly consider" any objection of a eurozone national

---

[109] Commission, Proposal for a Regulation of the European Parliament and of the Council amending Regulation (EU) No 1093/2010 establishing a European Supervisory Authority (European Banking Authority), COM(2012) 512 final (Brussels 12 September 2012).

[110] Council Regulation (EU) No 1024/2013 of 15 October 2013 conferring specific tasks on the European Central Bank concerning policies relating to the prudential supervision of credit institutions; Regulation (EU) No 1022/2013 of the European Parliament and of the Council of 22 October 2013 amending Regulation (EU) No 1093/2010 establishing a European Supervisory Authority (European Banking Authority) as regards the conferral of specific tasks on the European Central Bank pursuant to Council Regulation (EU) No 1024/2013.

[111] Art 4(1)(b), (d)-(i) and Art. 6(4)-(6) *e contrario* Regulation (EU) No 1024/2013.

[112] Art 4(1)(i) Regulation (EU) No 1024/2013.

[113] Namely the review of systemic risks affecting the Member State's financial system (Art. 97(1) (b) CRD IV) and the subsequent imposition of specific capital, liquidity, operational or governance requirements addressing those risks (Art.104–105 CRD IV).

[114] Art. 6(4)-(6) Regulation (EU) No 1024/2013.

[115] Art. 5 Regulation (EU) No 1024/2013.

[116] Art. 5(1) Regulation (EU) No 1024/2013.

[117] Art. 5(2) Regulation (EU) No 1024/2013.

[118] Art. 5(5) Regulation (EU) No 1024/2013.

competent authority that seeks to address a macroprudential risk on its own.[119] These reforms empower the ECB to protect the eurozone from systemic risks, however the ECB's powers rely on ad hoc judgments, which may raise concerns about the consistent application of such powers.

Moreover, under the proposal for a special resolution mechanism (SRM), the ECB will have limited macroprudential powers, merely allowing it to cooperate with the SRM's single resolution board (SRB) in conducting an *assessment* of the extent to which banks and groups under its direct supervision are resolvable without the assumption of extraordinary public financial support,[120] and to notify the SRB of a supervised entity requiring resolution.[121]

MACROPRUDENTIAL REGULATION IN PRACTICE

Despite the difficult policy and institutional challenges of implementing a macro-prudential regulatory regime, the European Banking Authority has encouraged the EU member states to adjust their regulatory instruments and practices to take account of macroprudential objectives. The United Kingdom's FPC has taken the lead amongst EU states in this area by proposing a set of macroprudential regulatory levers or tools (i.e., countercyclical capital requirements and limits on distributions) that could be imposed by the FPC on the financial sector through the microprudential authorities. These levers include the following. **Capital requirements:** Capital requirements could be varied depending on the riskiness of assets at points in economic cycle. Countercyclical capital buffers could be designed to dampen the credit cycle (e.g., by imposing higher capital requirements during a boom); **Liquidity tools:** Financial institutions can be required to hold liquid assets, these are assets that can be easily turned into cash. Also, leverage ratios could be used to limit the amount of leverage relative to the value of assets. **Forward-looking loss provisions**: Financial institutions can be required to set aside provisions against potential future losses on their lending. **Collateral requirements**: Lending could be limited by imposing higher collateral restrictions, for example, if growth in lending appears to be unsustainable. An example is a loan to value requirement, which would limit the size of a loan relative to the value of the asset. Similarly,

---

[119] Art. 5(4) Regulation (EU) No 1024/2013
[120] Art 8(1) Commission Proposal of 10 July 2013 for a Regulation of the European Parliament and of the Council establishing uniform rules and a uniform procedure for the resolution of credit institutions and certain investment firms in the framework of a Single Resolution Mechanism and a Single Bank Resolution Fund and amending Regulation (EU) No 1093/2010 of the European Parliament and of the Council (COM(2013) 520 final).
[121] Art 16(1) Commission Proposal of 10 July 2013 for a Regulation of the European Parliament and of the Council establishing uniform rules and a uniform procedure for the resolution of credit institutions and certain investment firms in the framework of a Single Resolution Mechanism and a Single Bank Resolution Fund and amending Regulation (EU) No 1093/2010 of the European Parliament and of the Council (COM(2013) 520 final).

"haircuts" on repurchase agreements would limit the amount of cash that can be lent as a proportion of the market value of a set of securities. **Information disclosure**: Greater transparency could help markets work better. For example, in times of crisis, more information about different institutions' risk exposure could increase the flow of credit as uncertainty is reduced. **Stress tests**: Stress testing by either the FPC or the other regulators could allow the FPC to see how resilient the system would be under different, adverse scenarios.

As mentioned before, the area of macroprudential tools is one where there is relatively little evidence and research. Goodhart, in particular, has highlighted that it would be good if macroprudential authorities such as the FPC did more analysis to understand how the various tools will work.[122] In addition, he has highlighted the need to consider what happens if institutions fail to meet their prudential requirements, and whether a "ladder of sanctions" should be considered:

> The more that regulations are now tightened, to represent desirable conditions rather than irreducible minima, the more the question of designing ladders of sanctions, (slight initially, toughened steadily, and ultimately involving intervention by the State to take over the weakening institution), needs to be urgently addressed. The international bodies have always tended to shy away from proposing this, meaning it may have to be tackled by the national macro and microprudential authorities. Penalties for violation of CARs [capital asset ratios] have now apparently been built into the current proposals for CRD4 [capital requirements directive IV]; the details will need to be examined to consider how appropriate these may be.[123]

The UK Financial Policy Committee's thinking about macroprudential regulation has advanced significantly in comparison with other EU and U.S. regulators. In December 2011, the FPC published a discussion paper in which it presented some of the possible macroprudential tools that could be wielded by the FPC. There is a particular emphasis here on time-varying risks, countered through regulation which aims to deal with cyclicality in the economic cycle and within certain sectors of the economy.[124] One of the first tasks of the FPC was to recommend in March 2012 several macroprudential levers to the UK treasury, which would have to submit them for approval as secondary legislation before Parliament.

The Bank of England and the Financial Services Authority (FSA), however, recognized in a published paper in 2011 that the choice of macroprudential levers is far from straightforward, as they could impinge substantially on economic activity and there is little hard evidence about how they would work in practice. For example, the bank and FSA suggested that varying loan-to-value or loan-to-income

---

[122] C. A. E. Goodhart, "The Macroprudential Authority: Powers, Scope and Accountability" (September 2011) Morgan Stanley Research <www.oecd.org/daf/fin/financial-markets/48979021.pdf> accessed 23 July 2014.

[123] Ibid.

[124] Most recently, the UK published another paper analysing the use of macroprudential tools.

ratios on mortgage lending would directly limit risky lending, but would also be very difficult to calculate because of "the trade-off between financial stability benefits, economic activity, and societal preferences for homeownership."[125] Moreover, the paper notes that limiting or regulating bank remuneration or distributions to shareholders may have the effect of penalizing well-managed banks alongside weak institutions. Similarly, the paper also observes that imposing too stringent controls on trading and clearing infrastructure may have the effect of driving this activity to less tightly regulated jurisdictions.[126]

When considering macroprudential regulation in the EU, in general, an important issue will be whether or not harmonized EU regulatory rules will grant member-state supervisors adequate discretion in the use of macroprudential supervisory levers. For instance, it appears that the Capital Requirements Directive IV will not give host country supervisors discretion to apply additional capital charges for EU-based banks that are systemically important in the host country's market, but not classified as systemically important in the bank's home EU state. Therefore the well-established principle of home country control (also known as the EU "passport") may limit the ability of EU states to take effective macroprudential measures.

Structural Regulation

In addition, some countries are attempting to enhance regulation by reducing the taxpayer's direct exposure to bank failures by adopting structural reforms to the banking industry. For example, the UK Financial Services (Banking Reform) Reform Act's macroprudential regulatory approach for retail banking is more systematic. It derives largely from the recommendations of the report of the Independent Commission on Banking (the "ICB Final Report").[127] This commission was created with the mission to "create a more stable and competitive basis for UK banking in the longer term."[128] The ICB Final Report recommends the ring-fencing of retail banking operations.[129] The purposes of ring-fencing include allowing the firm to survive the failure of affiliated firms and protecting the firm from being taken advantage of by affiliated firms[130] – both of which are included in

---

[125] Bank of England, Report (December 2011) <www.bankofengland.co.uk/publications/Pages/fsr/2011/fsr30.aspx> accessed 23 July 2014.

[126] The Australian experience, in contrast, of requiring banks to hold capital against off-balance sheet exposures has been considered a macroprudential regulatory lever that could work effectively with limited downside effects.

[127] Independent Commission on Banking, Final Report Recommendations (2011) (sometimes called the "Vickers Report" after Sir John Vickers, the Commission's chair).

[128] Ibid. 7.

[129] Ibid. 233.

[130] *See* S. L. Schwarcz, Ring-Fencing (2013) 87 *Southern California Law Review* 69, 73.

the ring-fencing of UK retail banking.[131] Thus, UK retail banks must individually maintain minimum capital and liquidity requirements,[132] and their interactions with affiliates must be at arm's length.[133] The purposes of ring-fencing also include limiting a firm's risky activities.[134] To that end, UK retail banks are prohibited from engaging in proprietary trading operations and many traditional investment banking activities.[135] Even beyond that, however, the United Kingdom is currently considering imposing a ban on proprietary trading by affiliates of UK retail banks[136] – presumably to make it less likely that such affiliates could fail, which might imperil the retail banks.[137]

Under the US Dodd-Frank Act,[138] the Volcker rule represents another form of structural regulation that restricts banking groups with deposit-taking subsidiaries from engaging in proprietary trading, while the EU Commission has accepted most of the recommendations from the Liikanen Group[139] in proposing that Europe's largest banking groups segregate their risky trading activities into a separate subsidiary. The move toward structural regulation of banking groups is an important element of macroprudential regulation that will change the business models of global financial institutions.[140] Macroprudential regulation and supervision will also necessarily involve central banks, – which are repositories of macroeconomic and financial data – in monitoring systemwide risks and working closely with microprudential supervisors to ensure that innovations in financial risk taking do not undermine financial stability. Macroprudential regulation will require that the practice of financial supervision is linked to factors in the macroeconomy and broader financial system.[141]

---

[131] ICB Final Report, *supra* note 127, 237–38.
[132] Financial Services (Banking Reform) Act, 2013, cl. 33 § 4.
[133] ICB Final Report, *supra* note 127, at 12.
[134] Schwarcz, *supra* note 130, at 10–11.
[135] Section 4 of the UK Banking Reform Act, *supra* note 70, prohibits retail banks from "dealing in securities as a principal."
[136] *See* UK Banking Reform Act, *supra* note 70, § 4 (requiring the PRA to study a possible ban on proprietary trading). *See also* Parliamentary Commission on Banking Standards, Proprietary Trading, 2012–13, H.C. 1034, at 15–19.
[137] *See, supra* notes 128–9 and accompanying text.
[138] *See* Wall Street Reform and Consumer Protection Act of 2010, sec. 619.
[139] The Liikanen Group was established by the European Commission in 2011 to provide independent advice on structural reforms of the European banking sector. *See* European Commission website. The Liikanen Group emphasises the importance of ring-fencing the investment banking activities of the banking group if it is necessary for an efficient bank resolution regime.
[140] However, the European Banking Federation (EBF) contends that "there is no convincing evidence that structural reform has a direct influence on systemic risk and would make restructuring or resolution easier in the event of a crisis."
[141] For example, countercyclical capital requirements would base the determination of regulatory capital, in part, on the ratio of bank asset prices to the trend rate of economic growth.

THE RISKS OF UNSYSTEMATIC FINANCIAL REGULATION

Theoretical Insights

Good rulemaking needs a conceptual framework. Without the guidance provided by such a framework, the resulting rules run the risk of being "at best redundant and at worst" contradictory.[142] Moreover, the rulemaking process itself may end up being costlier.[143]

An unprincipled and ad hoc approach to financial regulation may carry even greater risks, including regulatory arbitrage. Financial institutions may reorganize in the wake of major financial reform to minimize the reform's impact.[144] Regulatory arbitrage has been cited as contributing to the financial crisis[145]; banks allegedly exploited loopholes in the regulatory framework, allowing them to keep lower capital buffers during the precrisis upswing, leaving them with too little capital during the crisis.[146]

There are other risks. For example, the regulation may give regulators and policymakers a false sense of security.[147] Although "individual regulated banks may be safer than they were before," the "overall system of credit creation may not."[148] Moreover, macroprudential regulation, thus far, has focused mostly on the "risks arising from the leverage on the balance sheet of banks."[149] This narrow focus may miss how unleveraged financial institutions, such as asset managers, contribute to risk in the financial system.[150] Unsystematic financial regulation can therefore be inadvertently harmful. In the context of this chapter's focus on macroprudential financial regulation, unsystematic regulation can not only increase systemic risk but also decrease economic efficiency. Set forth in the following section are some real-world examples.

---

[142] D. Mellinkoff, "The Language of the Uniform Commercial Code" (1967) 77 Yale L.J. 185, 185, 225.

[143] *See, e.g.,* Steven L. Schwarcz, "A Fundamental Inquiry into the Statutory Rulemaking Process of Private Legislatures" (1995) 29 *Georgia Law Review* 909, 917f. The proposed rules may be unrelated to the problem that spurred the rulemaking. Ibid. at 918. Or, crafting the proposals may require more policymakers than would otherwise be needed. Ibid. at 917–18. Further, any sunk costs of the rulemaking process can induce policymakers to enact unnecessary or even undesirable rules, to try to justify those costs. Ibid. at 918–19.

[144] L. R. Smith and V. M. Muñiz-Fraticelli, Strategic Shortcomings of the Dodd-Frank Act (2013) 58 *The Antitrust Bulletin* 617, 624 (2013).

[145] T. Berg, B. Gehra and M. Kunisch, "A Certification Model for Regulatory Arbitrage: Will Regulatory Arbitrage Persist under Basel III?" (2011) 21 Journal of Fixed Income 39, 39; C. Whitehead, "The Goldilocks Approach: Financial Risk And Staged Regulation" (2012) 97 Cornell L. Rev. 1267, 1275f.

[146] Ibid.

[147] *See* S. G. Hanson, A. K. Kashyap and J. C. Stein, "A Macroprudential Approach to Financial Regulation" (2011) 25 Journal of Economic Perspectives 3.

[148] Ibid.

[149] A. G. Haldane Bank of England, Speech at the London Business School: The Age of Asset Management (Bank of England, 4 April 2014) 13.

[150] *See* Ibid.

Real-World Examples

The Derivatives Safe Harbor

One example of how unsystematic macroprudential financial regulation might inadvertently increase systemic risk can be illustrated by the effort to limit systemic risk arising out of derivatives transactions. For decades, the U.S. Congress has been granting derivatives counterparties special rights and immunities in the bankruptcy process, including allowing them to exercise their contractual enforcement remedies against a debtor or its property – including closing out, netting, and setting off their derivatives positions and liquidating collateral in their possession – notwithstanding bankruptcy law's stay of enforcement actions.[151] These special rights and immunities, collectively called the "safe harbor," are not systematic but path dependent – the result of decades of sustained industry pressure on congress to exempt the derivatives market from the reach of bankruptcy law, with each exemption serving as an historical justification for subsequent broader exemptions.[152] Path dependence does not necessarily make the safe harbor bad; the relevant question is whether it fulfills its stated purpose of protecting against systemic risk.

The safe harbor does not appear to reduce systemic contagion, and might increase it. The factor most relevant to systemic contagion is interconnectedness.[153] The safe harbor was thought to enable large interconnected derivatives dealers to enforce their remedies against a failed counterparty, thereby minimizing the dealer's losses and reducing its chance of collapse.[154] If a dealer itself is a defaulting counterparty, however, it can backfire by enabling the dealer's other counterparties to enforce their remedies, thereby hastening the dealer's collapse.[155] This appears to have occurred in the case of Lehman Brothers.[156] The safe harbor also incentivizes systemically risky market concentration by enabling dealers and other parties to virtually ignore counterparty risk because, if a counterparty defaults, the dealer can simply foreclose on the collateral.[157]

Additionally, the potential for the safe harbor to amplify, rather than protect against, systemic risk, transcends the traditional derivatives market. That is because, at least in the United States, the language of the safe harbor has become so inclusive – using broad definitions of derivatives, and no longer requiring that they

---

[151] Steven L. Schwarcz, "Derivatives and Collateral: Balancing Remedies and Systemic Risk" 2015 *University of Illinois Law Review* 699 (special symposium issue on the changing role of secured financing in corporate restructurings); also available at <ssrn.com/abstract=2419460>.

[152] Ibid.

[153] Ibid.

[154] Ibid.

[155] Ibid.

[156] Ibid.

[157] Ibid.

be traded on financial markets or physically settled – that virtually any ordinary financial transaction can be documented to fall within it.[158] To gain the enforcement advantages provided by the safe harbor, ordinary financing transactions, including secured loans, increasingly are being couched as derivatives transactions.[159]

The Volcker Rule

The Volcker Rule[160] illustrates how unsystematic macroprudential financial regulation might decrease economic efficiency, if not also inadvertently increase systemic risk. The Volcker Rule limits proprietary trading, which was thought to be a cause contributing to the financial crisis.[161] As explained later here, that limitation might decrease the economic efficiency of firms that profited from proprietary trading. More significantly, that limitation might also inadvertently increase systemic risk because it is being applied to commercial banks but not to other financial institutions.[162]

Due to that selective application of the Volcker Rule, proprietary traders have been leaving commercial banks for firms like hedge funds and investment banks.[163] These are among the core financial firms that populate the rising shadow-banking sector, in which such firms are replacing traditional banks as the sources of financial intermediation.[164] To the extent proprietary trading causes losses,

---

[158] Ibid.

[159] Ibid.

[160] Dodd-Frank Act, 12 U.S.C. § 1851. The rule is named after former Federal Reserve Chairman Paul Volker – often cited as its principal designer. C. Whitehead, "The Volcker Rule And Evolving Financial Markets" (2011) 1 Harv. Bus. L. Rev. 39, 40.

[161] Ibid. 39. The Dodd-Frank Act defines proprietary trading as "engaging as a principal for the trading account of [a bank] in any transaction to purchase or sell, or otherwise acquire or dispose of, any security, any derivative, any contract of sale of a commodity for future delivery, any option on any such ... [aforementioned] financial instrument." 12 U.S.C. § 1851(h)(4). That definition, however, has been criticized as "raising critical questions." Whitehead, *supra* note 160, 48.

[162] Ibid. 44.

[163] *See, e.g.*, Deutsche Bank Loses Option Trader Saiers to Hedge Fund Alphabet Management <www.bloomberg.com/news/2010-07-14/deutsche-bank-loses-option-trader-saiers-to-hedge-fund-alphabet-management.html>; Top JPMorgan Prop Trader Leaves To Launch Hedge Fund <www.forbes.com/sites/halahtouryalai/2013/02/15/top-jpmorgan-prop-trader-leaves-to-launch-hedge-fund>.

[164] *See, e.g.*, Whitehead, *supra* note 160, 39 (discussing how commercial banks outsource various risks – for example, credit risks – to hedge funds because doing so decreases the cost of extending credit); Fed Chair Examines Hedge Funds and Other Non-Bank Financial Firms in the Shadow Banking System, New York: CCH Incorporated: Health and Human Resources, Apr. 26, 2012, at 9–11 (noting that the shadow banking system is highly connected with commercial and clearing banks; and that because of this interconnectedness, losses in the shadow banking system may easily spill into other sectors of the economy). *See also* S L Schwarcz, "Regulating Shadows: Financial Regulation and Responsibility Failure" (2013) 70 *Washington and Lee Law Review* 1781, 1783f.

however, these firms are poorer at absorbing the losses than commercial banks, which tend to have much larger equity cushions.[165] Indeed, during the last few decades, proprietary trading losses had a much larger impact on noncommercial banks: losses as a percentage of equity were 260.0 percent and 298.7 percent, respectively, at noncommercial banks Amaranth Advisors and Barings, whereas they were only 3.8 percent and 4.0 percent, respectively, at commercial banks UBS and Deutsche Bank.[166] The Volcker Rule thus may increase the risk of systemic failure by shifting the risk of proprietary trading to a frailer part of the financial system.

The Volcker Rule may also impair efficiency by denying commercial banks the revenue gained by proprietary trading. This could be especially troubling for U.S. banks that compete with foreign banks that are not restrained by a similar limitation.[167]

Bail-in Requirements

Bail-in provisions are intended to address the moral hazard problem of so-called too-big-to-fail financial institutions and the unfairness of having taxpayers subsidize excessive private sector risk-taking.[168] Bail-in provisions that result from unsystematic financial regulation could, however, have unintended consequences.

In December 2013, for example, the European Commission and the European Parliament agreed to their "final compromise" of the Bank Recovery and Resolution Directive (BRRD).[169] BBRD possesses a bail-in feature, in which creditors and shareholders of a distressed financial institution must "suffer appropriate losses and bear an appropriate part of those costs arising from the failure of the institution ... [to] give shareholders and creditors of institutions a stronger incentive to monitor the health of an institution during normal circumstances"[170] The bail-in provisions include replacing management at the failing institution, and

---

[165] *See* J. R. Barth, D. McCarthy, "What is the Likely Impact of the Volcker Rule on Markets, Businesses, Investors, and Job Creation?" (September 2013) 28 J. PRIVATE ENTER. 63, 68–69 (observing that although JPMorgan Chase bore losses of over $7.5 billion, its equity cushion was so vast by comparison that the losses did not pose a solvency problem), <search.proquest.com/docview/1365183741?accountid=10598> (study data taken from 1990 to 2013).

[166] Ibid. 63–74, 66.

[167] Ibid. 64.

[168] EU Bank Recovery and Resolution Directive (BRRD): Frequently Asked Questions <europa.eu/rapid/press-release_MEMO-14–297_en.htm> accessed 16 June 2014.

[169] Proposal for a Directive of the European Parliament and of the Council of 18 December 2013 on Establishing a Framework for the Recover and Resolution of Credit Institutions and Investment Firms, at 1, COD (2013) 2012/0150 (18 December 2013) <www.plesner.com/resources/934.pdf>; *see also* A New Era for Crisis Management, PricewaterhouseCoopers Hot Topic 2–3 (Jan., 2014) (although not in full force, the Directive's provisions might come into effect as soon as the first quarter of 2015), <www.pwc.com/et_EE/EE/publications/assets/pub/pwc-eu-bank-recovery-and-resolution-directive-triumph-or-tragedy.pdf>.

[170] Ibid. 26.

implementing a "restructuring plan" as compatible as possible with the plan submitted by the corporation prior to its failing.[171]

However, the BBRD leaves much in the discretion of the regulators, allowing regulators to keep in place the institution's management where "appropriate and necessary" and to exclude "certain kinds of unsecured liability."[172] Further, in "extraordinary circumstances,"[173] regulators may request funding from "alternative financing arrangements"[174] – that could even include a taxpayer-funded loan.[175]

Some have argued that this wide regulatory discretion may increase, rather than decrease, moral hazard.[176] The chance that the institution's creditors and share-holders will ultimately be bailed out by taxpayer funds may justify a decision by the institution's management to engage in high-risk, potentially profitable, activity.[177]

Furthermore, a bail-in itself might trigger a contagion effect,[178] in which "the failure of one institution either causes the creditors of others to withdraw funding in a manner akin to a classic bank run or sets off a general panic leading debt markets to freeze."[179] News of a bail-in might also lower market confidence in the value of assets held by the bailed-in bank (if such assets might be subject to a forced sale), spreading market uncertainty to other institutions holding the same or similar assets.[180] Bail-ins will also impose losses on the bailed-in bank's shareholders and creditors, some of which may themselves be banks or other systemically important financial institutions.[181]

---

[171] Ibid. 28.

[172] Ibid. 28.

[173] *See* Ibid. 30 ("where liabilities have been excluded and the resolution fund has been used to contribute to bail-in in lieu of these liabilities up to the permissible cap").

[174] Ibid. 145.

[175] Ibid. 145 (the alternative arrangement "shall be conditional on prior and final approval under the State Aid rules").

[176] *See* B. Krauskopf, et al., 'Some Critical Aspects of the European Banking Union' (2014) 29 Banking and Fin. Law Review, 217, 241.

[177] A. S. Boyd, 'Bail-ins – Just Another Self-Fulfilling Prophecy?' (2012) 27 Banking and Fin. Law Review 559, 603; *See also* Smith, Muñiz-Fraticelli, *supra* note 144, 632. Others (including the author) believe, however, that some discretion should always be associated with a bail-in/bail-out decision. Quantitative factors do not necessarily fit every situation. Indeed, if used as an automatic trigger, they could create an unnecessary panic when a firm nears the trigger. *See* European Banking Federation, Positioning in Respect of the FSB Consultation on Effective Resolution of Systemically Important Financial Institutions, (16 August 2011) 7; Boyd, *supra* at 604–05.

[178] Letter from Tom Naratil and Steve Hottiger on behalf of UBS AG to Financial Stability Board 2 (2 September 2011) <www.financialstabilityboard.org /press/c_110909ddd.pdf>.

[179] H. S. Scott, Interconnectedness and Contagion (2012) 16 <ssrn.com/abstract=2178475>.

[180] Letter from Naratil and Hottiger, *supra* note 178, 3 (*e.g.*, "forced markdowns of assets at one institution will likely reduce confidence in other institutions holding similar assets").

[181] *See* Boyd, *supra* note 177, 616. *See also* I. Anabtawi, Steven L. Schwarcz, "Regulating Ex Post: How Law Can Address the Inevitability of Financial Failure" (2013) 92 TEX. L. REV. 75, 117 (making this same observation about contingent equity as a bail-in mechanism); Steven L. Schwarcz, "Controlling Financial Chaos: The Power and Limits of Law" (2012) WIS. L. REV.

Thus, unsystematic financial regulation bears many risks. Some of these risks have already taken their toll on financial markets, contributing to the 2008 financial crises, while many more risks could theoretically help bring about the next crisis. Set forth in the next section is a systematic and functional regulatory framework, designed to provide the financial market both structure and security while also minimizing efficiency costs.

TOWARD MORE SYSTEMATIC FINANCIAL REGULATION

A more systematic financial regulatory framework should at least be more consistent and complete than an ad hoc approach. It also could help to counter, or at least to place into perspective, potential financial industry lobbying for only selective "tools."[182]

For these reasons, scholars and policymakers should engage the question of how microprudential and macroprudential regulation can made more systematic, and thus more consistent and complete. One of us does that through what he calls the "functional regulation" of finance: (a) improving the functioning of the components of the financial system – firms and markets – by identifying their functions and examining how microprudential regulation could be designed to correct market failures that impede those functions; and (b) examining how macroprudential regulation can operate to best protect the financial system's integrity as a network system.[183]

This functional approach addresses how financial regulatory rules should be substantively designed. It should not be confused with what is sometimes called a functional approach to financial supervision, in which the supervisory government agency's jurisdiction is based not on an entity itself (for example, a bank) but on the business being transacted by an entity (for example, government agency X would supervise a bank's lending activities and government agency Y would supervise the same bank's securities' underwriting activities).[184]

From a functional perspective, macroprudential regulation should have two goals: to limit the triggers of systemic shocks, and to mitigate the harm from systemic shocks that nonetheless occur by breaking the transmission and limiting

---

815, 837 ("automatic conversions of debt claims to equity interests might create counterparty risk by reducing the value of firms holding those claims").

[182] *Cf.* G. E. Moore, Principia Ethica (1971) 10–14 (distinguishing positive observations of what exist (in our case, such as tools in the toolkit) from normative analysis of what should be). This distinction between what exists and what should exist is especially meaningful when the former may result from lobbying.

[183] Steven L. Schwarcz, *Regulating Financial Change: A Functional Approach*, forthcoming, 100 Minnesota Law Review, Issue No. 4, available at http://ssrn.com/abstract=2469467

[184] *See, e.g.*, Group of Thirty, The Structure of Financial Supervision: Approaches and Challenges in a Global Marketplace (2008) 13 (explaining that under a functional approach, supervisory oversight is based on the business being transacted by the entity) <www.group 30.org/images/PDF/The%20Structure%20of%20Financial%20Supervision.pdf>.

the impact of those shocks.[185] It would be ideal to perfectly achieve the first goal, ex ante, eliminating the triggers of systemic shocks.[186] But the vulnerabilities of the financial system that can trigger systemic shocks cannot all be eliminated.

The classic vulnerability, for example, is maturity transformation: the asset–liability mismatch that results from the short-term funding of long-term projects.[187] This mismatch creates a "liquidity default risk" that borrowers will be unable to repay their lenders. According to some scholars, illiquidity is the fundamental source of financial failure.[188] A bank "run" is the typical (though far from the only) example of maturity transformation leading to a liquidity default. Maturity transformation was also at the core of the financial crisis.[189]

But maturity transformation is not merely a vulnerability but a benefit of the financial system – potentially lowering the cost of borrowing.[190] It is therefore unlikely to, and probably should not, be eliminated by regulation.

---

[185] *Regulating Financial Change, supra* note 183. *See also* Anabtawi and Schwarcz, *supra* note 181, 78 (also citing A D Hall, R E Fagan, *Definition of System*, 1 Gen. Sys. 18, 18 (1956), and D H Meadows, Thinking in Systems: A Primer 22 (Diana Wright ed., 2008)).

[186] *Cf.* Steven L. Schwarcz, Keynote Address: "Ex Ante Versus Ex Post Approaches to Financial Regulation" (2011) 15 Chapman Law Review 257, 258 (observing that "[o]nce a failure occurs, there may already be economic damage, and it may be difficult to stop the failure from spreading and becoming systemic").

[187] Economists sometimes refer to the short-term funding of long-term projects as a form of maturity transformation or as an asset-liability mismatch. *See, e.g.,* H. M. Ennis, T. Keister, "Bank Runs and Institutions: The Perils of Intervention" (2009) 99 Am. Econ. Rev. 1588, 1590 ("Money market funds and other arrangements perform maturity transformation by investing in long-term assets while offering investors the ability to withdraw funds on demand.").

[188] Awrey et al., *supra* note 14, 1 (observing that "[i]n the absence of liquidity constraints, ... market participants could rest easy in the knowledge that—whatever unforeseen contingencies might arise *ex post*—it will be possible for them to obtain refinancing").

[189] *See, e.g.,* G. Gorton and A. Metrick, Regulating the Shadow Banking System (2010) 1 <ssrn. com/abstract=1676947> (discussing sale and repurchase (repo) agreements in the context of the financial crisis of 2007–2009); D. Covitz, N. Liang and G. Suarez, The Evolution of a Financial Crisis: Panic in the Asset-Backed Commercial Paper Market (2009), Fed. Reserve Bd. Fin. and Discussion Series, Working Paper #2009-36, 1) <www.federalreserve.gov/pubs/ feds/2009/200936/200936pap.pdf> (arguing that maturity transformation "played a central role in transforming concerns about the credit quality of mortgage-related assets into a global financial crisis."). *See also* V. V. Acharya, S. Viswanathan, "Leverage, Moral Hazard, and Liquidity" (2011) 66 *Journal of Finance* 99, 103 (observing that short-term funding of long-term projects "played an important role in the financial crisis of 2007 to 2009 and the period preceding it"); K. Glazier, Bernanke: Financial Crisis Was a Structural Failure (13 April 2012) Bond Buyer <www.bond buyer.com/news/bernanke-speech-financial-crisis-structural-failure-1038520-1.html?partner=sifma> accessed 17 June 2013 (quoting Federal Reserve Board Chairman Ben Bernanke as saying that "a key vulnerability of the [disintermediated financial] system was the heavy reliance ... on various forms of short-term wholesale funding"); M. H. Wolfson, 'Minsky's Theory of Financial Crisis in a Global Context' (2002) 36 J. Econ. Issues 393, 394 (describing Minsky's theory that market fragility grows as debt levels rise and that the proportion of debt will increase as firms use short-term debt to fund long-term financial assets).

[190] *See, e.g.,* N. Roubini, Liquidity/Rollover Risk on US Assets? A Nightmare Hard Landing Scenario for the US $ and US Bond Market (21 December 2004) EconoMonitor

Another vulnerability of the financial system that can trigger systemic shocks is the system's failure to internalize harm. A market participant may well decide to engage in a risky but profitable transaction, even though doing so could increase systemic risk, because much of the harm from a possible systemic collapse would be externalized onto other market participants as well as onto ordinary citizens impacted by an economic collapse. A significant contributor to this vulnerability is the long-standing corporate law regime of limited liability, which can give investor–managers of firms strong incentives to take risks that could generate out-size personal profits, even if that greatly increases systemic risk – a concern that is especially problematic for the small and decentralized firms (such as hedge funds) that dominate the shadow-banking sector, in which equity investors tend to be active managers.[191]

There are additional reasons why we cannot realistically eliminate all the triggers of systemic shocks. For example, the very nature of the financial system – including that it exhibits the characteristics of, and effectively comprises, a high-risk system that is susceptible to "normal accidents"[192] – subjects it to unpredictable vulnerabilities.[193] Economists also argue that systemic problems are inevitable because it is impossible to monitor everything in the financial system.[194] Furthermore, we often lack empirical evidence on regulatory cause and effect.

It therefore is virtually certain that the financial system will face systemic shocks from time to time. Functional regulation should therefore be designed to also operate ex post, after a systemic shock is triggered, by breaking the transmission of the shock and limiting its impact.[195]

CONCLUSION

Macroprudential financial regulation has been fueled more by political and emotional reactions to the financial crisis than by logic. The result is regulation that is unsystematic and ad hoc, leaving regulators with an incomplete and sometimes inconsistent set of "tools." Without direction, however, regulators will almost certainly misuse these tools, which may be as likely to cause financial problems as to solve them. Indeed, engaging in any kind of rulemaking without a conceptual framework can increase the costs of rulemaking and lead to unintended, negative consequences.

<perma.cc/opzwZqEYeHE> (explaining that it is much less expensive to finance short-term debt than longer-term debt).

[191] *The Governance Structure of Shadow Banking, supra.*

[192] For an analysis of normal accident theory, *see* C. Perrow, Normal Accidents: Living with High-Risk Technologies (1999) 18.

[193] Anabtawi and Schwarcz (N 175). *Cf.* Awrey et al., *supra* note 14, 1 (contending that absent information costs and uncertainty, market participants would be able to write contracts that allocate risk in every potential future state of the world, thereby ex ante addressing potential future liquidity problems).

[194] Eugene N. White, Professor of Economics, Rutgers University (statement at Chatham House conference) (6 December 2013).

[195] Group of Thirty, *supra* note 184.

Policymakers and regulators often conflate the need for a conceptual macroprudential framework with the need for a unified macroprudential supervisory
scheme – or, at least, they assume that the latter obviates the need for the former.[196]
It is true that the nature of the administrative supervision can influence the degree
of regulatory consistency and completeness.[197] Nonetheless, even a unified supervisor will fail if it administers an ad hoc set of laws.[198]

---

[196] *Cf.* Progress Report to G20 (N 31) 4 (observing that although countries recognize the need for
a systemwide perspective, the "main disagreement is on the importance of carving out a
specific macroprudential [supervisory] framework").

[197] *Cf.* Financial Stability Board et al., Macroprudential Policy Tools and Frameworks: Progress
Report to G20 4 (2011) <www.imf.org/external/np/g20/pdf/102711.pdf> (observing that
although countries recognize the need for a system-wide perspective, the "main disagreement
is on the importance of carving out a specific macroprudential [supervisory] framework").
Even otherwise ideal macroprudential regulation can be misapplied by fragmented supervisory authorities, especially if some of the regulators lack a mandate to promote financial
stability. *Cf. supra* note 17 and accompanying text (observing that regulatory ambiguity is
compounded by fragmented supervisory authority).

[198] Similarly, even if a single regulatory authority is tasked with overseeing financial stability,
macroprudential regulation can fail if that authority lacks the power to adequately implement
that regulation. As examples, the Financial Services Oversight Council (FSOC) – the coordinating overseer of financial stability in the United States – lacks the power to directly regulate
entities or practices. *See* Financial Stability Oversight Council Authority, 12 U.S.C. § 5322
(2010) (laying out the structure and powers of the Financial Stability Oversight Council). In
contrast, the Financial Policy Committee – the United Kingdom's macroprudential regulator – has the power to direct the other financial regulators how to act on macroprudential
issues. *See* G. A. Walker, "U.K. Regulatory Revision – A New Blueprint for Reform" (2012) 46
INT'L LAW. 787, 793. *See also* Financial Services Act, 2012, c. 21, § 4 (Eng.). The UK system lays
out how the regulators will interact with one another, but does not elucidate how the primary
macroprudential regulator will approach or use macroprudential policies.

9

Rethinking the Law in "Safe Assets"

Anna Gelpern and Erik F. Gerding

INTRODUCTION

There is no such thing as a risk-free investment. Nonetheless, multitrillion-dollar global markets seem to operate on the assumption that some financial contracts have done away with risk for all practical purposes. When the assumption fails, the consequences are dire. During financial crises in the United States and Europe, investors abruptly lost confidence in AAA-rated mortgage-backed securities, Euro-area government debt, and other contracts once considered super-safe. Panic selling, firm failures, government rescues, and economic contraction followed.

This experience refocused policy, market, and academic attention on the problem of "safe assets." The term describes a variety of financial claims on public or private sector entities that are used as if they were risk-free. Government debt, central bank debt and money are publicly produced safe assets. Bank deposits, highly rated corporate debt, repos and asset-backed securities are privately produced safe assets. Although the idea has been part of risk-management strategies, asset pricing models and financial regulation for a long time, an influential strand of postcrisis economic thinking has recast safe assets as central to financial instability.[1] Some have gone further to define safe assets as a category apart from the others, an elementary particle of all financial activity that merits special protection in regulatory design.[2] This stands in contrast to the more traditional view that policy

We owe thanks to Longhao Wang, Marylin Raisch, Esther Cho, Nicholas Brock, and Katherine Incantalupo for research assistance, and to the organizers and participants in the conference "Reconceptualizing Global Finance and Its Regulation," workshop participants at Georgetown and UCLA law schools, Donald Langevoort, Adam Levitin, and Robert Thompson for valuable comments. We are especially grateful to the editors of this volume for their input and support.

[1] Caballero 2009; IMF 2012.

[2] Gorton, Lewellyn, and Metrick 2012.

makers should not create protected asset categories, and instead should encourage investors to manage the risk embedded in all financial contracts.[3]

Underlying the economic debate, safe assets pose a high-stakes legal problem. Statutes, regulations, administrative agency, and private contracting practices allow, encourage, and constrain both the production of these financial contracts and market actors' ability to use them as if they were safe. If safe assets are under or overproduced, or misused, or if safety is misperceived, the law is at least partly to blame. Yet the law makes only an episodic appearance in the writing on safe assets, usually as a source of distortion.[4] In our view, analysis and policy design suffer for lack of an overall legal framework for thinking about safe assets. Our chapter considers the legal dimension of safe assets, and points to the policy and regulatory implications to be examined in future work. This project complements the economic perspectives, but is not wedded to any one among them.

In the economic and policy literature, safe assets perform multiple functions. They are collateral for lending, a store of value, a baseline for pricing other investments, a hedge against risk, and a source of liquidity. In many respects, they are like money; however, the term "safe assets" covers a broader and more heterogeneous set of claims, including those that perform only part of money's functions. For example, some can be used for long-term savings, but not as a medium of exchange in transactions.

Nevertheless, as described by economists, all safe assets share three attributes. *First*, they represent an effort to minimize risk. When a single asset minimizes multiple risks – for example, credit, liquidity, and market risk – it may be used for multiple purposes. When multiple assets minimize similar risks, investors might substitute them for one another. *Second*, safe assets are used in a discontinuous way. For example, regulated firms are either permitted or forbidden to make certain investments.[5] Similarly, traders in large and active markets demand collateral that can change hands "no questions asked," without inquiring into its risk attributes; otherwise, it is unsuited for this purpose.[6] *Third* and related, safe assets are used across the financial system, and promote interconnectedness within it – in postcrisis regulatory parlance, they are apt to be systemically important financial contracts.[7] An abrupt loss of safety or a shift in perception shocks the system as a whole, and calls for government intervention.

---

[3] Hannoun 2011; Nouy 2012; Portes 2013.

[4] IMF 2012; BIS 2012; Gorton et al. 2012.

[5] Cf. Fisher 2013 at 67.

[6] Dang, Gorton, and Holmstrom 2013a.

[7] The analogy is to systemically important financial institutions and their kin. See e.g., "Financial Stability Board," *Policy Areas—Systemically Important Financial Institutions (SIFIs)* at www.financialstabilityboard.org/list/fsb_pa/tid_174/index.htm (last accessed on September 21, 2014). We have each written about contracts as a source of systemic risk elsewhere (e.g., Gerding 2013b; Gelpern 2009; Gelpern and Levitin 2009; Gelpern and Gulati 2013).

Together, the three attributes give safe assets pride of place in theories about financial crises: they help weave a coherent story. In the mid-2000s, some central banks dramatically increased purchases of highly rated foreign sovereign debt.[8] Financial institutions replaced sovereign debt in their portfolios with privately engineered safe assets, such as mortgage-backed securities.[9] When risk rematerialized, investors quickly lost confidence in the engineered assets, which magnified and transmitted shocks throughout the global financial system.[10] Governments intervened on a large scale. They bought "toxic" assets that had lost their safety from financial firms, and replaced them with cash and government debt (publicly produced safe assets).[11] Postcrisis financial reforms shifted attention to the role of regulation in the market for safe assets. Market, academic, and policy observers predicted that new prudential requirements would boost demand for some traditional safe assets, such as government debt, constrain the supply of others, such as bank debt or senior asset-backed securities, and push investors to use riskier assets as if they were safe.[12] The resulting imbalances would fuel the next crisis. As we note later in the chapter, this is far from the only plausible story of the crisis, but it is one that has gained considerable traction among economists and policy makers.

Two related fears motivate the economic literature: *first*, the fear that supply and demand imbalances in safe assets feed financial crises, and *second*, that the world may face a shortage of safe assets.[13] This puts safe assets squarely in the realm of macroprudential policy, with its objective of making the financial system as a whole more stable and resilient in the face of inevitable shocks (Group of Thirty 2010). In this chapter, we do not take a position on aggregate supply of and demand for safe assets, but consider the institutional mechanisms by which supply and demand might come about.

Legal tools mediate between the world in which every asset is risky, and the transactional and policy imperatives to act *as if* some assets are risk-free. The concept of safe assets is useful precisely because it abstracts from reality and thereby

---

[8] The relative importance of this debt as a savings vehicle and an exchange rate management tool for exporting countries is debated. See, e.g., C. Fred Bergsten and Joseph E. Gagnon, *Currency Manipulation, the US Economy, and the Global Economic Order*, Peterson Institute for International Economics Policy Brief (Dec. 2012); Roubini and Setser 2004; Setser 2008; Marc Labonte and Jared C. Nagel, *Foreign Holdings of Federal Debt*, Congressional Research Service RS22331 (June 2014).

[9] Bernanke, Bertaut, DeMarco, and Kamin 2011.

[10] Caballero 2009; IMF 2012.

[11] Caballero and Farhi 2014.

[12] BIS 2012; IMF 2012; Gorton et al. 2012; Ralph Atkins, "Crunch Feared if Collateral Rules Enforced: New Clearing Regulations Could Suck in $10tn of Safe Assets," *The Financial Times* (Feb. 5, 2013), www.ft.com/intl/cms/s/0/e7737740-6f85-11e2-b906-00144feab49a.html.

[13] Caballero 2009; Gorton et al. 2012; IMF 2012. See also Cardiff Garcia, "The decline of 'safe' assets," FTAlphaville (Dec 05, 2011, 09:23), http://ftalphaville.ft.com/2011/12/05/778301/the-decline-of-safe-assets/; Credit Suisse 2011. Some commentators vigorously dispute the shortage story. See, e.g., Portes 2013; Fisher 2013.

makes it actionable.[14] When it is embedded in legislation, regulation, and contracting practice, this concept anchors expectations, and coordinates dispersed market participants to select a limited number of *relatively* low-risk investments for key functions in the financial system. In other words, safe assets are legally constructed,[15] for good or ill. Legal analysis is therefore well-placed to inform the spectrum of macroprudential policy choices about safe assets: from fighting investor assumptions about safety at every turn, to reinforcing them with constitutional commitments.

This insight is hardly radical in law, but it stands in tension with the prevailing description of safe assets as an organic phenomenon. As we elaborate below, economists speak of poorly understood mechanisms and technologies to be discovered, like the Higgs boson particle in a supercollider, and of natural supply overwhelmed by demand.[16] We see law and regulation shape virtually all aspects of safe assets.[17] At a minimum, legislators, regulators, and the courts take a stand by simply allowing market participants to use assets as if they were safe, with consequences for financial stability. In practice, the law's role in safe assets is much more expansive. Our project is to describe this role in a reasonably comprehensive and systematic fashion, teasing out the implications for the macroprudential policy tool kit.

We offer a three-part framework for understanding the mechanisms by which the law fosters the production of safe assets, nurtures the development of the markets in safe assets, and promotes the continuing safety of safe assets in multiple states of the world. Our framework roughly tracks the three shared attributes highlighted earlier in this introduction. First, the law *makes* some assets less risky, for example, by mandating capital cushions for issuers of safe assets or giving investors in those assets repayment priorities. Second, the law *labels* some assets as safe, reducing or eliminating market participants' incentives to discover their risk attributes. Third, the state *guarantees* the safety of assets when it perceives them to be important for the financial system as a whole. The law authorizes and frames the design of such guarantees.

For any given asset, governments both recognize the safety attributes that arise through private ordering and enhance them with regulation, labeling, and guarantees. If all goes well, the three categories of tools feed a virtuous cycle: for instance, when low-risk assets are labeled safe, it increases demand, broadens the investor

---

[14] Safe assets might be seen as a variant of legal fiction – a widely held simplifying assumption, like corporate speech, tax citizenship, or dating a document "as of" a date different from the one on which it is signed. See Riles 2011 at 172–3; Riles 2010.

[15] Pistor 2013.

[16] See, e.g., Gorton et al. 2012 ("[T]he relatively constant demand for safe debt suggests an underlying transactions technology that is not well understood."); Caballero 2009 ("[T]hese institutions sought the profits generated from bridging the gap between this rise in demand and the expansion of its natural supply.").

[17] Our focus on the legal construction of financial markets follows Pistor 2013.

base, boosts liquidity, and reduces the cost of funding for their issuers. On the flipside, when the tools are misaligned, they can contribute to instability. At the extreme, investors might herd into risky assets mislabeled as safe, then flee in panic when the perception of safety vanishes, with spillover effects on the broader economy. The government may have no choice but to step in with guarantees ex post, creating distortions and moral hazard.

The potential for virtuous and vicious cycles highlights the importance of distinguishing among, and dynamically aligning, the risk attributes of safe assets, market perceptions of their safety, and the public safety net. Our framework helps clarify each policy dimension and identify the tools best suited to address it. It is deliberately simple: while we propose a set of basic analytical distinctions (labeling an asset "safe" need not make it safe), we do not imply a mechanistic correspondence between policy objectives and legal tools. To the contrary, in drawing the distinctions, we shed light on the pervasive overlaps, entanglements, and feedback effects in the institutional architecture of safe assets, and more broadly, of macroprudential regulation. Furthermore, while most of our examples come from recent crises and illustrate the consequences of policy failures in the United States and Europe, keeping the framework sparse allows us to draw conclusions that apply more broadly.

Another contribution of this chapter is to suggest that macroprudential policy need not require a brand new toolkit. Our approach emerges from a description of how the law constructed four categories of safe assets – government debt, bank debt, repurchase agreements, and asset-backed securities – and how the construction unraveled in crisis. Each time, poor coordination among long-established legal and regulatory tools, rather than the tools themselves, stood out as a problem.

This chapter proceeds as follows. After this introduction, Part II surveys recent literature on safe assets. In Part III, we use four asset categories considered "safe" to show how safe assets are made, labeled, and guaranteed. In conclusion, we sketch out tentative policy implications and a research agenda.

THE SAFE ASSET DEBATE

The phrase "safe asset" is sprinkled through economic research, policy papers, and law review articles going back decades.[18] Until very recently, the phrase was not used as a term of art to denote a general phenomenon, but rather to describe

---

[18] A search of IMF, NBER, and Westlaw databases located hundreds of mentions between 1980 and 2007. A search for the phrase "safe asset" in IMF eLibrary, which contains the IMF's periodicals, books, working papers and studies, and data and statistical tools (available at www.elibrary.imf.org/), resulted in forty-nine returns between 1980 and 2007 and thirty-six returns between 2008 and 2014; a search for the phrase "safe asset" or "safe assets" on National Bureau of Economic Research (NBER) Working Papers, a database segment consisting of working papers and articles published in journals (available at www.nber.org), resulted in eight articles and papers between 1980 and 2007 and eighteen articles and papers between 2008 and 2014;

investments that carried minimal risks, or as shorthand for modeling assumptions.[19] The words "safe," "riskless," or "risk-free" were often enclosed in quotation marks or preceded by "relatively."

By the mid-2000s, economists and policy makers focused on the flow of savings from countries with unmet development needs to the United States and Europe.[20] Some theorized that this "uphill" capital flow could be explained by developing countries' inability to create enough financial instruments that could serve as reliable stores of value for the savings;[21] though others blamed exchange rate management.

The onset of financial crises in the United States in 2007 and Europe in 2010 brought a shared sense of discontinuity, a sudden loss of safety for AAA-rated "supersenior" asset-backed securities and government debt, also described as a vanishing of secure investments.[22] In 2011, market and policy radars detected a new kind of asset scarcity, this time driven by postcrisis risk aversion in mature markets.[23] By 2012, fears of scarcity and abrupt loss informed a growing body of research describing a category of financial contracts with shared attributes as a "cornerstone" of the global financial system.[24] "Safe assets" became a term of art

and a search for the phrase "safe asset" on *WestLaw Law Reviews & Journals* database resulted in forty-nine articles between 1980 and 2007 and sixty articles between 2008 and 2014.

[19] The following examples are typical. In economics: John Lipsky, Peter Keller, Donald J. Mathieson, Richard N. Williams, *International Bond Markets, International Capital Markets : Developments and Prospects*, IMF Occasional Paper No. 23, 08 July 1983, p. 34 (describing "institutional investors seeking relatively safe assets"; Morris Goldstein and Geoffrey Woglom, *Market-Based Fiscal Discipline in Monetary Unions: Evidence From the U.S. Municipal Bond Market*, IMF Working Paper No. 91/89, 01 September 1991 (referring to safe assets as a baseline for bond interest rates); Garry J. Schinasi, Steven Riess Weisbrod, and Monica Hargraves, *Asset Price Inflation in the 1980's: A Flow of Funds Perspective*, IMF Working Paper No. 93/77, 01 October 1993, p. 21 (describing U.S. depository institutions taking on risk by "selling safe assets and retaining the relatively risky ones such as commercial mortgages"); Peter Diamond and John Geanakoplos, *Social Security Investment in Equities I: Linear Case*, Nat'l Bureau of Econ. Res., Working Paper No. 7103 (1999) ("We assume that the returns to the real assets are such that both risky and safe assets are held in equilibrium when the safe asset exists.") In law: Joseph Bankman and Thomas Griffith, *Is the Debate Between an Income Tax and a Consumption Tax A Debate About Risk? Does it Matter?*, 47 TAX L. REV 377–59 (1992) (considering the effects of taxation on investment choices, as when "the combination of taxable gains and nonrefundable losses will reduce the expected return of risky assets below the return of safe assets, causing all investors to purchase riskless assets"); Jonathan R. Macey and Elizabeth H. Garrett, *Market Discipline by Depositors: A Summary of the Theoretical and Empirical Arguments*, 5 YALE J. ON REG. 215–39 (1988) (arguing that deposit insurance distorts bank managers' incentives because "a managerial decision to shift the bank's loan portfolio from a set of relatively safe assets to a set of highly risky assets will not affect in any way the interest the bank must pay to attract deposits.").

[20] Bernanke 2005; Bernanke 2007; Summers 2004; Roubini and Setser 2004.

[21] Caballero 2006; Caballero, Farhi, and Gourinchas 2008.

[22] BIS 2012 at 59–60. See, e.g., John Carney, "How the crash of safe assets fueled the financial crisis," CNBC, www.cnbc.com/id/101327578#.

[23] See Cardiff Garcia, "The decline of 'safe' assets, FTAlphaville (Dec 05 2011 09:23), http://ftalphaville.ft.com/2011/12/05/778301/the-decline-of-safe-assets/; Credit Suisse 2011.

[24] IMF 2012.

with correspondingly large policy implications. This body of research is the departure point for our analysis; this part offers a summary overview.

Why Safe Assets? Lumping

A unitary safe asset phenomenon helps generate unifying theories to explain the buildup of financial instability precrisis, investor behavior in crisis, and postcrisis disruptions in critical financial markets. The safe assets literature thus represents an intellectual exercise in "lumping" certain investors and investments to explore related market dynamics. There are two broad strands of lumping, reflecting different policy concerns. Using the proponents' terminology, we refer to the strands as asset scarcity and transactions technology.

Asset Scarcity

Ricardo Caballero and colleagues have argued that demand from surplus countries for instruments to serve as a long-term store of value had knock-on effects in the U.S. financial system, which led to the crisis.[25] This account extends the authors' earlier work on asset scarcity in the emerging markets.[26] In that work, "insatiable" global demand for savings vehicles with minimal risk, such as U.S. Treasury securities, outstripped their supply. The imbalance put pressure on the U.S. financial system to produce more safe assets to fill the gap, feeding the boom in mortgage securitization, until the markets unraveled.[27] This line of inquiry focuses on safe assets as a store of value, with low credit and liquidity risks, and highlights the global dimension of supply and demand.

Global asset scarcity analysis gained momentum when researchers and policy makers sought to link theories of global imbalances with explanations of the financial crisis as a product of regulatory failure. A U.S. Federal Reserve Board study of precrisis capital flows into the United States[28] distinguished between government savers' appetite for U.S. Treasury and U.S. housing finance "Agency" debt,[29] and demand from European financial institutions for riskier engineered

---

[25] Caballero 2009.
[26] Caballero et al. 2008.
[27] Caballero 2009.
[28] Bernanke et al. 2011.
[29] "Agency debt" refers to securities issued or backed by Fannie Mae, Freddie Mac, or Ginnie Mae. Fannie Mae (the Federal National Mortgage Association or FNMA), and Freddie Mac (the Federal Home Loan Mortgage Corporation or FHLMC), are government-sponsored enterprises (GSEs), which were taken over by the U.S. government in 2008. Ginnie Mae (the Government National Mortgage Association or GNMA) has been wholly owned by the U.S. government since its establishment in 1968. See Ginniemae.gov, *Ginnie Mae & the GSEs* (last updated 2/25/2013), available at www.ginniemae.gov/consumer_education/Pages/ginnie_mae_and_the_gses.aspx.

assets. It pointed to European bank regulation as a potentially distinct ingredient in the demand for "private-label" mortgage-backed securities, and to flaws in the U.S. financial system, such as lax underwriting standards, that supported the private production of apparently safe assets to feed capital inflows from 2003 to 2007.[30]

To serve as a government savings vehicle, an asset must generally have low credit risk. Unless otherwise specified in the investment mandate, many different assets might fit the bill; the choices are not necessarily discontinuous. On the other hand, to attract regulated institutions, it helps if the asset enjoys regulatory privileges, such as exemptions or low capital charges. Regulation thereby creates new continuities and discontinuities: firms might substitute higher-yielding, riskier assets for safe ones that come with the same privileges, and might discriminate among assets with the same risk profile based on their regulatory treatment.

Economists have also invoked ideas about global asset scarcity to explain why investors flocked to the United States even as securitization markets unraveled, and later continued to buy U.S. Treasury debt when it lost its AAA rating from Standard & Poor's to domestic political battles.[31] They stress that investors not only try to minimize the risk of default and other loss of value over time, but also seek out "convenience attributes" in financial contracts – their money-like functions. In this view, demand begets demand: U.S. Treasuries make good safe assets because they can be turned into cash instantly at face value, for use in transactions, simply because so many actors use them in so many ways. Few other assets play this role globally. We return to the money feature later in this part.

Transactions Technology

Gary Gorton, Stefan Lewellyn, and Andrew Metrick engage in a different sort of lumping. Instead of looking at global supply and demand, they consider the ratio of safe assets to total financial assets in the U.S. economy after World War II. They observe that this "safe asset share" remained remarkably constant – roughly 30 percent to 35 percent – from 1952 to 2010, while the ratio of financial assets as a proportion of the U.S. economy more than doubled.[32] This leads them to conclude

---

[30] Private-label securities are not backed by Agency guarantees. The combination of regulatory benefit and yields above U.S. Treasury and Agency securities could have made it worthwhile for the regulated firms in Europe to issue short-term debt to finance their purchases of U.S. private label mortgage-backed securities. Bernanke et al. 2011.

[31] IMF 2012; Krishnamurthy and Vissing-Jorgensen 2012.

[32] Gorton et al. 2012. The authors make several crucial assumptions in calculating the safe asset share based on Federal Reserve Flow of Funds data. They start with total liabilities produced by the government and financial sector. They then make a series of adjustments including removing government liabilities held by other governmental entities, removing certain financial sector liabilities (such as mutual fund shares) on the theory that these are not information insensitive, and assume that 85% of mortgage-backed securities and other asset-backed securities are information insensitive and qualify as safe assets.

that safe assets are a necessary input in the financial system, part of a little-understood "transactions technology."[33]

The transactions technology view, as the term suggests, emphasizes trading over long-term savings (store of value) uses of safe assets, and focuses on their money-like characteristics. Gorton and coauthors define safe assets as "information-insensitive debt," or debt "immune to adverse selection in trading because agents have no desire to acquire private information about the current health of the issuer."[34] The ideal safe asset is assumed to have minimal credit risk and is highly liquid – so much so that it can be traded "no questions asked" – especially useful as collateral to reduce counterparty risk. By definition, its uses are binary: once it pays for investors to research its risk attributes, the debt no longer qualifies as safe. A related paper highlights the downside of information-insensitive debt: it is prone to crashes and amplifies shocks when the insensitivity is lost, which helps explain the crisis.[35]

The stability of the safe asset share suggests that the total amount of safe assets determines the size of the financial sector through some kind of transactions technology. The data in the paper suggest that safe assets appear to play a key role in the financialization of the U.S. economy since the late 1980s. However, the research does not link the safe asset share to economic growth.[36]

The safe asset share has implications beyond transactions technology. Like those who write about global asset scarcity, Gorton and coauthors argue that safe assets substitute for one another, and that supply–demand imbalances can push investors to look for safety in new places. Most of the writing on safe assets describes hydraulic qualities of this sort; their paper goes a step further. It argues that, since the safe asset share is constant and since the government cannot fill all demand, financial firms perform a socially valuable task when they issue debt that is traded "no questions asked." They argue that attempts to "squelch" safe asset production by banks or shadow banks would simply push demand into even darker, less regulated corners of the financial system.[37] We revisit this image of organic growth suppressed by regulation in Part III.

What Are the Uses and Attributes of Safe Assets? Splitting

The Global Financial Stability Report (GFSR), a flagship publication of the International Monetary Fund (IMF), takes much of the credit for raising the profile

---

[33] Gorton et al. 2012.

[34] Gorton et al. 2012.

[35] Dang et al. 2013a.

[36] Some researchers divide safe assets into claims of financial firms on one another ("inside liquidity") and claims on the real economy or the government ("outside liquidity"). Pierre-Olivier Gourinchas and Olivier Jeanne, *Global Safe Assets*, BIS Working Paper No. 399 (December 2012) *citing* Bengt Holmström and Jean Tirole, *Private and Public Supply of Liquidity*, 106 *Journal of Political Economy* 1 (1998).

[37] Gorton et al. 2012.

of "safe assets" as a term of art in a 2012 chapter entitled "Safe Assets: Financial System Cornerstone?"[38] Despite this "lumping" title, IMF researchers produced a detailed survey of the different users, uses and attributes of safe assets based on the economic literature and IMF data – an exercise in "splitting."

Use, user, and asset permutations in the GFSR catalog seem endless. IMF researchers identify five broad uses for safe assets: (i) as a store of value and portfolio capital cushion, (ii) as collateral in repo and derivatives markets, (iii) as an element of compliance with solvency and liquidity regulation, (iv) as a pricing benchmark for riskier assets, and (v) as a tool in monetary policy operations. Each of these uses requires slightly different safety attributes.[39] For example, an asset makes a good store of value if it has minimal credit, inflation, and exchange rate risk. High market liquidity is important for transactional uses: an asset can serve as collateral in a wide range of financial transactions when it has a deep market and is easy to value, among other factors. In contrast, uses that respond to government policy emphasize the safety attributes specified by the relevant authorities, which may be different from those valued by the market. As we elaborate later, safe assets can also be used to make other safe assets.[40]

Some uses may be accommodated with multiple assets, while some assets may have multiple safe uses. For example, government debt, bank debt, and highly rated private debt can all serve as collateral, especially in calm economic times. Bank deposits and repos both have been used for liquidity management. Meanwhile, government debt is used both for savings and liquidity management. A shock can reduce the number and volume of assets suitable for safe use and increase demand for the remaining assets with multiple safe uses. Hence, again, the demand for U.S. Treasury debt at the height of the financial crisis.

Safe asset users include banks, official reserve managers and sovereign wealth funds, pension funds, central banks and nonbank financial institutions, including market infrastructure entities such as clearinghouses. A single user may have multiple uses for safe assets. For instance, while banks are by far the largest holders of safe assets according to the GFSR, their holdings meet several distinct needs. These include capital preservation and managing maturity mismatches, meeting regulatory requirements, and participating as primary dealers in government securities markets.

A different spin on splitting comes courtesy of law scholars writing about "money claims."[41] Economists writing about safe assets sometimes fold money in with the lot, since it can perform many safe asset functions at once: it can serve as a savings vehicle, a pricing benchmark, a hedge, and collateral. In contrast, Morgan Ricks draws a bright line between money – short-term, highly liquid claims including

---

[38] IMF 2012; Portes 2013.
[39] IMF 2012 at 84.
[40] Krishnamurthy and Vissing-Jorgensen 2013; Gorton and Metrick 2010.
[41] Ricks 2012; Blair 2013; Ondersma 2013.

deposits and repo – and safe assets, which he defines as longer-term securities subject to market risk even when they have negligible credit risk.[42] Money claims entail maturity transformation and expose the system to bank-style runs.[43] The implication is that money should be a priority for policy intervention.

Finally, there are the ultimate splitters, safe asset skeptics, who suggest that the term "safe assets" masks an incoherent category comprising a range of uses and attributes of safety with little in common, none of which inherently attach to any particular financial contract.[44] Some argue further that safe asset scholarship is damaging, because by describing and ascribing social value to a unitary phenomenon, it discourages risk assessment and calls for public backing of certain markets.[45]

Although we recognize the analytical merits of splitting, our chapter focuses on a subset of traits shared by all the assets described here, and acknowledged by the splitters. Across diverse settings, all safe assets seek to reduce risk so much as to make it negligible, they are used in a binary fashion (safe or not) in critical markets, and are prone to lose their safety abruptly in crisis, triggering government rescues. For crisis prevention and resolution, it is important to understand how and why market actors come to use assets as if they were risk-free, how different safe assets can serve as building blocks and substitutes for one another, how perceptions of safety change, and how loss of safety invokes public backing. A unified category, however provisional, is a useful starting point for such analysis.

Where Do Safe Assets Come From? Public and Private Production

Governments and private firms can produce safe assets. The safety of public safe assets derives in key part from governments' unique fiscal and monetary powers. Debt issued by creditworthy private firms with a deep and liquid market may have the attributes of a safe asset. Public and private safe assets can also be made safer by contract, for example, using short maturities to enhance liquidity, tiering cash flows to reduce the risk of default, and requiring collateral to limit counter-party risk.[46]

Economists show that purely private safe assets are especially vulnerable to systemic risk. They tend to lose their safety together in response to a common shock, and are more prone to transmit shocks across the financial system as contracts and financial engineering unravel. When the supply of safe assets in

---

[42] Ricks 2012.
[43] Some economists effectively make a similar argument when they say that money is the only safe asset.
[44] Fisher 2013.
[45] Portes 2013.
[46] Gorton and Penacchi 1990; IMF 2012.

the economy shrinks, economic contraction may follow.[47] Governments respond with guarantees and central bank liquidity support.[48]

The distinction between public and private production of safe assets is thin in practice. Governments and private market actors routinely collaborate to make and maintain safe assets.[49] Governments guarantee private debts, turning them into safe assets. They offer regulatory incentives for firms to buy designated assets, such as government, housing, or small business debt, creating markets in public and private safe assets. Central banks support such markets when they buy the assets or accept them as collateral in policy operations. Private credit rating agencies fueled precrisis growth in securitization (privately produced safe assets); their assessments were also incorporated in regulation.[50] In addition, public and private safe asset issuers appear to step in for one another at different times in the credit cycle: in good times, private safe assets make up for scarce public ones; in bad times, public safe assets make up for the lost safety of private ones.[51]

In this collaboration, there is a distinction between domestic and global safe assets. Governments can produce domestic safe assets by some combination of public credit, printing money, and regulatory fiat.[52] Global safe assets must be accepted as such by market actors beyond a single government's control.[53] However, regulatory coordination can help broaden the acceptance of assets as safe.[54]

Policy Problems and Unanswered Questions

We conclude by taking stock of the common threads, which we will pick up in Part III. In economic research, the concept of safe assets has helped describe a plausible path of the global financial crisis. This research tells how global and national demand for savings and liquidity management tools might have encouraged purchases of U.S. Treasury securities, and how it might have led some investors to seek out financial contracts engineered to be safe in some states of the world, but highly unstable in others. It also describes the substitution of publicly produced assets for private ones in crisis, and suggests how asset scarcity might manifest itself going forward.

Many parts of this story are contested. Yet there is widespread agreement that financial stability is at stake when market participants and policy makers get safe assets wrong. Investors may have trouble identifying and finding enough safe assets;

---

[47] Greenwood et al. 2010.

[48] Gorton and Penacchi 1990.

[49] Cf. DESAN, MAKING MONEY: COIN, BANK CURRENCY, AND THE COMING OF CAPITALISM (2014), on money as a constitutional project.

[50] IMF 2012 at 83. Rating agencies' role in the market was amplified with "regulatory license" when ratings were incorporated in regulations. Partnoy 1999.

[51] Caballero and Farhi 2014; Gorton and Ordonez 2013; Greenwood et al. 2010).

[52] Reinhart and Sbrancia 2011.

[53] Mehrling 2013.

[54] See, e.g., "Capital Requirements Directive II (CRD II)" (treating Euro area debt as risk-free).

they may also misjudge safety and herd into risky assets. When safety is treated as binary, a small shift in sentiment can trigger a selling stampede with dramatic spillover effects. Some commentators go a step further and claim that retrenchment can contribute to safe asset shortages, which might reduce financing for the economy and dampen growth. This view underpins arguments that policy should cultivate safe asset markets, or, at the other extreme, that it should fight general assumptions about safety.

Policy diagnoses and prescriptions are tentative, at least in part because there is no coherent account of how safe assets come about. Institutional descriptions are fragmented and foggy. IMF's GFSR takes a strong stand by attributing many disruptions in the safe asset markets to government intervention "distorting the price of safety";[55] however, empirical evidence is insufficient to link supply and demand to any dominant factor, be it regulatory intervention, regulatory arbitrage, or hydraulic pressure from surplus country savings. The relationship between safe assets and economic growth is similarly uncertain. Different views of how safe assets work yield different diagnoses of the problem, and radically different policy prescriptions: issuing more government debt,[56] foregoing debt restructuring,[57] relaxing shadow bank regulation,[58] or stripping government debt of regulatory privileges.[59]

Our chapter focuses on one strand of unanswered questions. In Part III, we use four examples of safe assets to investigate the tools by which the law supports their creation and use, maintains their safety, and makes up for their failure.

FOUR SAFE ASSETS

Government debt, bank debt, repos, and asset-backed securities have all been used widely as if they were risk-free. Over the past decade, each of these asset categories has played a prominent role in financial crises. Below we consider the lessons of their rise and fall.

Government Debt

In some market and policy circles, October 18, 2010 marks the day when Euro-area government debt stopped being a safe asset – more important than the day Greece was found fudging its public accounts, or the day France lost its AAA credit rating.[60] The Franco-German Declaration made in Deauville on October 18

---

[55] IMF 2012 at 82.
[56] Poszar 2013.
[57] Blommestein 2012.
[58] Gorton et al. 2012.
[59] Nouy 2011; IMF 2012; Weidmann 2013.
[60] Orphanides 2014; Gelpern and Gulati 2013 at 380. For press commentary, see, e.g., Joshua Chaffin and Peter Spiegel, "Franco-German bail-out pact divides EU," *Financial Times* (October 24, 2010), www.ft.com/intl/cms/s/0/56984290-df96-11df-bed9-00144feabdc0.html;

committed to strengthen fiscal discipline and economic policy reform, and also to establish a crisis management regime with "adequate participation of private creditors."[61]

To the uninitiated, the leaders' pledge of fiscal probity, to be enshrined in EU treaties and institutions, would make Euro area government debt safer. But to the traders who sold on news from Deauville, the defining safety feature was Europe's political commitment to avoid debt restructuring in any part of the Euro area at all costs. This illuminates a core contradiction of sovereign debt as a safe asset.

Government debt may be the most commonly cited example of a safe asset. It may also be the most contradictory. At the start of 2014, the world's governments had over $44 trillion in outstanding debt, with the United States, Europe, and Japan accounting for more than three-quarters of the total.[62] On the one hand, this debt is a contract like any other. Its risk profile is a function of economic performance and market conditions, which support the debtor's ability to pay. Governments' unique ability to tax and print money makes their debt safer than most. Because governments are bigger and need more financing than most other domestic economic actors, the markets in their debt tend to be deeper and more liquid. But repayment also depends on the political priorities and constraints of the sovereign, often described as a willingness to pay. When a government fails to pay, creditors have very limited means to collect, because sovereign immunity puts most of the debtor's resources beyond their reach.[63] Theorists have struggled to reconcile governments' unique capacity to pay, the political limits on this capacity, and creditors' perennial willingness to hold sovereign debt despite weak enforcement and a rich record of defaults.[64]

Gillian Tett, "Get used to world without 'risk free' rate," *Financial Times* (September 1, 2011). www.ft.com/intl/cms/s/0/52a9169e-d4b6-11e0-a7ac-00144feab49a.html.

[61] "Franco-German Declaration, Statement for the France-Germany-Russia Summit" (October 18, 2010), www.eu0.dk/upload/application/pdf/1371f221/Franco-german_declaration.pdf.

[62] World DataBank, Gross Central Government Debt Position, http://databank.worldbank.org/data/Views/Reports/ReportWidgetCustom.aspx?Report_Name=Table-C2.-Gross-Central-Gov.-Debt-Position&Id=46819dee27 (last visited 9/14/2014).

[63] Weidemaier 2013.

[64] For a literature summary, *see* Sturzenegger and Zettelmeyer 2007; Reinhart and Rogoff 2011. The tension is of constitutional proportions. For example, the Fourteenth Amendment to the U.S. Constitution expressly enshrines U.S. Treasuries' status as "no questions asked" debt: "The validity of the public debt of the United States … shall not be questioned." The next sentence effects debt repudiation: it declares the debt of the Confederate States "null and void" as illegitimate. In 1935, the U.S. Supreme Court demonstrated that a government's control over payment media in the economy could strip its repayment promise of all value. *Perry v. United States* 294 U.S. 330 (1935). Euro area governments in 2011 "solemnly reaffirm[ed] their inflexible determination to honor fully their own individual sovereign signature… as … a decisive element for ensuring financial stability in the euro area as a whole" – and in the same breath blessed Greece's "exceptional and unique" recourse to debt restructuring. www.consilium.europa.eu/uedocs/cms_data/docs/pressdata/en/ec/123978.pdf.

Because so many other safe assets use sovereign debt as a component part, it is important to understand what makes sovereign debt work as a safe asset – and whether the safe asset universe might have a hollow core. Minimizing the risk attributes in sovereign debt by law is challenging because, as already noted, sovereigns have trouble making credible commitments to repay. Even when the promise is embedded in a foundational text, as in the U.S. Constitution and the European treaty complex, the penalty for walking away is uncertain at best.

Contractual tools such as priority, collateral, and indexation, common in private debt, might seem like a simple way out. Yet a scant few national governments issue subordinated, secured, or indexed debt on a significant scale – despite generations of proposals to that effect.[65] Seniority and collateralization ideas came back in the Euro area crisis as a substitute for, or a complement to, cross-guarantees among member states; however, they have not been adopted.[66] Some observers have suggested that demanding security or collateral is by definition inconsistent with the idea of government debt as risk-free. For example, when governments issue short-term debt to reassure skeptical investors, the tenor responds to perceptions of risk – by definition, that debt is not a safe asset. Similarly, when governments borrow in foreign currency and under foreign law, they bolster their repayment commitment and make the debt safer; however, the fact that investors demanded it suggests that the debt is information sensitive.[67]

On the other hand, when a sovereign's debt is otherwise treated as free from credit risk, its short-term debt can further minimize interest-rate risk over time and can be used more like money.[68] Put differently, short maturity can make already-safe government debt more like money, but it cannot turn risky promises into safe assets.

In sum, traditional contract tools might make some sovereign debt marginally safer; they do not make it information insensitive. The downside risk of these tools to the debtor is substantial: they can signal investor risk perceptions, become politically sensitive for the debtor, and, in the end, are likely to run up against the sovereign commitment challenge when it matters most.

The value of government debt, like money, heavily depends on legal and institutional arrangements that create demand for it. Banks have been required to hold their own government's debt as a licensing condition; laws, regulations, and supervision practices encourage banks and nonbank financial institutions to buy

---

[65] IMF 2004.

[66] See, e.g., Markus K. Brunnermeier et al., ESBies: "A realistic reform of Europe's financial architecture" (October 25, 2011), www.voxeu.org/article/esbies-realistic-reform-europes-finan cial-architecture; Jacques Delpla and Jakob von Weizsäcker, "The Blue Bond Proposal," *Bruegel Policy Brief Issue* 2010/03, www.bruegel.org/publications/publication-detail/publica tion/403-the-blue-bond-proposal/.

[67] See, e.g., Borensztein et al. 2006 at 23 (on "original sin") and Zettelmeyer, Trebesch and Gulati 2013 (describing Greek debt issuance under English law).

[68] Greenwood, Hanson and Stein 2010; Ricks 2012.

government debt.[69] Regulatory privileges, such as the labeling of government debt as zero-risk, or including it in the limited range of permitted investments for regulated firms, create demand for government debt. Such privileges take on outsize importance when governments cannot credibly commit to pay. When governments use safety labels to foster a market in their own debt, they create a captive pool of savings to meet their borrowing needs, reassure investors that they can sell the debt at any time, and raise the ultimate cost of default. In other words, they signal commitment to repay and relax it at the same time.[70]

The effectiveness of labeling is partly a function of social control. At one extreme a despot, who can make its subjects buy and hold its debt (or any other), makes it domestically "safe" at the stroke of a pen – even if no one but its subjects would use it. This raises the specter of distortion, or "financial repression."[71] At the other extreme, when governments have incomplete control over their debt markets, their debt might become more sensitive to private safety labels, such as credit ratings. Private labels can present a challenge for monetary authorities using freely traded government debt as a policy tool. For example, ratings, downgrades, and credit insurance triggers for some Euro area government debt threatened to undermine the efforts of the European Central Bank (ECB) to ease monetary conditions in parts of the currency union; they also contradicted public safety labels, such as the debt's eligibility as collateral in central bank lending and as an instrument of monetary policy.

Government debt represents a direct, express pledge of public credit. It also benefits from more subtle and indirect guarantees. For example, when the debt is denominated in the sovereign's own currency, the central bank can print money to repay the debt, even at the risk of diluting its value. As the preceding discussion of safety labels illustrates, governments can also guarantee a measure of liquidity by regulation. Thus risk-free treatment and safe asset status are serviceable approximations for domestic government debt. Making foreign government debt safe is far more difficult.

When a foreign government defaults, investors have limited recourse unless their own governments step in and substitute domestic safe assets (money, public debt) for the failed foreign ones. In a monetary union such as the euro area, financial

---

[69] For banks, see National Bank Act, Sec. 5159. See, e.g., David M. Gische, "The New York City Banks and the Development of the National Banking System 1860–1870," 23 AM. J. LEGAL HIST. 21, 38–9 (1979). For nonbank financial institutions, see "National Association of Insurance Commissioners," *U.S. Government-Related and Foreign Government Debt Holdings Within the U.S. Insurance Industry* (5/9/13), www.naic.org/capital_markets_archive_index.htm ("EU-based insurers are not required to hold any capital to support their holdings of any sovereign debt issued by the 27 countries in the European Economic Area, regardless of the creditworthiness of the country issuing the debt."); U.S. Securities and Exchange Commission (SEC), *Money Market Fund Reform; Amendments to Form PF,* 79 F.R. 47736.

[70] Desan *forthcoming* 2015; cf. Pistor 2013.

[71] MacKinnon 1973; Shaw 1973.

integration policies can translate into indirect backing of one sovereign's debt by another, in tension with express treaty commitments.[72] For example, extending the risk-free label to all member government debt supports financial integration and monetary policy transmission by encouraging firms across the union to buy the debts of all member governments on the same terms. However, when a member state defaults, the others may have to choose between bailing out the sovereign and bailing out their own banks – or do both.

Euro area government debt is a useful case study because going into the crisis it was widely perceived as part of the safe asset core, and used with little differentiation among the debt of member states.[73] It was labeled zero-risk as part of the political design; as such, it successfully promoted financial integration.[74] However, the framework for making all sovereign debt in the Euro area equally safe, and for guaranteeing it with common fiscal resources, turned out to be inadequate. For ECB President Jean-Claude Trichet, the crisis ended a unique "privilege," where "the signature of the advanced economies ... was untouchable – in that sense, there is no more risk-free asset. The investors and savers the world over are looking at every signature on the basis of its fundamentals."[75] Of course there never had been a risk-free asset, but rather a political project enshrined in law and institutions. Trichet, his colleagues, and successors stretched the ECB's authority in the name of the project. However, the ECB's capacity to label and backstop the safety of its policy instruments exceeded its capacity to make them fundamentally

---

[72] European treaties enshrined commitments to financial integration and against both debt mutualization (bailouts) and monetary financing of government debt. See *Consolidated version of the Treaty on the Functioning of the European Union*, at Title VIII: Economic and Monetary Policy. ECB intervention in government debt markets was framed as monetary policy and liquidity support, but was widely interpreted as central bank backing for government debt, which in turn threatened the ECB's credibility. See e.g., Irwin 2013. Governments in and outside monetary unions may have a strong interest in guaranteeing one another's debts to limit damage to trade and broader economic activity (Bulow and Rogoff 1988).

[73] See, e.g., IMF 2012 at 86–7 (stating that "prior to the [Eurozone] crisis, there was little price differentiation across assets of varied quality [of different euro area sovereign debt]" and "[a]fter the crisis, the differentiation in the perceived safety of various asset classes increased markedly.").

[74] "[M]ost importantly, the member states of the European Community are firmly committed to the principle that all claims on banks, central governments and the official sector within European Community countries should be treated in the same way." Basel Committee on Banking Regulations and Supervisory Practices, International Convergence of Capital Measurement and Capital Standards (1988) at 34, available at www.bis.org/publ/bcbsc111.pdf? noframes=1 [hereinafter Basel I] (allowing banks to assign a 0% risk weight to exposures to OECD member countries); Parliament and Council Directive 2006/49/EC. On the Capital Adequacy of Investment Firms and Credit Institutions (Recast), 2006 O.J. (I. 177) 201 ("CRD II"); National Bank Act, 12 U.S.C. § 24 (Seventh) (treating certain types of obligations as risk-free).

[75] UBS Center, *Jean-Claude Trichet: "There is no more risk-free asset"* (Published on December 18, 2012), www.youtube.com/watch?v=CS9EvBZ_UOc.

creditworthy. Its economic policy mandate, like that of most central banks, is limited by law and politics.[76]

Bank Debt

Bank debt is the simplest and most common safe asset after government debt; at $40 trillion, it is also comparable in volume.[77] Although they have not always done so, commercial banks today perform multiple functions simultaneously.[78] They pool popular savings, allocate credit, operate payment systems, issue money in the form of demand deposits, and transmit government monetary policy. In the process, they transform long-term illiquid assets (loans) into extremely short-term liabilities (demand deposits), and, at least in theory, act as repositories of investment information. Two of these functions require bank debt to have safe asset characteristics: to pool savings, bank debt must be a safe store of value; to serve as money, bank debt must be liquid, or usable at face value in transactions. These safety features are achieved with a mix of contractual and regulatory tools.

Two categories of bank liabilities are generally included in safe asset counts: insured retail deposits and other unsubordinated debt, often referred to as wholesale funding. The safety of retail deposits is typically framed as a consumer protection concern, as well as a matter of financial stability given the propensity of depositors to panic and withdraw deposits. The primary constituents of the safety measures are retail depositors, ordinary people with small amounts of savings and a stream of small-scale transactional needs. The safety of wholesale deposits is first and foremost a financial stability concern; the constituents are large firms, financial institutions, and local governments. However, significant losses by institutional depositors have knock-on effects on the real economy and the government fiscal and safety net.

In the first instance, all bank deposits are made safe by contract, when banks promise repayment on demand and at par. The maturity mismatch on bank balance sheets detracts from the credibility of this promise, as do the banks' fractional reserve holdings and highly leveraged capital structure. Individual banks must also contend with cyclical dynamics in credit markets, cognitive biases, and

---

[76] The ECB has sought to impose economic policy conditionality on its lending, but has done so indirectly and behind the scenes for the most part. See e.g., ECB, Press Release – "Technical features of Outright Monetary Transactions" (Sept. 2012), www.ecb.europa.eu/press/pr/date/2012/html/pr120906_1.en.html ("A necessary condition for Outright Monetary Transactions is strict and effective conditionality attached to an appropriate European Financial Stability Facility/European Stability Mechanism (EFSF/ESM) programme.").

[77] IMF 2012.

[78] Proposals to disentangle some of these functions are resurgent. See e.g., Wolf 2014 and Levitin (forthcoming).

collective action problems, which prompt them to take excessive risks and lever up in good times and retrench after crises.[79]

Regulation tries to address these vulnerabilities directly by policing the credit quality and composition of bank assets and reserve levels, mandating minimum levels of equity and subordinated debt, and shielding banks from other parts of the financial system. Requiring banks to hold specified assets has the dual effect of making bank debt safer, and labeling the debt of other issuers as safe (or at least safe enough to serve as ingredients of bank safety. Regulation thus becomes an exercise in portfolio construction, turning banks into "safety multipliers," for example, producing safe private assets (bank debt) from a kernel of public debt.[80] Structural measures, such as affiliation and transaction restrictions, try to insulate banks from risk elsewhere in the financial system. Marking the boundary between banks and other firms reflects recognition of banks' inherent fragility and social value, but also defines part of the safe asset universe.[81]

Efforts to engineer banks as safe issuers and to insulate them from outside risk are inevitably incomplete. Both private ordering and regulation can get the bank safety mix badly wrong. If banks can shift the costs of their risk taking onto the public ex post, they will take too much risk, so that their debt would become unsafe absent public intervention.[82] On the other hand, regulators might have perverse incentives of their own from time inconsistency and agency problems, including regulatory capture.[83] When depositors continue to use bank debt as if it were safe despite the fact that it is not made safe, it raises the pressure for intervention in crisis.

In addition to making banks into safer issuers, regulation tries to make deposits themselves safer with special resolution regimes and payment priorities. Dedicated legal regimes for bank insolvency are designed to work fast – within days and weeks, not months and years. A growing number of resolution regimes provide for depositor preference, which can extend beyond insured deposits, giving each depositor a senior claim in distribution.[84] For insured deposits, seniority matters less because

---

[79] Gerding 2013.

[80] Weymuller 2013.

[81] See, e.g., "Board of Governors of the Federal Reserve System et al, Agencies Issue Final Rules Implementing the Volcker Rule" (December 10, 2013), www.federalreserve.gov/newsevents/press/bcreg/20131210a.htm; U.K. "Independent Commission on Banking, Final Report Recommendations" (September 2011) ("Vickers Report"), available at webarchive.nationalarchives.gov.uk/20131003105424/https:/hmt-sanctions.s3.amazonaws.com/ICB%20final%20report/ICB%2520Final%2520Report%5B1%5D.pdf; Liikanen et al., "High-Level Expert Group on Reforming the Structure of the EU Banking Sector" (October 2012) ("Liikanen Report"), available at http://ec.europa.eu/internal_market/bank/docs/high-level_expert_group/repor t_en.pdf. Structural separation is also used to protect claims by contract and regulation outside banking, in, among other areas, asset securitization (Gelpern and Levitin 2009) and investment fund regulation (Morley 2014).

[82] Admati and Hellwig 2012.

[83] Gerding 2013.

[84] See, e.g., U.K. Parliament, *Financial Services (Banking Reform) Act 2013*, http://services .parliament.uk/bills/2013–14/financialservicesbankingreform.html (depositor preference

they are paid from the insurance fund or the state backstop; the guarantor then steps into the depositor's shoes. For uninsured deposits, seniority directly improves the likelihood and size of recovery.[85]

Bank debt is labeled safe when it is assigned low-risk weights, usually just below government debt, in capital adequacy regulation. This encourages regulated firms and other investors to buy bank debt. In a less tangible way, bank licensing, eligibility for insurance, and central bank liquidity support all convey the institutions' public importance, a level of safety and oversight, and a likelihood of public rescue in crisis. Some observers have suggested that designations of systemic importance – systemically important financial institutions (SIFIs), global systemically important banks (G-SIBs), and the like – promise public backing in distress. Others argue that enhanced prudential oversight that accompanies systemic designations raises the cost of doing business for the designated firms, and may either make them less competitive and therefore less safe, or limit the volume of safe debt they can issue.[86]

The safety of bank debt is guaranteed by the state through deposit insurance, liquidity support from the central bank as lender of last resort (LOLR), and ad hoc credit and liquidity support in crises. Deposit insurance may be the best-known example of public backing for a safe asset. It protects both depositors and banks. Government guarantees of repayment at par make deposits "default-free" in the eyes of the public and discourage runs.[87] The bank's promise of redemption on demand and the government's guarantee of that promise make deposits money-like.

Public backing for deposits can be direct (available as a first resort) or contingent (available only after exhausting some combination of bank equity, junior debt, affiliate guarantees, and an industry-financed insurance fund). It is at least partly explicit, specified up front in legislation and regulation. However, there is also a pattern of extending deposit insurance coverage ex post, in crisis, to more claims and claimants.[88] At the other extreme, some governments cannot afford to honor the original guarantee, and are forced to curtail coverage or choose among the claimants. Iceland and Cyprus are prominent recent examples.

The ubiquitous pejorative "bailouts" is often used to describe government payments on implicit credit guarantees. Big banks, national champion manufacturers, political subdivisions, and other entities whose failure would be macroeconomically and politically intolerable[89] are the usual beneficiaries. Crisis rescues

in U.K.); Council of the European Union, *Council Agrees Position on Bank Resolution* (June 27, 2013), www.consilium.europa.eu/uedocs/cms_data/docs/pressdata/en/ecofin/137627.pdf.

[85] Federal Deposit Insurance Corporation, *Resolution of Systemically Important Financial Institutions: The Single Point of Entry Strategy*, 78 F.R. 243 (December 2013).

[86] See, e.g., IMF, "How Big Is the Implicit Subsidy for Banks Considered Too Important to Fail?" (April 2014), www.imf.org/external/pubs/FT/GFSR/2014/01/pdf/c3.pdf.

[87] Ricks 2012.

[88] Gelpern 2009.

[89] Levitin 2011.

make the existence of flexible "bailout" authority apparent to the public, and shape expectations for the future.[90] They make beneficiaries' debt look safer going forward.

In addition to credit guarantees, central banks supply emergency liquidity to firms and, increasingly, asset markets. Although the general parameters of LOLR authority tend to be specified in advance by statute and regulation, the availability of emergency liquidity for any particular firm or asset market is uncertain: at least in theory, it depends on the authorities' determination that the firm is solvent.[91] Like deposit insurance, LOLR is designed to stem panics; it must be publicly known and trusted in advance. Unlike deposit insurance, which is paid out to the seniormost creditors of insolvent banks, LOLR support benefits the illiquid firms themselves. In theory, LOLR lends freely, against good collateral, at a high rate of interest.[92] In practice, the collateral and price constraints appear malleable.[93] As a result, the line between liquidity support and credit guarantees is fuzzy.

Liquidity and solvency support for banks presents three complications for purposes of our discussion. First, LOLR operations support two kinds of assets simultaneously: all claims on eligible institutions (for example, bank debt) and the assets accepted as collateral.[94] The decision to lend thus involves, at a minimum, two distinct policy choices affecting asset safety.

Second, the LOLR may not be able to ensure the liquidity of assets denominated in a currency it does not issue. For example, the Central Bank of Korea needs access to Japanese Yen and U.S. dollars to guarantee the liquidity of Korean banks' yen and dollar liabilities. Only a few governments and central banks can issue claims usable as safe assets beyond their borders.[95] To be credible, a LOLR that does not control the currency of the claims it must back makes institutional arrangements to overcome the liquidity constraint. These can take the form of a full-blown monetary union, as in the euro area, or intergovernmental arrangements, such as currency swap lines.[96]

---

[90] Financial Crisis Inquiry Commission Report 2011; Wilmarth 2010; Wilmarth 2011; Davidoff and Zaring 2009.

[91] Cecchetti 2007.

[92] Bagehot 1873.

[93] For example, Cecchetti and Disyatat 2010; Nakaso 2001.

[94] In effect, the LOLR commits to hold eligible assets on its books until they recover in value, or to absorb the losses – taking on both liquidity and credit risk. LOLR is thus both a lender and a buyer of last resort. Cf. Mehrling 2010.

[95] cf. Mehrling 2013.

[96] See, e.g., "Federal Reserve, Central Bank Liquidity Swap Lines" (Last update: August 2, 2013), www.federalreserve.gov/newsevents/reform_swaplines.htm; ASEAN+3 Macroeconomic Research Office, Chiang Mai Initiative, www.amro-asia.org/documents/; Chalongphob Sussangkarn, "The Chiang Mai Initiative Multilateralization: Origin, Development and Outlook," *Asian Development Bank Institute Working Paper Series* No. 230 (July 2010), http://www.adbi.org/files/2010.07.13.wp230.chiang.mai.initiative.multilateralisation.pdf.

Third, when the public credit guarantee is combined with a high level of public debt on bank balance sheets, the safety measures can become a channel for continual risk transmission or "the doom loop."[97] For example, when a fiscally strapped government rescues troubled banks, its debt on the balance sheet of the banks becomes riskier, and undermines confidence in the banks. In some cases, the mere perception that banks are a contingent liability of the sovereign can have a negative effect on both sovereign and bank finances. Where the size of the banking system exceeds the size of the domestic economy, a sovereign's capacity to back the banks falls in doubt. For bank and sovereign liabilities to remain safe, domestic guarantees must be reinforced from other sources, such as foreign governments.

Repos

Repos, or repurchase agreements, are the functional equivalent of a very short-term secured loan. In a repo transaction, the borrower sells a security to the lender and agrees to repurchase it for a higher price at a future date, typically overnight. The sale price is the loan principal. The difference between the sale and repurchase prices reflects implicit interest on the loan. The security being sold functions as collateral. The borrower typically sells it to the lender for less than its market price, which makes the loan effectively overcollateralized at the outset. The amount of overcollateralization, or the difference between the sale price and the market price of the security, is referred to as a "haircut." Lenders demand a larger haircut (more collateral) when they worry about the risk of repayment or a decline in the value of collateral. In bilateral repos, borrowers in need of short-term funding deal directly with short-term lenders. In triparty repos, agents intermediate between borrowers and lenders; they stand ready to manage and substitute collateral and, in some cases, to provide intraday financing. As of January 2014, the U.S. repo market stood at just over $3 trillion, with triparty and bilateral repos each representing approximately $1.4 trillion.[98] In the U.S. market, most bilateral repos use U.S. Treasury debt as collateral; most triparty repos use other assets.

---

[97] For example, Obstfeld 2013. See Peter Coy, "A Way to Break Out of Europe's 'Doom Loop'," *BusinessWeek* (June 2012), www.businessweek.com/articles/2012-06-26/a-way-to-break-out-of-europes-doom-loop; Silvia Merler and Jean Pisani-Ferri, "Hazardous tango: sovereign-bank interdependence and financial stability in the euro area Bruegel" (April 2012), www.bruegel .org/publications/publication-detail/publication/725-hazardous-tango-sovereign-bank-inter dependence-and-financial-stability-in-the-euro-area/.

[98] As of January 2014, the total U.S. repo market was estimated at $1,407 billion for tri-party repo, $1,394 billion for bilateral repo, and $306 billion GCF repo. Adam Copeland, Isaac Davis, Eric LeSueur, and Antoine Martin, *Lifting the Veil on the U.S. Bilateral Repo Market*, Liberty Street Economics (July 2014), http://libertystreeteconomics.newyorkfed.org/2014/07/lifting-the-veil-on-the-us-bilateral-repo-market.html#.VBSAHPldWSp. GCF repo is a trading and settle-ment service provided by the Depository Trust & Clearing Corporation (DTCC). DTCC, *GCF Repo Service*, www.dtcc.com/clearing-services/ficc-gov/gcf-repo.aspx.

Repos thus function as synthetic recreations of bank loans for the seller–borrower – or bank deposits for the buyer–lender. Owing to their short maturities and their use as cash-like "transactional reserves,"[99] policy commentary has focused on the deposit analogy. When they function like deposits, repos transform longer term and less liquid assets (collateral securities) into overnight claims. As noted earlier, triparty repos also involve substantial intermediation.

Repos are made safe by contract and statute. Short maturity reduces the probability of a payment default during the term of the contract. Collateral similarly reduces the probability of default, and promises higher recovery in the events of default under the contract. Like all contracts, repos benefit from the background law that assures their enforcement and the buyer–lender's rights in the collateral. Repos also get an extra layer of statutory protection that makes them safer than other secured loans, and allows the lender to focus on the value of the collateral to the exclusion of counterparty risk. In 1984, the U.S. Congress exempted repos from many of the key elements of the bankruptcy regime.[100] These exemptions meant that repo lenders were no longer subject to the automatic stay on enforcement; when a borrower filed for bankruptcy protection, the lender could keep the collateral without waiting for the bankruptcy process to unfold. Lenders could shift their focus from finding private information about their counterparties to valuing the collateral.

Bankruptcy exemptions improve the repayment prospects of repos, and reduce their "information sensitivity."[101] They also function as a safety label, communicating a policy view that repos were a distinct category of private contract entitled to special protections in public ordering.

The market practice of collateralizing repos with other safe assets such as highly rated government and corporate debt and asset-backed securities further reduces their information sensitivity, this time by reducing lenders' incentives to discover private information about the collateral. Such contractual safety engineering also makes the repos' ability to function as safe assets contingent on the safety of the collateral securities. This connection between different safe asset classes turned into a transmission line for contagion in financial crisis. Deterioration in the safety of asset-backed securities that served as collateral for repos led to a freezing of the repo market, as lenders demanded larger haircuts and even safer collateral in the form of government debt, or refused to lend altogether. This "run on repo"[102]

---

[99] Ricks 2012.

[100] Bankruptcy Amendments and Federal Judgeship Act of 1984, Pub. L. No. 98-353, § 391, 98 Stat. 333 (1984). In 1982, 1984, and 1990, Congress extended the exemptions to various types of derivatives contracts. Franklin R. Edwards and Edward R. Morrison, "Derivatives and the Bankruptcy Code: Why the Special Treatment?," *Yale Journal on Regulation*, Vol. 22 pp 101–33 (2005), at 105–9.

[101] Dang et al. 2013b.

[102] See, e.g., Adam Copeland, Antoine Martin and Michael Walker, *Repo Runs: Evidence from the Tri-Party Repo Market*, Federal Reserve Bank of New York Staff Reports Staff Report

proved catastrophic for financial institutions and markets that relied on repos for essential liquidity.

Repo safety is guaranteed indirectly and implicitly in normal market conditions. For example, the U.S. Federal Reserve has served as LOLR to some of the larger institutional borrowers in the repo markets.[103] The Federal Reserve also uses repos in open market operations. In doing so, it buys (accepts as collateral) Treasury securities, Agency debt, and Agency mortgage-backed securities.[104] The eligibility of these instruments as collateral for the Federal Reserve's repo operations supports their liquidity, and enhances their utility as collateral in the broader repo market. While the Federal Reserve did not formally pledge to support the repo market, past practice might reasonably lead market participants to expect such support. Financial crisis response bolstered such expectations.

Beginning in 2007, the Federal Reserve's backing for the repo markets became more explicit, extensive, and creative. Large financial institutions faced skyrocketing costs when attempting to borrow in the repo markets using Agency debt or mortgage-backed securities. Lenders demanded ever-deeper "haircuts," while spreads between interest rates on repos collateralized with Agency mortgage-backed securities and those collateralized with U.S. Treasury debt widened dramatically. Large financial institutions that financed themselves in the repo market faced liquidity and solvency threats. In response, the Federal Reserve invoked emergency authority dormant since the Great Depression to establish lending and guarantee facilities for frozen financial markets.[105] One of the facilities was expressly targeted at the repo markets. Under the Term Securities Lending Facility (TSLF), the Federal Reserve loaned U.S. Treasury securities to large financial institutions, secured by Agency debt and Agency mortgage-backed securities. The Federal Reserve effectively swapped the dealers' illiquid assets for government debt, which firms could then pledge as collateral to reduce their cost of borrowing in the repo markets. The program appears to have revived the repo markets, narrowing interest rate spreads between repos collateralized with U.S. Treasuries and Agency securities.[106]

Asset-Backed Securities

Asset-backed securities (ABS) repackage payment streams from a pool of underlying obligations, such as home mortgages, small business loans, or credit card debts. Although structures differ depending on the market and the asset being

---

No. 506 (July 2011 Revised August 2014), http://www.newyorkfed.org/research/staff_reports/sr506.pdf.
[103] Madigan and Nelson 2002.
[104] Fleming, Hrung, and Keane 2010.
[105] Johnson 2011.
[106] Fleming, Hrung, and Keane 2010.

securitized, the basic framework entails an originator (for example, a bank) transferring debt contracts to a special-purpose entity, which issues securities to investors, but has no other liabilities.[107] The originator gets cash up front, while the investors receive payment flows from the underlying contracts are secured by them. U.S. mortgage-backed securities (MBS) are the largest subspecies. At the end of 2013, outstanding mortgage-related securities in the United States stood at $8.8 trillion, down from $9.4 trillion in 2007. Of the total, Agency MBS represented $7.1 trillion, compared to $1.7 trillion in private-label (non-Agency) MBS – a stark difference from 2007, when Agency MBS stood at $5.8 trillion and private-label MBS at $3.6 trillion. Most of the total represents residential mortgage financing; commercial MBS were $626 billion in 2013.[108]

Asset-backed commercial paper (ABCP) is another variation on ABS that featured prominently in the crisis. ABCP programs repackage diverse assets, such as manufacturers' trade receivables, auto loans, and credit card debt, into securities that typically mature in less than six months.[109] Like banking, ABCP effects credit intermediation and maturity transformation. ABCP is an important source of short-term financing for U.S. manufacturing and service firms, and a favored investment of money market mutual funds.

Among the various private and public objectives advanced by different forms of securitization, one stands out for purposes of our discussion: the transformation of illiquid assets of mixed credit quality, such as mortgages and car loans, into tradable securities with superior prospects of repayment. These securities were often used as ingredients in another round (or rounds) of securitization, to produce another generation (or generations) of safe assets.[110]

Like repos, ABS can be made safe by contract, statute, and regulation. For example, private-label MBS contracts in the United States rearrange cash flows from pooled mortgages into different classes of securities (tranches) of different repayment priority.[111] MBS and ABCP issuers hold assets in excess of their repayment obligations, and obtain various forms of credit and liquidity insurance. Tiered capital structures, credit and liquidity support (as seen in banks[112]), short maturities (as seen in banks and repos), overcollateralization (as seen in repos), along with

---

[107] Arner, Lejot and Schou-Zibell 2008.

[108] SIFMA, US Mortgage-Related Issuance and Outstanding (xls) (Last Updated 9/08/2014), www.sifma.org/research/statistics.aspx.

[109] For background on asset-backed commercial paper, see generally Covitz, Liang and Suarez 2013; Wells Fargo, A Primer on Asset-Backed Commercial Paper (2014), www.wellsfargoad vantagefunds.com/assets/pdf/fmg/icm/primer_abcp.pdf; Blackrock, Understanding ABCP (2013), www.blackrock.com/cash/literature/whitepaper/understanding-abcp-a-primer.pdf.

[110] Schwarcz 1994; Gelpern and Levitin 2009.

[111] cf. Gorton and Penacchi 1990.

[112] In banks, credit and liquidity support is provided by the public sector; the capital structure is substantially specified by regulation.

passive management and restructuring constraints, come together in bundles of contracts that turn middling IOUs into apparently safe and liquid debt.[113]

Statutory and regulatory intervention complements contractual safety features. For example, like repos, ABS are designed to escape debt write-offs in bankruptcy. Unlike repos, they are not exempt by statute, but are allowed to work around it to achieve "bankruptcy remoteness." ABS issuers in the United States are typically organized as trusts, a form that makes them ineligible to file for bankruptcy.[114] The assets underlying ABS are sold, not pledged, by the originator; "true sale" is intended to minimize the risk of implicating the assets in the originator's bankruptcy.

Risk retention requirements seek to improve the repayment prospects of ABS by aligning sponsor and investor incentives. In the United States and the European Union, financial reform required sponsors to retain five per cent of the risk in their ABS, subject to exemptions for certain categories of underlying assets, to encourage them to investigate and monitor asset quality.[115]

Some ABS are made safer with minimum underwriting standards, which improve the quality of the securitized asset pools. Such standards have long been imposed as a condition of Fannie Mae and Freddie Mac backing; more recently, they were introduced as an alternative to risk retention under the Dodd-Frank Act.[116]

ABS are labeled safe in several ways, again with a mix of private and public tools. In the run-up to crisis, these contract bundles were designed to the specifications of private credit rating agencies. Once labeled with a rating, they could be sold to investors with varying risk appetites, including risk-averse banks, insurance firms, pension and money market funds, which bought the seniormost tranches. The resulting liquidity made ABS more attractive as repo collateral and as hedging tools. They could also be repackaged into new tranched and rated ABS. After the bubble burst, industry leaders criticized the "dilution" in ratings in the run up to

---

[113] Cf. Bratton and Levitin 2013.

[114] 11 USC §109(a) ("Who may be a debtor") (2006); "In Re Secured Equipment Trust of Eastern Air Lines," 38 F.3d 86 (2nd Cir. 1994).

[115] EBA, Final Draft Regulatory Technical Standards, EBA/RTS/2013/12 and EBA/ITS/2013/08 (17 December 2013), available at www.eba.europa.eu/documents/10180/529248/EBA-RTS-2013–12 +and+EBA-ITS-2013–08+(Securitisation+Retention+Rules).pdf.; Comptroller of the Currency et al., *Credit Risk Retention* (Proposed Rule), Federal Register Vol. 76, No. 83 at 24090 (April 29, 2011).

[116] See, for example, 12 CFR § 1026.43 "Minimum standards for transactions secured by a dwelling." A mortgage that meets the "qualified mortgage" requirements of the Consumer Financial Protection Bureau is exempt from the proposed Dodd-Frank risk retention requirement ("skin in the game") for securitization. See id. (defining "qualified mortgage"); Office of the Comptroller of the Currency et al., Credit Risk Retention; Proposed Rule, 78 F.R. 57928 (September 20, 2013). See also North and Buckley 2012 (describing securitization reform under the Dodd-Frank Act).

the crisis: by January 2008, there were 64,000 AAA-rated structured finance instruments in the world, and only twelve AAA-rated companies.[117]

Regulatory labeling of ABS takes the form of listing them as permitted investments for regulated firms.[118] By the 1990s in the United States, changes in statutes, regulations, and regulatory interpretations first enabled federally regulated banks to buy Agency MBS, and then clarified that they could also hold investment-grade private label ABS.[119] Regulated firms in and outside the United States that were limited to investment-grade securities relied on credit rating agencies to define eligible ABS tranches.

Policymakers also labeled ABS safe by assigning lower risk weights to investment-grade tranches for purposes of capital adequacy. For example, Agency RMBS in the United States have long carried a risk weight of 20 percent, one-fifth of the risk assigned to other loans to private borrowers. Regulated firms had to hold less equity against these investments because they were deemed safe by law. This encouraged a measure of herding into ABS.[120] It also encouraged regulatory arbitrage: banks created and bought securities to reduce their regulatory capital requirements, rather than to transfer credit risk.[121]

As noted earlier in this section, most MBS in the United States are backed by housing finance agencies, which absorb the credit risk of the mortgages they securitize. Investors in Agency MBS retain interest rate risk. MBS securitized through government-owned Ginnie Mae had a measure of express government backing ex ante. Fannie Mae and Freddie Mac had implicit U.S. government guarantees, which became explicit ex post in crisis.

When higher-than-expected mortgage default rates exposed the models underlying private-label MBS as flawed, market participants lost confidence in a wide

---

[117] Lloyd Blankfein, "Do not destroy the essential catalyst of risk," *Financial Times* (February 8, 2009), www.ft.com/intl/cms/s/0/0a0f1132-f600-11dd-a9ed-0000779fd2ac.html.

[118] See, e.g., National Association of Insurance Commissioners, *Analysis of Insurance Industry Investment Portfolio Asset Mixes* (2011), www.naic.org/capital_markets_archive/110819.htm. In 2007, a substantial proportion of all Agency securities and Agency MBS were in the hands of regulated financial institutions or local government agencies. Board of Governors of the Federal Reserve System, Flow of Funds Accounts of the United States, Flows and Out-standings Third Quarter 2007 p. 88 (Dec. 6, 2007).
See also Acharya, Kulkami, and Richardson 2011 (citing 2008 report on regulated firms holding investment grade collateralized debt obligations).

[119] The Secondary Mortgage Market Enhancement Act of 1984 (SMEEA) (Pub. L. No. 98–440, § 105(c), 98 Stat. 1691) and the Riegle Community Development and Regulatory Improvement Act of 1994 (Pub. L. No. 103–325, 108 Stat. 2160) both amended 12 U.S.C. §24 (Seventh) to enable or expand the capacity of national banks to purchase asset-backed securities. (Fein 2010) For an analysis of SMEEA provisions on bank purchases of mortgage-backed securities, see Adelman 1985 See generally McCoy and Renuart 2008, Wilmarth 2009.

[120] Viral Acharya and others argue that large complex financial institutions herded into tail-risk, creating and buying investment-grade asset-backed securities for regulatory capital arbitrage, driven by government guarantees (Acharya, Cooley, Richardson, and Walter 2010, Richardson, Ronen and Subrahmanyan 2011, Gerding 2013 at 322–6).

[121] Id.

range of securitized instruments.[122] Some regulated firms had to sell ABS that had lost their investment-grade rating quickly, and at a loss. Deteriorating credit quality and lost liquidity reinforced each other: even the seniormost ABS tranches could no longer be bought and sold "no questions asked." The critical role of MBS in housing finance, and the pervasive use of ABS in banks and the money markets, led the U.S. government to step in with ex post guarantees. The Troubled Asset Relief Program (TARP) was initially proposed as a way to buy distressed ABS from financial firms, a form of credit support; however, it was not used that way.[123] Instead, the U.S. Federal Reserve used its emergency authority to launch more facilities styled as liquidity support. Two of the facilities stood ready to lend to banks against ABS and ABCP.[124] Another facility, already mentioned in the context of repo guarantees, loaned U.S. Treasury securities to primary dealers in exchange for illiquid Agency-backed MBS and other repo collateral that had lost its safety.[125] In addition, the Federal Reserve used Agency MBS in interest rate-setting open market operations, as part of its monetary stimulus to the economy in crisis.[126] By March 31, 2010, the Federal Reserve held $1.06 trillion in Agency mortgage-backed securities.[127]

Four Safe Assets Summarized

In each of the four case studies in this part, financial contracts become safe assets with the help of three distinct but overlapping sets of tools. They are *made* less risky with a mix of contract terms, issuer balance sheet engineering, underwriting standards, and repayment priorities. They are *labeled* safe by regulation and credit rating agencies (private information intermediaries). Issuers are *guaranteed* through deposit insurance schemes, central bank liquidity support, and emergency rescues. In addition, assets may benefit from implicit public backing when they are used in

---

[122] For data on the scope of the mortgage-backed securities crisis that examines credit default swap indexes and ratings downgrade information, see Brunnermeier 2009. Brunnermeier traces how the crisis spread from mortgage-backed securities to other structured products, such as asset-backed commercial paper.

[123] The Troubled Asset Relief Program (TARP) was created by the Emergency Economic Stabilization Act, P.L. 110–343, 12 U.S.C. 5311 et seq. For use of TARP funding, see CRS, Troubled Asset Relief Program (TARP): Implementation and Status, R41427 (June 27, 2013); U.S. Treasury, TARP Programs, www.treasury.gov/initiatives/financial-stability/TARP-Pro grams/Pages/default.aspx.

[124] Term Asset-Backed Securities Loan Facility (TALF) www.federalreserve.gov/newsevents/ reform_talf.htm; Asset-Backed Commercial Paper Money Market Mutual Fund Liquidity Facility (AMLF) www.federalreserve.gov/newsevents/reform_amlf.htm.

[125] Term Securities Lending Facility (TSLF) and TSLF Options Program (TOP) www.federalre serve.gov/newsevents/reform_tslf.htm.

[126] Agency Mortgage-Backed Securities (MBS) Purchase Program www.federalreserve.gov/newse vents/reform_mbs.htm.

[127] Johnson 2011.

TABLE 1 *The Safety Toolkit,* Public and *Private*

	Made Safe	Labeled Safe	Guaranteed Safe
Issuer	• Capital adequacy and other loss-absorbency requirements • Activity and investment restrictions • Affiliation restrictions • Risk retention requirements • *Tiered liabilities* • *Portfolio construction* • *Negative covenants* • *Passive management*	• Licensing • Primary dealer designation • *Credit ratings*	• LOLR liquidity • Ad-hoc crisis intervention • *Affiliate guarantees (ex ante and ex post)* • *Insurance and other credit enhancement*
Asset	• Margin, collateral rules • Bankruptcy exemptions • Underwriting standards/ Ability to repay • Shadow NAV • *Short maturity* • *Collateral*	• Permitted investments and exemptions • Assigned risk weights • Stable NAV accounting • *Credit ratings* • *CDS trigger*	• Deposit insurance • Central bank collateral policies • Monetary policy instrument • Ad-hoc crisis intervention • *Collateral* • *Insurance and other credit enhancement* • *Ex post guarantees*

central bank policy operations. Our examples also reaffirm that safe asset construction is a public–private undertaking.[128] Table 1 illustrates.

Four additional implications follow from the case studies. First, public and private ordering do not always appear in the same sequence in the safe asset market. For example, market practice has led the development of some safe asset classes, such as ABCP, outpacing the law's recognition of those assets as safe. Similarly, when the U.S. Congress enacted bankruptcy exemptions for repos in 1984, it responded to market participants' widespread use of this instrument as if their design had lowered counterparty risk. Yet markets also react to legal reforms that label assets as safe, make those assets safer, or guarantee them. After Congress exempted repos from key provisions of the bankruptcy code, repo markets enjoyed significant growth.[129]

Second, safe assets beget safe assets – but safety pyramids can unravel. Economists make this observation about privately constructed safe assets. Because such assets come about through asset repackaging, liability tiering, and contractual linkages, their capacity to transmit asset and counterparty risk appears intuitive.

---

[128] Cf. Pistor 2013.
[129] Acharya and Öncü 2012 at 330.

However, even with the basic building blocks of the safe asset universe, government and bank debt, mechanisms that "crowd in" safety in good times can beget vicious cycles in bad times.

What distinguishes some governments from all other safe asset producers and backers is their ability to act countercyclically when private issuers cannot. Not all governments have this ability. Some cannot credibly make, label, or guarantee safety for lack of fiscal, political, or institutional capacity, and must rely on external support or look outside for safe assets. Unlike the asset scarcity literature, this observation is by no means directed at emerging market economies: the crisis in Europe has demonstrated its broad applicability.

Third, in the process of safe asset construction, the law creates continuities and discontinuities among asset classes that might not otherwise exist. For example, exempting repos from the bankruptcy process makes them more like bank deposits, enhancing their liquidity and reducing their information sensitivity – but it creates a gap between repos and functionally equivalent secured loans. Investors might reasonably respond to the exemption by shifting away from bank deposits and secured loans into repos. Labeling similarly divides safe assets from all others: regulations permit banks and insurance companies to hold AAA-rated asset-backed securities, but not tranches in the same issuance one notch below investment grade. This creates potential for cliff effects. For example, regulated financial firms were forced to sell downgraded ABS in apparent fire sales in the crisis. Discontinuities and cliff effects can generate cascading losses of safety for interlinked safe assets, for example repos with ABS as collateral, money market funds invested in ABCP, or banks invested in the distressed debt of a sovereign.

Fourth, safe asset construction is fraught with distributional consequences. The process of selecting, labeling, reinforcing, and guaranteeing safe assets privileges some issuers, users, and uses over others. Guarantees shift public resources away from other uses to support safe assets; bankruptcy exemptions take from the debtor and nonexempt creditors; while portfolio mandates and regulatory labels redirect investment, lowering the cost of funds for some economic actors and raising it for others. Some researchers have attempted to quantify the subsidies embedded in safe asset labels, but the work is only starting (see e.g., Korte and Steffen 2014).

POLICY IMPLICATIONS AND A RESEARCH AGENDA

This chapter is part of a larger project on legal tools in macroprudential policy. We rethink the concept of "safe assets," which has attracted policy and academic attention among economists over the past five years. The law is conspicuously absent in the prevailing accounts of safe assets. Our objective has been to identify the institutional mechanisms by which safe assets emerge, become systemically important, and lose their safety.

In this chapter, we consider four case studies – government debt, bank debt, repos, and asset-backed securities – in an effort to tease out common features and policy tools that shape the safe asset universe. In each case, the law plays three distinct roles. First, it seeks to reduce the risks embedded in the asset. This is hard, uncertain, and time-consuming work. *Making* assets safer requires constant monitoring and supervision; this regulatory work is prone to agency problems that worsen at different times in the credit cycle.[130] In contrast, *labeling* assets as safe can be instantaneous. However, it is also risky for the government. Labeling by law establishes market expectations of safety, and encourages herding into the asset. If they are not backed by private contract, oversight or government guarantees, labelled assets can become unstable and vulnerable to runs. When governments *guarantee* safe assets, they may extend credit or liquidity support, or both. Like labeling, guarantees can arise on the spot. However, they are both economically and politically fraught, with public resources directly on the line. Labeling and guarantees also account for the discontinuous character of safe assets. At best, making can lead to safer assets; labeling and guarantees promise absolute safety for all practical purposes – but are not always credible.

Many questions for future research emerge from this description. First, for monitoring purposes, it is important to understand when relatively safe assets come to be treated in markets as if they were risk-free. The respective contributions of the three tools identified in this chapter, and of public and private ordering, to this market treatment remain to be investigated. The relative efficacy of the three tools and the interactions among them require further study. As part of the broader project, it is also important to establish how the three tools should work at different points in the credit cycle. Finally, it is critical not to lose sight of the implications of safe assets for social distribution. Designating financial contracts as "safe" might channel financing in their direction on a massive scale, while labeling and ex post rescues can entrench expectations of public support in some quarters, but not others.

We end with a paradox. Safe asset critics are right in one sense: for all its recent importance, the term covers a broad range of claims that can have little in common. Nonetheless, for as long as market participants treat some financial contracts *as if* they were safe, and do so on a large scale, they implicate financial stability and the public purse. The law enables both the production and the use of safe assets. It can hardly stay on the sidelines.

---

[130] Gerding 2013.

III

Reconceptualising Cross-Border Finance

10

Competing for Renminbi

Financial Centers in the Context of Renminbi Globalization

Wei Shen

Internationalization of Renminbi is a clear policy and an irreversible direction of the Chinese government. The use of Renminbi as a global payment currency is growing rapidly. In April 2014, Renminbi was the seventh most used currency, up from the thirteenth one year ago, with 1.4 percent of transfers, up from 0.6 percent in January 2013, according to Swift.[1] However, Renminbi still languishes below the Hong Kong dollar and the Norwegian krone even though China is the largest trading nation in the world. Meanwhile, financial centers are spotting the potential offered by Renminbi to improve their competitive positions in the postfinancial crisis era. Major financial centers are making aggressive moves to gain market share in lucrative Renminbi trading. The race is on to build a strong and differential Renminbi market proposition based on capability, timezone, reach, market, expertise, and relationships.[2] This chapter is an attempt to understand how Renminbi, as a non-freely-convertible currency, is being internationalized (Section "Internationalization of Renminbi") and how major financial centers are competing for Renminbi-related businesses (Section "Financial Centers' Competition in Renminbi Businesses"). In addition, the chapter tries to comprehend the difficulty in internationalizing Renminbi (Section "Opportunities and Challenges Ahead").

INTERNATIONALIZATION OF RENMINBI

Presently, Renminbi is freely convertible for trade in goods and services, but is still restricted for cross-border portfolio investment purposes due to capital account controls. China is taking steps to internationalize Renminbi by broadening the use of Renminbi among international investors. More channels are now available for

---

[1] James Kynge, "The Paradox of China's Push to Build a Global Currency", *Financial Times*, 17 June 2014 (online).

[2] Youssef Cassis, Capitals of Capital: The Rise and Fall of International Financial Centres 1780–2009 (Cambridge: Cambridge University Press 2006) 2.

offshore Renminbi funds to be repatriated to China. Renminbi earned offshore can be channeled back to China through investment, trade, and lending.

Cross-border Investment in Renminbi

Controls on inflows of Renminbi are gradually eased albeit with various restrictions. More channels have been opened up for the use of Renminbi funds in the Chinese market. Foreign investors may participate in equity private placements and equity transfers into domestic-listed companies by using offshore Renminbi.[3] Further, with approval from the Ministry of Commerce, foreign-invested holding companies, foreign-invested venture capitals, and private equity investment enterprises are allowed to accept Renminbi investments made by foreign investors. Previously, qualified overseas limited partners could only set up Renminbi funds in Pudong New District, Shanghai by way of foreign exchange investment. The real effect of this regulatory change may be limited as stringent requirements are imposed on the eligibility of foreign investors using offshore Renminbi to invest into the domestic capital market.[4] Foreign central banks and some foreign financial institutions are also allowed to invest in the onshore interbank bond market from August 2010.

Introduced in 2002, the Qualified Foreign Institutional Investors (QFII) scheme allows foreign investors to bring foreign currency into China and buy domestic stocks, bonds, and money market instruments. Starting in September 2009, the upper limit on portfolio investments by individual QFII was raised from US$70 million to US$200 billion,[5] and the principal lock-up period for medium- and long-term investments by pension funds, insurance funds, and open-end funds was decreased to three months from six to twelve months; while the principal lock-up period for other institutions was decreased from three years to one year. China Securities Regulatory Commission (CSRC), China's securities regulator, awarded US$16 billion of quotas to foreign securities investors in 2012, equivalent to the total granted during the past six years. The list of 201 license holders, at the end of 2012, is diverse and includes Goldman Sachs Group Inc., UBS AG, Stanford University, and various central banks like Norges Bank, the central bank in Norway.[6] All of these moves indicated China's acceleration of the opening up of its capital markets to foreign investors.[7]

---

[3] The Measures for the Administration of Strategic Investments in Listed Companies by Foreign Investors, Art 11.

[4] Ibid.

[5] "Dim Sum Bond Sales Double as New Elite Back Global Yuan", *South China Morning Post*, 30 November 2012 (online).

[6] Shanghai Stock Exchange, "QFII Facts and Figures", available at http://english.sse.com.cn/investors/introductiontoQFII/QFIIfactsandfigures.

[7] The QFII program is still tiny compared to the size of China's entire share market, which has a capitalization of 24 trillion yuan.

However, there are still some uncertainties in relation to the QFII program. First, investors want greater clarity regarding taxation under QFII, in particular, the capital gains tax for the program. Second, foreign investors have thus far been limited in the amount and types of bonds they can buy under QFII. Third and the largest concern is whether the equity market in China is attractive enough to lure a greater influx given the fact that China's equity market has been the world's worst performer in 2013, that is, Shanghai stocks having declined by 10.8 percent in 2013.[8]

The Chinese government started the Renminbi Qualified Foreign Institutional Investor (RQFII) scheme in December 2011 with an initial quota of US$20 billion. Initially, RQFII was launched to complement the QFII scheme. Different from the QFII, RQFII licence holders can, subject to the quota, invest Renminbi held offshore into China's domestic equity and interbank bond markets. The availability of RQFII scheme is a tool to encourage the use of Renminbi for international investment.

The quota of RQFII was increased to US$70 billion in 2012. CSRC indicated in early 2013 its plan to increase the quota for both the dollar-denominated QFII scheme and the Renminbi-denominated RQFII scheme as much as tenfold. At present, these two schemes account for 1.6 percent of the funds invested in the mainland's yuan denominated A-shares.[9] Under the RQFII scheme, foreign investors are allowed to use offshore Renminbi to buy into mainland securities and bonds: 80 percent of the granted quota must be invested in the domestic bond market with the remainder in mainland stocks. The fixed investment ratio between debt and equity of 80:20 is likely to be eliminated, allowing foreign investors to put more money into stock markets.[10]

Currently, the RQFII scheme is only open to Hong Kong units of mainland financial institutions (insurers) or Hong Kong-listed mainland fund managers to invest their offshore yuan in the domestic equity and bond markets. Only twenty-two licences were granted by June 2012. CSRC in March 2013 relaxed restrictions to enable foreign funds based in Hong Kong and offshore branches of Chinese banks to apply for a RQFII quota. Chinese regulators plan to allow individual and non-Chinese institutional investors to join the RQFII,[11] which will further help channel offshore Renminbi deposits back into mainland China.[12] In addition, the RQFII

[8] Jeanny Yu, "BlackRock Plans to Apply for New QFII Quota", *South China Morning Post*, 19 July 2013, B3.

[9] Ray Chan, "China Steps Up Opening of Markets with Tenfold Boost to Foreign Investors", *South China Morning Post*, 15 January 2013 (online).

[10] Ray Chen, "Relaxation of RQFII Rules in Sight", *South China Morning Post*, 25 February 2013 (online).

[11] Ibid. At the outset of the program in 2011, only the Hong Kong units of Chinese brokerages and fund managers had been allowed to participate.

[12] PBOC is in the preparation for trials of the qualified domestic individual investor, or QDII2, scheme, which is part of a major initiative in 2013 to increase outbound investment by the private sector. Ray Chan, "China Steps Up Opening of Markets with Tenfold Boost to Foreign Investors", *South China Morning Post*, 15 January 2013 (online). The scheme is to allow

scheme has been extended beyond Hong Kong to other offshore Renminbi-trading centers such as London, Singapore, and Taiwan.

Although RQFII fund managers have expressed a willingness to seek a larger quota to bring their offshore yuan back to the mainland, large-scale investors remain cautious and few of them want to invest directly in A-shares, for example, by setting up a pure equity fund.[13] The structural problems and banking systemic risks in the mainland often keep foreign capital cautious about investing in equities. In addition, returns on RQFII funds in 2012 were unattractive, averaging three to four percent, compared with a more than twenty-two percent rise in the Hang Seng Index. The heavy involvement of retail investors makes domestic stock markets more volatile. The volatility may present a challenge to offshore institutional investors, given their freedom to invest more heavily in China. Compared to the U.S. dollar (the use of which accounts for 86 percent of the foreign exchange market), the Renminbi merely accounts for less than one percent of trade in the foreign exchange market.[14] This suggests that a globalized yuan has a long way to go.

Cross-Border Trade in Renminbi

The Chinese government has been actively encouraging offshore use of Renminbi in a bid to break the dominance of the U.S. dollar as the de facto currency of global trade given that China is nominally the world's largest exporter. Getting more businesses to use Renminbi for trade settlement increases China's influence in the global economy. The transformation of Renminbi will touch every company trading with China. For those trading with Chinese companies, Renminbi

---

individual mainlanders to invest in overseas capital markets to boost outbound investment. The initial quota could be around 50 billion yuan and may require people to have more than 500,000 yuan to invest overseas. Currently, individual mainlanders can invest only through QDII with a quota of US$85 billion to 107 institutions. Some new products such as stock options, warrants, and more exchange-traded funds that track Hong Kong stocks would be introduced. However, the new scheme is unlikely to have an immediate impact on Hong Kong stocks as wealthy mainlanders have already invested in Hong Kong stocks through fund products under the existing QDII quota or grey channels. The technical difficulty is that the scheme would be functioning only if some prerequisites are satisfied such as the full convertibility of the capital account and further loosening of foreign exchange controls on the mainland side. Jeanny Yu, "Investors Wary of New QDII Prospects", *South China Morning Post*, 21 January 2013 (online).

[13] According to data compiled by the *South China Morning Post*, the five Hong Kong-based RQFII fund managers that posted the best investment returns in 2012 all chose to invest their granted quota in the domestic bond market rather than the equity market. The average investment return of the top five bond funds was 4 percent while the Shanghai Composite Index was only 3.2 percent. Jeanny Yu, "Bigger QFII Quotas Unlikely to Draw Investors", *South China Morning Post*, 17 January 2013 (online).

[14] Alice Ross, "Banks Report Growth in Trade in Renminbi", *Financial Times*, 16 October 2012 (online).

represents an urgent challenge. Failure to grasp the pace of change could be at the expense of their business.

Cross-border trade transactions denominated in Chinese currency have surged from almost zero in mid-2009 to US$20 billion worth of China's cross-border trade by the end of June 2010,[15] and further to US$150 billion or so in the first half of 2011.[16] In the second quarter of 2011 alone, more than ten percent of China's trade settlement was paid in Renminbi, compared with one percent for the same period in 2010.[17] As a result of the gradual relaxation of capital control rules on the use of Renminbi in cross-border trade transactions, seven percent of Chinese external trade was settled in Renminbi in 2011.[18] Trade in Renminbi in 2012 was on track for US$425 billion, up almost thirty percent from the year before,[19] and reached 16.5 percent of the People's Republic of China (PRC) total trade in the second quarter of 2013.[20] It appears that Renminbi is increasingly being used as a trade settlement currency, with daily trading volume doubling in 2013.[21]

Among others, cost saving may be the key reason for international traders – especially small- and medium-sized enterprises – settling or invoicing in Renminbi with Chinese trading partners. As Deutsche Bank pointed out, trading in Renminbi could lower prices by nearly five percent.[22] China's central bank indicated that foreign importers could save two to three percent on their invoices if they paid in Renminbi.[23] Moreover, American and other foreign companies can have more competitive pricing from their Chinese suppliers if they accept yuan payments as this eliminates the fees that are necessary to convert dollars to yuan, along with any risk of exchange-rate fluctuations.

In July 2009, the first pilot scheme for cross-border trade settlement in Renminbi was put in place. According to the Administrative Rules for the Pilot Scheme for Settlement of Cross-border Trade in Renminbi, promulgated by the People's Bank of China (PBOC, China's central bank) on 1 July 2009, cross-border trade

[15] Jamil Anderlini, "China Increases Foreign Access to Domestic Interbank Bond Market", *Financial Times*, p.18 August 2010, p.1.
[16] Robert Cookson, "Banks Warned on HK Renminbi Trade", *Financial Times*, 10 November 2011, p 24.
[17] May Chan, "HK In Big Sell on Yuan Services", *South China Morning Post*, 15 September 2011, B3.
[18] James Blitz, "China Set to Back UK Renminbi Trading", *Financial Times*, 8 September 2011, p.1.
[19] Mike Rees, "Renminbi's Rapid Rise Concentrates Minds", *Financial Times*, 19 December 2012 (online).
[20] Barry Eichengreen and Masahiro Kawai, "Issues for Renminbi Internationalization: An Overview", (January 2014) ADBI Working Paper Series No. 454, p.5.
[21] John Noble, "European Central Bank and China Strike Currency Swap Deal", *Financial Times*, 10 October 2013 (online).
[22] Alice Ross, "Banks Report Growth in Trade in Renminbi", Financial Times, 16 October 2012 (online).
[23] Nicole Hong, "Yuan Hits Milestone in Trade Deals," *The Wall Street Journal*, 4 December 2013, C2.

transactions (both imports and exports) between certain approved areas of the mainland and selected areas outside the mainland became eligible for settlement in Renminbi. Enterprises in designated pilot areas and offshore enterprises are entitled to use Renminbi to settle any current account items[24] between them. The qualification is that only approved pilot enterprises in the designated pilot areas are eligible to receive Renminbi funds as payment for exports of goods from the mainland. The scheme was expanded to cover twenty provinces and cities in the mainland in June 2010, and later to the entire nation in August 2011, and all countries and regions overseas. Starting from October 2010, overseas institutions were allowed to apply for Renminbi accounts for trade settlement. The number of Chinese exporters eligible for cross-border settlement rose from 365 to 67,359.[25]

The booming of the offshore Renminbi market does not suggest that the Renminbi-denominated transactions and the internationalization of Renminbi are free of legal risks. By contrast, the world's largest banks have taken steps to protect themselves from the risk of a collapse of the offshore Renminbi market in Hong Kong even though the chance of encountering such a risk is extremely slim. In February 2012, Swift, the global payments system operated by almost 10,000 banks implemented a plan that would allow its members to complete trades with each other even if the offshore Renminbi market became completely illiquid. Banks using the Swift network to process transactions in foreign exchange markets, money markets, and derivatives may specify that their offshore Renminbi trades are subject to a special "disruption event agreement." This is prepared by the International Swaps and Derivatives Association and gives banks the right to postpone payments and settle their transactions in U.S. dollars, rather than in the Chinese currency if the offshore Renminbi trades become "illiquid, inconvertible, or nontransferrable."[26]

Other technical hurdles and risks may also put some foreign companies off in settling in Renminbi in cross-border trade. For example, hedging products for multinational companies remain very limited. The process of switching payment systems takes effort and time. In addition, Renminbi needs to overcome a number of challenges including inertia and systems set up to invoice only in U.S. dollars. Some Chinese companies may be using trade finance as a way to borrow money more cheaply offshore, thereby evading strict restrictions on lending at home. Chinese regulators cracked down on credit growth by preventing financial institutions from disguising corporate loans as interbank loans. A Chinese company can

---

[24] Opposite to capital account items, current account items often refer to and include payments for imports and exports of goods, cross-border service trade, and other current transfers into and outside the mainland.

[25] Rahul Jacob, Robert Cookson and Robin Kwong, "Hong Kong Becomes a Lab for a Currency Experiment", *Financial Times*, 18 January 2011, p 7.

[26] Robert Cookson, "Banks Prepare for Disruption on Offshore Renminbi Trade", *Financial Times*, 15 February 2012, p.22.

circumvent the capital control rule by getting a yuan-denominated letter of credit from its Hong Kong subsidiary, and using the proceeds to obtain a loan in Hong Kong for a lower interest rate. China's benchmark interest rate is six percent and the rate in Hong Kong is 0.5 percent. Savvy Chinese businesses are using letters of credit as a way to borrow at a lower rate outside of China.

Although seven percent of Chinese external trade is now settled in its national currency,[27] most of the Renminbi trade settlement is for imports by China through which foreign traders can acquire Renminbi. By contrast, there is little settlement in Renminbi of China's exports. This one-way pattern of trade settlement can be interpreted in various ways. First, the recipients of exports from China may have limited amounts of Renminbi or are not willing to reduce their holdings given their anticipation of Renminbi's appreciation. Second, China's trade and financial integration with global markets will make it more difficult to tightly manage the currency's external value.

In May 2013, sixteen percent of the mainland's cross-border trade was settled in yuan, up from less than one percent in 2009.[28] Total remittances of yuan for cross-border trade settlement were 318.1 billion yuan in June 2013.[29] Yuan trades between counterparts based outside China rose to eighteen percent of the deals in the currency settled in Hong Kong. Importers and exporters used yuan for 8.7 percent of their financing agreements with trade partners in October 2013, up from 4.4 percent a year earlier. This is a milestone as the use of yuan in trade finance overtook the euro and the yen. Therefore, yuan has become the secondmost used currency in trade finance. This matches China's status as the largest trading nation in the world in 2012 and demonstrates China's progression in the opening up of its economy. Nevertheless, yuan is still well behind the U.S. dollar, which backs eighty-one percent of trade finance.[30] It rarely changes hands outside China. Renminbi is currently being used to pay for just 0.8 percent of all global transactions, lagging behind currencies of smaller economies, including the Thai baht and Swedish krona. Since most of the trade finance in China occurs with Hong Kong, Singapore, and Taiwan, it seems fair to say that Renminbi's growing use is a regional phenomenon.

Dim Sum Bonds

In January 2007, Hong Kong's financial markets took another great leap by welcoming mainland financial institutions issuing Renminbi bonds in Hong Kong

[27] James Blitz, "China Set to Back UK Renminbi Trading", *Financial Times*, 8 September 2011, p 1.
[28] Jeanny Yu, "Hong Kong RMB Deposits Seen Surging on Qianhai Reforms", *South China Morning Post*, 20 July 2013 (online).
[29] Kanis Li, "Hong Kong Lenders Pay More for Yuan Deposits", *South China Morning Post*, 9 July 2013 (online).
[30] Nicole Hong, "Yuan Hits Milestone in Trade Deals," *The Wall Street Journal*, 4 December 2013, C1.

as long as the necessary approvals were obtained from competent authorities in the first place. This move was followed by the gradual opening of qualified Renminbi bond issuing business to mainland nonfinancial institutions and Hong Kong companies.

Different from Renminbi retail bonds, the issue of "dim sum" bonds, yuan-denominated bonds issued in Hong Kong, is a faster and more efficient way of raising Renminbi funds as the execution timeline is between four and six weeks on average. They are nicknamed "dim sum bonds" partly because they are often smaller than yuan bond issues on the mainland. The dim sum bond market is subject to international legal and regulatory standards and offers much simpler tax and repatriation rules for those seeking to exit investments. The first "dim sum" bonds, in the amount of Renminbi 1.38 billion, were issued by Hopewell Highway Infrastructure Ltd. in July 2010. McDonald's issuance of dim sum bonds in August 2010 attracted significant international attention. Issuance of dim sum bonds in the first eleven months of 2013 stood at US$9.7 billion. The better outlook for Renminbi and the improved liquidity are essential reasons why issuers are willing to tap into the market.

The most challenging aspect of dim sum bonds is its short tenor that is usually below three years. This means that a third of outstanding dim sum bonds or Renminbi 80 billion of a total Renminbi 244 billion are due by the end of 2012.[31] As dim sum bonds are debt products, a short tenor imposes pressures on refinancing – there should be a steady supply of debt that needs to be refinanced until 2014. The heavy bond supply together with illiquidity will be likely to create more pressure on dim sum bond yields to rise. The case may be opposite, driving yields lower than before if investors expect Renminbi to appreciate more sharply against the U.S. dollar and investors pour more capital into the dim sum bond market. However, this is not likely to happen given the outlook of Renminbi evaluation against the U.S. dollar in the long term. Up to now, the longest tenors are five to ten years for the bonds issued by China Development Bank (CDB). Although CDB considered thirty-year notes, the market feedback was not positive since only a few life insurance companies had placed orders.[32] Dim sum bonds have other weaknesses. Issuance of dim sum bonds is confined to banking and financial institutions. Most issuers are Chinese firms. It has also been reported that a large portion of cross-border Renminbi settlement is used for cross-border arbitrage between Chinese companies and their Hong Kong subsidiaries.[33] These factors show the limited potential of dim sum bonds right now.

---

[31] Robert Cookson, "Investors Weigh Prospects for Rally in Dim Sum Bonds", *Financial Times*, 10 February 2012, p.21.

[32] Jeanny Yu, "China Development Bank Issuance to Lift Confidence in Dim Sum Bonds", *South China Morning Post*, 8 November 2013 (online).

[33] Robert Cookson, "Renminbi Threat to Dollar Could be Stalling", *Financial Times*, 24 November 2011 (online).

Under a pilot scheme, promulgated on 16 August 2010, offshore Renminbi clearing banks and other eligible offshore institutions are allowed to invest in the onshore interbank bond market. This is a great step in diversifying the investment products available to investors holding Renminbi. The scheme also represents a small but significant step in the opening of capital account items by the Chinese government and is only the first of many steps in the expected full liberalization of the mainland's capital account market. One big step along the way may be the introduction of PRC rules that render capital account remittance permissible.

FINANCIAL CENTERS' COMPETITION IN RENMINBI BUSINESSES

Hong Kong

Since 2004, Hong Kong has been the testing ground for a variety of initiatives to promote the global use of Renminbi. In terms of the numbers, no other financial center has mounted a challenge to Hong Kong's status as the largest offshore Renminbi hub. It is at the forefront of China's attempts to turn Renminbi into a globally accepted form of payment, and a well-established currency channel in and out of China itself. Hong Kong is the largest offshore deposit base of Renminbi with more than Renminbi 700 billion and the largest trading center for Renminbi outside China. Daily trading volume is around US$12 billion to US$13 billion of Renminbi, more than double the US$5 billion exchanged daily in London. Hong Kong is also home to the majority of Renminbi-denominated investment assets. Since the launch of dim sum bonds, Hong Kong has developed a globally recognized asset class, with a number of funds and a FTSE-managed index. Hong Kong has the most established Renminbi clearing system, with the advantage of its proximity to China.

The Renminbi banking business was launched in Hong Kong in 2004, which has widely been regarded as a notable move in internationalizing Renminbi as well as developing Hong Kong's financial market because Renminbi-related activities in the offshore market were quite limited. Overseas investors can make use of Hong Kong's banking services to tap into the Chinese market. Since 2004, Hong Kong banks have been able to offer deposit-taking, currency exchange, and remittance services to their customers. The scope of Renminbi banking business in Hong Kong was later extended to debit and credit card services in April 2004, and to check services in December 2005. The Hong Kong Interbank Market initiated a Renminbi settlement system in 2006 to provide check clearing, Renminbi square position, remittance processing, and bank card payment services. The last quarter of 2010 witnessed a boost in Renminbi-denominated financial transactions due to the approval granted in mid-2010 to financial institutions in Hong Kong to open Renminbi accounts and for Hong Kong banks to access the onshore interbank market; an array of Renminbi-denominated bond issuance activities, a currency swap line between the PBOC and the Hong Kong Monetary Authority (HKMA), Hong Kong's de facto central bank, providing the latter with Renminbi liquidity in order to further encourage it to permit local banks and firms to do business in Renminbi. Both corporate and individual customers can open Renminbi deposit accounts with Hong Kong banks that participate in any or all types of Renminbi business after having entered into settlement agreements with the clearing bank, and transfer Renminbi funds between different accounts, whether maintained with the same bank in Hong Kong or not. The cap on the amount of Renminbi that a company can purchase has been removed. Hong Kong banks have extended Renminbi loans to corporate customers. Hong Kong banks are taking advantage of lending opportunities to Chinese borrowers amid tight credit conditions on the mainland and high borrowing costs Chinese borrowers are more willing to pay.

Since 2004, the development of Renminbi banking business in Hong Kong has already surpassed the initial goals of facilitating cross-border tourists' spending and strengthening the economic connection between Hong Kong and the mainland. The most significant contribution Hong Kong has made to the ultimate internationalization of the Renminbi has been the creation of an offshore Renminbi interbank market, which has resulted in the emergence of a two-tier market in Hong Kong. Daily turnover of yuan interbank settlements in Hong Kong hit 390 billion yuan (equivalent to HK$494 billion) in May 2013, surpassing HK$487 billion of interbank payments denominated in Hong Kong dollars.[34] This was the first time settlement of yuan interbank payments surpassed that of Hong Kong dollars. In 2010, the average daily turnover of yuan payments through Hong Kong's clearing platform was 5.3 billion yuan and surged to an average of 213 billion yuan per day in 2012.[35] The robust growth of yuan cleared by the Real Time Gross Settlement System is a sign of a significant increase in offshore yuan commercial and trade activities conducted in Hong Kong.

The interest rate on yuan deposited in Hong Kong is determined in a dynamic way. Bank of China (Hong Kong), the yuan clearing bank in Hong Kong, sets the interest rate. The Bank raised the rate it offered banks with yuan business in Hong Kong to 0.648 percent per year from 0.629 percent. It now offers the banks fixed deposits of one to three months. The interest rate on these deposits is published daily. The one-month rate is 2.2 percent a year, 2.3 percent a year for two month deposits, and 2.4 percent a year for three-month deposits.[36] The flexibility offered by the clearing bank is useful for banks to allocate their holdings in the currency and to promote the development of Hong Kong as an offshore yuan center. However, customers with yuan deposits in Hong Kong are unlikely to get higher

---

[34] Gary Cheung, "Yuan Clearing Beats Volume in Hong Kong Dollars", *South China Morning Post*, 17 January 2013 (online).

[35] Ibid.

[36] Kanis Li, "No Extra Interest for Retail Yuan Deposits", *South China Morning Post*, 4 March 2013 (online).

interest on deposits because the rate on retail deposits is based on the demand and supply of yuan in Hong Kong. What the bank pays on deposits is determined by such factors as the channels for the bank to reinvest the yuan, the difference between the interest it earns through these channels, and the interest it pays on deposits. Therefore, an interbank rate that banks charge each other for short-term loans is a more important determinant of the interest paid on yuan deposits than the rate Bank of China (Hong Kong) offers. In addition, the availability of offshore yuan in the market will offset the effect of Bank of China (Hong Kong)'s increase in the interest rate. As a matter of fact, the retail interest rates are benchmarked to the interbank rates. HKMA launched the world's first offshore yuan interbank rate fixing.[37] Hong Kong banks enjoy their flexibility of fixing interest rates to counter changing economic dynamics.

In order to fight off competition from Singapore, which is also trying to establish itself as an offshore Renminbi trading hub, the HKMA allowed banks to waive some paperwork required for Renminbi trade settlements starting in April 2012 as the troublesome document-reviewing procedures have pushed some local clients to Singapore for offshore Renminbi trade settlement. When the banks have "reasonable assurance" that squaring Renminbi transactions through the clearing bank are for "eligible yuan trade transactions", banks can proceed without reviewing the supporting documents. "Reasonable assurance" is deemed to be available if the company is listed for at least three years in Hong Kong, on mainland China, Taiwan, London, or New York or any other jurisdiction belonging to the Financial Action Task Force, and that have had a relationship with the banks for more than three years.[38] The document reviewing process can also be waived if a company or its subsidiary has a business relationship with the bank for more than three years and the company has been in a mainland-related trading business for more than five years, with the relevant trading volume representing thirty percent or more of the company's overall trade, and the mainland-related transaction value not exceeding Renminbi 5 million.[39]

Renminbi bonds issued in Hong Kong have become the key element in shaping Hong Kong as an offshore Renminbi center compared to other international financial centers such as London and Singapore. Hong Kong has made great attempts to widen the range of Renminbi products available to foreign investors so as to sharpen its competitive edge against Singapore and London. The launch of the first yuan-denominated initial public offering (IPO) by Hopewell in October 2012 marked a watershed in Hong Kong's efforts to emerge as an offshore yuan hub,

---

[37] Enoch Yiu, "Yuan Funding Rules Eased To Shore Up HK's Offshore Lead", *South China Morning Post*, 26 July 2013, B3.

[38] Wei Shen, "Rational or Irrational? Chinese Capital Control Rules in the Context of Internationalizing Renminbi" in M Wong & W Chan (eds.), *Investing in Asian Offshore Currency Markets: The Shift from Dollars to Renminbi* (Palgrave Macmillan, 2013) 117.

[39] Lulu Chen, "Regulator Gives Yuan Payments New Push", *South China Morning Post*, 3 April 2012, B4.

processing eighty percent of yuan payments in September 2012.[40] Hong Kong Stock Exchange showed its ambition to drive dual-currency trading. Harvest Global Investments launched the first dual-currency, exchange-traded fund on the Hong Kong Stock Exchange in October 2012.[41]

Hong Kong now is truly the largest offshore yuan business center in the world. By the end of April 2013, Hong Kong's yuan deposit pool amounted to 836.6 billion yuan, up sixteen percent year on year and the number of settlement banks and institutions reached 209.[42] Deposits of yuan in Hong Kong have risen to 920 billion as of February 2014. Yuan deposits in Taiwan have risen to 268 billion yuan in 2013 while Singapore had Renminbi deposits of 200 billion by the end of 2013. Deposits of Renminbi in South Korea rose to a record of 49 billion yuan.[43] As of the end of June 2013, Hong Kong had amassed the world's biggest pool of yuan deposits outside the mainland China, at 698 billion yuan, followed by Singapore with 100 billion yuan, Taiwan 71 billion yuan, and London 12 billion yuan.[44] Of about one trillion yuan in deposits outside mainland China, about 700 billion yuan is in Hong Kong, making it the world's most important offshore Renminbi market.[45] This 700 billion yuan deposited in Hong Kong accounts for more than ten percent of the city's deposit base.[46]

London

London, the world's largest foreign-exchange trading center, is also showing its ambition to develop itself as a leading offshore yuan hub. London sees the potential benefits to be reaped from becoming the number one center for anything that Renminbi can be used for outside of Asia, including deposits, foreign exchange transactions, debt and loans, and dim sum bonds. Over the past two years, the British government has been in discussion with the Chinese government as to what role London could play in offshore yuan trading. A working group was formed by HSBC, Standard Chartered, ICBC, and BOC in January 2012 with the aim of ironing out the technical issues involved in promoting the yuan business in London.[47] George

[40] Ray Chan and Lulu Chen, "Hong Kong Trumps Singapore in Yuan Hub Race with Hopewell IPO", *South China Morning Post*, 25 October 2012 (online).
[41] Ibid.
[42] Ibid.
[43] Anjani Trivedi and Fanny Liu, "Taiwan Takes Aim at Yuan Products", *The Wall Street Journal*, 18 April 2014, C3.
[44] Denise Tsang, "New Free-trade Zones Force Hong Kong to Sharpen Its Game", *South China Morning Post*, 12 September 2013 (online).
[45] George Chen and Nick Edwards, "Beijing Eases Entry for Foreign Banks in Milestone Plan", *South China Morning Post*, 9 July 2013 (online).
[46] Jeanny Yu, "Hong Kong RMB Deposits Seen Surging on Qianhai Reforms", *South China Morning Post*, 20 July 2013 (online).
[47] Enoch Yiu, "London Pushes Ahead with Yuan Ambitions", *South China Morning Post*, 3 December 2012 (online).

Osborne, the UK Chancellor of the Exchequer, sought to reinforce London's position as a global Renminbi hub by rolling out the red carpet for Chinese banks looking to expand in London and breaking down regulatory barriers so that Chinese banks could carry on wholesale operations through branches in London.[48] Osborne's strategy is to make London "a home of Chinese banks, Chinese bonds and Chinese finance".[49] If this strategy is put in place, Chinese banks can significantly scale up their activity in Britain. Mark Carney, Bank of England governor, stressed that "helping the internationalization of the Renminbi is a global good, consistent with London's historic role".[50]

According to Swift, a banking payment provider, sixty-two percent of Renminbi payments outside of China take place in London, and forty-seven percent of yuan global payments, excluding mainland China and Hong Kong, are from Europe.[51] London is also the largest hub for foreign exchange trading, with about forty-one percent market share.[52] More multinational companies are now willing to hold yuan deposits or yuan investment products in order to bet on its appreciation. London now is hosting twenty-eight percent of the yuan trade settlement worldwide, the second largest yuan pool outside China, merely next to Hong Kong. Yuan deposits in the City of London reached 109 billion yuan by the end of April 2012.[53] According to data released by Swift, London has been increasingly dominant as the center for trading offshore Renminbi, with London's share of the market outside China and Hong Kong growing from fifty-four percent in January 2013 to sixty-two percent by October 2013.[54] Renminbi foreign exchange trading amounted to a daily US$5.3 billion according to the Bank of International Settlements.[55] London has a forty-one percent share of the global foreign exchange market and handles more than sixty percent of Renminbi trade outside Asia; but this only amounts to half the volumes traded in Hong Kong.

London won a licence allowing investors to invest in stocks and bonds in Renminbi. London asset managers are the only ones in the West able to invest directly in Chinese stocks and shares in Chinese currency through the RQFII

[48] George Parker, Sam Fleming and Patrick Jenkins, "UK Opens Doors to Chinese Banks With Special Terms for Lenders", *Financial Times*, 14 October 2013 (online).
[49] Ibid.
[50] George Parker and Jamil Anderlini, "Britain Trumpets Welcome to Chinese", *Financial Times*, 24 October 2013 (online).
[51] Jeanny Yu, "China and UK in Talks over London Yuan Clearing Bank", *South China Morning Post*, 22 February 2014 (online).
[52] Jenny Anderson, "Britain Gains Renminbi Trading Deal", *New York Times*, 27 March 2014, B11.
[53] Enoch Yiu, "London Pushes Ahead with Yuan Ambitions", *South China Morning Post*, 3 December 2012 (online).
[54] Josh Noble, "European Central Bank and China Strike Currency Swap Deal", *Financial Times*, 10 October 2013 (online).
[55] George Parker, Sam Fleming and Patrick Jenkins, "UK Opens Doors to Chinese Banks With Special Terms for Lenders", *Financial Times*, 14 October 2013 (online).

program. In 2013, the initial quota was £8.2 billion, or US$13.57 billion.[56] This would help UK financial groups attract China-related investments. Given the great appetite on both sides, the British government has been in negotiations with the Chinese government about the granting of quotas to financial institutions in the City of London that would give their offshore yuan deposits access to the Chinese market. The Chinese government is considering allowing companies in London and Singapore to participate in the RQFII scheme. However, no London-based company has been approved yet. To obtain an RQFII, a foreign firm needs approval from China's securities and foreign exchange regulators.

China is to grant London-based investors the right to use their yuan to buy up to 80 billion yuan worth of mainland stocks, bonds, and money market instruments according to the agreement reached by the Chinese and British governments.[57] London-based institutional investors will be able to apply for licences to invest yuan directly into the mainland under the RQFII scheme. The approval for London to participate in the RQFII scheme is the first time the program has expanded beyond Asia (mainly Hong Kong). This gives London more opportunities as it can now develop and provide more Renminbi-denominated products for investors. In practice, it may take time for investors to qualify for their share of the quota and allocate funds.

The City of London is promoting the use of yuan by domestic companies and investors. More British firms are now trading with Chinese companies showing a preference for settlement in yuan partly because their trading partners in China prefer to be paid in yuan and would offer a discount for the same, which roughly saves up to two percent in costs compared with settlement in U.S. dollars. The key problem is a lack of awareness among companies of the benefits of trading directly with Chinese companies in Renminbi. To take one example, the use of Renminbi in international trade may help reduce invoices by nearly five percent.

The Bank of England and the PBOC reached an agreement on March 26, 2014, according to which the clearing and settlement of Renminbi trades in London are now allowed. Two central banks will sign a memorandum of understanding and a bank will be designated as the clearing bank. This is the most recent step that the UK has taken to step up its efforts to attract Chinese investment. Clearing and settlement is part of the essential plumbing of finance. Clearing of payments is necessary to turn the promise of payment, like an electronic request, into the actual movement of money from one bank to another. In an offshore Renminbi center, a clearing bank acts as a settlement agent for interbank payments, and can help with loans, trades in goods and services, and financial instruments like foreign exchange. Having a clearing bank in London will encourage more UK firms to use the

---

[56] Jenny Anderson, "Britain Gains Renminbi Trading Deal", *New York Times*, 27 March 2014, B11.

[57] Reuters, "China to Extend RQFII Scheme to London", *South China Morning Post*, 16 October 2013 (online).

Renminbi as a currency for international trade, allowing investors to cut the risk from making overseas payment in Chinese currency. Having a clearing bank in London burnishes London's position as the global center for foreign exchange trading as China's rise shifts international financial flows. Currently, London is relying on Hong Kong's infrastructure for clearing offshore trade in the Renminbi. In December 2013, Standard Chartered signed an agreement with the Agricultural Bank of China to provide clearing and settlement services in London for the first time, subject to the PBOC's approval. The clearing bank gives London the infrastructure to compete with Hong Kong and Singapore.

London is the major financial center hosting offshore bonds denominated in Renminbi. It is also the second largest offshore yuan spot FX trading center with a market share of twenty-six percent, right after Hong Kong with a fifty-six percent market share.[58] It accounts for sixty-two percent of global trading in Renminbi outside China and Hong Kong.[59] However, London is far behind Hong Kong. As George Osborne, UK Chancellor, has said, London is only in a "developing status" as the Western hub for Renminbi business.[60] London, as the largest offshore U.S. dollar market, is able to offer international Renminbi services compared to other regional financial centers. London's concern lies in the fact that it is home to international banks that have more extensive networks that are well-prepared to meet the yuan needs of global customers.

London is keen to maintain its role as the main offshore Renminbi trading center outside Asia but is facing severe competition from Frankfurt and Luxembourg. With a clearing bank, London is equipped with the necessary mass of infrastructure, putting Britain at the front of the global race.[61] Almost at the same time, Germany and China signed a similar agreement. However, London is lagging behind in the field such as deposit taking. Luxembourg and Frankfurt are ahead on that front. London is also facing competition from Hong Kong. Renminbi deposits in London are still limited in the scale.

Taipei

China also signed an agreement with Taiwan on a clearing system for each other's currencies in September 2012, which not only drew both sides closer but also promoted trade to more than US$160 billion per year.[62] The landmark currency

[58] Jeanny Yu, "Britain and Beijing in Talks About Yuan Quotas", *South China Morning Post*, 29 September 2013 (online).
[59] Chad Bray, "Chinese Bank Buys Into London Trading", *New York Times*, 30 January 2014, B5.
[60] Alice Ross, "CCB Issues 'Dim-Sum' Bonds in London", *Financial Times*, 30 November 2012 (online).
[61] Philip Stafford and Delphine Strauss, "UK to Host Renminbi Clearing Bank", *Financial Times*, 27 March 2014, p.22.
[62] Reuters, "Bank of China Hopes to Begin Yuan Clearing Business: Taiwan Cenbank", *South China Morning Post*, 12 December 2012 (online).

clearing pact signaled that nonmainland companies, institutions, and residents can now trade the currency and settle trade deals before the yuan becomes fully convertible. Under the pact on currency clearing, each side would name a clearing bank to handle direct conversions between the yuan and the Taiwan dollar. Taiwan in 2012 appointed Bank of Taiwan's Shanghai Branch as a clearing bank for Taiwan dollar transactions on the mainland.[63] Bank of China was appointed as the clearing bank for Renminbi transaction in Taiwan.[64] Bank of China plans to open its Taipei branch for carrying out its Renminbi clearing business in Taiwan.[65] A yuan clearing bank was also appointed in February 2013.[66] These clearing banks are equipped to provide "regionwide solutions" for customers seeking yuan products and services.

The establishment of the clearing banks enables residents on both sides to deposit and borrow money in each other's currencies. More than symbolic, residents in Taiwan are able to deal in yuan-denominated assets such as deposits, loans, and yuan investments. Banks in Taiwan began taking yuan deposits domestically in February 2013, and Taiwan's first yuan debt sale followed in the same month. Individuals who sell or buy Renminbi will be subject to a 20,000 yuan daily cap, similar to the rules in other yuan offshore markets such as Hong Kong. Daily yuan remittance to other accounts is capped at 80,000 yuan for each Taiwan resident.[67] Currently, Taiwan does not allow the free entry and exit of yuan. Foreign currency bond transactions are subject to a yield tax of as much as fifteen percent in Taiwan.[68] Further, mainland issuers are barred from the market. These restrictions are natural as Taiwan still maintains capital control rules. Taiwan should remove restrictions on mainland companies and its currency so that it can become an offshore hub for Renminbi.

Singapore

Before the Renminbi business opened to Singapore, banks from other countries tried to have a bite of the Renminbi market through Hong Kong. For instance, CBS, the largest bank in Singapore by market capitalization, held deposits of 14 billion yuan in Hong Kong by the end of 2012, up from 13 billion yuan one year

[63] Daniel Ren, "Yuan Trade to Start in Taiwan in Weeks", *South China Morning Post*, 26 January 2013 (online).

[64] Ibid.

[65] Reuters, "Bank of China Hopes to Begin Yuan Clearing Business: Taiwan Cenbank", *South China Morning Post*, 12 December 2012 (online).

[66] Kanis Li, "Big Investors Stay Wary on China Equities Despite RQFII Rules Change", *South China Morning Post*, 25 March 2013 (online).

[67] Daniel Ren, "Yuan Trade to Start in Taiwan in Weeks", *South China Morning Post*, 26 January 2013 (online).

[68] Bloomberg, "Taiwan Must Ease Rules to Become Yuan Hub: SinoPac", *South China Morning Post*, 19 July 2013, B5.

earlier. CBS's income from yuan products provide to customers jumped sixty percent year on year in January and February 2013.[69]

China's current three offshore clearing banks are Bank of China (Hong Kong), Bank of China's Taiwan branch, and Industrial and Commercial Bank of China's branch in Singapore. BOCHK clears about 700 billion yuan everyday, while the other banks each clear about 200 billion yuan a day. HSBC and Standard Chartered are the two biggest underwriters in offshore yuan bonds with market shares of 17.1 percent and 18 percent respectively.[70]

China designated ICBC as the sole clearing bank authorized to handle offshore Renminbi transactions in Singapore,[71] which completed the last step that was necessary to prepare Singapore for its role as Southeast Asia's hub for Renminbi. Together with Hong Kong and Taipei, bringing Renminbi to Singapore was an important milestone that quickly made Renminbi a regional "trade invoicing currency" in Asia. This step has also widened the currency net in the East Asian region. Banks in Singapore including branches of foreign banks such as Standard Chartered and Citigroup can skirt the multiple custodial relationships with banks in Hong Kong to access the currency at Bank of China's branch, the sole designated offshore clearing bank. As the opening of Renminbi accounts in Singapore is now possible, this effectively allows for the creation of a pool of liquidity in Renminbi thereby pushing for trade carried out across Southeast Asia in Renminbi. A Renminbi clearing bank in Singapore allows greater financing of trade flows through Singapore where banks such as United Overseas Bank are increasingly working with Chinese companies in order to expand their business presence into Singapore and ASEAN countries. ICBC's move paves the way for the start of an offshore deliverable market similar to the ones in Hong Kong and Taiwan. An offshore Renminbi center in Singapore will become an entrepôt for ASEAN and other economies trading with China.

Singapore joined Hong Kong and London as a financial center where investors can apply for a quota under China's RQFII scheme. Holders of RQFII licences can use Renminbi that they hold offshore to invest indirectly in domestic Chinese assets, from bonds to stocks to money market funds. The expansion of the RQFII quota amounts to Renminbi 400 billion of which only Renminbi 130 billion has been allocated. This is the latest step of the Chinese government's broad and long term goal of improving access to China's domestic financial markets. Singapore

---

[69] Kanis Li, "Big Investors Stay Wary on China Equities Despite RQFII Rules Change", *South China Morning Post*, 25 March 2013 (online). It is also reported that DBS employs 90 people in its dealing room in Hong Kong, mostly serving mainland corporates, and about seventy percent of dealing room revenues are generated by yuan-related transactions, compared to twenty percent of revenue they contributed three or four years ago.

[70] Jeanny Yu, "China and UK in Talks over London Yuan Clearing Bank", *South China Morning Post*, 22 February 2014 (online).

[71] Jeremy Grant, "ICBC Named Sole Singapore Renminbi Clearer", *Financial Times*, 8 February 2013 (online).

may become the second offshore jurisdiction hosting Renminbi-denominated IPO. Li Ka-shing-backed Dynasty REIT may become the second offshore yuan offering outside mainland China and the first such IPO in Singapore.[72]

Summary

Financial centers are facing some technical and institutional challenges while moving forward to development Renminbi-denominated markets. They also face the problem that Renminbi trading remains a small slice of global foreign exchange markets. The global pool of liquidity needs to increase in multiple places if Renminbi business is to flourish. Growing Renminbi business generally would be good news for the globalization of Renminbi. These financial centers have their own competitive edges.

Hong Kong has a good start in terms of its trade finance and hedging instruments. Singapore has strengths with regard to its private banking, Asian trade, and treasury management. London has become the second largest offshore yuan hub worldwide, and the largest Western hub for Renminbi with US$238 billion worth of yuan transferred in and out of the market. London's share of the market is Renminbi 15 billion; only a drop in the ocean of the City of London's capital markets. This again will propel London to the center of the global financial market as a London-based eurodollar market did in the 1950s.[73] London's advantages include possessing a Hong Kong-complementary timezone and strengths in investment, foreign exchange, and capital raising activities. The shortcomings London has to overcome swiftly are Renminbi liquidity and credibility. London can benefit from the establishment of a cross-border interbank payment (CIP) system,[74] which would allow banks in London to clear yuan transactions directly with the PBOC instead of through clearing banks in Hong Kong. Singapore and Taiwan are the

---

[72] Ray Chan and Lulu Chen, "Hong Kong Trumps Singapore in Yuan Hub Race with Hopewell IPO", *South China Morning Post*, 25 October 2012 (online).

[73] The eurodollar market was a reaction to exchange controls imposed in 1957 amid a crisis of confidence in Britain's economy. The exchange control rules prevented the use of sterling for trade between parties outside the UK, threatening to diminish the role of the City's banks. As a result, some London banks started accepting dollar deposits and using them to fund dollar-denominated loans to clients in Britain or abroad. The new market was a commercial initiative rather than a regulatory one.

[74] CIP system is expected to be launched in 2014 and will be a different environment for market participants and financial centers. CIP system is different from the clearing system Hong Kong, Singapore and Taiwan now have, CIP system does not involve any intermediate clearing bank and would enable a more fluid transfer of activity from one center to the others. There are two consequences of relying more on the CIP system. First it changes the global yuan clearing model and can improve cross-border yuan settlement efficiency. Second, Shanghai can become a more prominent international center. The establishment of the CIP system will be a key infrastructure development for China's internationalization of yuan. The enhancement of channels for cross-border flows of yuan is conducive to the wider use of yuan and the further development of the offshore yuan center.

third and fourth largest offshore yuan hubs with US$127 billion and US$79 billion, respectively, in and out of the market in June 2013. The United States and Australia rank after with US$66 billion and US$26 billion, respectively, in June 2013.[75]

Technical issues within the Renminbi market include the absence of a recognized benchmark yield curve needed to create hedging products. More complicated products may favor London or Singapore. Compared to Singapore, which is dominant in Asian FX trading or London that is the clear global market leader, Hong Kong's shortcoming is obvious. Futures trading may gravitate to London while Renminbi investment might move to the fund management center of Singapore. Although banks in Hong Kong including HSBC and Standard Chartered are trying to make more Renminbi-denominated investment products, there remains a critical constraint to the growth of Renminbi financial products in Hong Kong. The Chinese government has controls preventing money flowing in and out of the mainland for investment purposes. Capital flows require approval on a case-by-case basis. On the other hand, investors have less incentive in holding Renminbi if it cannot be invested in the mainland. Therefore, low-yielding deposit accounts and bonds are overall less attractive to foreign investors.

One way to avoid messy competition is to deepen cooperation. The Hong Kong and Singapore bourses in December 2013 signed a memorandum of understanding (MOU) on cooperation in developing yuan business.[76] They agreed to connect their data centers and work closely on technology and regulatory issues. The MOU will pave the way for significant connectivity and infrastructure development around the usage of the yuan in capital markets outside China. The MOU is to build on Hong Kong's position as the premier offshore yuan center by developing closer links with Singapore and helping regional investors deploy a growing pool of investable offshore yuan. This understanding is beneficial as it may make it easier for investors to operate in both markets. Both markets need to further liberalize the ability of their investors to buy and sell yuan. Signing the MOU will also accelerate the already strong momentum in the internationalization of the yuan.

In terms of liquidity, a noteworthy development is that China has been or is in the process of entering into deals with various countries thereby allowing direct trading between its own currency and foreign currency so as to eliminate the need for foreign counterparties to first buy and sell dollars. China has had such direct trading with Malaysia, Russia, and Australia. China's plan is to see one third of its foreign trade settled in Renminbi by 2015.[77] For instance, China and Japan signed a pact to promote the use of their currencies for bilateral trade and investment flows

---

[75] Enoch Yiu, "Yuan Funding Rules Eased to Shore up HK's Offshore Lead", *South China Morning Post*, 26 July 2013, B3.
[76] Enoch Yiu, "HK Teams with Singapore on Yuan Business," *South China Morning Post*, 16 December 2013, B3.
[77] Sophie Yu, "China Looking at Direct Yuan Trade with Australian Dollar", *South China Morning Post*, 8 April 2013 (online).

in December 2011. Trade between the two economies amounted to about US$300 billion in 2010 while bilateral financial flows were estimated to be less than US$100 billion, and Renminbi-denominated trade accounted for less than one percent of the total value of trade between Japan and China.[78] A unique feature of the agreement with Japan was to allow the Bank of Japan to hold Renminbi sovereign debt as foreign exchange reserves and to promote the issuance of Renminbi-denominated bonds by Japanese companies.

A number of central banks have already included Renminbi in their foreign currency reserves. The Reserve Bank of Australia in April 2013 invested about five percent of its reserves in Renminbi-denominated assets such as Chinese government debt.[79] The Nigerian central bank had included as much as ten percent Renminbi in its external reserves holdings.[80] Central banks in Malaysia, Mongolia, Chile, and Venezuela also added yuan to their reserve portfolios.

By the end of October 2013, China signed twenty-three bilateral Renminbi-denominated swap arrangements.[81] The most recent swap arrangement is between China and European Central Bank (ECB). The arrangement is valid for three years and allows the ECB to access at most 350 billion yuan while the PBOC can get as much as €45 billion from the ECB when needed. The swap line allows central banks to purchase and subsequently repurchase Chinese currency and euros from each other. The swap line is available to all eurozone counterparties via national central banks. European companies with Renminbi-denominated bills are able to turn to the ECB for liquidity if they cannot find it on the market. While the ECB has yet to publish technical details, this will probably take place at market rate plus a small markup. This would allow the PBOC to provide up to €45 billion in liquidity inside the mainland. This is also good for China to diversify away from the U.S. dollar.

The Bank of England and the PBOC have made a three-year deal to swap sterling and yuan when needed. It was China's first pact with a G7 member and a major developed economy.[82] This is a three-year currency swap line of up to

---

[78] Ben McLannahan, "Sluggish Start for Yen/Renminbi Market", *Financial Times*, 29 November 2012 (online).

[79] Josh Noble, "China Bond Markets Open Slowly to Outsiders", *Financial Times*, 24 October 2013, 20.

[80] Jenny Anderson, "Britain Gains Renminbi Trading Deal", *New York Times*, 27 March 2014, B11.

[81] China started to establish swap lines with other central banks even before it internationalizes Renminbi. It arranged six of them with other ASEAN plus three economies under the Chiang Mai Initiative in the early 2000s to deal with country-specific liquidity crunches. Details are available at http://en.wikipedia.org/wiki/Chiang_Mai_Initiative. However, the swap arrangements under Chiang Mai Initiative were dollar-local currency swaps, under which China would provide U.S. dollars in exchange for the local currency of the counterparty economy.

[82] Danny Lee and Olivia Rosenman, "Tibet Win in Britain Stiffens Beijing's Resolve with EU", *South China Morning Post*, 15 July 2013, A6.

200 billion yuan to promote financial stability and bilateral trade.[83] The swap line with China facilitates two-way currency flows and enabled the Bank of England to supply yuan for other currencies when there is a shortage in London. Signing a swap has witnessed a jump in yuan business, with daily spot trading rising by 240 percent to US$2.5 billion.[84] Britain also made some technical agreements with Hong Kong authorities to investigate clearing and settlement systems, and to develop new products denominated in Renminbi.[85]

OPPORTUNITIES AND CHALLENGES AHEAD

Dominance of the global economy goes hand-in-hand with dominance of the global monetary system. In a global context, changes in the international reserve currency also represent shifts in global powers. Of the currencies of the world's six largest economies, Renminbi is the only one that has not attained reserve currency status. Along with China's economic growth, Renminbi, at least in theory,[86] will attain reserve currency status sooner than later. Although many may expect Renminbi to match China's important status, the currency itself is not ready to challenge the dominance in the global monetary system enjoyed by the U.S. dollar.

The global demand for yuan seems to be on an inevitable upward trend. More Asian and European central banks are increasing their yuan holdings to diversify their currency holdings in the face of U.S. dollar depreciation, high volatility in the euro, and continuing appreciation of Renminbi. One indication of Renminbi's growing stature is the fact that banks in Asia look into their holdings of Renminbi when they lend dollars to corporate borrowers so that they can get a sense of comfort. This shows the investors and banks' faith in both the stability and the long term appreciation prospects of Renminbi. In addition, both central banks and sovereign wealth funds are now increasing their holdings of yuan assets. This bullish position of Renminbi is attributed to the fact that Renminbi was the most profitable trade during the first six months of 2013 for several Singapore-based hedge funds in a counterintuitive bet, which guaranteed a spread of three percent.[87] The low volatility has also added to the appeal of the trade. Seen from this angle, China has emerged as a source of global liquidity.

[83] Jane Cai and Enoch Yiu, "London Confident on Yuan Role", *South China Morning Post*, 25 July 2013, B2.

[84] Jeanny Yu, "Britain and Beijing in Talks About Yuan Quotas", *South China Morning Post*, 29 September 2013 (online).

[85] "China and the City", *Financial Times*, 17 January 2012, p.10.

[86] Menzie Chinn and Jeffrey Frankel, "Will the Euro Eventually Surpass the Dollar as Leading International Reserve Currency?", in Richard Clarida (ed), *G7 Current Account Imbalances: Sustainability and Adjustment* (Chicago: University of Chicago Press 2007) (suggesting that economic size is an important determinant of the extent of international use of a national currency).

[87] Henry Sender, "Hedge Funds Gain from Renminbi Strength", *Financial Times*, 1 August 2013 (online).

It appears that the dollar bloc in East Asia has been displaced by an emerging new currency bloc based on China's Renminbi.[88] As a matter of fact, seven out of ten countries in the region such as South Korea, Indonesia, Taiwan, Malaysia, Singapore, and Thailand have started to track Renminbi more closely than the U.S. dollar after the financial crisis, and especially after China's resumed floating in June 2010.[89] For instance, Taiwan is considering putting Renminbi into its foreign exchange reserves portfolio.[90] South Korea recently allowed its commercial banks to tap into a Renminbi swap arrangement with China.[91] China Construction Bank launched a Renminbi clearing service in Sydney in February 2014. Meanwhile, Bank of China announced a new clearing arrangement in conjunction with the Australian Securities Exchange's Austroclear system. These arrangements bring potentials that can create a seismic shift in the international monetary and financial landscape.[92] Some ASEAN member states have seen a rising role of Renminbi in their exchange rate policy and reserve holdings. The increasing use of Renminbi as a reference currency is largely due to China's rise as a major trading partner to most East Asian economies with an increase in its share of Asian economies' trade from two percent in 1991 to twenty-two percent in 2012.[93] China's trading partners have more incentives to stabilize their exchange rates against Renminbi. It is likely that this trend may expand to some trading partners in other regions which may discover that they would do well to follow Renminbi more closely. This appears to be a win–win scenario where China may reduce its dependence on the dollar while other countries enjoy the advantages of tighter trade and financial links with China by

[88] Arvind Subramanian and Martin Kessler, "China's Currency Rises in the US Backyard", *Financial Times*, 21 October 2012 (online).

[89] Ibid. Hong Kong, Vietnam and Mongolia are three exceptional cases following the US dollar more closely than Renminbi. Hong Kong dollar's exchange rate is still linked to the U.S. dollar. When Hong Kong dollar pushes up against the upper limits of its trading band of US$1 to HK$7.75, HKMA, sold HK$4.67 billion and HK$3.9 billion on 19 October and 24 October 2012 respectively to halt the rise of the Hong Kong dollar against the US dollar up to 7.7501. HKMA's move suggested that it would continue to defend the HK dollar peg in the future, at least before Renminbi becomes fully convertible. Rahul Jacob, "HK Moves Again to Halt Currency Rise", *Financial Times*, 23 October 2012 (online). The recent stronger HK dollar is largely caused by the strong inflow of capital into the Hong Kong-dollar market when the global investors' appetite towards Hong Kong's stock market is turning bigger. The link of Hong Kong dollar to the U.S. dollar was put in place in 1983 when China and the UK negotiated the future arrangement of Hong Kong after it is turned over to China.

[90] Reuters, "Bank of China Hopes to Begin Yuan Clearing Business: Taiwan Cenbank", *South China Morning Post*, 12 December 2012 (online).

[91] Jeremy Grant, "ICBC Named Sole Singapore Renminbi Clearer", *Financial Times*, 8 February 2013 (online). The Republic of Korea was the first counterparty to the swap arrangement with China in December 2008 for Renminbi 180 billion, with a maturity of 3 years. Korea and China renewed the arrangement in 2011, doubling the amount of the swap to Renminbi 360 billion.

[92] Philip Stafford and Delphine Strauss, "UK to Host Renminbi Clearing Bank", *Financial Times*, 27 March 2014, p.22.

[93] Reuters, "Bank of China Hopes to Begin Yuan Clearing Business: Taiwan Cenbank", *South China Morning Post*, 12 December 2012 (online).

participating in various bilateral or regional swap arrangements, thereby shaping a new monetary integration framework in Asia.[94]

It has to be pointed out that the internationalization of Renminbi is a policy-oriented development. The Chinese government sets the pace and guides the market due to the capital account controls, exchange rate intervention, interest rate caps, financial market development constraints, and heavily regulated macro-economic policies. Different from the eurodollar market,[95] the Renminbi's internationalization is controlled by the Chinese government rather than the private sector's appetite. The eurodollar market was built on the dollar's preeminence, which by the end of the 1950s had become the leading international currency, used to settle and invoice more than eighty percent of international trade. By 1970, US $385 billion was held outside the United States, where it could easily be enticed into offshore banks. The market for offshore dollar deposits grew at more than twenty-five percent a year throughout the 1970s, and quadrupled its size between 1977 and 1987. A quarter of the U.S. dollar balance sheet is located offshore.[96] The Renminbi however has had limited international use thus far. Renminbi is hardly seen in the international payment system even though the use of Renminbi has increased to fourteen percent of China's total trade.

Whether China will obtain reserve currency status for Renminbi is unknown; but if it will, the journey will be a long one. A reserve Renminbi will be fully convertible on both capital and current accounts, which may expose China to global capital as well as global financial crises. Free capital flows may also destabilize domestic banks, create liquidity bubbles in a good economy, or choke off the credit supply when the economy deteriorates. To a certain extent, a freely convertible Renminbi may be a source of economic volatility. The government is likely to lose control over the technical difficulty of maintaining Renminbi as a currency peg in the face of massive capital inflows. Meanwhile, the increasing demand for Renminbi may push up its value and make an export-orientated growth model less sustainable. The internationalization process of Renminbi will have a more global horizon despite Renminbi's lack of convertibility and modest size of use at the global level. In the long run, the effects could be larger as China's capital account becomes more open.

It was pledged by the ruling Communist Party in its 18th National Congress's Third Plenum in November 2013 to further promote free movement of capital in

---

[94] Carsten Hefeker and Andreas Nabor, "Yen or Yuan? China's Role in the Future of Asian Monetary Integration" HWWA Discussion Paper 206 (2002); George M. von Furstenberg and Jianjun Wei, "The Chinese Crux Monetary Union in East Asia" (2002), available at http://en .wikipedia.org/wiki/George_M._von_Furstenberg.

[95] Youssef Cassis, *Capitals of Capital: The Rise and Fall of International Financial Centres 1780–2009* (Cambridge: Cambridge University Press 2006) 219–35.

[96] Benjamin J. Cohen, "Monetary Governance and Capital Mobility in Historical Perspective", in Rainer Grote and Thilo Marauhn (eds.), *The Regulation of International Financial Markets: Perspectives for Reform* (Cambridge: Cambridge University Press 2006) 48–50.

and out of China for investment purposes and to make the exchange rate more market based.[97] The PBOC has outlined its plan to focus on the reform of convertibility.[98] It is likely that as part of the Renminbi exchange rate formation mechanism the foreign exchange policy will be further liberalized, with the daily trading ban for the yuan gradually widened, at least doubling in size first and eventually being eliminated; and the capital account is increasingly open with the bond market leading the way.[99] Similarly, China will steadily push forward market-based liberalization of interest rate. Renminbi's internationalization, that is, the yuan's convertibility, is more likely to be dependent on China's own speed of liberalizing its financial and currency markets.[100] The more quickly China liberalizes its currency and strengthens its financial market development, the more quickly Renminbi will broaden its horizon.[101]

[97] Bloomberg, "More Convertible Yuan Next Goal, China's Central Bank Chief Says", *South China Morning Post*, 18 November 2012 (online).

[98] Ibid.

[99] Credit Agricole Report, cited in Toh Han Shih, "Winds of Change 'to Blow Through' China's Economy", *South China Morning Post*, 27 November 2012 (online).

[100] It has been reported that the State Council is working on an operational plan to achieve full convertibility, and the plan will outline steps towards a market-based exchange rate system and capital account liberalization. Jane Cai, "Yuan Heads for Key Level Against Dollar", *South China Morning Post*, 5 June 2013 (online).

[101] Some market observers estimated that a full convertibility of Renminbi is likely to take place within five years. "Dim Sum Bond Sales Double as New Elite Back Global Yuan", *South China Morning Post*, 30 November 2012 (online).

11

"Market Quality" and Moral Hazard in Financial Market Design

David C. Donald

INFRASTRUCTURE DESIGN MATTERS

An alluring idea that contradicts common experience runs as follows: the most efficient institutions are the most competitive, so efficient institutions naturally prevail. Its most important corollary for regulatory policy – that such self-policing efficiency obviates the need for most regulation – has recently shown itself to be dangerous.[1] As Douglass North has observed, "Institutions are not necessarily or even usually created to be socially efficient; rather they, or at least the formal rules, are created to serve the interests of those with the bargaining power to devise new rules."[2] It may be that while *socially* efficient institutions do not naturally arise and thrive, institutions of *mercenary* efficiency (designed primarily to serve the maker's material benefit) do. Does this apply to financial market infrastructure? A step toward answering this question is to decide whether the concept of "market quality" we use to measure such infrastructure entails a market being socially efficient or merely efficient in a mercenary sense for certain market participants. History teaches us that choices among infrastructure options can create winners and losers. Bridges reduce the need for ferries, and highways for rail and canal. At the end of the nineteenth century, refrigerated cars on the railroad from Chicago meant dressed meat could be shipped to the East Coast, obviating the butcher facilities

The author would like to thank the Hong Kong Research Grants Council for the generous funding of this work under the Theme Based Research Project, "Enhancing Hong Kong's Future as a Leading International Financial Centre" (T31–717/12-R).

[1] With regard to the OTC derivatives market in the lead up to the global financial crisis, Awrey explains, "This rationale was grounded in the conviction that rational and fully informed market participants – utilizing sophisticated quantitative methods and the innovative financial instruments these methods made possible – had both eliminated uncertainty and effectively mastered risk." Dan Awrey, "Toward a supply-side theory of financial innovation," *Journal of Comparative Economics* 41 (2013) 401–419, p. 402.

[2] Douglass North, *Institutions, Institutional Change and Economic Performance.* Cambridge University Press, 1990, p. 16.

that had been established around eastern cities' rail stations.[3] At the end of the twentieth century, express couriers robbed traditional postal services of their urban-rural cross-subsidies, and the internet dramatically reduced the business of both post and courier. As Schmid observes, "Technological change is not some benign process where everyone gains. Even if the change has the potential to be Pareto-better, it may not be so in practice. Thus, change is a function of which competing interests can control the process and this is affected by institutions that influence whose preferences count."[4] History shows us that the same applies to the design and use of infrastructure. However, while we readily understand why someone should not dam a river to irrigate fields upstream of her competitor, we might think less about what impact financial market design has on the allocation of liquidity.

Some changes arise from technological innovation, as with highways and railroads; others arise from government intervention, such as in the breakup of the telecommunications monopolies. Recent changes in the financial industry have arisen from both, and this has not been – as might be expected – simple government action to facilitate the use of technological innovation. Rather than tracking technological progress, the course of development more closely follows the interests of the market participants who control market structure design. This is exemplified in the case of the 1975 legislation that ordered the creation of a U.S. "national market system,"[5] which included both front- and back-office aspects. The opposing centripetal and centrifugal forces that this legislation initiated are still in play today. On the one hand, it mandated open competition in the business of matching securities trades (dominated by securities exchanges for over a century), which eventually brought about a cheaper, but radically fragmented market.[6] On the other, it required that the securities traded on exchanges be immobilized in a depository and registered in the latter's name (rather than the shareholder's), which has created a highly centralized system of holding, transferring and registering shares.[7] Major broker-dealers lobbied against, and stalled the full introduction of active competition for trade matching until the development of their business plans made it a profitable prospect. On the contrary, improvements in computer and information technology should have, but did not, obviate the need

---

[3]   A. Allan Schmid, *Conflict and cooperation: institutional and behavioral economics*. Blackwell, 2004. Pp. 207–208.

[4]   Ibid., p. 207.

[5]   Securities Acts Amendments of 1975, Pub. L. 94–29, June 4, 1975, 89 Stat. 97 (1975). The 1975 Amendments instructed the SEC to eliminate the system of fixed commissions, if appropriate. 15 U.S.C. § 78f(e)(1). This was part of a "national market system program" designed to allow trades and information to flow freely between all national and regional exchanges. 15 U.S.C. § 78k-1; S. REP. NO. 94–75, at 180 *et seq.* (1975). The two prongs of the national market program were to open up isolated, uncompetitive pockets of trading and price information to all market participants and also create a national system for clearing and settlement. 15 U.S.C. § 78q-1; S. REP. NO. 94–75, p. 183 *et seq.* (1975).

[6]   This is discussed in Part III.B.

[7]   This is discussed in Part III.A.

for broker-dealers to retain their central role in the holding and voting of listed securities. Issuers and investors, who have only minimal input into the design of financial market infrastructure, have generally been the losers, while the large broker-dealers who both design and own the infrastructure, have usually been the winners.

While these two developments pulled the market in different directions (one centralizing and the other fragmenting) and related to technological change in different ways (one following the trend and the other fighting it), they display a solid correlation with the interests of the largest broker-dealers. The immediate implementation of the 1975 decree that an overflow of paperwork be managed by an immobilization in depositories meant that an entity controlled by the largest banks and broker-dealers became the "registered owner" of nearly all listed shares. This infrastructural change created good business opportunities for those broker-dealers who could take them up.

Immobilization of shares in a central depository meant that a number of large banks and broker-dealers became indirect legal owners of 99 percent of U.S. listed securities. The change forced issuers and shareholders to transfer their valuable, mutual relationship to the control of the financial industry. The rights and information the market participants gained from this new position could then be sold back to shareholders and issuers in the form of a new business called "corporate actions." As will be discussed in Part III.B, competition for trade matching was held at bay until the New York Stock Exchange (NYSE) became interested in going public, and this, combined with developments in the technology for alternative matching venues, made the business of alternative trading venues viable. This meant that the exchanges (with their new mix of ownership) lost market share while broker-dealers large enough to invest in the creation of alternative trading venues (whether dark or lit) had new sources of revenue. The scale of operations of these broker-dealers also allowed them to finance powerful computer systems profitably to navigate the complexity of the new, fragmented markets. Smaller brokers were faced with an arms' race in trading hardware, and if they did not have the size to set up their own matching pools, they could also be forced into becoming customers of their competitors. Investors were presented with a market in which the fees for a given trade were indeed lower, but both the number of trades and the prices at which they were struck became suspicious. In each instance, those with control over the design of market infrastructure reaped benefits and those without such control suffered losses. Mercenary efficiency for some was achieved, but whether this entailed social efficiency is highly questionable.

Markets designed mainly to create rents for the largest participants are not socially efficient. Both regulators and academics frequently assess markets for quality, yet transfers of wealth due to opportunistic infrastructure appear to fall outside the parameters of such assessments. The concept of "market quality" applied in such assessments, which are generally limited to assessing the smooth operation of the machine itself, is too narrow to catch design hazard. The concept of market quality as conventionally applied includes (i) the cost of trading, (ii) the speed and accuracy with which information is impounded in price (efficiency), (iii) the increments at which a security may be priced (tick size), (iv) the average spread between best ask and bid, and (v) the intraday volatility of the market. Questions such as whether the machine is doing what its ultimate end users – borrowers and investors – seek from finance are not generally asked. While it is very useful to uncover drag and imbalance within the mechanism, such (predominately quantitative) studies bracket out both ultimate impact on investors and issuers, and the opportunity costs of the current model. "Social" efficiency is out of the picture, so proposals for alternative arrangements face the high hurdle of showing some inherent design flaw. This situation is unfortunate, given that market participants are likely to design such infrastructure to their own benefit, even if due only to the natural biases of their informational repertoire and perspective. Neither issuers nor investors (whether retail or institutional) have much say in this process. While, as discussed in Part III, official decisions affecting market design are open for consultation, the asymmetry of information in this area is so high that financial market infrastructure borders on being a black box known in detail only to its operators. The efficacy of the notice and comment process for such purpose is therefore questionable.

Where interests are strong, information asymmetry high, and the benefits (and detriments) accruing from the infrastructure design adopted are substantial, it is unacceptable that our understanding of "market quality" be limited to assessing whether the current model performs well for its immediate users. It must be designed in the interests of the ultimate users: investors and ventures. *Social*, not simply *mercenary*, efficiency should be our goal. This article shows why a more inclusive concept of market quality is necessary and proposes such adjustment. Part II reviews our methods for assessing "market quality," showing that measures of cost, efficiency and volatility are too limited for a fully accurate assessment. Part III presents two examples of how market insiders have designed financial market infrastructure in ways that created business opportunities for themselves while generating considerable negative externalities for issuers, investors, and brokers whose size did not allow them to capitalize on the new opportunities. Part IV offers a revised concept of market quality designed to achieve social efficiency in markets.

MEASURES OF MARKET QUALITY

Efficiency: Prices Promptly and Accurately Reflect Public Information

When we speak of an "efficient market," we generally mean this in the sense of Eugene Fama's "semi-strong" form of efficiency: that "current prices 'fully reflect' all obviously publicly available information."[8] The efficient market theory as formulated by Fama has been closely examined by leading scholars for decades. Some of the most important assumptions on which the theory depends[9] were brought out and examined as the institutional "mechanisms of market efficiency" by Gilson and Kraakman.[10] They found that "the prompt reflection of publicly available information in a security's price had to be the outcome of institutional and market interactions whose proper functioning necessarily depended on the character of those institutions."[11] This brought legal work on securities regulation in sync with the economic analysis of price movement, foreshadowed the creation of the "law and finance" movement, and in many ways also ushered in the new field of market microstructure analysis.[12] One assumption necessary for market efficiency regards the rationality of investor decision-making, and in this area, the work of Tversky and Kahneman[13] and later Shiller[14] unfolded the many biases that channel the way in which investors react to such information. Thus our understanding of the process of price creation has become broad and rich, stretching from the various legal institutions of the financial markets to the vagaries of the human mind.

Detailed knowledge of how information is ultimately impounded in the price created on a securities market, and whether it is done efficiently, could help us understand whether an alternative market design should be sought. However, it is not generally employed in this manner, but rather to test the efficiency of price creation in a particular, given market. For example, in a recent study on the market quality effects of high frequency trading (HFT), Brogaard, Hendershott, and Riordan examine the price impact of HFT on the Nasdaq Stock Market.[15]

[8] Eugene F. Fama, "Efficient Capital Markets: A Review of Theory and Empirical Work," *The Journal of Finance*, 35 (1970): 383–417, 404. Shiller points out that this concept – albeit formulated intuitively rather than rigorously – has been a common understanding for over a century, as evidenced by the work of 1889 work of Gibson and the 1929 work of Laurence. Robert J. Shiller, *Irrational Exuberance*. Princeton University Press, 2009, 2nd ed., p. 178.

[9] A market without transaction costs, in which all available information is costless for all participants, and all agree on the implications of the information for the relevant security. Fama, "Efficient Capital Markets," *supra* note 8, p. 387.

[10] Ronald J. Gilson & Reinier Kraakman, "The Mechanisms of Market Efficiency," *Virginia Law Review*, 70 (1984) 549. Also see by the same authors, "Market Efficiency after the Financial Crisis: It's Still a Matter of Information Costs," *Virginia Law Review*, 100 (2014) 313.

[11] Ronald J. Gilson & Reinier Kraakman, "The Mechanisms of Market Efficiency Twenty Years Later: The Hindsight Bias," *Journal of Corporation Law*, 28 (2003) 715, 716.

[12] Paul G. Mahoney, "Market Microstructure and Market Efficiency," *Journal of Corporation Law*, 28 (2003): 541.

[13] Amos Tversky & Daniel Kahneman, "Judgment Under Uncertainty: Heuristics and Biases," *Science*, 185 (1974) 1124–1131.

[14] Robert J. Shiller, "Do Stock Prices Move Too Much to Be Justified by Subsequent Changes in Dividends?," *American Economic Review* 71 (1981) 421–436.

[15] Jonathan Brogaard, Terrence Hendershott & Ryan Riordan, "High frequency trading and price discovery," European Central Bank Working Paper Series No. 1602 (2013).

They find that HFT can bring information into a securities price up to four seconds faster than ordinary trading, which when taken alone is understood to mean that HFT benefits market quality.[16] Because HFT are faster to sell during this period, they drain the market of liquidity, but because they are even faster to buy when available information advises (supplying liquidity), the authors find the overall impact of HFT to be beneficial.[17] The SEC cites this study as indication that HFT improves market quality, although it expresses reservations about the adverse selection costs to non-HFT.[18] In this, and other studies of HFT, a mystery arises as to why HFT provides liquidity and trades against the price trend when placing limit orders (passive trading), but takes liquidity while trading with the trend when placing market orders (aggressive trading). The fact that the active and passive trading of HFT are not generally studied as parts of a strategic or functionally determined whole is too limited a focus and a reason why traditional measures of market quality do not uncover moral hazard designed into market structure.

As will be discussed in Part III.B, Clark-Joseph hypothesizes that this combination is a strategy of "exploratory trading" through which an HFT participant learns of profit opportunities when its passive orders are triggered by other traders.[19] This raises questions well beyond whether HFT has assisted prices in more quickly impounding available information; it exemplifies how a combination of fragmented market design and speed can allow traders with a sufficient technological endowment to beat others on the basis of the market's design, rather than on estimations of a security's value. Markets designed so the sophisticated can game suckers do not engender the kind of trust that makes markets efficient. As North and Buckley rightly argue, "[t]he real question for policy makers concerns the extent to which management, institutional or individual incentives and efficiencies align with the incentives and efficiencies that serve the long-term economic interests of the nation. A sustainable policy must serve the public interest rather than the efficiency or profit interests of only some market participants such as financial institutions."[20]

Cost: Fees and Spread Size

It was the cost of trading in an environment of fixed brokerage commissions that led the U.S. government to order competition in the activity of trade matching, initially

---

[16] Ibid., p. 32.

[17] Ibid., p. 32.

[18] US Securities and Exchange Commission, "Equity Market Structure Literature Review Part II: High Frequency Trading," (2014) p. 24, available at www.sec.gov/marketstructure (last accessed July 2014). More study of such adverse selection costs would of course lead to an analysis of the market structure's benefits and detriments for the various participants, bringing us closer to an analysis of social efficiency.

[19] Adam D. Clark-Joseph, "Exploratory Trading" (2013), available at www.nanex.net (last accessed July 15, 2014).

[20] Gill North & Ross Buckley, "A Fundamental Reexamination of Efficiency in Capital Markets in Light of the Global Financial Crisis," UNSW *Law Journal* 33 (2010) 714, 739.

in the form of an antitrust suit and eventually through amending the Securities Exchange Act.[21] The coordinated effort to protect fixed, minimum commissions was one of the clearest and most egregious examples of intermediary influence in the history of the U.S. financial system.[22] Thirty-five years after the 1975 amendments first mandated the national market system, and about ten years after the introduction of full competition, Angel, Harris and Spatt could observe that "[v]irtually every dimension of U.S. equity market quality is now better than ever. Execution speeds have fallen ... Retail commissions have fallen substantially and continue to fall. Bid-ask spreads have fallen substantially and remain low ...."[23] It is customary to understand low trading costs as a characteristic of good market quality. Here quality is not just a matter of a commodity becoming cheaper to buy, but conceived as an integral element of liquidity itself. Lower costs are understood to enhance the ability of "market participants ... better ... to hold the assets most suited to them, and informed participants ... to trade on their private information and impound it into asset prices."[24] Direct costs of trading include the fees paid to brokers and exchanges and the difference (spread) between the best ask and bid prices, which difference goes to a trader making market in a given security. An indirect determinant of the spread is the minimum tick size, or denomination unit in which securities are priced, given that the spread would be measured in units of tick size.

The logic according to which decreases in trading costs are understood as positively correlated with increases in market quality should be understood against the background of inflated fees extracted through the cartel situation mentioned above, and does not consider the possibility that excess trading might not contribute to market quality, provided it does not bring excessive volatility, which is a separate item of evaluation. This leaves advocates of a financial transaction tax to curb (rather than force a fiscal contribution from) financial activity[25] in qualitative disagreement with most market specialists, who would not draw a line between

[21] Senate Report 94–75, p. 2; Chis Welles, *The Last Days of the Club*. E.P. Dutton & Co., 1975, pp. 86–121.

[22] This is discussed in Welles, *Last Days, supra* note 21, pp. 3–22; Kathryn Judge, "Intermediary Influence," *University of Chicago Law Review*, Forthcoming; Columbia Law and Economics Working Paper No. 477 (May 27, 2014). pp. 19–20, available at SSRN: http://ssrn.com/abstract=2430163.

[23] James J. Angel, Lawrence E. Harris & Chester S. Spatt, "Equity Trading in the 21st Century," Marshall School of Business Working Paper No. FBE 09–10 (February 23, 2010), available at SSRN: http://ssrn.com/abstract=1584026, p. 5.

[24] Jonathan Brogaard, Terrence Hendershott, Stefan Hunt & Carla Ysusi, "High-Frequency Trading and the Execution Costs of Institutional Investors," *The Financial Review* 49 (2014) 345–369, 367.

[25] For example Joseph Stigliz and John Maynard Keynes. See Joseph E. Stigliz, "Using Tax Policy To Curb Speculative Short-Term Trading," *Journal of Financial Services Research*, 3 (1989) 101–115; John Maynard Keynes, *The General Theory of Employment, Interest and Money*, edited by Thomas Cate (1945).

speculative trading that provides liquidity and "excessive" speculation, on condition that the price is not "manipulated" and volatility remains within acceptable limits. The fact that more trading is equated with more liquidity, and low cost trading facilitates more of it, can also lead economists to conclude that market fragmentation, which has made pre- and post-transaction market transparency and regulatory oversight significantly more difficult, improves market quality because studies show that "fragmented stocks generally have lower transaction costs and faster execution speed."[26] This is of course a somewhat circular argument, given that competition (fragmentation) was introduced to lower costs, and a natural means of competition among venues in an age of accelerating computing speed is to offer faster execution speed. The circle closes when the immediate result of introducing competition among matching venues is understood as convincing evidence that the changes have led to good market quality.

Excessive Volatility: Intraday

Although the term "volatility" can be defined in many ways,[27] when it is used to assess market quality it is generally a measure of the variance in a security's price or return during a given period as seen against other, similar periods for the same security or securities,[28] normally during the same day. Studies of market quality focus on short-term volatility, which can be measured as price or return variance during a matter of seconds, minutes, or hours. Some volatility always exists because of the spread between the best bid and best ask established by limit (passive) orders, so that when a market (aggressive) order is executed, the price will drop (or rise) and then revert back following execution to the next bid or ask limit order queued. As volatility is more common when the order book is thin, volatility is also correlated with low liquidity securities or markets. For any security, the brief volatility through drop (or rise) and mean reversion, – which is unrelated to any information regarding the value of the security traded – offers professional traders an opportunity to profit.[29] Too much volatility, however, damages trust in the efficiency of price creation.[30]

Because professional, proprietary traders can view volatility as a profit opportunity unrelated to the fundamental value of a security, and because HFT is composed almost entirely of professional, proprietary traders whose algorithms are designed to

---

[26] Maureen O'Hara & MaoYe, "Is market fragmentation harming market quality?," *Journal of Financial Economics* 100 (2011) 459–474, 460.

[27] *See* e.g. Stephen J. Taylor, "Stock price volatility," *The New Palgrave Dictionary of Economics.* 2nd ed, 2008.

[28] Terrence Hendershott & Pamela C. Moulton, "Automation, speed, and stock market quality: The NYSE's Hybrid," *Journal of Financial Markets* 14 (2011) 568–604, 591.

[29] Robert A. Schwartz & Reto Francioni, *Equity Markets in Action: The Fundamentals of Liquidity, Market Structure & Trading.* John Wiley & Sons, 2004, p. 95.

[30] Ibid., p. 100–101.

reap such benefits,[31] much of the analysis of HFT's impact on market quality examines its impact on volatility. For example, Breckenfelder finds on the Stockholm stock exchange (NASDAQ OMXS) "deteriorating market quality for stocks facing competition between HFTs" as evidenced by the fact that "intraday hourly volatility increases by 20 percent, five-minute volatility by 9 percent and maximum intraday volatility by about 14 percent."[32] This volatility is also connected to another problem for market quality because Breckenfelder's evidence shows that "trend chasing . . . increases significantly for stocks for which there is competition between HFTs,"[33] and such momentum trading is contrary to efficient price discovery. As observed above, some volatility generated by the mere interaction of orders is always present, and the extent of such volatility is a function of the orders placed, including orders that "chase the trend," as Breckenfelder puts it. Using a stylized model in which HFT and ordinary traders interact in this manner, Hoffmann shows that ordinary traders face a much higher adverse selection risk by having their orders picked off by HFT chasing the trend, which forces ordinary traders into an "arms race" for speed to protect themselves.[34] Although the related measures of efficiency, volatility, and cost (as a factor of execution fees, spread, and tick size) do provide a good picture of what is happening in a market, they do not ordinarily include in their assessment the kind of conclusions reached by Hoffmann, and do not tell us whether a given market design is fair for all stakeholders using the market.

Fairness is an elusive state of affairs, particularly when one is looking to draw lines in a competitive market that is already subject to rules on the misuse of nonpublic information and the application of unsupported price pressure (market manipulation). One obvious place to look for unfairness is in a market design created by a group of people who have clear conflicts of interests between their own profit incentive and the public good. If a market designed and controlled by broker-dealers generates returns for this group at the expense of stakeholders with lesser control over its design, such as investors and issuers of securities, this would appear to be an *abuse of trust* that regulators should closely scrutinize and probably eliminate. The next Part examines the construction of two central aspects of our modern securities markets: the depository indirect holding system for securities settlement and the introduction of competition between multiple matching venues, such as regulated exchanges, alternative trading platforms, dark pools, and internalization. In both historical accounts, there is evidence that influential

---

[31] Michael Lewis, *Flash Boys: A Wall Street Revolt*. W. W. Norton & Company, 2014, p. 98.

[32] Johannes H. Breckenfelder, "Competition between High-Frequency Traders, and Market Quality," NYU Stern Microstructure Meeting 2013 (November 1, 2013) p. 3, available at SSRN: http://ssrn.com/abstract=2264858.

[33] Ibid.

[34] Peter Hoffmann, "A dynamic limit order market with fast and slow traders," *Journal of Financial Economics*, 113 (2014) 156–169.

broker-dealers worked for the creation of a financial market infrastructure that maximizes business opportunities for themselves.

BUILDING BUSINESS OPPORTUNITIES INTO MARKET INFRASTRUCTURE

Creating the Indirect Holding System[35]

The currently dominant depository model of securities settlement is based on the "immobilization" of share certificates in the vaults of a depository bank and "book-entry" transfers on the accounts containing credits against such immobilized securities.[36] This model was used from the 1870s as a main market feature for transferring securities in Vienna, Austria,[37] albeit the securities in question were bearer rather than registered notes. In the United States, the depository model was introduced following a major market failure in the late 1960s (the "paper crunch" or "paper blizzard") caused by the inability of clerks to register the growing volume of securities transfers manually.[38] This was the largest crisis that had hit the U.S. securities markets since the crash of 1929; it forced the NYSE to run on limited hours for over a year and eventually led to the collapse of about a hundred brokerage firms.[39] It was the impetus for the Securities Acts Amendments of 1975[40] and the beginning of America's version of the "big bang." The U.S. Congress chose the solution of obviating paperwork altogether by ordering the immobilization of security certificates in the vaults of a central depository, which was raised to the status of a self-regulatory organization (SRO),[41] and transferring claims against the depository's accounts rather than the shares themselves.

---

[35] The rise of the indirect holding system and the issues this entails are presented in more detail in David C. Donald, "Heart of Darkness: The Problem at the Core of the US Proxy System and Its Solution," *Virginia Law & Business Review*, 6 (2011) 41–100.

[36] Committee on Payment and Settlement Systems [CPSS] & Technical Committee of the International Organization of Securities Commissions [IOSCO], Recommendations for Securities Settlement Systems 45–47 (2001).

[37] *See* Theodor Heinsius et al., Depogestz – Kommentar zum Gesetz Über die Verwahrung und Anschaffung von Wertpapieren Vom 4. Februar 1937 (1975) § 5 margin no. 1.

[38] U.S. Securities and Exchange Commission, "Study of Unsafe and Unsound Practices of Brokers and Dealers," (December 1971) (hereinafter "Unsafe Practices Study"), p. 28. Also *see* Chris Welles, *The Last Days*, pp. 172 *et seq.* (1975).

[39] S. Rep. No. 94–75, p. 183 (1975); Joel Seligman, *The Transformation of Wall Street: A History of the Securities and Exchange Commission and Modern Corporate Finance.* Aspen, 2003, 3rd ed. p. 1366.

[40] Securities Acts Amendments of 1975, Pub. L. 94–29, June 4, 1975, 89 Stat. 97 (1975).

[41] The depository was made at, the Depository Trust Company (DTC) and the market's shares were registered in the name of its depository, "Cede & Co.," with "Cede" being short for "certificate depository." See Rules, By-laws and Organization Certificate of the Depository Trust Company (version of Sept. 2009), available at www.dtcc.com/legal/rules_proc (hereinafter "DTC Rules"), Rule 6.

This "indirect holding system"[42] introduced general use of the concepts "registered" and "beneficial" ownership into the parlance of U.S. securities regulation, for the market intermediary became the registered (legal) owner of virtually all traded shares, while the previous owners of the shares (shareholders) became mere beneficiaries, with contractual (and likely equitable) rights against the intermediary. In order to cement the financial intermediaries into this position of centrality, the U.S. commercial law had to be significantly amended, even at the expense of doctrinal incoherence (i.e., declaring an *in personem* relationship to be *in rem*). In 1995, substantial amendment of the Uniform Commercial Code turned the contractual relationship against a custodian into a property right with purely *in personem* characteristics.[43] The direct relationship of shareholding between issuers and investors was severed, and the intermediary now became a broker not only of trades in shares, but also of share ownership, information flows, corporate announcements to members, and the exercise of voting rights. No legal right between issuers and shareholders exists and few legal questions regarding shares can now be answered without reference to the financial intermediary. After being installed in the U.S., the indirect holding system was then exported through transplanting the important characteristics of the amended UCC Article 8 into a Hague "Convention on the Law Applicable to Certain Rights in Respect of Securities Held with an Intermediary"[44] and, in particular the 2009 UNIDROIT "Convention on Substantive Rules for Intermediated Securities."[45]

This result was far from inevitable. Indirect holding was not the only solution at hand. Congress had instructed the SEC to investigate the paper crunch,[46] and the Commission called the stakeholders together in 1970 to discuss available options.[47] Two competing models of securities settlement were proposed. One was the indirect holding through a central depository. Another was a "Transfer Agent

---

[42] This is the term used by the National Conference Of Commissioners On Uniform State Laws when amending the Uniform Commercial Code to meet the needs of the new settlement system. *See* UCC, Article 8 Prefatory Note, at Sec. 1.C "Evolution of the Indirect Holding System."

[43] UCC § 8–503(b) (2005) ("An entitlement holder's property interest with respect to a particular financial asset under subsection (a) is a pro rata property interest in all interests in that financial asset held by the securities intermediary . . ."). An "entitlement holder" may take action against a third party who has unjustly received the holder's security entitlement only if the securities intermediary holding the account has entered insolvency proceedings, it doesn't have sufficient interests in the relevant asset to satisfy all its outstanding security entitlements because it violated a duty to maintain such amounts, and the transferee of the security entitlement did not give value for or obtain control of the entitlement, or acted in collusion with the securities intermediary, and the trustee or liquidator fails to take action to recover the asset. UCC § 8–503(d), (e) (2005).

[44] Conférence de la Haye de Droit International Privé, Convention on the Law Applicable to Certain Rights in respect of Securities held with an Intermediary (2006).

[45] Institut International pour L'Unification du Droit Privé (UNIDROIT), Convention on Substantive Rules for Intermediated Securities (2009).

[46] The Securities Investor Protection Act of 1970, Pub. L. 91–584, 84 Stat 1636, (1970) codified in 15 USC §78 aaa *et seq.*

[47] See SEC, "Unsafe Practices Study," *supra* note 38, p. 68.

Depository," (TAD),[48] which would have been decentralized, like the then newly introduced National Association of Securities Dealers Automated Quotation (NAS-DAQ) system. The TAD would have linked issuers' transfer agents[49] in a computer network so that transfers of uncertificated (dematerialized) securities could be electronically recorded by book entry.[50] In this model, the "account" on which transfers took place would also have been the "register" in which the securities were originally created by the issuer, so that transfers would have been purely electronic, but the relationship between issuers and their shareholders would have remained unchanged. It would have required only minimal clarification in commercial law, given that there would be no distinction between the claim and the security because the dematerialized claim *was* the security.[51] This model was advocated by transfer agents and corporate secretaries, not exactly a dream team for powerhouse lobbying in Washington. On the other hand, the depository model was advocated by the Banking and Securities Industry Committee (BASIC), which represented the largest U.S. investment banks and broker-dealers, and was chaired by the chairman of Morgan Guaranty (one of the creators of Euroclear, a successful depository-based settlement entity located in Brussels).[52] A prototype of this model was already in operation as the NYSE Central Certificate Service. In its 1971 Report, the SEC explained that most market participants backed the TAD, but were concerned that it could not be implemented quickly and safely, given the state of the law and of technology in 1971.[53] In backing BASIC's proposal, the SEC noted:

> The many points of difficulty in the delivery and transfer process manifestly call for attack on various fronts: the expansion of facilities, the removal of artificial stumbling blocks; the modernization of those processes through the improvement of clearance procedures, the immobilization of the certificate through the advancement of the development of depositories, such as the NYSE Central Certificate Service, the development of machine readable certificates, and, hopefully, the ultimate achievement of a certificateless society.[54]

---

[48] Ibid., p. 180.

[49] See 17 CFR § 240.17Ad.

[50] See SEC, Unsafe Practices Study, *supra* note 38, pp. 191 *et seq.*; Welles, *Last Days*, *supra* note 21, pp. 320 *et seq.*

[51] This is the model the UCC Drafting Committee supported in the 1978 amendments of Article 8, UCC, which would have allowed "changes in ownership ... to be reflected by changes in the records of the issuer." (UCC, Article 8 Prefatory Note, Sec. I.B. "The Uncertificated Securities System Envisioned by the 1978 Amendments.") Uncertificated securities are transferred simply by registering the transfer on the books of the issuer. (UCC § 8–301) Thus the "delivery" of uncertificated securities, which is an essential element of the transfer, takes place either by registering the name of the transferee on the securityholders' list or by a third party declaring to hold the share on behalf of the transferee. (UCC § 8–301(b))

[52] SEC, "Unsafe Practices Study", *supra* note 38, pp. 184 *et seq.*

[53] See SEC, "Unsafe Practices Study", *supra* note 38, pp. 168, 173.

[54] Ibid., pp. 168, 203 ("... the ultimate objectives of the certificateless society and the standardization of documents used in the clearing, settlement and delivery process").

Congress then instructed the SEC to carry this industrial policy into the economy by taking the steps necessary so that the market's securities would be immobilized in a depository.[55] An indirect holding system works best with complete monopoly because then maximum liquidity exists in the accounts held with the central depository, and between 1970 and 1990 this was largely achieved.[56] While the "certificateless society" did on its own arrive in the 1990s because electronic book entries replaced nearly all paper certificates, the financial industry was not about to cede its newfound position of power. As mentioned above, the UCC was amended in 1995, but it had been previously amended in 1978 to accommodate the transfer of uncertificated securities for the favored TAD system. The substantial amendments of 1995 reversed course in order to ensure the robust treatment of claims against the accounts of a financial intermediary in the indirect holding system. When, at the time that these amendments to the UCC were being considered, transfer agents and corporate secretaries launched a "direct registration system" (DRS) to return shareholders to their position as legal, registered owners, brokers argued that the system as designed presented "unreasonable delays" in allowing "shareholders to 'recover' their shares" out of direct registration and transfer them into the broker's accounts for trading purposes.[57] The SEC followed the advice of the broker-dealers in concluding that the proposed, new system should become a function of the depository they owned,[58] and never acknowledged awareness that the brokers might have a conflict of interests in advocating a system insuring their own centrality. In reaching its decision, the SEC merely concluded that bringing DRS into DTC created a "more efficient mechanism."[59] The question that should have been posed

---

[55] As amended, § 17A Exchange Act requires the SEC to "use its authority . . . to end the physical movement of securities certificates in connection with the settlement among brokers and dealers of transactions in securities . . ." (15 U.S.C. § 78q-1(e) (2000)).

[56] When considering BASIC's 1971 argument to make NYSE's Central Certificate Service the core of the U.S. clearing and settlement infrastructure, the SEC explained that in the case of a centralized system based on the immobilization of certificates, "for maximum effectiveness, the depositories would have to encompass close to the maximum number of transactions effected in the marketplace in which it is designed to serve." *See* SEC, "Unsafe Practices Study," *supra* note 38, p. 187. In 1980, the SEC repeated this opinion as a criterion for registering clearing agencies. *See* Regulation of Clearing Agencies, SEC Release No. 16900, (June 17, 1980), published in Vol. 20 SEC Docket p. 434 (July 1, 1980).

[57] SEC Release No. 34-41862, "The Depository Trust Company; Notice of Filing of Amendment and Order Granting Accelerated Approval of a Proposed Rule Change Relating to Implementation of the Profile Modification System Feature of the Direct Registration System," 64 *Federal Register* 51162, 51163 (September 21, 1999).

[58] Ibid.

[59] Ibid., p. 51165. The analysis applied by the SEC in this context also employs an overly narrow measure of market quality that excludes important aspects of how and why the market exists. When assessing securities settlement, regulators ask whether the system at hand allows robust transfer of ownership interests in securities quickly and cheaply. They do not ask whether the means of transfer preserves the exercise of rights in such security by the owner. The history of designing securities settlement structures has shown that the actual content of rights in securities is happily sacrificed for the possibility of transferring the securities in a seamless

is, efficient for *whom?* Today, DRS has become a bridge between two mutually exclusive options among which a shareholder must choose: corporate law rights or liquidity. In the DRS, shareholders can hold uncertificated shares as the registered owner with full shareholder rights in databanks managed by transfer agents for issuers, but in order to be transferred, such shares must then be pulled (upon payment of a fee) into a broker's account where they are reregistered in the name of Cede & Co. so that a claim on a DTC account can be traded.[60] The "direct" side of the DRS offers a sort of safe deposit box for untransferable shares and the side in which the shares are registered in the name of Cede & Co. is the liquid side, connected to the market because registered in the name of a financial intermediary. The immediate relationship between companies and their members has become an irretrievable historical artifact for U.S. listed companies. While the ability of the financial industry to spin straw into gold through immobilization and absorption of DRS presents an admirable feat of lobbying prowess, for issuers and shareholders it has been grim, but this process has a name which the SEC is apparently unable to guess.

The National Market System

The second purpose of the 1975 amendments was then to introduce competition for matching trades in securities, that is, break down the concentration of the regulated securities exchanges, particularly the NYSE. This is the centrifugal force in the program, and has led to the current state of market fragmentation into exchanges, dark pools, and other matching platforms. At the time the legislation was adopted, the NYSE had a longstanding rule in force that no NYSE exchange participant could execute a trade off-exchange.[61] Although a major thrust of the 1975 amendments was to counteract such rule, that is to prevent an exchange from "limit[ing] or condition[ing] the ability of members to effect transactions in securities otherwise than on such exchanges," the SEC also had power to exempt violators from its application.[62] Seligman reports that in early 1978, while the SEC was considering whether to adopt a proposed rule that would prohibit the NYSE's restrictions on broker execution, the composition of the SEC changed through the appointment of new commissioners, and "the NYSE orchestrated a lobbying campaign . . . [with]

---

fashion. The shape of the product is conformed to the means of distribution. I discuss this problem at some length in Donald, "Heart of Darkness," *supra* note 35, pp. 82–86.

[60] SEC Release No. 34-37931, "The Depository Trust Company; Order Granting Accelerated Approval of a Proposed Rule Change Relating to the Procedure to Establish a Direct Registration System," 61 *Federal Register* 58600 (November 15, 1996).

[61] In its most recent form, this was Rule 390, which was finally repealed in 2000. See SEC Release No. 34-42758, "Self-Regulatory Organizations; New York Stock Exchange, Inc.; Order Approving Proposed Change To Rescind Exchange Rule 390," 65 *Federal Register* 30175 (May 10, 2000) ("Rule 390 Release").

[62] 15 U.S.C. § 78k-1(c)(4).

nineteen of the twenty-two largest securities firms" and a number of New York politicians.[63] The SEC then put the proposed rule on hold and instead approved a rule change allowing a number of OTC stocks to qualify for exchange listing, thus allowing member brokers to trade in those shares.[64] Although members of the U.S. House of Representatives strongly criticized the SEC in 1980 for its reversal against the thrust of the legislation,[65] the NYSE was able to keep the restrictive rule in place until 2000.[66] This is why we think of the "national market system" as something that arose with Regulation National Market System in 2005,[67] a regulation that codified, updated and completed the piecemeal provisions issued between 1975 and 2003. Unlike the centripetal forces of central securities settlement, which transferred rents to the financial industry and was immediately adopted in spite of being seen as a second-best solution, the centrifugal forces of competition for matching trades was put on hold for a quarter century. This was not a factor of technological development, as can be understood by the facts that modern data transmission did not lead to the creation of an issuer-friendly TAD system and alternative trading venues do not require technology at all to offer lower fees and better service. These developments do, however, track the interests of the central market participants.

When in 2000, the NYSE did finally allow off-exchange trading by its members, this was not the result of an SEC order instructing that the NYSE abrogate its noncompetition rule. Instead, given that the NYSE was moving toward its desired goal of a public listing, SEC Chairman Arthur Levitt suggested that it would be more appropriate if a public, for-profit company were to open up to off-exchange trading, and the NYSE did later decide to eliminate the rule.[68] Such restrictions would not be necessary for the project that the NYSE was to undertake. During the next five years, the NYSE merged with exchanges and "electronic communication networks" (ECNs) in the U.S. (Archipelago Holdings, Inc., the Pacific Stock Exchange) and with stock and futures exchanges in Europe (Euronext NV) to create an international network of linked trading facilities. Although this strategy may have been in the medium term less successful than hoped (after an unsuccessful attempt to be acquired by Deutsch Börse the NYSE was purchased in 2013 by a company originally set up as an electronic exchange for energy derivatives, Intercontinental Exchange Group Inc),[69] the exchange's compliance with the 1975

---

[63] Seligman, *Transformation, supra* note 39, p. 518.

[64] Ibid., p. 519.

[65] Ibid., p. 520.

[66] SEC, "Rule 390 Release."

[67] SEC Release No. 34–51808, "Regulation NMS," 70 *Federal Register* 37496 (June 29, 2005) ("Reg NMS").

[68] Seligman, *Transformation, supra* note 39, p. 708.

[69] See the Intercontinental Exchange Group Inc Form 10-K for the period ending December 31, 2013, at http://ice.q4cdn.com/223e9074-ded8-480e-b429-aea663b57cd1.pdf (accessed July 15, 2014).

Act tracked what appears to be its own perception of its business needs, not social efficiency as conceived by the U.S. Congress. The most recent business trend has been one of large broker-dealers having less need of exchanges (Archipelago, for example, was first backed by Goldman Sachs and Merrill Lynch[70]), and thus designing financial market infrastructure accordingly. The path of one of the first ECNs, Instinet, is instructive. Instinet was founded in 1969 as a network to serve institutional investors, allowing them to trade NSADAQ listed shares directly with each other,[71] but the company really began to grow in the 1980s when it changed its business model to seek out the business of large broker-dealers on the electronic network, and these institutions were able to have their trades matched on the ECN at spreads well under what retail investors received from NASDAQ market makers.[72] At this time, NASDAQ market makers were setting the spreads they offered to retail investors at artificially high, informally agreed levels.[73] The SEC reacted by requiring full disclosure of spreads on both sides of this two-tiered market, and by reorganizing the regulation of NASDAQ market makers.[74] A private antitrust suit was also filed against JP Morgan, Merrill Lynch and Solomon Smith Barney, among other leading investment banks.[75] This was the period in which the U.S. national market system was maturing, and the opportunities for institutions with the capital to invest in appropriate technology became apparent.

The U.S. securities markets in 2014 can boast trading costs at historical lows and "efficiency" so high that information is impounded into prices before a human trader can even blink his eye, while turnover has increased dramatically. All the traditional metrics of market quality are booming, and all the assessment criteria boxes have been ticked, but this surging flow of orders occurs on hundreds of platforms constituting a market so complex that even institutional investors can feel like mice running in a maze built by the cat. Clark-Joseph, using data from the Chicago Mercantile Exchange shows that HFT can place small, passive orders as bait that yields information on price resilience when triggered by a large trade, and design algorithms to "trade ahead of predictable demand innovations," beating slower traders to execution and reaping the difference between what the market was for the large trade and what it became after the HFT trade got ahead of it.[76] Breckenfelder, using data from the Swedish exchange, finds that HFT traders in competition to get ahead of such demand innovations ("trend chasing") increase

---

[70] Mark Lewis, "Reuters Gambles with Instinet IPO," *Forbes* (April 9, 2001).

[71] See www.instinet.com/history.html (accessed July 15, 2014).

[72] Seligman, *Transformation, supra* note 39, p. 702.

[73] See Seligman, *Transformation, supra* note 39, pp. 698–701; Judge, "Intermediary Influence," pp. 18–19.

[74] Seligman, *Transformation, supra* note 39, pp. 701–703.

[75] Seligman, *Transformation, supra* note 39, p. 701.

[76] Clark-Joseph, "Exploratory Trading," pp. 36–37. Discussed at some length with more examples in Louis, *Flash Boys*, p. 243.

destabilizing short-term volatility.[77] Hoffmann explains how such techniques – given the fact that slow traders likely suffer adverse selection due to HFT strategies – leads to an "arms race" in which brokers are forced to build up their technological arsenal or perish, a socially undesirable outcome.[78] The race for speed has also led to accidents, including a four-minute, 6 percent, drop of the U.S. equity markets,[79] erroneous trades bringing one of the largest institutional brokers to the edge of insolvency,[80] and glitches that can both stop an IPO and affect other stocks with similar names on the NASDAQ Stock Market.[81]

In addition to presenting opportunity for unequal competition between those with and those without large computing power, and placing the infrastructure under unsafe levels of stress (as would pressure in a water main, too much weight on a bridge, or excessive speed on a highway), a complex and fragmented market constitutes moral hazard for entities like investment banks that both trade securities and operate infrastructure. Such entities do not enjoy the supervision and reputational bonding that arises in stock exchanges when all major market participants are either members or shareholders. In 2014, the New York State Attorney General filed fraud charges against Barclays plc and one of its subsidiaries for using a dark pool trading venue to trap unwary institutional traders.[82] The Complaint alleges that, "contrary to Barclays' representations that it implemented special safeguards to protect clients from "aggressive," "predatory," or "toxic" high-frequency traders, Barclays has operated its dark pool to favor high-frequency traders. Barclays has actively sought to attract such traders to its dark pool, and it has given them advantages over others trading in the pool."[83] This straightforward case of moral hazard arises from a conflict of interests and power over an environment that is not transparent to the public. Like many predatory behaviors that the law forbids, it is both dangerous and ordinary, and it can arise because the market has been fragmented into sideshows set up to chase new business opportunities of uncertain value. This affects market quality, and assessments of market quality must take the risks inherent in such structural designs and the behavior they encourage into their assessments.

Algorithmic trading presents a fundamental risk that is rarely raised in assessments of market quality, but that all forms of law requiring licensing aim to

---

[77] Ibid.

[78] Hoffmann, "Fast and slow traders," *supra* note 34, p. 164.

[79] Staffs of the U.S. Commodity Futures Trading Commission and the U.S. Securities and Exchange Commission, "Findings regarding the market events of May 6, 2010," September 30, 2010, available at www.sec.gov/news/studies/2010/marketevents-report.pdf (accessed July 15, 2014).

[80] Michael Mackenzie, Philip Stafford and Arash Massoudi, "Traders urge action after Knight fiasco," *The Financial Times* (August 5, 2012).

[81] Telis Demos, "IPO software behind BATS' failure," *The Financial Times* (March 26, 2012).

[82] Complaint, "The People of the State of New York versus Barclays Capital, Inc and Barclays plc," June 25, 2014.

[83] Ibid., pp. 1–2.

prevent: decisions that affect public safety should be made by a qualified and duly licensed person, not an insentient being or someone incapable of prudent reflection. Computers guided by algorithms make thousands of decisions a second without intelligence or reasoned judgment. This can lead to more than just bad trades. As Zigrand, Cliff, and Hendershott explain, the interaction of automated trading on different markets or among competing traders on the same market and the programming of automated risk management systems can generate a number of "feedback loops" that are able to lead traders in highly undesirable directions, multiplying market instability.[84] Echoing Breckenfelder's findings on trend chasing among HFT, Zigrand et al observe that, "the less diversity that market participants show, the more in unison they act and so the stronger the feedback loops."[85] An algorithm that initiates defensive trades by trader A when security prices fall or when the volume of trades increase could misread liquidity-seeking sales by trader B, and the latter's computers, if similarly programmed, could then misinterpret the trades executed by trader A, which could then trigger more sales, increasing the sales volume and price drop, which information would then trigger trader A's algorithm to execute further defensive trades, and so on. It is true that the damage cause by such feedback loops could be reduced by writing a second trigger into an algorithm so that instructions would be reversed or aborted were some additional exogenous criterion not to be present following one or two rounds of sales, but even if this were effective, the loops would still lead to choppy volatility, which could be used against slower traders caught in the trend. As irrational and dishonest as humans can sometimes be, the removal of human decision-making from the execution of most trades allocating capital within an economy should raise a large, red flag in any assessment of market quality.

MARKET QUALITY FOR SOCIALLY EFFICIENT INFRASTRUCTURE

Major market participants design financial infrastructure in their own favor because they can. First of all, they own nearly all the detailed information on market design, given that scholarship in this area is usually limited to measuring the market quality indicators discussed in Part II. Second, they have a special relationship with regulators because they use the infrastructure most intensely and for this reason are best placed to understand the (mercenary) efficiency issues. Third, given their business ties to the infrastructure, they have the greatest incentive to make their voice heard, and apparently dedicate the funds necessary to do so, such as through participating in consultations or undertaking lobbying. Fourth, it appears that neither regulators nor academics take seriously the moral hazard of

---

[84] Jean-Pierre Zigrand, David Cliff and Terrence Hendershott, "Financial stability and computer based trading," 2001. pp. 13–17. Available at www.bis.gov.uk/assets/bispartners/foresight (accessed July 15, 2014).

[85] Ibid., p. 17.

allowing broker-dealers to design the securities markets they operate for a profit. Fifth, as argued here, the assessment aimed at uncovering flaws in market quality investigates whether the internal operation of the machine is smooth and not overly costly. Regulators do not throw themselves in the admittedly tricky and difficult evaluation as to whether the social function of a financial market – to allocate the capital of investors to the borrowers able to provide the highest return – is met.

Social efficiency should be reintroduced as a measure of good financial infrastructure. Equity markets should be understood as, "a means by which the expertise of the intermediary enables savers to derive the benefits of diversification and liquidity while minimizing the disadvantages resulting from the loss of information and control."[86] Issues of unequal treatment, bias, and incentives should be included as measures of market quality. Dealing with potential moral hazard requires no great innovation. The law presents numerous tools for countering conflicts of interests, actual and potential, through introducing independent members of decision-making bodies, discounting the voice of interested parties, or deliberately amplifying the voice of minority stakeholders. The operation of the financial system greatly depends on its structure, and the design of this structure should not continue to be an occasion for powerful market participants to build in self-enriching business opportunities at the expense of other stakeholders.

---

[86] The Kay Review of UK Equity Markets and Long-Term Decision Making, Final Report, Ref: BIS/12/917, July 2012.

12

Cross-Border Banking: Reconceptualizing Bank Secrecy

Ruth Plato-Shinar

INTRODUCTION

Cross-border banking has become the prevailing reality. This fact is reflected twice over: Many banks operate outside their homeland by opening branches and subsidiaries in foreign countries. At the same time, they provide services in their home countries, not only to local citizens but also to foreign customers.

One of the predominant characteristics of the banking activity, including the cross-border activity, is bank secrecy. However, banking secrecy is not an absolute value. Aside from the bank's obligation to maintain the affairs of its client secret, different legal systems acknowledge exceptions to the doctrine of bank secrecy; Exceptions that require the bank to disclose to third parties information regarding its customers.

Banks that operate in foreign countries are subject to the disclosure obligations that apply in those countries. These obligations may be different from the disclosure obligations that apply in the home country of the bank; and a bank that operates in a foreign jurisdiction must take this into account and organize its business accordingly. This is the territorial subordination to the disclosure obligations of the foreign country, and it is an understandable result of the bank operating in the foreign jurisdiction.

But, in recent years, it appears that even banks that provide services in their native state, may find themselves subject to disclosure obligations of a foreign country, due to the provision of services – in the home country of the bank – to citizens of the foreign country. In other words, the duties of disclosure of the foreign country have extraterritorial applicability even on banks outside their country of origin. This is the extraterritorial subordination to the disclosure obligations of the foreign country.

In recent years, an ever progressive process of erosion of the status of banking secrecy can be noticed, and this is particularly evident with regard to cross-border banking. The list of exceptions under which banks are required to disclose information about their customers is becoming more widespread, and applies to the banks both in their territorial and extraterritorial subordinations to the disclosure obligations of foreign jurisdictions. Banks that are engaged in cross-border activities find themselves subject to an ever growing number of disclosure obligations, a phenomenon that influences not only the right of privacy of the customer, but also that of the bank itself, and in a more comprehensive view – even the global banking system and the international markets.

In this article I will analyze the erosion of the status of bank secrecy against the expansion of cross-border banking, highlighting the difficulties and problems emerging due to the extraterritorial obligations of disclosure.

CROSS-BORDER BANKING

Banking today is a cross-border business: Banks open branches, subsidiaries, and agencies throughout the world and conduct their activities globally.[1] At the same time, their local branches provide services to a growing number of foreign clients.

Cross-border banking is subject to far-reaching controls in an increasingly tightened regulatory environment. Strict compliance with local and foreign provisions is only one of the main issues with which banks must deal with most utmost diligence. Banks with cross-border activity are confronted with a multitude of country-specific regulations, and find it more and more complicated to fulfill their compliance obligations. They have no choice but to establish a holistic cross border framework, in order to minimize the risks that such an international activity bears, including legal and reputational risks.[2]

Banks that operate in foreign countries find themselves subject to a different legal environment than that which prevails in their homeland. Despite the process of globalization and efforts of legal harmonization, the law remains a state matter and therefore can vary, sometimes quite alarmingly, from country to country. This is also true with regard to the rules of banking secrecy: Significant differences in banking secrecy rules, particularly extensive disclosure obligations that do not exist in the country of origin of the bank, may pose considerable difficulties for a bank that wishes to carry out international operations.

---

[1] In this regard see: E. Cerutti, G. Dell'Ariccia, M. S. M. Peria, "How Banks Go Abroad: Branches or Subsidiaries?," 31 *Journal of Banking and Finance* (2007) 1669. Gillian G. H. Garcia, "Sovereignty Versus Soundness: Cross-Border Interstate Banking in the European Union and in the United States: Similarities, Differences and Policy Issues," 27 *Contemporary Economic Policy* 109 (2009).

[2] Roger McCormick "Legal Risk in the Financial Markets," 138 (Oxford University Press, 2006).

Moreover, in recent years, following the global financial crisis that hit many countries, forcing them to look for other sources of income, countries now devote more effort than in the past to the collection of tax from their citizens. They turn to financial institutions in other jurisdictions to divulge unreported bank accounts of their citizens, accusing these financial institutions of assisting in tax evasion.[3] Following this increasing phenomenon, a significant risk in holding the money of foreign residents has developed in the global banking system. If in the past financial institutions did not habitually check whether their foreign clients declared and reported their financial income in their home countries, such behavior may now impose on institutions a serious legal risk, in the form of heavy fines and damage to reputation. The legal and reputational risks[4] associated with cross-border financial services have noticeably increased in recent years to the extent that they could threaten the continued existence of some institutions and also undermine the economies of some countries. The reason for this is not only tighter foreign supervision, but also systematic enforcement of the supervisory rules. The result is a growing challenge for banks and financial institutions in striving to manage the required standards with operating in a highly globalized and competitive environment.[5]

Financial regulators throughout the world have understood the need to address these risks, by obliging the banks to take proper precautions. Hence, for example, the Swiss Financial Regulator (FINMA) has obliged the Swiss banks and financial institutions to analyze and address legal risks for cross-border business that not only arise out of supervisory rules, but also from foreign regulation and legislation. In principle, cross-border banking activities "must be considered in order to identify, measure, assess and manage the risks arising out of them. They include, in particular, tax laws and the associated criminal law. It is particularly important to establish whether and under what circumstances the foreign legal frameworks and the authorities charged with enforcing them view acts or omissions by financial institutions as aiding and abetting tax crimes. This is also relevant even if the activities concerned are solely carried out in Switzerland. No effective risk mitigation can take place without analysing this issue and the related risks to which the institution and its staff are exposed."[6]

Banks are required to conduct a thorough assessment of the legal framework and the risks associated with their cross-border business. Subsequently, suitable measures to mitigate or eliminate risk should be taken. The financial supervisors expect

---

[3]   See chapter D *infra*.

[4]   For the definition and meaning of these terms see McCormick, *supra* note 2, at pp. 95–121.

[5]   FINMA Position Paper on Legal and Reputational Risks in Cross-Border Financial Services, at p. 5 (October 2010), available at www.finma.ch/e/finma/publikationen/Documents/position spapier_rechtsrisiken_e.pdf.

[6]   FINMA: Legal and Reputational Risks in Cross-Border Financial Services, FAQ's, Answer No. 1 (19 June 2012), available at www.finma.ch/e/faq/beaufsichtigte/pages/faq-grenzuebers chreitendes-geschaeft.aspx.

institutions to duly observe foreign supervisory legislation, and to define an appropriate model for each individual target market.[7]

BANK SECRECY

Bank secrecy is one of the most important attributes of the banking industry. Bank secrecy is one of the key obligations imposed on the bank vis-à-vis its customers, by virtue of which the bank is prohibited from disclosing to third parties information relating to its customers. Bank secrecy embodies not only the customer's interest but also the interest of society as a whole, since the right to privacy is one of the basic human rights, in particular when it comes to the financial affairs of the individual.[8]

Despite the incontestable importance of bank secrecy, it is not an absolute principle. Aside from the need to protect the customer's privacy, there are conflicting interests that undermine the legal and moral basis of bank confidentiality; and consequently justify certain exceptions to the rule, under which a bank is obligated to disclose information associated with its customers.

Generally speaking, the exceptions to the principle of bank secrecy can be divided into two groups. One group includes exceptions aimed at preventing crime and maintaining public order. This group includes, inter alia, provisions with regard to the prohibition on money laundering and financing of terror, and to combatting tax evasion. This group of exceptions also contains provisions that provide access to banks records by financial regulators, in order to enable them to carry out their supervisory role. Originally, the exceptions in this group provided access to bank records for domestic authorities only. However, lately, their scope has changed and they now provide access to foreign authorities as well, a subject that will be broadly dealt in the section Bank Secrecy and Disclosure Requirements of Foreign Authorities in this chapter.

The second group of exceptions to the principle of bank secrecy includes provisions aimed at trade and economic development. The need to improve payment ethics, to better assess credit risks, to increase commercial certainty, and to enhance competition in the provision of credit to private and corporate clients, are considered as interests that justify a violation of financial privacy. This group of exceptions includes provisions that enable banking information to reach private bodies, mostly through its disclosure to credit bureaus and rating agencies.

In recent years, the aforementioned exceptions have undergone a gradual process of expansion, which renders bank secrecy subordinate to a growing number of obligations of disclosure by virtue of the law. More and more countries have changed their laws in ways that undermine bank secrecy, and require the banks

---

[7] FINMA Position Paper, *supra* note 5, at p. 3.
[8] Ruth Plato-Shinar, "Bank Secrecy in Israel," 29 *Comparative Law Yearbook of International Business* 269, 269 (2007).

to provide extensive information about their customers. This trend has significantly escalated both in terms of the number of the laws that oblige the disclosure of the information, and in terms of the scope to which the recipients of the information are permitted to make use thereof. Enhanced technologies for using, maintaining and transferring personal electronic data have contributed to the flow of information, thus transforming the banks into an "information industry," and replacing money with "information standards."[9]

BANK SECRECY AND DISCLOSURE REQUIREMENTS OF FOREIGN AUTHORITIES

General Review

Recently, the phenomenon of the weakening of the power of bank secrecy has deepened, not only on the national level, but also – and especially – on the international level. Banks are forced to disclose and transfer information not only to the authorities in their country, but also to foreign authorities. This trend is becoming more vigorous as cross-border banking spreads wider.

Throughout the world, the legislation in relation to crimes of an international character such as money laundering, financing of terror, and organized crime, is rapidly evolving. It requires the acceleration of international cooperation, since these crimes are cross-border and the struggle against them often requires the assistance of law enforcement authorities in other countries. A similar approach is currently developing in the field of taxation and fiscal offenses. Previously, the issue of taxation was perceived as a national affair. The conventional approach was that a state is not permitted to enjoin other states to assist in tax collection from its citizens. Most international conventions that were signed in the past, with the purpose of formalizing international legal assistance regarding financial crimes, excluded the tax topic and did not apply to it. [10]But lately, a significant change in the attitude of the international community can be noticed. Tax crimes, like other financial crimes, are seen as a strategic, political, and economic threat to the interests of both developed and developing countries.[11]Based on this acknowledgment, various countries, mainly the United States, demand other countries to cooperate with them against tax evaders. Such demands create difficulties, especially in countries where tax evasion is not considered as a money laundering offense.

---

[9] Virginia Boyd, "Financial Privacy in the United States and the European Union: A Path to Transatlantic Regulatory Harmonization," 24 Berkeley J. Int'l L. 939, 939 (2006).

[10] Yael Grossman, Roni Belkin, Sally Licht, "Anti-Money Laundering in Theory and Practice," 658–659 (Israel, 2013, in Hebrew).

[11] OECD: Center for Tax Policy and Administration: Tax and Crime, available at www.oecd .org/ctp/crime/abouttaxandcrime.htm.

In general, law enforcement authorities of one state cannot enforce their authority in the territory of another country, without that country's consent. They cannot undertake an investigation, search, or seizure in the territory of another state, unless the latter agreed to that action. Law enforcement agencies seeking to obtain evidence and information in the territory of another state have to work within international conventions and interstate agreements, and are dependent on the cooperation of the local law enforcement authorities in the country where the information is obtainable.

The awareness of the importance of international cooperation between law enforcement agencies in different countries is increasing, but the actual implementation raises many difficulties. Experience shows that requests for legal assistance through formal interstate channels may be both a lengthy and complicated process. Difficulties in carrying out international investigations are due, not only to differences in legislation between the countries, but also to differences in the working methods of their law enforcement agencies and the differences in their priorities. Cooperation within the channel of intelligence is relatively fast. However, the fact that intelligence information is transferred between countries with relative ease, is not enough. The transfer of information is just the beginning of the process: Intelligence information has to be translated into admissible evidence, and this requires investigations, obtaining documents, collection of additional data, and submitting formal requests for international legal assistance. The result of this complicated process is that in many cases it is actually impossible to finish the investigation and bring the offenders to trial.[12]

In order to circumvent these difficulties, the enforcement authorities in different countries began to explore other tactics: to directly approach banks in foreign countries and demand from them information about their clients who are citizens of the applying country. A striking example of this process is the U.S. law, which I shall review in the next subsection.

The American Law

The United States has, in recent years, markedly increased its struggle against American tax evaders who possess financial property outside its borders. For this purpose it has developed unique methods of obtaining evidence from outside its territory; methods that undermine the sovereignty of other countries. Thus, it requires from banks in other countries, to provide information on their clients who are American citizens. In this chapter, I will review several milestones that illustrate the development of this issue.

---

[12] Grossman et al., *supra* note 10, at pp. 660–661.

Court Orders

One of the methods exercised by U.S. authorities to obtain information directly from foreign banks operating outside the U.S., is the use of judicial orders.[13] A good example in this regard is the case of *In re Grand Jury Proceedings versus Bank of Nova Scotia*.[14]

This case dealt with a Canadian bank that had branches in the United States and the Bahamas. A Federal Grand Jury conducting a tax and narcotics investigation against one of the bank's clients, issued a *subpoena* on the bank, calling for the production of certain records related to that client, that were maintained at the bank's branch in the Bahamas. The subpoena was served on the bank's branch in Miami. The bank declined to produce the documents, asserting that compliance with the subpoena without the customer's consent or an order of the Bahamian Courts would violate Bahamian Bank Secrecy Laws, and would expose the bank to prosecution under the Bahamian Bank Secrecy Law. The bank also showed that the American government could obtain an order of judicial assistance from the Supreme Court of the Bahamas allowing disclosure, if the subject of the investigation is a crime under Bahamian Law as well. Nevertheless, the American Court ruled that the bank's failure to comply with the judicial order constituted contempt of court.

In addition, there are also cases where the American courts required American customers of foreign banks to sign a waiver or authorization under the foreign financial privacy law, authorizing disclosure of their account's information;[15] This was done even though the courts in the foreign jurisdiction where the information was located, have ruled that such waivers were not effective under their law.[16]

In addition to orders that require information about a specific customer of the bank who is suspected of committing an offense, in recent years the U.S. authorities increasingly used another type of judicial order – *John Doe Summons*. Under these summons the foreign bank is required to provide "bulk" information about its American customers, enabling the U.S. authorities to go "fishing" for U.S. citizens whose identity was not known to the authorities.[17]

---

[13] The American Restatements details a list of considerations that a U.S. court should take into account in deciding whether to order production of information located abroad. See: Restatement (Third) of the Foreign Relations Law of the United States § 442 (2002).

[14] In re Grand Jury Proceedings versus Bank of Nova Scotia, 691 F. 2d 1384 (11th Cir. 1982), 740 F. 2d 817 (11th Cir 1984), cert denied, 469 US 1106 (1985). See also: Linde v. Arab Bank, PLC, 463 F.Supp.2d 310)E.D.N.Y. 2006), appeal dismissed (Court of Appeals, 2nd Circuit 2013) (tort action of terror victims' families dealing with terror financing). Compare to: First National Bank of Chicago, 699 F. 2d 341(7th Cir. 1983) (refusing to compel disclosure where foreign statute clearly provided that release of the requested information, even with the consent of the customer, would result in criminal punishment under the law).

[15] See for example: United States versus Ghidoni, 732 F2d 814 (11th Cir 1984). Doe v. United States, 487 US 201 (1988).

[16] See for example: Re ABC Ltd [1984] CILR 130 (Grand Court of Cayman Islands).

[17] This kind of summons was used in the UBS affair described later on in this chapter. For further cases in which *John Doe summons* was used see, for example: "U.S. Department of

Qualified Intermediary Program

The idea that foreign banks operating outside the U.S. are expected to cooperate with the U.S. Tax Authorities was already reflected in American legislation in 2000, by the launching of the Qualified Intermediary Program (QIP).[18]

This program was designed to encourage foreign financial institutions to voluntarily cooperate with the American Internal Revenue Service (IRS) by offering them reduced paperwork and reduced disclosure obligations. Under the program, banks and financial institutions, who operate outside the United States, are invited to enter into a Qualified Intermediary (QI) Withholding Agreement with the IRS.

Generally speaking, under the QI Agreement, the financial institution has to detect the financial activity of its clients (domestic and foreign) who hold American securities, given that the profits on these securities are committed on U.S. Income Tax. The financial institution maintains its own records about its customers. However, it is responsible for reporting income to the American authorities, as regards American citizens who agreed to this disclosure. As to both American customers who did not approve the income reporting, and non-American customers, the financial institution is responsible for a 30 percent withholding tax, which is anonymously delivered to the American authorities.

Formally, the aforementioned mechanism of the QI Agreement does not violate the accepted rules of banking secrecy, since it does not oblige disclosure of personal information without the customer's consent. However, at least for U.S. customers, the severe withholding sanction creates heavy pressure that might result in a forced consent to the disclosure, which thereby constitutes a de facto infringement of bank secrecy.

Justice: Court Authorizes Service of John Doe Summons Seeking the Identities of U.S. Taxpayers with Offshore Accounts at Canadian Imperial Bank of Commerce's First Caribbean International Bank," (April 30, 2013), available at www.justice.gov/opa/pr/2013/April/13-tax-488.html. Robert W. Wood, "IRS Issues John Doe Summonses to Citibank, Chase, BoA, Mellon, HSBC-Tax Prosecutions Coming," (November 13, 2013), available at www.forbes.com/sites/robertwood/2013/11/13/irs-issues-john-doe-summonses-to-citibank-chase-boa-mellon-hsbc-tax-prosecutions-coming/. "United States Department of Justice: Court Authorizes IRS to Seek Records from UBS relating to U.S. Taxpayers with Swiss Bank Accounts," (January 28, 2013), available at www.justice.gov/usao/nys/pressreleases/January13/Wegelin SummonsPR.php. See also Laura Szarmach, "Piercing the Veil of Bank Secrecy? Assessing the United States' Settlement in the UBS Case," 43 *Cornell International Law Journal* 409, 417–419 (2010).

[18] 26 U.S.C. §§1441–43; Treas. Reg. §1.1441–1(e)(5); Revenue Procedure 2000–12, 2000–4 I.R.B. 387; available at www.irs.gov/pub/irs-drop/rp-00–12.pdf. See also: IRS: Qualified Intermediaries, available at www.irs.gov/Businesses/Corporations/Qualified-Intermediaries-(QI). "US Senate: Offshore Tax Evasion; The Effort to Collect Unpaid Taxes on Billions on Hidden Offshore Accounts," at pp. 13–17 (February 26, 2014), available at www.hsgac.senate.gov/subcommittees/investigations/hearings/offshore-tax-evasion-the-effort-to-collect-unpaid-taxes-on-billions-in-hidden-offshore-accounts.

The USA PATRIOT Act

Another important piece of legislation that allows U.S. authorities to obtain information from foreign banks operating outside the U.S., is the USA Patriot Act, enacted after the terror attack of September 2001.[19] The primary purpose of the act is to combat against terrorism, and it relates to the prohibition of money laundering and financing terror as well.[20]

The act contains a special due diligent regime for accounts maintained at financial institutions in the United States for foreign customers or foreign banks.[21] In addition, it authorizes the Attorney General or the Secretary of the Treasury, to obtain information from any foreign bank that maintains a correspondent account in the United States for records associated to such accounts, including records outside the United States relating to the deposit of funds into the foreign bank.[22] In this regard, it is worth noting that the USA PATRIOT Act allows government prosecutors to share confidential information that is related to non-U.S. governments, businesses or persons, with any U.S. law enforcement agency for any law enforcement purpose.[23]

The UBS Affair

The UBS affair is a good example to show how U.S. authorities took advantage of American law provisions in order to pressurize a foreign bank that refused to cooperate with them.

In 2007, the IRS launched an investigation into U.S. citizens who held money in UBS in Switzerland. In addition, the bank itself was suspected of actively helping American clients to evade taxes and defraud the U.S. tax authorities. In July 2008 the bank was required, by virtue of a *John Doe Summons*, to provide information on 19,000 of its American clients. In 2009, a historic agreement was reached between the American Justice Department and the bank, under which the bank admitted helping clients avoid paying U.S. tax; agreed to pay the American government a fine of 780 million dollars; and also delivered the names of 250 of its American clients.

However, one day after the bank admitted assisting in tax evasion, the U.S. government filed suit against the bank, requiring it to disclose the names of an additional 52,000 clients. Because the bank argued, inter alia, that the delivery of

---

[19] Uniting and Strengthening America by Providing Appropriate Tools Required to Intercept and Obstruct Terrorism Act of 2001 (USA PATRIOT Act), Pub. L. No. 107–56, 31 USC §§ 5311–5331 (2002).

[20] The USA PATRIOT Act, Title III – International Money Laundering Abatement and Anti-Terrorist Financing Act of 2001.

[21] See in particular §§ 311, 312, 313, 319(b)(2) of the USA PATRIOT Act.

[22] USA PATRIOT Act § 319(b). For critical analysis of this section see: IMF: "The Impact of the USA Patriot Act of 2001 on Non-US Banks," at pp. 12–14 (May 2002), available at www.imf.org/external/np/leg/sem/2002/cdmfl/eng/tompki.pdf.

[23] USA PATRIOT Act § 203. The IMF Report, ibid, at pp. 14–17. See also USA PATRIOT Act § 314.

the requested information would adversely affect the sovereignty of Switzerland, the conflict moved into the interstate level, a process that was supposed to take a long time.[24] However, in view of the bank's concern that the U.S. authorities would restrict its businesses in the United States, in August 2009 the bank agreed to a settlement, under which the bank produced the names of 4,500 additional Americans who held accounts in its branches in Switzerland, in return for a withdrawal of the proceedings.

The UBS affair was only the beginning of the story. In the wake of this affair criminal investigations against fourteen additional Swiss banks were launched, and further investigations were planned against approximately another 300 Swiss banks.[25] In summer 2013, following intense pressure by the U.S. government, a formal agreement between the governments of the USA and Switzerland was signed, which brought an end to the status of Switzerland as a tax haven for U.S. citizens.

Under the agreement, Swiss banks (except those against which a criminal investigation had already been authorized) may request a Non-Prosecution or Non-Target Agreement, and then be immune against criminal proceedings by U.S. authorities.[26] However, in consideration for this amnesty, the banks are required to name their American customers and provide detailed information regarding their accounts, name culpable employees, and specify any offshore promoters they worked with. In addition, the Non-Prosecution Agreement imposes heavy penalties on the banks, ranging from 20 percent to 50 percent of the total sum of their American clients' assets.[27] To these payments one should add administrative and legal costs of dealing with the U.S. authorities, which could run into millions of francs themselves.[28]

The analysis of the UBS affair may prove useful in predicting the outcome of inevitable future disputes over confidential client information between the United States government and other banks and governments around the world.[29] The UBS

---

[24] Bradley J. Bondi, "Don't Tread On Me: Has the United States Government's Quest for Customer Records from UBS Sounded the Death Knell for Swiss Bank Secrecy Laws?," 30 *Northwestern Journal of International Law & Business* 1, 7–13 (2010). Szarmach, *supra* note 17, at pp. 410–412 (2010).

[25] Matthew Allen, "Degrees of Sin" (December 9, 2013), available at www.swissinfo.ch/eng/business/US_tax_deal_could_prove_deadly_for_small_banks.html?cid=37501974.

[26] U.S. Department of Justice: "First Deadline Approaches for Participation in the Program for Non-Prosecution Agreements or Non-Target Letters for Swiss Banks," (December 12, 2013), available at www.justice.gov/opa/pr/2013/December/13-tax-1311.html.

[27] Joint Statement between the U.S. Department of Justice and the Swiss Federal Department of Finance (August 29, 2013), available at www.justice.gov/iso/opa/resources/8592013829164 213235599.pdf.

[28] Matthew Allen, "US Tax Deal Could Prove Deadly for Small Banks," (December 9, 2013), available at www.swissinfo.ch/eng/business/US_tax_deal_could_prove_deadly_for_small_banks.html?cid=37501974. Giles Broom, "Switzerland Urges Banks to Meet U.S. Disclosure Deadline," (December 9, 2013), available at www.bloomberg.com/news/2013–12–09/switzer land-urges-banks-to-meet-u-s-disclosure-deadline.html.

[29] On U.S. investigations against banks in additional countries see: Michael B. Nelson, "More Foreign Banks under U.S. Grand Jury Investigation," (May 8, 2012), available at http://assetprotectionworld.com/more-foreign-banks-under-u-s-grand-jury-investigations.

case is particularly interesting because it referred to a country where bank secrecy was not only a characteristic of the banking and finance segment, but a key element of the local culture as a whole.[30] Nevertheless, the Swiss government and the Swiss banks decided to surrender to American demands. If it happened in Switzerland, there is a strong likelihood that it may happen in other countries as well.

Following the settlement with UBS, the IRS launched an Offshore Voluntary Disclosure Program, allowing Americans to disclose their assets abroad and pay a reduced penalty. This program created a flood of voluntary disclosures. The procedure of the voluntary disclosure obliged American citizens to provide complete and detailed information about all their foreign bank accounts. As a result, the U.S. authorities accumulated prima facie evidence of tax evasion in additional banks, not only in Switzerland but in other offshore jurisdictions as well.[31]

Foreign Account Tax Compliance Act

The American authorities were not satisfied with heavy punishment for past cases. In order to prevent similar incidents in the future, they enacted in 2010 the Foreign Account Tax Compliance Act (FATCA).[32]

The primary focus of FATCA is to identify noncompliance by U.S. taxpayers using offshore accounts. FATCA requires foreign financial institutions (FFI) to disclose information about accounts held by U.S. individuals or companies in which U.S. individuals hold a substantial stake. FFI that refuses to provide this information will face a sanction of 30 percent tax withholding of all U.S. source payments that are due to the FFI or its customers. Foreign banks who wish to have access to U.S. capital markets, have no choice but to cooperate and sign an FFI Agreement with the IRS.[33]

Under the FFI Agreement, the FFI is required to identify its "U.S. accounts" and to report certain information with respect to each of them (including the account balance) on an annual basis directly to the IRS. Any account holder that fails to provide the information required to determine whether the account is a U.S.

---

[30] For elaboration about the Swiss bank secrecy see: Michèle Moser, "Switzerland: New Exceptions to Bank Secrecy Laws Aimed at Money Laundering and Organized Crime," 27 CASE W. RES. J. INT'L L. 321, 324 (1995); Eric M. Victorson "United States v. UBS AG: Has the United States Successfully Cracked the Vault to Swiss Banking Secrecy?," 19 Cardozo J. Int'l & Comp. L. 815, 842 (2011). Swiss law contains strict prohibitions against foreign attempts to obtain confidential Swiss banking information. Article 273 of the Swiss Criminal Code (available in English at www.admin.ch/ch/e/rs/311_0/a273.html) criminalizes as espionage certain disclosure of business secrets to foreign governments under the premise that such disclosure may harm the Swiss economy.

[31] Victorson, ibid, at pp. 822–825.

[32] The FATCA is part of the Hiring Incentives to Restore Employment Act, P.L. 111–147, 124 Star. 71 (2010). It is added in chapter 4 of Subtitle A of the Internal Revenue Code (IRC), and new Sections 1471 through 1474. See the internet site of the IRS: www.irs.gov/Businesses/Corporations/Foreign-Account-Tax-Compliance-Act-(FATCA).

[33] IRC § 1471.

account, or the information required to be reported by the FFI, will be sanctioned by the imposition of a withholding tax of 30 percent. If foreign law prevents the FFI from reporting the required information without a waiver from the account holder, and if the account holder fails to provide such a waiver, the FFI is required to close the account.[34]

The American authorities intend to implement FATCA through the use of various models of intergovernmental agreements (IGAs):

According to Model 1 IGA, the partner jurisdiction agrees to oblige its FFIs to identify U.S. accounts and report specified information about them to the local authorities in the partner jurisdiction. The partner jurisdiction then delivers this information to the IRS.[35] Model 1 comes in a reciprocal version (Model 1A), under which the United States will share counterpart information, and a nonreciprocal version (Model 1B).

According to Model 2 IGA, the partner jurisdiction agrees to direct all the FFIs located in the jurisdiction to register with the IRS and report information concerning U.S. accounts directly to the IRS. Model 2 comes in two versions: Model 2A with no Tax Information Exchange Agreement (TIEA) or Double Tax Convention (DTC) required; and Model 2B for countries with a preexisting TIEA or DTC.[36]

Recently, new opinions were voiced in the U.S. Senate for a stricter approach than that of the FATCA, in order to increase U.S. tax enforcement.[37]

Additional Steps

The U.S. government is not the only one requiring extraterritorial information from foreign banks. Similar steps are taken by other countries such as Germany and the UK, whose tax authorities have launched investigations regarding the property of their citizens, held in banks outside the country.[38] In the absence of appropriate legislation such as FATCA, the authorities in those countries have no power to

---

[34] Ibid. See also: Ian M. Comisky, Matthew D. Lee, "The Foreign Account Tax Compliance Act: An End to Bank Secrecy?," 25 *Journal of Taxation and Regulation of Financial Institutions* 5 (2013). J. R. Harvey "Offshore Accounts: Insider's Summary of FATCA and its potential Future," 57 Villanova Law Rev 471 (2012).

[35] See the internet site of the IRS: www.irs.gov/Businesses/Corporations/FATCA-Governments. U.S. Department of Treasury Resource Center: Foreign Account Tax Compliance Act (FATCA), available at www.treasury.gov/resource-center/tax-policy/treaties/Pages/FATCA .aspx.

[36] Ibid.

[37] United States Senate: Permanent Subcommittee on Investigations: "Offshore Tax Evasion: The Effort to Collect Unpaid Taxes on Billions in Hidden Offshore Accounts," (February 26, 2014), available at www.hsgac.senate.gov/subcommittees/investigations/reports.

[38] Nelson, *supra* note 29. Philipp Wittrock, "The 'Singapore Connection': German Tax Investigators Set Their Sights on UBS," (August 10, 2012), available at www.spiegel.de/international/ germany/german-authorities-investigate-ubs-in-relation-to-tax-evasion-a-849366.html.

oblige the foreign banks to provide information. Therefore, they focus on personal investigations against suspected customers.

However, there are foreign banks (especially those who have already experienced the strict approach of the American authorities by way of investigation or financial sanctions) that voluntarily decided to adopt a strict approach regarding their European customers as well. Although these banks have not been required to do so by the European Tax Authorities, nevertheless, in order to mitigate the legal risks involved, they require their European customers to provide documents proving that the money deposited in the foreign bank was reported to the tax authorities in their homeland.[39]

Recently, the extraterritorial disclosure obligations bear another form: bilateral interstate agreements for the exchange of information in tax matters, in accordance with the standard model developed by the OECD.[40] Under this model, jurisdictions obtain information from their financial institutions and exchange that information with other jurisdictions.[41] The implementation of this model at the national level requires many countries to amend their law in order to enable the authorities to gather the financial information and exchange it with foreign authorities, thus widening the exceptions to the bank secrecy doctrine.

SUMMARY

In the wake of recent developments described in this article, a new era has been conceived for cross-border banking. The bank secrecy doctrine has been diminished, and its role has been replaced by extraterritorial disclosure requirements.

Extraterritorial disclosure can be divided into two main categories. The first category is the subordination of banks to disclosure requirements of a foreign country, and includes the transfer of banking information directly to the authorities of that country. The second category is the subordination of banks to disclosure obligations imposed by their home state, where the banking information is delivered to the local authorities and they, in turn, forward the information to their foreign counterparts.

Recent measures taken by the United States and other countries around the world highlight the process of the erosion of bank secrecy, specifically vis-à-vis governments. Whereas customer information remains relatively confidential in relation to private third parties, the situation is different when the information is sought by governments

---

[39] This is the situation, for example, in Israel, especially as regarding to customers who use the "hold-mail" service. See: Irit Avisar "Banks' Gates are Closing to Tax Evaders," Globes (February 23, 2014, in Hebrew).

[40] OECD: "Standard for Automatic Exchange of Financial Account Information," (February 13, 2014), available at www.oecd.org/ctp/exchange-of-tax-information/automatic-exchange-of-financial-account-information.htm.

[41] OECD: "Automatic Exchange of Information: What it is, How it works, Benefits, What Remains to be Done," (2012), available at www.oecd.org/ctp/exchange-of-tax-information/automaticexchangeofinformationreport.htm.

and official authorities. It is very likely that this trend will continue and become even stronger under the guidance of the OECD and similar bodies, who aim to combat money laundering, financing of terrorism, organized crime, tax evasion, and in the future – possibly other additional offenses as well. If, in the past, cooperation was forced upon governments (such as in the case of Switzerland and the UBS affair), currently the spreading model is of interstate agreements for the reciprocal exchange of information, made voluntarily. If this trend continues, it will not take too long until customer information will be freely delivered to authorities in other jurisdictions with which their homeland maintains cooperative agreements, and bank secrecy vis-a-vis governments may become an historical anachronism.

The end result is a serious infringement of the customer's financial privacy. Even if, in those cases where banks do not provide personal information about a client without his consent, banking secrecy is maintained de jure; nevertheless, the mechanisms used to obtain the client's consent for the disclosure create forced consent and infringement of banking secrecy de facto. This situation is especially severe with respect to accounts that already exist in the system, as opposed to the opening of new accounts, because it unilaterally constitutes a change of the game rules.

This process of tightening cross border disclosure obligations places the banks in a complicated situation as well. Providing information to law enforcement agencies, especially when the information is designated for foreign agencies, may undermine not only the public's confidence in the doctrine of bank secrecy, but also in the banks themselves. In addition, obedience to the new regime of extraterritorial disclosure, and the efforts to mitigate the legal and reputational risks as well as the operational risks that derive from such a regime, generate enormous costs for the banks. For small banks, that may not be able to afford such expenses, this could mean either a merger or liquidation. Furthermore, increased regulation and enforcement, as well as restrictions that banks voluntarily undertake upon themselves, lead to a massive withdrawal of funds by clients, who are unwilling to declare their deposits. The result of such withdrawals, apart from the damage to the bank itself, may be, at the state level – a flourishing of underground organizations offering the public alternative, unreported channels. And at the global level – a flow of funds from reporting countries to havens not covered by international cooperation agreements, thus causing a relocation of deposits to the benefit of the least compliant havens.[42]

In conclusion, the process of the erosion of bank secrecy due to extraterritorial disclosure requirements, and the transformation of the banks into gatekeepers of foreign governments, will have a far-reaching impact, not only on cross-border banking, but also on the global economy as a whole.

---

[42] Niels Johannesen and Gabriel Zucman, "The End of Bank Secrecy? An Evaluation of the G20 Tax Haven Crackdown," 6 *American Economic Journal: Economic Policy* 65 (2014). OECD: "Measuring OECD Responses to Illicit Financial Flows from Developing Countries," (2013), available at www.oecd.org/dac/governance-development/IFFweb.pdf.

13

Liability for Transnational Securities Fraud, *Quo Vadis?*

Amir N. Licht

INTRODUCTION

Globalization of securities markets is not a new phenomenon. Although commentators often invoke recent advances in computer and telecommunication technology in connection with globalized securities markets, these are but facilitating factors in a trend that has been with us for well over a century. As of mid-2014, roughly six percent of some 43,600 firms listed on the world's stock exchanges were foreign.[1] The sheer number of foreign firms and their share among the total number of companies traded on a particular market vary greatly. They are especially high in global and regional financial centers such as New York, London, Hong Kong, and Luxembourg. Inflows of cross-listings signify that firms find their foreign destination market a valuable asset worth the costs, both one-off and ongoing, that this transaction entails. This makes cross-listing a topic of prime importance for policy and lawmakers in both home and host markets of cross-listed firms.

Why firms prefer certain stock exchanges over others when they decide to internationalize their capital market presence has been a vexing question for academics for more than three decades. Even today, this question is anything but settled. Of particular interest in this regard are factors that could be amenable to policy measures, especially legal reforms, because regulators may be able to employ such measures to improve their country's relative position in the global capital market. This chapter focuses on a particular legal institution – namely, civil liability for transnational securities fraud. This institution has attracted much scholarly attention as a pivotal component in the institutional environment that foreign firms may consider valuable. According to the "legal bonding theory," which is discussed later, becoming exposed to such liability consequent to a foreign

[1] Author's calculations based on data from the World Federation of Exchanges available at www.world-exchanges.org. For further details see Part II given later.

listing may be used by corporate insiders as a credible signal for committing to improved corporate governance.[2]

Many believe that the U.S. federal regime of securities fraud liability serves precisely as a credible commitment mechanism of this sort. In support of this view commentators cite a combination of factors, including in particular the U.S. class action mechanism and, until recently, the willingness of American courts to apply this regime expansively in terms of its extraterritorial reach. In 2010, however, the United States Supreme Court significantly curtailed this extraterritorial reach in its landmark decision in *Morrison v. National Australia Bank*.[3] Surprisingly discarding forty years of elaborate jurisprudence on this subject, the court held that only investors who traded on U.S. markets can sue for securities fraud. Regardless of their nationality, investors who traded securities of cross-listed firms in other venues were excluded from getting redress for fraud under the U.S. regime.

This chapter evaluates the state of affairs with regard to liability for transnational securities fraud in the post-*Morrison* era, to find that it is in a state of flux. Indeed, the *Morrison* decision has relatively little to do with this situation beyond helping to expose the severe limitations from which civil liability for securities fraud already suffers. The current U.S. liability regime may be ineffectual in deterring securities fraud and in supporting good corporate governance through legal bonding. In contrast, public enforcement emerges as a potent institution in this regard in various countries around the world, although its effectiveness hinges on informal institutional prerequisites.

THE WORLD OF CROSS-LISTINGS

Trends

Companies can expand their capital market presence in various ways.[4] Cross-listing refers to a transaction in which the firm, on its own initiative, makes its securities available for trading on a foreign market. This could be done with or without raising of new capital, where in the former case the listing is accompanied by an issuance of new securities. In large financial centers such as London and New York, and increasingly in other countries as well, foreign firms can choose from a menu of modes of listing. Each mode of listing may entail different regulatory requirements in terms of disclosure and other corporate governance measures, due either

---

[2] For an excellent survey *see* G. Andrew Karolyi, *Corporate Governance, Agency Problems and International Cross-Listings: A Defense of the Bonding Hypothesis*, 13 EMERGING MARKETS REV. 516 (2012).

[3] 130 S. Ct. 2869.

[4] For an excellent survey *see* G. Andrew Karolyi, *The World of Cross-Listings and Cross-Listings of the World: Challenging Conventional Wisdom*, 10 REV. FIN. 99 (2006); *see also* Thomas O'Connor & Kate Phylaktis, *Cross-Listing Behaviour*, in SURVEY OF INTERNATIONAL FINANCE 248 (H. Kent Baker and Leigh A. Riddick, eds. 2012).

to legal requirements or to the stock exchange's listing rules that are deemed part of the listing agreement. Because securities are often denominated in the firm's home currency, financial intermediaries may facilitate trading in these securities in the host market by establishing a depositary receipt facility, of which the most well-known are American Depositary Receipts (ADRs).[5]

Liberalization of foreign exchange and international capital movements during the early 1980s caused the number of cross-listed firms around the world to swell more than sixfold. According to a study by Fernandes and Giannetti, this number rose from less than 400 in 1980 to some 2,500 in 1997.[6] After 1997 there were between 2,400–2,500 cross-listed firms and as noted earlier, in 2014 a similar number of foreign firms were cross-listed in exchanges followed by the World Federation of Exchanges. Table 1 provides details about the number of domestic and foreign firms in some thirty prominent markets around the world in April 2014.[7] One may note the particularly high share of foreign firms in numerous markets, ranging from the mammoth NYSE on the one hand to the much smaller Irish Stock Exchange on the other hand. Indeed, it is not uncommon to find a high share of cross-listed firms even in relatively small and peripheral exchanges such those in Lima, Santiago, or Oslo.

Recent research shows that trends in cross-listings have been anything but monotonic. In addition to substantial variation in the proportion and the number of firms listed in any foreign exchange, Fernandes and Giannetti's data show an increasing concentration of foreign listings in the top two world exchange countries: the United States and the United Kingdom. Until 1990, UK and U.S. exchanges jointly held less than forty percent of the total number of foreign listings. By the end of 2006, these major international exchanges had increased their market share to approximately sixty percent. Importantly, the number of foreign firms increased relative to the number of domestic companies in the United States and the United Kingdom (as opposed to the remaining stock exchanges in their sample). In 1988, foreign listed firms represented 5.6 percent of the firms listed in the United States and the United Kingdom, whereas in 2006 these firms accounted for more than 17 percent. Equally interestingly, while in 1980 the London Stock

---

[5]   Unless otherwise stated, I will use "cross listing" and "foreign listing" interchangeably. The literature also uses "dual listing" and "multiple listing" as similar, though not identical, terms. With a similar caveat, I will also use "listing" and "trading" interchangeably.

[6]   *See* Nuno Fernandes & Mariassunta Giannetti, *On the Fortunes of Stock Exchanges and Their Reversals: Evidence from Foreign Listings*, 23 J. FIN. INTERMEDIATION 157 (2014).

[7]   The World Federation of Exchanges publishes data on some sixty markets, in which more than 43,000 firms are listed and cross-listed. For presentation in Table 1 I selected markets that may have special importance inter alia as global or regional financial centers, as emerging markets, etc. For the full dataset see World Federation of Exchanges ("WFE") Statistics, available at www.world-exchanges.org/statistics/monthly-reports (last visited June 2, 2014). Note that the WFE's membership is not universal. For example, the London Stock Exchange is not a member such that Table 1 does not cover it.

TABLE 1 *Number of Listed Companies – April 2014*

Exchange	Total	Domestic Cos	Foreign Cos	Share Foreign/ Total
Americas				
BM&FBOVESPA [Brazil]	370	359	11	3%
Lima SE	267	213	54	20%
NASDAQ OMX	2675	2367	308	12%
NYSE Euronext (US)	2393	1870	523	22%
Santiago SE	305	226	79	26%
TMX Group [Canada]	3844	3765	79	2%
Total region	**9,854**	**8,800**	**1,054**	11%
Asia – Pacific				
Australian SE	2043	1940	103	5%
Hong Kong Exchanges	1667	1575	92	6%
Japan Exchange Group – Tokyo	3427	3415	12	0%
Korea Exchange	1808	1793	15	1%
National Stock Exchange India	1690	1689	1	0%
New Zealand Exchange	165	142	23	14%
Singapore Exchange	766	477	289	38%
Taiwan SE Corp.	871	807	64	7%
Total region	**12,437**	**11,838**	**599**	3%
Europe – Africa – Middle East				
BME Spanish Exchanges	3289	3256	33	1%
Deutsche Börse	706	627	79	11%
Euronext	1066	938	128	12%
Irish SE	52	43	9	17%
Johannesburg SE	379	318	61	16%
Luxembourg SE	229	23	206	90%
Moscow Exchange	257	256	1	0%
NASDAQ OMX Nordic Exchange	757	731	26	3%
Oslo Børs	213	168	45	21%
SIX Swiss Exchange	274	237	37	14%
Tel Aviv SE	485	469	16	3%
Wiener Börse	99	80	19	19%
Total region	**7,806**	**7,146**	**660**	7%
Total	**30,097**	**27,784**	**2,313**	5%

Source: World Federation of Exchanges (www.world-exchanges.org/statistics/monthly-reports).

Exchange dominated the market for foreign listings with some 26 percent share, with U.S. exchange following with about 14 percent, these markets changed places and by 2006, U.S. markets had 35 percent of cross-listings whereas London had just below 25 percent. Several European exchanges, that in 1990 had a 7–13 percent share of foreign listings, have lost ground dramatically toward 2006 – a change that the authors relate to differences in corporate governance.

Sarkissian and Schill put the aforementioned trends in yet a more general context.[8] Using an especially broad sample of cross-listing transactions during a fifty-seven-year period of 1950–2006, these authors show that listings cluster in time, forming foreign listing waves. Waves in a host market often reflect waves in a home market with which it shares a particular affiliation. For example, the United Kingdom's popularity in the 1950s as a host market reflected an increase in listings from South Africa, whose firms tended to list in the United Kingdom. Overall, Sarkissian and Schill interpret their evidence as consistent with cross-listing activity being motivated by shocks in market pricing efficiency and economic proximity, but not shocks in the stringency of market institutions. From firms' point of view, cross-listing decisions are largely motivated by economic synergies between countries rather than pricing efficiency or institutional differences between markets. Consistent with a growing number of prior studies, Sarkissian and Schill also observe that cross-listing firms experience temporary valuation gains that fail to prove durable in the long run.[9]

Motivations

The academic literature has advanced a series of theoretical accounts about factors that could motivate cross-listing. These theories have evolved over time. The first theories to appear dealt with financial aspects of cross-listing. Starting in the early 1990s, studies about other business motivations for cross-listing also emerged. It was only toward the late 1990s that theories about governance ("bonding") motivations were first articulated in detail. One should note at the outset that these accounts are not mutually exclusive. In fact, it is quite likely that several motivations are simultaneously at work in any firm's cross-listing decision-making process. The following provides brief references to these theories[10]; bonding theories are further elaborated in the next part.

Financial Gains: Cross-listings were originally thought of as a means for lowering firms' cost of capital – that is, for enabling firms to get more money from investors

---

[8] *See* Sergei Sarkissian & Michael J. Schill, *Cross-Listing Waves*, J. Fin. Quantitative Anal. (forthcoming).

[9] *See also* Juan Carlos Gozzi et al., *Internationalization and the Evolution of Corporate Valuation*, 88 J. Fin. Econ. 607 (2008); Sergei Sarkissian & Michael J. Schill, *Are There Permanent Valuation Gains to Overseas Listing?*, 22 Rev. Fin. Stud. 371 (2009); Sergei Sarkissian & Michael J. Schill, *The Nature of the Foreign Listing Premium: A Cross-Country Examination*, 36 J. Banking & Fin. 2494 (2012).

[10] For detailed descriptions of these theories *see* Amir N. Licht, *Genie in a Bottle? Assessing Managerial Opportunism in International Securities Transactions*, 2000 Colum. Bus. L. Rev. 51 (2000); *see also* Olga Dodd, *Why Do Firms Cross-List Their Shares on Foreign Exchanges? A Review of Cross-Listing Theories and Empirical Evidence*, 5 Rev. Behavioral Fin. 77 (2013); G. Andrew Karolyi, *Why Do Companies List Abroad?: A Survey of the Evidence and Its Managerial Implications*, 7 NYU Salomon Bros. Center 1 (1998).

when they offer their stock to the public. This effect could stem from two related sources – segmentation gains and diversification gains, the former being a more prominent explanation.[11] Segmentation occurs when similar assets in different markets have different prices, barring transaction costs. In this view, the popularity of investing in emerging market stocks largely lies in potential segmentation gains. Such markets may exhibit barriers to foreign investment due to regulatory limits on foreign holdings in domestic corporations, informational barriers, and so forth. In the past, foreign exchange restrictions may have also engendered capital market segmentation but these barriers have been largely dismantled by end of the millennium. Additionally, cross-listing brings foreign stocks closer to investors, and offers several other straightforward advantages that stem from lower transaction costs.

Liquidity: Cross-listing may contribute to share value by increasing stock liquidity, for example, thanks to increased trading hours and trading venues. Expected returns positively correlate with liquidity, measured in terms of the bid-ask spread. Narrower spreads following cross-listing generate improved liquidity, which increases share value.[12] Enhanced inter-market competition might lower the spread and therefore improve liquidity, but multimarket trading might also decrease liquidity by fragmenting order flows among the markets. Management surveys indicate the importance of the liquidity motivation,[13] but the net result depends on the circumstances of each security.[14]

Shareholder base: By cross-listing its stocks, a firm could expand its potential investor base more easily than if it traded on a single market. As cross-listing brings foreign securities closer to potential investors, it increases investor awareness of the securities. This familiarity could lower expected returns.[15] In business management terminology this aspect is referred to as "firm visibility" – a broad notion encompassing frequent mentioning of the firm in the financial press and closer monitoring of its securities by securities analysts.

---

[11] *See*, for example, René M. Stulz, *Globalization of Corporate Finance and the Cost of Capital*, 8 J. APPLIED CORP. FIN. 30 (1999); Gordon J. Alexander et al., *Asset Pricing and Dual Listing on Foreign Capital Markets: A Note*, 42 J. FIN. 151 (1987); Robert C. Stapleton & Marti G. Subrahmaniam, *Market Imperfections, Capital Market Equilibrium and Corporation Finance*, 32 J. FIN. 307 (1977).

[12] *See* Yakov Amihud & Haim Mendelson, *Asset Pricing and the Bid-Ask Spread*, 17 J. Fin. Econ. 223 (1986); Yakov Amihud & Haim Mendelson, *Liquidity and Asset Prices: Financial Management Implications*, 17 Fin. Mgmt. 5 (1988).

[13] *See* Franck Bancel & Usha R. Mittoo, *European Managerial Perceptions of the Net Benefits of Foreign Stock Listings*, 7 EUR. FIN. MGMT. 213 (2001); Franck Bancel & Usha R. Mittoo, *Why do European firms go public?*, 15 EUR. FIN. MGMT. 844 (2009).

[14] *See* K.C. Chan et al., *Information, Trading and Stock Returns: Lessons from Dually-Listed Securities*, 20 J. Bank. & Fin. 1161 (1996).

[15] *See* Robert C. Merton, *A Simple Model of Capital Market Equilibrium with Incomplete Information*, 42 J. FIN. 483 (1987).

Visibility: The putative benefits of increased visibility in the host country go well beyond the expected increase in shareholder base. In addition to greater demand for its stock, listing abroad provides a firm with greater access to foreign money markets and makes it easier to sell debt there. A firm becomes more credible by providing information to the local capital market, and, in turn, this continuous flow of information allows the capital market to make faster, more accurate decisions.[16] The latter aspect substantially overlaps with the "reputational bonding" theory advanced by Siegel and discussed further in the following section.[17]

Marketing motivations: Using cross-listings for marketing reasons relates to the visibility rationale. According to this reasoning, foreign listing can boost corporate marketing efforts by broadening product identification among investors and consumers in the host country. The listing, it is claimed, creates greater market demand for the firm's products as well as its securities.[18]

Technical issues: Effecting a securities transaction abroad is still more complicated and expensive than effecting it domestically. Cross-listing can improve a firm's ability to effect structural transactions abroad such as foreign mergers and acquisitions, stock swaps, and tender offers.[19] Relatedly, cross-listing also facilitates and enhances the attractiveness of employee stock ownership plans (ESOPs) for employees of large multinational corporations. Local listing in the foreign market provides foreign employees with an accessible exit mechanism for their stocks.

Corporate governance (bonding). Cross-listing on a foreign market signifies an entry into the host country's capital market. The latter market operates in a different institutional environment than that of the firm's home county. Institutional differences may include different financial institutions, different informational intermediaries (such as analysts and rating agencies), different market norms, and, importantly, a different legal environment. A cross-listing brings the firm under the jurisdiction of that market's capital market regulators. Any or all of such institutional differences may induce an improvement in the firm's corporate governance. In a proactive version of this account, firms may cross-list in higher-corporate-governance market with a view to self-improve on this front and thus lower their cost of capital.[20]

---

[16] See, for example, Edward B. Rock, *Greenhorns, Yankees, and Cosmopolitans: Venture Capital, IPOs, Foreign Firms, and U.S. Markets*, 2 Theor Inq L 711 (2001).

[17] *See* Jordan Siegel, *Can Foreign Firms Bond Themselves Effectively by Renting U.S. Securities Laws?*, 75 J. Fin. Econ. 319 (2005).

[18] *See* H. Kent Baker, *Why U.S. Companies List on the London, Frankfurt, and Tokyo Stock Exchanges*, 6 J. Int'l Sec. Markets 219 (1992).

[19] *See* G. Andrew Karolyi, *DaimlerChrysler AG, the First Truly Global Share*, 9 J. Corp. Fin. 409 (2003).

[20] *See* Rene M. Stulz, *Globalization of Corporate Finance and the Cost of Capital*, 8 J. Applied Corp. Fin. 30 (1999); John E. Coffee, Jr., *The Future as History: The Prospect for Global Convergence in Corporate Governance and Its Implications*, 93 Nw. U. L. Rev. 641 (1999).

BONDING, LEGAL BONDING

Within the multitude of theories about likely motivations for cross-listing, the bonding theory has become the dominant account and engendered substantial literature, especially in its version that focuses on legal improvements. The notion that issuers may want to improve their corporate governance by subjecting themselves to a better corporate governance regime through cross-listing – say, on an American market – is appealingly elegant. However, it should be handled with care. This part first contextualizes the legal bonding theory in a broader analytical framework. Next, it elaborates the legal complexity entailed by cross-listing, focusing on disclosure issues. Finally, this part briefly discusses some recent evidence.

Institutions, Frontiers, and Bonding

A research tradition inspired by North and others has established the importance of institutions for economic development.[21] Assuring that one's property is secured from opportunistic abuse provides incentives for investment and for complex trade. Establishing credible commitment mechanisms thus is a central challenge for economic agents, be they political potentates or corporate insiders.[22] A legal system that is well-designed in terms of the rules it promulgates to protect investors and is well-functioning in terms of actually enforcing investor protection rights may provide actors with means for making such commitment.[23] In the absence of such an institutional environment, good-type agents with good projects may find it difficult to distinguish themselves from the opportunistic crowd. Unless, however, they can find an institutional substitute. Legal bonding may provide such a substitute.

The issue may be theorized within the conceptual framework advanced by Djankov, Glaeser, La Porta, Lopez-de-Silanes, and Shleifer.[24] According to these

[21] *See*, for example, DOUGLASS NORTH, INSTITUTIONS, INSTITUTIONAL CHANGE, AND ECONOMIC PERFORMANCE (1990).

[22] *See*, respectively, Douglass C. North & Barry R. Weingast, *Constitutions and Commitment: The Evolution of Institutional Governing Public Choice in Seventeenth-Century England*, 49 J. ECON. HIST. 803 (1989); OLIVER WILLIAMSON, THE ECONOMIC INSTITUTIONS OF CAPITALISM (1985); OLIVER WILLIAMSON, THE MECHANISMS OF GOVERNANCE (1996). On commitment mechanisms in general, *see* Kenneth A. Shepsle, *Discretion, Institutions, and the Problem of Government Commitment*, in SOCIAL THEORY FOR A CHANGING SOCIETY 245 (Pierre Bourdieu & James S. Coleman eds., 1991). On institutional commitment mechanisms in international investment, *see* Witold J. Henisz, *The Institutional Environment for Multinational Investment*, 16 J.L. ECON. & ORG. 334 (2000); Witold J. Henisz & Oliver E. Williamson, *Comparative Economic Organization – Within and Between Countries*, 1 BUS. & POL. 261 (1999).

[23] *See* Simon Johnson et al., *Tunnelling*, 90 AM. ECON. REV. 22 (2000); for a summary *see* Rafael La Porta, Florencio Lopez-de-Silanes & Andrei Shleifer, *The Economic Consequences of Legal Origins*, 46 J. ECON. LIT. 285 (2008).

[24] *See* Simeon Djankov et al., *The New Comparative Economics*, 31 J. COMP. ECON. 595 (2003); *see* also Bruno Dallago, *Comparative Economic Systems and the New Comparative Economics*, 1

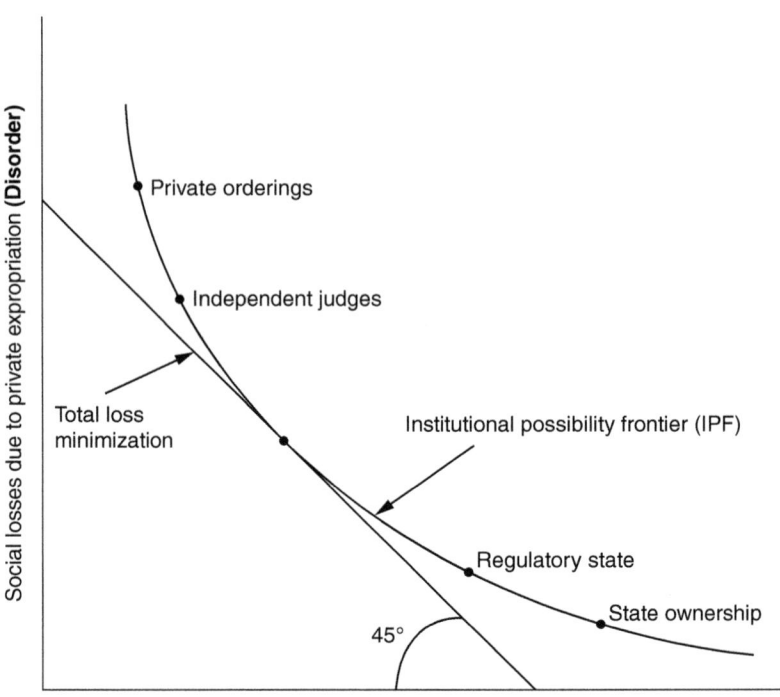

FIGURE 1 Institutional Possibilities
Source: Simeon Djankow, Edward Glaeser, Rafael La Porta, Florencio Lopez-de-Silanes,
& Andrei Shleifer, *The New Comparative Economics*, 31 J. COMP. ECON. 595, 599 (2003).

authors, institutions function to control the twin dangers of dictatorship and disorder that every society faces when it strives to secure property rights, broadly defined to include a wide range of entitlements. In this setting, countries are located on different points on an institutional possibility frontier. Each point on the frontier represents a combination of institutional strategies for dealing with social power (dictatorship) and disorder, including private orderings, private litigation, and regulation.

Figure 1 graphically depicts the notion of institutional possibilities. On the x-axis, the social losses from dictatorship, as opposed to the gross amounts of such activities as taxation and government expropriation, are measured relative to a world with perfect property rights. On the y-axis, the social losses from disorder are measured relative to a perfect property rights benchmark.[25] The authors provide a pertinent illustration for the present discussion:

[25] Djankov et al., *supra* note 24, at 599.

To illustrate these categories, take the example of social control of securities issues. Suppose that society wants to have broad and liquid securities markets and, to this end, deems it desirable that firms issuing equity disclose accurate information about their circumstances. This society has four basic institutional strategies for the enforcement of good conduct. First, the market discipline solution relies on the incentives of issuers themselves, or of their underwriters, to disclose the truth about the securities because they need to establish a reputation for credibility to raise funds in the future. Second, the society can rely on private suits by buyers of securities who feel that they have been cheated by the issuers, under the general doctrines of contract or tort. For this, the society needs a court and a judge. The question for the court is whether the issuer disclosed inaccurate information or failed to disclose material information. Third, the society can designate a public regulatory agency, which mandates what should be disclosed by security issuers, inspects their books and disclosures, and penalizes issuers and underwriters who break its rules. Between private litigation and full-scale regulation, the regulator can establish the rules for security issuance, but leave the enforcement of these rules to private litigation by the wronged investors. Fourth, the society can nationalize security issuance. A company wishing to raise capital must relinquish the inspection, disclosure, and sale of securities to the state.[26]

Since any institutional possibility frontier entails an inevitable trade-off between institutional approaches, societies may wish to overcome this trade-off by shifting their frontiers toward the origin point. Djankov et al., for instance, argue that common law countries tend to be located on a frontier that is closer to the origin in comparison to civil law countries – a feature that (according to the authors) represents general superiority of the former over the latter.[27] However, exogenous factors such as historical heritage, physical endowments, and culture may hinder a country from pushing its frontier or even from moving too far along the frontier, because any point on it may constitute an equilibrium.

Against this backdrop, individual actors may wish to escape their home country's institutional possibility frontier and exploit another country's better frontier. Subjecting oneself to the other country's laws is one way to achieve this. What is not feasible for an entire society may be for individuals and firms who can migrate to another country's institutional environment. Specifically, by cross-listing on a better-regulated market firms can legally bond themselves and their insiders to better corporate governance as they become subject to a better legal regime, as

---

[26] Djankov et al., *supra* note 24, at 601.

[27] Djankov et al., *supra* note 24, at 605. Although, as noted, the framework advanced by Djankov et al. relates to these authors' work on legal origins, the issues are conceptually distinct such that (fortunately), we can abstract here from the scholarly controversy over the institutional role and impact of legal origins. *See* Edward Glaeser & Andrei Shleifer, *Legal Origins*, 117 Q. J. Econ. 1193 (2002); *compare*, for example, Nuno Garoupa & Carlos Gómez Ligüerre, *The Syndrome of the Efficiency of the Common Law*, 29 B.U. Int'l L.J. 287 (2011); Daniel M. Klerman et al., *Legal Origin or Colonial History?*, 3 J. Legal Analysis 379 (2011).

Stulz and Coffee have argued.[28] Civil liability based on class action litigation plays a key role in this account in ensuring that the foreign entrants in fact comply with the legal rules of the host market.[29] Coffee thus claimed:

> All that is necessary for the [legal] bonding hypothesis to have validity is that the defendant's perceived risk of liability rises at least marginally with its entry into the U.S. markets... If, as a result, the controlling persons of the foreign issuer provide superior disclosure or consume less private benefits of control... then the value of the public shares in such companies should logically rise (and it does).[30]

While theoretically sound, the legal bonding hypothesis coincides with additional, equally plausible theories on the factors that may motivate firms' cross-listing decisions. Siegel has advanced a theory and supporting empirical findings on "reputational bonding," showing that cross-listed firms may invest in reputational assets in lieu of weakly enforced laws.[31] In this theory, reputational intermediaries such as analysts, investment bankers, and institutional shareholders screen the foreign issuer's compliance with legal rules and additional market norms, especially with regard to full and timely disclosure. This bonding theory expands on the general theory of reputation as a credible commitment device.[32]

I have criticized the legal analysis underlying several elements of the early version of the bonding hypothesis, which leave liability for securities fraud as the only plausible basis for legal bonding.[33] Liability due to public enforcement by the Securities and Exchange Commission (SEC), however, has not been a primary source of threat in light of an ostensibly lenient, "hands-off" approach toward foreign issuers.[34] This renders public enforcement a noncredible basis for legal

---

[28] See Stulz, *supra* note 20; Coffee, *supra* note 20. The image of Ulysses tying himself to the ship's mast so as not to heed the Sirens' call immediately comes to mind. Jensen and Meckling formalized this notion in their agency theory, in which agents may want to incur bonding costs in order to facilitate contracting at the shadow of opportunism. *See* Michael C. Jensen & William H. Meckling, *Theory of the Firm: Managerial Behavior, Agency Costs and Ownership Structure*, 3 J. FIN. ECON. 305 (1976).

[29] *See* Rafael La Porta, Florencio Lopez-de-Silanes & Andrei Shleifer, *What Works in Securities Laws?*, 61 J. FIN. 1 (2006).

[30] John C. Coffee, Jr., *Racing Towards The Top?: The Impact of Cross-Listing and Stock Market Competition on International Corporate Governance*, 102 COLUM. L. REV. 1757, 1796 (2002).

[31] *See* Siegel, *supra* note 17.

[32] *See* Douglas W. Diamond, *Monitoring and Reputation: The Choice between Bank Loans and Directly Placed Debt*, 99 J. POL. ECON. 689 (1989); Douglas W. Diamond, *Reputation Acquisition in Debt Markets*, 97 J. POL. ECON. 828 (1989); Benjamin Klein & Keith B. Leffler, *The Role of Market Forces in Assuring Contractual Performance*, 89 J. POL. ECON. 615 (1981); for a survey *see* Jonathan M. Karpoff, *Does Reputation Work to Discipline Corporate Misconduct?* In THE OXFORD UNIVERSITY HANDBOOK OF CORPORATE REPUTATION 361 (Michael L. Barnett & Timothy G. Pollock eds. 2012).

[33] *See* Amir N. Licht, *Cross-Listing and Corporate Governance: Bonding or Avoiding?*, 4 CHI. J. INT'L L. 141 (2003).

[34] *See* Licht, *supra* note 33; Natalya Shnitser, *A Free Pass for Foreign Firms? An Assessment of SEC and Private Enforcement Against Foreign Issuers*, 119 YALE L.J. 1638 (2010); *compare*

bonding and would thus narrow the basis of liability-based legal bonding to civil liability. More importantly, I have also emphasized that any form of regulation that would support legal bonding arguably to attract foreign issuers to U.S. markets is also likely to exert an opposite, deterrent effect. This is because corporate insiders who stand to benefit from noncompliance would rather avoid more stringent regulation – hence, the "avoiding hypothesis." The upshot of what is discussed earlier is that in addition to the several different motivations for cross-listing even bonding-motivated cross-listing is susceptible to the effect of several, sometimes conflicting, factors. Stulz thus acknowledges that "some firms will choose stronger securities laws than those of the country in which they are located and some firms will do the opposite."[35]

Complex Legal Regimes

Before moving to the empirical assessment the legal bonding theory, this section takes another look at the complexity of the legal regime that firms become subject to consequent to a foreign listing. The key insight is that cross-listing firms may be able to exceed their home country institutional possibility frontier but they cannot leave it entirely behind them. The level of impact exerted by each legal system varies across different issue areas.[36] Certain topics may effectively be influenced by one legal system, while others may be influenced by both systems, to a different degree by each. This relative level of influence varies with the extent to which an issue area is company oriented or rather transaction oriented (trading oriented).

Consider a security that is cross-listed on two markets in two jurisdictions. In such a scenario, two potential sources of law affect the security and all the stakeholders related to it: the legal regime of the domestic (home) market and the regime of the foreign (host) market. As a general matter, the domestic market will be the country where the company is incorporated and headquartered. In most cases it is also where the lion's share of trading takes place.

Traditionally, the location of an issue area along the second dimension would depend on the extent to which the issue is classified as relating to either "company law" or "securities regulation." The more a certain subject could be classified as a "company law" issue, the more it would be governed by a single legal regime, usually the home market. On the other hand, the more an issue could be classified as a "securities regulation" one, the more likely it is that both systems would have a

Coffee, *supra* note 30, at 1794–95; Roger Nelson Silvers, *The Valuation Impact of SEC Enforcement Actions on Non-Target Foreign Firms*, Working Paper (2012); *see* also Jordan I. Siegel & Yanbo Wang, *Cross-Border Reverse Mergers: Causes and Consequences*, Harvard Business School Strategy Unit Working Paper No. 12–089 (2013).

[35] Rene M. Stulz, *Securities Laws, Disclosure, and National Capital Markets in the Age of Financial Globalization*, 47 J. Acct. Res. 347, 349 (2009).

[36] The following draws on Amir N. Licht, *Regulatory Arbitrage for Real: International Securities Regulation in a World of Interacting Securities Markets*, 38 Va. J. Int'l L. 563 (1998).

claim to regulate it. The distinction between "company law" and "securities regulation" has never been clear-cut.[37] However, during the last decade this distinction had become even fuzzier as host markets began to intervene in corporate governance issues that used to be the realm of the home country – for instance, with regard to board composition in terms of the share of independent directors.

A graphic presentation may be useful for illustrating the abstract argument. Consider a two-dimensional space where one dimension stands for the issue area. An issue may be entirely company related – for example, the definition of the bundle of rights attached to the security or the structure and operation of company institutions such as the board of directors, committees, etc. Alternatively, an issue area may be entirely transaction related such as rules concerning insider trading. Finally, it could be a combination of both aspects. The second dimension represents the level of influence by each of the two potentially applicable legal systems. Legal impact may stem solely from one system, or from the other, or be a combination of both.

Figure 2 depicts this model. The x-axis represents the sources of law. An issue area governed solely by domestic law would lie on the left-hand side of the space; vice versa for issues regulated entirely by the host country. If both the domestic and foreign legal systems claim an interest in regulating the issue it would lie in some midpoint along this axis. The y-axis represents the nature of the issue. A purely issuer-oriented subject would lie at the top area of the space; purely transaction-oriented issues would lie along the bottom. Mixed issues would lie in the midrange.

To get a feeling about the working of this presentation model, consider the core of company law. As noted earlier, by convention this issue is generally governed by the issuer's home country (domestic) law. Therefore, it is located in the upper left corner of the square as depicted by box no. 1. Next, consider disclosure duties owed by the company and its insiders with regard to a non-U.S. firm that is cross-listed in the United States. The scope of U.S.-mandated disclosure varies according to the type of cross-listing (so called "levels"), such that box no. 2, which represents this issue, may be located on nearly any point along the x-axis. Finally, consider insider trading. This is a purely transaction-related issue, so it lies along the bottom of the square. Since insider trading can take place in any of the markets where the stock trades, each country is expected to prescribe some laws with regard to it. To be sure, the particular manner of regulation may vary from strict prohibition coupled with severe sanctions to open tolerance of the conduct, but some policy is likely to exist in both countries. Box no. 4 is thus depicted in the middle of the bottom side of the space.[38]

---

[37] For a discussion of this distinction *see* Amir N. Licht, *International Diversity in Securities Regulation: Roadblocks on the Way to Convergence*, 20 CARDOZO L. REV. 227 (1998).

[38] For brevity, other points depicted in Figure 2 are not elaborated on. *See* Licht, *supra* note 36.

Legend
1 - Company law (corporate governance)
2 - Disclosure
3 - Takeover regulation

FIGURE 2 Sources of Law Affecting Cross-Listed Firms
Based on Amir N. Licht, *Regulatory Arbitrage for Real: International Securities Regulation in a World of Interacting Securities Markets*, 38 VA. J. INT'L L. 563, 620 (1998).

The Evidence

Substantial evidence suggests that a U.S. cross-listing could be beneficial, especially for firms from emerging economies.[39] Evidence directly in support of legal bonding is limited, however. The empirical challenge of identifying causality is considerable. One has to show that it is the legal system that "makes the bonding stick" – both by setting better rules *and* by inducing compliance with these rules. The former element may be difficult to show but is at least observable: one could

[39] *See* Karolyi, *supra* note 2 for a detailed survey of this evidence. *See*, in particular, Ugur Lel & Darius P. Miller, *International Cross-listing, Firm Performance and Top Management Turnover: A Test of the Bonding Hypothesis*, 63 J. FIN. 1897 (2008) (top management turnover); Michael R. King & Dan Segal, *The Long-Term Effects of Cross-Listing, Investor Recognition, and Ownership Structure on Valuation*, 22 REV. FIN. STUD. 2293 (2009) (investor recognition); Luzi Hail & Christian Leuz, *Cost of Capital Effects and Changes in Growth Expectations around U.S. Cross-Listings*, 93 J. FIN. ECON. 428 (2009) (cost of capital); Laurent Frésard & Carolina Salva, *The Value of Excess Cash and Corporate Governance: Evidence from U.S. Cross-Listings*, 98 J. FIN. ECON. 359 (2010) (value of excess cash); Ryan T. Ball, Luzi Hai, & Florin P. Vasvari, *Equity Cross-Listings in the U.S. and the Price of Debt*, Working Paper (2013) (price of debt).

compare the laws of two countries and try to rank them. This is no small feat in its own right and scholarly debates rage over such rankings.[40] The latter element, of the compliance mechanism, is even more elusive. Legal bonding implies that compliance obtains because of the legal system – due to deterrence – as opposed to voluntary compliance. A good deal of the literature assumes, but does not show, that beneficial effects associated with a U.S. cross-listing can be attributed to legal bonding. In tandem, there is substantial evidence for the reputational bonding and the avoiding hypotheses. This section briefly points to the evidence.

Firstly, the multiplicity of possible financial or strategic motivations for cross-listing described earlier may lead to identification problems due to endogeneity beyond any corporate governance factors.[41] Evidence for the avoiding hypothesis has been accumulating recently.[42] The main challenge, however, concerns the need to disentangle legal bonding from reputational bonding. Some studies ignore this distinction and refer simply to "bonding."[43] Several other studies cite both legal and reputational bonding and assume that both play a causal role in engendering the observed beneficial effect.[44] Yet other studies find direct evidence consistent with reputational bonding irrespective of legal bonding.[45]

A handful of studies tackle the empirical challenge systematically. Doidge, Karolyi, Lins, Miller, and Stulz argue that "direct U.S. securities laws and

[40] For a brief discussion in the cross-listing context *see* Licht, *supra* note 33. *See*, generally, Holger Spamann, The "Antidirector Rights Index" Revisited, 23 REV. FIN. STUD. 467 (2010); *see also* Priya P. Lele & Mathias M. Siems, *Shareholder Protection: A Leximetric Approach*, 7 J. CORP. L. STUD. 17 (2007); Mathias M. Siems, *Shareholder Protection Around the World (Leximetric II)*, 33 DEL. J. CORP. L. 111 (2008); John Armour et al., *How Do Legal Rules Evolve? Evidence From a Cross-Country Comparison of Shareholder, Creditor, and Worker Protection*, 57 AM. J. COMP. L. 579 (2009).

[41] *See* Karolyi, *supra* note 2; Hail & Leutz, *supra* note 39.

[42] *See* Craig Doidge et al., *Private Benefits of Control, Ownership, and the Cross-listing Decision*, 64 J. FIN. 425 (2009); Craig Doidge, Andrew Karolyi & Rene M. Stulz, *Why Do Foreign Firms Leave U.S. Equity Markets?*, 65 J. FIN. 1507 (2010); Ole-Kristian Hope, Tony Kang & Yoonseok Zang, *Bonding to the Improved Disclosure Environment in the US: Firms' Listing Choices and their Capital Market Consequences*, 3 J. CONTEMP. ACCT. ECON. 1 (2007).

[43] *See*, for example, Franck Bancel, Madhu Kalimipalli & Usha R. Mittoo, *Cross Listing and Long Term Performance of ADRs: Revisiting European Evidence*, 19 J. INT'L FIN. MKTS INSTITUTIONS & MONEY 895 (2009); Michael Melvin & Magali Valero, *The Dark Side of International Cross-Listing: Effects on Rival Firms at Home*, 15 EUR. FIN. MGMT. 66 (2009).

[44] *See* Arturo Bris et al., *A Breakdown of the Valuation Effects of International Cross-Listing*, 13 EUR. FIN. MGMT. 498 (2007); Craig Doidge et al., *Why Are Foreign Firms Listed in the U.S. Worth More?*, 71 J. FIN. ECON. 205 (2004); Ball et al., *supra* note 39; Hail & Leutz, *supra* note 39; Lel & Miller, *supra* note 39.

[45] *See* Frésard & Salva, *supra* note 39; Steven Crawford, *The Role of Market Forces and Legal Institutions in Bonding Cross-Listed Firms*, Working Paper, Rice University (2009); John Ammer et al., "Why Do U.S. Cross-Listings Matter?," Board of Governors of the Federal Reserve System, International Finance Discussion Paper 930 (2008); *see also* Natasha Burns et al., *Cross-Listing and Legal Bonding: Evidence from Mergers and Acquisitions*, 31 J. BANKING FIN. 1003 (2007); King & Segal, *supra* note 39; Kate Litvak, *The Relationship among US Securities Laws, Cross-listing Premia and Trading Volumes*, Working Paper (2009).

enforcement are more important constraints in the extraction of private benefits than is the scrutiny of financial analysts."[46] These authors find that analyst coverage increases invariably for all types (so-called "levels") of foreign listings, regardless of the firm's involvement in the U.S. capital market, suggesting that such coverage does not explain cross-listing benefits. Two parallel studies exploit a legal reform that made it easier for cross-listed firms to delist and deregister from the American market.[47] Their findings suggest that the market reacted more negatively to this reform with regard to firms from countries with weak disclosure and governance regimes. While the listing mechanism is legally based and may be instrumental for long-term bonding, it still leaves open the question which mechanism may induce compliance – whether it is legal deterrence or reputational motivations. In an illuminating review of the legal bonding theory circa 2012, Karolyi thus tentatively observes: "A proper verdict about the bonding hypothesis, especially of its purer 'legal' form, has not yet been fully rendered. I think a more complete understanding of the enforcement mechanisms around the world, their financial needs as inputs and the full scope of legal outcomes is still needed."[48]

To foreshadow the next section, the U.S. Supreme Court's decision in *Morrison* provided an opportunity to address the legal bonding theory. In a joint study with Siegel, Poliquin, and Li, we examined the reactions of market participants to this case, which denied the right to sue for securities fraud in a U.S. class action from investors who traded outside the United States, thus practically shielding cross-listed firms from civil liability toward such investors.[49] Surprisingly, we fail to find negative reactions to this exclusionary effect. In fact, our findings even suggest the possibility of a positive reaction, which is inconsistent with the legal bonding theory.[50] Investor behavior after the case further suggests that having this cause of action is not a significant concern in choosing a trading venue. In a study that appeared after a preliminary version of this study came out, Gagnon and Karolyi also examine the economic consequences of *Morrison*. These authors, too, fail to find in their sample a significant change in firms' market value on the oral argument focal event. This is in contrast to what the legal bonding hypothesis implies and is therefore not inconsistent with our results in this respect. Finally, in

---

[46] Doidge et al., *supra* note 42, at 428.

[47] *See* Nuno Fernandes, Ugur Lel & Darius P. Miller, *Escape from New York: The Market Impact of Loosening Disclosure Requirements*, 95 J. FIN. ECON. 129 (2010); Doidge et al., *supra* note 42.

[48] G. Andrew Karolyi, *Corporate Governance, Agency Problems and International Cross-Listings: A Defense of the Bonding Hypothesis*, 13 EMERGING MARKETS REV. 516, 524 (2012).

[49] *See* Amir N. Licht et al., *What Makes the Bonding Stick? A Natural Experiment Involving the U.S. Supreme Court and Cross-Listed Firms*, Harvard Business School Strategy Unit Working Paper No. 11-072 (2014).

[50] The staff of the U.S. Securities and Exchange Commission has repeated some of our analyses using their data and obtained consistent results. SECURITIES AND EXCHANGE COMMISSION (SEC), STUDY ON THE CROSS-BORDER SCOPE OF THE PRIVATE RIGHT OF ACTION UNDER SECTION 10(B) OF THE SECURITIES EXCHANGE ACT OF 1934 (2012).

line with our broad-based findings on trading patterns, Bartlett in a uniquely detailed dataset on institutional investors' trading fails to find any significant change in their choice of trading venue, suggesting that they may not sufficiently value a private right of action for securities fraud.[51]

CIVIL LIABILITY AS AN ENFORCEMENT MECHANISM

In light of the foregoing discussion, this part addresses the role enforcement plays in the efficacy of the complex legal regime that applies to cross-listed firms. Indeed, enforcement may not only be significant but is outright crucial for the legal regulation of such firms. In terms of formal regulation – namely, the content of legal rules – there has been a sweeping trend of convergence in recent years in relation to securities regulation. For example, the adoption of the International Financial Reporting Standards (IFRS) by nearly all of the important market economies except the United States has eliminated much of the cross-country variability in financial reporting. Directives of the European Union ("E.U."), especially on disclosure and on market abuse, have worked further to eliminate such variability, at least in terms of the "law on the books" in E.U. Member States. Against this backdrop, compliance with formal regulation – and in particular, the mechanisms that may induce such compliance – becomes a key issue for policy makers. The first section of this part explains the importance of enforcement for effective regulation. The next section focuses on civil liability as a private enforcement mechanism against securities fraud. The final section points to problems in and challenges to civil liability in the current legal environments.

Enforcement: The Importance of Being Earnest

Disclosure helps in mitigating agency problems and is therefore generally believed to be desirable. More accurate and timely disclosure also helps market participants to better price financial assets.[52] Firms in certain circumstances may have some incentive to make voluntary disclosure,[53] but on the whole, securities regulation

---

[51] *See* Robert P. Bartlett, "Do Institutional Investors Value the 10b-5 Private Right of Action?" Evidence from Investor Trading Behavior Following *Morrison v. National Australia Bank Ltd.* UC Berkeley Public Law Research Paper No. 2171006 (2012).

[52] For surveys *see* Anne Beyer et al., *The Financial Reporting Environment: Review of the Recent Literature*, 50 J. ACCT. & ECON. 296 (2010); Luca Enriques & Sergio Gilotta, *Disclosure and Financial Market Regulation*, in THE OXFORD HANDBOOK ON FINANCIAL REGULATION (Eilís Ferran, Niamh Moloney, & Jennifer Payne, eds. forthcoming).

[53] *See* Stephan Hollander, Maarten Pronk, & Erik Roelofsen, *Does Silence Speak? An Empirical Analysis of Disclosure Choices during Conference Calls*, 48 J. ACCT. RES. 531 (2010); Abby Kim, *The Value of Firms' Voluntary Commitment to Improve Transparency: The Case of Special Segments on Euronext*, 25 J. CORP. FIN. 342 (2014); *see* specifically with regard to cross-listed firms Ole-Christian Hope, Tony Kang, & Joung W. Kim, *Voluntary Disclosure Practices by Foreign Firms Cross-Listed in the United States*, 9 J. CONTEMP. ACCT. ECON. 50 (2013).

regimes impose mandatory disclosure requirements and rely on deterrence to curb fraud. Consistent with these general insights, committing to better disclosure is a central theme in several theories on motivations for cross-listing. The underlying notion is that more extensive disclosure is beneficial to investors as a means for mitigating agency costs and, therefore, to the firm and to its insiders.[54] Evidence further shows that cross-listings are associated with improving firms' informational environment.[55]

Enforcement and reputation stand out as particularly important among the mechanisms that can make firms' commitment to better disclosure credible. From Bentham to Becker and beyond,[56] conventional analysis implies that vigorous expected enforcement should increase compliance. The efficacy of enforcement depends on a well-functioning legal system, including public authorities that investigate breaches and impose punishments and a civil liability system that provides injured parties with effective remedies against wrongdoers.[57] Enforcement thus may be conceptualized as a third dimension for assessing the legal regime that applies to cross-listed firms, in addition to the two dimensions depicted in Figure 2.

As the theory of institutional possibility frontiers implies and evidence confirms, countries vary in the legal duties they promulgate and in the apparatus they deploy to enforce them, especially with regard to investor protection.[58] In contrast, reputation relies on self-discipline that leads actors credibly to commit to lawful (or cooperative, or otherwise nonopportunistic) behavior by creating reputational assets.[59] Evidence indeed shows that firms' noncompliance entails both legal and reputational costs.[60] To make things more complex yet, enforcement and

---

[54] *See* Khaled Amira & Mark L. Muzere, *Competition among Stock Exchanges for Equity*, 35 J. BANKING FIN. 2355 (2011); Thomas J. Chemmanur & Paolo Fulghieri, *Competition and Cooperation Among Exchanges: A Theory of Cross-Listing and Endogenous Listing Standards*, 82 J. FIN. ECON. 455, 457 (2006); Steven Huddart, John Hughes & Markus Brunnermeier, *Disclosure Requirements and Stock Exchange Listing Choice in an International Context*, 26 J. ACCT. & ECON. 237 (1999); Oren Fuerst, *A Theoretical Analysis of the Investor Protection Regulations Argument for Global Listing of Stocks*, Int'l Center for Fin. at Yale, Working Paper (1998); for a policy analysis *see* Amir N. Licht, *Stock Exchange Mobility, Unilateral Regulation, and the Privatization of Securities Regulation*, 41 VA. J. INT'L L. 583 (2001).

[55] *See*, for example, Nuno Fernandes & Miguel A. Ferreira, *Does International Cross-Listing Improve the Information Environment?*, 88 J. FIN. ECON. 216 (2008); Shingo Goto, Masahiro Watanabe, & Yan Xu, *Strategic Disclosure and Stock Returns: Theory and Evidence from US Cross-Listing*, 22 REV. FIN. STUD. 1585 (2009).

[56] JEREMY BENTHAM, AN INTRODUCTION TO THE PRINCIPLES OF MORALS AND LEGISLATION (J.H. Burns & H.L.A. Hart eds., 1970) (1789); Gary S. Becker, *Crime and Punishment: An Economic Approach*, 76 J. POL. ECON. 169 (1968).

[57] *See*, generally, Bernard S. Black, *The Legal and Institutional Preconditions for Strong Securities Markets*, 49 UCLA L. REV. 781 (2001).

[58] *See* La Porta et al., *supra* note 29; Howell E. Jackson & Mark J. Roe, *Public and Private Enforcement of Securities Laws: Resource-Based Evidence*, 93 J. FIN. ECON. 207 (2009).

[59] *See* Diamond, *supra* note 32; Klein & Leffler, *supra* note 32.

[60] *See* Karpoff, *supra* note 32.

reputation as compliance-inducing mechanisms interact with one another.[61] Specifically, enforcement measures – both public enforcement steps implemented by regulators and private enforcement through litigation – may be needed for triggering the imposition of reputational penalties by market participants.[62]

Putting reputational mechanisms aside and focusing on legal enforcement, several studies analyze the role of public versus private enforcement in disclosure regimes. Both types of enforcement engender deterrence, which is needed to overcome insiders' inclination to hide or delay bad news because they may fear getting sued.[63] Between these two types, a growing body of evidence now shows that a solid infrastructure of public enforcement, that in turn relies on informal social institutions of law-abidingness, are needed for making a country's disclosure regime efficacious.

Jackson and Roe thus show that the scope of regulatory staff and budget positively affects financial market outcomes.[64] In an especially important study, Christensen, Hail, and Leuz investigate the implementation of market abuse and transparency directives in E.U. Member States, finding positive effects, which are larger in countries that implement and enforce the directives more strictly. These effects are also stronger in countries with traditionally stricter securities regulation and with a better prior track record of implementing regulation and government policies.[65] These authors obtain consistent results with regard to the adoption of IFRS accounting standards – namely, that beneficial (market liquidity) effects are limited to five E.U. countries that concurrently made substantive changes in reporting enforcement.[66] There is little evidence of liquidity benefits in IFRS countries without substantive enforcement changes even when they have strong legal and regulatory systems. At the firm level of analysis, Daske, Hail, Leuz, and Verdi argue that capital market benefits to more transparent firms accrue only to

---

[61] *See* Edward M. Iacobucci, *On the Interaction between Legal and Reputational Sanctions*, 43 J. LEGAL STUD. 189 (2014); Scott Baker & Albert Choi, *Managing Reputation with Litigation: Why Legal Sanctions Can Work Better than Market Sanctions*, Working Paper (2013).

[62] *See* John Arrmour, Colin Mayer, & Andrea Polo, *Regulatory Sanctions and Reputational Damage in Financial Markets*, Working Paper, Saïd Business School (2011); with regard to private enforcement through securities class actions *see* Brian Carson McTier & John K. Wald, *The Causes and Consequences of Securities Class Action Litigation*, 17 J. CORP. FIN. 649 (2011); Mark L. Humphery-Jenner, *Internal and External Discipline Following Securities Class Actions*, 21 J. FIN. INTERMEDIATION 151 (2012); *See*, generally, Karpoff, *supra* note 32.

[63] *See* Douglas J. Skinner, *Why Firms Voluntarily Disclose Bad News*, 32 J. ACCT. RES. 38 (1994); S.P. Kothari, Susan Shu & Peter Wysocki, *Do Managers Withhold Bad News?*, 47 J. ACCT. RES. 241 (2009).

[64] Jackson & Roe, *supra* note 58.

[65] *See* Hans B. Christensen, Luzi Hail & Christian Leuz, *Capital-Market Effects of Securities Regulation: Prior Conditions, Implementation, and Enforcement*, ECGI Finance Working Paper No. 407/2014 (2013).

[66] *See* Hans B. Christensen, Luzi Hail & Christian Leuz, *Mandatory IFRS Reporting and Changes in Enforcement*, 56 J. ACCT. ECON. 147 (2013).

firms from countries where the rule of law prevails.[67] Bhattacharya and Daouk similarly show that the cost of equity actually rises when some countries enact an insider trading law, but do not enforce it, indicating that sometimes "no law is better than a good law (that remains a dead letter)."[68] Finally, Bushman and Piotroski find that firms in countries with strong public enforcement are more conservative, but private enforcement (disclosure and litigation) has no impact on conservative financial reporting.[69]

This is all nice and well, but of relatively little relevance for cross-listed firms. That is, it is now undisputed that vibrant public enforcement is pivotal for the efficacy of a securities regulation regime. In a cross-listing setting, such enforcement in theory could come from the issuer's home-country regulator as well as it host-country regulator, wherein the more stringent enforcement regime would dominate.[70] As noted earlier, however, public enforcement against foreign issuers in the United States is minimal at best, even if some sporadic enforcement might take place occasionally.[71] While there could have been an idiosyncratic enforcement action vis-à-vis foreign issuers in other jurisdictions, I am not aware of any systemic enforcement efforts of this type. The upshot is that host-country public enforcement cannot be relied on as a legal bonding mechanism, leaving private enforcement as the remaining candidate for this task.

Private Enforcement and its Predicaments

In their study entitled *What Works in Securities Laws*, La Porta, Lopez-de-Silanes, and Shleifer argued that it is mandating disclosure and facilitating private enforcement through civil liability rules that benefit stock markets (while discounting the role of public enforcement).[72] In connection with cross-listing and legal bonding Coffee argued that the market appreciates civil liability as "a powerful engine of

---

[67] *See* Holger Daske et al., *Mandatory IFRS Reporting Around the World: Early Evidence on the Economic Consequences*, 46 J. ACCT. RES. 1085 (2008).

[68] *See* Utpal Bhattacharya & Hazem Daouk, *When No Law is Better than a Good Law*, 13 REV. FIN. 577 (2009); *see also* Bhattacharya & Hazem Daouk, *The World Price of Insider Trading*, 57 J. FIN. 75 (2002); Mark DeFond, Mingyi Hung & Robert Trezevant, *Investor Protection and the Information Content of Annual Earnings Announcements: International Evidence*, 43 J. ACCT. & ECON. 37 (2007); Mark Humphery-Jenner, *Strong Financial Laws Without Strong Enforcement: Is Good Law Always Better than No Law?*, 10 J. EMPIRICAL LEGAL STUD. 288 (2013).

[69] *See* Robert M. Bushman & Joseph D. Piotroski, *Financial Reporting Incentives for Conservative Accounting: The Influence of Legal and Political Institutions*, 42 J. ACCT. & ECON. 107 (2006); see also Ole-Kristian Hope, *Disclosure Practices, Enforcement of Accounting Standards, and Analysts' Forecast Accuracy: An International Study*, 41 J. ACCT. RES. 235 (2003).

[70] *See supra* Figure 2 and accompanying text.

[71] *See supra* note 34 and accompanying text.

[72] *See* La Porta et al., *supra* note 29.

private enforcement (e.g., the contingent fee-motivated plaintiffs bar) [that] stands ready to enforce U.S. legal rules."[73] Coffee further underscored the qualities of the U.S. class action in this regard:

> Very few other jurisdictions recognize the class action, and virtually none has any experience with it in the securities law context. Equally important, U.S. law accepts the contingent fee and the practice of awarding relatively high fee awards to the successful attorney in a class action. Finally, the "American Rule" on fee shifting, under which each side generally bears its own expenses, means that an unsuccessful plaintiff does not face liability for the defendant's typically greater expenses. All these elements combine to create an entrepreneurial system of private enforcement in the United States that is not paralleled elsewhere.[74]

Securities fraud class actions are a mixed blessing, however. To begin on a positive note, McTier and Wald present evidence consistent with the notion that securities class actions draw attention to agency problems in the firms, which are then at least partly resolved.[75] Humphery-Jenner similarly argues that class actions may be conducive to mitigating agency problems by promoting disciplinary takeovers, CEO turnover and pay-cuts, and may harm CEOs' future job-prospects.[76] Several studies associate litigation risk (namely, exposure to securities class actions) with more timely disclosure of bad news.[77] This evidence predominantly refers to U.S. firms.

On the other hand, securities class actions have engendered a vast literature criticizing their merit and general desirability as a means for imposing civil liability in the secondary market.[78] In the United States, a 1995 legal reform to the civil liability regime has reduced the problem of meritless "strike-suits," that are filed solely to extract settlements for their nuisance value to the firm. Yet the reform

---

[73] *See* Coffee, *supra* note 30, at 1788.

[74] Coffee, *supra* note 30, at 1780.

[75] *See* McTier & Wald, *supra* note 62.

[76] *See* Humphery-Jenner, *supra* note 62.

[77] *See* Laura Field et al., *Does Disclosure Deter or Trigger Litigation?*, 39 J. Acct. & Econ. 487 (2005); Dain C. Donelson et al., *The Timeliness of Bad Earnings News and Litigation Risk*, 87 Acct. Rev. 1967 (2012); *See* also Douglas J. Skinner, *Earnings Disclosures and Stockholder Lawsuits*, 23 J. Acct. & Econ. 249 (1997).

[78] *See*, for example, Janet Cooper Alexander, *Rethinking Damages in Securities Class Actions*, 48 Stan. L. Rev. 1487 (1996); John C. Coffee, Jr., *Reforming the Securities Class Action: An Essay on Deterrence and its Implementation*, 106 Colum. L. Rev. 1534 (2006); Paul G. Mahoney, *Precaution Costs and the Law of Fraud in Impersonal Market*, 78 Va. L. Rev. 623 (1992); Paul G. Mahoney, *The Development of Securities Law in the United States*, 47 J. Acct. Res. 325 (2009); Joel Seligman, *Rethinking Private Securities Litigation*, 73 U. Cin. L. Rev. 95 (2004); *see*, generally, Steven A. Ramirez, *The Virtues of Private Securities Litigation: An Historic and Macroeconomic Perspective*, 45 Loy. U. Chi. L.J. 669 (2014). Note that Coffee thus seems to be of two minds with regard to the desirability of securities class actions against cross-listed firms. For a discussion *see* John C. Coffee, Jr., *Law and the Market: The Impact of Enforcement*, 156 U. Pa. L. Rev. 229 (2007) (hereinafter Coffee 2007).

yielded mixed results, such that the general desirability of class-action-based antifraud liability remains debatable.[79]

The most fundamental difficulty in securities class actions regarding secondary market transactions stems from the "circularity problem."[80] Briefly, for any transaction in the secondary market affected by fraud by the issuers or its insiders, one investor's loss is the counterparty's gain (hence "circularity"). Current public shareholders end up paying past shareholders – where the two groups at least partially overlap – for insiders' misdeeds, either by way of compensation or through insurance policies, which in either case are funded from the company's coffers (hence again "circularity"). In any event, it is virtually undisputed that insiders who committed fraud rarely have to pay anything directly. Caskey estimates attorneys pocket about half of the direct costs paid by the firm.[81] Lack of effective deterrence is further suggested by the finding that managers in the same companies repeatedly violate the securities laws and that insurers provide a set of products to such firms.[82]

In the domestic U.S. context scholars thus call for radical reforms in the securities fraud civil liability regime. For example, Fox goes as far as to argue that an issuer not publicly offering securities at the time of a disclosure violation (namely, fraud) should have no liability.[83] Rose calls for consolidating the enforcement authority now shared between federal regulators, state regulators, and class-action lawyers in a federal agency, such as the SEC, and to grant that agency exclusive authority to prosecute national securities frauds.[84] Without

---

[79] For a review *see* James D. Cox & Randall S. Thomas, *Mapping the American Shareholder Litigation Experience: A Survey of Empirical Studies of the Enforcement of the U.S. Securities Law*, 6 Eur. Company & Fin. L. Rev. 164 (2009).

[80] *See*, for example, James D. Cox, *Making Securities Fraud Class Actions Virtuous*, 39 Ariz. L. Rev. 497 (1997); Donald C. Langevoort, *Capping Damages for Open-Market Securities Fraud*, 38 Ariz. L. Rev. 639 (1996); Jennifer H. Arlen & William J. Carney, *Vicarious Liability for Fraud on Securities Markets: Theory and Evidence*, 1992 U. Ill. L. Rev. 691; Paul G. Mahoney, *Precaution Costs and the Law of Fraud in Impersonal Markets*, 78 Va. L. Rev. 623 (1992); for a summary *see* Merritt B. Fox, *Civil Liability and Mandatory Disclosure*, 109 Colum. L. Rev. 237 (2009); *Compare* James J. Park, *Shareholder Compensation as Dividend*, 108 Mich. L. Rev. 323 (2009); Jill E. Fisch, *Confronting the Circularity Problem in Private Securities Litigation*, 2009 Wis. L. Rev. 333; *see also* Lawrence E. Mitchell, *The "Innocent Shareholder": An Essay on Compensation and Deterrence in Securities Class-Action Lawsuits*, 2009 Wis. L. Rev. 243.

[81] *See* Judson Caskey, *The Pricing Effects of Securities Class Action Lawsuits and Litigation Insurance*, 30 J. L. Econ. & Org. 493 (2014).

[82] *See*, generally, Tom Baker & Sean J. Griffith, Ensuring Corporate Misconduct: How Liability Insurance Undermines Shareholder Litigation (2010); for consistent evidence in cross-listed firms *see* Siegel, note 17.

[83] *See* Cox, *supra* note 80.

[84] *See* Amanda M. Rose, *The Multienforcer Approach to Securities Fraud Deterrence: A Critical Analysis*, 158 U. Pa. L. Rev. 2173 (2010); *compare* James J. Park, *Rules, Principles, and the Competition to Enforce the Securities Laws*, 100 Calif. L. Rev. 115 (2012); Genevieve Beyea, *Morrison v. National Australia Bank and the Future of Extraterritorial Application of the U.S. Securities Laws*, 72 Ohio St. L.J. 537 (2011).

delving into the details of these ideas, it is clear that they reflect deep misgivings about the current U.S. regime.[85]

Civil Liability in Cross-Listed Firms

All of the earlier discussions hold a fortiori with regard to firms cross-listed in the United States, in addition to legal issues that are unique to imposing transnational civil liability for securities fraud on such firms. The latter factor will be discussed in the following section. Legal scholar who addressed the appropriateness of the current class-action-based civil liability for cross-listed firms have unsurprisingly coalesced around a consensus that it is undesirable. Citing the weaknesses of the current U.S. regime – in particular, the circularity problem – Langevoort has opined that "a case can be made for some pull back in terms of antifraud liability exposure in private actions" against cross-listed firms.[86] In a comprehensive and insightful analysis of this subject, Fox argues that the U.S. regime should not as a general matter be imposed upon any genuinely foreign issuer, even where the claimant is a U.S. investor purchasing shares in a U.S. market or where the issuer engages in significant conduct in the United States relating to the misstatement.[87] The only exception, he argues, would be a foreign issuer that has agreed, as a form of bonding, to be subject to the U.S. regime. Determining a foreign issuer's "national identity" is key in applying this theory. Recognizing this challenge, Guseva in a similar spirit calls for adopting a regulatory approach that takes into account the foreign issuer's home-country institutions.[88]

These views are backed by evidence on the securities fraud liability that cross-listed firms may face in the United States. Siegel's field work on cross-listed firms examined in detail the actual operation of the civil liability regime among firms and securities lawyers, confirming that in these firms, too, virtually all cases end in settlement that is paid by insurers.[89] In a recent study of markets' reaction to the

---

[85] A heated debate has been raging in the United States with regard to the fraud on the market doctrine. Though the issue is related to the present discussion it exceeds the present scope. Recently, the U.S. Supreme Court decided to keep this doctrine intact, with a minor procedural modification. See *Halliburton Co. v. Erica P. John Fund, Inc.*, 573 U.S. ____ (2014).

[86] See Donald C. Langevoort, *U.S. Securities Regulation and Global Competition*, 3 Va. L. & Bus. Rev. 191, 199 (2008); see also Coffee 2007, *supra* note 78.

[87] See Merritt Fox, *Securities Class Actions against Foreign Issuers*, 64 Stan. L. Rev. 1173 (2012); see also Merritt B. Fox, *Securities Disclosure in a Globalizing Market: Who Should Regulate Whom*, 95 Mich. L. Rev. 2498 (1997); Merritt B. Fox, *The Political Economy of Statutory Reach: U.S. Disclosure Rules in a Globalizing Market for Securities*, 97 Mich. L. Rev. 696 (1998).

[88] See Yuliya Guseva, *Cross-Listings and the New World of International Capital: Another Look at the Efficiency and Extraterritoriality of Securities Law*, 44 Geo. J. Int'l L. 411 (2013); compare Steven M. Davidoff, *Rhetoric and Reality: A Historical Perspective on the Regulation of Foreign Private Issuers*, 79 U. Cin. L. Rev. 619 (2010).

[89] See Siegel, note 17.

filing of class actions against foreign firms, Gande and Miller find in their extended sample a negative market response estimated at some $73 billion for 1996–2008.[90] As noted earlier, in a joint study with Siegel and others, we find that when the *Morrison* Court signaled its intention to deny non-U.S. trades a federal cause of action for securities fraud, market participants responded with indifference or even positively and did not seem to change their trading patterns to secure such a cause of action by trading in U.S. markets.[91] This evidence suggests that market participants do not consider the U.S. class-action-based private enforcement regime of civil liability a valuable mechanism for ensuring full disclosure and good corporate governance more generally.

Implementing civil liability through a U.S.-style class-action mechanism is controversial among policy makers in other countries as well. Several other countries during the last decade have adopted some type of class actions, and a small number among them have adopted a full-fledged "American-style" class-action mechanism. These reforms deal with mass torts in general and are not limited to securities fraud liability.[92] However, in the securities area, governments that responded to the study that the Dodd-Frank Act instructed the SEC to conduct after the *Morrison* decision cited different approaches to implementing civil liability for securities fraud. The British Government in particular voiced fundamental disagreement "as to the desirability and appropriateness of even having a private right of action against an issuer for securities fraud," citing the circularity problem and high costs.[93] Against this backdrop, and having replicated the gist of our findings by its staff, the SEC responded to Congress's mandate by providing a detailed review of several options that Congress might take but eschewed any explicit recommendation in favour of extending U.S. securities fraud liability beyond the scope that the *Morrison* Court has delineated.[94]

Private Enforcement Post-*Morrison*

The *Morrison* decision has been nothing short of a watershed event for the regulation of global capital markets. In *Morrison*, the U.S. Supreme Court discarded, in harsh terms, forty years of jurisprudence on the international application of the federal civil liability regime for securities fraud. The court's novel territorial test indeed responded to well-reasoned calls for scaling back the scope of this liability,

---

[90] *See* Amar Gande & Darius P. Miller, *Why Do U.S. Securities Laws Matter to Non-U.S. Firms? Evidence from Private Class-Action Lawsuits*, Working Paper (2012); *see also* Elaine Buckberg & Max Gulker, *Cross-Border Shareholder Class Actions Before and After* Morrison, NERA Economic Consulting, Working Paper (2011).

[91] *See* Licht et al., *supra* note 49.

[92] *See* Deborah R. Hensler, *The Future of Mass Litigation: Global Class Actions and Third-Party Litigation Funding*, 79 GEO. WASH. L. REV. 306 (2011).

[93] *See* SEC, *supra* note 50, at 24.

[94] *See* SEC, *supra* note 50.

yet it did so in a manner that reflected deeper currents in U.S. law with regard to the United States' regulatory role on the global scene and, not less importantly, about the role of courts and on statutory interpretation.[95] Lower U.S. courts took cue from *Morrison* and applied it forcefully to ensure that only U.S.-located full transactions would be covered by the U.S. civil liability regime.[96] With respect, this judicial approach at times exhibits a certain zeal that even exceeds the textualist interpretation that the Supreme Court insisted on in *Morrison*.[97]

In assessing the road ahead with regard to transnational civil liability for securities fraud, scholars have looked introspectively at remaining avenues within American law. Buxbaum's thorough analysis of the law post-*Morrison* identifies two such avenues: litigation brought in U.S. federal courts under foreign securities laws, and participation in Federal Account for Investor Restitution (FAIR) fund distributions ordered by the SEC.[98] Both of these ways are fraught with difficulties and neither of them provides an equal substitute for pre-*Morrison* law. One may note in particular that the distribution to injured investors of amounts recovered as penalties through the FAIR fund mechanism depends on an SEC public enforcement action and on the SEC's discretion.[99] In light of the deficiencies of the current U.S. class action regime, one is hard pressed to argue for expanding it further. One might further conjecture that the "foreigners need not apply" atmosphere, which characterizes post-*Morrison* decisions in lower federal courts, could also affect future litigation based on foreign securities laws in American courts.

In tandem, commentators have also looked extrospectively, with regard to non-U.S. jurisdictions, to see if non-U.S. traders might find a substitute there for the loss of U.S. federal civil remedies after *Morrison*. Realistically, the chances for that are

---

[95] Compare *Kiobel v. Royal Dutch Petroleum Co.*, 133 S. Ct. 1659 (2013).

[96] *See*, as of this writing, *City of Pontiac Policemen's & Firemen's Ret. Sys. v. UBS AG*, No. 12–4355 (2d Cir. 2014) and cases cited therein.

[97] In *City of Pontiac* the United States Court of Appeals for the Second Circuit rejected the so-called "listing theory," holding that *Morrison* bars Exchange Act Section 10(b) claims with respect to the purchase or sale of securities on foreign exchanges when those same securities are cross-listed on a U.S. exchange. This decision, while showing fidelity to *Morrison*'s territorial approach, is inconsistent with the very language of Section 10(b), which runs afoul of the judicial deference to Congressional statutory language called for by *Morrison*. Separately, the Second Circuit ruled that *Morrison* also applies to criminal cases. *See United States v. Vilar*, 729 F.3d 62 (2d Cir. 2013); *see also* Zachary D. Clopton, Bowman *Lives: The Extraterritorial Application of U.S. Criminal Law After* Morrison v. National Australia Bank, 67 N.Y.U. ANN. SURV. AM. L. 137 (2011).

[98] *See* Hannah L. Buxbaum, *Remedies for Foreign Investors Under U.S. Federal Securities Law*, 75 L. & CONTEMP. PROBS. 161 (2012); *see also* Linda J. Silberman, Morrison v. National Australia Bank: *Implications for Global Securities Class Actions*, in EXTRATERRITORIALITY AND COLLECTIVE REDRESS 363 (Duncan Fairgrieve & Eva Lein eds., 2012); Marco Ventoruzzo, *Like Moths to a Flame? International Securities Litigation after* Morrison: *Correcting the Supreme Court's "Transactional Test,"* 52 VA. J. INT'L L. 405 (2012).

[99] *See*, generally, Barbara Black, *Should the SEC Be a Collection Agency for Defrauded Investors?*, 63 BUS. LAW. 317 (2008); Verity Winship, *Fair Funds and the SEC's Compensation of Injured Investors*, 60 FLA. L. REV 1103 (2008).

not great. A more likely outcome, at least in the foreseeable future, is a fragmentation of civil liability litigation among several jurisdictions under their different regimes of mass claim litigation.[100] As Walker, a Canadian, puts it in light of an international survey she conducted: "[E]veryone, at least outside the United States, seems also to agree that they do not want to adopt U.S.-style class actions in their legal systems."[101]

Canadian courts indeed loomed as a potential forum for global securities fraud litigation after the twin decisions in *Imax*, which certified a global class of shareholders that alleged statutory and common law misrepresentation claims.[102] While recovery under the statutory claims is significantly capped, recovery under common law ones need not be, but the latter depends crucially on avoiding the need to show individual reliance. In early 2014, however, in a decision that also related to the *Imax* litigation, the Court of Appeal for Ontario determined that common law negligent misrepresentation claims could not be certified as class actions on the basis of "fraud on the market" or "efficient market" theories.[103] Hopes for reaching mega settlements in Ontario instead of the Southern District of New York thus diminished accordingly.

The European Union has been another arena for interesting developments about securities fraud liability in connection with broader reform programs on mass litigation. Commentators pointed out the Dutch procedure of collective arbitration in this regard.[104] Yet there is consensus that that procedure, while allowing for the grouping of claimants from several jurisdiction, cannot substitute the U.S. class-action-based regime for securities fraud. Importantly, resistance to this mode of liability in European and in other civil law jurisdiction is principled, as this mode is at odds with basic conceptions of individual autonomy in private law in these jurisdictions.[105]

---

[100] *See*, with regard to Australia, Peta Spender & Michael Tarlowski, *Adventures on the Barbary Coast*: Morrison *and Enforcement in a Globalised Securities Market*, 35 MELB. U. L. REV. 280 (2011).

[101] *See* Janet Walker, *Who's Afraid of U.S.-style Class Actions?*, 18 SW. J. INT'L 509, 509 (2012); *see* also Hensler, *supra* note 92.

[102] *Silver v. IMAX Corporation* [2009] O.J. Nos. 5573; 5585 (S.C.J.). *See* Tanya Monestier, *Is Canada the New Shangri-La of Global Securities Class Actions?*, 12 NW. J. INT'L L. & BUS. 305 (2012); *see* also Poonam Puri, *Securities Litigation and Enforcement: The Canadian Perspective*, 37 BROOKLYN J. INT'L L. 967 (2012).

[103] *See Green v. Canadian Imperial Bank of Commerce*, 2014 ONCA 90.

[104] *See*, for example, Silberman, *supra* note 98; *see* also Wulf A. Kaal & Richard W. Painter, *Forum Competition and Choice of Law Competition in Securities Law After* Morrison v. National Australia Bank, 97 MINN. L. REV. 132 (2012); Michael Palmisciano, Note: *Going Dutch: The Effects of Domestic Restriction and Foreign Acceptance of Class Litigation on American Securities Fraud Plaintiffs*, 53 B.C. L. REV. 1847 (2012); *see*, generally, S.I. STRONG, CLASS, MASS, AND COLLECTIVE ARBITRATION IN NATIONAL AND INTERNATIONAL LAW (2013).

[105] *See* Manning Gilbert Warren III, *The U.S. Securities Fraud Class Action: An Unlikely Export to the European Union*, 37 Brook. J. Int'l L. 1075 (2012); *see* also Antonio Gidi, *The Recognition of U.S. Class Action Judgments Abroad: The Case of Latin America*, 37 BROOK. J. INT'L L. 893 (2012);

CONCLUSION

This chapter has sought to evaluate the state of affairs with regard to liability for transnational securities fraud, in particular, subsequent to the U.S. Supreme Court's seminal decision *Morrison*. In a word, this liability is in a state of flux. The notion that investors who were harmed as a result of a breach of the duty of full disclosure deserve compensation looks compelling, if not self-evident. That the law should implement procedural and substantive rules for helping injured claimants whose claim is too small to pursue individually also sounds hard to quarrel with, and indeed countries around the world are in the process of developing such rules. These policy goals are worth pursuing regardless of whether such civil liability may also serve as a mechanism for legal bonding to improve corporate governance in firms, though the issues are closely related, of course.

Civil liability for securities fraud – in a domestic setting and a fortiori in a transnational setting – nonetheless entails an especially vicious combination of difficulties that for now defies satisfactory solutions. Without derogating from the need to continue efforts toward reform in the civil liability context, this chapter underscores the importance of public enforcement for protecting the integrity of securities markets. More progress in this direction may be achieved by each country improving its own public enforcement institutions. In addition, although regulatory cooperation is not challenge-free either, investing in regulatory cooperation likely will enhance the effectiveness of domestic enforcement institutions.[106]

Dana M. Muir, Junhai Liu & Haiyan Xu, *The Future of Securities Class Actions against Foreign Companies: China and Comity Concerns*, 46 U. MICH. J.L. REFORM 1315 (2013).

[106] *See*, generally, Chris Brummer, *Post-American Securities Regulation*, 98 CAL. L. REV. 327 (2010); Pierre-Hugues Verdier, *Mutual Recognition in International Finance*, 52 HARV. INT'L L.J. 56 (2011); Pierre-Hugues Verdier, *The Political Economy of International Financial Regulation*, 88 IND. L.J. 1405, 1405 (2013); David Zaring, *Finding Legal Principle in Global Financial Regulation*, 52 VA. J. INT'L L. 683, 685 (2012); Sean J. Griffith, *Substituted Compliance and Systemic Risk: How to Make a Global Market in Derivatives Regulation*, 98 MINN. L. REV. 1291 (2014); *see also* Amir N. Licht, *Games Commissions Play: 2x2 Games of International Securities Regulation*, 24 YALE J. INT'L L. 61 (1999).

IV

Addressing Too-Big-To-Fail and Shadow Banking

14

Large Systemic Banks and Fractional Reserve Banking

Intractable Dilemmas in Search of Effective Solutions

Emilios Avgouleas

INTRODUCTION

Banks have been a ubiquitous feature of economic life since at least the eighteenth century[1] and well before neoclassical economics incorporated capital in its growth models, chiefly though J. M. Keynes's writings. In modern times the concept of availability of capital has been updated, or even stretched, to be closely associated with the concept of financial sector development and attendant levels of access to (external) finance.[2] Yet, while the value of an enlarged financial sector remains disputed, given its perennial fragility due to its preponderance to generate booms and busts,[3] the economic and social utility of a savings-based economy is not.

I owe a debt of gratitude for conversations I had in the context of drafting this paper to Charles Goodhart.

[1] The best example is the Bank of Scotland, part of the Lloyds Group today, which was established in Edinburgh in 1695 with the purpose of conducting commercial banking operations. For the history of the Bank of Scotland that set up as a rival to the Bank of England albeit with different focus as the former was established to manage government debt see http://en.wikipedia.org/wiki/Bank_of_Scotland.

[2] For a collection of the most important research substantiating the role of finance in economic growth see A. Demirguc-Kunt and R. Levine (eds, *Financial Structure and Economic Growth: A Cross-Country Comparison of Banks, Markets, and Development* (MIT Press, 2003). It seems that the findings of the cited studies in the MIT volume were not as instructive as those researchers made us believe. So in their own subsequent writings they have themselves admitted that the indicators they used were very crude and it is still unclear which of the key properties of the financial system provide the best measure of its development and contribution to economic growth. See for a summary of the findings and conclusions of contemporary financial development research see M. Cihak, A. Demirguc-Kunt et al., "Measuring Financial Development" VOX column, 25 April 2013, available at www.voxeu.org/article/measuring-financial-development.

[3] On the value of financial stability in fostering growth see D. Arner, *Financial Stability, Economic Growth, and the Role of Law* (CUP, 2007). See also T. Beck, "The Role of Finance Economic Development: Benefits, Risks, and Politics" in D. C. Mueller, *The Oxford Handbook of Capitalism* (OUP, 2012), online, chapter 6.

This is not just the experience of older societies but even more so it is a widespread and largely unchallenged – probably because it is true – assumption of modern societies.

For example, one of the least mentioned utilities of savings-based economies is that banking (and capital markets) operating in a competitive environment and outside government interventions on their lending decisions and other capital allocation decisions can facilitate individuals' economic and social mobility.[4] Affording individuals or small enterprises access to credit and savings services that might not have been available otherwise, whether by means of mainstream banking, or community banking, or even microfinance schemes, can help mobilize individuals' or communities' creative talents. Moreover granting to the poor access to saving accounts facilitates their forward planning and to some extent alleviates any future short-term income shocks that may experience (e.g., unemployment), making them more proactive and entrepreneurial.[5] These benefits accrue to societies in addition to those flowing from the ability of the financial system to finance long-term development or infrastructure projects with strong social utility.

Arguably, financial sector development is not a goal in itself, it is rather a means to an end. Yet in the past thirty years financial markets have developed into a thick and complex web of claims and counterclaims, tradable assets, and risks. The transformation that banks have undergone in the past three decades has made the struggle to keep them safe, ever harder, and more challenging.

Whether operating under the principle of limited or unlimited liability, on a purely domestic or international basis, as mainstream lenders or as part of complex organizations, within a free banking environment or under the protective "wings" of the lender of last resort, banks have never been straightforward creatures. They normally operate on the basis of a fractional reserve system, trading on the basis of a large multiple over shareholders' equity and only keeping small reserves against their liabilities, that is, money entrusted (lent) to them by depositors and bondholders. Fractional reserve banking presupposes a strong amount of trust in the safety of individual banks and the stability of the entire financial system. But such confidence can easily evaporate either because of trouble within a bank or developments in other parts of the financial system or even outside the financial system in the wider national and international economy.[6]

The pace of bank business transformation has been unprecedented in the past three decades. This is a period that roughly coincides with global trade liberalisation,

---

[4] See R. Rajan, L. Zingales, *Saving Capitalism from the Capitalists: Unleashing the Power of Financial Markets to Create Wealth and Spread Opportunity* (Princeton, 2004).

[5] For analysis and extensive relevant bibliography see E. Avgouleas, "International Financial Regulation, Access to Finance, Systemic Stability, and Development", (2008) *LAWASIA Journal* 62–76.

[6] The risk of a confidence shock spreading throughout the financial system (contagion) is in fact the fundamental rationale of banking regulation. See C. Goodhart, et al. *Financial Regulation: Why, How and Where Now?* (Routledge, 1998).

and effective and rapid communications, normally defined as the era of globalization. This era in global banking has two distinct phases, the period between 1990 and 2008 and the period post-2008. During the first phase the biggest banks gradually moved to a purely multifunctional–universal bank model and global geographic coverage of operations, as banks became increasingly transnational.

The second phase is exclusively defined by a tidal wave of regulatory reforms at the national, regional, and global level. One of the most important consequences of the Global Financial Crisis (GFC) was that, due to the threat of systemic disruption, it became impossible to tolerate the failure of even medium-sized investment banks, like Lehman Brothers. National treasuries had to put together expensive bail-out plans in order to rescue severely undercapitalized banks in crisis from going bankrupt and thus reinforcing a vicious chain effect of panic, contagion, and instability. Some of these bailouts proved very expensive, though the final cost was not the same in all jurisdictions. Ensuing reforms have aimed at remedying the perceived causes of the GFC and prevent the reoccurrence of a crisis of such magnitude.

The notion of market discipline aiding financial stability in the financial sector is sometimes stretched to a breaking point for two all-pervasive reasons. First, shareholders normally care little for financial stability threats and much more about their returns on equity (ROE). Secondly, most modern financial institutions are too complex to be properly subjected to the rigors of market discipline. Even when shareholders and creditors have the right incentives to be effective monitors, balance sheet complexity will remain a challenging obstacle.[7] Moreover, any reliance on market discipline acting as a restraint to the operations of large and/ or interconnected banks entirely evaporated, reinforcing moral hazard (normally called too-big-to-fail (TBTF).

This chapter intends to provide a balanced, all-encompassing, and in-depth discussion of the social utility of big banks in a fractional reserve banking system in the post-2008 context utilizing a very wide array of empirical and theoretical works. It will, thus, discuss the dilemmas surrounding the famed demolition of the TBTF bank in the postreform era. To this effect, the chapter will explain that while well calibrated structural reforms and special resolution regimes can certainly help to alleviate the TBTF problem in the banking sector, they will not eliminate it. At the same time, implementation of the suggested alternative of full-reserve, limited-purpose, or narrow-banking models would, in practice, create more problems than it would solve.

Arguably, until the present model of fractional reserve banking is radically overhauled, mostly through effective regulatory systems and structural reforms that

---

[7] For analytical discussion see E. Avgouleas and J. Cullen, "Market Discipline and EU Corporate Governance Reform in the Banking Sector: Merits, Fallacies, and Cognitive Boundaries", 41 *Journal of Law and Society* 28–50 (2014).

refocus global finance on long-term growth objectives, societies may have to provide a form of fiscal backstop to big (mostly ring-fenced or separated) commercial banks. This may be the social cost that has to be paid for the benefit of fractional reserve banking. It ought not to be confused with the abuses surrounding the TBTF subsidy in the pre-2008 era.

This chapter is divided in five sections. The first section is the present introduction. The second section will discuss the historical emergence of the multifunctional banks, also called megabanks, as the dominant model of bank organisation. The third section will provide an in depth evaluation of the costs and benefits of large multifunctional (TBTF) banks with special reference to the economics of bank organisation and the TBTF subsidy utilising an extensive range of empirical and theoretical studies. To this effect, the section will provide a balanced discussion of the risks and challenges posed by the existence of large multifunctional banks, which, in the absence of an effective structural regulation and a failure proof resolution framework are bound to be TBTF. The fourth section provides a critical evaluation of the remedial regulatory and policy reforms that have already been implemented or are under way to deal with the TBTF problem. It will also discuss the Kotlikoff and Kay proposals for a full reserve (narrow – limited purpose) banking system. Section V provides the conclusion.

EMERGENCE OF THE MEGABANK MODEL

Introductory Remarks

Outside Continental Europe, chiefly Switzerland and Germany, the business model of financial conglomeration that is best manifested by megabanks emerged as late as the 1990s as a result of three factors. First, financial innovation both eroded the traditional boundaries between commercial and investment banking, as a host of derivatives products and financing techniques could be used by both kinds of institutions and created a strong movement towards disintermediation. The latter meant that profit margins became ever thinner for traditional lenders that did not normally engage in capital market activities. At the same time, investment banks needed an ever larger capital and funding base in order to compete successfully under the new conditions. That larger capital and funding base could be ensured through the merger of an investment bank with a lending institution. Such mergers were seen at the time as the apex of capital optimization in the banking sector; investment banking would bring higher profit margins and commercial banking the wide, cheap, and safe funding basis ensured through acceptance of retail and commercial deposits.

The second reason was the global, and possibly misguided, trend toward financial liberalization, which lied at the heart of economic globalization, together with trade liberalization. International financial liberalization was achieved through the abolition of national controls over cross-border capital flows and of restrictions over foreign entry to domestic financial services markets. Globalization, in turn, presented big banks and their public regulators with two important challenges: first, how to build big institutions that could compete successfully at the global stage, and, second, by which means this global industry could be regulated? The latter was achieved through the nearly universal endorsement of the prudential regulation standards[8] issued in the last two decades by the Basel Committee on Banking Supervision (BCBS).

The third reason was deregulation of the financial services industry in the western world. First, in the United Kingdom, where, unlike the United States, segregation between commercial and investment banking institutions was informal, so called "big bang" of 27 October 1986 meant the disappearance of traditional stock jobbers.[9] This created a chain reaction, which gradually led to the acquisition of most of the traditional discount houses and merchant banks, either by foreign competitors or large UK commercial banks. The latter meant a huge shift of business culture for the big UK banks, which eventually culminated to the disastrous business policies followed by the Royal Bank of Scotland and the Halifax Bank of Scotland two decades later.

Repealing Glass-Steagall

The United States had in place the last relics of depression era legislation, so called Glass-Steagall Act,[10] until 1999. The core sections of the Banking Act of 1933, which referred to banks' securities operations and were defined as the Glass-Steagall Act, were sections 16, 20, 21, and 32. Section 16, as amended by the Banking Act of 1935, generally prohibited Federal Reserve member banks from purchasing securities for their own account. Sections 16 and 21 also forbade deposit-taking institutions from engaging in the business of "issuing, underwriting, selling, or distributing, at wholesale or retail, or through syndicate participation, stock, bonds, debentures, notes or other securities", except holdings of U.S. treasury bills and other public sector debt obligations. The Act (section 20) also prohibited member banks from affiliating with a company "engaged principally" in the "issue, flotation, underwriting, public sale,

---

[8] Professor J. J. Norton was the first legal scholar who identified and seriously examined the emerging global consensus for banking regulation. Norton's work set the course for many subsequent studies. See J. J. Norton, *Devising International Bank Supervisory Standards* (The Hague: Martinus-Nijhoff, 1995), and Norton (ed.), *Bank Regulation and Supervision in the 1990s* (Kluwer Law, 1991); Norton *and* I. Fletcher, *International Banking Regulation and Supervision: Change and Transformation in the 1990s* (Kluwer Law International, 1994).

[9] On the disappearance of the LSE's stock jobbers and their business culture see Bernard Attard, "Making a Market, The Jobbers of London Stock Exchange, 1800–1986", (2000) 7 *Financial History Review* 5.

[10] Banking Act of 1933, 48 Stat. 162, codified in several sections of the United States Code, now repealed.

or distribution at wholesale or retail or through syndicate participation of stocks, bonds, debentures, notes, or other securities". In fact, cognizant of the scope for conflicts of interest section 32 prohibited a member bank from having interlocking directorships or close officer or employee relationships with a firm "principally engaged" in securities underwriting and distribution, even if there was no common ownership or corporate affiliation between the commercial bank and the investment company.

By the time of its formal repeal in 1999,[11] Glass-Steagall type restrictions had been seriously eroded,[12] especially as regards the ability of commercial banks to acquire securities affiliates,[13] and the trend towards megamergers between financial services institutions had already set in. Considerable effort was put into debunking the historical underpinnings of the Glass-Steagall Act and to showing that the risks and abuses were not as great as its proponents claimed.[14] Yet, the pressure to repeal Glass Steagall did not originate from investment banks but it was more commercial banks' desire to acquire a slice in lucrative securities underwritings to boost their income.

But since mid-1990s the motives for the repeal of the act had become even more sinister and mostly referred to serious gains in terms of stock prices that accrued to megamergers,[15] especially those hailed by "learned" market analyst as augmenting income in the long-term and creating massive economies of scale especially on the sell side.[16] This trend was culminated in the merger of Citicorp (a banking company) with Travellers, a financial conglomerate with several insurance subsidiaries and the securities firm (Salomon Smith Barney) to produce Citigroup. This

---

[11] Gramm-Leach-Bliley Financial Services Modernization Act, Pub. L. No. 106–102, 113 Stat. 1338 (1999). For today's reader that has the benefit of hindsight it seems inexplicable that so few U.S. senators opposed at the time the repeal of Glass-Steagall Act. *See* "Glass-Steagall Act: The Senators And Economists Who Got It Right", *Huffington Post*, 11 May 2009, available at www.huffingtonpost.com/2009/05/11/glass-steagall-act-the-se_n_201557.html.

[12] Bank Holding Company Act of 1956, Pub. L. No. 511, 70 Stat. 133.

[13] For example, in June 1988 the U.S. Supreme Court (by denying certiorari) upheld a lower court's ruling accepting the Federal Reserve Board's April 1987 approval for member banks to affiliate with companies underwriting commercial paper, municipal revenue bonds, and securities backed by mortgages and consumer debts, as long as the affiliate does not principally engage in those activities.

[14] For example, G. Benston, *The Separation of Commercial and Investment Banking* (New York, OUP, 1990).

[15] For an overview of this phase in the history of American banking see L. Baxter "Betting Big: Value, Caution and Accountability in an Era of Large Banks and Complex Finance", 31 *Review of Banking and Financial Law* 784–800 (2011–12), pp. 765–877.

[16] For the timeline of long efforts to repeal the Glass-Steagall Act and an uncorroborated estimate of the cost of lobbying for the final repeal of the Act in 1999 see Editorial, "The Long Demise of Glass-Steagall, A chronology tracing the life of the Glass-Steagall Act, from its passage in 1933 to its death throes in the 1990s, and how Citigroup's Sandy Weill dealt the coup de grâce", Available at www.pbs.org/wgbh/pages/frontline/shows/wallstreet/weill/demise.html.

merger preceded and probably "coerced" the repeal of Glass-Steagall Act.[17] It was followed by the subsequent merger of JP Morgan with Chase Manhattan in 2000. These mergers made megabanks a menacing reality both to competitors and consumers and the financial system.[18]

The EU "Levels" the Playing Field

The same drive toward deregulation, by means, in this case, of harmonization legislation with the explicit intent of levelling the playing field between continental European universal banking and the informally segregated model operated in Britain and in some other EU member states, meant that EU legislation actively promoted the universal bank model.[19] Thus, it fostered the creation of several megabanks in the United Kingdom and rest of Europe, of a size at least similar to that of their U.S. counterparts.

Liberalization and the dismantling of barriers between commercial and investment banking also meant a large number of cross-border mergers and acquisitions,[20] creating large complex financial conglomerates with very strong international business, asset, and deposit base. A major EU measure, ostensibly designed to counteract market risks associated with securities and other activities, was the Capital Adequacy Directive (the CAD).[21] In fact the CAD had as much to

[17] See for the influence of the Citigroup merger on the repeal of Glass-Stegall Act and the enactment of the Gramm-Leach-Billey Act. See A. E. Wilmarth "The Dark Side of Universal Banking: Financial Conglomerates and the Origins of the Subprime Financial Crisis", 41 *Connecticut Law Review* 963 (2009), pp.972–975.

[18] The figures that this consolidation represented in the United States are staggering: "More than 5,400 mergers took place in the U.S. banking industry from 1990 to 2005, involving more than $5.0 trillion in banking assets. In seventy-four of those mergers, both the acquiring bank and the target bank had assets exceeding $10 billion. As a consequence of the bank merger wave, the share of U.S. banking assets held by the ten largest banks more than doubled, rising from twenty-five percent in 1990 to fifty-five percent in 2005. The three largest U.S. banks – Citigroup, Bank of America (BofA) and JP Morgan Chase (Chase) – expanded rapidly after 1990, and each bank held more than $1.5 trillion of assets at the end of 2007. Wachovia, the fourth largest U.S. bank, also grew rapidly, and its assets exceeded $780 billion at the end of 2007. Ibid. pp. 975–976. (notes omitted).

[19] The chief example of such EU legislation is the Second Banking Directive 89/646/EEC [1989] OJ L 386/1, replaced by Directive 2006/48/EC [2006] OJ L 177/1 relating to the taking up and pursuit of the business of credit institutions. The Second Banking Directive allowed deposit-taking European Banks to also engage in the kind of investment market activities that were usually reserved, at least outside of Germany, for securities firms and non-deposit taking investment banks.

[20] For the full discussion see R. Cranston, *Principles of Banking Law* (OUP, 2nd ed., 2002), chapter 3.

[21] Directive on the capital adequacy of investments firms and credit institutions, 93/6/EEC [1993] OJ L141/1. See M. Hall, "The Measurement and Assessment of Market Risk: a Comparison of the European Commission and Basle Committee Approaches", *BNL Quarterly Rev.*, no 194, Sept. 1995, 183; G. Walker, "The Law of Financial Conglomerates", (1996) 30 *Int'l. L* 57. CAD has since been supplanted by EU legislation and EU banks and

do with competitive concerns as with addressing problems of risk. There was much criticism of the earlier approach of protecting the universal bank from competition from nonbank securities firms.[22]

"UNBUNDLING" THE TBTF BANK CONUNDRUM

Introductory Remarks

It is widely argued that the reason for the oligopolistic and highly concentrated structure of banking markets is that bigger institutions enjoy funding advantages. As explained later this assertion is largely true and also amounts to a clear distortion of competition. At the same time, it is not clear how detrimental is the impact of these distortions on customer welfare. Either way in order to unpick the different elements of the TBTF bank conundrum we best consider first how these banks became TBTF. The rationales for the historical trend toward repeal of legislation that controlled conglomeration and to some extent size have already been discussed. However, it would be unreasonable to assume that the push toward conglomeration was disconnected from two key shareholder concerns: first, organizational advantages, that is, attainment of economies of scale and scope, and, secondly, capital optimization, namely, maximization of ROE.

In the case, of TBTF banks the aforementioned shareholder considerations are inextricably linked to the well-documented funding advantage that TBTF banks enjoy, so-called TBTF subsidy. Thus, in the next few paragraphs I, first, discuss claims and counterclaims in relation to the social utility of TBTF banks. Then, I turn, to discuss the nature of the TBTF subsidy and the validity of economies of scale and scope assumptions about TBTF banks and the impact of TBTF banks on competition with the aid of contemporary empirical studies. In this context, I also look at the role of ROE optimization by means of increased leverage of what essentially were failure proof organizations.

Benefits and Disutilities of TBTF Banks

The universal banking model acquired strong supporters among the economics profession in the 1990s and 2000s.[23] It was argued that permitting banks to conduct

---

investment firms' capital requirements are regulated today by Regulation (EU) No 575/2013 of the European Parliament and of the Council of 26 June 2013 on prudential requirements for credit institutions and investment firms [2013] OJ L 176/18, normally called the EU Credit Requirements Regulation (CRR).

[22] For example, E. Dimson and P. Marsh, *The Debate on International Capital Requirements* (London, City Research Project, Subject Report 8, 1994).

[23] JR Barth, G Caprio, Jr, and R Levine, "Bank Regulation and Supervision: What Works Best?", NBER Working Paper No. W9323, November 2002.

securities and insurance activities presented several advantages[24]: (a) exploitation of economies of scale and scope in gathering and processing information about firms, (b) risk diversification, (c) building a diversified base of activities leads to a more stable source of income and thus more stable banks, and (d) building reputation capital with clients, and increasing the franchise value of banks and thereby augment incentives for banks to behave prudently.[25] Also it was suggested that restricting the kind of activities a bank may undertake hinders bank development[26] and thus economic growth.

Arguably, greater diversification of earnings may be associated with more stable, safer, and ultimately more valuable financial institutions. The lower the correlations among the cash-flows from a firm's various financial intermediation activities, the greater the benefits of diversification.[27] In principle this should have produced higher credit quality and higher debt ratings (lower bankruptcy risk), therefore lower cost of capital than faced by narrower, more focused firms. Likewise, greater earnings stability should bolster share prices. Key to the business of banking is risk processing and absorption. And confidence in a bank requires it to be safe. Diversification is then needed to be able to absorb risks augmenting bank safety.

But the recent crisis has proven beyond doubt that these welfare gains did not materialize. I postulate that this is due to three reasons none of which is directly related to the TBTF subsidy that will be discussed in the ensuing paragraphs: (a) TBTF banks suffered severe agency problems; (b) homogenization induced by rational herding and externally imposed capital regulations;[28] and (c) cultural changes.

Agency problems within TBTF banks are caused by three factors. First, shareholders have quite different objectives to those of creditors who will absorb the cost of bank bankruptcy,[29] independently or in addition to any taxpayer costs. Secondly, adverse compensation incentives made bank employees aggressive risk seekers. Thirdly, complexity was a very strong barrier for shareholders or creditors who

---

[24] See J. R. Barth, R. D. Brumbaugh and J. A. Wilcox, "The Repeal of Glass-Steagall and the Advent of Broad Banking", (2000) 14 *Journal of Economic Perspectives* 191; S. Claessens, D. Klingebiel, "Competition and Scope of Activities in Financial Services", World Bank, mimeo, April 2000.

[25] For the perceived relationship between franchise value and bank management's incentives to behave prudently see M. Keeley, "Deposit Insurance, Risk, and Market Power in Banking", (1990) 80 *American Economic Review* 1183–1200; R. S. Demsetz, M. R. Staidenberg and P. E. Strahan, "Banks with Something to Lose: The Disciplinary Role of Franchise Value", (1996) 2 *Economic Policy Review* 1.

[26] Barth, Caprio and Levine (2002), *supra* note 23, pp 31–32.

[27] Saunders and Walter (2011).

[28] See E. Avgouleas, *Governance of Global Financial Markets, the Law, the Economics, the Politics* (CUP, 2012), chapters 2 and 3.

[29] A. Admati and M. Hellwig, "The Leverage Ratchet Effect", Rock Center for Corporate Governance at Stanford University Working Paper 146, June 2013, available at www.gsb .stanford.edu/sites/default/files/research/documents/Leverage%20Ratchet%20Effect.pdf.

would be willing to exercise market discipline.[30] Fourthly, lax capital regulations and lack of leverage checks, created incentives to massively expand bank balance sheets through reckless lending,[31] not just in order to inflate profits and pay packages but also for job retention and career advancement purposes.[32] The cumulative impact of agency problems, complexity, and herding was that TBTF multifunctional banks eventually became, apart from a systemic threat, a serious financial system governance and integrity risk.

Management's and shareholders' opportunistic behavior and a marked shift in organizational ethics and culture, which degraded the role of proper risk controls and risk divisions within the bank,[33] and inherent complexity within the multifunctional bank business model eventually meant that TBTF multifunctional banks became very hard to manage[34] and regulate. This assumption explains why TBTF (multifunctional) banks have been at the heart of most contemporary financial scandals, whether it is with respect to rotten advice given to consumers and investors in the context of the subprime crash or the LIBOR[35] and Forex markets' ringing[36] or alleged money laundering.[37]

---

[30] E. Avgouleas and J. Cullen, "Excessive Leverage and Bankers' Pay: Governance and Financial Stability Costs of a Symbiotic Relationship", 20(2) *Columbia Journal of European Law*, 2014/5, forthcoming, available at http://papers.ssrn.com/sol3/papers.cfm?abstract_id=2412869.

[31] See Parliamentary Commission on Banking Standards, "An accident waiting to happen": The failure of HBOS, Fourth Report of Session 2012–13 HL Paper 144, HC 705, 4 April 2013, paras 28, 30, 39. [Hereinafter, *Parliamentary Report* 2013].

[32] Avgouleas and Cullen, Excessive Leverage (2014/5).

[33] The Parliamentary Report on the failure of the HBOS characteristically notes: "The risk function in HBOS was a cardinal area of weakness in the bank. . ." The degradation of the risk function was an important factor in explaining why the high-risk activities of the Corporate, International, and Treasury Divisions were not properly analyzed or checked at the highest levels within the bank. (Para 64). The weaknesses of group risk in HBOS were "a matter of design, not accident. . . (Para 65)" (emphasis added). Parliamentary Report 2013, *supra* note 31.

[34] Ibid., at Para 53.

[35] See "The LIBOR scandal: The rotten heart of finance – A scandal over key interest rates is about to go global", *The Economist* 7 July 2012, available at www.economist.com/node/21558281; Kristen Dooley, "The LIBOR Scandal", note in 32 *Review of Banking and Financial Law* 2–12 (2013), available at www.bu.edu/rbfl/files/2013/09/The-LIBOR-Scandal.pdf.

[36] "Foreign exchange allegations 'as bad as Libor', says regulator", *BBC*, 4 February 2014, quoting Martin Wheatley, the head of the UK's Financial Conduct Authority, available at www.bbc .co.uk/news/business-26041039. See also J. McGeever, "TIMELINE-The FX 'fixing' scandal", Reuters, 31 March 2014, available at http://uk.reuters.com/article/2014/03/31/swiss-forex-investi gation-events-idUKL6N0M71KO20140331; J. Moore, "RBS boss warns Forex scandal could be bigger than Libor rigging", *The Independent*, 18 July 2014, available at www.independent.co .uk/news/business/news/rbs-boss-warns-forex-scandal-could-be-bigger-than-libor-rigging-9616316.html.

[37] United States Senate, Permanent Subcommittee on Investigations, "HSBC Exposed U.S. Financial System to Money Laundering, Drug, Terrorist Financing Risks – Senate Subcommittee Holds Hearing and Releases Report", Monday, 16 July 2012, available at www.hsgac.senate .gov/subcommittees/investigations/media/hsbc-exposed-us-finacial-system-to-money-launder ing-drug-terrorist-financing-risks. The outcome of the investigation was reported by the BBC as follows: "HSBC to pay $1.9bn in US money laundering penalties", *BBC*,

The trend toward homogeneization, on the other hand, had two potent sources. The first was capital regulations, which provided ample opportunity for regulatory arbitrage inducing symmetric (gaming) behavior by big banks to minimize capital retention. The second was the use of similar risk measurements and risk mitigation techniques, the latter also based on Basel standards.[38] The cumulative effect of regulatory and industry harmonization of capital and risk measurement techniques was homogenization of different business divisions' income streams, which became dependent on the same markets (e.g., housing) even if the markets and the products sold were much different (e.g., cash mortgages, ABS, CDOs, or CDSs over the ABS).[39] Eventually, all multifunctional banks adopted a "follow the leader" strategy,[40] making them very vulnerable to the first change in the financial winds in 2007, that is, the subprime mortgage crisis.

A third explanation is a shift in the culture and ethics of the industry[41] that was possibly due to the "contamination" of big commercial banks by the operating and management style of investment banks that led to weakened risk management controls and a persistent focus on ROE.[42] Not a direct consequence of conglomeration but indicative of the casual attitude to risk that it created was the excessive use by banks of asset securitization and the adoption of the hazardous originate-to-distribute model, which meant that megabanks were the principal promoters of subprime mortgages and the key drivers behind their growth to disastrous levels.[43] The notion that risk could be endlessly diversified through "originate-to-distribute" led to a serious relaxation of credit risk controls by originator banks.[44]

Apart from the havoc wreaked on global financial stability and economic welfare by badly shaken TBTF banks during the 2008 turmoil, another major welfare loss

---

11 December 2012, available at www.bbc.co.uk/news/business-20673466. For similar incidents see J. Schneider, "FBI Says Cartel Used Bank of America to Launder Money", *Bloomberg*, 9 July 2012, available at www.bloomberg.com/news/2012–07–09/fbi-says-cartel-used-bank-of-america-to-launder-money.html.

[38] K. Alexander, J. Eatwell, A. Persaud and R. Reoch, "Financial Supervision and Crisis Management in the EU", Study for the European Parliament Committee on Economic and Monetary Affairs, Brussels, Dece. 2007, sections 1 and 2.

[39] Parliamentary Report 2013, *supra* note 31, Pars 42–43.

[40] A. G. Haldane, "Rethinking the Financial Network", Speech to the Financial Student Association, Amsterdam, 28 April 2009, pp. 3–4, available at www.bis.org/review/r090505e.pdf.

[41] The terrible fall in standards of customer care and the unethical behavior associated with recent banking scandals like Libor are very well documented in the Report of the Parliamentary Commission on Banking Standards, "Changing banking for good", *Vol. II*, HL Paper 27-II HC 175-II, 19 June 2013.

[42] For a discussion of the impact of this shift in cultural attitudes in the banking industry see in this volume W. Blair, "Reconceptualizing the Role of Standards in Supporting Financial Regulation", this volume, Chapter 21; R. Buckley, "The Changing Nature of Banking and Why it Matters", this volume, Chapter 2.

[43] Wilmarth, *supra* note 17, pp. 1017–1022.

[44] E. Avgouleas, "The Global Financial Crisis, Behavioural Finance and Financial Regulation: In Search of a new Orthodoxy", (2009) 9 *Journal of Corporate Law Studies* 121.

that may be attributed to conglomeration is that the financial system did not innovate in a way that would enhance growth and manage household risks. Instead financial innovation was driven by tax and regulatory arbitrage and obfuscated bank balance sheets undermining market discipline and regulatory monitoring. Thus, it increased risk, which was warehoused in opaque parts of the system, and within large multifunctional banks.[45]

Having more or less explained the rationale for size and conglomeration in banking markets I turn now to examine whether such arguments hold true on the basis of economic theory (economics of the bank industrial organization) and empirical studies.

Economics of Industrial Organization and the TBTF Bank

Saunders and Walter note that, on the basis industrial economics theory, "the structural form of firms pursuing economic activity should follow the dictates of institutional comparative advantage. If there are significant economies of scale that can be exploited, it will be reflected in firm size".[46] If there are significant economies of scope that can be exploited – either in terms of costs or revenues – it will be reflected in the range of activities in which successful firms are engaged. In principle, if productive linkages can be built across geographies or client segments or business lines, it too will be reflected in the breadth and geographic scope of the underlying drivers of the structure of financial intermediaries.[47] Namely, in a pure market-driven context, optimum institutional structure is driven by the production functions of financial intermediaries, on the one hand, and preference functions of end users, on the other. Thus, in theory, distortions in markets for financial intermediation in the form of taxes, explicit or implicit subsidies, and regulatory constraints will alter structural optimization and create efficiency losses in the financial system.[48]

Building Size: The Economies of Scale Assumption

In terms of revealed preferences banks present a paradox compared to other forms of business organization: they prefer to combine many different activities instead of focusing on maximization of competitive advantage. This paradox also

---

[45] See E. Avgouleas, "Regulating Financial Innovation: A Multifaceted Challenge to Financial Stability, Consumer Protection, and Growth" in E. Ferran, N. Moloney, J. Payne (eds.) *Oxford Handbook on Financial Regulation* (Oxford University Press, 2015) chapter 23, forthcoming.

[46] A. Saunders and I. Walter, "Financial Architecture, Systemic Risk, and Universal Banking", 26 *Fin. Markets and Portfolio Mgt* 39–59 (2012), p. 48.

[47] Ibid., pp. 41–49.

[48] Ibid.

distinguishes banks from other financial services firms, for, example nonbanking financial institutions like mutual funds and finance companies. The latter often choose to specialize and therefore are much more transparent. Adjusting for scale and operating efficiency the range of activities engaged in by financial intermediaries can have both cost and revenue benefits.[49] Sources of scale and scope economies include the following:

  i.   Information technology-related economies
  ii. Reputation and marketing/brand name-related benefits
  iii. (Financial) Innovation-related economies
  iv. Diversification benefits[50]

Information technology-related economies particularly refer to back-office efficiencies and distribution network-related benefits, at the same time transaction processing offers distinct scale economies. Information technology developments facilitate an increasing array of financial products and services to be offered through the same distribution network, and thus allow for cross selling.[51] Reputation and brand name or marketing-related economies might be present in the joint marketing of products to customers.[52]

On the basis of the foregone discussion, economies of scale within financial conglomerates should have been an undisputable fact. Yet the empirical evidence is as contradictory as the theoretical literature is straightforward.[53] Scale and scope economies in banking have been studied extensively. In general, studies are divided into those which are agnostic,[54] strongly positive, or strongly negative. The result of earlier studies was that economies of scale were exhausted at relatively small-size banks (under ten billion USD in assets).[55] Yet more recent studies point at more persistent scale economies. Wheelock and Wilson (2009)[56] and Feng and Serletis (2010)[57] find increasing returns to scale.

---

[49] Ibid., p. 50.

[50] A. Boot, "Restructuring in the Banking Industry with Implications for Europe" in 8(1) 2003 EIB Papers (Europe's Changing Financial Landscape: Recent Developments and Prospects), 108, pp. 110 *et seq.*

[51] Ibid.

[52] Ibid.

[53] Ibid.

[54] A. N. Berger, R. S. Demsetz and P. E. Strahan, "The Consolidation of the financial Services Industry: Causes, Consequences and Implications for the Future", 23 *Journal of Banking and Finance* 135–194 (1999), concluded that, in general, the empirical evidence cannot readily identify substantial economies of scale or scope.

[55] For an excellent discussion of these studies see Boot, *supra* note 50, pp. 23–26.

[56] D. C. Wheelock and P. Wilson, "Are U.S. Banks Too Large?", Working Paper 2009–054 (2009), Federal Reserve Bank of St. Louis.

[57] G. Feng and A. Serletis, "Efficiency, Technical Change, and Returns to Scale in Large US Banks: Panel Data Evidence from an Output Distance Function Satisfying Theoretical Regularity", 34 *Journal of Banking and Finance* 127–138 (2010).

These more recent studies use a different methodology, correcting to some extent possible flaws in earlier studies,[58] but more importantly they utilize more advanced IT technology and wider availability of data, given how much more transparent banks have become since 2008. This is important because it is unclear whether earlier researchers had access to information about efficiencies and profitability of individual business division within banks, figures that all big bank management prefers to obfuscate. To this effect, and challenging earlier assumptions, the most recent studies show that size in banking is linked to economies of scale in a variety of contexts[59] and especially improves banks operating costs, understood as noninterest costs like employee remuneration, cost of premises, IT infrastructure etc.[60] Naturally, evidence of economies of scale is higher in efficiently run versus inefficient banks,[61] exhibiting the value of good and sensible management.

Conglomeration and Economies of Scope

Unlike most success stories in financial services where focus tends to reap supra-competitive rewards, for example, Goldman Sachs, Euroclear, Blackstone, banks tend to diversify the scope of their activities. As explained earlier, this is in part in order to diversify sources of income. But this is not the only purpose. In the period before 2008 it was consistently argued that conglomeration in the financial sector was motivated by and presented distinct economies of scope. According to Saunders and Walter, "revenue economies of scope in financial intermediation arise when the all-in cost to the buyer of multiple financial services from a single supplier is less than the cost of purchasing them from separate suppliers. This includes search, monitoring, and contracting costs".[62] Financial intermediaries

---

[58] For example, L. J. Mester, "Scale Economies in Banking and Financial Regulatory Reform", Note in: The Region. Federal Reserve of Minneapolis, Sept. 2010, available at www.minneapolisfed.org/publications_papers/pub_display.cfm?id=4535.

[59] J. Hughes and L. Mester, "Who Said Large Banks Don't Experience Scale Economies? Evidence from a Risk-Return-Driven Cost Function", 22 *Journal of Financial Intermediation* 559–85 (2013); D. C. Wheelock and P. W. Wilson, "Do Large Banks Have Lower Costs? New Estimates of Returns to Scale for U.S. Banks", 44 *Journal of Money, Credit, and Banking* 171–99 (2013).

[60] It is suggested that quantitatively a 10 per cent increase in assets is associated with 0.3 to 0.6 per cent decline in noninterest expense scaled by income or assets, depending on specification. A. Kovner, J. Vickery and L. Zhou, "Do Big Banks Have Lower Operating Costs?", 20(2) *Federal Reserve Bank of Economic Policy Review*, March 2014, 1–44, pp. 221–22. The authors of the aforementioned study have found evidence that lower operating costs are a source of scale economies because large banks spread overheads associated with IT and accounting systems and marketing over a larger asset or revenue base. Id. pp. 2, 12–18, 21 with extensive tables. It is the present author's view that such detailed studies would not have been possible to prior to 2008. In addition the authors of the aforementioned study are researchers based in the NY Fed, which means they had access to an extensive range of unpublished (nonconfidential) data than authors of earlier studies.

[61] Hughes and Mester, *supra* note 59.

[62] Saunders and Walter, *supra* note 46, p. 51.

that are diversified could achieve cost reductions by cross-selling as well as selling a broader rather than narrower range of products. At the same time, shared IT platforms, client database, branch networks, as well as data mining constitute a fixed cost that be spread better in a bigger organization.

Accordingly, like economies of scale, cost-related scope economies should be directly observable in production functions of financial services suppliers and in aggregate performance measures.[63] Yet, unlike the mixed to positive picture offered by the aforementioned studies on the relationship between bank size and economies of scale, most empirical studies[64] have failed to find significant cost economies of scope in the banking, insurance or securities industries. On the contrary, there is evidence of diseconomies of scope, which emanate from three sources: new product costs,[65] the diversification discount,[66] and organization complexity that leads to inefficient management and regulatory supervision.

Significant cost-scope economies or diseconomies should be reflected on investor valuations of financial intermediaries and these valuations should, in principle, be an important factor (alongside financial stability and consumer welfare) in choosing optimal institutional structures in banking. Yet a strong line of studies point to the opposite direction revealing the existence of a persistent discount in valuations of financial conglomerates. The more recent studies, starting with Laeven and Levine (2007)[67] confirm the existence of a diversification discount in banks that combine lending and nonlending financial services, mostly reflecting potential agency problems and inefficiencies associated with cross-subsidies. Schmid and Walter (2009)[68] confirm the Laeven and Levine (2007) results, and verify that this discount is indeed caused by diversification, and not by inefficiencies that already existed before the diversification.[69]

Rajan, Servaes, and Zingales (2000)[70] showed that the interrelation between activities within the conglomerate is of crucial importance. Diversified firms can trade at a premium if the dispersion between activities is low. High dispersion induces inefficiencies, which add credence to the hypothesis that focus adds value

[63] Ibid.

[64] For a comprehensive overview of these studies see Boot, *supra* note 50, pp. 24–26.

[65] For example, it has been observed that when financial services firms add new product lines and the product range widens, unit-costs seem to go up and not down. Ibid.

[66] The most common meaning of this term is that due to conglomerate's opaque balance sheets and complex business activities capital markets value the whole of the business less than the sum of its parts. This is in line with corporate finance theory that tells us that investors can choose to diversify and that this does not need to be done at the firm level.

[67] L. Laeven and R. Levine, "Is There a Diversification Discount in Financial Conglomerates?", 85 *Journal of Financial Economics* 331–367 (2007).

[68] M. M. Schmid and I. Walter, "Do Financial Conglomerates Create or Destroy Economic Value?" 18 *Journal of Financial Intermediation* 193–216 (2009).

[69] Both studies, using large data panels, have attempted to ascertain whether or not functional diversification is value enhancing or value destroying in the financial services sector and estimate the value-reduction effect at about 20%. Ibid.

[70] R. Rajan, H. Servaes and L. Zingales, "The Cost of Diversity: The Diversification Discount and Inefficient Investment", 55 *Journal of Finance* 35–80 (2000).

to the business of banking. Evidence from capital markets' reaction to financial sector mergers reinforces this view. DeLong (2001) examined shareholder gains from focused versus diversifying bank mergers in the United States between 1988 and 1995.[71] Focused mergers, in terms of kind of activity undertaken by the merger firms and geographic dispersion, were found to result in a positive effect on the immediate postannouncement share prices. Activity-diversifying mergers had no positive announcement effects.[72]

The consequences of the rise in agency costs in financial conglomerates have been evident in the already discussed Libor, FX rigging, and money-laundering scandals. Impossible to manage and too complex to regulate banking conglomerates turned into a constant integrity and efficiency risk for the financial system. While the spotlight has fallen on rotten cultures and ethics within the "chastened" banks, banking conglomerates were likely to encounter several of the revealed abuses, even in the absence of infractions of ethical standards. Simply put, the broader the range of financial firm activities, in the presence of imperfect information, the greater the probability that the firm will encounter conflicts of interest.

Agency costs due to complexity that conglomeration brings means that sooner or later business lines' diversification will destroy shareholder and franchise value through a marked rise in agency costs and inefficient use of capital. Namely, conglomerates tend to use capital inefficiently and this is independently of the colossal conduct costs that the scandals discussed earlier brought about in the form of payment billions of dollars in regulatory fines and other sanctions.[73] Managerial discretion to engage in value-reducing projects, cross-subsidization of marginal or loss-making projects that drain resources from healthy businesses, misalignments in incentives between central and divisional managers seem to be as responsible.[74] In addition, as Boot[75] accurately argues that conglomeration proved an excellent technique to bury trade-related losses in the group balance sheet and it was, thus, mostly favored by senior bank management that came from the investment banking side.[76]

---

[71] G. DeLong, "Stockholder Gains from Focusing versus Diversifying Bank Mergers", 59 *Journal of Financial Economics* 221–242 (2001).

[72] Ibid. In the author's view these results may indicate the presence of scale rather than scope economies in banking.

[73] A very good study by the LSE Bank conduct costs project run by R. McCormick has indicated that conduct costs for the ten world-leading banks in the period between 2008–2012 have neared 150 billion GBP. See for the requisite table the period between 2008–2012 http://blogs .lse.ac.uk/conductcosts/bank-conduct-costs-results/.

[74] P. G. Berger, E. Ofek, "Diversification's Effect on Firm Value", 37 *Journal of Financial Economics* 39–65 (1995).
The bulk of value erosion in conglomerates is usually attributed to overinvestment in marginally profitable activities and cross-subsidization. Id.

[75] Boot, *supra* note 50, pp. 16–20.

[76] In the present author's view Bob Diamond's ascent to the top of Barclays PLC is only one instance of proven domination of senior management jobs in big universal banks by investment bankers in the 2000s.

These findings make shareholder preference for conglomeration, or, at least, no resistance to, it even more puzzling. I argue that there is a twofold explanation for this seeming departure from shareholder self-interest maximization. First, conglomeration renders the biggest parts of the financial group TBTF, incentivizing, thus, shareholders to seek leverage and take advantage of the TBTF subsidy. Secondly shareholder preference for/nonresistance to conglomeration in the financial sector may be evidence of the prevalence of bounded rationality even within sophisticated capital market actors.

The TBTF Subsidy and Bank Competition

Evidence of the TBTF Subsidy

In general, big systemic banks, so-called too-big-to-fail banks enjoy a strong advantage in terms of costs of funding, which smaller institutions do not. There have been numerous quantitative studies of the "subsidy" provided by the implicit government bail-out guarantee to the larger banks that are too-big-to-fail. The first in a line of several such studies was by Andy Haldane who made the bold claim that direct and indirect state subsidies to big banks amounted to 25 percent of world GDP.[77] This was followed by several others providing similar conclusions, for example, Ueda and Weder-Di Mauro, 2011[78]; Li et al. 2011,[79] with the latest authoritative study finding that the funding discount enjoyed by TBTF banks could rise to as high as (-)1.21 percent.[80] The TBTF funding subsidy constitutes a clear distortion of competition.

Taking advantage of lower funding costs, larger banks can cut margins aggressively, offering new clients better lending terms, to edge out smaller competitors (Hakenes and Schnabel, 2011),[81] a clear distortion in terms of playing field. Yet it is unclear if this is the sole or even the main reason for the very high levels of

---

[77] A. G. Haldane, "On Being the Right Size", Institute of Economic Affairs, 21 Beesley Lecture, 25 October 2012, p. 4 et seq., available at www.bankofengland.co.uk/publications/Documents/speeches/2012/speech615.pdf. In fact, Haldane argues that any economies of scale in TBTF banks comes due to the funding advantage ensured by the TBTF subsidy. However, the Kovner et al. study cited in note 57 earlier, which found strong evidence of economies of scale in big banks, measured noninterest operating costs.

[78] K. Ueda and B. Weder Di Mauro, "Quantifying the Value of the Subsidy for Systemically Important Financial Institutions", IMF Working Paper 12/128, (2011).

[79] Z. Li, S. Qu and J. Zhang, "Quantifying the Value of Implicit Government Guarantees for Large Financial Institutions. Moody's Analytics Quantitative Research Group" (January 2013).

[80] See J. Santos, "Evidence from the Bond Market on Banks' 'Too-Big-To-Fail' Subsidy", 20 *Federal Reserve Bank of New York, Economic Policy Review* (Special Issue: Large and Complex Banks), March, 2014.

[81] R. Gropp, H. Hakenes, and I. Schnabel, "Competition, Risk-shifting, and Public Bail-Out Policies", 24 *Review of Financial Studies* 2084–2120 (2011).

concentration experienced by banking markets in most major economies where banking products and services are offered by a small group of very large banks. Thus, I provide below a more in-depth analysis of issues of competition in the banking sector.

Bank Competition and Systemic Stability: How Much Competition Is Too Much?

As explained earlier, the banking industry has been building size for at least two decades and the recent forced mergers and acquisitions, in order to avoid bank collapses, have only intensified this phenomenon. It is, however, unclear whether banking markets present highly oligopolistic structures because banking is an industry that offers its services more efficiently through large-size institutions, or because regulatory controls and licensing requirements are so expensive as to deter new entrants from entering the market, especially in the market for retail banking services where the margins for profit can be quite low.

There are two basic hypotheses in the literature on the relationship between financial stability and competition: the *franchise value paradigm* (competition-fragility view) and the *risk-shifting hypothesis* (competition-stability view).[82] The competition-fragility view contends that an increase in competition will hurt bank stability by eroding the franchise value.[83] Based on empirical findings and theoretical simulations these studies postulate that less competitive banking systems are less fragile because the numerous lending opportunities, high profits, capital ratios, and charter values of incumbent banks make them better placed to withstand demand- or supply-side shocks, and provide disincentives for excessive risk taking.[84]

The competition-stability view holds that competition leads to less fragility, because the market power of banks results in higher interest rates for customers, making it more difficult for them to repay loans.[85] This increased the possibility of loan defaults, increasing risk for bank portfolios, making the financial system less stable.[86]

---

[82] For analytical discussion of the two hypotheses see M. López-Puertas Lamy, "Commercial banks versus Stakeholder banks: Same business, same risks, same rules?", mimeo, 2012, pp. 3–6, available at www.globalcube.net/clients/eacb/content/medias/events/research_awards_2012/cooperative_banks_vs_commercial_banks_Lamy_monica.pdf.

[83] F. Allen and D. Gale, "Competition and Financial Stability", 36 *Journal of Money, Credit and Banking* 453–480 (2004); E. Carletti, "Competition and Regulation in Banking" in A Boot, A Thakor, (eds.) *Handbook of Financial Intermediation and Banking* (Amsterdam: Elsevier, 2008), chapter 14.

[84] Ibid.

[85] Boyd and De Nicoló, *infra* note 88.

[86] Ibid.

Most recently, Martinez-Miera and Repullo (2010) suggest a nonlinear relationship between bank competition and financial stability, arguing that heightened competition may reduce a borrower's probability of default (referred to as the risk-shifting effect), but it may also reduce interest payments from performing loans, which serve as a buffer to cover loan losses (referred to as the margin effect). They find evidence of a U-shaped relationship between competition (measured by the number of banks) and bank stability. In highly concentrated markets, the risk-shifting effect dominates and more competition reduces bank risk, while in very competitive markets the margin effect dominates, and increased competition erodes bank franchise value and hence increases risk.[87]

Overall empirical evidence with respect to whether competition enhances or reduces bank stability is mixed. While some researchers find that the risk of bank failure increases in less competitive markets,[88] others find that risk decreases with a rise in the market power of incumbent banks.[89] Berger et al. (2009), using a variety of risk and competition measures from twenty-three countries, provide limited support to both the competition-fragility and competition-stability views.[90] Specifically, they find that market power increases credit risk, but banks with more market power face less risk, overall, which also is in accord with the conclusions of the Jimenez et al. study.

The view that "too much" competition could undermine instead of fostering financial stability is clearly upheld by IMF experts:[91] "Limited competition and strong regulation, which limits banking activities and requires banks to have more equity (i.e., shareholder funds) and more secure investments, can lead to a more secure banking system".

Ratnovski accurately postulates that this is due to problems of corporate governance. Shareholders face inverse incentives, as they normally wish to pursue profitability at the expense of safety and creditors, turning thus into weak corporate monitors.[92] Moreover, complexity of bank business provides yet another obstacle to strengthening shareholders' role as monitors[93] and it may be also

---

[87] D. Martinez-Miera, R. Repullo, "Does Competition Reduce the Risk of Bank Failure?", CEPR Working Paper DP6669/2009.

[88] See J. H. Boyd and G. De Nicoló, "The Theory of Bank Risk Taking and Competition Revisited", 60 *Journal of Finance* 1329–1343 (2005); J. Boyd, G. De Nicoló, A. Al Jalal, "Bank risk taking and competition revisited: New theory and new evidence", mimeo, Carlson School of Management, University of Minnesota, 2006.

[89] G. Jiménez, J. A. López and J. Saurina, "How does competition impact bank risk taking?" Federal Reserve Bank of San Francisco, Working Paper 2007–23, Sept. 2007, available at www.frbsf.org/publications/economics/papers/2007/wp07–23bk.pdf.

[90] A. N. Berger, L. F. Klapper, R. Turk-Ariss, "Bank competition and financial stability", 35 *Journal of Financial Services Research* 99–118 (2009).

[91] L. Ratnovski, "Competition Policy for Modern Banks'", International Monetary Fund, WP/13/126, 2013, available at www.imf.org/external/pubs/ft/wp/2013/wp13126.pdf.

[92] Ibid.

[93] See also Avgouleas and Cullen, *supra* note 7.

an obstacle to shareholders' pushing for more competition if they do not have an accurate picture of which part of the bank's business has the highest potential.

Experience shows that Canada and Australia, which were among the least-affected countries by the GFC, were dominated by very few big banks, due to previous crises and older rounds of baking sector consolidation, which increased bank resilience.[94] It is disputed, however, that these oligopolies made markets less competitive especially when it came to pricing consumer products. For example, a 2013 IMF paper on the matter shows Australia and Canada presenting medium intensity levels of competition.[95]

But these observations ought not to be taken too far and up to the point that consumer welfare is detrimentally affected. They just mean that measures to increase competition in banking presuppose that the banking system is already robust to ameliorate any systemic stability impact that enhanced competition may have. As explained in the Vickers Report the banking industry in the United Kingdom (and in other countries) presents higher levels of concentration after the crisis than before, given the merger of major commercial banks in the aftermath of the crisis (e.g., Lloyds Bank with Halifax Bank of Scotland).[96] This ought to be a matter of concern for regulators because the concentration of retail accounts has reached such a level as to restrict consumer choice.[97] More recently, the United Kingdom's Competition and Markets Authority has conducted a review of the industry and reached some "damning" conclusions.[98] CMA is now moving toward a "root and branch" review of the conditions of competition in the UK banking industry.[99]

---

[94] N. Arjani and G. Paulin, "Lessons from the Financial Crisis: Bank Performance and Regulatory Reform", Bank of Canada Discussion Paper 2013–4 December 2013, pp. 1–5. Others, on the other hand, like ex IMF chief economist Simon Johnson argue that Canadian banks were more undercapitalized and leveraged than U.S. banks and what made them more stable was the fact that Canadian banks paid a very low premium to have their mortgages insured by the federal government. Peter Boone and Simon Johnson, "The Canadian Banking Fallacy", blog entry, 25 June 2010 http://baselinescenario.com/2010/03/25/the-canadian-banking-fallacy/.

[95] Ratnovski, *supra* note 91.

[96] Independent Commission on Banking, "Final Report – Recommendations", September 2011, p. 16–18 and chapters 6–8, available at https://hmt-sanctions.s3.amazonaws.com/ICB%20final%20report/ICB%2520Final%2520Report%5B1%5D.pdf.

[97] Ibid. pp. 154–156.

[98] The CMA found that: "Essential parts of the UK retail banking sector lack effective competition and do not meet the needs of personal consumers or small- and medium-sized enterprises (SMEs)". CMA, "CMA consulting on provisional decision to launch an in-depth investigation", 18 July 2014, www.gov.uk/government/news/personal-current-accounts-and-small-business-banking-not-working-well-for-customers.

[99] See CMA, "Competition and Markets Authority case Personal current accounts and SME banking", 1 August 2014, www.gov.uk/cma-cases/review-of-banking-for-small-and-medium-sized-businesses-smes-in-the-uk.

Capital Structure "Optimization" and Excessive Leverage

There is ample evidence to show that funding advantages allowed TBTF institutions to expand their balance sheets through leverage and there is sufficient evidence to show that too-big-to-fail banks are prone to take much riskier assets than other banks.[100] It is, however, unclear whether in the absence of leverage restrictions, elimination of TBTF subsidy will radically alter bank management behavior. While Admati, Hellwig, and others[101] accurately point out that bankers are addicted to leverage but they might have overlooked another important element. Shareholder pressure on bank management to build leverage and thus maximize ROE may be the only survival and career-advancement strategy even for the most prudent of bank managers if their competitors are doing the same. I have written on this matter elsewhere[102] and the discussion has been upheld and furthered by the *Financial Times* in a recent editorial,[103] so no more will be said here.

Was Glass Steagall Successful?

While the arguments of its critics proved to have shaky foundations, the financial stability benefits of Glass Steagall have been beyond much doubt. Apart from the crisis in the Savings & Loans sector of the late 1980s and early 1990s, which saw 747 thrift failures (out of 3,234)[104] but did not in the end infect systemic financial institutions covered by the Act, the U.S. financial sector suffered no major crisis during the life the Act. During the same period the United States saw the failure of only one systemic institution, the Continental Illinois Bank and Trust Company in 1984.

At the same time, it is hypothesized that the Act, by adding focus, which led to creating high level skills and impetus in the search of new revenues, was, in part, responsible for the progressive dominance of U.S. investment banks in rapidly evolving offshore and onshore capital markets worldwide. The gradual liberalization and integration of global markets since the 1970s also meant that American securities firms progressively dominated the competitiveness tables edging out European universal banking behemoths and their Asian counterparts, which had

---

[100] G. Afonso, J. Santos, J. Traina, "Do 'Too Big To Fail' Banks Take on More Risk?", 20 *Federal Reserve Bank of New York, Economic Policy Review* (March 2014) Special Issue: Large and Complex Banks; M. Brandao, L. R. Correa, and H. Sapriza. 2013. "International Evidence on Government Support and Risk Taking in the Banking Sector", International Monetary Fund Working Paper no. 13/94.

[101] Admati and Hellwig, *supra* note 29.

[102] Avgouleas and Cullen, Excessive Leverage (2014/5).

[103] M. Arnold, "Tale of Two Banks Exposes Pay as Wrong Target of Critics – UK's Co-op is opposite extreme to Wells Fargo of US", *FT*, 14 April 2014, available at www.ft.com/cms/s/0/a9a41d96-c3e1-11e3-a8e0-00144feabdc0.html#axzz3C5WYTP7K.

[104] Saunders and Walter (2011), pp. 43–45.

traditionally enjoyed intimate relationships with domestic corporates and governments.[105] Glass Stegall is also credited the impetus for the development of "global buy-side" markets, comprising insurance companies, pension funds, and other institutional investors, by U.S. investment banks that provided buy-side participants with new investment alternatives. It is validly assumed that had Glass Steagall not been in place after 1933, the lack of competitive pressure would have affected their global competitiveness and drive to innovate that U.S. investment banks subsequently showed, especially after the mid-1970s.

It is, therefore, unsurprising that the true impetus to amend and eventually repeal the Act did not come from the SEC regulated broker-dealer sector but rather it was the result of pressure by large U.S. commercial banks[106] whose participation in global capital markets and especially in the lucrative securities underwriting market was restricted even after the 1956 amendments, which allowed commercial banks to maintain a limited purpose securities subsidiary. Commercial banks, which already competed "vigorously with investment banks in government bond, foreign exchange, and other traded markets as well as corporate advisories" argued that Glass Steagall restrictions on their securities activities placed them at a competitive disadvantage. Namely, the principal factor behind the disastrous repeal of Glass Steagall was greedy commercial bank shareholders rather than a nepharious Wall Street conspiracy.

Summary of Findings

The presence of significant economies of scale associated with bank size are not a sufficient reason to allow banks to expand their balance sheets, normally though leverage, to the point that they threaten financial stability. But even if there is a trade-off between efficiencies-driven bank size and financial stability, the studies discussed earlier showed no evidence of any efficiencies attained through conglomeration. On the contrary, as Glass Steagall's impact on the competiveness of the U.S. investment banking sector and the examples of important financial services firms like Blackrock, Euroclear, and large hedge funds have shown, focus pays off in banking as in most other industries. In contrast, conglomeration, in the name of unproved income diversification, seems to bring intolerable costs. These include the diversification discount and over-stretching management and regulatory ability to the point that universal bank behemoths become a constant social and financial stability risk.

---

[105] Ibid. Saunders and Walter accurately note: "By the early 1990s American investment banks basically dominated their industry worldwide, with a market share approaching 75% in terms of transactions volume. As a consequence, investment banking developed into one of the top U.S. export industries". Id.

[106] Saunders and Walter name as the principal agitators Morgan Guaranty Trust Company, Bankers Trust, Chase Manhattan and Citicorp. Saunders and Walter (2011), pp. 45–47.

Moreover, all evidence points to the direction that systemic risk cannot be contained in large diversified banks. On the contrary a number of studies, e.g., Richardson, Smith, and Walter (2010)[107] conclude that "expansion to multiple functions – the LCFI (large, complex financial institution) model – produces greater systematic risk".[108] Their conclusion echoes an extensive line of studies pointing to the same direction, including more recently De Jonghe (2010)[109] and theoretical work by Wagner (2010).[110] It follows that, in the absence, of any strong evidence in favour of conglomeration, structural reform is a good way to respond to interconnectedness in financial markets. This is an issue that I will further discuss in the next section.

DEALING WITH THE TBTF BANK

Special Resolution Regimes and Structural Reform

Implementation of special resolution schemes and structural reform rather than enhanced competition have been the main prongs of government and regulators' approach to resolving the TBTF problem. Special resolution regimes for financial institutions, in general, as is the case with the EU Bank Resolution Directive, or just for systemically important institutions, as is the case with the Dodd Frank OLA, target TBTF moral hazard from two very important routes.

First, by removing legal obstacles to resolution, by means of derogation from general company and insolvency law safeguards and procedures, and by minimizing the risk of contagion, special resolution regimes purportedly secure the orderly failure of a TBTF bank, without damaging confidence in the financial system or disrupting the provision of essential payment and other services by the failing institution. Secondly, through the use of bail-in clauses, special resolution regimes attempt to force TBTF bank funders (shareholders & creditors) to internalize the risk of failure of systemic banks,[111] namely, to curb the externalities caused by risk-seeking banks. It is expected that such bail-in regimes will make bank shareholders and more importantly creditors better corporate monitors minimizing excessive risk seeking.[112]

---

[107] M. Richardson, R.C. Smith and I. Walter, "Large Banks and the Volcker Rule" in V. Acharya et al. (eds.), *Regulating Wall Street: The Dodd-Frank Act and the New Architecture of Global Finance* (Willey, 2010), 181–212.

[108] Ibid.

[109] O. De Jonghe, "Back to the Basics in Banking? A Micro-Analysis of Banking System Stability", 19 *Journal of Financial Intermediation* (2010) 387–417.

[110] W. Wagner, "Diversification at Financial Institutions and Systemic Crises", 19 *Journal of Financial Intermediation* 373–386 (2010).

[111] One of the Act's explicit aims, as stated in its preamble, is: "to protect the American taxpayer by ending bailouts". Thus, under section 204(a) (1) of the Dodd Frank Act creditors and shareholders bear all the losses of the financial company that has entered OLA.

[112] See T. F. Huertas, "The Case for Bail-ins", chapter in A. Dombrat and P. Kenadjian, *The Bank Recovery and Resolution Directive* (Berlin, De Gruyter, e-book, 2013). For some scepticism as to the possible adverse effects of triggering the bail-in process E. Avgouleas and C. Goodhart,

Structural reform, on the other hand, has, in general, taken two forms. First, the Vickers model that seeks to both shelter (ring-fence) the commercial banking part of the group from risks arising in the investment banking part of the group and battle interconnectedness, by virtue of the limitations it imposes on the activities the ring-fenced bank can undertake.[113] The commercial banking subsidiary will remain part of the group subject to strict corporate governance safeguards. The second model (the Volcker Rule) amounts to an outright restriction on licensed commercial bank groups to engage in proprietary trading and shadow banking activities, namely, the riskiest parts of investment banking business. Thus, the Volcker Rule (s. 619 of the Dodd Frank Act) includes a ban on "proprietary trading" and "investing" and "sponsoring" a "covered fund", a term that extends to a variety of shadow banking vehicles and beyond. A banking entity "invests" in a "covered fund" if it acquires or retains any equity, partnership, or other ownership interest in a hedge fund or a private equity fund.

Both Volcker rule and Vickers separation models present some distinct advantages when it comes to battling interconnectedness. In addition, revised Basel capital and liquidity requirements are bound to add further resilience and insert a more long-term perspective in the funding sources of commercial banks.

Yet structural reform may not resolve, on its own, the TBTF conundrum. While structural separation of different forms of banking is essential for financial stability yet the optimum model is rather elusive. For example, both the Vickers and Volcker models of structural separation are characteristically discomforted by the most challenging part of banking: wholesale lending. Also the circumstances surrounding the already discussed repeal of Glass Steagall and the EU "level the playing field" legislation have shown how vulnerable is structural legislation to political economy risks. There is always the possibility that due to groupthink or regulatory capture, driven by industry self-interest, one day politicians will turn back the clock to recent structural reforms and conglomeration and financial stability risk will re-emerge.

Finally, fractional reserve banking works on trust and any important endogenous or exogenous shock is capable of triggering a panic, in the absence of fiscal backstops. To this effect a discussion of the advantages and disadvantages of the alternative full reserve banking and of the two best-known models of narrow/limited purpose banking, both proposed by prominent economists, is very apposite here.

"A Critical Evaluation of Bails as Bank Recapitalisation Mechanisms", CEPR, DP 10015/14, available at http://papers.ssrn.com/sol3/papers.cfm?abstract_id=2478647.

[113] The best example is the UK's new ring fencing regime based on the recommendation of the Vickers Report which were implemented by means of the Financial Services (Banking Reform) Act 2013, c. 33.

Full Reserve Narrow/Limited Purpose Banking

Chamley, Kotlikoff, and Polemarhakis have argued that "[b]anks collapse for one reason – they are leveraged. Hence, limiting proprietary information, that is, providing much more disclosure and transparency, and eliminating leverage are the key to having a stable, well-functioning financial system".[114] Thus Kotlikoff[115] and Chamley[116] have proposed a full reserve alternative.[117] The essence of their proposal is that all limited liability financial intermediaries should be treated identically, regardless of organizational form. Namely, all commercial banks, investment banks, insurance companies, hedge funds, private equity funds, credit unions would have to operate as mutual fund holding companies that issue 100 percent equity-financed open- and closed-end mutual funds. Total lack of leverage would mean that different institutions and the financial system as whole would never fail. Shadow banking vehicles will be allowed to carry leverage but as they would be unlimited liability entities, any losses would fall on their owners.

Full reserve limited purpose banking is not without its own intractable problems. For example, how would full reserve limited purpose banks defend themselves from a depositor flight when competing "shadow banks" offer reasonable and safely higher interest, while they are themselves constrained to do so by the fact that their reserves would be fully invested in low yielding instruments? Moreover, not all "shadow banks" will be the same. What if imprudent depositors start chasing illusionary high returns from Chinese type investment trusts, rendering unregulated retail shadow banks the order of the day. Of course, Kotlikoff et al. note that

---

[114] C. Chamley, L. J. Kotlikoff, H. Polemarhakis, "Limited Purpose Banking – Moving from 'Trust Me' to 'Show Me' Banking", mimeo May 2012, available at www.kotlikoff.net/content/limited-purpose-banking-moving-trust-me-show-me-banking.

[115] L. J. Kotlikoff, *Jimmy Stewart Is Dead: Ending the World's Ongoing Financial Plague with Limited Purpose Banking* (John Wiley and Sons, 2010).

[116] See C. Chamley and L. J. Kotlikoff, "Limited Purpose Banking – Putting An End to Financial Crises", *Financial Times*, The Economists' Forum, 27 January 2009, available at http://people.bu.edu/Kotlikoff/newweb/LimitedPurposeBanking1-27-09.pdf.

[117] Their proposal has been summarized as follows:

1. All financial companies protected by limited liability can market just one thing – mutual funds.
2. Mutual funds are not allowed to borrow, explicitly or implicitly, and, thus, can never fail.
3. Cash mutual funds, which are permitted to hold only cash, are used for the payment system.
4. Cash mutual funds are the only mutual funds backed to the buck.
5. Tontine-type mutual funds are used to allocate idiosyncratic risk.
6. Pari-mutuel mutual funds are used to allocate aggregate risk via direct or derivate betting.
7. The Federal Financial Authority (FFA) hires private companies working only for it to verify, appraise, rate, custody, and disclose, in real time, all securities held by mutual funds.
8. Mutual funds buy and sell FFA-processed and disclosed securities at auction. This ensures that issuers of securities, be they households or firms, receive the highest price for their paper. Chamley et al. (2012).

shadow banking entities will have to be unlimited liability vehicles. However, this, in effect, means very little. Will regulators be able to check if owners' equity is enough to cover the shadow banks' liabilities? If yes then the "shadow banks" are now "regulated banks" in some jurisdictions. Then how are we supposed to avoid – disastrous in this case – regulatory arbitrage by shadow banks in the absence of a global regulatory system and a global regulator, which may be politically unfeasible for some time?

Professor Kay has suggested a different form of full reserve narrow banking. This would involve the spinoff of big banks' proprietary trading business, because this business differs only in scale from their treasury operations, which are both necessary and legitimate.[118] As a result, Kay proposed a division between narrow banks accepting retail deposits, which should preferably be invested in risk-free government bonds and would only provide payment and other utility banking services and all other financial business. The latter could be deregulated and freed from microprudential regulation.

Professor Kay's model also presents intractable difficulties. First, under the Kay model most forms of lending that could create an asset bubble such as mortgage or big business lending would be conducted by the unregulated or quasiregulated sector, perpetuating the risks that led to the global financial crisis, such as the too-big-to-fail problem.[119] Also, leaving risky lending to the unregulated sector would mean that unequipped financing vehicles would have to assume risks that commercial banks are much better equipped to handle.

Another loophole of Kay's model is the constantly fluctuating state of sovereign bond markets. As the Asian and Eurozone crises have shown, these assets are as unsafe as any. In addition, there may be inadequate supply of such instruments to cover the entire stock of insured deposits in any given country, as is the case with the United Kingdom.[120]

Arguably, there is no way around either problem, and Kay's suggestion for the government to issue additional gilts to on-lend to narrow banks "would essentially mean the nationalization" of credit risk. Finally, Kay's model is even more vulnerable to unlicensed competitors (e.g., money market funds) offering higher interest rates to existing and potential depositors as the suggested narrow banks' assets would attract the traditionally lower sovereign bond yields rather than the superior corporate bond interest rates.

---

[118] J. Kay, "Narrow Banking, The Reform of Banking Regulation", Report for the Centre for the Study of Financial Innovation, September 2009, available at www.johnkay.com/papers/ JK_NarrowBanking.pdf.

[119] Kay suggested that funds for these activities would be raised from wholesale markets, securitizations and own capital, instead of retail deposits. Ibid.

[120] Financial Services Authority (FSA), "A Regulatory Response to the Global Banking Crisis: Systemically Important Banks and Assessing the Cumulative Impact", Discussion Paper 09/4, October 2009, pp. 23–24.

Yet, what is discussed earlier does not mean that the introduction of narrow banking vehicles, which combine both equity and debt financing through the capital markets, in parts of the financial system, would be out of place. On the contrary, especially when it comes to credit markets like mortgage lending, where leverage has a massive impact on the real economy, and a feedback effect on financial stability, due to the volatility of housing markets, if their rates were competitive, such narrow banking vehicles would remove a very substantial source of instability from the financial system.

CONCLUSION

Saunders and Walter have observed that in a pure market context, optimum institutional structure in the financial sector should be driven by the production functions of financial intermediaries and the preferences of end users.[121] In practice financial institutions become larger or smaller, broader or narrower than what is optimal for the intermediation tasks to be performed. This is mostly due to distortions in markets for financial intermediation in the form of taxes, explicit or implicit subsidies, and regulatory constraints.[122] Two prominent such distortions are the TBTF subsidy and the preferential tax treatment of debt that affects the structure of bank capital.[123] Lots of questions had been left unaddressed for a long time. Is bigger better? Is broader better? Both questions have no easy answers. We need to consider them in the context of financial stability, client welfare, shareholder value, regulatory effectiveness, and oversocial utility.

Issues of financial stability and consumer welfare ought to be addressed first. As explained earlier there are strong arguments against excessive competition in the banking sector, as margins could be eroded leading to reckless risk taking. As regards consumer welfare, a good example is the TBTF subsidy. This amounts to abuse of stronger competitive position. So in theory there ought to be welfare losses emanating from the discussed funding cost squeeze on competition. While these are still to be measured,[124] it may also be the case that the TBTF subsidy translates into gains for consumers, as banks pass on their funding advantage to their customers, primarily in the shape of lower interest rates. In addition, the subsidy

---

[121] Saunders and Walter (2011), p. 48.
[122] Ibid.
[123] A. R. Admati, P. M. DeMarzo, M. F. Hellwig and P. C. Peiderer, "Fallacies, Irrelevant Facts, and Myths in the Discussion of Capital Regulation: Why Bank Equity is Not Expensive", Rock Center for Corporate Governance at Stanford University, Working Paper No. 86/2010.
[124] For example, it is argued that is should measured in terms of losses of potential competition. See H. Liu, P. Molyneux, J. O. S. Wilson, "Competition and Stability in European Banking: A Regional Analysis", Working Paper, September 2010, available at http://papers.ssrn.com/sol3/papers.cfm?abstract_id=1670744.

makes TBTF banks more attractive to capital market investors and thus easier to raise fresh capital.[125] Therefore, whether bigger and broader is better in banking has no easy answers, notwithstanding the all-pervasive issue of moral hazard and the ever present threat of shifting the burden of imprudent bank management to the taxpayers via expensive bailouts.[126]

TBTF banks were rightly castigated as the main culprits of the GFC and attempts to put an end to them and thus to public bailouts are properly guided from a public-interest perspective. Moreover, the preservation of fractional reserve banking faces colossal challenges beyond the possibility of a run. The quest for optimal bank organization and ending the TBTF problem may not be separated from the fact that such banks operate on the basis of a fractional reserve system that may require fiscal backstops to eliminate the possibility of multiple runs.[127] By offering a clear model of limited purpose banking, Kotlikoff, Kay and others have rightly highlighted leverage as the problem. However, as explained already, full reserve limited purpose/narrow banking model is fraught with intractable problems itself. These refer to the economics and mechanics of credit supply being very vulnerable to both predatory and bona fide competitors offering better rates. Accordingly, it is the duty of epistemic and regulatory communities to identify one or a number of optimal structural models, which ought to also target the boundary problem[128] and foster long-term growth.[129] Higher capital requirements and especially leverage controls have lots of potential to make banks more stable and the establishment of tailor-made resolution regimes amounts to a significant step to avert the panic that followed the collapse of Lehman Brothers.

Nonetheless, assumptions about the power of post-2008 resolution regimes to internalize the cost of bank failures, eliminating TBTF moral hazard and attendant competitive distortions, contain a considerable amount of wishful thinking, until proven otherwise. Especially in the context of big international bank resolution, limited fiscal backstops will remain, under different guises.[130] Perhaps this limited fiscal prop on ring-fenced or segregated banks is the cost that society is asked to pay for the benefit of fractional reserve banking. And this

---

[125] Both points are intellectual loans from a previous paper I authored jointly with Charles Goodhart and he deserves most of the credit for raising them.

[126] Saunders and Walter (2011).

[127] See also D. Schoenmaker, "A Fiscal Backstop to the Banking System", Duisenberg School of Finance Mimeo, June 2014.

[128] An excellent exposition of the border problem is offered in C. Goodhart, "How Should We Regulate the Financial Sector?", in A. Turner et al., *The Future of Finance and the Theory that Underpins It* (LSE, 2010), chapter 5, pp. 176–179.

[129] E Avgouleas, "The Reform of 'Too-big-To-Fail' Bank – A New Regulatory Model for the Institutional Separation of 'Casino' from 'Utility Banking'", University of Manchester Working Paper, February 2010, available at http://papers.ssrn.com/sol3/papers.cfm?abstract_id=1552970.

[130] Avgouleas and Goodhart, *supra* note 112.

will probably remain the case until another organizational form emerged, which would replace fractional reserve banks as providers of liquidity (virtually) on demand and would answer, at the same time, most of the questions raised so far regarding financial stability, competition, and consumer welfare. Hopefully, any such model would bring within the regulatory umbrella, even in part, shadow-banking activities and would accentuate the importance of long-term growth finance for financial stability.

15

Turning the Tide? How European Banking and Financial Services Legislation are Making Waves on the Enforcement Front

Dalvinder Singh and James Hodges

INTRODUCTION

The financial crisis highlighted the need for reform to the regulation and supervision of banks and other financial institutions.[1] As a response, the European Commission has, since 2010, proposed approximately forty new sets of rules to improve the regulation and supervision of the financial services sector across the EU.[2] In seeking to address questions such as those of financial stability, depositor and investor protection, and the recovery and resolution of failing financial institutions, these changes are not only relevant to the EU's sizeable banking and financial services sector, but have wider societal implications.[3] These reforms are also inextricably linked with broader questions of European economic and political integration.

The European agenda is, at this juncture, focused on institution building and the harmonization of rules and regulations, to improve the safety and soundness of financial firms and to strengthen the integrity of markets as a whole at the

---

[1] For example, Ben S. Bernanke, Chairman, Board of Governors of the Federal Reserve System, "Monetary Policy and the Housing Bubble", Annual Meeting of the American Economic Association, Atlanta, Georgia (3 January 2010) <www.federalreserve.gov/newsevents/speech/bernanke20100103a.htm> accessed 17 July 2014 ("...it is essential that we learn the lessons of the crisis so that we can prevent it from happening again. Because the crisis was so complex, its lessons are many, and they are not always straightforward. Surely, both the private sector and financial regulators must improve their ability to monitor and control risk taking. The crisis revealed not only weaknesses in regulators' oversight of financial institutions, but also, more fundamentally, important gaps in the architecture of financial regulation around the world").

[2] European Commission, *A new financial system for Europe: Financial reform at the service of growth*, State of Play: 27.06.2014 <http://ec.europa.eu/internal_market/publications/docs/financial-reform-for-growth_en.pdf> accessed 16 July 2014.

[3] In the U.S. context, see Adam J. Levitin, "The Politics of Financial Regulation and the Regulation of Financial Politics: A Review Essay", (2014) 127 *Harv. L. Rev.* 1991.

European level.[4] Those reforms do not, however, consider adequately the approach to enforcement as a separate policy consideration to ensure firms and individuals in the financial services industry comply with those requirements. It is suggested here that the reforms should also include formal consideration of enforcement policy at both the Member State level and the European Central Bank (ECB) level to ensure both prudential requirements and conduct risk requirements are enforced consistently. It is argued that, given the level of discretion to interpret the provisions provided to EU Member States under CRD IV,[5] further technical guidance is required on the approach to those administrative measures and penalties to reduce the risk of enforcement arbitrage. It is suggested here that the European Single Rulebook and Single Supervisory Handbook need to be complemented with a single enforcement handbook to properly govern financial services.

THE EUROPEAN REGULATORY LANDSCAPE PRE FINANCIAL CRISIS[6]

The regulation of financial institutions operating within the EU is complex. In their home EU Member State, financial institutions are subject to both national and European legislation. In addition, financial institutions that operate in multiple states (both within the EU and globally) are subject to the regulatory regimes of those foreign states in which they operate. From the 1980s and early 1990s, European financial services regulation sought to promote cross-border operations by facilitating the establishment of branches in other EU Member States by "passporting" home EU Member State authorizations and by harmonizing technical standards.[7] Such initiatives aimed to promote trust between EU Member States by underpinning the process of "passporting" home state authorizations through a range of minimum administrative prudential regulation and supervision

---

[4] In particular, the European Banking Authority is leading an initiative to develop a Single Rulebook, which aims to provide a unified regulatory framework of prudential rules for the EU financial sector and to complete the single market in financial services.

[5] Regulation (EU) No 575/2013 of the European Parliament and of the Council of 26 June 2013 on prudential requirements for credit institutions and investment firms and amending Regulation (EU) No 648/2012 [2013] OJ L176/1 (CRR); Directive 2013/36/EU of the European Parliament and of the Council of 26 June 2013 on access to the activity of credit institutions and the prudential supervision of credit institutions and investment firms, amending Directive 2002/87/EC and repealing Directives 2006/48/EC and 2006/49/EC [2013] OJ L176/338 (CRD IV).

[6] Peter Kerstens, Political Officer for Financial Services Policy, DG for Internal Market and Services, "An Introduction to the European Architectural Landscape", (Workshop hosted by the Industry and Parliamentary Trust, London, 6 March 2014).

[7] European Commission, *Completing the Internal Market: White Paper from the European Commission to the European Council* COM (1985) 310 final; Single European Act [1987] O.J. L169/1; Second Council Directive 89/646/EEC of 15 December 1989 on the coordination of laws, regulations and administrative provisions relating to the taking up and pursuit of the business of credit institutions and amending Directive 77/780/EEC [1989] O.J. L386/1.

for banks and investment businesses seeking to operate across borders. The EU agenda in the late 1990s shifted attention to securities markets and later to banking, insurance, and pensions markets.[8] The agenda focused on their relative competitiveness, efficiency, and the interests of investors with an agenda to minimize implicit barriers and achieve a higher level of financial services integration.[9] This mirrored similar concerns in the United States, and prompted the dismantlement of barriers for banking and nonbanking activities on both sides of the Atlantic, albeit in the United States later than in the EU with the Gramm-Leach Bliley Act 1999.[10] This deregulatory and reregulatory trend continued until the financial crisis of 2007/08.

Then, the financial crisis. Although termed the "Global Financial Crisis", it is more accurately described as, at least, two separate but interconnected crises. The first, the "U.S. subprime mortgage crisis" saw the collapse of the U.S. housing market and sent shockwaves across world financial markets through the international trade in financial instruments derived from such mortgages. The second, the "European sovereign debt crisis", highlighted the potential "vicious circle"[11] that may exist between states and their domestic banks. Certain EU Member States were exposed materially as lender of last resort to their domestic banks, whilst those domestic banks, in turn, held considerable amounts of sovereign debt issued by their home EU Member State and were thereby exposed to the creditworthiness of that state.[12] Common to both crises were problems of financial interconnectedness (although arising at different levels of the financial system) and of inherent structural weakness.

RECENT REGULATORY REFORMS OF THE
EU FINANCIAL SERVICES SECTOR

In response, fundamental reforms to the global financial system have been proposed. The G20, in adopting an "in it together" approach, has been instrumental in

---

[8] European Commission, *Financial Services: Implementing the Framework for Financial Markets: Action Plan*, COM (1999) 232, 11 May 1999 (known as the 'Financial Services Action Plan'); European Commission, *Commission White Paper of 1 December 2005 on Financial Services Policy 2005–2010*, COM (2005) 629; Alexandre Lamfalussy, *Final Report of the Committee of Wise Men on the Regulation of European Securities Markets* (Brussels, 15 February 2001); Ross Cranston (ed.), The Single Market and the Law of Banking (Lloyds of London Press, 2nd ed., 1995).

[9] For example, EC Directive 2004/39/EC of the European Parliament and of the Council of 21 April 2004 on markets in financial instruments amending Council Directives 85/611/EEC and 93/6/EEC and Directive 2000/12/EC of the European Parliament and of the Council and repealing Council Directive 93/22/EEC, [2007] O.J. L145/1 (MiFID).

[10] Financial Services Modernization Act of 1999 (the Gramm-Leach-Bliley Act) 15 U.S.C. §6801.

[11] Various parties have coined the term "vicious circle", for example, see European Central Bank, Euro Area Statement, 29 June 2012 ("…it is imperative to break the vicious circle between banks and sovereigns").

[12] A high-level timeline of the European sovereign debt crisis is set out at <www.bbc.co.uk/news/business_13856580> accessed 14 July 2014.

establishing the core elements of this new global regulatory framework.[13] Key objectives of these reforms include addressing the structural weaknesses high-lighted earlier, but also promoting a more stable financial system and encouraging better international coordination. To that end, the reforms have targeted the resilience of financial institutions (for example, through tougher prudential requirements), financial institutions that are "too-big-to-fail", and the regulation of the "shadow banking" sector and of derivatives trading.[14] In addition, the EU has adopted measures to strengthen another source of structural weakness, the adoption of the euro across multiple EU Member States within the euro area.[15] The passing of legislation to effect these internationally promulgated reforms is now well advanced at the EU level.[16] These reforms are primarily structural and institutional, and can be grouped under three broad headings:

(A) Creating a **new regulatory architecture for the safety and soundness of the EU financial services sector** – This has included further har-monization of rules governing the financial services sector, and from a supervisory perspective, the establishment of three new European Supervisory Authorities,[17] and a European Systemic Risk Board to identify macroprudential risks;[18]

[13] G20, *Declaration: Summit on Financial Markets and the World Economy*, 15 November 2008.
[14] The G20's financial regulatory reform agenda is coordinated by the Financial Stability Board. See, Financial Stability Board, *Press Release: Financial Stability Board reports to G20 leaders on financial regulatory reform progress*, 5 September 2013; Financial Stability Board, *Press Release: Meeting of the Financial Stability Board in Moscow on 8 November*, 8 November 2013; Financial Stability Board, *Press Release: FSB Plenary meeting in London*, 31 March 2014, each available at <www.financialstabilityboard.org/list/fsb_publication/index.htm> accessed on 17 July 2014.
[15] Eilis Ferran, European Banking Union: Imperfect, But It Can Work', *Legal Studies Research Paper Series, Paper No.* 30/2014, April 2014.
[16] European Commission, *A new financial system for Europe: Financial reform at the service of growth*, State of Play: 27.06.2014 <http://ec.europa.eu/internal_market/finances/policy/map_re form_en.htm> accessed 16 July 2014.
[17] Regulation (EU) No 1093/2010 of the European Parliament and of the Council of 24 November 2010 establishing a European Supervisory Authority (European Banking Authority) amending Decision No 716/2009/EC and repealing Commission Decision 2009/78/EC, OJ L 331, 15 December 2010; Regulation (EU) No 1095/2010 of the European Parliament and of the Council of 24 November 2010 establishing a European Supervisory Authority (European Securities and Markets Authority), amending Decision No 716/2009/EC and repealing Com-mission Decision 2009/77/EC, OJ L 331, 15 December 2010; Regulation (EU) No 1094/2010 of the European Parliament and of the Council of 24 November 2010 establishing a European Supervisory Authority (European Insurance and Occupational Pensions Authority), amending Decision No 716/2009/EC and replacing Commission Decision 2009/79/EC, OJ L 331, 15 December 2010; Proposal for a Directive of the European Parliament and of the Council amending Directives 2003/71/EC and 2009/138/EC in respect of the powers of the European Insurance and Occupational Pensions Authority and the European Securities and Markets Authority, /*COM/2011/0008 final – COD 2011/0006*/, 19 January 2011.
[18] Regulation (EU) No 1092/2010 of the European Parliament and of the Council of 24 Novem-ber 2010 on the European Union macroprudential oversight of the financial system and establishing a European Systemic Risk Board, OJ L 331, 15 December 2010.

(B) Promoting a <u>**safer and more responsible financial services sector in**</u> <u>**the EU**</u> – Tools for achieving this have included imposing stronger prudential requirements on banks,[19] reforming executive remuneration and board structures,[20] and adopting a new crisis prevention, management, and resolution framework[21]; and

(C) Establishing a <u>**"banking union"**</u> to support the single currency within the euro area – This is based on three key pillars, being a single supervisory mechanism,[22] a single resolution mechanism,[23] and a common deposit guarantee scheme.[24]

Each is considered in more detail in the following section.

A New Regulatory Architecture

A key objective of the European Commission has been to promote financial stability. In 2011, three new European Supervisory Authorities (the European

---

[19] See, in particular, development of: (i) a Single Rule Book of prudential requirements for banks capital, liquidity and leverage under CRD IV and CRR; (ii) an enhanced framework for securities markets under Directive 2014/65/EU of the European Parliament and of the Council of 15 May 2014 on markets in financial instruments and amending Directive 2002/92/EC and Directive 2011/61/EU, OJ L 173, 12 June 2014 (MiFID 2) and Regulation (EU) No 600/2014 of the European Parliament and of the Council of 15 May 2014 on markets in financial instruments and amending Regulation (EU) No 648/2012, OJ L 173, 12 June 2014 (MiFIR); and (iii) an enhanced framework to prevent market abuse under Directive 2014/57/EU of the European Parliament and of the Council of 16 April 2014 on criminal sanctions for market abuse (market abuse directive), OJ L 173, 12 June 2014 (MAD) and Regulation (EU) No 596/2014 of the European Parliament and of the Council of 16 April 2014 on the market abuse (market abuse regulation) and repealing Directive 2003/6/EC of the European Parliament and of the Council and Commission Directives 2003/124/EC, 2003/125/EC and 2004/72/EC, OJ L 173, 12 June 2014 (MAR).

[20] CRD IV, Articles 92–95.

[21] Directive 2014/59/EU of the European Parliament and of the Council of 15 May 2014 establishing a framework for the recovery and resolution of credit institutions and investment firms and amending Council Directive 82/891/EEC, and Directives 2001/24/EC, 2002/47/EC, 2004/25/EC, 2005/56/EC, 2007/36/EC, 2011/35/EU, 2012/30/EU and 2013/36/EU, and Regulations (EU) No 1093/2010 and (EU) No 648/2012, of the European Parliament and of the Council, OJ L 173, 12 June 2014.

[22] Regulation (EU) No 1024/2013 of the European Parliament and of the Council of 15 October 2013 conferring specific tasks on the European Central Bank concerning policies relating to the prudential supervision of credit institutions, OJ L 287/63; Regulation (EU) No 1022/2013 of the European Parliament and of the Council of 22 October 2013 amending Regulation (EU) No 1093/2010 establishing a European Supervisory Authority (European Banking Authority) as regards the conferral of specific tasks on the European Central Bank pursuant to Council Regulation (EU) No 1024/2013, OJ L 287/5, 29 October 2013.

[23] European Commission, STATEMENT/14/119 on Finalizing the Banking Union: European Parliament backs Commission's proposals (Single Resolution Mechanism, Bank Recovery and Resolution Directive, and Deposit Guarantee Schemes Directive), 15 April 2014.

[24] Directive 2014/49/EU of the European Parliament and of the Council of 16 April 2014 on deposit guarantee schemes, OJ L 173, 12 June 2014.

Banking Authority, the European Securities and Markets Authority, and the European Insurance and Occupational Pensions Authority)[25] and the European Systemic Risk Board[26] were established to improve cross-border cooperation, consistent enforcement of rules, and systemic oversight within the EU. To support a level playing field across the Single Market, the European Commission has also proposed further harmonization of legislation to establish a Single European Rulebook of prudential requirements for all financial institutions within the EU. Whilst financial services legislation was historically promulgated through EU directive, recent reforms have generally been implemented through regulation. Regulations are directly effective in EU Member States without further enactment and so their use seeks to avoid "gold plating" by EU Member States and to promote greater consistency across EU Member States.

A Safer and More Responsible Financial Services Sector

Based on commitments undertaken by the G20, recent EU legislation has established revised prudential requirements for banks, building societies, and investment firms. These reforms implement in the EU the recommendations promulgated by the Basel Committee on Banking Supervision in December 2010 (Basel III).[27] At its core, CRD IV imposes enhanced capital adequacy requirements on banks, including through the increased holding of core tier-one capital. CRD IV also imposes additional capital requirements against countercyclical risk, imposes new rules for counterparty risk, and establishes new tests for liquidity and leverage coverage. There are also further enhanced capital buffer requirements

---

[25] Regulation (EU) No 1093/2010 of the European Parliament and of the Council of 24 November 2010 establishing a European Supervisory Authority (European Banking Authority) amending Decision No 716/2009/EC and repealing Commission Decision 2009/78/EC, OJ L 331, 15 December 2010; Regulation (EU) No 1095/2010 of the European Parliament and of the Council of 24 November 2010 establishing a European Supervisory Authority (European Securities and Markets Authority), amending Decision No 716/2009/EC and repealing Commission Decision 2009/77/EC, OJ L 331, 15 December 2010; Regulation (EU) No 1094/2010 of the European Parliament and of the Council of 24 November 2010 establishing a European Supervisory Authority (European Insurance and Occupational Pensions Authority), amending Decision No 716/2009/EC and replacing Commission Decision 2009/79/EC, OJ L 331, 15 December 2010; Proposal for a Directive of the European Parliament and of the Council amending Directives 2003/71/EC and 2009/138/EC in respect of the powers of the European Insurance and Occupational Pensions Authority and the European Securities and Markets Authority, /*COM/2011/0008 final – COD 2011/0006*/, 19 January 2011.

[26] Regulation (EU) No 1092/2010 of the European Parliament and of the Council of 24 November 2010 on the European Union macroprudential oversight of the financial system and establishing a European Systemic Risk Board, OJ L 331, 15 December 2010.

[27] Basel Committee on Banking Supervision, *Basel III: International framework for liquidity risk measurement, standards and monitoring* (Bank of International Settlements, December 2010); Basel Committee on Banking Supervision, *Basel III: The liquidity coverage ratio and liquidity risk monitoring tools* (Bank of International Settlements, January 2013).

for systemically important financial institutions.[28] CRD IV came into effect on 1 January 2014 (although certain provisions will be phased in up to 2019).

CRD IV also addresses the remuneration of bank executives. It imposes various requirements on banks, including the adoption of a global remuneration policy, the establishment of independent remuneration committees, and special rules on variable remuneration.[29] Whilst variable remuneration structures (for example, bonuses, performance shares, and share options) are commonly used to align senior managers' interests with those of shareholders, such structures have also been identified as a potential cause of excessive risk taking. Similarly, the nonbinding nature of a substantial body of corporate governance (based on voluntary codes of conduct) has been criticized as being ineffective in promoting sound corporate governance practices. Significantly, focus in each case is on the incentives and levers that influence the behavior of bank executives, not on the personal responsibility of those individuals for that conduct itself.

In relation to variable remuneration, CRD IV provides that the variable component of a bank executive's remuneration must not exceed 100 percent[30] of the fixed component of his or her remuneration. If the EU Member State so provides, that ratio may be increased up to 200 percent, provided that certain conditions are fulfilled. EU Member States may also allow banks to apply a discount rate on up to twenty-five percent of the remuneration if it is deferred for at least five years.[31] This new regime has applied to remuneration paid from 1 January 2014, irrespective of when the relevant contract was entered into.[32] As to the question of its effectiveness, to the extent that these reforms increase the proportion of remuneration that is fixed, then arguably they do mitigate the structural concern that excessive variable remuneration promotes risk taking. There is, however, evidence already that major banks are seeking to structure around the new requirements, with HSBC, for instance, adopting "fixed pay allowances" to reduce the ratio of variable to fixed remuneration.[33] This is an area where economic and political considerations interplay. Public hostility toward what is perceived as excessive pay for bank executives and employees, being balanced against concerns that such measures may prejudice the global competitiveness of EU banks in attracting the most talented employees. Whilst the impact of these reforms will only become clear over time, they do demonstrate the importance placed on bank corporate

---

[28] For further details see European Commission, *A comprehensive EU response to the financial crisis: substantial progress towards a strong financial framework for Europe and a banking union for the eurozone*, MEMO/14/57, 24 January 2014.

[29] CRD IV, Articles 92–95.

[30] Or lower percentage, if an EU Member State so provides.

[31] CRD IV, Article 94(g)(iii).

[32] CRD IV, Article 162(3).

[33] Jamie Robertson, "Bankers' bonuses: Shareholders wary of making allowances", (*BBC News*, 24 April 2014) <www.bbc.co.uk/news/business-27145092> accessed on 16 July 2014.

governance and remuneration in promoting financial stability, and hence the need for increased regulation in these areas.

A final core element of promoting a safer and more responsible financial services sector is the Bank Recovery and Resolution Directive,[34] which received agreement between the European Parliament and EU Member States in December 2013. Again, the focus is on ensuring financial stability. The Directive will apply to all EU Member States, and aims to ensure that failing banks are wound down in a predictable and efficient manner, whilst minimizing the use of public funds. As a first step, all banks must prepare recovery plans to set out how they will deal with their own financial distress. The Directive also gives regulatory authorities broad powers and tools to ensure that failing banks are restructured so as to preserve financial stability and minimize recourse to public funds.

A "Banking Union" within the European Union

Another key issue faced by EU Member States following the financial crisis was the imbalance in their respective abilities to weather the crisis. The fragmented response of EU Member States to the European sovereign debt crisis highlighted the lack of centralized mechanisms at the EU level to resolve the crisis. This absence of a coordinated approach was seen as particularly damaging to the euro area given its shared single currency. Indeed, arguably, this imbalance has been more destabilizing for the governance mechanisms of the EU than the crisis itself. As a result, in addition to the regulatory and supervisory initiatives detailed earlier, specific measures have been enacted to maintain confidence within the euro area. The establishment of a "banking union", compulsory within the euro area and open to all other EU Member States, seeks to promote a more centralized and coordinated response to any future financial crisis, as well to break the potentially dangerous negative feedback loops between the banks and the sovereign debt markets. It also represents part of the European Commission's further efforts toward deeper economic and monetary union.

There are three main pillars to the "banking union". First, a "Single Supervisory Mechanism" was formally adopted by the EU in October 2013.[35] The ECB, in its capacity as the European Banking Authority (EBA), will now have responsibility for banking supervision within the "banking union"; its objective being to safeguard

---

[34] European Commission, *Commissioner Barnier welcomes trilogue agreement on the framework for bank recovery and resolution*, MEMO 13/1140, 12 December 2013.

[35] Regulation (EU) No 1024/2013 of the European Parliament and of the Council of 15 October 2013 conferring specific tasks on the European Central Bank concerning policies relating to the prudential supervision of credit institutions, OJ L 287/63; Regulation (EU) No 1022/2013 of the European Parliament and of the Council of 22 October 2013 amending Regulation (EU) No 1093/2010 establishing a European Supervisory Authority (European Banking Authority) as regards the conferral of specific tasks on the European Central Bank pursuant to Council Regulation (EU) No 1024/2013, OJ L 287/5, 29 October 2013.

the financial soundness of individual financial institutions and to protect consumers of financial services.[36] In so doing, responsibility for banking supervision will be centralized at the European level, although the ECB will only have direct supervision over significant banks (estimated to be around 130 banks, representing approximately eighty-five percent of the total banking assets within the euro area).[37] Macroprudential supervision will be undertaken by another new authority, the European Systemic Risk Board.[38] Second, a "Single Resolution Mechanism" is to be established, so that if a bank were to get into difficulty, the resolution process would be managed by a single "resolution authority" funded by a levy raised from all euro zone banks.[39] Finally, a common deposit guarantee scheme (with a limit of up to one hundred thousand euros)[40] is to be implemented across the euro area, and to be guaranteed by a single fund.[41]

The reforms detailed earlier concentrate on the structures and institutions of the EU financial services market and have various objectives. They seek to avoid excessive risk taking, for example, through holding insufficient capital or through remuneration and bonus structures. They seek to avoid moral hazard by improving resolution techniques to reduce the exposure of public funds as the lender of last resort, and they seek to promote financial stability through the orderly resolution of failing financial institutions. But, noticeably, they do not address questions of responsibility for the financial crisis. Even the reforms to bank executive remuneration, are one step removed from the question of individual responsibility by addressing the rewards for behavior, not the behavior itself.

We argue in the following part of the chapter that further policy elaboration is required to make a coherent set of middle-ground administrative penalties and measures as advocated in CRD IV, in order to reduce the risk of enforcement arbitrage between EU Member States and regulatory authorities taking either an overaccommodative or underaccommodative approach to enforcement. In particular, it is suggested that the European Single Rulebook and Single Supervisory Handbook should be complemented with a single enforcement handbook to promote consistency.

---

[36] Gerard Hertig, Ruben Lee and Joseph A McCahery, "Empowering the ECB to Supervise Banks: A Choice-Based Approach", (2010) 7 ECFR 171.

[37] An outline of the scope of regulation is set out on the European Central Bank website at <www.ecb.europa.eu/ssm/html/index.en.html> accessed on 17 July 2014.

[38] Regulation (EU) No 1092/2010 of the European Parliament and of the Council of 24 November 2010 on the European Union macroprudential oversight of the financial system and establishing a European Systemic Risk Board, OJ L 331, 15 December 2010.

[39] European Commission, STATEMENT/14/119 on Finalising the Banking Union: European Parliament backs Commission's proposals (Single Resolution Mechanism, Bank Recovery and Resolution Directive, and Deposit Guarantee Schemes Directive), 15 April 2014.

[40] Some EU Member States have a higher coverage limit, notable Italy and France.

[41] Directive 2014/49/EU of the European Parliament and of the Council of 16 April 2014 on deposit guarantee schemes, OJ L 173, 12 June 2014.

DO THE REFORMS ADEQUATELY ADDRESS QUESTIONS
OF ACCOUNTABILITY OF FIRMS AND INDIVIDUALS
FOR THE FINANCIAL CRISIS?

A major call, both during and after the financial crisis, has been to ensure powers exist to hold those at the helm of the large financial institutions accountable for their part in the crisis. A number of culprits responsible for the financial crisis are clearly evident, including failings of governments, central banks, financial regulators, and the firms and individuals that either were rescued with state support or merged during the crisis. However, apportioning responsibility on private actors only addresses one part of the complex picture underpinning the root causes. Indeed, the reason for the large number of culprits is arguably the "intellectual capture" that surrounds monetary policy, risk management, financial regulation, and prudential supervision. It is beyond the scope of this chapter to explore those issues further. Focus here is devoted instead to enforcement sanctions against private actors, namely financial firms and individuals.

The life cycle of financial institutions shows evidence of opportunities to address less material failures and forms of noncompliance, where the failure to address them could lead to a culture of mismanagement as a whole (rather than breaches of prudential requirements). The weakness of the EU single financial services market agenda is its reliance on the EU Member States to determine the sanction (if any) for compliance failures. Whilst it is not suggested that the EU single financial services market agenda has not addressed matters of regulatory sanctions, it has left, in many ways, the administration of the sanctions to the discretion of each EU Member State. We suggest this leads to an uneven playing field when it comes to enforcement sanctions and so a risk of inconsistent public enforcement. Moreover, such enforcement is more likely to express itself in the form of supervisory warnings and threats rather than formal publicized penalties or administrative measures.

In this context, this chapter assesses the extent to which the reforms proposed by CRD IV will address some of those themes. It will be suggested that given gaps in the legislation, inconsistency of approach is inevitable and thus will result in an uneven playing field.

THE EU MOVES TO A COHERENT ENFORCEMENT APPROACH?

The EU financial services regulators are not without a range of enforcement powers and sanctions, far from it.[42] Still, the thought of a single overarching approach to

---

[42] Committee of European Banking Supervisors, Review Panel titled "Mapping supervisory objectives and powers, including early intervention measures and sanctioning powers", CEBS 2009/47, March 2009; See also EU Commission, Impact Assessment, Accompanying the document Proposal for the Directive of the European Parliament and the Council, on the access to the activity of credit institutions and the prudential supervision of credit institutions

enforcement and sanctions poses tremendous challenges for the discrete ways regulation and supervision are undertaken in the members of the European Union.[43] The cultures and traditions of regulation, supervision, accountability, and enforcement differ considerably as well as whether responsibilities are allocated to a single, dual, or multiple set of regulators and supervisors. It highlights that there are not only country-specific cultural approaches that need to be appreciated but also, as noted earlier, different approaches between the different business lines that make up the financial services industry. However, under the EU agenda of more consistency of approach to the oversight of financial services, enforcement must also be tackled like the prudential and conduct risk requirements outlined in the first part. Whilst what is explained earlier may improve compliance with more robust prudential requirements and conduct risk requirements, it is suggested that a coherent deterrence approach is needed to complete the enforcement objectives. The move to a "single supervisory regime" will improve EU Member State compliance. Compliance will, however, only be entirely consistent when the deterrence part of the enforcement model is also coherently addressed. Whilst an EU Member State can fulfil compliance with prudential requirements, if it needs to exercise some form of deterrence action, it will be dependent on what range of sanctions that EU Member State has at its disposal and its willingness to take the appropriate course of action that could lead to a situation of over or under enforcement from a deterrence viewpoint. The evidence provided by the 2009 review and the 2011 impact assessment clearly indicate significant gaps in the enforcement arsenal of EU Member States and a lack of a credible deterrence in the enforcement of administrative penalties and administrative measures. It highlights, in particular, gaps and divergences of approach between EU Member States in what regulators can and cannot do when faced with similar problems at banks. This also depends on whether the relevant bank is, for all intents and purposes, a going concern or a gone concern.

The adoption of CRD IV sets out a number of reforms to the enforcement regime in EU Member States to address the divergence between EU Member States in the way that they deal with failures at banks as well as individuals responsible for those failures.[44] It first provides the basis to develop administrative penalties and criminal penalties.[45] It also requires EU Member States to put in place administrative measures that can be exercised to deal with forms of

---

and investment firms and amending Directive 2002/87/EC of the European Parliament and of the Council on the supplementary supervision of credit institutions, insurance undertakings and investment firms in a financial conglomerate, (COM (2011) 453 final), 20.7.2011, SEC (2011) 952 final.

[43] The point here is the financial services industry is not a single homogenous grouping, let alone a single industry, but a complex set of different industries where a single enforcement approach would need to be broad enough to achieve the objectives of the distinct industries.

[44] CRD IV, Section IV, Supervisory powers and powers to impose penalties, Art. 64.

[45] CRD IV, Art. 65(1).

noncompliance. EU Member States can rely on existing penalty regimes to build up a coherent set of penalties and fill in gaps with new penalties to deal with the different forms of noncompliance likely to arise. Article 65(2) enables EU Member States to apply the penalty in accordance with national law provisions that also apply to members of the management body, such as for example, shareholders' powers to dismiss directors.[46] In this respect, the financial regulator will have to be mindful of such procedural rights when exercising those powers.

The forms of administrative measures that EU Member States need to have in place, as a minimum, are listed and the matters to be taken in to account in deciding the size of the penalty or extent of the administrative measures are provided.[47] The first set of reforms includes those to deter unauthorized regulated activities or unauthorized acquisition of a qualifying holding in a credit institution.[48] In respect of those administrative measures, EU Member States are required to publish a statement about the matter; exercise a cease and desist order; and adopt a procedure to calculate the penalty to be applied on the firm and individuals responsible.[49] In those instances, the regulator may well address such problems using a combination of administrative and civil sanctions. In extreme cases, individuals found to be managing such unregulated businesses could also be criminally prosecuted for fraud or dishonesty.

The other administrative measures to improve the regulators' ability to deal with the different forms of noncompliance include[50]: false statements to acquire authorization;[51] failure to report changes to acquired holdings[52]; governance arrangements[53]; misreporting information to the regulator about own funds[54]; misreporting data,[55] large exposure,[56] liquidity,[57] or leverage ratio[58]; failure to hold the appropriate liquid assets[59]; exceeding exposure limits[60]; mismanaging securitization risks;[61] and appointment of members of the management body without the suitable experience, skill, and knowledge.[62] In response to such matters, the EU

---

[46] CRD IV, Art. 65(2); Companies Act 2006, s.168.
[47] CRD IV, Art. 66.
[48] CRD IV, Art. 66 (1) (a)-(d).
[49] CRD IV, Art. 66 (2) (a)-(f).
[50] CRD IV, Art. 67 (1) (a).
[51] CRD IV, Art. 67 (1) (b).
[52] CRD IV, Art. 67 (1) (c).
[53] CRD IV, Art. 67 (1) (d).
[54] CRD IV, Art. 67 (1) (e).
[55] CRD IV, Art. 67 (1) (f).
[56] CRD IV, Art. 67 (1) (g).
[57] CRD IV, Art. 67 (1) (h).
[58] CRD IV, Art. 67 (1) (i).
[59] CRD IV, Art. 67 (1) (j).
[60] CRD IV, Art. 67 (1) (k).
[61] CRD IV, Art. 67 (1) (l).
[62] CRD IV, Art. 67 (1) (p).

Member State may withdraw authorization,[63] impose a temporary prohibition on individuals from the industry,[64] or impose pecuniary penalties on the firm or relevant individuals.[65]

In respect of these types of failure, the regulator may not address those problems with deterrence options. Instead it may opt for more of a compliance-based approach and negotiate to ensure adherence, or the threat of sanctions may be enough to make the regulated respond. When deciding the size of the administrative penalties and/or the severity of the administrative measures, the regulator is specifically required to take into account the following: the gravity of the breach; the level of responsibility of the firm or individual; the level of profit or loss avoided as a result of the breach; losses sustained by investors; the level of cooperation offered; and the risk posed to the stability of the system.[66]

EU Member States are required to report administrative penalties to the EBA, which will give the single supervisory authority a better understanding of the level of enforcement penalties administered across the EU.[67] The utility of this is, however, called in to question since it should also extend to administrative measures so that the EBA can get a better picture of the enforcement of those matters across the EU as a whole. Whilst some of the administrative measures may not be publicized rightly in the public interest since they could pose external spillover risks, the confidential reporting of such matters to the EBA is not the same. The risk of enforcement inconsistency remains since some EU Member States may exercise more punitive administrative measures in comparison to others when breaches are identified at banks.

CRD IV makes significant changes to the enforcement regime but it also confers significant discretion on EU Member States to interpret the provisions and discretion on the regulators to make decisions on a day to day basis. Therefore, it will not necessarily improve the level of consistency across the EU. It is suggested that additional regulatory guidance from the EBA is needed to reduce the divergence of approach and so reduce the risk of enforcement arbitrage by booking the more risky business in jurisdictions where there is a greater probability of underenforcement compared to a jurisdiction where there is likely to be overenforcement. The level of enforcement is still reliant on the level of resources that the local regulator has to investigate such matters, so will again lead to the risk of enforcement arbitrage by firms that are aware of the differing approaches to the supervision of risk. Moreover, the enforcement sanctions associated with breach of prudential requirements are not likely to be initiated, or even publicized, unless the institution's viability is in doubt and it forms part of the move toward resolution.

---

[63] CRD IV, Art. 67 (2) (c).
[64] CRD IV, Art. 67 (2) (d).
[65] CRD IV, Art. 67 (2) (e)–(g).
[66] CRD IV, Art. 66 (1) (c)–(d); Art. 67(2) (e)–(g); Art. 70(a)–(h).
[67] CRD IV, Art. 69 (1)–(4).

The administrative penalties and measures focus on the authorization of regulated activities, prudential requirements, and internal management controls and, in so doing, concentrate on the safety and soundness of institutions. Those measures are necessary and are not called in to question, but do require consistency across the EU. Moreover, since mismanagement of conduct risk generally exists before signs of prudential risk emerge, it is argued that the move to reform administrative penalties and administrative measures should be extended to all areas of financial services. The level of public enforcement of prudential requirements is miniscule in comparison to its conduct of business counterpart. With such focus on prudential requirements and internal management controls, the enforcement agenda is not being addressed appropriately to improve consistency and to avoid the risks of under or overenforcement, as described by Mann.[68]

The move to introduce formally a criminal sanctions regime to support administrative sanctions and measures across the EU and to address the failure experienced over recent years is a response to the call from society to ensure that those individuals found culpable are exposed to the risk of imprisonment or criminal financial penalties. Criminal sanctions provide the traditional deterrent against acts that are considered morally wrong by society. The punishment prescribed by the criminal justice system tries to achieve a broad range of goals that are not necessarily attainable with one sanction, such as restraint, retribution, rehabilitation, education, denunciation, compensation, or just deserts.[69] Indeed, the introduction of a criminal sanctions regime will not necessarily mean we will see those considered culpable put behind bars, for it is incredibly difficult to succeed in securing criminal prosecutions. For similar reasons, it is unlikely to find regulators exercising their powers to revoke a bank's licence or ban individuals from working in the industry. In the regulatory context, a greater overlap between criminal, administrative, and civil sanctions exists under the auspices of administrative powers.[70] The growth in the use of administrative sanctions is nevertheless based on a systematic process of decriminalizing regulatory offences, which has curtailed the use of criminal sanctions for all but the most serious offences.[71] It is only in

---

[68] Kenneth Mann, "Punitive Civil Sanctions: The Middleground between Criminal and Civil law", (1992) 101 Yale L. J. 1795.

[69] For a detailed examination of criminal sanctions see James Gobert and Maurice Punch, *Rethinking Corporate Crime* (London: Butterworths, 2003) at pp. 214–252; Hazel Croall, *Understanding White Collar Crime* (Milton Keynes: Open University Press, 2001) at pp. 123–142.

[70] For the use of criminal sanctions see Sanford H. Kadish, "Some observations on the use of criminal sanctions in enforcing economic regulations" (1963) 30 U. Chi. L. Rev. 423; "Developments in the law. Corporate crime: regulating corporate behavior through criminal sanctions",(1979) 92, Harv. L. Rev., 1227.

[71] John C. Coffee Jr., "Paradigms lost: The blurring of the criminal and civil law models – And what can be done", (1992) 101 Yale L. J. 1875; Laura J. Kerrigan et al. "Project: The decriminalization of administrative law penalties: Civil remedies, alternatives, policy, and constitutional implications", (1993) 45 Admin. L. Rev. 367.

more recent times that we have seen a reemergence of criminal sanctions to complement other sanctions.

Given what is stated earlier, it is argued that the powers provided in CRD IV require the single supervisory authorities to develop better guidance for EU Member States, and for the ECB to flesh out a more consistent application of enforcement sanctions.

COMPLEMENTING THE EUROPEAN SINGLE RULEBOOK AND THE SINGLE SUPERVISORY HANDBOOK WITH A SINGLE ENFORCEMENT HANDBOOK

The proposal in this chapter is to create an enforcement handbook to complement the European Single Rulebook and the Single Supervisory Handbook. It is suggested that the latter two are focused on a compliance-orientated and remedial model of enforcement. The remedial approach is interpreted to mean putting in place corrective measures to deal with, inter alia, capital, liquidity, governance, and internal control shortcomings. It is reliant on the EBA, in terms of rule design, and the ECB to undertake part of the work of prudential supervision on its own and to work with EU Member States to ensure banks comply with requirements set out, for instance, in CRD IV and the capital requirements regulation (CRR). The process of the EBA assisting with rule convergence and compliance is an example of that model.[72] This approach will also identify inconsistencies in approach and put in place mechanisms to iron out those inconsistencies through the development of technical standards, guidance, and recommendations. Moreover, the process of peer review by the EBA of supervisory compliance with their standards and guidelines is another illustration. It is yet to develop, however, standards, guidance, or recommendations on the enforcement sanctions set out in CRD IV.

The responsibility conferred on the ECB to fulfil the single supervisory role also lends itself to more of a compliance-based model of enforcement, consisting of a remedial approach to supervisory matters (with the exception of the most punitive of sanctions, withdrawal of authorization).[73] The aforementioned mechanisms, such as the Single Rulebook and Single Supervisory Handbook, provide a considerable level of support to the ECB and a centralized supervisory agenda. Moreover, the ECB is also expected to work closely with the national regulators of EU Member States not within the eurozone through formal memoranda of understanding.[74]

---

[72] See for instance the process of peer review undertaken by the EBA similar to the IMF and World Bank financial sector assessment process. For example, EBA, Report on the Peer Review of The EBA Guidelines 31 Regarding Credit Concentration Risk, 2014.

[73] Art. 4(1) of Regulation (EN) No. 1024/2013.

[74] Art. 3(6) of Regulation (EN) No. 1024/2013.

The ECB is conferred a range of investigatory, information gathering, and enforcement powers to support its supervisory work that it can exercise directly or indirectly.[75] It is conferred responsibilities that amount to it being the competent authority of those banks deemed significant.[76] The ECB can exercise directly supervisory, investigatory, and enforcement powers, or initiate powers indirectly with the support of national supervisory authorities acting on its behalf. There are benefits gained by the ECB's ability to utilize the national supervisory authorities in their supervisory tasks given the latter's understanding of the respective banks operating in the relevant EU Member State. In addition, the ability of the ECB to share staff from national supervisory authorities through exchanges and secondments enables the ECB to build up its own understanding of the institutions on a day to day basis. It therefore will have, for all intents and purposes, the powers of national supervisory authorities at its disposal. The recent decision by the ECB to assess a number of banks to determine whether they could in the future be classified as significant is a good example of it exercising its discretion.[77] It also illustrates the way the ECB can ask the national authorities to provide it with the information to make such an assessment and to form its view. The ECB's use of national authorities to inform its decisions does, however, require a consistent approach to ensure that disproportionate relationships are not established based on the political bargaining power of respective EU Member States. The ECB will need therefore to develop its own approach to supervision policy so that it can be judged against that policy in the exercise of its responsibilities.[78] The tools and tasks of supervision and the discrete approaches of national supervisory authorities require policy coherency to bring them together.

Whilst there is a significant degree of consistency in the approach to supervision, there is still room for enforcement arbitrage given the multiple layers of oversight at a regional and EU Member State level and the reality of participating and nonparticipating EU Member States within the framework of centralization. This reflects the reliance the ECB will have on national resources and approaches to

---

[75] Chapter III. The ECB will also have to think about separating the functions of supervision and investigation to avoid conflicts of interest spilling in to the decision making process regarding potential enforcement decisions. The reliance on the EU Member States' national authorities will need to be coordinated accordingly as well.

[76] ECB, List of credit institutions, www.ecb.europa.eu/ssm/list/html/index.en.html; ECB, The list of significant supervised entities and the list of less significant institutions, September 2014 www.ecb.europa.eu/pub/pdf/other/ssm-listofsupervisedentities1409en.pdf?59d76de0c5663687 f594250ebf228c6b.

[77] Decision of The European Central Bank, Identifying the credit institutions that are subject to the comprehensive assessment, (ECB/2014/3), (2014/123/EU) 4 February 2014.

[78] Danièle Nouy, "Launch of the SSM – what will change in banking supervision and what are the imminent impacts on the banking sector?" (Third FIN-FSA Conference on EU Regulation and Supervision, Helsinki, 5 June 2014).

fulfil part of its mandate.[79] But more significantly, the regulation requires the ECB to exercise its responsibilities in accordance with relevant EU law. This is interpreted to mean it is required to apply relevant EU law as it emanates from primary and secondary legislation. The ECB is required therefore to comply with the interpretation of the provisions of directives adopted by EU Member States. CRD IV also enables national authorities to interpret enforcement sanctions in line with national law thereby exacerbating the risk of enforcement arbitrage. This is so despite the decision to take a consistent approach to the interpretation of CRD IV. The result could be that the ECB may be required to apply different interpretations to similar sets of circumstances depending on how the relevant EU Member State has exercised its discretion. Indeed, the area of administrative enforcement sanctions is one area that could lend itself very easily to differing interpretations due to the precision with which they are drafted and so lead to different outcomes.[80] In order to remedy in part the gap identified here, the move to creating a single enforcement handbook would start the process of minimizing inconsistency.

This chapter therefore advocates the move toward a single enforcement book to improve interpretation of administrative enforcement powers at the level of the centralized bodies, EU Member States, supervisory bodies, and the regulated. The development of a single enforcement handbook would serve several purposes in line with Diver's work on the precision of administrative rules.[81] The process of articulating standards and guidelines around administrative sanctions enables the centralized bodies to articulate the aims, objectives, and principles that they would like to associate with this part of their responsibilities. The process of providing guidance on the use of enforcement sanctions would also assist a process of consistency of application of administrative sanctions. Such guidance would need to reflect the interpretation of the enforcement sanctions and so provide a more centralized approach to what is considered reasonable behavior. Indeed, the approach taken to address behavior needs to clarify the opacity surrounding "what is reasonable and unreasonable" whilst not unnecessarily disabling the use of those sanctions to address individual behavior. The guidance could also assist national authorities and EU Member States to gauge which type of enforcement sanction to

---

[79] There is also the risk the ECB relies on the supervisory authority to exercise enforcement decisions rather than take such decisions itself. However, the risk of such an approach would be to show itself to be reluctant to intervene and give the impression it is underenforcing and using more carrots than sticks. In a similar vain to Ayres and Braithwaite's analogy of central banks acting as a "Benign Big Gun" where they have a considerable arsenal of tools and powers but rarely utilize them, the argument runs that the presence of the powers is enough to ensure compliance. As we have seen that is sadly not always the case.

[80] The classic work in this area is by, Colin S. Diver, "The Optimal Precision of Administrative Rules", (1983) 93 Yale L. J. 65.

[81] Ibid. There are challenges to articulate the precision of administrative sanctions but this has not prevented financial regulators from formulating a better understanding of this area.

apply, whether administrative, civil, or criminal. This would assist the authorities to determine the level of recourse that it will need to devote to deal with a matter. The centralized authorities would also be able, through a process of transparency of practices, to gauge better areas of under and overenforcement when relying on national supervisory authorities to execute certain enforcement sanctions. The ECB as a supervisor would be able to gauge whether it is taking a consistent approach to such matters across the EU and not simply being influenced by national interests. The move to a single enforcement handbook would also lead to better coordination of enforcement powers between going concern and gone concern. It can readily be linked to other circumstances as well, namely the powers of early intervention. The whole enforcement life cycle can then be addressed as a whole rather than incrementally in separate places. Contacting the parts together also means better levels of accountability since it enables the central authorities to identify whether national authorities could address problems earlier with the application of administrative sanctions prior to it snowballing into a risk of the bank being put into resolution. The EBA's process of peer review of rule compliance and frequency of use could equally apply to the compliance with, and frequency of use of, administrative sanctions. The review work would offer the centralized bodies the opportunity to understand better the level of resources they need to devote to such areas.

CONCLUSION

The move toward greater levels of consistency in rule compliance with the adoption of a single regulatory regime and the centralization of regulatory and supervisory policy and oversight of significantly important banks makes a more consistent approach to enforcement policy necessary to deal with "middle-ground" failures that can arise when a bank is a going concern but not at the point of resolution. The task of developing a coherent enforcement strategy is imperative to improve the consistency of approach and to achieving consistent supervisory objectives. The task is nevertheless onerous due to the complex way enforcement can be administered in each EU Member State. Neither that hurdle nor the complexity of the financial services industry itself should, however, prevent taking the opportunity to address enforcement in the financial services industry and to consider the feasibility of forming a single enforcement approach.

16

Shadow Banking or "Bank's Shadow": Reconceptualizing Global Shadow Banking Regulation

Yingmao Tang

INTRODUCTION

Regulating shadow banking is a new development. In the November Seoul Summit 2010, G-20 leaders requested the Financial Stability Board (FSB) to develop recommendations for strengthening the regulation of the shadow banking system. In 2011, the FSB released policy papers to report its recommendations.[1] The FSB also releases shadow banking monitoring reports on an annual basis.[2]

Why is it important to regulate the shadow banking system? Firstly, shadow banking activities were one of the causes of the global financial crisis in 2008.[3] The negative impacts of shadow banking entities or activities such as securitization and money market funds have been widely discussed. Secondly, there is a concern of systemic risk arising from the shadow banking system.[4] Thirdly, regulatory arbitrage may become even more serious if the shadow banking system is left unregulated while new banking regulations such as Basel III are introduced.

The FSB has a broad definition of shadow banking. According to the FSB, shadow banking refers to "credit intermediation involving entities and activities outside the regular banking system."[5] To make it easy for each member country to monitor shadow banking entities and activities, the FSB breaks the shadow banking

---

[1] See, *Shadow Banking: Scoping the Issues*, Financial Stability Board (FSB) (April 12, 2011); *FSB Report with Recommendations to Strengthen Oversight and Regulation of Shadow Banking*, FSB (October 21, 2011) [hereinafter *FSB 2011 Recommendation*].

[2] For the latest report, *see, Global Shadow Banking Monitoring Report 2013*, FSB (November 14, 2013) [hereinafter *FSB 2013 Monitoring Report*].

[3] See, Zoltan Pozsar et al., *Shadow Banking*, STAFF REPORTS NO. 458, NEW YORK FED, 1 (2010) (REVISED 2012) available at www.newyorkfed.org/research/staff_reports/sr458.html.

[4] See, Steven L. Schwarcz, *Regulating Shadow Banking*, 31 REV. BANKING & FIN. L. 619, 638 (2012) (discussing the rationale for regulating shadow banking including minimizing systemic risk as well as maximizing economic efficiency to address information failure, rationality failure, principal-agent failure and incentive failure).

[5] See FSB 2011 Recommendation, *supra* note 1, at 1.

sector into nine major subsectors. These subsectors include, for example, investment funds, broker-dealers (e.g., investment banks), structured finance vehicles, finance companies, money market funds, and hedge funds.[6]

The proposed regulation of shadow banking may have a positive impact. However, I will argue in this chapter that the FSB's approach has at least two fundamental flaws. First, by focusing only on nonbanking sectors, the FSB overlooks the possibility that regular banking may well be the source of issues arising from the shadow banking system. Secondly, by focusing exclusively on nonbanking financial sectors, the FSB overlooks the possibility that shadow banking may well include those that are not part of traditional financial entities or activities.

I will use China's experience to support the aforementioned argument. I will show that Chinese regulators take a much broader view of the shadow banking system compared to the FSB. The shadow banking system in China not only includes nonbank financial entities or activities outlined by the FSB, but also includes activities within the regular banking system. For example, offerings of wealth management products by commercial banks are considered to be part of shadow banking in China. The shadow banking system in China also includes a wide range of entities and activities relating to the so-called "Internet finance."

As a secondary point, I will argue that the FSB's approach is a simplistic view of global financial regulation. It reflects the view of developed economies based on lessons learned from the recent global financial crisis. But, as will become clear from the discussion concerning China, this view lacks appreciation of the complexity of the financial world.

This chapter is divided into four parts. Part 1 explains how China's view of shadow banking is different. Part 2 discusses the recent development of reregulating wealth management products in China. Part 3 discusses the recent development of regulating Internet finance activities in China. Part 2 and Part 3 are intended to show why China takes a different approach to shadow banking. Part 4 discusses lessons that may be learned from China.

How Is China Different?

The FSB's definition of shadow banking clearly excludes regular banking activities. The rationale is that regular banking activities have been subject to strict regulation in the past few decades. This overlooks the fact that financial players may conduct banking activities by using entities that are not subject to stringent banking regulation. The recharacterization of the regulation of shadow banking that is proposed in this paper is thus intended to reduce regulatory arbitrage by leveling the playfield between the regular banking and shadow banking sectors.

---

[6] See *FSB 2013 Monitoring Report, supra* note 2, at 14.

In addition, the FSB provides a useful breakdown of the shadow banking sector, which clearly includes only financial entities or activities. According to the FSB, there are nine major subsectors of the shadow banking system. Among these nine subsectors, three subsectors are fund-related entities, including money market funds, hedge funds, and other investment funds; three other subsectors include broker-dealers, finance companies, and structured finance vehicles; the remaining three subsectors are country-specific entities including Dutch Special Financial Institutions, U.S. funding corporations, and U.S. financial holding companies. Under the FSB's approach, nonfinancial entities or activities are not part of the shadow banking system. The FSB explicitly uses the term "other financial intermediaries" or OFIs to refer to the shadow banking system.[7]

In comparison, the shadow banking sector in China includes both regular banking activities and nonfinancial entities or activities. For example, certain wealth management products offered by commercial banks are considered part of the shadow banking system in China.[8] The shadow banking system in China also includes Internet finance. The term "Internet finance" is used to include a wide range of Internet-related entities or activities such as online "peer to peer" (P2P) lending, online "crowdfunding" and online third-party payment tools.[9]

The idea of wealth management products is straightforward and does not require explanation. The concept of Internet finance, however, is quite new and still evolving in China. The types of Internet finance entities or activities available today vary greatly in terms of the services that they offer. For example, online P2P platforms provide services through the Internet to match lenders and borrowers typically on a one-on-one basis.[10] In contrast, online crowdfunding platforms assist one borrower to

---

[7] *See FSB 2013 Monitoring Report, supra* note 2, at 7.

[8] It was widely reported that the State Counsel of China promulgated a circular in December 2013 [hereinafter *Circular No. 107*] to regulate the shadow banking sector in China. According to news reports, Circular No. 107 provides a clear scope of the shadow banking in China, which includes, among others, certain wealth management products offered by commercial banks, private lending between or among individuals and Internet finance entities or activities. However, Circular No.107 has not been made available to the public so it is unclear whether what news reports indicate is consistent the actual language of the circular. *See* Daile Xia, *Yin zi yin hang sheng si ling: 107 hao wen de zhen shih an yi [Death Warrant of Shadow Banking: True Meaning of Circular No. 107]*, PEKING UNIVERSITY LAW REVIEW, at www.pkulawrev.com/?p=995 (Jun. 22, 2014). *See, also,* Shusong Ba, *Ying cong jin rong jie gou yan jin jiao du ke guan ping gu ying zi yin hang [Objective Evaluation of Shadow Banking from the Perspective of Financial Institution Development]*, Issue No. 4, ECONOMIC REVIEW, 27 (2013) (discussing four different views of the scope of the shadow banking in China, the narrowest of which include wealth management services offered by banks and the broadest of which also include private lending).

[9] Xia, *id.* (discussing the scope of China's shadow banking defined by Circular No. 107). *See, also,* SHEN Wei, *Shadow Banking System in China – Origin, Uniqueness and Government Response*, JOURNAL OF INTERNATIONAL BANKING LAW AND REGULATIONS, Issue 1, 2013, at 20–23 (P2P and private lending are part of the shadow banking in China).

[10] In China, there are about 2000 P2P platforms in 2014 with a lending balance of around RMB 100 billion. "Lending Club" in the United States is often cited by Chinese scholars as an

raise funds from a number of lenders to finance a project such as making a movie.[11] Third-party payment tools are those offered by entities other than commercial banks. Online third-party payment tools typically allow people to transfer money from their bank accounts to their payment accounts at online payment service providers and allows people to conduct a variety of transactions such as making payments to settle online purchases, buying money market funds, securities products, insurance products, or even transferring funds between or among individuals.

Similar Internet finance activities can offer very different services as well. For example, online P2P service platforms may simply provide services relating to online information dissemination (e.g., borrower and project information) and online information gathering (e.g., lenders' information and requests); However they may also provide other services relating to evaluation of borrowers' credit, credit enhancement for borrowers, or even fund pooling.

The aforementioned section demonstrates that, in comparison to the FSB's approach, China is quite a unique case in how it defines its shadow banking system. To summarize, firstly, the shadow banking system in China captures activities in the regular banking sector such as those relating to wealth management products. Secondly, the shadow banking system in China captures nonfinance entities or activities utilizing new technology tools. This is in contrast to the FSB's approach that draws a clear distinction between regular banking and nonbanking sectors and between financial and nonfinancial sectors. It is clear that China does not appear to "respect" those fine lines.

What has caused China to take this unique approach? The two main arguments raised in this regard are that banking regulation may be inadequate so it may be necessary to strengthen banking regulation in the form of the proposed regulation of shadow banking within the regular banking sector. Furthermore, financial regulation may be inadequate so it may also be necessary to strengthen financial regulation in the form of proposed regulation of shadow banking in the nonfinancial area. These arguments are explored in the next two sections.

Wealth Management Products, "Ponzi Scheme" and "Bank's Shadow"

Chinese commercial banks started to offer wealth management products only a few years ago. The Industrial and Commercial Bank of China (ICBC), the largest

example of P2P platform. *See*, Bing Peng & Jing Li, *Fei fa ji zi yu P2P wang dai [Illegal Fund Raising and P2P Online Lending]* (May 2014) (Unpublished manuscript, on file with Internet Finance and Law); *China Shadow Bankers Go Online as Peer-to-Peer Sites Boom*, Bloomberg News, at www.bloomberg.com/news/2012–07–23/china-shadow-bankers-go-online-as-peer-to-peer-sites-boom.html (Jul. 24, 2012).

[11] For Chinese examples of "crowdfunding" platforms, *see*, for example, Shijie Feng, *Zhong chou wang luo rong zi ping tai de yun ying mo shi he fa lv feng xian [An Analysis of Operational Model and Legal Risks of "Crowdfunding" Online Financing Platforms]* (2014) (unpublished master thesis, Peking University) (on file with author).

commercial bank in China and also top ten in the world, indicated in its initial public offering (IPO) in 2007 that the development of wealth management products was one of its future strategies not its current strength.[12] However, wealth management products have developed rapidly in recent years. For example, these products offered by commercial banks increased fourteen times from RMB 500 billion (USD 82 billion) in early 2008 to RMB 7 trillion (USD 1 trillion) by the end of 2012.[13]

The fast growth of wealth management products has not developed in a regulatory vacuum. In 2005, the China Banking Regulatory Commission (CBRC) issued the 2005 *Wealth Management Product Rule* to regulate these products.[14] This begs the question, if wealth management products are already subject to banking regulation, why would China be concerned about these products being part of the shadow banking system?

To be sure, wealth management products offered by nonbank financial institutions such as trust companies and securities companies (broker-dealers) are already captured by the FSB's definition to the extent these products raise any concern from the shadow banking perspective. What makes China different is the offerings of wealth management products by commercial banks themselves. Some of these products are considered part of the shadow banking system in China. While under the FSB's definition, regular banking activities such as offerings of wealth management products by commercial banks would not be part of the shadow banking system.

The FSB's rationale, as well as the rationale of the 2005 Wealth Management Product Rule, is that wealth management is a service in nature and should be treated as such by banking regulation. Customers give their money to banks, banks invest customers' money according to their contracts with customers, customers receive profits or take losses for those investments, and banks charge customers service fees. Banks typically do not take losses of those investments. To the extent that banks and customers will share profits and losses, wealth management contracts will make it clear. As a result, the rule of thumb is that bank regulations often treat wealth management products as off-balance sheet items. The offer of a wealth management product to customers on the one hand and the investment of proceeds received from the offering on the other hand would be generally considered as two integrated elements of a wealth management product. This is also the case for the 2005 Wealth Management Product Rule.

---

[12] *See*, ICBC's IPO prospectus (2006), available at http://static.sse.com.cn/disclosure/listedinfo/announcement/c/2006–10–26/601398_20061026_2.pdf.

[13] Jing Lin & Kun Zhang, *Ying zi yin hang ti xi de feng xian te zheng yu jian guan ti xi cui sheng* [*Risk Characteristics of Shadow Banking System and Supervision System Creation*], Issue No. 7, FINANCE, 53 (2013).

[14] *Shang ye yin hang ge ren li cai ye wu guan li zan xing ban fa* [Provisional Measures of Administration of Commercial Bank Individual Wealth Management Business] (promulgated by CBRC, Sep. 24, 2005, effective Nov. 1, 2005) (P.R.C.).

However, this is not the case for all such products offered by Chinese commercial banks in recent years; and this is certainly not the case for wealth management products offered by commercial banks in cooperation with trust companies. The development of these products as the result of cooperation between commercial banks and trust companies shows that commercial banks in China have ventured beyond this arrangement. As a consequence, the regulatory treatment of these products has changed completely within a few years.

In one scenario, wealth management services turn into a way of self-dealing by commercial banks. The way this works is that a bank raises money from selling wealth management products to customers, and then lends money to a trust company in the form of an "entrusted loan." In an "entrusted loan," a bank typically instructs a trust company how the loan should be invested. The trust company then uses the "entrusted loan" to buy loans and other assets from the same bank.[15] In essence, customers' money will be invested in loans and other assets of the same bank that offers wealth management products to these customers. As long as the loans and other assets generate enough profits to pay investment returns to customers and expenses or fees to the trust company, this model will work economically.

This model obviously takes the advantage of China's interest rate regulation. The interest rate regulation allows banks to make profits by borrowing money from the public at a regulated low interest rate and lend money to corporate and other borrowers at a higher interest rate. The investment returns offered by wealth management products are higher than the regulated interest rates for savings account. This model will work as long as there is room or spread between investment returns offered by banks to customers purchasing wealth management products and returns generated from making loans and other assets. This model also takes advantage of the off-balance sheet treatment of "entrusted loans," which is considered part of the overall wealth management services.

In addition, banks would also be able to make more loans to generate more profits after the loans and other assets underlying the wealth management products are off its balance sheet. In other words, wealth management products enable banks to "double-dip" bank regulations that allow off balance sheet treatment of certain bank

---

[15] *Zhong guo yin jian hui guan yu jin yi bu gui fan yin xin he zuo you guan shi xiang de tong zhi* [Circular Regarding Further Strengthening Cooperation between Banks and Trust Companies] (promulgated by CBRC, Dec. 14, 2009, effective Dec. 14, 2009) art. 5 (P.R.C.) [hereinafter 2009 *Circular*] (prohibiting investments of wealth management products based on cooperation between banks and trust companies in loan assets of banks issuing wealth management products, which suggests that the prohibited investments existed in practice; *Zhong guo yin jian hui guan yu gui fan yin xin li cai he zuo ye wu you guan shi xiang de tong zhi* [Circular Regarding Standardizing Certain Matters Relating to Banks and Trust Companies Cooperation Business] (promulgated by CBRC, Aug. 5, 2010, effective Aug. 5 2010) art. 4 (P.R.C.) [hereinafter 2010 *Circular*] (imposing cap on so called financing type cooperation wealth management business based on cooperation between banks and trust companies, which business include "entrusted loans," "sales of loan assets" and others.

business or assets (e.g., off-balance sheet treatment of "entrusted loan" under the cover of wealth management products as well as loan assets sold to trust companies.)

This model raises a number of issues. The self-dealing nature of this model obviously raises an ethical issue as well as a transparency issue for the issuing bank. Has the bank disclosed this to the customers? Does the bank need approval from the customers? More importantly, it appears that this model may not work economically at all times. In practice, banks either provide guarantees in favor of trust companies for loans and other assets that are sold to trust companies, or to make commitments to repurchase those loans and other assets from trust companies under certain conditions.[16] This means that banks might not be able to move loans and other assets from their balance sheets to the balance sheets of trust companies. This raises a "true sale" issue that is often seen in securitization deals where off-balance sheet treatment of underlying assets or bankruptcy remoteness of the sponsoring entity is subject to challenge.

In another scenario, rather than investing in its own loans and other assets, commercial banks can allow trust companies to invest in a wide variety of potentially risky financial instruments. These financial instruments include, for example, loans and other assets of other commercial banks,[17] as well as debt instruments offered by trust companies in the form of the so-called "trust products" that are further invested in risky debt instruments offered by real-estate developers or local government investment platforms.[18]

These risky investments raise consumer protection issues. Even if a consumer agrees in writing to take losses arising from these risky investments, does the consumer clearly understands what he or she agrees to? These risky investments also raise issues for banks themselves as banks may agree to take losses arising from these investments.

There are many other scenarios or models of cooperation between commercial banks and trust companies in offering wealth management products and investing offering proceeds that will not be discussed here.

---

[16] *Zhong guo yin jian hui guan yu gui fan shang ye yin hang li cai ye wu tou zi yun zuo you guan wen ti de tong zhi* [Circular Regarding Standardizing Certain Issues Relating to Commercial Bank Wealth Management Business Investment Operations] (promulgated by CBRC, Mar. 25, 2013, effective Mar. 25, 2013) art. 8 (P.R.C.) [hereinafter 2013 *Circular*] (prohibiting the provision by commercial banks of guarantee or undertaking of repurchase of commercial banks each in respect of loan assets invested by wealth management products, which indicates that commercial banks provided guarantee for or committed to repurchase loan assets).

[17] Article 1 of the 2013 *Circular* uses the term "non-standard debt instruments" to refer to a wide range of debt instruments invested by wealth management products. These "non-standard debt instruments" are defined to be debt instruments that are not traded on open markets, and include loans, "trusted loans," "entrusted loans," receivables, equity investments with repurchase obligations, and so on.

[18] Article 8 of the 2009 *Circular* requires trust companies that cooperate with commercial banks to conduct thorough due diligence on projects sponsored by local governments, which indicate that wealth management products offered by commercial banks in cooperation with trust companies are invested in projects sponsored by local governments.

After a few years of rapid development of these products, problems started to surface. Certain wealth management products were in default because underlying investments suffered losses as a result of failures to make payments by ultimate investees such as real-estate developers, local governments, or other investee entities. One senior regulator has described certain wealth management products as Ponzi schemes.[19] Some scholars label shadow banking in China as "bank's shadow."[20] As such, soon after commercial banks started to offer wealth management products, the original regulatory framework of such products was brought into question. As a result, between 2008 and 2013, the CBRC issued a number of rules to gradually reregulate these wealth management products in two areas.

The first area is consumer protection. For example, a qualified investor concept was introduced in 2009 that requires banks to screen customers if underlying investments are made in potentially risky equity instruments.[21] Other consumer protection measures such as information disclosure, account separation and risk management are also emphasized in this rule.[22]

The second area is accounting and regulatory treatment. This includes both the regulatory treatment of investments underlying the wealth management products and the regulatory treatment of wealth management products in general. Since 2010, the CBRC has explicitly required banks to move investments underlying wealth management products from off balance sheet back to balance sheet.[23] The trust companies are required to do the same. Other restrictions have also been imposed: for example, the CBRC requested commercial banks and trust companies in 2010 to reduce by 25 percent each quarter the balance of "entrusted loans" or loans made by banks to trust companies using funds raised from offering wealth management products.[24]

The reregulation of bank-offered wealth management products in China, whether aiming at consumer protection or regulatory capital adequacy, clearly shows that the regular banking system is not immune from the risks arising from shadow banking. China may be an extreme case in the sense that within only a few years the Chinese regulator managed to somehow completely change the regulatory treatment of certain wealth management products. China's experience suggests that if we exclude regular banking activities from the shadow banking sector, we run the risk that shadows may well be within the banks themselves. Risks arising

---

[19] Gang Xiao, *Regulating Shadow Banking*, CHINA DAILY, October 12, 2012, at Page 8. A Ponzi scheme refers to a fraudulent operation where the operator of the scheme pays returns to its investors from new capital paid by new investors, rather than from profit earned by the operator.

[20] *See*, for example, YIN JIANFENG & WANG ZENGWU, YING ZI YIN HANG YU YIN HANG DE YING ZI [SHADOW BANKING AND BANK'S SHADOW] (1st ed. 2013)

[21] 2009 *Circular*, *supra* note 15, art. 6.

[22] *See*, for example, 2013 *Circular*, *supra* note 16, art. 3, 4.

[23] 2010 *Circular*, *supra* note 15, art. 7.

[24] 2010 *Circular*, *supra* note 15, art. 1.

from shadow banking activities within the regular banking system include inadequate consumer protection regulation, over regulation (e.g., those relating to interest rate regulation) and deregulation (e.g., a blank off-balance sheet treatment of wealth management products). Moreover, these factors provide an opportunity for regulatory arbitrage.

Internet Finance

I now turn to another example to show how China's approach to shadow banking is different by examining its approach to Internet finance. The term "Internet finance" is loosely used to refer to a wide range of entities or activities that take advantage of the Internet and other information technology tools to facilitate financing activities.

In typical Internet finance activities, Internet and IT technologies are used to facilitate the loan-making process, such as bringing lenders and borrowers together or making it easy to review credit of borrowers or the creditworthiness of a project. In these Internet finance activities, whether P2P or crowdfunding, the common issue facing Chinese regulators, as with those in other countries, is whether the existing framework can be used to regulate these new entities or activities.

In this regard, China's case is not unique. China's problem is its lack of a regulatory framework to regulate these financing activities while such frameworks exist in other jurisdictions. For example, securities rules regarding the registration of public offerings of securities and related exemptions have been applied to P2Ps and crowdfunding in jurisdictions outside China.[25]

These Internet finance activities, however, do raise issues that are quite often seen in China but do not arise in other jurisdictions. For example, P2Ps and crowdfunding often turn into illegal fund-raising activities where they are used as platforms to raise and pool funds from the public, thereby becoming credit intermediating entities.[26] Operators of certain platforms even conduct frauds under the cover of P2Ps or crowdfunding by raising funds from the public and then

---

[25] For example, the SEC in the U.S. found in 2008 that the offering of instruments by P2P platforms such s "Prosper" would be subject SEC's jurisdiction. *See, Person- to Person Lending: New Regulatory Challenges as Industry Grow,* (July 2011), GAO Access, available at http://www.gao.gov/new.items/d11613.pdf. In the UK, a rule entitled "Crowdfunding and the Promotion of Non-Readily Realizable Securities Instrument 2014" was released by the Financial Conduct Authority in March 6, 2014, under which P2P online lending activities would be subject to the jurisdiction of the FCA. *See, Crowdfunding and the Promotion of Non-Readily Realizable Securities Instrument 2014,* (Mar. 6, 2014), FCA Access, available at http://www.fca.org.uk/your-fca/documents/policy-statements/ps14-04.

[26] Xiaopu Zhang, *Hu lian wang jin rong jian guan de yuan ze: tan suo xin jin rong jian guan fan shi* [*Principles for the Regulation of Internet Finance: Exploring New Financial Regulatory Model*] (Mar. 2014) (Unpublished manuscript, on file with Internet Finance and Law). Also *See* Peng, *supra* note 10.

absconding with the funds.[27] In this regard, Chinese regulators' concern for illegal fund raising by P2P or crowdfunding justifies the inclusion of these entities or activities in the scope of the shadow banking system.

However, not every attempt of Chinese regulators is successful or receives support from the public. One example is the recent proposed regulation of online third-party payment tools such as Alipay.

Alipay is associated with Alibaba, which is an online business-to-business and business-to-consumer company like Amazon.com. To resolve the issue of lack of trust between online sellers and buyers in China, Alibaba has developed escrow services for buyers. Rather than making payments directly to sellers, online buyers make payments to their escrow accounts at Alipay. Alipay releases escrow money to sellers only after buyers confirm receipt of goods. To wire money to the escrow accounts at Alipay, buyers would either transfer money from their bank accounts to the escrow accounts directly, or transfer money from their personal accounts at Alipay to escrow accounts at Alipay. The money in their personal accounts at Alipay come either from customers' bank accounts or from transfers from personal accounts of other customers at Alipay.

As a third-party payment entity, Alipay is subject to a third-party payment regulation issued by the People's Bank of China (PBOC) in 2010.[28] This regulation applies to nonfinancial entities engaging in payment services. Over 200 third-party payment entities have received licenses from the PBOC. Alipay is obviously one of the most famous ones because of its affiliation with Alibaba. Alibaba is the largest e-commerce platform in China with 255 million annual active buyers and 8 million active sellers.[29] Twelve billion seven hundred million orders were placed on Alibaba last year generating five billion packages, which accounts for more than half the packages delivered in China.[30] About 80 percent of these transactions were settled through Alipay.[31] On November 11, 2013, China's Singles' Day, 254 million orders were processed by Alibaba and USD 5.8 billion was settled through Alipay within just one day.[32]

What has made Alibaba and Alipay even more famous was the success of Yu E. Bao in 2013, a money market fund offered by Tian Hong Fund Management Company using Alipay as the only sales channel. The cooperation between Alibaba

---

[27] It was reported that over 100 P2P platforms ceased operations in 2013 and operators of these platforms simply run away. *See*, Peng & Li, *supra* note 10.

[28] *Fei jin rong ji gou zhi fu fu wu guan li ban fa* [The Administration Measures of Non-Financial Entity Payment Services] (promulgated by PBOC, Jun. 14, 2010, effective Sep. 1, 2010) (P.R.C.).

[29] *See* Alibaba's Form F-1 (filed with the SEC, Jun. 16, 2014), at 4, available at www.sec.gov/Archives/edgar/data/1577552/000119312514236860/d709111dfia.htm.

[30] *Id.*

[31] *Id.* at 25 ("In fiscal year 2014, 78.3% of the GMV on our *retail* market places were settled through Alipay").

[32] *Id.* at 7, 75.

and the fund company allowed Alibaba's online customers to use money in their accounts at Alipay to subscribe for Yu E. Bao. Yu E. Bao turned out to be an immense success. By March 31, 2014, Yu E. Bao had 810 million subscribers and RMB 540 billion worth of assets. This ranked it third in the world, only next to Fidelity and Vanguard money market funds.[33]

Chinese commercial banks and regulators feel the pressure from Yu E. Bao and Alipay. Commercial banks are concerned about the loss of saving deposits. Regulators are concerned about the potential liquidity and other issues that Yu E. Bao, as a money market fund, may face; like what we saw in the U.S. right before the 2008 financial crisis.

In March 2014, commercial banks imposed daily and monthly limits on the amounts that could be transferred by automatic payments from customers' bank accounts to their accounts at Alipay.[34] In April 2014, the PBOC and the CBRC jointly issued a circular requiring commercial banks to conduct additional customer verification procedures prior to establishing an automatic link between their bank accounts and their accounts with Alipay.[35] These new regulations appear to be successful as they only require actions on the part of commercial banks. Alipay and other third-party payment service providers simply have to accept the result.

However, as the regulators became more aggressive in regulating online payment activities, they start to face strong public criticism. In March 2014, the PBOC also released a proposed regulation that prohibits individuals from using their funds at their Alipay accounts to make purchases exceeding RMB 5,000 (USD 804) in any single transaction or over RMB10,000 (USD 1,609) in aggregate purchases per month. It is unclear when the draft regulation will become final. But the PBOC clearly encountered very strong criticism from online shoppers due to the inconvenience this proposed regulation could cause upon them.[36]

To give a hypothetical example, without this regulation, thirty-year-old Xiaoming, the plumber, could have a big flat screen TV delivered to his home easily after a few clicks on the computer mouse while shopping at Alibaba. If the draft regulation becomes effective, Xiaoming may not be able to use his Alipay account to make the payment because the TV may cost more than RMB 5,000 – the limit imposed by the PBOC. He will have to use his online bank account to complete the purchase, which may be disadvantageous since online banking services of big banks are not as convenient as Alipay. Xiaoming may also feel that he can no longer buy and sell Yu E. Bao because of this proposed regulation. Yu E. Bao does not set any minimum purchase threshold. Xiaoming can use any balance, even a single

---

[33] Yan Liu, *Jian guan yu e bao: zhen wen ti yu jia wen ti* [*Regulating Yu E. Bao: Real or Phony Issues*] (Jun. 2014) (Unpublished manuscript, on file with author).

[34] *See, supra* note 29, at 26.

[35] *Id.*

[36] *See, for example*, Ifeng Finance, *Yang hang xian e yin zheng yi* [The Restriction by PBOC Raised Controversy, available at http://finance.ifeng.com/a/20140320/11934409_0.shtml.

dollar remaining in his Alipay account, to buy corresponding shares in Yu E. Bao. Other money market funds have minimum purchase thresholds that can sometimes are as high as RMB 10,000.

In my view, Chinese regulators have every reason to strengthen regulation of online third party payment tools such as Alipay. Millions of potential users and investors may be involved. These payment tools can be used in a wide range of activities including the buying of insurance policies, trading securities, and even conducting direct transfers between individuals. These tools certainly have the potential to pooling funds for credit intermediation. In addition, the fast growth of mobile phone payment applications may raise additional issues and concerns.[37]

It appears that Chinese regulators did not expect that the proposed regulation would cause Xiaoming and others to feel angry given that these people are the people whom the regulators intend to protect. This suggests that there must be something erroneous about the approach of the Chinese regulators; otherwise, why would the public protest against the proposed regulation? The proposed regulation may perhaps be viewed by the public as a way to protect the interests of large state-owned banks that are unable to offer convenient banking and payment services. Consequently, the legitimacy of this proposed regulation is being challenged.

It is too early to determine the effects of the proposed regulation of Internet finance activities and entities. Scholars have argued for more room before imposing regulatory requirements such as reserve, capital, or liquidity requirements.[38] The background to the proposed regulation shows the complexity of financial activities brought about by the Internet and how they are intertwined with China's unique circumstances. These unique circumstances include, for example, the fact that China has such a large number of online and mobile phone users and financiers, while its physical shopping facilities are inadequate and its banking services are underdeveloped. Most of all, it is a fast-moving society that makes it extremely difficult to balance regulation and innovation.

From the perspective of shadow banking regulation, the inclusion of certain Internet finance activities by Chinese regulators within the scope of shadow banking is justified to the extent that Chinese regulators have a right to be, at a minimum, suspicious about the potential credit intermediation role that may be played by Internet finance. However, the regulation of Internet finance is much more complicated as we see from the Alipay situation.

---

[37] It was widely reported that PBOC issued an urgent circular on March 13, 2013 (Circular of Suspending the Offline Barcode Payment Businesses of Companies such as Alipay) to suspend the offline barcode payment services and virtual credit card services offered by third-party payment companies such as Alipay. *See*, for example, Sina Finance, *Jin liu cheng wang you ren wei yang hang zan ting er wei ma zhi fu guan li bu qia dang* [Almost 60% internet users consider the suspension of barcode payment services as an inappropriate action], at http://finance.sina.com.cn/money/bank/bank_hydt/20140314/163418512202.shtml.

[38] Liu, *supra* note 33.

What Can We Learn from China?

The successful reregulation of wealth management products and the not-so-successful regulation of certain Internet finance activities in China illustrate the uneasy course of financial regulation in this country. From the perspective of shadow banking regulation, China's experience indicates at least a possibility that the regulation of shadow banking may be much more complicated that what the FSB seems to suggest.

As a useful starting point, the FSB gives us a pragmatic definition and breakdown of the shadow banking system. However, it is difficult to generalize a principle that can be applied anywhere in the world. Any principle or doctrine is likely to be incomplete given the complexity of the world we live in.

China's experience provides us with useful lessons for thinking about global financial regulation, in particular, the regulation of the shadow banking system. What we can take away from China's experience is that shadow banking can exist anywhere as long as there is potential for regulatory arbitrage between banking and nonbanking activities. This means that shadow banking can be seen within the regular banking sector as long as there are possibilities for regulatory arbitrage. Shadow banking may also exist in areas that are not subject to traditional financial regulation. If we take the view that stringent bank regulations are the bench mark so that any entities or activities that side-step these regulations to achieve the same credit intermediation purpose would look suspicious, then we should not bind ourselves to the doctrinal concept of "regular banking" or "financial entities or activities."

However, the idea that shadow banking can exist anywhere does not mean that such activities should all be regulated or regulated in the same way. China's case suggests that regular banking may well be the source of shadow banking activities, whether facilitated through offerings of wealth management products or conducting Internet finance activities. This means that regulatory treatment of wealth management products and Internet finance, both of which may be labeled as shadow banking activities, could well be very different.

The story behind the proposed regulation of Internet finance tools shows the lack of appreciation by Chinese regulators of the convenience that technological development brings to the ordinary public. The popularity of Alipay and Yu E. Bao is largely the result of the inability of traditional banks to offer the same services. The rapid increase in E-commerce in China is largely the result of a lack of physical shopping facilities in the country. This is especially true in the third- or fourth-tier cities in China: cities outside Beijing, Shanghai, and other capital cities or provinces. People in the third- or fourth-tier cities have nowhere to shop other than online. Alibaba and Alipay bring to those people the shopping and finance tools they need.

As such, it may well be that Chinese regulators living in big cities do not realize that the proposed regulation would make it more difficult for ordinary people to shop and finance activities as part of daily living. This is quite different from developed economies such as U.S. or European countries where ordinary people like Joe the plumber would generally be able to access shopping and financial services even if they did not go online.

I agree with Chinese regulators' broad view of the scope of shadow banking because certain Internet finance tools do raise concerns. However, I certainly do not believe that they should be subject to the same level of regulation. We should not impose regulations on Internet finance tools if such regulation would cause them to become much like a regular banking entity that is unable to offer any affordable services of high quality to the ordinary public. As a final note, it is important to emphasize that shadow banking is not necessarily "bad" banking or "risky" banking; therefore, labeling Internet finance as shadow banking should not mean that it is to be subject to the same level of banking regulation as regular banks.

To conclude, the FSB's approach should be only a starting point. The FSB attempts to draw a distinction between regular banking and nonbanking sectors and between financial and nonfinancial sectors. This distinction may not be clear in the real financial world. In this regard, there is much to learn from China's experience. We should be suspicious about any line that is drawn when we rethink regulating shadow banking. However, we should also be suspicious about the role of shadow banking regulation when we use it to regulate new financial entities, activities or tools that may change our idea of traditional banking or financing.

17

Shadow Banking and Its Regulation: The Case of China

Robin Hui Huang

INTRODUCTION

Shadow banking has been widely identified as one of the major causes of the global financial crisis of 2008 and as such, has become a focus of financial regulatory reform worldwide. Great efforts are being made to improve the regulation of shadow banking at a national and global level. Due to the complexity of shadow banking, however, there is still much debate about what shadow banking is, let alone how to regulate it.

China, now as the second largest economy in the world, presents an interesting case for study due to its unique political and economic system. In January 2014, the Chinese central government, namely the State Council, promulgated an important document with respect to the regulation of shadow banking in China, entitled *Guowuyuan Bangongting Guanyu Jiaqiang Yingzi Yinhang Jianguan Youguan Wenti de Tongzhi [Circular of the General Office of the State Council on Relevant Issues of Strengthening the Regulation of Shadow Banking]* (State Council Circular No. 107, 2013) (hereinafter Circular No. 107).[1] It has the highest legal force among all documents China has promulgated towards shadow banking to date, and sets out an overarching regulatory framework for shadow banking in China. Hence, the discussion of this chapter will be focused on this document.

Although the term "shadow banking" has become widely used, there is no consensus over its definition at the international level. The term is generally believed to be coined by economist and investment manager Paul McCulley, who used it to refer to "the whole alphabet soup of levered up nonbank investment

---

[1] *Guowuyuan Bangongting Guanyu Jiaqiang Yingzi Yinhang Jianguan Youguan Wenti de Tongzhi* [Circular of the General Office of the State Council on Relevant Issues of Strengthening the Regulation of Shadow Banking] (State Council Circular No. 107, 2013) (hereinafter Circular No. 107).

conduits, vehicles and structures."[2] Other commentators have since redefined and expanded the meaning of "shadow banking." Economists of the Federal Reserve in the United States, for instance, have broadly described shadow banking as "financial intermediaries that conduct maturity, credit, and liquidity transformation without access to central bank liquidity or public sector credit guarantees," so that shadow banking may include "finance companies, asset-backed commercial paper conduits, limited-purpose finance companies, structured investment vehicles, credit hedge funds, money market mutual funds, securities lenders, and government-sponsored enterprises."[3]

It is worth noting that some commentators have used other terms that are synonymous with shadow banking. For instance, Mr Tim Geithner, the then president of Federal Reserve Bank of New York, used the term "parallel banking system" in a 2008 speech[4]; the International Monetary Fund used the term "near-bank entities" in a 2008 report.[5] In a sense, these alternative terms are more neutral than shadow banking, as the latter has a pejorative connotation to the extent that operating in the shadows implies inappropriateness. Nevertheless, shadow banking has been used by most commentators, perhaps to highlight the problem and the need to address it.

In the newly issued Circular No. 107, the Chinese government also uses the term "shadow banking" [Yingzi Yinhang], and describes it as "credit intermediation entities and activities outside the traditional banking system." This is broadly similar to the way Financial Stability Board (FSB) defines shadow banking.[6]

Further, the Circular No. 107 classifies shadow banking into three categories: (1) credit intermediation entities that do not have financial licenses and that are completely unregulated, such as internet finance companies and third-party wealth management entities; (2) credit intermediation entities that do not have financial licenses and that are subject to an inadequate level of regulation, such as financing guarantee companies and petty loan companies; and (3) entities that hold financial licenses and that have activities that are not adequately regulated, such as money market funds, securitization, and some types of wealth management businesses.[7]

It is not entirely clear about the size and structure of China's shadow banking for two main reasons. First, due to the broad nature of shadow banking, different

---

[2] Paul McCulley, "Teton Reflections: Pimco Global Central Bank Focus," *PIMCO* (September 2007) 2.

[3] Zoltan Pozsar et al., *Federal Reserve Bank of New York Staff Report No 458, Abstract to Shadow Banking* (2010).

[4] Tim Geithner, "Reducing Systemic Risk in a Dynamic Financial System," Remarks at the Economic Club of New York, New York City, June 9, 2008, available at www.newyorkfed.org/newsevents/speeches/2008/tfg080609.html.

[5] International Monetary Fund, *Global Financial Stability Report: Financial Stress and Deleveraging, Macrofinancial Implications and Policy* (October 2008) 19.

[6] Financial Stability Board, *Shadow Banking: Scoping the Issues* (April 2011).

[7] Circular No. 107, s1.

institutions use different criteria to make estimates. Second, it is extremely difficult, if not impossible, to assess some components of China's shadow banking system, such as private lending. According to the FSB, the scale of China's shadow banking in 2011 was about RMB four trillion, while several Chinese institutions estimated it to be in the range of RMB twenty to thirty trillion.[8] Hence, there is a great need for improvements in the availability of data and other related qualitative information. Despite the big differences in the assessment of shadow banking activities in China, there appears a consensus that China's shadow banking plays a significant role in its financial system and, if left unregulated, may become a major source of systemic risk in the future.

SHADOW BANKING MARKETS IN CHINA

Historical Development

The rise of shadow banking is one of the most important developments in China's financial system over the past few years. According to the FSB, in 2012, China has a growth rate in shadow banking asset of forty-two per cent, which is the highest rate in the world.[9] China's shadow banking system has grown significantly in diversity and breadth. To understand the rapid growth of shadow banking in China, one needs to examine both supply-side and demand-side aspects.

On the supply side, the contributing factors mainly include gains in efficiency and regulatory arbitrage. This needs to be assessed against the broad background of China's macroeconomic policy. Although China's shadow banking system existed before the global financial crisis of 2008, it started to grow rapidly after that. This is in stark contrast with the U.S. situation where the shadow banking system developed before, and finally contributed to, the global financial crisis of 2008. This is mainly because the Chinese government has tightened its monetary policy in the postcrisis era, making it much more difficult to get finance through the traditional loan business of commercial banks.[10] As a result, shadow banking has become an increasingly important alternative source of liquidity in China.

The inefficiency of China's traditional banking system is a major factor behind the rapid growth of shadow banking in China. For a variety of reasons, China's commercial banking sector has a high level of monopoly. The banking market has long been dominated by large state-controlled banks, which generally favor

---

[8] Yingwei Zhao, *Woguo Yingzi Yinhang de Xinyong Fenxian Juji—Jiyu Lici Jinrong Weiji de Shijiao Fenxi* [A Comparison of Shadow Banking Credit Risk Aggregation From the Perspective of Global Financial Crises in the Past] (2013) 11 Caijing Kexue [Finance and Economics Science].

[9] FSB, *Global Shadow Banking Monitoring Report 2013* (Basel 14 November 2013) 12.

[10] Hui Huang, "China's Legal Responses to the Global Financial Crisis: From Domestic Reform to International Engagement," (2010) 12(2) *Australian Journal of Asian Law* 157.

state-owned enterprises or large firms in extending loans. Hence shadow banking is needed to supply liquidity to disadvantaged firms such as private micro and small-sized firms.

What is more, regulatory arbitrage provides incentives for banks to engage in shadow banking businesses. Traditional banks need to comply with strict pruden-tial regulation requirements, including the capital adequacy ratio, the ratio of loan balance versus deposit balance, the deposit reserve ratio, and limits on the total loan value. But nonbank financial institutions are not subject to the same level of restriction. Traditional banks thus cooperate with nonbank financial institutions, notably trust companies, to offer wealth management products. As banks do not hold these loans on their balance sheets, this business can help them enhance profit and circumvent relevant regulatory requirements.

The development of shadow banking is also fuelled by financial market innov-ations and technological advancements. China has been encouraging financial innovation, such as securitization and wealth management products, in an attempt to further stimulate the development of its financial markets. Technological advancement facilitates shadow banking by expanding the time and space for conducting financial transactions, reducing transaction costs, and improving the efficiency in allocating financial assets. The concept of Internet finance has recently become a very hot topic in China, giving rise to a wide variety of related products.

The analysis of the development of China's shadow banking system would not be complete without looking at the stimulus from the demand side as well. Due to strict control over the interest rate paid on deposits by traditional banks, Chinese investors are increasingly attracted to shadow banking that can offer much higher rates of return. In 2004, China started to relax its interest rate control policy by allowing banks to set their loan rates at a discount of 10 percent of the official base rate issued by the central bank, namely People's Bank of China. This reform process has been accelerated in recent years. The government control over the loan rate was further relaxed to allow a discount of 20 percent in June 2012 and then 30 percent in July 2012, culminating in a complete abolishment of the lower limit on the loan rate in July 2013. On the other hand, however, the deposit rate is still subject to tight control, because it has greater impact on the cost of capital for banks and its reform may need to take longer time than that of the loan rate. In June 2012, the deposit rate given by commercial banks was allowed for the first time to be higher than the official base rate by up to 10 percent. As of the time of writing, this cap has remained unchanged.

Current Situation

Although shadow banking is a global phenomenon, the shadow banking system in China has its distinctive features, which makes it substantially different from its counterparts overseas. This part will examine the composition, players and sophistication of the Chinese shadow banking system, and compare it with its U.S. counterpart.

Composition and Players

Some commentators have come up with a taxonomy of the shadow banking system participants, divided them into three subgroups.[11] The first is the government-sponsored shadow banking subsystem consisting of the government-sponsored enterprises such as the Federal Home Loan Bank System, Fannie Mae and Freddie Mac. The second is the "internal" shadow banking subsystem, where large banks use a range of off-balance sheet securitization and asset management techniques to conduct lending with less capital than if they had retained loans on their balance sheets. The final subgroup is the "external" shadow banking subsystem, namely a global network of shadow banks where the origination, warehousing, and securitization of loans are conducted mainly from the United States while the funding and maturity transformation of structured credit assets conducted mainly from various offshore financial centers.

Amongst the aforementioned three subgroups of shadow banking participants, the first and third subgroups are the main players in the U.S. shadow banking, including investment banks, hedge funds, money market mutual funds, structure investment vehicles, and government-sponsored enterprises. The shadow banking system in the United States has long established its footprint in the capital markets. For instance, monetary market funds can operate independently from traditional banks, while repo and securitization markets are open to all participants, including banks and nonbanks. The U.S. shadow banking is therefore more market-based, operating in parallel to and to a large extent, in competition with traditional banks.

In contrast, China's shadow banking system has grown in heavy reliance on traditional banks to perform basic functions of credit intermediation. Due to historical and political reasons, traditional banks have long had a predominant position in the Chinese financial system, enjoying absolute advantages in terms of the branch network, scale and marketing channel. Without banks' active involvement in liquidity provision, product distribution, credit guarantee, and investment recommendation, the shadow banking system would not have reached the level of development today. Hence, the relationship between the shadow banking system and the traditional banking system is more collaborative than competitive. This is well illustrated by the business model of wealth management products in China (WMPs).[12]

---

[11] Zoltan Pozsar, Tobias Adrian, Adam Ashcraft, and Hayley Boesky, "Shadow Banking," (2013) Federal Reserve Bank New York Economic Policy Review.

[12] For a more detailed discussion of WMPs, see Yingmao Tang, "Shadow Banking or 'Bank's Shadow': Re-conceptualizing Global Shadow Banking Regulation," Chapter 16 of this book.

Level of Sophistication

The U.S. shadow banking system grows in a developed financial system and utilizes highly sophisticated financial tools to offer complex financial products such as securitized loans, asset-backed commercial paper, repurchase agreements, and money market funds. These techniques may contribute to the build-up of high, yet simultaneously disguised, leverage in the financial system. In contrast, the Chinese financial system is far less developed than its U.S. counterpart, and shadow banking is not dominated by complex derivatives. As the traditional banks in China cannot meet the financing need of certain kinds of firms, particularly small and medium-sized private enterprises, shadow banking mainly involves direct lending to the real economy with a modest level of leverage, such as WMPs and private lending activities [Minjian Jiedai].

Securitization, for instance, is a well-established practice in the U.S. financial markets, performing the important function of converting illiquid assets into liquid assets. At the moment, however, the business of securitization is still in the stage of experimentation in China. Many of shadow banking products in the United States can also be seen as advanced versions of relevant products in China.[13] For example, WMPs correspond to the monetary market mutual funds (MMFs) in the United States. They play a similar role in providing shadow deposits and share a common origin in regulatory arbitrage. The development of MMFs in the United States started as a response to the Federal Reserve Board's (FRB) interested rate caps on savings deposits in commercial banks required under the Glass-Steagall Act. Like WMPs, MMFs offered investors, particularly small investors, a higher return than what was available on savings deposits. MMFs have continued to grow even after the interest rate cap was abolished later. Despite their similar role and origin, WMPs are less sophisticated than MMFs, which are highly liquid and use various accounting techniques to manage and report its net asset value per share.[14]

SHADOW BANKING REGULATION IN CHINA

As discussed previously, China's shadow banking is still in the initial stage of development and is less sophisticated than its counterparts overseas, notably the United States. This means that the level of risk posed by shadow banking in China may be lower than that in the United States, but there are still significant risks that require adequate regulatory attention in order to reduce the likelihood of them

[13] Zengting Yuan, *Zhongwai Yingzi Yinhang Tixi de Benzi yu Jianguan* [The Nature and Regulation of Shadow Banking in China and Overseas] (2011) 1 Zhongguo Jinrong [China Finance].

[14] International Organization of Securities Commissions, "Policy Recommendations for Money Market Funds," (October 2012).

causing a new financial crisis.[15] In September 2012, Mr Gang Xiao, the then Chairman of Bank of China and the current Chairman of China Securities Regulatory Commission, was reported to opine that China's shadow banking would be the greatest risk in the Chinese financial system in the next five years.[16] This highlights the great need for an effective regulatory regime for China's shadow banking system. The Circular No. 107 represents a good effort made by the Chinese government in this regard.

To start with, the Circular No. 107 has a balanced view over the benefits and risks of shadow banking. It states that the advent of shadow banking is the necessary product of financial development and financial innovation, and that as a beneficial supplement to the traditional banking system, shadow banking plays a positive role in serving the real economy and enriching investment channels for Chinese people. It is also recognized that as demonstrated in the global financial crisis of 2008, shadow banking is prone to systemic risk due to the complex, hidden, vulnerable, and contagious nature of shadow banking risk. Hence, the Circular No. 107 adopts the overarching policy that tries to maximize the benefits of shadow banking while at the same time minimizing its negative effects and risks.[17]

Further, the Circular No. 107 provides substantive guidance on how to regulate the shadow banking system in China. Specifically, it covers significant components of China's shadow banking, including the WMPs offered by various financial institutions,[18] the business of trust companies,[19] cross-sector products and cooperation,[20] private lending businesses,[21] financing guarantee businesses,[22] private investment funds[23] and internet finance activities.[24] It is worth noting that securitization does not feature as prominently as is the case with the Dodd-Frank Act, because as discussed earlier, securitization is still in its infancy in China and thus does not pose systemic risk.

It should be noted that as the Circular No. 107 is a policy document in nature, the aforementioned guidance is couched in very general terms. It basically sets out

---

[15] Hongqian Qi and Baomin Huang, *Woguo Yingzi Yinhang de Fazhan Jiqi Fenxian Fangfan* [The Development of China's Shadow Banking and its Risk Containment] (2013) 30(6) Shenzhen Daxue Xuebao (Renwen Shehui Kexue Ban) [Journal of Shenzhen University (Humanities & Social Sciences)].

[16] Liping Deng, Xiao Gang: *Weilai Wunian Zuida Fenxian shi Yingzi Yinhang* [Xiao Gang: The Biggest Risk is Shadow Banking in The Next Five Years] Meiri Jingji Xinwen [Everyday Economic News] (13 September 2012), available at http://bank.hexun.com/2012–09–13/145786733.html.

[17] Circular No. 107, s 1.

[18] Circular No. 107, s 3(2).

[19] Circular No. 107, s 3(3).

[20] Circular No. 107, s 3(4).

[21] Circular No. 107, s 3(5).

[22] Circular No. 107, s 3(6).

[23] Circular No. 107, s 3(8).

[24] Circular No. 107, s 3(7).

broad policies, leaving relevant agencies to make specific implementing rules in the future.[25] An in-depth assessment of China's shadow banking regulation would not be possible before the promulgation of the implementing rules. In the process of issuing implementing rules, the coordination and cooperation between relevant regulatory agencies will become critically important, and hence the following section will focus on the institutional structure of shadow banking regulation in China.

The Chinese Practice and Problems

In order to truly appreciate how China has responded to the shadow banking system and the key issues that may have an impact on China's financial regulation in the future, it is necessary first to have an overview of how China's financial regulation is structured. The current financial regulatory framework in China has the defining feature of being sectors-based, with separate regulators for banking, securities, and insurance, namely the China Banking Regulatory Commission (CBRC), the China Securities Regulatory Commission (CSRC) and the China Insurance Regulatory Commission (CIRC).[26]

Together with the central bank, the Peoples' Bank of China (PBOC), the previously mentioned three highly specialized and mutually independent regulatory commissions make up China's financial regulatory framework, collectively referred to as *Yihang Sanhui* (one bank, three commissions). The PBOC has responsibility for monetary policy and the stability of the financial system generally. The CBRC, the CSRC, and the CIRC are the authorities responsible for regulating the banking, securities, and insurance sectors respectively. This sector-based regulatory model corresponds to the segmentation of financial services and markets in China, a policy commonly known as *Fenye Jingying, Fenye Jianguan* (separate operation, separate regulation).

Against this sectors-based regulatory background, the Circular No. 107 sets out more detailed guidance on the institutional structure of shadow banking regulation in China. In general, it adopts an entity-based approach to dividing regulatory responsibility among different regulatory bodies: whoever approves the establishment of the shadow banking entity shall be responsible for regulating it.[27]

First, for shadow banking entities that fall clearly under the statutory sectors-based regulatory framework, their shadow banking businesses shall be regulated by the sectoral regulators separately. For instance, the WMPs offered by banks are subject to the supervision of the CBRC; the WMPs offered by securities and futures

---

[25] Circular No. 107, s 5(5).
[26] For a more detailed discussion, see Hui Huang, "Institutional Structure of Financial Regulation in China: Lessons from the Global Financial Crisis," (2010) 10(1) *The Journal of Corporate Law Studies* 219.
[27] Circular No. 107, s2(1).

firms, as well as private equity investment funds, are regulated by the CSRC; the WMPs offered by insurance companies are regulated by the CIRC. Responsibility for regulating cross-sector WMPs and third-party payment businesses falls on the PBOC.[28]

Second, some shadow banking entities are regulated by local governments in accordance with a uniform set of rules promulgated by the relevant departments of the central government. For instance, the CBRC is responsible for coordinating an interdepartment meeting to make relevant rules applicable to the businesses of financing guarantee companies, while the actual supervision should be carried out by the local governments. Similarly, the supervisory rules on petty-loan companies are to be made by the CBRC in consultation with other agencies such as the PBOC, and the provincial governments are the day-to-day supervisor.[29] This central-local cooperative supervisory arrangement is also applicable to other shadow banking businesses.[30]

Finally, for shadow banking issues to which no regulatory body has been clearly designated, greater research efforts shall be made to find solutions. For instance, the PBOC is tasked with making rules, in collaboration with other relevant departments, on the WMPs offered by third parties, securitization by nonfinancial institutions, and Internet financial businesses.

Although the Circular No. 107 makes great efforts to clarify the division of regulatory responsibilities, it does not come without problems however. The development of shadow banking has significantly changed the way the financial markets operate in China, posing a serious challenge to China's traditional sectoral regulation under which regulatory responsibility is divided along the traditional line of banking, securities, and insurance. As discussed earlier, the Circular No. 107 adheres to the general policy of "separate operation, separate regulation" in establishing the institutional architecture for shadow banking regulation, but this has a number of inadequacies.

On the one hand, the same or similar financial products are subject to different regulators, creating the issue of regulatory inconsistency and thus the opportunity for regulatory arbitrage. A strong example is the regulatory arrangement for the WMPs offered by various financial institutions: albeit being similar financial products, they are subject to different regulators. On the other hand, many shadow banking products, such as securitization, are cross-sector in nature, and do not fit neatly into the traditional classification of banking, securities, and insurance businesses which underpin China's current sector-based regulation. This also explains why the Circular No. 107 fails to specify regulators for certain new and innovative shadow banking businesses, and calls for more research on those issues.

---

[28] Circular No. 107, s2(2).
[29] Circular No. 107, s2(3).
[30] Circular No. 107, s2(4).

In short, there is a mismatch between China's regulatory structure and the underlying market it regulates, which has affected the efficacy of the regulation by creating regulatory inconsistency, gaps, and overlaps. Hence, it is crucial for China to have a more effective regulatory framework for shadow banking.

International Experiences

The preceding analysis has identified a number of structural problems with China's regulatory regime for shadow banking. In quest of a solution to the problems stated earlier, what follows here is a comparative analysis of the three major regulatory models currently in use around the world.

The Sectors-Based Model

The U.S. financial regulation is typical of this model, under which the different financial sectors of banking, securities, and insurance are subject to separate statutes, and supervised by separate regulatory agencies, with boundaries divided institutionally or functionally.

In the wake of the global financial crisis, the United States has enacted the Dodd-Frank Wall Street Reform and Consumer Protection Act (Dodd-Frank Act),[31] which, amongst other things, establishes the Financial Stability Oversight Council (FSOC) as an important measure to safeguard U.S. financial stability. The FSOC is empowered to designate nonbank financial entities and identify nonbank financial activities as systemically significant. A nonbank financial company may be designated as a nonbank systemically important financial institution (SIFI), if the FSOC determines that U.S. financial stability could be threatened by material financial distress at the company, or the nature, scope, size, scale, concentration, interconnectedness, or mix of the activities of the company.[32] The scope of the nonbank SIFI is broad, including (1) any U.S. or foreign company that is "predominantly engaged in financial activities" other than a bank-holding company; (2) a foreign banking organization that is treated as a bank-holding company in the United States; and (3) certain other types of entities subject to bank or bank-like regulation.[33] Similarly, in identifying particular activities as posing systemic risk, the FSOC must find that "the conduct, scope, nature, size, scale, concentration, or interconnectedness of such activity or practice could create or increase the risk of significant liquidity, credit, or other problems spreading among bank holding

---

[31] Pub. L. No. 111–203 (2010).

[32] Dodd-Frank Act, s 113.

[33] Dodd-Frank Act, s 106. It is worth noting that under s 170 of the Dodd-Frank Act, the Federal Reserve Board of Governors can promulgate regulations to exempt certain classes of nonbank financial companies from its supervision.

companies and nonbank financial companies, financial markets of the United States, or low-income, minority, or underserved communities."[34]

It should be noted that the entity designation has different regulatory implications from the activity designation. If a nonbank entity is designated as a nonbank SIFI, it will automatically subject to the oversight of the Federal Reserve Board (FRB) as if they were banks. In contrast, if the FSOC identifies an activity as systemically significant, this will not automatically trigger new prudential constraints on the activity. Rather, the FSOC will make nonbinding reform proposals to the primary regulator or regulators that oversee the activity or to the Congress, and the latter can reject the proposals with relevant explanations.

The FSOC has so far been focused on the task of identifying SIFIs. In April 2012, it approved a rule setting forth a three-stage process by which a nonbank SIFI will be identified. This rule contains substantive criteria, including both quantitative and qualitative metrics, as well as procedural matters such as the voting mechanism the FSOC uses to make a designation decision, the right of the proposed nonbank SIFI to challenge the decision, and the procedure for holding a nonpublic hearing.

In sum, the Dodd-Frank Act does not fundamentally change the "sectoral regulation" model of financial regulation in the United States, but just makes some technical adjustments.

The "Integrated Regulation" Model

This model was best represented by the United Kingdom until its reform in April 2013. The United Kingdom was the first jurisdiction in the world – soon followed by some countries including Germany, Japan, and South Korea – to adopt this model in setting up a powerful and nearly universal regulator for its financial services industry, namely the Financial Services Authority (FSA). The FSA was a super regulator in terms of its unusually broad regulatory mandate: it was mandated to not only regulate a diversity of businesses, including banking, securities, and insurance, but was also charged with both prudential and business conduct regulation.

The "Twin-Peaks" Model

Australia is the champion of this model, being the first to establish a financial regulatory framework comprised of two main regulators. The first regulator, the Australian Securities and Investment Commission (ASIC), has responsibility for business conduct regulation across banking, securities, and insurance. The second regulator in the Australian regime, namely the Australian Prudential Regulatory

---

[34] Dodd-Frank Act, s 120.

Authority (APRA), is responsible for prudential regulation, ensuring the financial soundness of all licensed financial institutions except for securities firms that are regulated by the ASIC.

As the Australian regulatory regime consists of two separate regulators with different mandates in relation to prudential regulation and business conduct regulation respectively, it is vividly named the "twin-peaks" model, or the "object-ives-based regulation" model. It is noteworthy that apart from the ASIC and the APRA, some other agencies perform certain regulatory functions in the financial markets, most notably the Reserve Bank of Australia, the central bank in Australia. It is responsible for monetary policy and financial stability, but no longer has any direct banking regulatory responsibilities.[35]

Suggestions for China

As shown earlier, there are three major structural models of financial regulation at the international arena: (1) the "sectoral regulation" model; (2) the "integrated regulation" model; and (3) the "twin-regulators" model. Naturally, each regulatory model has its own advantages and disadvantages. However, an objective assessment of each approach, in isolation from their jurisdictional financial landscapes, is hardly meaningful. Thus, this section will put the assessment into the Chinese context with a view to finding an appropriate solution to the problems confronting China's financial regulation.

The Chinese financial regulatory regime is broadly similar to the United States, both adopting the traditional sectoral structure with a multiplicity of regulators. In the short term, China may learn from the U.S. practice to improve its regulation of shadow banking without radically changing the overarching structural model. As discussed earlier, under the Dodd-Frank Act, the FSOC is created to improve interagency cooperation and prevent things falling down the cracks amongst various regulators. In particular, it has power to designate nonbank SIFIs for enhanced supervision and regulation by the FRB. Hence, the FRB has authority to supervise all firms that could pose a threat to financial stability, even those that

---

[35] In this sense, the Australian financial regulatory system is composed of three regulators, namely the ASIC, the APRA, and the Reserve Bank of Australia, and therefore it is sometimes classified as not two-but "three-peaked." This is in contrast with the Netherlands, the other country with the "twin peaks" model. In the Netherlands, prudential regulation is combined with financial stability regulation in a single agency (i.e., the Dutch central bank called 'De Nederlandsche Bank'), with conduct of business regulation being assigned to a separate agency called "Autoriteit Financiele Markten" (Financial Markets Authority). For a more detailed comparative study of the Australian and Dutch practices, see Hui Huang, "Insti-tutional Structure of Financial Regulation in China: Lessons from the Global Financial Crisis," (2010) 10(1) *The Journal of Corporate Law Studies* 219; Robin Hui Huang and Dirk Schoenmaker (eds.), *Institutional Structure of Financial Regulation: Theories and International Experiences* (Routledge, forthcoming).

do not own banks. This effectively extends the Federal Reserve's consolidated supervision to all large, interconnected financial groups whose failure could have serious systemic effects. As a result, financial firms will not be able to escape regulatory oversight simply by manipulating their legal structure.

The mentioned reforms seem to be a pragmatic response to the problems with the U.S. financial regulation as highlighted by the 2008 global financial crisis. Indeed, the Dodd-Frank Act stops short of holistically addressing the structural inadequacies of the U.S. financial regulation, and its structural model remains sectors-based with separate regulators responsible for each financial sector. But the reform has the advantage of being quick and measured to deal with the pressing issues in practice.

The U.S. approach merits consideration in the context of China. On the one hand, the PBOC can be authorized to supervise all systemically important financial institutions; on the other hand, an interagency oversight council on shadow banking can be created to bring together regulators from across markets and other relevant agencies to coordinate and share information, and to identify gaps in the regulation of shadow banking.[36] In order to promote efficiency and continuity, the council may set up a standing committee composed of the PBOC and the three sector-specific regulatory agencies, namely the CBRC, the CSRC, and the CIRC. As with the case of the Dodd-Frank Act, this solution can be a practical expedient for China in the short term.

More importantly, the short-term recommendation is based on a realistic appraisal of the present needs of China's financial markets. While the U.S. current regulatory regime is said to be suboptimal for its financial markets, it may well be a suitable model for the less developed Chinese markets. As discussed before, China's shadow banking system is still in its infancy on the basis of relatively unsophisticated financial tools. Thus, the U.S. model should be adequate to meet the challenges China's financial regulatory regime currently faces.

The U.S. reform under the Dodd-Frank Act does little more than just fine-tuning regulatory authorities within the preexisting regulatory framework, which has proved to be an antiquated system for a well-developed economy like the United States. In fact, legitimate concerns have been raised over the U.S. extension of banking regulation to nonbank SIFIs. First, the banking regulator, namely the FRB, has virtually no experience regulating entities that are not banks or bank holding companies. Second, as nonbank SIFIs will be regulated by both the FRB and their traditional sectoral regulators, this increases complexity and the costs of compliance, and risks imposing conflicting requirements. More regulators does not necessarily mean greater oversight: turf wars and coordination failures can lead to

---

[36] Dasong Yuan, "International Financial Regulatory Reforms to Strengthen the Regulation of Shadow Banking," (2012) 2 *Faxue Yanjiu [Chinese Journal of Law]* 194, 207; Jianjun Li and Guangning Tian, "An Analysis of the Top Tier Design of the Reform of the Regulation of Shadow Banking," (2011) 8 *Hongguan Jingji Yanjiu [Macro-Economic Research]*.

even more gaps. In short, the U.S. reform may make its regulatory structure even more complicated, fragmented, and incoherent.[37]

In the intermediate or long run, therefore, China cannot rely on the U.S. experience, but instead needs to consider the twin-peaks model or to a lesser extent the integrated regulation model. The twin-peaks and integrated regulation models attempt to thoroughly overhaul the regulatory structure, taking a novel approach to financial regulation. They are better adapted to the realities of modern financial markets than the sectoral structure, dispensing with the traditional boundaries between banking, securities and insurance. Both represent genuine efforts to modernize financial regulation to deal with the issues created by financial moderation and innovation as is exemplified by many shadow banking entities and activities. In this sense, they point out the right direction for financial regulatory reforms in the future.

The key difference between the integrated regulation and the twin-peaks models is that while the former assigns all regulatory responsibilities to a single regulator, the latter divides responsibilities and creates two separate regulators: one for prudential regulation and the other for business conduct regulation. Compared to the integrated regulation model, the twin-peaks model has a number of competitive advantages. Hence, the twin-peaks model has attracted increasing attention as a template for reform in many countries, particularly after the global financial crisis of 2008.[38] These latest international developments should shed light on the debate over the future development of China's financial regulation.

CONCLUSION

This paper presents a preliminary investigation of the incidence and regulation of shadow banking in China, as a contribution to the international discourse on the important issue. Evaluating the size of the shadow banking system in China is not straightforward due to the confusion about what shadow banking is, as well as the lack of relevant data and information. Nevertheless, some tentative conclusions can be drawn from the analysis carried out in this paper.

Shadow banking has grown rapidly in China over the past few years, which exhibits distinctive features in terms of driving forces, components, players, and risk

---

[37] Edward F. Greene and Elizabeth L. Broomfield, "Promoting risk mitigation, not migration: a comparative analysis of shadow banking reforms by the FSB, USA and EU," (2013) 8(1) *Capital Markets Law Journal* 6, 27.

[38] For a more detailed discussion of the advantages of the twin-peaks model vis-à-vis the integrated regulation model and the recent reforms towards the twin-peaks model in various jurisdictions such as the United Kingdom and South Africa, see Hui Huang, "Institutional Structure of Financial Regulation in China: Lessons from the Global Financial Crisis," (2010) 10(1) *The Journal of Corporate Law Studies* 219; Robin Hui Huang and Dirk Schoenmaker (eds.), *Institutional Structure of Financial Regulation: Theories and International Experiences* (Routledge, forthcoming).

profiles. Despite the various differences between China's shadow banking and its overseas counterparts, they give rise to similar regulatory concerns, including systemic risk and regulatory arbitrage. From a regulatory standpoint, however, the important benefits of shadow banking should not be disregarded.

China's regulatory responses to shadow banking, as embodied in the recently issued Circular No. 107, appear to be based on a balanced view of the benefits and risks of shadow banking. It provides for both institutional structure and substantive guidance in relation to the regulation of shadow banking in China. The substantive guidance is useful, but its workability depends very much on implementing rules to be issued by various agencies. The institutional structure of shadow banking regulation thus becomes very important in coordinating the rule-making and enforcement efforts of those agencies. To this end, Circular No. 107 clarifies the regulatory arrangements for shadow banking within the existing sectoral regulatory structure. While this may work in the short term, China should consider a more fundamental reform towards the twin-peaks model in the long term.

v

The Role of Culture and Ethics in Global Finance

18

Promoting Capital Markets Professionalism: An Emerging Asian Model

Brian W. Tang

"Publicity is justly commended as a remedy for social and industrial diseases. Sunlight is said to be the best of disinfectants; electric light the most efficient policeman."

Justice Louis D. Brandeis, *Other People's Money*, 1914[1]

INTRODUCTION: CAPITAL MARKETS PROFESSIONALISM AS A LYNCHPIN TO MARKET INTEGRITY

The quality of our global capital markets relies upon quality due diligence and disclosure by experienced practitioners outside and within our listed companies. Transparency through disclosure is the regulatory foundation upon which our modern capital markets were established to allow companies seeking cost-effective capital to access "other people's money." It is really quite amazing to think that capital markets investors globally are willing to make decisions worth trillions of dollars without actually visiting the investee companies' premises nor meeting with management – in essence, they rely on written information provided by company management and research analysts.

Institutional and retail investors, internationally and within domestic markets, rely on capital markets integrity to give them confidence to price, invest, and trade in those trillions of dollars of securities and their corollary derivatives. Especially in emerging and transitional economies where concerns about corporate corruption and fraud remain high, the professionalism of such capital markets practitioners and gatekeepers, who are paid directly or indirectly by the issuers of such securities, is the lynchpin of market integrity relied upon by issuers and investors alike.

Data in this chapter, other than in the conclusion, is as of July 2014.

[1] Louis Brandeis, *Other People's Money And How the Bankers Use It* (1914), a collection of essays that originally appeared in Harper's Weekly that was first published as a book in 1914, and reissued in 1933 in the lead-up to the passing of the U.S. securities regulation that has formed the basis and philosophy of much securities and capital markets regulation globally.

Since the global financial crisis (GFC), there has been a tremendous growth of financial legislation and regulation around the world to prevent similar crises from recurring and to address certain improprieties.

Regulations and active enforcement play an important role in promoting behavioral change. Given the ever-increasing international market competition, the size and complexity of institutions and organizational dynamics and the emergence of post-GFC financial scandals, there is now also an emerging recognition that more regulation alone is not enough.

This chapter will address the following:

(a) A brief overview of the legislative and regulatory reaction to the GFC and the increasing focus on addressing misconduct in the key international financial centers (IFCs) of New York, London, and Hong Kong

(b) Shifting from compliance gatekeepers to capital markets professionalism[2]

(c) Practical challenges faced in exercising capital markets professionalism, with a focus on Hong Kong

(d) Lessons from other industry-led initiatives to promote good culture and practices relating to the capital markets

(e) Directions for a new Asian initiative promoting capital markets professionalism: the Asia Capital Markets Institute.

A BRIEF OVERVIEW OF THE LEGISLATIVE AND REGULATORY REACTION TO THE GFC

Initial Priority Focused on Prudential Standards to Address Systemic Issues

The GFC, with its subprime mortgage and credit and liquidity crisis, resulted in, among other things, the collapse of Lehman Brothers, the effective nationalization of Northern Rock, RBS and AIG, and forced takeovers of Washington Mutual, Bear Stearns and Merrill Lynch. In the wake of this, the initial wave of prudential regulation focused on systemic risk, financial stability, liquidity and capital levels, including the designation of "too-big-to-fail" (TBTF) institutions.[3]

---

[2] For the purpose of this chapter, "capital markets professionals" is defined to focus on those who are involved in the due diligence and preparation of disclosure relied upon by the capital markets. While there are principles that may be applicable to other functionalities within financial institutions (e.g., traders), it may have much less application to others (e.g., commercial lenders). See for example, Brian Tang "Integrity of capital markets relies on professional conduct." (SCMP, May 13, 2014) www.scmp.com/comment/article/1511232/integrity-capital-markets-relies-professional-conduct.

[3] See for example, Emilios Avgouleas, "Large Systemic Banks and Fractional Reserve Banking, Intractable Dilemmas in Search of Effective Solutions," (Chapter 14, this book), *ibid.*

An avalanche of legislation and regulation also followed. For example, the US Dodd-Frank Wall Street Reform and Consumer Protection Act (Dodd-Frank) addressed wide-ranging issues in its 849 pages and 396 rule-making requirements. Law firm Davis Polk reported that, as of July 1, 2014, 280 Dodd-Frank rulemaking requirement deadlines have passed, of which 127 (45.4%) have been missed.[4] In other words, notwithstanding one description of its length to date being fifteen times longer than Herman Melville's novel Moby Dick,[5] five years from the GFC, there are still more regulations to come.

Subsequent Scandals In the Banking Sector and Capital Markets

The increasing lack of trust in financial institutions and its participants did not arise from the GFC alone. The following is a brief and indicative survey as of June 30, 2014 outlining various major conduct-related scandals that have since arisen:

- Misleading investors about residential mortgage-backed securities (RMBSs) and collateralized debt obligations (CDOs) that fueled the GFC – Bank of America Corp settled with Fannie Mae by paying U.S. $11.6 billion,[6] and Citibank and JPMorgan Chase settled with U.S. regulators by paying U.S.$7 billion and U.S.$13 billion respectively[7]
- Foreclosure abuses – ten banks settled by paying U.S.$8.5 billion following the four largest U.S. banks and Ally Financial settling the prior year by paying U.S.$25 billion[8]
- "London Whale" trading scandal – JPMorgan Chase paid more than U.S.$1 billion to U.S. and British regulators for internal controls and risk management breakdowns that led to its failure to disclose the true extent of its U.S.$6.2 billion trading loss[9]

---

[4] Davis Polk Dodd-Frank Progress Report (July 1, 2014) www.davispolk.com/Dodd-Frank-Rule making-Progress-Report.

[5] "Overhaul Grows and Slows," (*Wall Street Journal*, May 2, 2011) http://online.wsj.com/news/articles/SB10001424052748703346704576295873060349068?mod=ITP_moneyandinvesting_0&mg=reno64-wsj&url=http%3A%2F%2Fonline.wsj.com%2Farticle%2FSB10001424052748703346704576295873060349068.html%3Fmod%3DITP_moneyandinvesting_0.

[6] See for example, "Bank of America to pay $9.3 billion to settle mortgage bond claims," (*Reuters*, March 16, 2014) www.reuters.com/article/2014/03/26/us-bankofamerica-settlement-fhfa-idUSBREA2P23720140326.

[7] See for example, "Citigroup to pay $7 billion to settle U.S. mortgage probe," (*Reuters*, July 14, 2014) www.reuters.com/article/2014/07/14/us-citigroup-settlement-doj-idUSKBN0FJ13120140714.

[8] See for example, "Big Banks Settle Mortgage Hangover," (*Wall Street Journal*, January 7, 2013) http://online.wsj.com/news/articles/SB10001424127887324391104578227292446942824.

[9] See for example, "The London Whale" (*Bloomberg*, October 17, 2013) www.bloomberg.com/quicktake/the-london-whale/.

- London Interbank Offered Rate (LIBOR) rate-rigging scandal – European Commission fined eight big banks U.S.$2.3 billion for participating in "illegal cartels,"[10] with U.S. suits still ongoing against banks allegedly falsely inflating or deflating their interest rates to profit from trades, or to give the impression that they were more creditworthy than they actually were, as well as ongoing investigations into the fixing of foreign currency exchange markets and commodities price manipulation
- Money-laundering and sanctions violations – in joining banks such as Standard Chartered, ING and RBS, HSBC paid the then-largest fine of U.S.$1.9 billion for what a U.S. Senate subcommittee described as "actively circumvented U.S. safeguards... designed to block terrorists, drug lords, and rogue regimes"[11]
- Insider trading – the Manhattan U.S. District Attorney has convicted eighty-one people for insider trading in the last four and a half years,[12] including imprisoning the founder of hedge fund The Galleon Group, Raj Rajaratnam, and former McKinsey head and Goldman Sachs board member, Rajat Gupta and having SAC Capital Partners plead guilty to insider trading, paying a U.S.$1.8 billion fine and converting from a hedge fund to a family office[13]
- Private bank tax evasion scandal – fourteen banks have reportedly been under criminal investigation by the U.S. Department of Justice for assisting with tax evasion,[14] to which UBS has already settled by paying U.S. $780 million[15]
- Asian investment banking hiring practices – U.S. Securities and Exchange Commission (SEC) is reportedly investigating at least six banks for potential breaches of the Foreign Corrupt Practices Act (FCPA) relating to the hiring of children of senior officials in exchange

---

[10] See for example, "Big Banks Fined $2.3B Over Illegal Libor Cartels, More Fines On The Way" (*Forbes*, December 4, 2013) www.forbes.com/sites/halahtouryalai/2013/12/04/big-banks-fined-2-3b-over-illegal-libor-cartels-more-fines-on-the-way/.

[11] U.S. Permanent Sub-Committee on Investigations of the U.S. Senate Committee on Homeland Security and Governmental Affairs, "HSBC Exposed US Financial System to Money Laundering, Drug, Terrorist Financing Risk" (Press release, July 16, 2012) www.hsgac.senate .gov/subcommittees/investigations/media/hsbc-exposed-us-finacial-system-to-money-launder ing-drug-terrorist-financing-risks.

[12] For example, "Rengan Rajaratnam cleared, U.S. insider trading streak snapped," (*Reuters*, July 8, 2014): www.reuters.com/article/2014/07/08/us-usa-insidertrading-rajaratnam-idUSKBN0 FD1QU20140708.

[13] See for example, "SAC Record $1.8 Billion Insider Plea Caps 7-Year Probe," (*Bloomberg*, April 11, 2014) www.bloomberg.com/news/2014-04-10/sac-judge-approves-record-insider-trading-accord-with-u-s.html.

[14] See for example, "Remaining 'hit list' banks sweat over US verdicts," (*SwissInfo*, May 22, 2014) http://origin.swissinfo.ch/eng/remaining–hit-list–banks-sweat-over-us-verdicts/38637818.

[15] See for example, "UBS Agrees To Pay $780 Million," (*Forbes*, February 18, 2009) www.forbes .com/2009/02/18/ubs-fraud-offshore-personal-finance_ubs.html.

for business,[16] which has led to JPMorgan's former China head being arrested by Hong Kong's Independent Commission Against Corruption (ICAC)[17]

It seems little wonder that the 2014 Edelman Trust Barometer continues to rank the financial services industry as the least trusted industry globally.[18]

Concerns About TBTF, Lack of Accountability, and Loss of Trust

While the prudential measures sought were designed to address global financial stability, before long, legislators and regulators began expressing concerns regarding TBTF resulting in moral hazard and a lack of accountability.

United States – Shifting Focus from TBTF

According to Financial Times research as of March 2014, Wall Street banks and their foreign rivals paid out U.S.$100 billion in U.S. legal settlements in the last five years.[19]

In February 2013, Senator Elizabeth Warren gave voice to the growing public concern that "'too-big-to-fail' has become 'too big for trial.'"[20]

In March 2013, U.S. Attorney-General Eric Holder voiced his own concern that "the size of some of these institutions becomes so large that it does become difficult for us to prosecute them when we are hit with indications that if we do prosecute – if we do bring a criminal charge – it will have a negative impact on the national economy, perhaps even the world economy... I think that is a function of the fact that some of these institutions have become too large."[21]

[16] See for example, "Regulators Step Up Probe Into Bank Hiring Overseas," (*Wall Street Journal*, May 6, 2014) http://online.wsj.com/news/articles/SB10001424052702303417104579546190553220338.

[17] See for example, "JPMorgan ex-chief arrested by ICAC" (*The Standard*, May 22, 2014) www.thestandard.com.hk/news_detail.asp?art_id=145618&con_type=1.

[18] 2014 Edelman Trust Barometer for Financial Services Industry www.edelman.com/insights/intellectual-property/2014-edelman-trust-barometer/trust-in-business/trust-in-financial-services/.

[19] "Banks Pay Out $100 bn in US fines" (*Financial Times*, March 25, 2014) www.ft.com/intl/cms/s/0/802ae15c-9b50-11e3-946b-00144feab7de.html.

[20] Elizabeth Warren's comments at the Senate Banking Committee hearing on February 14, 2013 can be seen at: www.youtube.com/watch?v=mavB1lbtIow, where she contrasts that "[t]here are district attorneys and United States attorneys out there every day squeezing ordinary citizens on sometimes very thin grounds and taking them to trial in order to make an example." In September 2013, Senator Warren and others were seeking to pass a 21st Century Glass–Steagall Act so that "big banks would still be big—but not too big to fail or, for that matter, too big to manage, too big to regulate, too big for trial, or too big for jail": "The 21st Century Glass–Steagall Act would reduce the risk of another crash" (*Boston Globe Op Ed*, September 18, 2014) www.warren.senate.gov/?p=op_ed&id=242.

[21] Eric Holder, selected transcript (*American Banker*, March 6, 2013): www.americanbanker.com/issues/178_45/transcript-attorney-general-eric-holder-on-too-big-to-jail-1057295-1.html.

The practice of deferred prosecution agreements (DPA) also started receiving more attention, including from members of the bench (which is tasked with ratifying many such DPAs), such as when U.S. District Judge Jed Rakoff provocatively asked in a speech: "Why have no high-level executives been prosecuted in connection with the financial crisis?"[22]

Not long after her arrival as SEC chairman, Mary Joe White stated that she would reconsider seeking admissions of wrongdoing as part of enforcement settlements,[23] and in March 2014, Eric Holder clarified that "[t]here is no such thing as too big to jail."[24] In the following months, two major foreign banks became the first banks since the GFC to plead guilty to a U.S. financial crime and paid ever-increasing fines: Credit Suisse pleaded guilty for aiding U.S. tax evasion and was fined U.S.\$2.6 billion, and BNP Paribas pleaded guilty for U.S. sanction violations and was fined a record U.S.\$8.9 billion, plus faces a temporary suspension to its interbank, and oil and gas dollar clearing facilities.[25]

Various U.S. regulators are increasingly turning their attention to the issue of financial institution culture. In November 2013, Federal Reserve Bank of New York head William Dudley observed that "'too-big-to-fail' is not the only problem with large banks,"[26] and that "[t]here is evidence of deep-seated cultural and ethical failures at many large financial institutions."[27] To that end, Thomas J. Curry, the head of the Office of the Comptroller of the Currency (OCC), has proposed a rule that would make its "heightened expectations" for big banks enforceable, including

[22] Jed S Rakoff, "Why Have No High Level Executives Been Prosecuted In Connection With The Financial Crisis?" (November 15, 2013) http://clsbluesky.law.columbia.edu/2013/11/15/why-have-no-high-level-executives-been-prosecuted-in-connection-with-the-financial-crisis; although his decision to reject an SEC settlement with Citibank was overruled, his role was credited in changing public and SEC opinion: "Overuled, Judge still left a mark on SEC agenda" (*New York Times*, June 4, 2014) http://dealbook.nytimes.com/2014/06/04/appeals-court-overturns-decision-to-reject-s-e-c-citigroup-settlement/?_php=true&_type=blogs&_r=0.

[23] Mary Jo White, "Deploying the Full Enforcement Arsenal" (September 26, 2013) www.sec.gov/News/Speech/Detail/Speech/1370539841202#.U70VpaiwrIU.

[24] Eric Holder "There is no such thing as too big to jail" http://video.cnbc.com/gallery/?video=3000272622. For a review of DPAs, see for example, Gibson Dunn's half-yearly Updates on Corporate Non-Prosecution Agreements (CAN) and Deferred Prosecution Agreements (DPA) www.gibsondunn.com/Search/Pages/PublicationsSearch.aspx?k=(%22Publication%20Practice%22%3A%22White%20Collar%20Defense%20and%20Investigations%22%20AND%20%22Publication%20Topic%22%3A%22Deferred%20and%20Non-Prosecution%20Agreements%22%20AND%20%22Publication%20Type%22%3A%22Client%20Alert%22).

[25] See for example, "Not too big to jail," (*Economist*, May 24, 2014) www.economist.com/news/finance-and-economics/21602692-big-financial-firm-pleads-guilty-criminal-charge-and-lives-tell. While these are significant milestones in terms of criminal pleas and fines, it has not been without controversy in the acknowledgment that they are both not US banks: see for example, "No way to treat a criminal," (*Economist*, July 5, 2014) www.economist.com/news/leaders/21606279-french-bank-deserved-clobbering-americas-legal-system-looks-extortion.

[26] "Regulators Size Up Wall Street, with Worry," (*New York Times*, March 12, 2014) http://dealbook.nytimes.com/2014/03/12/questions-are-asked-of-rot-in-banking-culture/?_php=true&_type=blogs&_r=0.

[27] William Dudley, "Ending Too Big To Fail," (November 7, 2013) www.newyorkfed.org/newsevents/speeches/2013/dud131107.html.

that boards show a "willingness to provide a credible challenge to bank management's decision-making."[28]

United Kingdom – Focus on Financial Institution Conduct and Culture

While the GFC very significantly impacted the UK public perception of banks due to major bank nationalizations, it was the scandal relating to the alleged widespread manipulation of LIBOR, which was administered by the British Banking Association (BBA) that caused the UK parliament to convene a joint Commission on Banking Standards in July 2012 "to consider and report on

- professional standards and culture of the UK banking sector, taking account of regulatory and competition investigations into the LIBOR rate-setting process
- lessons to be learned about corporate governance, transparency and conflicts of interest, and their implications for regulation and for Government policy

and to make recommendations for legislative and other action."[29]

After much publicized testimony by many of the City's leading bankers, the resulting report on Changing Banking for Good[30] published in June 2013 reinforced many of the nearly concurrent findings of the Salz independent review of Barclays' business practices[31] that blamed "cultural shortcomings." The report recommended, among other things, criminal liability for reckless senior bankers as part of a revamp of the "senior persons' regime" and "support[ed] the creation of a professional standards body to promote higher professional standards in banking."[32]

In September 2013, United Kingdom's six largest banks invited Sir Richard Lambert to conduct a Banking Standards Review, whose report was published in May 2014 and recommended the establishment of a Banking Standards Review Council (BSRC).[33]

---

[28] US Office of the Comptroller of the Currency (Press release, January 16, 2014) www.occ.gov/news-issuances/news-releases/2014/nr-occ-2014-4.html.

[29] UK Joint Parliamentary Commission on Banking Standards (JPCBS), www.parliament.uk/business/committees/committees-a-z/joint-select/professional-standards-in-the-banking-industry/.

[30] JPCBS, Changing Banking for Good (June 19, 2013) www.parliament.uk/business/committees/committees-a-z/joint-select/professional-standards-in-the-banking-industry/news/changing-banking-for-good-report.

[31] Anthony Salz, "Salz Review: An Independent Review of Barclays' Business Practices," (April 2013) www.barclays.com/content/dam/barclayspublic/documents/news/875-269-salz-review-04-2013.pdf.

[32] JPCBS, Changing Banking for Good, *ibid*, Paragraph 601.

[33] Banking Standards Review (May 19, 2014) www.bankingstandardsreview.org.uk/assets/docs/may2014report.pdf.

ıditionally, the United State's more "rules-based" regulatory drafting and ını .pretive approach (as demonstrated by the very technical and precise general accepted accounting principles, GAAP, with narrow safe harbors) underlines its more individualistic rights-based jurisprudence, and when coupled with the availability of contingency fees, gives rise to the substantial risk and fear of class-action litigation. This is contrasted with the European and United Kingdom's predilection toward the "principles-based" approach that vests more discretion in its participants.[34]

The Financial Services Authority (FSA) recognized the need to "focus on business models, strategies, risks, and outcomes than primarily on systems and processes,"[35] and bifurcated its prudential and conduct roles into the Prudential Regulatory Authority (PRA) and the Financial Conduct Authority (FCA) respectively effective April 1, 2013. Since then, FCA Chief Executive Officer Martin Wheatley has been very focused on "modelling integrity through culture" when regulating markets,[36] and in June 2014 joined the UK Treasury and Bank of England in announcing its "Fair and Effective Markets Review."[37]

These are sentiments that have also been echoed more broadly by leading figures at the Inclusive Capitalism Conference[38] hosted by the City of London in May 2014. International Monetary Fund (IMF) Managing Director Christine Lagarde observed that "regulation and supervision by themselves are still not enough" and "we also need to turn our attention to the culture of financial institutions and to the individual behavior that lies beneath."[39]

Hong Kong – Focus on Capital Markets Gatekeepers

Hong Kong is one of the world's leading venues for raising of capital through initial public offerings (IPOs).[40] Although Asian financial institutions and capital markets

---

[34] See for example, John C Coffee Jr, "Gatekeeper Failure and Reform: The Challenge of Fashioning Relevant Reforms," Columbia Law and Economics Working Paper No. 237 (September 2003) http://papers.ssrn.com/sol3/papers.cfm?abstract_id=447940.

[35] Financial Services Authority "The Turner Review – a Regulatory Response to the Global Banking Crisis," (March 2009) www.fsa.gov.uk/pubs/other/turner_review.pdf.

[36] Martin Wheatley, "Modelling integrity through culture," (November 19, 2013) www.fca.org .uk/news/firms/modelling-integrity-through-culture.

[37] The focus of the review will be on misconduct that has arisen in fixed-income, currency and commodity markets, including associated derivatives and benchmarks: see "Fair and Effective Markets Review announced by Chancellor of the Exchequer," (Press release, June 12, 2014) www.gov.uk/government/news/fair-and-effective-markets-review-announced-by-chancellor-of-the-exchequer.

[38] Conference on Inclusive Capitalism: Building Value, Renewing Trust: www.inclusivecapital ism.org.

[39] Christine Lagarde, "Economic Inclusion and Financial Integrity—an Address to the Conference on Inclusive Capitalism," (May 27, 2014) www.imf.org/external/np/speeches/2014/052714 .htm; see also William Blair, "Reconceptualizing the Role of Standards in Supporting Financial Regulation," (Chapter 21, this book); *ibid*.

[40] According to, PwC's IPO Centre, Hong Kong raised the most money and had the most number of IPOs in the five years ended December 2012: PwC "Which Market? An overview of

were fortunately not as heavily affected by the GFC, Hong Kong has had its own share of capital markets misconduct and scandals, such as Hontex International's shares being suspended within three months of its IPO due to an overstatement of sales and profits.[41] The Securities and Futures Commissions' (SFC) thematic inspections of sponsors have also determined that the levels of sponsor due diligence have often proven "inadequate."[42]

Hong Kong's regulators are very focused on holding its capital markets gatekeepers accountable. This arises primarily due to jurisdictional enforcement limitations where, like IFCs such as Singapore and to a certain extent London, many issuers and their assets are based offshore.[43]

While U.S. commentators have historically focused on external gatekeepers such as public accountants, lawyers, research analysts, and ratings agencies,[44] and the United Kingdom and Hong Kong on listing sponsors,[45] there is an increased recognition of the importance of internal gatekeepers as well, with SEC's Mary Jo White calling directors "essential gatekeepers."[46]

In 2013, Hong Kong underwent tremendous regulatory changes. As of January 1, listed company directors face personal civil liability for nontimely disclosure of price-sensitive information (PSI).[47] As of October 1, the new IPO sponsor regime became effective,[48] requiring the appointment of sponsors and notification to the Hong Kong Stock Exchange (HKEx) at least two months prior to the first filing, and requiring all deal team members to be named and sponsor withdrawals to be noisy. Effective April 1, 2014, corporate issuers and their IPO sponsors are also required to make their first draft A-1 prospectus filings available for public scrutiny on the HKEx website at the same time as its submission to regulators. Returned filings would result in a public "naming and shaming" of inadequate actors and an

London, New York, Hong Kong and Singapore stock exchanges," p.3 (September 2013) www.pwc.com/en_GX/gx/audit-services/publications/assets/pwc-which-market.pdf.

[41] See "Hontex ordered to make $1.03 billion buy-back offer over untrue IPO prospectus," (SFC Press release, June 20, 2012); www.sfc.hk/sfcPressRelease/EN/sfcOpenDocServlet?doc no=12PR63.

[42] See for example, SFC "Report on Sponsor Theme Inspection Findings," (March 2011) www.sfc.hk/sfc/doc/EN/speeches/public/surveys/11/Sponsor%20report_FINAL.pdf.

[43] The proposed Shanghai-Hong Kong Stock Connect also provides unprecedented market access opportunities for Hong Kong's financial and investor communities, along with regulatory challenges regarding how best to ensure accountability of participants located outside Hong Kong.

[44] For example, John C. Coffee Jr., *Gatekeepers: The Role of the Professions and Corporate Governance*, Oxford University Press, Oxford (2006).

[45] While the United Kingdom and Hong Kong have listing sponsor regimes, underwriters of securities offerings in the United States have a due diligence defence against material misstatements or omissions under section 11 of the U.S. Securities Act of 1933.

[46] Mary Jo White, "A Few Things Directors Should Know About the SEC," (June 24, 2014) www.sec.gov/News/Speech/Detail/Speech/1370542148863#.U8CWZ6iwrIV.

[47] Securities and Futures (Amendment) Ordinance 2012 (Amendment Ordinance) (Ord. No. 9 of 2012 gazetted May 4, 2012) www.gld.gov.hk/egazette/pdf/20121618/es1201216189.pdf.

[48] SFC, "Consultation Conclusions on regulation of IPO sponsors" (December 12, 2012); www.sfc.hk/edistributionWeb/gateway/EN/consultation/conclusion?refNo=12CP1.

eight-week moratorium imposed on any subsequent submission. Hong Kong's Financial Services and Treasury Bureau (FSTB) is also seeking to overhaul public accountant oversight[49] while the SFC was considering seeking Legislative Council confirmation regarding criminal liability of IPO sponsors.[50]

In June 2014, SFC Executive Director of Intermediaries James Shipton highlighted an important broadened securities supervisory approach that focuses on the "important component for ensuring right decisions are made and the right levels of professionalism – acting conscientiously and skilfully – exist in the culture of the organization."[51]

SHIFTING FROM COMPLIANCE GATEKEEPERS TO CAPITAL MARKETS PROFESSIONALISM

Capital Markets Participants and Gatekeepers

In general, capital markets participants and gatekeepers are attributed to include

(i) external gatekeepers, such as:
   a. IPO sponsors (including, in the case of Hong Kong, global financial institutions, boutiques, securities firms, and regional and mainland financial institutions)[52]

---

[49] In June 2014, FSTB issued a public consultation to review an overhaul of public accountant oversight to vest investigatory and enforcement powers held by the Hong Kong Institute of Certified Practicing Accountants (HKICA) to the independent Financial Reporting Council (FRC): Financial Services and Treasury Bureau, "Consultation on Proposals to Improve Regulatory Regime for Listed Entity Auditors," (June 20, 2014) www.fstb.gov.hk/fsb/ppr/con sult/doc/consult_rpirrlea_e.pdf.

[50] See Hong Kong Administration, "Sponsor Regulation and Other Investor Protection Initiatives," CB(1)1128/12–13(04) (June 3, 2013) www.legco.gov.hk/yr12–13/english/panels/fa/papers/ fa0603cb1–1128–4-e.pdf.

[51] James Shipton, "Importance of capital markets professionalism and the role of regulators" (June 17, 2014) www.sfc.hk/web/EN/files/ER/PDF/Speeches/James%20Shipton_20140617.pdf. To that end, Shipton outlined three aspects of culture on which the SFC would increase scrutiny:

   (i) ethical culture – focussing not just on traditional control systems and procedures frameworks but also "control culture" – the "human element," incentives and disincentives
   (ii) leadership culture – examining decision-making structures and the delivery and distribution mechanism of the "tone from the top" and those in authority by engaging more directly and proactively with business and operational leaders rather than through legal, compliance and third parties
   (iii) culture of professionalism – looking at business models to see if there is alignment of their control priorities and culture with their business strategy and decision-making processes, and whether these principles are in fact embedded in businesses and operations, as opposed to a "surrender of an ethical standard for a legal one" that is "subject to biased interpretations and/or 'opinion shopping'"

[52] UK sponsors are similarly recognized as playing "a unique and critical role in the listing regime, providing expert guidance to premium listed issuers and applicants for Premium

    b. public accountants

    c. securities research analysts

    d. credit-ratings agencies (for debt and structured transactions)

    e. lawyers[53]

(ii) internal "corporate disclosure professionals" (whose additional corporate governance responsibilities arise from companies receiving "other people's money"), such as:

    a. directors (especially independent non-executive directors)

    b. statutory officers such as company secretaries[54]

    c. other senior executives such as CEOs, CFOs, general counsel,[55] compliance officers, and investor relations officers

It is the reputational capital of such gatekeepers that provides some of the critical efficiencies of the capital markets – loss of trust and confidence in such gatekeepers would increase transactional costs, the cost of capital, and systemic risk.

Listing on the interpretation of our rules, to help them meet their obligations, and also as a first line of defence, giving us important confirmations of a premium listed issuer's ability to meet certain obligations which helps us meet our objectives": David Lawton, "Regulatory Developments and Changing Market Structure" (February 27, 2014) www.fca.org.uk/news/regulatory-developments-and-the-changing-market-structure.

[53] Many lawyers may reject their characterization as gatekeepers on grounds that it impinges upon the lawyer's role as advocate and transaction engineer. *Yet see SEC v. WorldCom*, 2003 WL 22004827 (S.D.N.Y Aug. 26, 2003): "[B]oards of directors, outside auditors and outside counsel are the gatekeepers of behavior standards who are able to prevent damage before it occurs if they are alert, and above all if they are willing to act when necessary. A common denominator in many of the major frauds has been the failure of these gatekeepers to stop improper practices at the outset." Mainland China is proving a fascinating area of development: not only have underwriters unusually sued their own counsel who happen to be two of China's most prominent law firms ("China: Forest Fire," The Lawyer, October 14, 2013) www.thelawyer.com/analysis/market-analysis/regions/asia-pacific-analysis/china-forest-fire/3010905.article), Chinese law firms have been fined and suspended by the China Securities Regulatory Commission (CSRC) for inadequate IPO due diligence: ("Jingtian & Gongcheng Fined Over IPO Due Diligence," *American Lawyer*, March 13, 2014) www.americanlawyer.com/id=1202646712080/Jingtian–Gongcheng-Fined-Over-IPO-Due-Diligence?slreturn=20140611230736.

[54] David W. Smith described corporate secretaries as "gatekeepers and filters of governance and other challenges facing corporations" ("Society of Corporate Secretaries & Governance Professionals – In A Challenging Time," (*Metropolitan Corporate Counsel*, April 5, 2010)) www.metrocorpcounsel.com/articles/12390/society-corporate-secretaries-governance-profes sionals-challenging-time). In Hong Kong, the Corporate Governance Code has been observed to "seek to preserve the independence of the company secretary as an in-house gatekeeper" ("Independence of the Company Secretary," CSj, April 2013, p 10); in the words of Carina Wessels, President of Corporate Secretaries International Association (CSIA), a "gatekeeper for good governance" ("Forging a Global Profession," CSj, June 2014, p 15).

[55] This is more prevalent in the United States where in-house lawyers are more involved in disclosure related matters and are required by SOX to do "up the ladder reporting."

The new Hong Kong IPO sponsor regime codified the HKEx Listing Rule requirement that sponsors conduct due diligence with "professional skepticism"[56] in relation to the accuracy and completeness of statements, representations, and information provided.

"Professional skepticism" is a phrase borrowed from accounting literature;[57] yet are investment bankers and many of the other capital markets participants "professionals?"

What Does It Mean To Be a Professional?

Professionals have long been recognized as a highly educated elite group within society that serve and advise their clients who are the principals.

Arising as self-regulated guilds, there appear to be three essential elements of true professionals:

(a) First, professionals have knowledge and expertise in a specialized area on which their judgment is relied upon.

(b) Second, professionals apply such knowledge and expertise to the factual circumstances presented and exercise their judgment in rendering their advice. Certain roles have been recognized under common law to owe fiduciary duties of care and loyalty to clients.[58] Yet, beyond serving the best interests of the client to keep them satisfied, a professional may form, and need to deliver, an opinion that the client may not like to hear. How does a professional such as a doctor, accountant or lawyer have that willingness, skill and courage to do so in circumstances where the client may otherwise seek a more "desirable opinion" elsewhere?

(c) This is linked to the third element, namely that all true professions also serve a public interest, which can form an important source of intrinsic motivation.[59]

---

[56] New paragraph 17.6(b) of the SFC Code of Conduct for Persons Licensed by or Registered with the SFC (Code of Conduct) sets out the meaning of "professional skepticism" as "making a critical assessment with a questioning mind and being alert to information, including information from experts, that contradicts or brings into question the reliability of such statements, representations and information."

[57] See for example, ICAEW resources on "Professional skepticism and other key audit issues," www.icaew.com/en/technical/audit-and-assurance/professional-scepticism.

[58] For example, while professionals such as lawyers, doctors and the clergy have long been recognized under common law as owing fiduciary duties, US underwriters have vehemently denied such a relationship and duties: see for example, "Fiduciary Duty To IPO Clients Hangs By Thread In NY Appeal," (*Law 360*, May 24, 2013) www.law360.com/articles/444653/fiduciary-duty-to-ipo-clients-hangs-by-thread-in-ny-appeal – the matter did not go to trial and was settled: "Goldman Sachs finally ends litigation over 1999 eToys IPO," (*Reuters*, September 19, 2013) www.reuters.com/article/2013/09/19/us-goldmansachs-etoys-settlement-idUSBRE98I0VL20130919.

[59] See for example, research into the area of public service motivation (PSM) has found that "monetary incentives were irrelevant for public and private practitioners when strong

This analysis corresponds with the research of the Carnegie Foundation for the Advancement of Teaching exploring the role of higher education to prepare professionals.[60]

Professionals such as doctors, lawyers, and accountants have traditionally been instilled with pride in their specialized technical expertise and, in exercising their professional judgment, must address the conflict and balance business self-interest with client service excellence and responsibility to a broader community of stakeholders who rely upon their work.

What Is the Capital Markets Professionals' Public Purpose?

Hong Kong's SFC Code of Conduct General Principles 1, 2, and 7 expressly require all licensed persons to act "in the best interests of its clients and the integrity of the market." In January 2014, the SFC Appeals Tribunal expressly recognized this "dual obligation of the sponsor, an obligation not only to the client but, equally importantly, to the integrity of the market."[61]

Capital markets integrity is relied upon by investors to give them confidence to price, invest, and trade in securities. Importantly, this includes "mom and pops" who directly and indirectly (through fund managers, pension funds, and insurance companies) rely on market integrity to invest and save for their livelihoods and retirement and as a means to participate in capital and wealth accumulation beyond earnings from their labor.[62]

---

professional norms were in place": N. Belle and P. Cantarelli "Public Service Motivation: The State of the Art" (December 2–3, 2010), p12 citing 2007 research of LB Anderson.

[60] Anne Colby and William M Sullivan "Formation of Professionalism and Purpose: Perspectives from the preparation for the Professions Program," *University of St. Thomas Law Journal*, Vol. 5, No. 2 (September 2008) http://carnegiehighered.org/article/formation-of-professionalism-and-purpose-perspectives-from-the-preparation-for-the-professions-program/. Based on a comparative framework of five professions (namely, the clergy, law, engineering, nursing and medicine), its Preparations for the Professions Program (PPP) identified three universal strands of professional education that it metaphorically designated as three formative apprenticeships:

(1) Intellectual training to learn the academic knowledge base and the capacity to think in ways that are important to the profession (*knowledge* or *cognitive* apprenticeship)

(2) A skill-based apprenticeship of practice: the craft know-how that marks expert practitioners of the domain (*practical* apprenticeship)

(3) An apprenticeship to the ethical standards, social roles, and responsibilities of the profession, grounded in the profession's fundamental purposes (*professionalism* apprenticeship)

[61] *Sun Hung Kai Internatonal v SFC*, Securities and Futures Appeals Tribunal (SFAT) Application No.3/2013 (January 27, 2014), p.14. www.sfat.gov.hk/english/determination/AN-3-2013-Determination.pdf.

[62] This issue seems particularly important in light of the research findings and subsequent discussions generated by Thomas Piketty's observations and forecast that the average annual rate of return on capital exceeds the annual rate of growth of the economy: Thomas Piketty, *Capital in the Twenty-First Century* (Harvard University Press, 2014).

In the words of the SFC Appeals Tribunal, "the route to ensuring such trust must rest principally on the sponsor,. . . on the conduct of an objective, professional and scrupulous investigation of all material relevant to the listing and the initial public offering: in short on the conduct of reasonable due diligence."[63]

This professional shared value of market integrity in the exercise of quality due diligence and disclosure is also critical to corporate issuers to raise cost-efficient capital from "other people's money" to finance their growth.[64]

More prominent focus on this shared public purpose will provide practitioners with principles that give more guidance in making professional judgments on pivotal capital markets issues such as "material information or omissions," "price sensitive information," and "reasonable due diligence" that are not issues easily resolved through literal rule compliance.

While it may not be surprising that the "public interest" role of global finance and capital markets is increasingly being advocated by global spiritual leaders such as Pope Francis,[65] mainstream authorities such as Bank of England Governor and Financial Stability Board (FSB) Chairman Mark Carney is a strong advocate that "a top-down approach is insufficient. Employees of the financial institutions need a sense of broader purpose, grounded in strong connections to their clients and their communities."[66] Perhaps with an eye toward the challenge of addressing traders, structurers and others in the wholesale financial industry who do not face and therefore may not consider the needs nor impact on the ultimate individual end-user, Mr. Carney described this challenge as the "need to create a sense of the systemic."[67]

In the narrower context of capital markets professionals, I would suggest a less abstract and more practical approach to encapsulate the shared value of market integrity: in the exercise of judgment regarding appropriate due diligence and disclosure, and notwithstanding that they are in fact being paid directly or indirectly by the issuer company and/or employer issuing the securities, capital market professionals should ask themselves: "Would you like your mother, your grandmother, or their fund manager to know about these facts to allow them to make an investment decision?"

---

[63] *Sun Hung Kai International, supra* note 61, p14.

[64] It has been observed that the UK equity market structure no longer focuses on capital formation: Kaye Review of UK Equity Markets and Long Term Decision Making (July 2012) www.publications.parliament.uk/pa/cm201314/cmselect/cmbis/603/60302.htm.

[65] Pope Francis said: "It is important that ethics once again play its due part in the world of finance and that markets serve the interests of peoples and the common good of humanity": "Pope: It's 'intolerable' markets have the power to decide people's fate," (*Catholic News,* June 16, 2014) www.catholicnews.com/data/stories/cns/1402463.htm.

[66] Mark Carney, "Rebuilding trust in global banking," (February 25, 2013) www.bankofcanada.ca/2013/02/rebuilding-trust-global-banking/.

[67] Mark Carney, "Inclusive capitalism: creating a sense of the systemic," (May 27, 2014) www.bankofengland.co.uk/publications/Pages/speeches/2014/731.aspx.

PRACTICAL CHALLENGES FACED BY GATEKEEPERS IN
EXERCIZING CAPITAL MARKETS PROFESSIONALISM, WITH
A FOCUS ON HONG KONG'S RECENT DEVELOPMENTS

Traditionally, one did not learn professionalism merely by studying it at university. Apprentices learned the exercise of professional judgment beyond rule compliance on the job under the tutelage of their practicing masters, with their collective professional peers and elders to look to for guidance. In recent decades, a myriad of practical complexities have arisen that challenge the best-intentioned and most skillful capital markets professionals and gatekeepers from effecting quality due diligence and disclosures, and have eroded professional practices and standards.

Hyper-Competitive Financial Markets

Citibank's former CEO Chuck Prince encapsulated well the competitive dynamic and mindset, and corollary risk of financial market bubbles, when he said just before the outbreak of the GFC: "As long as the music is playing, you've got to get up and dance."[68]

Globally, the market for public auditors remains highly concentrated in the Big Four. Hong Kong IPO underwriters and law firms, however, face tremendous commercial competition and pressure. With less listings of large state-owned enterprizes that characterized Hong Kong's global league table leadership years earlier, many factors conspire that makes it a really tough market for rational economic actors to make their resource-allocation decisions, that in turn increases pressure toward a "race to the bottom"[69]:

- The size of issuer offerings (and corollary fees) is getting smaller.
- More listing candidates are smaller privately-owned enterprises (with increasing corollary risks of irregularities and fraud).
- The number of joint bookrunners (JBRs) on each deal seems to be increasing, thereby decreasing the proportion and amount of fees earned and allowing for issuer arbitrage among JBRs of opinions where no one wants to appear to be "the bad guy."[70]

---

[68] "Citibank Chief Stays Bullish on Buy-Outs," (*Financial Times*, July 9, 2007) www.ft.com/cms/s/80e2987a-2e50-11dc-821c-0000779fd2ac.html.

[69] "See for example, "Forget Fees: IPO sponsor boom risks fraud," (*FinanceAsia*, June 17, 2014) www.financeasia.com/News/387962,forget-fees-ipo-sponsor-boom-risks-fraud.aspx; "WH Group's aborted HK IPO leaves dozens of banks empty-handed," (*Financial Times*, April 30, 2014) www.ft.com/intl/cms/s/0/21755612-d041-11e3-af2b-00144feabdco.html#axzz37RJtOEKw.

[70] The record 29 appointed JBRs competing for the same pot of fees arguably hindered rather than helped WH Group's initially aborted IPO: see for example, "Chinese pork giant

- There are many new market participants who have gained significant market share of the number of deals.[71]
- IPOs seem to rely more on cornerstone investors rather than bookbuilding, thereby reducing the traditional underwriting fees earned and increasing the market overhang.[72]
- Liability risks are rising, as well as, anecdotally, corollary transactional and compliance costs, which in turn squeezes already tight margins.
- Globalization and international competitiveness also raises the spectre of regulatory arbitrage, as demonstrated by the heated debates regarding the listing venue of Alibaba's IPO and corporate governance standards.[73]

In addition, there is increasing concern about the sufficiency of remuneration, and D&O insurance, of directors and corporate secretaries to address the tasks and risks involved.[74]

John Coffee has observed that "if the gatekeeper faces excessive risks that it cannot pass on to its client in its fees, the market for gatekeeping services may simply fail."[75] If rewards are perceived as not being commensurate for such services and risks, and the appeal of being a gatekeeper wanes (whether as financial intermediaries consider being mere distributors rather than IPO sponsors[76] or good board director candidates are unwilling to step forward), how might that impact the quality of future gatekeepers and the overall market integrity and growth?

WH Group pulls Hong Kong IPO citing weak demand," (SCMP, April 29, 2014) www.scmp .com/business/china-business/article/1500070/chinese-pork-giant-wh-group-pulls-hong-kong-ipo-weak-demand; "Too Many Bankers Hurt Hong Kong IPOs as Bacon Maker WH Drops 26," (*Bloomberg*, July 23, 2014) www.bloomberg.com/news/2014–07–22/too-many-bankers-hurt-hong-kong-ipos-as-bacon-maker-wh-drops-26.html.

[71] According to Dealogic data, the role of Chinese investment banks as joint bookrunners have arisen, such that based on the number of deals (as opposed to the traditional league table of size of deals), as of YTD June 13, 2014, the top five joint bookrunners for Hong Kong IPOs were all Chinese investment banks.

[72] "Brokers call for tighter regulations on cornerstone investors in listings," (SCMP, June 26, 2014) www.scmp.com/business/money/markets-investing/article/1540591/brokers-call-tighter-rules-cornerstone-investors.

[73] On the debate on the listing venue for what may be the world's largest ever IPO, see for example, "Loss of Alibaba IPO Spurs Calls for Reforms of Hong Kong Listing Rules," (SCMP, September 27, 2013) www.scmp.com/business/companies/article/1318917/loss-alibaba-ipo-spurs-calls-reforms-hong-kong-listing-rules.

[74] See for example, comments of Hong Kong Institute of Directors chairman Kelvin Wong in "SFC to tighten check for misconduct," (SCMP, January 25, 2014) www.scmp.com/business/companies/article/1412887/sfc-tighten-check-misconduct.

[75] Coffee, *supra* note 44, p. 61.

[76] "New Filing Regime Weighs on Issuance," (*FinanceAsia*, July 6, 2014): www.financeasia.com/News/388426,new-filing-regime-weighs-on-hk-issuance.aspx.

Internal Organizational Dynamics and Culture

Global financial institutions have grown in size and complexity, and are often accused of being silo-ed, with regulatory and risk matters and responsibilities delegated or "externalized" as compliance issues for compliance and risk-management departments. This extends to the frequent bifurcation between investment banking coverage (country and industry marketing) and execution (corporate finance assuming documentation responsibility).[77] It should further be recalled that many investment and merchant banks were originally organized as partnerships, like traditional professions such as lawyers and accountants, which fostered a greater shared sense of identity and responsibility.[78] However, an unintended corollary to corporatization and globalization of firms that provide professional advisory services to increase scale and efficiency has placed pressure on the traditional master-apprenticeship model that instilled professionalism:[79] managers of professional advisory services in Asia must satisfy shareholders if they are part of publicly listed entities as well as their respective head offices to meet their financial targets or else risk downsizing or closing.

Economist Intelligence Unit reported that finance executives surveyed in 2013 still "struggle to see the benefits of greater adherence to ethical standards." with "53% think that career progression at their firm would be difficult without being flexible on ethical standards. The same proportion thinks their firm would be less competitive as a consequence of being too rigid in this area."[80]

Corporate governance challenges in Asia reflect those in many emerging markets where issuers are often family and state-owned: corporate disclosure professionals may have to work with the CEO who may also be the board chairman, controlling shareholder, and company founder, and who may be resistant toward full disclosure of developments that minority shareholders would appreciate.[81]

---

[77] In Hong Kong, even the requisite corporate finance advisor required to be appointed after an IPO until the publication of the first full financial statements is called a "compliance adviser."

[78] See for example, the IPO of Goldman Sachs has been attributed as one reason for its "organizational drift": Steven G. Mandis, *What Happened to Goldman Sachs: An Insider's Story of Organizational Drift and Its Unintended Consequences* (Harvard Business Review Press, 2013).

[79] See for example, "Law firms: A Less Gilded Future," (*Economist*, May 5, 2011) www.econo mist.com/node/18651114; Christopher J Whelan, "The Paradox of Professionalism: Global Law Practice Means Business," *Penn State International Review*, Vol. 27, No. 2, 2009 http://papers .ssrn.com/sol3/Delivery.cfm/SSRN_ID1334119_code599.pdf? abstract id=1334119&mirid=1; MJ Schlesinger, BH Gray and KM Perreira, "Medical professionalism under managed care: the pros and cons of utilization review," *Health Affairs*, 16 No.1 (1997): 106–24. www.ncbi.nlm .nih.gov/pubmed/9018948#.

[80] Economist Intelligence Unit "A Crisis of Culture – Valuing Ethics and Knowledge in Financial Services," (November 25, 2013) www.economistinsights.com/sites/default/files/ LON%20-%20SM%20-%20CFA%20WEB.pdf.

[81] This is in contrast with the corporate governance issues in the United States and United Kingdom being focused on management agency issues and alignment with shareholders of widely held listed companies.

As mentioned earlier, regulators are increasingly looking into decision-making, culture, and incentives at financial institutions and listed companies alike,[82] as well as promoting structural corporate governance changes[83] and whistle-blowing.[84]

How may a financial institution and listed corporate senior management demonstrate the requisite commitment and steps taken to effect the requisite cultural changes?

Anticipating and Meeting Regulatory Expectations

The SFC appears to be increasing oversight and pressure in three parallel prongs:

(a) SFC Corporate Finance division created a Corporate Regulation team in December 2013 to focus on corporate behaviour and disclosure when reviewing listing applications and listed company continuous disclosure on a transactional basis.[85]

(b) SFC Enforcement division has been very active in actions against perceived misconduct. In June 2013, the Court of Final Appeal in the *Tiger Asia case* recognized SFC's expanded final asset freezing powers under section 213 of the Securities and Futures Ordinance (SFO) "as protector of the collective interests of the persons dealing in the market who have been injured by market misconduct"[86] in circumstances where neither Tiger Asia nor its executives had yet been convicted of any offence under insider dealing or market misconduct. In January 2014, the SFC Appeals Tribunal in the *Sun Hung Kai International case*[87] fined the IPO sponsor HK$12 million and suspended it for twelve months from advising on IPOs for, among other things, lack of "professional skepticism."

(c) SFC Intermediaries division is conducting supervisory oversight of licensed entities and individuals with its new focus on institutional culture.[88]

---

[82] See *supra* note 55; note that the SFC also established a Corporate Regulation team to focused on disclosure and corporate misconduct: see SFC, "Corporate Regulation Newsletter," (Issue No. 1, July 2014) www.sfc.hk/edistributionWeb/gateway/EN/news-and-announcements/news/doc?refNo=14PR85.

[83] See for example, the FCA's new independent director voting requirements for premium listed companies with a controlling shareholder under The Listing Rules (Listing Regime Enhancements) Instrument 2014 that came into force May 16, 2014.

[84] See for example, SEC Officer of the Whistleblower created by Section 922 of Dodd-Frank www.sec.gov/whistleblower.

[85] See *supra* note 86.

[86] *SFC v Tiger Asia Management LLC* (2013) 16 HKCFAR 324, para 16 http://legalref.judiciary .gov.hk/lrs/common/ju/ju_frame.jsp?DIS=87093&currpage=T.

[87] *Sun Hung Kai International, supra* note 61.

[88] See *supra* note 55.

The renewed regulatory focus on books and records[89] also increases the burden and compliance costs of participants to ensure a paper trail of what has been and should be done.

How comfortable are capital markets professionals with their level of awareness of regulatory directions and developments, and vice versa, regarding the regulatory awareness of market dynamics and practicalities?

Expectations on Gatekeepers Regarding Corruption and Fraud Detection

Corruption and fraud are issues often faced in emerging markets, and the Chinese government has been initiating a major antigraft crackdown that is impacting Chinese listed SOEs.[90]

Gatekeepers are traditionally not expected to undertake forensic investigations, but will suffer reputational as well as litigation costs if issues subsequently arise, especially with the increase in critical short seller report publications.[91] Do most capital markets professionals have sufficient rudimentary forensic skills to identify all relevant "red flags" and the client-management skills to address any identified issues with their clients, superiors, and colleagues?

Quality Disclosure Problem

There is increasing regulatory emphasis on what the SEC calls "disclosure effectiveness"[92] and what the SFC calls "meaningful disclosure"[93] to avoid volume and clutter and to focus on disclosure that investors really want.

International Accounting Standards Board (IASB) has a Disclosure Initiative that focuses on the quality disclosure problem, namely the "understandable risk-aversion on the part of preparers, auditors and regulators [that] leads to a ticking-the-box mentality,"[94] and IASB Chairman Hans Hoogervorst recognizes that

---

[89] See for example, *Sun Hung Kai International, supra* note 61.

[90] For example, removal of Song Lin as chairman of one of China's largest SOE conglomerates China Resources: see for example, "China's Anticorruption Campaign Spills Over Into New Sectors," (*Wall Street Journal*, April 23, 2014) http://blogs.wsj.com/chinarealtime/2014/04/23/chinas-anticorruption-campaign-spills-over-into-new-sectors/.

[91] See reports of firms such as Muddy Waters, Citron Research, Emerson, Kerrisdale Capital and Anonymous Analysts.

[92] Keith F Higgins, "Disclosure Effectiveness: Remarks Before the American Bar Association Business Law Section Spring Meeting," (April 11, 2014) www.sec.gov/News/Speech/Detail/Speech/1370541479332#.U7iEj6iwrIU.

[93] See for example, SFC, "Corporate Regulation Newsletter," (Issue No. 1, July 2014).

[94] Hans Hoogervorst "Breaking the Boilerplate," (June 27, 2013); www.ifrs.org/Alerts/Conference/Documents/2013/HH-Amsterdam-June-2013.pdf; www.ifrs.org/Features/Pages/Video-of-Hans-Hoogervorst-speech-Breaking-the-boilerplate.aspx. IASB is responsible for developing International Financial Reporting Standards (IFRS).

"material improvements will require behavioural change to ensure that financial statements are regarded as tools of communication rather than compliance."[95]

This is complicated by the sheer diversity of investors to identify and determine how best to give them what they want. These range from retail investors (who may favor simplicity) to hedge funds (who may favor more detailed information for "edge"), as well as "long only" institutional funds (who may be subject to the pressures of herding and some of whom may not be able to exercise the "Wall Street walk" relating to index stocks regardless of disclosure standards).

How does one form a consensus and encourage appropriate behavioral change on the part of preparers?

Lack of Guidance and Focus on Professional Judgment and Professional Skepticism

While the SFC code of conduct requires that SFC licensed capital markets professionals at all times balance acting "in the best interests of its clients and the integrity of the market" in their exercise of professional judgment and professional skepticism, is there sufficient guidance, support, and encouragement for capital markets professionals to make those determinations (especially given their source of fees/compensation)?[96] Is the existing mode of "compliance training" sufficient to address these issues of culture, practices, and standards? And can the prisoner's dilemma that prevents seeking and reaching a consensus regarding practices that may assist as a defence of reasonable diligence or material disclosure to a court and/ or regulator be overcome, notwithstanding the long term benefit to firms and the industry as a whole?

Regulatory and Policy Challenges to Quality Due Diligence and Disclosure Posed by State Secrets and Personal Data Privacy

Due diligence and disclosure have become even more complicated in Asia especially in light of increasing concerns and regulation relating to personal data privacy[97] and China's state secrets regime. Capital markets professionals can and

---

[95] International Accounting Standards Board, "Feedback Statement: Discussion Forum – Financial Reporting Disclosure," (May 28, 2013) www.ifrs.org/Alerts/PressRelease/Pages/IASB-pub lishes-Feedback-Statement-on-Disclosure-Forum.aspx.

[96] In its audit inspection of 20 Australian audit firms, the Australian Securities and Investments Commission (ASIC) was also critical when it concluded that "insufficient professional skepticism was applied," ASIC Audit Inspection Program Report for 2011–2012, Report 317 (December 2012), para 41; www.asic.gov.au/asic/pdflib.nsf/LookupByFileName/rep317-pub lished-4-December-2012.pdf/$file/rep317-published-4-December-2012.pdf.

[97] See for example, "China charges GSK-linked investigators for illegally obtaining private information," (*Reuters*, July 14, 2014) www.reuters.com/article/2014/07/14/us-china-gsk-investi gators-idUSKBN0FJ05G20140714; Ana Swanson, "China's Chilling Crackdown on Due-Diligence Companies," (*The Atlantic*, October 23, 2013) www.theatlantic.com/china/arch

have been put between a rock and a hard place, as vividly demonstrated by the accounting industry, where the nondisclosure to the SEC of their Chinese company clients' audit papers held in Mainland China on the grounds of state secrets has resulted in the SEC's suspension of the Big Four auditors operating in China.[98] Concerns regarding state secrets have also been linked to the PRC Ministry of Finance's proposed new regulations that would ban overseas auditors from sending accountants onshore to audit Mainland Chinese companies, notwithstanding the cross-border nature of any capital raising, and in effect requires the critical gatekeepers and capital markets professionals to be PRC licensed audit firms and accountants.[99] These are important issues that will require a combination of diplomacy, regulatory coordination, and capital markets professionals' input on the potential impact on aspects such as securities pricing and the cost of capital, and emphasizes the need for and benefit of a cross-jurisdictional approach that promotes professionalism regardless of location of licensing regime.

LESSONS FROM VARIOUS INDUSTRY-LED INITIATIVES TO PROMOTE GOOD CULTURE AND PRACTICES RELATING TO THE CAPITAL MARKETS

Unlike the traditional professions, the financial services sector has always been heavily regulated.

In Hong Kong, Monetary Authority (HKMA) Chief Executive Norman Chan espoused focus on the three Cs of competence, control, and culture in its regulation of banks.[100] Of the three layers of parameters that help shape behavior and values, after statutes, rules and regulations, he identified the second as "normally in codes of conduct issued by the various professional or industry bodies."[101]

---

ive/2013/10/chinas-chilling-crackdown-on-due-diligence-companies/280787; "Dun & Bradstreet Fined, Four Sentenced in China," (*Wall Street Journal*, January 9, 2013) http://online .wsj.com/news/articles/SB10001424127887323482504578230781008932240.

[98] See SEC Initial Decision Release No. 553 Administrative Proceeding File Nos. 3-14872, 3-15116 In the Matter of BDO China Dahua CPA Co., Ltd., Ernst & Young Hua Ming LLP, KPMG Huazhen (Special General Partnership), Deloitte Touche Tohmatsu Certified Public Accountants Ltd., and PriceWaterhouseCoopers Zhong Tian CPAs Limited (January 22, 2014) www.sec.gov/alj/aljdec/2014/id553ce.pdf; note the distinction in EY's analysis between information held in Hong Kong and information held in Mainland China: "Ernst & Young produces audit working papers in Hong Kong and appeals order over Mainland papers," (SFC Press release, June 23, 2014) www.sfc.hk/edistributionWeb/gateway/EN/news-and-announcements/news/doc?refNo=14PR78.

[99] See for example, "China's ban on overseas auditors raises concern over transparency," (SCMP, May 19, 2014) www.scmp.com/business/china-business/article/1515191/chinas-ban-overseas-auditors-raises-concern-over.

[100] Norman TL Chan, "The Power of the Three Cs," (October 12, 2012) www.hkma.gov.hk/eng/ key-information/speech-speakers/ntlchan/20121012-1.shtml.

[101] *Ibid*, para 156–17. For example, the Hong Kong Association of Banks (HKAB) Code of Banking Conduct regarding services to personal customers endorsed by the HKMA.

However, there is currently no equivalent body for IPO sponsors nor, other than separate industry trade associations representing the different practitioners,[102] for capital markets professionals in general to provide industry guidance and give life to the SFC's Code of Conduct, the breach of which could result in SFC imposed fines and license suspensions.

Lessons can be learned from various interesting models that exist in that space between regulatory rules, supervision and enforcement, and those issued, supervised, and enforced by self-regulated organizations (SROs),[103] which have themselves been subject to recent criticism.[104]

Regulating the Accounting Profession and Standard-Setting

The accounting profession, like most professional bodies, was historically wholly self-regulated. It is one of the most internationalized professions, given the cross-border nature of capital flows and investment, and with its emphasis on "professional skepticism," has the same shared public interest of market integrity as other capital markets professionals. Mark Steward, SFC Enforcement division's executive director, reflected the regulator's perspective when he observed that "[t]he sponsor's functions are similar to the auditor's: the sponsor too performs an assurance role in respect of the information in the IPO prospectus."[105]

Since the collapse of Enron, Worldcom and Parmalat, regulatory oversight regarding accountants and standard-setting have increased dramatically.[106] Due to historical reasons and different regulatory philosophies, accountants around

---

[102] For example, HK Institute of Company Directors (HKIoD), HK Institute of Chartered Secretaries (HKICS), HK Institute of Certified Practicing Accountants (HKICPA), HK Investor Relations Association (HKIRA), Law Society of Hong Kong.

[103] For example, U.S. Financial Industry Regulatory Authority (FINRA) is an SRO whose predecessor National Association of Securities Dealers, Inc (NASD) was created as a result of the 1938 Maloney Amendment to the US Securities Exchange Act that regulates trading in securities and licensing of individuals and firms.

[104] For example, "FINRA weighs tougher stance," *Wall Street Journal*, June 19, 2014 http://online .wsj.com/articles/wall-street-watchdog-finra-under-pressure-to-toughen-sanctions-1403219509. Even the SRO status of stock exchanges has been queried: "Policing of Exchanges Questioned," (*Wall Street Journal*, October 2, 2013) http://online.wsj.com/news/articles/ SB10001424052702304906704579111483532305624. Note that the CFA Institute is more optimistic: *Self-Regulation in Securities Markets: Transitions and New Possibilities* (August 2013) www.cfapubs.org/doi/pdf/10.2469/ccb.v2013.n11.1: this is presumably in the context of investment advisors and in light of the possible imposition of fiduciary duties: "Ruling Near on Fiduciary Duty For Brokers," (*Wall Street Journal*, April 13, 2014): http://online.wsj.com/news/ articles/SB10001424052702304679404579459831342132534.

[105] SFC Executive Director of Enforcement Mark Steward, Asian Chief Audit Executive Leadership Forum 2014 (July 3, 2014) http://www.sfc.hk/web/EN/files/ER/PDF/Speeches/ MS_20140703.pdf.

[106] See for example, U.S. Public Company Accounting Oversight Board (PCAOB) was established by Sarbanes-Oxley Act (SOX).

the world face a myriad of national approaches,[107] complicated by a multitude of international standard-setting boards, and different extents of regulatory oversight.[108]

In general, three main types of accountant-related standards can be distinguished:

(i)   Financial reporting standards – technical standards on preparing financial statements

(ii) Audit and assurance standards – requirements and explanatory guidance on auditor responsibilities in audit engagements

(iii) Ethical and professional standards – standards and guidance on the quality of conduct regarding professional work, integrity, objectivity, and independence

In addition to standard-setting, regulatory oversight has also been sought over areas such as the following:

(a) Registration and licensing[109]
(b) Investigation of complaints
(c) Enforcement for breach
(d) Inspection for supervision of systems
(e) Continuing professional education.

Hong Kong is undergoing its own regulatory review of public audit oversight. The Financial Services and Treasury Bureau (FSTB) issued a public consultation in June 2014 to review an overhaul of public accountant oversight to vest investigation and enforcement powers held by Hong Kong Institute of Certified Practicing Accountants (HKICPA) to the independent Financial Reporting Council (FRC).[110] That analysis and discussion will provide valuable insight and ideas for other capital markets professionals and the financial industry as a whole.

Voluntary Standards Markets for Standards-Setting

Chartered Institute for Securities & Investment (CISI) and British Standards Institute (BSI) are exploring a "new combined approach" through the voluntary standards market for financial services. This is "a commercial system in which actual and potential buyers and suppliers of products and services rely on

---

[107] See for example, Deloitte and Financial Reporting Council, Report on Independent Audit Oversight (September 2013) www.frc.org.hk/en/index.php.

[108] See for example, Fayez Choudhury, "Shared Standard Setting in the Public Interest: A Strong Model," (June 24, 2014) www.ifac.org/global-knowledge-gateway/viewpoints/shared-standard-setting-public-interest-strong-model#. See also David Zaring, "Financial Regulation's Overlooked Networks," (Chapter 5, this book), *ibid*.

[109] Registration can be of institutions and/or individuals.

[110] Financial Services and Treasury Bureau (FSTB), "Consultation on Proposals to Improve Regulatory Regime for Listed Entity Auditors," (June 20, 2014) www.fstb.gov.hk/fsb/ppr/consult/doc/consult_rpirrlea_e.pdf.

conformity assessments"[111] carried out against standards and can consist of self-certification, second-party or third-party independent verification and certification.

The International Organization for Standardization (ISO) has technical committees that develop standards, whereby ISO management system standards may be certified by independent bodies (which may in turn be accredited) and is subject to annual audit. ISO's technical committee for financial services (ISO/TC 68) has to date focused more on technology-based standards. More recently, ISO guidelines for compliance management are being developed.[112]

The proposed UK Banking Standards Review Council (BSRC) could arguably be a variant of this model. UK banks who sign up to the proposed new voluntary industry code of practice commit to continually improving their culture and report to the public annually on progress made. The BSRC, with an independent board and funded by bank members, will also produce an annual report highlighting the progress and shortcomings of both the industry and individual banks.

Industry Association Model of Standard-Setting

International Capital Markets Association (ICMA) was founded in 1969 and promotes best market practice through developing industry guidelines, rules, recommendations, and standard documentation. Primarily a pan-European association, ICMA is recognized as an SRO and focuses on debt capital market development that is less subject to national competition than equity capital markets. It also has an ICMA Centre at Henley Business School of the University of Reading that provides executive education.

Banking and merchant banking industry associations in several other Asian jurisdictions have published due diligence guidelines[113] and the U.S. National Investor Relations Institute has published standards of practice for investor relations disclosure.[114]

---

[111] CISI, BSI and Long Finance, "Backing Market Forces: How to Make Voluntary Standards Market Work for Financial Services Regulation," (November 2013); Alderman Professor Michael Mainelli and Ciara von Gunten "Backing market forces: voluntary standards markets and the regulation of financial services" (CISI.org, November/December 2013).

[112] Project Committee ISO/PC271 is chaired by GRC Institute Managing Director Martin Tolar to develop ISO 19600 as guidelines as opposed to a specification that provides requirements: see for example, "Clayton Utz Insights: New international compliance standard on the way," (August 29, 2013): www.claytonutz.com/publications/edition/29_august_2013/20130829/new_international_compliance_standard_on_the_way.page.

[113] For example, The Association of Banks in Singapore (ABS) IPO Due Diligence Guidelines (www.abs.org.sg/pdfs/Publications/ABS_IPO_Due_Diligence_Guidelines.pdf) and Association of Merchant Bankers of India (AMBI) Due Diligence Manual (www.ambi.org.in/). The Hong Kong Sponsor Due Diligence Guidelines (http://duediligenceguidelines.com/) were drafted by an informal grouping in the wake of the new sponsor regime.

[114] U.S. National Investor Relations Institute (NIRI), *Standards of Practice for Investor Relations Vol III – Disclosure* (April 23, 2012) www.niri.org/Main-Menu-Category/resource/publications/Standards-of-Practice-for-Investor-Relations.aspx.

Voluntary Individual Accredited Educational Model

Many industry associations impose continuous professional education requirements on their membership,[115] but other than traditional professions such as the law and accounting, relatively few that relate to the capital markets have a threshold educational requirement that is in addition to university qualifications.[116]

The most well-known is the CFA Institute, which focuses on postgraduate education and credentials for buy-side investment managers, and whose Code of Ethics and Standards of Professional Conduct is also used by the Chartered Alternative Investment Analysts Association (CAIA) for its educational offering to alternative investment professionals. In the aftermath of the GFC, CFA Institute launched its Future of Finance initiative[117] and effective July 1, 2014, expressly requires all members to "[p]romote the integrity and viability of the global capital markets for the ultimate benefit of society."[118]

CISI is one of the few sell-side organizations that also has completion of its self-run educational requirements for its main levels of membership.[119] Since April 2013, CISI has developed and expanded its online Integrity Matters test for entry level brokers and traders to raise awareness of ethical dilemmas and issues:[120] this has been described as making London "the first global financial centre to require a separate, upfront ethics test."[121]

This model has been arguably been adopted by Hong Kong's Private Wealth Management Association (PWMA) with its Enhanced Competency Framework (ECF).[122] As a voluntary individual accreditation scheme to promote Hong Kong as a center for private wealth management, the ECF was developed under a public-private collaboration[123] and successful candidates will receive a Certified Private Wealth Professional (CPWP) certification by PWMA.

---

[115] For example, HKIoD.

[116] In relation to corporate disclosure professions, one example is HKICS, which requires completion of its International Qualifying Scheme (IQS) for its main membership category. The HKEx Listing Rules do not require listed company secretaries to be HKICS members.

[117] CFA Institute, Future of Finance Initiative www.cfainstitute.org/learning/future/pages/index .aspx?WPID=Strategic_Home&PageName=Homepage.

[118] CFA Institute Code of Ethics and Standards of Professional Conduct www.cfainstitute.org/ ethics/codes/ethics/pages/index.aspx.

[119] Hong Kong Securities and Investment Institute (HKSI) administers the SFC's licensing examinations and offers Continuous Professional Training (CPT) trainings on a non-exclusive basis.

[120] See for example, "Trade body rolls out compulsory integrity tests for bankers," (*Reuters*, April 2, 2013) http://uk.reuters.com/article/2013/04/02/uk-britain-banks-integrity-idUKLNE 93100O20130402.

[121] "Would-be brokers must take ethics test," (*Financial Times*, April 1, 2013) www.ft.com/intl/ cms/s/0/3b622fb0–9707–11e2-a77c-00144feabdc0.html#axzz37RJtOEKw.

[122] "Private Wealth Management Association announces the launch of the Enhanced Competency Framework in Hong Kong," (*Press release*, June 24, 2014): http://www.pwma.org.hk/ Uploads/53a8e9e774216.pdf.

[123] The ECF Task Force was chaired by HKMA, and comprised representatives of PWMA (whose members comprise 27 private banks), the Hong Kong Institute of Bankers (HKIB),

Australian Model of Professional Standards Legislation and Liability Caps for SROs

In Australia, occupational associations can seek to be covered by the Professional Standards Scheme to cap the civil liability of such association members across Australia on a mutual recognition basis by applying to Professional Standards Councils (PSCs) established in each state and territory as independent statutory bodies. For such associations and its members to qualify for the Scheme, PSCs take into account various requirements, including the code of ethics and conduct, complaints handling and disciplinary system, risk management strategies, continuing professional education, as well as minimum insurance standards.

Hailed as an innovation to promote consumer protection, to improve professional services and to help associations, as of June 30, 2014, the PSCs administered twenty-six schemes in relation to seventeen occupational associations[124] ranging from lawyers, accountants, engineers, surveyors, and even IT. While the statutory liability cap is certainly an incentive for associations to opt into the scheme, this approach has yet to gain broad global acceptance.[125] It should also be noted that the PSC recently devoted its first white paper to the professionalization of financial services.[126]

DIRECTIONS FOR A NEW ASIAN INITIATIVE PROMOTING CAPITAL MARKETS PROFESSIONALISM — ASIA CAPITAL MARKETS INSTITUTE

Quality and efficient capital markets are vital to fuel the growth and development in Asia as well as nurture the savings of its populace.

By adapting some of the above industry-led initiatives to promote good culture and practices, Asia Capital Markets Institute (ACMI) was launched[127] based on the following principles.

Hong Kong Securities and Investment Institute (HKSI) and Treasury Markets Association (TMA). The training for the ECF modules on Technical, Industry and Product Knowledge would be conducted by HKSI, and the Ethics and Compliance module by HKIB.

[124] Professional Standards Councils *Annual Report 2013–2014*, p. 19: www.psc.gov.au/sites/default/files/PSC6520%20PSC%20Annual%20Report%202014_accessible_v4.pdf.

[125] For a review of auditor liability caps, see for example, Nili Karoko-Eyal, "Setting a Statutory Cap on Auditors' Liability: What Method Should be Used?" 10: 1 *Rutgers Business Law Review* (2013) 56.

[126] Professional Standards Councils, *White paper – Professionalisation of Financial Services*, (August 2014) www.psc.gov.au/sites/default/files/NEW-PSC%20Whitepaper_final.pdf.

[127] ACMI organized its Launch Summit at the Exchange Auditorium on June 17, 2014 with keynote speakers comprising SFC's James Shipton and HKEx Listing Department MD and COO Grace Hui. There were two panels: the primary market panelist faculty on the panel on business of bringing companies public comprise heads of corporate finance from Deutsche Bank and CICC, the Asia head of CFA Institute and a litigator and council member of FSDC, and the secondary market panelist faculty on panel on the role of corporate disclosure professionals included the chairman of HKIoD, HKICPA Corporate Governance Working

Practitioner-Led and Multidisciplinary Education-Based Approach

To exercise good judgment and provide good advice and guidance on prospectus and continuous disclosure, deal structure, corporate governance issues, and securities pricing, capital markets professionals must be equipped and encouraged to be willing to face and ask hard questions, and advise clients on what they need to hear, rather than merely what they want to hear.

Asia's and the global capital markets would benefit from an educational platform to promote peer learning from senior practitioners (in following the professions of old) who are proud of their profession and willing and able to share their experiences and expertise as practitioner faculty[128] in a community of practice (CoP)[129] to raise the bar across the industry and help hone reasonable judgment, communication and tactical skills, to give voice to their shared values of market integrity, and better connect professionals to the communities who rely upon them.

Listing sponsors are recognized by the UK FCA as experts that need "on the job" experience and training.[130] Technical skills of capital markets professionals that can be honed include due diligence techniques such as effective financial due diligence, third-party due diligence, detecting "red flags" of fraud, and instilling professional skepticism to "ask the hard questions."[131]

Since the exercise of judgment for due diligence and disclosure is more of an art than a science, capital markets professionals will benefit from a multidisciplinary approach:

(a) Developing situation awareness based on social psychology research regarding sometimes unconscious social phenomena such as uncritical obedience to authority,[132] peer conformity,[133] and bystander

---

Group co-convenor and Hysan's company secretary, HKSI's technical director and BlackRock Asia head of corporate governance. Launch Supporting Organizations included HKIoD, HKICS, HKSI, ICMA, Chinese Securities Association of Hong Kong, Chamber of HK Listed Companies and HKIRA.

[128] This is modeled on the U.S. legal profession's Practicing Law Institute (PLI).

[129] See the work of cognitive anthropologists Jean Lave and Etienne Wenger on situated learning and communities of practice.

[130] The UK FSA is proposing "changes that clarify our expectation of the sponsor regime as an 'expert regime', putting in place clearer expectations around the relevant 'on-the-job' experience of sponsors will need in order to reflect the expert nature of the role, and also the minimum level of knowledge and ability that we expect sponsors to retain through their teams": Lawton, *supra* note 52.

[131] The auditing profession provides a lot of resources: see for example, Steven M Glover and Douglas Prawitt, "Enhancing Auditor Professional Skepticism," www.thecaq.org/docs/research/skepticismreport.pdf.

[132] See for example, the 1963 Stanley Milgram's experiment and research in the wake of the Holocaust.

[133] See for example, the Asch conformity experiments and research by Solomon Asch in the 1950s.

inhibition[134] that can negatively influence voicing of or acting upon the shared value of market integrity[135]

(b) Learning and development skills on client management, influencing and building resilience of capital markets professionals to individually and collectively develop techniques to give voice to their values both within their organizations and with respect to their clients.[136]

An education-based industry-wide approach focused on individual commitment[137] and habit through practice[138] will encourage the taking of personal responsibility to help address the issue of inter and intrainstitutional competition through individual excellence rather than a "race to the bottom" or a "tick the box" compliance mentality.

Senior management would be pleased to learn of research that demonstrates that appropriate intrinsic and prosocial motivation, such as having the shared value of market integrity, can not only improve employee creativity, problem solving, and persistence, but also benefit risk management.[139]

It is hoped that the marketplace will also increasingly recognize the demonstrated commitment and accreditation to benefit both individuals in their career prospects (including mobility across the capital markets spectrum), as well as their institution and employers in raising their reputational branding with issuer and investor clients, regulators, and shareholders alike.

As a policy matter, regulators who are serious about instituting a more systemic focus on professionalism and culture across the industry should consider following the example of the New York State Bar Association (NYSBA) for New York attorneys[140] and require that licensed person continuous professional learning requirements include a mandatory professionalism and ethics component.

---

[134] See efor example, the 1973 "Good Samaritan" experiment and research of JM Darley and CD Batson.

[135] See for example, the programs developed by Philip Zimbardo, who conducted the 1973 Stanford Prison experiment and research: http://heroicimagination.org/public-resources/situational-awareness.

[136] See for example, Giving Voice to Values (GVV) curriculum funded by Babson College, and developed with The Aspen Institute Business & Society Program as incubator and as founding partner along with Yale School of Management: see www.babson.edu/academics/teaching-research/gvv/pages/curriculum.aspx.

[137] See for example, principles behind initiatives such as the MBA Oath: Max Anderson and Peter Escher, *The MBA Oath: Setting a Higher Standard for Business Leaders* (Portfolio, April 29, 2010).

[138] See for example, psychology research-based interventions developed by Philips Zimbardo as part of the Heroic Imagination Project: http://heroicimagination.org/.

[139] See for example, AM Grant and JW Berry, "The necessity of others is the mother of invention: Intrinsic and prosocial motivations, perspective-taking, and creativity," (2011) *Academy of Management Journal*, 54, 73–96 http://www.selfdeterminationtheory.org/SDT/documents/2011_GrantBerry_AM.pdf.

[140] New York State Bar Association (NYSBA) requires twenty-four continuing legal education (CLE) credit hours during each biennial reporting cycle, of which at least four must be from the Ethics and Professionalism category: www.nycourts.gov/attorneys/cle/attorney_faqs.shtml.

Multistakeholder Platform

A multistakeholder collaborative platform would break down the existing silos and, working with existing industry groups, bring together the various capital markets professionals across the spectrum to give voice to their shared value of market integrity. These would comprise sponsor investment bankers,[141] accountants, lawyers, and credit-rating agencies, together with the listed company corporate disclosure professionals such as directors, officers, and senior management such as CEOs, CFOs, corporate secretaries, general counsel, and investor relations officers who collectively are ultimately responsible for ensuring the timely disclosure of material price-sensitive information for investors to make informed investment decisions.

Involving other important capital markets stakeholders is critical to assist in honing their collective interests in market integrity and growing the pie; these include the following:

(a) Regulators and stock exchanges whose rules and expectations need be met and who wield the sticks in the event of non-compliance.
(b) Investors who are the main "public interest" beneficiaries of the due diligence and disclosure conducted and who wield the promise of carrots for client service excellence.
(c) Specialists (such as advisors on internal controls, private investigations, and asset valuations) whose consulting expertise may be called upon to improve the process.
(d) Venture capital and private equity promoters and State and family business owners who participate in and drive the entry and exit of public companies to better appreciate the qualities and benefits of professionalism in conjunction with accessing "other people's money."

Signposts for Industry-Wide Guidelines, Practices, and Documentation Standardization

Capital markets professionals would benefit from regulatory support and leeway for industry-led efforts to set signposts for guidance and good practices in areas such as the following:

(a) Practical techniques and story sharings from experience to "give life" to the SFC Code of Conduct and its equivalents to assist in addressing conflicts of interest and the exercise of reasonable professional judgment[142] regarding issues and practices such as "materiality" for an

---

[141] Research analysts would of course need to be excluded due to maintain their independence.
[142] There is much that can be discerned from the accounting industry's experience. For example, Institute of Chartered Accountants of Scotland (ICAS) has developed a "Professional

investment decision and "price-sensitive information," and drafting of
quality disclosure.

(b) Industry-wide practices,[143] increased use of technology for online collaborative and active learning and as commitment devices, as well as
standardized documentation where appropriate to improve efficiencies
and reduce overall transactional costs in areas such as

- due diligence, such as third party due diligence and site inspections
- listed company internal controls[144]
- joint book-running practices
- cornerstone investor practices[145]
- record-keeping.

(c) Developing and responding to legislative and regulatory initiatives to
promote innovation to responsibly "grow the pie" in our competitive
and ever-increasingly interconnected global capital markets to the
benefit of all key stakeholders.[146]

CONCLUSION – THE BEGINNING OF AN ASIAN JOURNEY TOWARD A "RACE TO THE TOP"?

Human capital is the software that drives the service industry that is at the heart of
IFCs, and HKMA's Norman Chan has described "the race to become an IFC is a
battle of soft power."[147]

In June 2014, the FCA's Martin Wheatley went so far as to observe that:

"[A]ll around the world, reform of conduct is dominating industry – to the point
that we're seeing financial centres actively competing on issues like market integrity and cleanliness... Improved conduct, stability, better consumer outcomes,

Judgment Framework for Financial Reporting: An international guide for preparers, auditors,
regulators and standard-setters," (August 2012) http://icas.org.uk/pjf.pdf.

[143] The industry response to the new predeal research rules, to which the author was an active
participant, is an example of a successful co-ordinated industry initiative in Hong Kong, for
example, Anthony Dapiran "Regulating Pre-deal Research," (*LexisNexis*, February 15, 2012)
http://law.lexisnexis.com/webcenters/hk/At-Issue/Regulating-pre-deal-research.

[144] See HKEx, Consultation Paper on Internal Controls Section of its Corporate Governance
Code (June 20, 2014) www.hkex.com.hk/eng/newsconsul/hkexnews/2014/140620news.htm.

[145] For example, see "Brokers call for tighter rules on cornerstone investors in listings," (South
China Morning Post, June 26, 2014) www.scmp.com/business/money/markets-investing/art
icle/1540591/brokers-call-tighter-rules-cornerstone-investors.

[146] As of mid-2014, there are many initiatives and public consultations, such as Financial Services
Development Council (FSDC) research policy report on "Positioning Hong Kong as an
International IPO Centre of Choice," (June 18, 2014) www.fsdc.org.hk/sites/default/files/
IPO4-2%20%28Final%2017-6-2014%29.pdf.

[147] Norman TL Chan, "The Power of the Three Cs," *supra* note 100. Hopefully, this provides
Hong Kong, with its history of capital markets professionals immersed in the rule of law, with a
unique and continuing role as China's global financial center.

trust, confidence: I'd argue these are strong indicators of a non-zero sum game, where all participants are victorious – like a good marriage or partnership."[148]

If he is correct, it would help prevent regulatory arbitrage and provide an excellent opportunity in Asia to reinforce and instill a "sense of vocation and responsibility"[149] in capital markets professionals. An important component of this would be to highlight and reinforce the disclosure paradigm's historical and normative basis of professionalism under which major securities and fundraising legislation such as the U.S. Securities Act of 1933 and Securities Exchange Act of 1934 were enacted, and upon which paradigm many securities regimes globally are implicitly based.[150]

This is a particularly critical and busy time for Asia. Chinese companies remain one of the world's more important sources of capital markets fundraisers, with the IPO of Alibaba on the New York Stock Exchange (NYSE) being the largest ever in the United States and indeed the world.[151] Along with its ongoing SOE reform efforts,[152] the China Securities Regulatory Commission (CSRC) is in the process of transitioning Mainland China's domestic A-share markets into a disclosure-based

---

[148] Martin Wheatley, "Good Conduct and Market Integrity," (June 2, 2014) www.fca.org.uk/news/good-conduct-and-market-integrity.

[149] Mark Carney, "Inclusive capitalism: creating a sense of the systemic," (May 24?, 2014) www.bankofengland.co.uk/publications/Pages/speeches/2014/731.aspx.

[150] See for example, Justin O'Brien, *Culture Wars: Rate Manipulation, Institutional Corruption, and the Lost Normative Foundations of Market Conduct Regulation*, 37 SEATTLE U. L. REV. 375 (2014) http://digitalcommons.law.seattleu.edu/cgi/viewcontent.cgi?article=2209&context=sulr, who provides some timely insights from the era of James M. Landis and Joseph Kennedy, critical architects of the U.S. securities legislation and the SEC's first two chairmen. For example, O'Brien quotes Baldwin Bane, the chief of securities division of Federal Trade Commission (FTC), the Securities Act's initial regulator, who said in 1931: "It would be idle to pretend that. . .[the Securities Act] does not ask something of the security world, but it also promises much in return—the opportunity of creating a true and honorable profession by the assumption and adequate discharge of public responsibilities.," *ibid.*, p418.

[151] The U.S.$25 billion IPO of Chinese e-commerce company Alibaba on the NYSE was the largest in history, overtaking the US IPOs of Visa (2008) and Facebook (2012) and the concurrent Hong Kong and Shanghai IPOs of Chinese SOEs Agricultural Bank of China (2010) and Industrial and Commercial Bank of China (2006): see "Alibaba Claims Title For Largest Global IPO Ever With Extra Share Sales," (*Forbes*, September 22, 2014) www.forbes.com/sites/ryanmac/2014/09/22/alibaba-claims-title-for-largest-global-ipo-ever-with-extra-share-sales/. The company which previously held the title was also a Chinese company, Agricultural Bank of China.

[152] Third Plenum of the Communist Party of China's 18th Central Committee announced in November 2013 that market forces would play a "decisive" role in the allocation of resources: "CPC acknowledges market's 'decisive' role," (*Xinhua*, November 12, 2013) http://news.xinhuanet.com/english/china/2013–11/12/c_132882359.htm. China's SOE reforms includes pilots to attract private investment for "mixed ownership" SOEs and granting more SOE board autonomy to hire professional management (such as the chief accountant and board secretary): see for example, "Reform move for state enterprises runs up against old obstacles," (SCMP, July 19, 2014) www.scmp.com/business/article/1556564/reform-move-state-enterprises-runs-against-old-obstacles.

registration system.[153] International investors can now invest directly in certain Shanghai Stock Exchange listed companies via the HKEx through the pilot Shanghai-Hong Kong Stock Connect,[154] and a direct listing framework has been announced to allow companies from China to list on the Singapore Stock Exchange (SGX).[155] Singapore has joined Malaysia and Thailand in implementing the Association of South East Asian Nations (ASEAN) Disclosure Standards Scheme to facilitate greater regional fundraising activity through harmonizing documentation for cross-border offerings of securities,[156] and the SGX also plans to establish three independent listing committees, increase enforcement powers, as well as publish a practice note or handbook on issuer manager duties and standards to maintain the quality of listing submissions.[157]

As a fledgling industry-wide multistakeholder educational initiative to promote capital markets professionalism in client service excellence and to give voice to shared values of market integrity, ACMI is a work-in-progress and has benefitted from many senior industry professionals and stakeholders who have already stepped forward to support and to act as its faculty.

And even as emerging online capital marketplaces (also known as internet finance, crowdfunding and peer-to-peer lending) threaten to disrupt traditional capital markets, banking and entrepreneurial finance business models and processes,[158] ACMI's approach can and should be applied to these new platforms and actors that seek to democratise finance by digitally tapping "other people's money"

---

[153] China Securities Regulatory Commission, "CSRC Releases Opinions on Further Promoting the IPO System Reform," (November 30, 2013) www.csrc.gov.cn/pub/csrc_en/newsfacts/release/201402/t20140214_243817.html.

[154] See Joint Announcement of China Securities Regulatory Commission and Securities and Futures Commission (10 April 2014) www.sfc.hk/edistributionWeb/gateway/EN/news-and-announcements/news/doc?refNo=14PR41.

[155] See Joint Annouuncement of China Securities Regulatory Commission and Singapore Stock Exchange, SGX and China Securities Regulatory Commission establishing direct listing framework (November 25, 2013) www.sgx.com/wps/wcm/connect/sgx_en/home/higlights/news_releases/SGX+and+China+Securities+Regulatory+Commission+establishing+direct+listing+framework.

[156] See for example, ASEAN Equity Securities Disclosure Standards www.theacmf.org/ACMF/upload/asean_equity_standards_1_apr_2013.pdf and ASEAN Debt Securities Disclosure Standards www.theacmf.org/ACMF/upload/asean_debt_standards_1_apr_2013.pdf. As at 1 April 2013, Singapore, Malaysia and Thailand have announced the implementation of the Scheme under their respective jurisdictions.

[157] See Singapore Stock Exchange, Consultation Paper on Reinforcing the SGX Listings and Enforcement Framework (17 September 2014) www.sgx.com/wps/wcm/connect/4f659a93–81b5–4081–9393–047de90878c7/Consultation+Paper+on+Reinforcing+the+SGX+Listings+and+Enforcement+Framework.pdf?MOD=AJPERES.

[158] According to Goldman Sachs, *The Future of Finance: The Socialization of Finance* (March 13, 2015), 4: "The socialization of finance [defined as the impact of technology and changing behavior on financial services markets] is attacking over $4 trillion in addressable revenue and $470 billion in profit."

to support entrepreneurship, especially if new asset classes are to be created from such Fintech innovations.[159]

While audacious in scope, ACMI remains humble in recognizing that promoting capital markets professionalism is neither easy nor a panacea.

Only if enough industry participants are willing to work together with regulators and other stakeholders in seeking to balance the following:

(a) Addressing enforcement "sticks" and supervisory expectations as deterrents against rule violations and misconduct by institutions and individuals[160]

(b) Creating new "carrots" to encourage, reward and offset the market pressures against good judgment and the risks of failure of the gatekeeping market[161]

(c) Drafting constructive signposts to help guide good judgment and behavior,[162]

will practitioners be able to regain pride in being capital markets professionals and to help restore market and regulatory trust and confidence in the same.

---

[159] See Brian W Tang, "For capital marketplaces to create a new asset class, trust and professionalism are key", *The FINTECH Book* (forthcoming, Wiley, 2016). See also, for example, the European Crowdfunding Network's updated Code of Conduct and Charter of Crowdfunder's Rights as of 1 July 2015: www.eurocrowd.org/2015/07/ecn-releases-updated-code-of-conduct-and-charter-of-crowdfunders-rights/ .

[160] IOSCO has been reported to want to seek greater uniformity of governmental penalties of wrongdoing: "Global regulator reviews corporate penalties, seeks more uniformity," (*Reuters*, July 11, 2014) http://uk.reuters.com/article/2014/07/11/uk-iosco-sanctions-review-idUKKBNoF GoUT20140711.

[161] For example, initiatives that promote a "comply or explain" approach to listed company environmental, social and governance (ESG) reporting such as being considered by the Hong Kong and Singapore stock exchanges in 2015, and promoted by the UN Sustainable Stock Exchanges initiative, hope that such disclosure will facilitate the market to reward and favourably price companies who demonstrate ESG commitment.

[162] For example, ASIC provided a Conduct Risk Calculator to 19 investment banks in February 2015 based on their 3 Cs message of Communication, Challenge and Complacency: http://asic.gov.au/about-asic/corporate-publications/newsletters/asic-market-supervision-update/asic-market-supervision-update-previous-issues/market-supervison-update-issue-57/ .

19

Competitiveness of Financial Centers in Light of Financial and Tax Law Equivalence Requirements

Dirk Zetzsche

INTRODUCTION

Financial centers are best explained using *Arner's* hub and spoke model.[1] This explanation for financial centers essentially relies on scale economies. Given the clients' needs for base and specialized financial services, base services are provided locally while specialized services are centered in order to justify the costs for specialization. Centers provide the expertise and infrastructure to offer these specialized services. From the specialization results a service industry which coordinates their interests to further their business. While this model to a certain extent explains why financial centers exist, it does not explain where financial centers are located, and why some financial centers flourish while others fail.

Most commentators refer to nonlegal means when explaining a financial center's success or failure. In particular, economic and social factors like language, financial literacy of the workforce, technical capabilities, infrastructure, reputation, and geographical location are some of the features considered in the literature.[2] For instance, *Arner* maintains that the development of "financial centres is an

Dr. iur. (Düsseldorf); Dr. iur. habil (Düsseldorf); LL.M. (Toronto). The author is thankful to comments provided by John Armour, Douglas Arner, Dan Awrey, Andreas Engert, Erin O'Hara, Todd Henderson, Sebastiaan Hooghiemstra, Thomas Marte, Jennifer Payne, Christina Preiner, Roberta Romano, Klaus Schroeder, Tobias Tröger, Kristin van Zwieten, as well as participants at conferences and workshops at the University of Hongkong, Oxford University, the University of Liechtenstein and the University of Mannheim.

[1] *See* Douglas W. Arner, *The Competition of International Financial Centres and the Role of Law*, in: ECONOMIC LAW AS AN ECONOMIC GOOD, ITS RULE FUNCTION AND ITS TOOL FUNCTION IN THE COMPETITION OF SYSTEMS 193, 203 (K. Meesen, ed., 2009).

[2] *See* Ishan Erdem Kayral/Mehmet Baha Karan, *The research on the distinguishing features of the international financial centers*, 2 J. APPL. FIN. AND BANK. 217 (2012); The Global Financial Centres Index (GFCI) defines five broad areas of competitiveness: Business Environment, Financial Sector Development, Infrastructure, Human Capital and Reputational and General Factors, see Z/Yen Group, GFCI 16, 22 September 2014, available at www.longfinance.net/images/GFCI16_22September2014.pdf (last visited Oct 5, 2014).

evolutionary process of strategically building sophisticated human and institutional infrastructure to support the searching for economic opportunities."[3] According to *Arner,* language capacity, economic education, and cultural openness to financial innovation are decisive to the development of a financial center.[4] These commentators assume that financial centers adjust their laws to the intermediaries' demands, turning the race to the bottom into a standard recipe for financial center success.[5] Disclosure to investors' matters only in so much as it assists them in defining which financial center caters most to their demands.

In contrast, this chapter takes the view that law and regulation do shape financial center development. As a starting point we assume, in line with *Arner's* model, that market access and interconnectedness are key conditions for the development and importance of financial centers.[6] Given that more and more rules and regulations set the framework for cross-border financial services, market access today requires a sophisticated legal framework. At the heart of cross-border financial regulation lies the equivalence principle. Under the equivalence principle either the foreign financial services provider or financial product must be regulated and supervised in its respective home country in a substantively similar way to that of the respective intermediary or product in the investor's, client's or counterparty's home jurisdiction. The equivalence principle is meant to provide a "level-playing field" of home and host jurisdictions and prevent regulatory arbitrage[7]; the "level-playing-field" is a political term for curbing the attraction of certain financial centers (that have for long employed the race-to-the-bottom standard recipe).

In contrast to political expectations, this chapter argues that the equivalence principle is likely to *increase* competitiveness among financial centers. It is structured as follows: Part II investigates the equivalence principle's purpose and origin in international supervisory agreements. Part III presents an example of the principle's implementation in European financial law. Part IV argues that while tax

---

[3] Arner, *supra* note 1, at 193.

[4] Arner *supra* note 1, at 193. *See* also Douglas Arner, Financial Stability, Economic Growth and the Role of Law (2007).

[5] If regulation is discussed, strict regulation is assessed as a disadvantage for financial centers, *see* Michael A. Goldberg, Robert W. Helsley, Maurice D. Levi, *On the Development of international financial centers,* 22 Ann. Reg. Sc., Festschrift Issue 81 (1988) (discussing the stringency of financial regulation as one of four development factors).

[6] Arner, *supra* note 1, at 203.

[7] *See* FSB, The Chairman, Progress of Financial Reforms 2 (15 April 2013), available at: www.g20ys.org/upload/files/Progress_on_G20_Financial_Reforms.pdf; FSB, Structural Banking Reforms, Cross-border consistencies and global financial stability implications 15 (27 October 2014), available at: www.financialstabilityboard.org/publications/r_141027.pdf; FSB, Strenghtening Oversight and Regulation of Shadow Banking, Regulatory framework for haircuts on non-centrally cleared securities financing transaction 2 (14 October 2014), available at: www.financialstabilityboard.org/publications/r_141013a.pdf. On European banking and financial law *see,* for example, recital 59 of the European Market Infrastructure Regulation (EMIR) and recital 5 of the Directive on Managers of Alternative Investment Funds (AIFMD).

arbitrage was one reason to rely on low-tax financial centers in the past, global tax law initiatives have been intensified, and domestic tax laws increase the burden associated with foreign intermediation. This means that tax arbitrage is unlikely to provide a sound reason for relying on foreign financial intermediaries in the future, that is, tax arbitrage does not offset whatever effect the equivalence principle has on financial centers. Part V presents some basic assumptions on how the equivalence principle is likely to transform the role of financial centers in the coming years. These amount to the underlying argument that if the equivalence principle removes the stigma of a race to the bottom, financial centers may attract new business. Moreover, while expertise and infrastructure have always been bundled in financial centers, they may have been used for imposing the least regulatory burden possible. Under equivalent legal conditions the same expertise may be used to optimize the regulatory burden within the limits provided by equivalence. Inexpensive and fast implicit coordination of market participants in financial centers can substitute costly and lengthy explicit coordination by legal means in distribution countries. Implicit coordination is likely to be used to increase the understanding of the rules promulgated by distribution countries and to reduce intermediary-related agency costs. Investors and clients benefit from better information and lower transaction costs than in distribution countries. Part VI summarizes and concludes.

THE EQUIVALENCE PRINCIPLE IN INTERNATIONAL FINANCIAL REGULATION

The Proliferation of Financial Law

While much ink has been spilled over corporate law theory and economics (including takeover law), financial law literature often focuses on disclosure rules.[8] However, literature focusing on disclosure reflects the situation prior to the financial crisis. The stream of regulation following the financial crisis of the late 2000s has led to the present state of the law including various authorization and organizational requirements for financial intermediaries, many of them inhibiting the free development of financial markets and cross-border financial services by setting legal requirements for market entry. These requirements pertain to all kinds of financial services being offered to all types of clients. We refer to this trend as proliferation of financial law. It has at least two consequences.

First, the proliferation of financial law reduces the importance of private contracting (including company, trust and agency law). For example, prior to the crisis private equity funds and their managers were traditionally organized using ordinary

---

[8] *See*, for instance, on the equivalence of International Accounting Standards and US-GAAP in the context of the Prospectus Directive Pierre Schammo, EU PROSPECTUS LAW: NEW PERSPECTIVES ON REGULATORY COMPETITION IN SECURITIES MARKETS 142–192 (2011).

(non-regulated) company law vehicles. After the crisis, private equity has become a "regulated industry" with the Dodd-Frank Act in the United States[9] and the Directive on Alternative Investment Fund Managers (AIFMD) in the EEA[10] imposing authorization requirements, a minimum organizational set-up and permanent reporting to and supervision by competent authorities.

Second, the proliferation of financial law is likely to impact on the development and status of financial centers. The enhanced requirements of financial regulation as a precondition for market access influence the position and strategies of financial centers. With market access being conditioned by stricter regulation the importance of other success factors – like the social, geographical, and cultural environment – is likely to be diminished. The way in which the proliferation of financial law demands modifications to accepted explanations for financial center development and the way in which financial centers may respond to this new trend is examined throughout this chapter.

Pro Loco Requirements of the New Financial Law

In 2008 the G20 in Washington committed to submitting all important financial actors to appropriate regulation.[11] To ensure effective supervision the EU/EEA Member States implemented a pro loco requirement. This can be demonstrated on all three levels of financial regulation. First, *intermediary regulation* requires the head office of the financial intermediary to be at the same place as the registered seat. Letter Box Entities are prohibited. Second, a set of *product regulations* – for example, product intervention rules, limits of leverage and limits on the use of derivatives at least in the retail sector – shall reduce the impact of financial

---

[9] Title VI of the Dodd-Frank Wall Street Reform and Consumer Protection Act, Pub. L. No. 111–203 (2010) eliminated the private adviser exception from the Investment Advisers Act 1940. In turn, all advisers to private funds with more than $150 mio. in assets under management within the United States are required to register with the SEC. (Note that the U.S. Congress voted to exempt advisers to private equity funds with the Small Business Capital Access and Job Preservation Act, H.R. 1105 (2013); the bill requires the Senate's approval before coming into law).

[10] Directive 2011/61/EU of the European Parliament and of the Council of 8 June 2011 on Alternative Investment Fund Managers and amending Directives 2003/41/EC and 2009/65/EC and Regulations (EC) No 1060/2009 and (EU) No 1095/2010 (Text with EEA relevance), O.J. L174/1 (2011). On details of the authorization and organization requirements of the AIFMD *See* the contributions in Zetzsche (ed.), THE ALTERNATIVE INVESTMENT FUND MANAGERS DIRECTIVE (WoltersKluwer: 2012).

[11] G20, Declaration of the Summit on Financial Markets and the World Economy (Nov. 15, 2008), available at: www.g20.utoronto.ca/2008/2008declaration1115.html#regulation (last visited October 31, 2014) ("A review of the scope of financial regulation, with a special emphasis on institutions, instruments, and markets that are currently unregulated, along with ensuring that all systemically-important institutions are appropriately regulated, should also be undertaken").

intermediaries on financial stability and enhance investor protection.[12] Third, *sales regulation* requires disclosure to local investors/clients in line with local standards.[13]

While national treatment for international financial intermediaries has long been the norm in financial law – for example, a U.S. firm acting in Germany must comply with German laws when providing their services in Germany – equivalence goes beyond these requirements. Equivalence requires that law and supervision of the intermediary, the product and the distribution materials *in the intermediary's home country* must be equivalent to the respective law and regulation in the host country where the services are provided or distributed.

The Equivalence Principle

The equivalence principle was implemented in the early 1990s to regulate cross-border market access under the General Agreement on Tariffs and Trade (GATT). It functioned to break the deadlock after countries insisted that their health and product safety standards be observed during the negotiations.[14]

The Concept

Under the equivalence principle of financial regulation,[15] the host country's regulator reviews the foreign intermediaries' home country regulation and its enforcement whether it is substantively and sufficiently similar to the law and regulation in the home country, in order that the regulation and supervision may substitute in function, albeit not formally, the host country's regulation and enforcement without incurring significant risk for investors/clients/counterparties and/or the

---

[12] *See* Art. 25 (3) AIFMD (giving competent authorities the power to limit the leverage used by AIF); Art. 50 UCITSD (restricting the use of exposure from derivatives for UCITS); Art. 31, 31 (a) and 32 MiFIR (giving competent authorities extensive powers to intervene in relation to the sale of particular products).

[13] *See*, on details, Dirk Zetzsche, *Joint Principles of European Asset Management Law*, in: THE ALTERNATIVE INVESTMENT FUNDS DIRECTIVE – EUROPEAN REGULATION OF ALTERNATIVE INVESTMENT FUNDS 747, 749 (D. Zetzsche, ed., 2012); Dirk Zetzsche, *Drittstaaten im Europäischen Bank-und Finanzmarktrecht* (transl: Third Countries in European Banking and Financial Law), in: FINANZMARKTREGULIERUNG ZWISCHEN INNOVATION UND KONTINUITÄT (transl: Financial Regulation between Innovation and Continuity) 47, 74–125 (G. Bachmann and B. Breig, eds., 2014).

[14] *See* Michael Trebilcock, Robert Howse, and Antonia Eliason, THE REGULATION OF INTERNATIONAL TRADE 288–290 (4th Ed., 2012).

[15] *See* Tzung-bor Wei, *The Equivalence Approach to Securities Regulation*, 27 NORTHW. J INT'L L. AND BUS. 255, 257 (2007) (with regard to securities regulation); Eilis Ferran and Look Chan Ho, CORPORATE FINANCE LAW 417–419 (2nd Ed. 2014) (deeming equivalence the practical substitute for convergence, aiming at substantial rather than full convergence of securities laws); Rolf Weber and Rolf Sethe, *Äquivalenz als Regelungskriterium im Finanzmarktrecht* (transl: Equivalence as regulatory criterion in financial law), 110 SCHWEIZERISCHE JURISTEN-ZEITUNG 569.

financial system of the host country. As a consequence of equivalent laws and enforcement, financial intermediaries may be exempted from some or even all additional requirements of the host country law. Although these intermediaries are regulated and supervised by their home country, they are treated – de facto – as host country firms.

In this way equivalence avoids a one-size-fits-all market access regime that may incur double costs for intermediaries. Equivalence is meant to provide a dynamic system that grants privileges to countries with stronger, and penalizes those with weaker financial regulation and enforcement.

According to Ferran and Ho,

"equivalence' refers to a foundational degree of similarity that is needed for concessionary arrangements to function. ... [E]quivalence is best understood as implying a holistic test with benchmarks that focus on high comparability between regulatory and supervisory outcomes, rather than rigid line-by-line examinations of similarities and differences, and a quest for exact mirroring of practices and philosophies."[16]

The joint understanding of equivalence encompasses functional and cost equivalence. *Cost equivalence* requires that the costs imposed on intermediaries by the host country's law and supervision is comparable with the costs imposed on intermediaries by the home country's law and supervision, that is, that submitting to a home country's law does not yield an (unfair) competitive advantage. If *functionally equivalent* – as opposed to formal equivalence – the rules of the home and the host countries, although they differ in form and substance, produce similar results, hence equivalence is an outcome-based approach. The formal similarity or dissimilarity of rules and standards theoretically does not matter. Different means may achieve the same result.[17] The rules and regulations of home and host country must simply fulfill the same objective and achieve the same level of protection.

While the equivalence principle is intuitive, the devil lies in the details. In applying the equivalence test, (1) the home and host country need to determine the objectives of rules and regulation, and (2) the assessor compares the results of each country's legislation and supervision. Both steps are laden with significant uncertainty regarding the authority of sources relied on and the assessment methods.

---

[16] Ferran and Ho, *id.*, at 417.

[17] *See* recital 48 of Rating Regulation (EU) 462/2013: While "a third-country regulatory regime does not have to have identical rules as those provided for" in European law, "in order to be considered equivalent to or as stringent as the Union regulatory regime, it should be sufficient that the third-country regulatory regime achieve the same objectives and effects in practice." Pursuant to recital 75 of the CSD Regulation, "when assessing the relevant rules of third countries, a proportionate, outcomes-based approach should be taken, focusing on compliance with applicable Union rules and, where relevant, international standards. Conditional or interim recognition may also be granted where there are no areas of substantive difference that would have foreseeable detrimental effects on Union markets."

How host regulators determine equivalence is thus subject to discussion. A market-based test apparently worked in the comparison of IAS and US-GAAP accounting standards,[18] but whether market tests can be applied beyond disclosure rules to intermediary and product regulation remains uncertain.

The Future of Global Financial Regulation?

The equivalence principle exists twice in competing approaches to international financial law. The first position seeks the middle ground between harmonization and competition,[19] and the second between convergence and diversity. While the former discussion refers to how international financial law should develop, the latter refers to the ideal outcome of the development process.

BETWEEN COMPETITION AND HARMONIZATION Under the *competition approach*,[20] countries try to attract financial business by tailoring their financial law according to the needs of financial intermediaries. Proponents of the competition approach argue that regulatory competition eventually pushes a country's legal environment toward market preferences that are likely to most efficiently meet intermediary *and* investors' demands. At the same time the competition approach retains the openness of a legal regime for innovation and reduces the risk of a) regulatory errors, and b) intermediaries responding simultaneously to incentives provided by regulation – which comes with a type of systemic risk prompted by regulation.

Regulators, however, frequently question whether competition among jurisdictions leads to a race to the top. In particular, the ever-present risk of fraud would require robust enforcement while competition concerns may prompt lenient treatment by the legislature, regulators and the courts. The intensity of enforcement toward foreign intermediaries by home enforcement agencies compared with national champions in the home courts is uncertain. At least in tax matters, some countries have until recently nurtured a lax approach toward other countries' tax affairs. It is purported that the same is true for investor, client, and counterparty protection. Financial centers also create externalities: Profits are accrued by home intermediaries while foreign investors, clients, etc., bear the risk of the

---

[18] Christian Leuz, *IAS versus U.S. GAAP: Information Asymmetry-Based Evidence from Germany's New Market*, 41 J. ACC'T RES. 445 (passim).

[19] Wei, *supra* note 16, at 255–257 (on securities regulation).

[20] *See*, instead of many, Roberta Romano, *The Need for Competition in International Securities Regulation*, 2 THEORETICAL INQUIRIES L. 1565, 1571 (2001) (passim); Roberta Romano, *Against Financial Regulation Harmonization: A Comment*, in LAW AND ECONOMICS OF FINANCIAL INSTITUTIONS 27 (Peter Nobel, K. Krehan and A. Tanner, eds., 2010) (arguing that harmonization increases systemic risk).

intermediaries' failure. This may prompt a morally hazardous situation in which regulatory concern about the risks created by interconnectedness of financial intermediaries, that is, systemic risk, is curbed by domestic interests.

Under the *harmonization approach*, countries should try to harmonize financial law using top-down measures. Full harmonization eliminates additional costs for doing cross-border business. Once achieved harmonization would offer many benefits, including the prevention of a "race to the bottom" due to regulatory arbitrage, reduced information, and transaction costs, the internalization of externalities across countries, as well as enhancing scale economies and the mobility of market participants. On the downside, full harmonization leads to a lesser recognition of national particularities and lesser innovation.

Even among promoters of harmonization the Catch 22 question that has remained subject to discussion is which standard should function as role model for convergence. Statements on the apparent benefits of U.S.-style regulation and supervision experienced a lukewarm reception in other parts of the world. The question is of significance since the regulatory model determines the cost distribution of harmonization. Regulators have found themselves burdened with a collective action problem: While they expected the world as a whole to benefit from a sufficient level of harmonization and supervisory cooperation, all regulators – focusing on their territory and "their" intermediaries – waited for others to bear the costs of harmonization.

BETWEEN CONVERGENCE AND DIVERSITY Equivalence also represents an intermediate position in the discussion as to whether convergence or diversity is preferable.[21]

Convergence of financial regulation increases the systemic risk of synchronized behavior of regulated intermediaries with potentially unwanted consequences. On the upside, convergence reduces complexity in cross-border settings and facilitates transaction and information flows freely among intermediaries and regulators as all actors use the same terminology. Convergence also prevents negative externalities that may be exploited by sophisticated entities by providing services to many markets simultaneously. Finally, convergence may present an option to developing economies about which regulation they want to adopt.

Diversity is costlier to manage for financial intermediaries that offer cross-border services. However, diversity also creates knowledge about which rules work under which circumstances. Regulators may choose the system adequate for their

---

[21] *See,* instead of many, Roberta Romano, *For Diversity in the International Regulation of Financial Institutions: Critiquing and Recalibrating the Basel Architecture,* 31 YALE J. REG. 1 (2014) (arguing that Basel approval of mortgage backed securities ("MBS") lead to a concentration in MBS risk in bank's balance sheet).

jurisdiction, avoiding costs stemming from a one-size-fits-all approach and making the regulatory system for that jurisdiction more robust.

In this discussion equivalence requires convergence of objectives, but allows for diversity with regard to details as long as the outcome – the level of investor protection and financial stability – is substantively similar.

Equivalence and Risk Symmetry

Equivalence is particularly suitable for dealing with the risk of regulatory arbitrage.

The risk of regulatory arbitrage is low as long as the home and the host country's financial services attach the same level of importance to investor protection and systemic risk prevention. Whether this is the case depends on the demand for and supply of financial services within the home and host country. For example, in some financial centers supply and demand of financial services could be equally high[22] while the intermediaries in other countries primarily provide supply-side financial services (hereafter referred to as production country) or demand-side services (referred to as distribution country). Where demand and supply is even we may expect balanced regulation and supervision that takes both intermediaries' and investors'/clients' needs into account.

However, if either the production or the distribution component of financial services is of greater importance, the government and the regulators have incentives to overly protect intermediaries in production countries, or investors in distribution countries. In the latter case that constitutes an imbalance in supply and demand within one country, the equivalence principle leads to a balance of supply and demand by legal means: An intermediary from a production country is likely to be subject to laxer laws and enforcement than intermediaries in the distribution countries. In this case the equivalence principle requires home country regulators and enforcement agencies to at least adopt rules and enforcement that are substantively similar to the laws and regulation of the host country.

The risk asymmetry argument does not lead to a reduction of standards if intermediaries of distribution countries offer services in the production countries. In the absence of equivalence restricted by (overly) strict and costly investor protection requirements, intermediaries from distribution countries are unfit to compete with intermediaries from production countries. Besides the risk asymmetry argument, equivalence also improves the competitiveness of distribution countries. This double impact explains the appeal of equivalence for governments from distribution countries.

---

[22] For instance, Liechtenstein intermediaries offer services to thousands of trusts and foundations. Both demand (by foundations and trusts) and supply (by intermediaries) are important for Liechtenstein regulators.

Financial Crisis, G20 and FSB: The Rise of Equivalence

Drawing on the compromising capacity of equivalence in the GATT negotiations, the European Commission has promoted equivalence as third way between competition and harmonization[23] while U.S. commentators have viewed equivalence as either a roadmap toward convergence[24] or an easy exit for jurisdictions promoting lax regulation and enforcement.[25]

The crisis has changed the global landscape. Regulators have realized that without coordinated efforts individuals can take advantage of the regulators' collective action problems and put the financial system at risk. In Washington in 2008 the G20 committed to fundamental reform to strengthen the resilience of the international financial system.[26] At the Pittsburg summit in 2009 the G20 directed the Financial Stability Board to stick to their commitment to coordinate national efforts.[27] While focusing on the resilience of financial institutions, the G20 defines the openness of the global financial system as second priority, given its importance for the "strength and sustainability of global growth."[28] The G20 summit in St. Petersburg in 2013 agreed that

---

[23] *See* Fritz Bolkestein (then Commissioner for the Internal Market and Taxation), *EU-US Regulatory Cooperation on Financial Markets : A Matter of Necessity*, speech before in front of the European American Business Council, Washington D.C., 24 February 2003, available at: http://europa.eu/rapid/press-release_SPEECH-03-96_en.htm (last visited 1 November 2014); Alexander Schaub (then Director–General, DG Internal Market of the European Commission), Testimony before the Committee on Financial Services, U.S. House of Representatives, 13 May 2004, available at: http://ec.europa.eu/internal_market/finances/docs/general/2004-05-13-testimony_en.pdf (last visited 1 November 2014).

[24] *See* Donald T. Nicolaisen, *A Securities Regulator Looks at Convergence*, 25 Nw. J. Int'l L. and Bus. 661, 665 (2004–05) (arguing that a single accounting standard – IFRS – will greatly benefit investors and detailing "a variety of approaches to increased convergence").

[25] *See* Wei, *supra* note 16, at 259 (citing statements from the Congress hearing on accounting standards convergence).

[26] *See* G20, *supra*, note 12.

[27] G20, Leaders' Statement: The Pittsburg Summit (2009), 16–18 ("16. To make sure our regulatory system for banks and other financial firms reins in the excesses that led to the crisis. Where reckless behavior and a lack of responsibility led to crisis, we will not allow a return to banking as usual. 17. We committed to act together to raise capital standards, to implement strong international compensation standards aimed at ending practices that lead to excessive risk-taking, to improve the over-the-counter derivatives market and to create more powerful tools to hold large global firms to account for the risks they take. Standards for large global financial firms should be commensurate with the cost of their failure. For all these reforms, we have set for ourselves strict and precise timetables. 18. To reform the global architecture to meet the needs of the 21st century. After this crisis, critical players need to be at the table and fully vested in our institutions to allow us to cooperate to lay the foundation for strong, sustainable and balanced growth. 19. We designated the G-20 to be the premier forum for our international economic cooperation. We established the Financial Stability Board (FSB) to include major emerging economies and welcome its efforts to coordinate and monitor progress in strengthening financial regulation.")

[28] Financial Stability Board, The Chairman, *Financial Reform – Progress and Challenges*, Letter of 17 February 2014 to G20 Finance Ministers and Central Bank Governors, at 1, available at www.financialstabilityboard.org/publications/r_140222.pdf (last visited Oct 31, 2014).

"jurisdictions and regulators should be able to defer to each other when it is justified by the quality of their respective regulatory and enforcement regimes, based on similar outcomes, in a non-discriminatory way, paying due respect to home country regulation regimes."[29]

In Spring 2014 the FSB's Chairman promoted "outcomes-based approaches to resolving cross-border issues," construing the G20 commitment as an endorsement of the equivalence principle:

> "To realise fully the benefits of an open system, the FSB recommends that the G20 commit to an approach characterised by: ... Deferring to each other's market regulatory regimes where they achieve equivalent outcomes"[30].

Under the FSB's outcomes-based approach, different jurisdictions need not have identical market regulations, as long as the outcomes are similar. Using the OTC derivatives markets as a test case, the FSB suggests reviewing how far flexible outcomes-based approaches resolve cross-border market regulation issues in other fields of financial regulation.[31]

Leaving the discussion on convergence versus diversity behind, the crisis and its regulatory consequences have paved the way for convergence. Two results are particularly noteworthy from the perspective of this chapter. First, equivalence is posited as the future of international financial integration. For the moment, the voices against convergence and in favor of diversity have been disregarded.

Second, mutual recognition and reciprocity disputes are settled within the G20/FSB forum. Hence, concerns about political strategies with the equivalence assessment as bargaining tool are limited to countries not represented by the G20/FSB. Important financial centers such as Hong Kong, the Cayman Islands, Ireland, Luxembourg, Liechtenstein, Singapore and Switzerland and others are not present at the G20 (although Singapore, Hong Kong, and Switzerland are members of the FSB). Accepting some generalizations, one could argue that the most important distribution countries have used the G20 to coordinate their efforts vis-à-vis financial centers, with the United States and the United Kingdom (under the impression of the financial crisis) simultaneously taking both sides, given the importance of New York, London, and Chicago for international finance.

EQUIVALENCE IN EUROPEAN BANKING AND FINANCIAL LAW

In this section we demonstrate that the equivalence principle is deeply ingrained in financial regulation.

The equivalence principle unites the European Member States' ambitions to impose higher standards on foreign providers of financial services and the

---

[29] G20 Leaders' Declaration, St. Petersburg, September 6, 2013, 71, available at www.g20
.utoronto.ca/2013/2013–0906-declaration.html (last visited Oct 31, 2014).
[30] Financial Stability Board, The Chairman (*supra* note 19) at 1.
[31] Financial Stability Board, *id.*, at 3–4.

European Union's international obligations under the agreement establishing the World Trade Organisation (WTO), including the General Agreement on Trade in Services (GATS). The GATS' two core principles of (1) most favored nation and (2) equal treatment as service providers located in the home country prohibit outright discrimination of third countries' service providers.[32] Equivalence is all European countries can ask for.

Some Examples

Consequently, under various EU provisions, the European Commission "may adopt an equivalence decision (...), stating that the legal and supervisory framework of a third country ensures that [financial service providers] authorised or registered in that third country comply with legally binding requirements which are equivalent to the requirements resulting from [European financial law] and which are subject to effective supervision and enforcement in that third country."[33] These requirements are most widely spread over pan-European market infrastructure regulation, extending to rating agencies, central securities depositaries, central counterparties, and trade repositories.[34]

We also find equivalence requirements in other parts of European financial law, albeit inconsistently and, generally speaking, less restrictively than for the regulation of market infrastructure.

For instance, while the Directive on Alternative Investment Funds Managers (AIFMD) provides full-fledged regulation for third-country managers and third-country investment funds based on the equivalence principle,[35] the Directive on Undertakings for Collective in Transferable Securities (UCITSD) foregoes an equivalence test for third-country managers. The MiFID governing managers of individual portfolios of financial instruments takes an intermediate stance. The equivalence principle is nevertheless deeply ingrained in European asset management law, as the details reveal: European UCITS management companies investing in third-country investment funds and bank deposits may do so only if the third-country fund is regulated equivalently to European funds, and if the "credit institution is subject to prudential rules equivalent to those laid down in Community law."[36] Under Article 19 (6) MiFID asset managers may provide execution-only services with regard to third-country securities if these securities are admitted to trading on a European regulated market or in an equivalent third-country market. Pursuant to Art. 46 MiFIR, a third-country firm may not provide

---

[32] For details on the WTO/GATS framework for financial services *See* Zetzsche, *Drittstaaten, supra* note 14, at 66–73.
[33] See, for example, Art. 5 (6) of Rating Regulation.
[34] *See* Art. 5 (6) of Rating Regulation; Art. 25 (9) CSD Regulation; Art. 25 (6), 75 EMIR.
[35] *See* Art. 36–42 AIFMD.
[36] *See* Recital 40 and Art. 50 (1) e) and f) UCITSD.

investment services to eligible counterparties and to professional clients unless they are registered as equivalent third-country firms.[37] The European Securities and Markets Authority (ESMA) assesses equivalence under the conditions of Art. 47 MiFIR. Under Art. 24 (4) MiFID the laxer regulation for transactions with eligible counterparties also pertains to third-country counterparties that are equivalently regulated.

In European banking law, credit exposures to investment firms, credit institutions, clearing houses and exchanges from third countries shall be treated equally as exposures to an European institution only "if the third country applies prudential and supervisory requirements to that entity that are at least equivalent to those applied in the Union."[38] If third-country public sector institutions, including central, regional, and local banks and governments, are equivalently governed and supervised as within the EU/EEA, European banks may use the same exposure calculations as they use for European public banking institutions.[39] Similarly, investment funds that are equivalently supervised as European AIF and UCITS may be treated as AIF and UCITS in banks' capital requirement calculations.[40] Internal rating-based approaches of banks regulated and supervised equivalently in their home jurisdictions only count as such for purposes of European prudential regulation of banks.[41] Finally, the consolidated supervision of third-country bank parent undertakings may be treated as a consolidated supervision under European law only when the parent undertaking is under consolidated supervision by a third-country supervisory authority that is equivalent to European consolidated supervision.[42]

While particularly older European legislation vests national competent authorities with the powers to assess equivalence,[43] since the financial crisis the majority of European legislation entitles the European Commission to make a decision as to whether a third country applies supervisory and regulatory arrangements at least equivalent to those applied in the Union subject to a specified examination procedure.

Elements

The core elements of the European equivalence test are the duality of equivalent substantive law and equivalent enforcement by the third country authorities.[44]

---

[37] *See* also Recital 42 MiFIR.

[38] Art. 107 (3) and (4) CRR.

[39] Art. 114 – 116 CRR.

[40] Art. 4 (1) No. 7 and 132 CRR.

[41] Art. 142 (2) CRR.

[42] Art. 127 CRD IV.

[43] In particular, see Art. 24 (4) MiFID on eligible counterparties and Art. 127(1) CRD IV on consolidated supervision.

[44] *See* Art. 5 (6) Rating Regulation; Art. 25 (9) CSD Regulation; 25 (2) b), (6) EMIR; Art. 28 (4), 47 (1) MiFIR; Art. 4 (1) subp. 3 Prospectus Directive; Art. 7 (2) Short Selling Regulation.

In particular, European law necessitates that the financial intermediary is subject to legally binding rules that are equivalent to those set out in European law, and that the intermediary is subject to (1) authorisation or registration and (2) effective supervision and enforcement on an ongoing basis.

In addition, cooperation agreements must ensure that European authorities or national competent authorities of the Member States rely on the information gathered by the (effective) supervision in the third country.[45] These agreements must specify "(a) the mechanism for the exchange of information between [the ESAs] and the relevant supervisory authorities of the third countries concerned; and (b) the procedures concerning the coordination of supervisory activities."[46] Furthermore, the data exchanged must be subject to professional secrecy rules as well as adequate data protection.[47] Hence, equivalence accounts for nothing if not paired up with formal supervisory cooperation with European authorities. The latter is negotiated centrally on behalf of all EU/EEA states by the European Commission and the ESAs.

Some European legislation supplements the equivalence principle with two wider policy goals: combatting money laundering,[48] and tax avoidance by requiring a tax information exchange agreement (TIEA) as a precondition for market access.[49] These additional requirements reflect a stakeholder perspective on a financial system that exceeds the common duality of protecting both investors/ clients, etc., and financial stability.[50]

Anticircumvention Rules

An apparently easy exit for entities seeking to avoid equivalence requirements could be the outsourcing of most, if not all, of its activities to less regulated third countries. However, European financial law reduces incentives of outsourcing by setting conditions for outsourcing that come close to those for entities performing services within the EU-/EEA-borders. For instance, under Art. 15 MiFID Implementing Regulation 2006/73/EC, service providers must be authorized or registered to provide that service in their home country and must be subject to prudential

---

[45] *See* Recital 17 and Art. 5 (6) Rating Regulation; Art. 25 (4) c) and (10) of CSD Regulation; Art. 55 – 57, 115 CRD IV; Art. 68 Solvency II; Art. 76 EMIR; Art. 88 MiFID II; Art. 47 (2) MiFIR; Recital 39, Art. 38 Short Selling Regulation; Recital 69, Art. 26 Market Abuse Regulation; Recital 63, 69, 74, Art. 34 (2) b), 35 (2) a), 36 (1) b), 37 (7) d), 40 (2) a), 42 (1) b) AIFMD.

[46] Recital 17 and Art. 5 (6) Rating Regulation.

[47] For example, Art. 63 MiFID.

[48] For example, Art. 25 (2) d) EMIR; Art. 39 (2) MiFID II.

[49] For example, Art.21 (6) d), 35 (2) c), 37 (2) f) AIFMD, Art. 39 (2) e) MiFID II.

[50] *See* on the stakeholder orientation of European financial law Zetzsche, *Investment Law as Financial Law: From Fund Governance over Market Governance to Stakeholder Governance?*, in: THE EUROPEAN FINANCIAL MARKET IN TRANSITION 337 (Birkmose, Neville, Sørensen, eds., 2012).

supervision, while the national competent authority must have entered into an cooperation agreement with the supervisory authority of the service provider. Under European law governing alternative investment funds managers, outsourcing of portfolio and risk management services is limited to six requirements that de facto result in an equivalence assessment of the delegate's jurisdiction, including that the delegate must be regulated and authorized, that the delegate's home authority must have entered into a supervisory agreement with the national competent authority of the AIFM, that the delegation must not prevent the effectiveness of supervision of the AIFM, that the delegate is qualified and capable of undertaking the functions in question, that it was selected with all due care, and that the AIFM is in a position to effectively monitor the delegated activity at any time.[51] We find similar outsourcing restrictions in all market infrastructure and asset management legislation,[52] as well as in crucial parts of banking (such as external calculations of exposures[53]).

Another circumvention of regulation could be tried by setting up a branch within the EU/EEA of intermediaries regulated and authorized by third-country authorities. The right to set up branches is guaranteed by WTO and GATS.[54] However, domestic law may impose certain conditions to ensure financial stability. European financial law regulates the set-up of branches. For example, under Art. 39 (2) MiFID II, where a branch is required as a condition to provide services to customers in one Member State under domestic law, the branch shall acquire prior authorisation by the competent authorities of that Member State subject to six conditions[55] that include many of the conditions that the third country would have

---

[51] Art. 20 (1) d) AIFMD in conjunction with Art. 78 (3) AIFMD Level 2. see Zetzsche, *Drittstaaten, supra* note 14, at 91.

[52] Art. 20 (1) c) AIFMD in conjunction with Art. 78, 79 b) AIFMD Level 2; Art. 13 (1) d) UCITSD; Art. 19 (6) CSD Regulation; Art. 35 EMIR.

[53] Art. 190 (3), (4) regarding outsourcing of data collection for calculating capital requirements, Art. 316 (1) a) CRR regarding the calculation of the basic indicator.

[54] For details, *see* Zetzsche, *Drittstaaten, supra* note 14, at 66–73.

[55] *See* Article 39(2) MiFiD: "(. . .) (a) the provision of services for which the third-country firm requests authorisation is subject to authorisation and supervision in the third country where the firm is established and the requesting firm is properly authorised, whereby the competent authority pays due regard to any FATF recommendations in the context of anti-money laundering and countering the financing of terrorism;

(b) cooperation arrangements, that include provisions regulating the exchange of information for the purpose of preserving the integrity of the market and protecting investors, are in place between the competent authorities in the Member State where the branch is to be established and competent supervisory authorities of the third country where the firm is established;

(c) sufficient initial capital is at free disposal of the branch;

(d) one or more persons are appointed to be responsible for the management of the branch and they all comply with the requirement laid down in Article 9(1);

(e) the third country where the third-country firm is established has signed an agreement with the Member State where the branch is to be established, which fully comply with the standards laid down in Article 26 of the OECD Model Tax Convention on Income

to meet in an equivalence assessment. In particular, "the provision of services for which the third country firm requests authorisation is subject to authorisation and supervision in the third country where the firm is established and the requesting firm is properly authorised." Furthermore the third country must engage in anti-money laundering and countering the financing of terrorism, and agree to tax information exchange under Art. 26 of the OECD Model Agreement.

To sum up, although European law lacks consistency with regard to some fields of European financial law, it is fair to say that both outsourcing and branching work smoothly as long as the third country meets the equivalence threshold.

The Rest of the World

U.S. regulation refers to the same concept as "substituted compliance." U.S. law, however, relies on "substituted compliance" to a far lesser extent than European law on equivalence. In line with the G20/FSB commitment, certain foreign swap providers may apply for an exemption from U.S. federal laws based on their compliance with substantively the same rules and regulations as well as supervision by a foreign regulator that has similar enforcement powers and capacity as the U.S. Commodity Futures Trading Commission ('CFTC').[56] Substituted compliance was also proposed for the cross-border recognition of foreign broker-dealers and stock exchanges.[57] In many other cases, such as the management of investment companies, foreign intermediaries offering products to U.S. clients are left with but one choice: full compliance with U.S. regulations. In this case, foreign intermediaries must establish and capitalize subsidiaries and ask for authorizations from U.S. authorities.

> and on Capital and ensures an effective exchange of information in tax matters, including, if any, multilateral tax agreements;
> (f) the firm belongs to an investor-compensation scheme authorised or recognised in accordance with Directive 97/9/EC.

[56] The comparability determinations of the Commodity Futures Trading Commission ('CFTC') would permit substituted compliance with non-U.S. regulatory regimes as compared to certain swaps provisions of Title VII of the Dodd-Frank Act and the Commission's regulations, *see* CFTC, Cross-Border Guidance (7/2013), available at www.cftc.gov/LawRegulation/Dodd FrankAct/Rulemakings/Cross-BorderApplicationofSwapsProvisions/index.htm (last visited October 31, 2014). *See* Sean J. Griffith, *Substituted Compliance and Systemic Risk: How to Make a Global Market in Derivatives Regulation*, 98 U. MINN. L. REV. 1291, 1293–4 (2014) (arguing that "Regulatory uniformity, in general, is a highly suspect means of addressing systemic risk" and "that a better approach to derivatives regulation would be to adopt a more supple regulatory super-structure that encourages a diversity of approaches to achieve the objective of minimizing systemic risk").

[57] Steven M. Davidoff Solomon, *Rhetoric and Reality: A Historical Perspective on the Regulation of Foreign Private Issuers*, 79 U. Cin. L. Rev. 619, 633 (2010) (citing and discussing the COMMITTEE ON THE REGULATION OF U.S. CAPITAL MARKETS IN THE 21ST CENTURY, U.S. CHAMBER OF COMMERCE, REPORT AND RECOMMENDATIONS (2007) that proposed substituted compliance for the regulation of foreign broker-dealers and stock exchanges).

The equivalence concept is also prevalent, for instance, in Australia[58] and Asia.[59]

EQUIVALENCE IN TAX LAW

From the policy perspective, financial risk is an externality. As with other externalities imposing costs/risks on others, financial risk may be challenged by regulation *or* taxation. Notwithstanding that most jurisdictions opt for regulation instead of taxation,[60] a brief look at the taxation of cross-border financial services could provide some insights as to how competition may take place in the future.

One oft-cited reason for the attraction of certain financial centers is taxation. If low taxation in home countries persists, while host countries charge high taxes, a stricter level of financial regulation as a precondition for market access will not induce financial centers to transform. These centers will attract clients based on tax competition rather than competition for the best regulatory environment. This is particularly true if low taxation is mixed with low transparency in tax matters, so that requesting the services of an intermediary from a certain home country furthers nontransparent, low-rate taxation (and sometimes illegal tax evasion).

Hence, it is crucial for the impact of financial law equivalence on competition that tax evasion is limited and that the effective tax rate for clients relying on foreign financial services is similar to that under which clients of domestic financial intermediaries are taxed. In this section we will show that both conditions are met. We draw this conclusion from major strains of development in international tax law on the level of investors/clients as well as on the level of structures used for shifting tax burdens across borders.

The Investor Level: Automatic Information Exchange in Tax Matters

On the investor level incentives provided by tax law to move income across borders are reduced by the automatic information exchange in tax matters. Since March

---

[58] Ferran and Ho, *supra* note 16, at 417–418 (citing examples from Australian securities laws).

[59] The Asia Region Funds Passport (ARFP) proposes a pan-Asian scheme for collective investment schemes in Australia, Singapore, South Korea, New Zealand, the Philippines and Thailand. The proposal sets substantive requirements for collective investment schemes and operators to be eligible for the passport; see *Asia-Pacific Economic Cooperation, Consultation Paper: Arrangements for an Asia Region Funds Passport* (2014), available at: www.treasury.gov .au/~/media/Treasury/Consultations%20and%20Reviews/Consultations/2014/Asia%20Region% 20Funds%20Passport/Key%20Documents/RTF/Consultation-Paper.ashx (last visited November 5, 2014); the Asean Capital Markets Forum (ACMF) initiated a framework for cross-border offering of ASEAN collective investment schemes which fulfil a set of common standards (equivalence), see *ACMF, Standards of Qualifying CIS*, available at: www.theacmf.org/ ACMF/upload/standards_of_qualifying_cis.pdf (last visited November 5, 2014); ACMF, Handbook for CIS Operators of ASEAN CISs, August 25, 2014, available at: www.theacmf.org/ ACMF/upload/asean_cis_handbook.pdf (last visited Nov 5, 2014).

[60] Donato Mascinadaro and Francesco Passarelli, *Financial Systemic Risk: Taxation or Regulation?*, 37. J. BANK. FIN. 587 (2013) (concluding that if the majority chooses a tax, then it is likely to be too low. If it chooses regulation it will possibly be too harsh.).

2010, the U.S. *Foreign Account Tax Compliance Act* (FATCA)[61] has required foreign financial intermediaries to report to the U.S. Internal Revenue Services the data on financial accounts held by U.S. residents as well as data on foreign entities in which U.S. residents hold a substantial ownership interest. If foreign financial intermediaries do not document their FATCA status, U.S. withholding agents will withhold thirty percent on certain payments to these entities.[62] In addition, information about noncompliant foreign intermediaries is reported to the IRS (which may follow up on this information and prompt investigations).

In order to avoid multiple standards across jurisdictions after the FATCA implementation, following demands by France and Germany, the OECD supported by the G20[63] endorsed the OECD's Standard for Automatic Exchange of Financial Account Information in Tax Matters[64] (hereafter referred to as GATCA – Global FATCA). According to the OECD standard, governments enter into, and financial institutions must support, the automatic exchange of detailed account information across countries that have adopted the standards with other jurisdictions on an annual basis. "On 29 October 2014, 51 jurisdictions ... signed a multilateral competent authority agreement to automatically exchange information based on Article 6 of the OECD Multilateral Convention."[65] An extension of the standard for developing countries is under way.[66]

Investors and clients whose intermediary is subject to FATCA and GATCA reporting requirements will be taxed for their foreign income at their home country's taxation level. In the absence of a Double Taxation Agreement (DTA), tax could be collected by the clients' home country in addition to taxes levied upon the income by the foreign jurisdiction. If the intermediary opts for FATCA noncompliance, the withholding requirement amounts to a thirty-percent penalty on the clients' income. U.S. clients will only accept the penalty if their personal tax

---

[61] FATCA refers to Subtitle A, chapter 4 of the U.S. Internal Revenue Code, 26 U.S.C. §§ 1471–1474 ("TAXES TO ENFORCE REPORTING ON CERTAIN FOREIGN ACCOUNTS"). FATCA was enacted by the Hiring Incentives to Restore Employment (HIRE) Act on 18 March 2010.

[62] 26 U.S.C. § 1471 (b) (3).

[63] *See* OECD: "On 6 September 2013, the G20 Leaders committed to automatic exchange of information as the new global standard and fully supported the OECD work, with G20 countries, aimed at presenting such a single standard in 2014." Available at www.oecd.org/tax/exchange-of-tax-information/automaticexchange.htm (last visited Oct 31, 2014).

[64] OECD, Standard for Automatic Exchange of Financial Information in Tax Matters, published July 21, 2014, available at: www.oecd.org/ctp/exchange-of-tax-information/standard-for-automatic-exchange-of-financial-information-in-tax-matters.htm (last visited Oct 31, 2014).

[65] *See* OECD, Multilateral Competent Authority Agreement on Automatic Exchange of Financial Account Information, available at: www.oecd.org/ctp/exchange-of-tax-information/multilateral-competent-authority-agreement.pdf (last visited Oct 31, 2014).

[66] *See* OECD, OECD and G20 pursue efforts to curb multinational tax avoidance and offshore tax evasion in developing countries, publ. 22 Sept 2014, available at: www.oecd.org/ctp/oecd-and-g20-pursue-efforts-to-curb-multinational-tax-avoidance-and-offshore-tax-evasion-in-developing-countries.htm (last visited Oct 31, 2014).

rate is higher than thirty percent. The 30 percent rate is strategically set since the effective personal tax rate of wealthy US residents (top 1% of the U.S. households) is 29.6 percent.[67]

Hence, under FATCA (and most likely GACTA as well) beneficial tax treatment in the financial intermediary's home country does not provide incentives to opt into cross-border intermediation. Quite the opposite is true, given that cross-border income generates additional administrative expenses for reporting and tax advice on the side of investors and clients. All in all, investors and clients bear higher tax costs for foreign than domestic financial intermediation.

The Entity Level

Instead of accepting levies on the investor and client level, clients and investors could transfer their profit-yielding assets into vehicles and shift them to countries with beneficial tax treatment. While this is and always will be an option – among more than 100 jurisdictions, some will always provide amenable tax conditions – it is argued that the OECD's BEPS project as well as general antiavoidance rules in national tax legislation and DTAs render such tax-based transfers more costly and thus less appealing to investors. In addition, the tax laws of some countries discriminate against foreign financial intermediation.

BEPS

The OECD's project on Base Erosion and Profit Shifting (BEPS) "looks at whether ... the current rules allow for the allocation of taxable profits to locations different from those where the actual business activity takes place."[68] The OECD initiative is based on the policy perception that BEPS "constitutes a serious risk to tax revenues, tax sovereignty and the trust in the integrity of tax systems of all countries" and brings with it "a negative impact on investment, services and competition, and thus on growth and employment globally."[69] In turn, OECD member states encourage efforts to develop "instruments to put an end to or neutralise the effects of ... arbitrage."[70] The OECD seeks a "borderless digital economy" and "a new set of standards to prevent double non-taxation." The OECD BEPS project comes with "closer international co-operation, greater transparency, data and reporting requirements."

---

[67] The Distribution of Household Income and Federal Taxes, 2010. The U.S. Congressional Budget Office (CBO). Report, December 4, 2013. Available at www.cbo.gov/publication/44604 (last visited Oct 31, 2014).

[68] OECD, website, available at: www.oecd.org/tax/beps-about.htm (last visited Nov 4, 2014).

[69] OECD, Meeting of the OECD Council on the Ministerial Level, Declaration on Base Erosion Profit Shifting, Paris 19–20, 2013, at 2 (2013).

[70] OECD, idem, at 3.

The OECD's report on BEPS is likely to be accompanied with proportionate and dissuasive penalties albeit that sanctions for noncompliance of certain countries and entities have not been disclosed.[71] Penalty taxes such as the thirty percent withholding tax on noncomplying financial institutions in FATCA are one likely option.

Investors and clients may respond to the BEPS initiative in one of two ways: They may either move their business beyond the BEPS borders. However, this option is only viable if their personal seats are also beyond the BEPS borders, as they cannot reap the profits from this income without falling under the radar of FATCA and GATCA. Given that more than eighty percent of the world's economy shall be subject to automatic information exchange, moving away may involve taking residence in some less appealing places on this planet and restrictions on personal freedoms, including the freedom to travel, open bank accounts and hold investments in OECD countries.

Alternatively, investors/clients comply with the BEPS rules and accept the tax level applicable to the "business activity" in the business' home country.[72] In the latter case, tax will not be a factor that benefits foreign financial intermediaries.

Antiavoidance Rules

The second measure that deems vehicle-based tax structuring less appealing belongs to the general antiavoidance rules that we find in national tax legislation[73] as well as in certain clauses of DTAs.[74]

For instance, the limitation on benefits clauses that we often find in U.S.-style DTAs[75] shall ensure that the benefits granted under the DTA are restricted to those

---

[71] See OECD, *Addressing Base Erosion and Profit Shifting* (Feb 2013), *available at*: 10.1787/9789264192744-en (last visited Nov 13, 2014); OECD, *Action Plan on Base Erosion and Profit Shifting* (July 2013), *available at*: 10.1787/9789264202719-en (last visited Nov 13, 2014).

[72] In the context of Double Taxation Agreements, the scope of the term "business activity" is subject to controversy. It is unlikely that the BEPS initiative comes to uniform results.

[73] *See*, for example, s. 42 of the German Abgabenordnung ("Tax Ordinance"), stating that by abusive tax structures may not circumvent the tax legislation. General tax avoidance regulations have also been imposed, for instance, by regulations implementing s. 701 of the U.S. *Internal Revenue Code* (on partnership taxation) and s. 245 of the Canadian *Federal Income Tax Act*. At times, though, it is difficult to identify when a detailed rule is designed as antiavoidance rule. *See* Lawrence Zelenak, *Codifying Anti-Avoidance Doctrines and Controlling Corporate Tax Shaleters*, 54 SMU L. Rev. 177, 178 (2001).

[74] German DTAs often contain antiabuse clauses that reserve the right to apply national antiabuse provisions, such as s. 42 of the German Abgabenordnung (idem). See, for example, Art. 23 (1) of the DTA Germany – The Netherlands of 12 April 2012. In addition to these general anti-avoidance rules and the limitation on benefits-clauses preferred by the U.S. DTA standard, controlled foreign company rules establish a third method to combat tax avoidance. Under these provisions certain benefits do not accrue to entities controlled from certain jurisdictions with (perceived) harmful tax practices. *See* OECD, Adressing BEPS (*supra* note 72), at 52.

[75] *See*, for instance, Art. 28 of the DTA U.S.A. – Germany.

parties which the agreeing countries had in mind when entering into the DTA. Generally speaking, from the U.S. perspective mutual trade and business should benefit from the DTA.[76] For these activities U.S. DTAs erase double taxation for entities with links to both treaty countries and impose an "active trade or business" test.[77] Despite being formally a privately held corporation, or partnership, respectively, the test means that the making or management of investments disqualifies the corporation, or partnership, respectively, from benefiting from the DTA because managing investments is neither a trade nor a business activity but an investment activity. U.S. foreign and international tax law in turn shall not grant corporate (nor partnership) tax treatment to investment funds since these are not substantively similar to U.S. corporations or partnerships in terms of their business activities.[78]

In addition to these general antiavoidance rules and the limitation on benefits-clauses preferred by the U.S. DTA standard, controlled foreign company rules establish a third method to combat tax avoidance. Under these provisions the deferral on corporate income tax does not accrue to income generated by foreign entities controlled by a tax resident if the entity is located in a jurisdiction with (perceived) harmful tax practices. The latter include, for the most part, jurisdictions with lower tax rates than the rate in the country of the tax resident, or jurisdictions that do not cooperate fully in tax matters.[79]

General or specific antiavoidance rules, be they of statutory or contractual nature, suffer from two flaws: 1) a lesser degree of legal certainty, given that the distinction between legal use of structural options and illegal abuse of these options is far from clear,[80] and 2) a weak factual basis to make the abuse case, given that the motive of the taxpayer to enter into the structure must be assessed in hindsight.

In light of the automatic data exchange stemming from both the FATCA/GATCA and the BEPS initiatives, the tax authorities have better chances of gaining from the informational advantage the taxpayers previously had. It is reasonable to assume that general antiavoidance rules will be more frequently enforced if tax

---

[76] *See* on the macro-economic anti-competitive effects of double taxation *Schönfeld/Häck*, Einleitung ¶7, in: DBA Commentary (J. Schönfeld and X. Ditz, eds., 2013).

[77] See Nancy H. Kaufman, *Common Misconceptions: The Function and Framework of "Trade or Business Within the United States,"* 25 VAND. J. TRANSN'L L. 729 (1993).

[78] However, open-ended, widely held investment funds, such as UCITS, which cannot be used for structuring tax burdens, may rely on exemptions granting the power to tax regulators to grant treaty benefits to entities that albeit they do not pass the active trade or business test cannot be used for tax structuring. *See* Tomi Viitala, *Taxation of Investment Funds in the European Union* (2004), p. 315.

[79] *See* the overview of 65 countries provided by DITS, *The Guide to Controlled Foreign Company Regimes* (Jan 2014), *available at*: www.deloitte.com/content/dam/Deloitte/global/Documents/Tax/dttl-tax-guide-to-cfc-regimes-210214.pdf (last visited Nov 13, 2014).

[80] *See* Ralf Dremel, Artikel 1 Rn. 85 et seq., in: DBA Commentary (J. Schönfeld and X. Ditz, eds., 2013). The uncertainty spurs the discussion as to whether general anti avoidance rules are compatible with the rule of law, see Rebecca Prebble and John Prebble, *Does the Use of General Anti-Avoidance Rules to Combat Tax Avoidance Breach Principles of the Rule of Law?*, 55 St. Louis Univ. L. J. 21 (2010).

authorities gain better insight into the overall structure and its connections to various countries. Using foreign intermediaries for tax purposes only is in turn more costly, and hence less likely. Again, we find that tax incentives have become less convincing in explaining cross-border financial intermediation.

Investment Funds Taxation

In some cases foreign financial intermediation may even be more costly to investors than domestic intermediation. The treatment of investment funds in DTAs may provide an example to support the argument.

For a long time investment funds have been neglected in international tax agreements. As a consequence they were dealt with under the rules applicable to their legal form. For instance, if an investment fund was formed using a partnership, corporate, or contract form, the law governing the taxation of partnerships, corporations, or the contract was applied to the investment fund. According to this principle, particularities of the business of managing investments on behalf of investors were disregarded for tax purposes. This can result in differing tax treatment for different legal forms used by fund investors despite the same business (investment) activity. Among others things, investment funds as intermediate entity can be 1) entirely disregarded as a taxable entity and thus regarded as "transparent," 2) deemed a taxable, but not taxed, entity or 3) taxed at the corporate tax rate applicable in one country.[81] Depending on the fund vehicle's tax treatment, different tax results are triggered at the asset and the investor level. For instance, profits and losses generated by assets of a transparent investment fund accrue immediately on the investors' income, while an intermediate taxable entity may function as a tax layer that allows profits to be discounted against losses delaying taxation to the time of profit distribution to investors. In the absence of distributions, taxation may be delayed for some time. The more taxation based on the legal form became the more doubtful, the more investment funds were used for treaty shopping, that is, using investment funds for optimizing the tax burden for investors by using multiple (shell) vehicles in multiple countries and channeling income from an underlying business and investment activity through the vehicles to the investors. Depending on the combination of vehicles and countries, the tax burden could be reduced or even eliminated (double nontaxation).[82]

Together with the limited purpose of the DTA, which should further trade and business, the potential for tax structuring explains the restrictions that some domestic tax laws impose on foreign investment funds. For some tax laws as well as some DTAs, foreign investment funds do not benefit from privileges that are granted to

[81] *See* Andreas Oestreicher and Markus Hammer, *Taxation of Income from Domestic and Cross-Border Collective Investment,* 2014 (Springer), p. 26 et seq.
[82] *See* on double nontaxation in the context of German cross-border taxation *Schönfeld/Häck,* Einleitung ¶12–21, in: DBA Commentary (J. Schönfeld and X. Ditz, eds., 2013).

domestic investment funds. For example, U.S. tax law treats foreign investment funds as Passive Foreign Investment Companies (PFIC).[83] This status leads to a top marginal tax rate and an interest charge on retained profits, unless (among other things) the PFIC subjects itself to the Securities and Exchange Commission as well as the U.S. Internal Revenue Services or the shareholders pay taxes on retained profits. To the same extent, while German investment funds are exempted from withholding tax on corporate dividends, taxes are withheld on dividends paid to foreign investment funds including investment funds that have essentially the same investment strategy as UCITS. With regard to similar provisions in France and Poland, the ECJ maintained that this discrimination against foreign financial intermediaries violates Art. 63 of the Treaty on the Functioning of the European Union.[84]

Equivalence through the Backdoor

Although the former initiatives do not explicitly cite equivalent taxation as their motive, the underlying rationale is clear: If taxes become too low, legal structures lose their cross-border recognition for tax purposes or are made subject to a penalty tax. To the extent that tax authorities take their home country's tax level as a benchmark for an appropriate tax level,[85] the general antiavoidance rules require a de facto taxation level that is substantively similar to their own, that is, equivalent. Admittedly the equivalence principle is far less pronounced and less enforceable than in financial regulation. However, the implicit condition of equivalent taxation as a precondition for cross-border recognition of legal structuring limits the potential of financial centers to compete with low taxes. We conclude that tax effects will not accrue to the appeal of financial centers in the future. At the same time, domestic tax laws impose an equivalence principle for measuring the fairness of taxation in foreign jurisdictions.

SOME (UN)INTENDED CONSEQUENCES

The financial and tax law equivalence will prompt some intended but also some unintended consequences for the competitiveness of financial centers.

---

[83] *See* 26 U.S. Code § 1297.

[84] ECJ, 10 April 2014, Case C-190/12 (Emerging Markets Series of DFA Investment Trust Company); ECJ, 12 May 2012, Cases 338/11 – 347/11 (Santander Asset Management SGIIC SA).

[85] *See* s. 2 (2) No. 1 of the *Außensteuergesetz* (German foreign tax law) (defining low tax countries as countries that impose overall personal tax that is a third lower than German personal income tax); s. 8 (3) of the Außensteuergesetz (defining low tax countries as countries that impose overall corporate tax lower than the German corporate tax rate of twenty-five percent, prior to DTAs and withholding tax discounts).

Regulatory Level on the Rise

In order for cross-border financial services to work smoothly the EU/EEA area must mutually recognize third-country regimes. From the perspective of the host country of financial services there is little incentive to mutually recognize a home country's regime if it does not protect investors and the financial system as a whole to the same extent as the host country's laws and regulation.

Some EU/EEA countries primarily adopt the role of home countries of financial intermediation (for instance, Luxembourg) while other countries primarily adopt the role of host countries (for instance, Germany). In light of this differing perspective, the EU/EEA home country's discretion to respond to equivalence requirements by optimizing their own legal framework is limited: European financial law and – due to the active role of the European Court of Justice[86] – domestic tax laws of EU/EEA Member States provide a minimum level of harmonization. These minimum regulations provide European home countries of financial intermediaries with little choice to opt into lax regulation. At the same time the European Supervisory Authorities ESMA, EBA, and EIOPA (the ESAs) ensure that national competent authorities enforce European rules. In turn, not the EEA member states, but only third countries have the option of responding to equivalence requirements with either "comply" or "not comply."

Noncompliance is not an attractive option for financial centers since most financial intermediation is based on market access to distribution countries. There are few funds to manage, if clients from wealthy countries cannot channel their funds to the center.[87] If any financial link to the EU/EEA zone more or less depends on equivalence as is argued here, home countries of significant financial intermediaries that look for EU/EEA market access are forced into adopting equivalent regulations and enforcement.

We also expect the regulatory level to rise across borders in line with the distribution country's standards. First, distribution countries are likely to set high entry levels. Services that create either major income or major risks are most likely to be subjected to the most stringent equivalence test. Second, financial centers seeking market access are likely to adopt (more) restrictive financial regulation and supervision. This does not pertain to all services at the same time, but the trend is imminent and intact.

---

[86] While the European directives governing taxation provide a mere minimum framework, the European Court of Justice performs as pacemaker of European tax harmonization, relying on the four Basic Freedoms provided by the Treaty on the Functioning of the European Union. *See*, for example, on exit taxation of individuals ECJ of 11 March 2004, Case C-9/02 (Lasteyrie du Saillant) and on exit taxation of corporations ECJ of 29 November 2011, Case C-371/10 (National Grid Indus).

[87] Physical transfer comes along with risks long overcome by electronic payment and settlement systems. More importantly, it does not allow for large-scale financial intermediation necessary for rendering a place where intermediaries are located a financial center.

Given that equivalence with the lowest EU/EEA jurisdiction in many cases ensures market access to the whole EU/EEA, the future equivalence level is the lowest regulatory level that one Member State of the EU/EEA accepts as equivalent. Experience shows that this would be the minimum level available under European law. In light of this, the centralization of the equivalence assessment for most financial services[88] in the hands of the European Commission and its supervision by the ESAs reflects a realistic view on the functioning of the Single Market.

Cost Effects

As intended by distribution countries, with a higher regulatory level comes higher costs for intermediaries based in low-regulation countries.

But this is only part of the picture. A centralized assessment reduces the costs for accessing the EU/EEA market[89] for third countries with equivalent legislation and supervision while centralized assessment increases the costs for countries with nonequivalent legislation. However, the cost reduction for equivalent third countries is likely to be significant since European law attaches in some important cases the privilege of cross-border activity *in all Member States* (European passport) to a positive outcome of the equivalence assessment.[90]

Given that the European Commission has a reputation to lose, it is unlikely that it will give in without clear gains on the European side. We thus predict a stricter rather than liberal approach to equivalence. Placing the equivalence assessment in the hands of the European Commission also ensures a greater level of legal certainty about when foreign intermediaries require authorizations. This is because Member States explicitly lobby for clarification important to their business models according to the European law. For instance, after some Member States experienced difficulties with the first generation of European third country rules the MiFID II stated that reverse solicitation of third-country services by EU/EEA investors and clients does not require authorization (nor an equivalence assessment) by EU authorities.[91]

---

[88] An exception to the rule are retail investment products. These remain within the jurisdiction of national competent authorities. See, for example, recital 109 of MiFID II.

[89] In the absence of a uniform assessment by the European Commission the national competent authorities assess the equivalence. Different assessments likely result in differing outcome for the same third country, requiring financial centers to bargain for access with multiple actors. In a world of country-by-country assessment market access to the Single Market is expensive.

[90] *See* for example Art. 20 (2) and Art. 17–19 Prospectus Directive; Art. 37 AIFMD; Zetzsche, *Drittstaaten, supra* note 14, p. 92, 102 et seq.

[91] For instance, Art. 42 MiFID II ("Member States shall ensure that where a retail client or professional client within the meaning of Section II of Annex II established or situated in the Union initiates at its own exclusive initiative the provision of an investment service or activity by a third-country firm, the requirement for authorisation under Article 39 shall not apply to the provision of that service or activity by the third country firm to that person including a

Equivalence as a Political Concept

Despite commentators' references to international standards,[92] equivalence remains a political concept that may be used for bargaining, particularly for countries with little, if any, influence on the level of the G20/FSB. Lobbying efforts will focus on European rather than national institutions, as there is more to gain from European than national recognition of a third country regime. The importance of national competent authorities will consequently diminish.

This concentration is a two-sided coin. On the one hand, it yields clear advantages both with regard to the relationship of Member States to each other and the relationship of Member States to important third countries. With regard to the inter-Member State relationship, the concentration lessens the risk of championism between one EU Member State (let us say for the sake of argument only: the UK) and particular third countries (let us say the Channel Islands or Hong Kong) for historical, cultural, or business reasons. Championism could result in an implicit tacit collusion to undercut the European equivalence standard in day-to-day practice and thereby harm the level-playing field approach of the Single Market. With regard to important third countries (let us say for the sake of argument only: the United States or China), concentration reduces the risk of extortion. Without concentration small and/or weak EU/EEA Member States face the risk of being forced into favorable conditions for market access of third-country intermediaries while its own firms do not receive the beneficial treatment on a mutual basis when accessing the third country's market.[93] The negotiation power of the European Union as a whole is most likely stronger than that of most Member States on a stand-alone basis.

On the other hand, the concentration of the equivalence assessment facilitates uniformism and national particularities may be disregarded. Moreover, it opens the door to politics with regard to the equivalence requirements. The equivalence is measured in a comitology proceeding that is influenced by political representatives of the EU Member States. We have seen unexpected correlations between third-country internal politics and the outcome of equivalence tests.[94] The political

---

relationship specifically relating to the provision of that service or activity. An initiative by such clients shall not entitle the third-country firm to market otherwise than through the branch, where one is required in accordance with national law, new categories of investment products or investment services to that client.")

[92] Ferran and Ho, *supra* note 16, at 417 (stating that "[i]nternational standards set by global bodies may be called into use as the benchmark for equivalency of outcomes").

[93] While the GATS' principle of reciprocity limits the risk in theory, day-to-day practice may differ from the letters of the agreements.

[94] For instance, the Swiss comitology proceeding on EMIR equivalence was delayed after the Swiss people decided in a poll to impose restrictions on immigration that could affect European individuals looking for work in Switzerland. *See* Neue Zürcher Zeitung online, "Brüssel lässt Schweizer Börse bangen"(Oct 4, 2014), available at: www.nzz.ch/schweiz/bruessel-laesst-schweizer-boerse-bangen-1.18397421.

interference is facilitated by the legal uncertainty surrounding the equivalence assessment. For example, the European Commission may, in the case of the rating regulation, "specify or amend the criteria for determining the equivalence of the regulatory and supervisory legal framework of third countries."[95]

Smaller countries may also feel disadvantaged by the European Commission's likely prioritization of third countries that are important for all of Europe rather than those which are solely important for them.

All in all, the political impact on the equivalence assessment creates uncertainty that reduces the incentives to invest in an equivalent law and supervision as a precondition for fair competition of financial centers.

Competition under Equivalent Conditions

If regulatory levels are on the rise and tax provides lesser incentives to enter inter cross-border financial intermediation, financial centers can maintain their function as production sites only if they focus on nonlegal competitive factors.

We hypothesize that nonlegal coordination among financial actors at financial centers, including regulators, supervisors, and financial intermediaries will assist financial centers in remaining competitive, despite equivalent regulation and a level playing field for tax. This may take one of two directions.

First, the coordination within financial centers could facilitate *circumvention of the equivalent standards*. For instance, intermediaries, regulators, and supervisors could collude to display equivalence formally, while in practice the enforcement of the rules is not equivalent. However, in light of the global benchmarking by international organizations such as the OECD and FSB,[96] and supervisory coordination by virtue of the FSB,[97] IOSCO, and others, coordination to circumvent equivalence – while not totally excluded – puts market access of the financial center and thus the center's lifeline at risk. We assume that few centers will adopt this short-sighted strategy, and even fewer that do so will succeed.

Second, while financial centers could do little about *systemic risk* (defined as the risk of being connected to the global financial system and interconnected with many other intermediaries),[98] financial centers could use nonlegal coordination for optimizing the level of *investor and client protection*. The (low cost, fast, and focused) implicit coordination among market actors at financial centers, if

---

[95] Recital 71 Rating Regulation.

[96] Financial Stability Board, The Chairman (*supra* note 29), at 1 (Committing to "[p]eer reviews and impact assessments to ensure consistent implementation when we get standards right and refinement of standards when we get them wrong.").

[97] Financial Stability Board, The Chairman (*supra* note 29), at 1 (Committing to "[e]nhanced co-operation to avoid domestic measures that fragment the global system.").

[98] As a precondition of their center function, financial centers must be connected to the world's financial markets. The greater the interconnectedness, the greater the systemic risk.

successful, could substitute the (expensive, slow, and necessarily general) explicit coordination of distribution countries by law.

The centers could thus forego mandatory law (where it does not hurt the equivalence assessment) and reduce intermediary-related agency costs that come naturally given the influence that intermediaries have upon regulators in financial centers. Note that this alternative – the enhancement of investor/client orientation – is not the same as adopting the laws of distribution countries in full, since the laws in distribution countries are influenced by nonclient interests pandering to the public or some special political constituency.

If equivalence hinders regulatory arbitrage (although equivalence will never have the capacity to abolish arbitrage entirely), financial centers will be keen to credibly signal their client orientation. If they can do this the lower intermediary-related agency costs may persuade new clients/investors to trust financial centers and benefit from the greater level of expertise and better infrastructure that the center offers. We expect the equivalence assessment and benchmarking by international organizations to be vital to the financial center's new procompliance strategy allowing for strategic compliance in order to signal expertise and focus on financial affairs where it matters for their client base. For instance, we view Singapore – as general Asian banking center competing with Hong Kong and the new centers on the Chinese main land – as one of the first and best-rated countries with regard to banks' capital requirements under Basel III.[99] Liechtenstein, the European center for family and estate structuring, was the first European country to implement the AIFMD (in December 2012) and an early volunteer for adopting the Automatic Information Exchange in Tax Matters.

The more financial centers focus on early adoption and early compliance, the more obvious it becomes to investors and clients that distribution countries lag behind. The tardiness of distribution countries is consistent with the lesser importance of financial service matters on the domestic agenda. Distribution countries simply care less about financial affairs, or they need time to coordinate the different constituencies given that the interest within distribution countries are not as well aligned as that in financial centers. Hence, early compliance acts as a signal indicating the financial centers' expertise and investor/client orientation!

We could also see the further rise in financial centers – to the detriment of the financial industries in, and counter to the political will in, distribution countries. With reputation and equivalence now being benchmarked by international standard setters, and assuming that benchmarking takes place in an unbiased fashion, the race-to-the-bottom, regulatory arbitrage argument that formerly constituted one of the main impediments to the centers' recognition by clients in distribution countries is likely to vanish. Originally designed to curb

---

[99] BCBS, Progress report on Basel III implementation 13 (April 2012), available at www.bis .org/publ/bcbs215.pdf.

the attraction of financial centers, equivalence requirements may well contribute to furthering their development.

CONCLUSION

To the extent possible under GATS, the equivalence standard is designed to avoid regulatory arbitrage and risk-shifting from production to distribution countries of financial services. This chapter has argued that, contrary to the distribution countries' expectations, the introduction of equivalence principles is likely to further rather than reduce the importance of financial centers for two reasons. First, the implicit coordination of government, supervisors, and intermediaries substitutes costly, lengthy, and overgeneralized explicit coordination of distribution countries by legal means and may result in an optimal level of investor protection (within the limits imposed by equivalence). Financial centers could thus move closer and more quickly toward striking a Golden Mean between clients' and intermediary's interests than distribution countries.[100] Second, international coordination efforts provide the opportunity to display and prove domestic prioritization of (certain specialist) financial service matters, while benchmarking makes the seriousness of the efforts and the advantages of the centers transparent. Together, both aspects render foreclosing the market based on an equivalent assessment difficult (while outright discrimination would violate the GATS).

All other conditions being equal, we would expect to see financial centers flourish under equivalence requirements.

---

[100] The lower costs for specialized services and better-balanced law and enforcement could even level out disadvantages stemming from tax legislation, so that clients from distribution countries prefer intermediaries from financial centers.

20

Human Rights Due Diligence as New Policy in Financial Institutions

Rolf H. Weber

INTRODUCTION

In the aftermath of the financial crisis of 2007/08 it has become evident that many elements of the international financial architecture need to be changed or adapted and that human behavior also requires closer scrutiny. Institutional structures alone neither explain nor determine human behavior. At a fundamental level, human beings steer the markets, including the impenetrable financial instruments that were one of the key reasons for the crisis. However, it is also human beings who suffer if the international financial system collapses.

As a consequence, the scope and limit of rule-making and norm setting should be taken into account when it comes to regulating human behavior.[1] The reconceptualizing or rethinking of the global financial regime must enshrine additional elements that are related to ethics, morality and fundamental values common in society. This assessment requires that an interdisciplinary approach extending the traditional law and economics understanding should also be included in this reconceptualization.

In the context of complex financial markets the general assumption is that human behavior can be guided rationally alongside the appropriate structures. But research has shown that human action includes incentives that are hardly explainable with economic charts and figures. People, when operating in the market, consider not only their individual profit maximization but also ethical principles such as fairness or avoiding conflicts.[2]

This contribution has benefited from the support of my research assistant MLaw Letizia Angstmann, University of Zurich.

[1] See also C Kaufmann, *Respecting Human Rights in Investment Banking: A Change in Paradigm*, in: K Wendt (ed.), *Responsible Investment Banking*, Springer, 2015 at 509 and 510.

[2] Ibid., at 509.

Ethical thinking, like legal rules, is focused on the individual, but operates as a social connecting tool at the same time. Ethics enshrines the foundational principles in law, particularly human rights. The corresponding intrinsic material values, which go beyond legal structures, must also be taken into account in the reconceptualization of the international financial architecture.

HUMAN RIGHTS COMPLIANCE AS GLOBAL TREND

Overview

Before the international community became aware of the necessity for a human rights agenda in the financial markets, several supranational efforts to expand the implementation of human rights among multinational enterprises (MNE) had already been established. A major project was the United Nations (UN) Global Compact, which is a policy initiative open to "businesses that are committed to aligning their operations and strategies with ten universally accepted principles in the areas of human rights, labor, environment and anticorruption."[3] Participating companies are meant to submit periodic reports about their compliance with the UN Global Compact. If they decide not to comply with these rules, they will be labeled as "noncommunicating." However, the only consequence of being labelled as "noncommunicating" is the expulsion from the Global Compact after twelve months of being labeled as such. There are no other legal ramifications.

The UN Global Compact was followed more than ten years later by the broader framework of the UN Guiding Principles on Business and Human Rights (UN Guiding Principles), which address state obligations and responsibilities of private actors related to human rights in the business environment. The UN Guiding Principles complement and amend the Global Compact, providing its participants (not only businesses but also states) with guidance as to how to fulfil their commitment to human rights.[4] When the Human Rights Council unanimously adopted the UN Guiding Principles on Business and Human Rights in 2011, it was the first document of its kind, marking a paradigm shift in the collaboration between states and businesses regarding the implementation of human rights. Even though the principles are not legally binding, they mark a change of perspective: the consideration of human rights shall no longer merely be an element of businesses' economic planning, but shall be an important objective in and of itself.[5]

Other international organizations also became active in the field of human rights and business:

---

[3] Overview of the UN Global Compact, available at: www.unglobalcompact.org/AboutTheGC/index.html.

[4] See the UN Guiding Principles and the Global Compact, available at: www.unglobalcompact.org/Issues/human_rights/The_UN_SRSG_and_the_UN_Global_Compact.html.

[5] See Kaufmann, *supra* note 1, at 512 and 513.

- The Organization for Economic Cooperation and Development (OECD) Guidelines for Multinational Enterprises are recommendations addressed to corporations operating in or from adhering countries. The forth part of the Guidelines sets out the parameters for the expected approach of enterprises to the issue of human rights. Additionally, paragraph 36 directly refers to the UN Guiding Principles.[6]
- Important action has also been taken by the International Labor Organization (ILO). The Tripartite Declaration of Principles Concerning Multinational Enterprises and Social Policy, adopted by the Governing Body in 1977 and revised in 2006 refers to the other international developments aiming at the respect of human rights by MNEs.

Financial Institutions in Particular

Compliance with human rights has also become an issue in the financial markets. The following initiatives are noteworthy: The risk management framework of the Equator Principles (EP) can be adopted by financial institutions "for determining, assessing and managing environmental and social risk in projects."[7] The EPs apply globally, to all industry sectors and to four financial products:

- Project finance advisory services;
- Project finance;
- Project-related corporate loans;
- Bridge loans.

The International Finance Corporation (IFC) acknowledges the responsibility of business to respect human rights.[8] The relevant human rights standards in this context are those set out in the International Bill of Human Rights and the eight core conventions of the ILO.[9]

The broadest and in the medium term probably most influential approach is the one chosen by the Thun Group. The Thun Group of Banks is an informal group of bank representatives that have been discussing the meaning of the UN's "Protect, Respect and Remedy Framework" as set out in the Guiding Principles for the activities of financial institutions, particularly banks. The name originates from the location in Switzerland where the group met for two workshops in May 2011 and

---

[6] See www.ilo.org/wcmsp5/groups/public/–ed_emp/–emp_ent/–multi/documents/publication/wcms_094386.pdf.

[7] See Equator Principles, available at: www.equator-principles.com/index.php/about-ep/about-ep.

[8] See paragraph 12 of IFC "Policy on Environmental and Social Sustainability," available at: www.ifc.org/wps/wcm/connect/7540778049a792dcb87efaa8c6a8312a/SP_English_2012.pdf?MOD=AJPERES.

[9] Ibid.

March 2012, but it does not constitute an official body of any kind.[10] In October 2013 the group released a "Discussion Paper for Banks on Implications of Principles 16 – 21" of the UN Guiding Principles.[11]

The Group involves banks that have a genuine interest in gaining a better understanding of the "Framework" and the "Guiding Principles" and in looking for methods by which they can be applied in financial institutions. The discussions of the Thun Group banks were supported by expert input from the University of Zurich Competence Centre for Human Rights, a member of the Swiss Centre of Expertise in Human Rights.[12]

The group states that its work is motivated by the aims of acting responsibly, of acting instead of waiting for legal requirements, and of acting jointly. The purpose is the implementation of a preventively designed framework. The group's banks see respecting human rights as "the right thing to do" and as an integral part of responsible business conduct. All of the contributing banks are committed to respecting human rights in their business actions. According to the Discussion Paper, the motivation for this commitment is twofold: it reflects responsible business practice by reducing related risks and emphasizes the banks' desire to manage their impacts on society responsibly.

The Thun Group, therefore, decided to proactively engage in ongoing debate around the Guiding Principles and their implementation. The participating banks agree that the Guiding Principles need to be realized in a way appropriate for each institution if they are to become operationally effective. At the same time the banks see opportunity in joint thinking on how to tackle this process. The Discussion Paper aims to support financial institutions in general and banks in particular in mapping and analyzing their potential adverse impacts on human rights and related risks for their own operations, including reputational, legal, operational and financial risks.[13]

Other Markets and Regional Initiatives

Other activities include the International Organization for Standardization (ISO), which has released Standards 26000. These provide guidance on how businesses and organizations can operate in a socially responsible way,[14] and the

---

[10] See UN Guiding Principles on Business and Human Rights: Discussion Paper for Banks on Implications of Principles 16–21, The Thun Group of Banks, October 2013, at 3; available at: www.credit-suisse.com/responsibility/doc/thun_group_discussion_paper.pdf. (cited as: Discussion Paper).

[11] Ibid.

[12] Ibid. see also a description at www.skmr.ch/de/publikationen/wirtschaft/thun-group-of-banks-ruggie.html?zur=110.

[13] See Discussion Paper, *supra* note 10, at 3.

[14] See www.iso.org/iso/home/standards/iso26000.htm.

Global Reporting Initiative (GRI), that builds trust, knowledge, and expertise among a diverse set of interests by using a multistakeholder international consultation method.[15]

The European Commission published "A renewed EU strategy 2011–2014 for Corporate Social Responsibility" that clarifies corporate social responsibility (CSR) standards and aims to strengthen its "soft law" nature through the concretization and implementation of the required action plans based on the Ruggie framework.[16] The vague arrangement of the strategy illustrates a general transnational problem: since international legal regulations are often loose and not institutionalized, the decay of sovereignty leads to a lack of standards.

All of these multilevel activities show that human rights compliance is a global trend. However, there are doubts among experts as to whether the current realization of human rights within business has the potential to reform mechanisms within international financial markets.[17] As mentioned, human beings are the center of cause and effect within the financial system. Accordingly, it is essential to address the human aspect when dealing with the question of a new perspective on global finance and its regulation.

POLICY DEVELOPMENTS

Ethics in General

Ethics is about acting morally. Accordingly, ethics addresses principles or rules that state something about good human action.[18]

Doctrine distinguishes three types of ethics:

- Descriptive or empirical ethics describes the multiple appearances of existing morals and customs of individuals, groups, institutions and cultures.
- Normative ethics examines existing attitudes toward morality and frames action-oriented norms.
- Metaethics critically scrutinizes ethical methods and extends them.

---

[15] See www.globalreporting.org/Pages/default.aspx.
[16] See Communication from the Commission to the European Parliament, the Council, the European Economic and Social Committee and the Committee of the Regions, A renewed EU strategy 2011–14 for Corporate Social Responsibility, Brussels, 25.10.2011 COM (2011) 681 final; see also R H Weber, "Corporate social responsibility as new challenge for the IT industry," *Computer Law and Security Review* 28, 2012, at 636 and 637.
[17] See M Dowell-Jones, "Financial Institutions and Human Rights," in: Blecher L, Kaymar Stafford N and Bellamy G C, (eds.), *Corporate Responsibility for Human Rights Impacts: New Expectations and Paradigms*, 2014, at 405.
[18] See for example, R H Weber, "Finanzmarktinstrumente im Dienste ethisch-sozialer Nachhaltigkeitskonzepte," in: AJP (4) 2014, at 513.

The objective for private and public agents, in acting ethically, has to be to display moral commitment as an indispensable basis of a questioning, emancipatory self-understanding that embraces freedom and humanity. Correspondingly, ethics has the following concerns:

- Reflective clarification for those affected by valid moral claims.
- Familiarizing with the critical assessment of practical procedures.
- Encouraging attention to issues of social responsibility and moral competence.

When assessing and determining the quality of actions, situations can arise where different ethical norms can come into conflict (collision) or where they can coexist (pluralism). In such cases, ethics should allow for the formulation of coordination goals and coordination forms.

Ethics is not simply an abstract discipline, its practice requires guidelines and goals. One important manifestation of applied ethics is business ethics, which aims at achieving social justice and the protection of human rights within economic activity. Ethics also fosters a long-term view of business relationships as developed in Confucian thinking.[19]

Consideration of Human Rights in Financial Institutions

Within the field of ethical behavior, human rights represent one aspect of what is considered to be morally correct government conduct vis-à-vis individuals. Recently this scope has been thought to be too narrow, and national and international enterprises are also being made accountable for their human rights impacts, as has been outlined earlier.[20]

The tendency to consider banks and financial sector institutions as subjects of the global human rights regime, particularly through the concept of complicity – that is, by providing funds to MNEs that may be involved in human rights infringements, merits increased attention by the international community.[21] However, the financial services industry operates a host of complex processes with a highly diverse range of products and services.[22] A broad range of individual, institutional and corporate clients use these services, and they cover all industry sectors. To be able to implement human rights across all aspects of banking operations will

---

[19] The Confucian perspectives on the grounds and content of human rights cannot be discussed in this contribution; for further details see J Chan, "A Confucian Perspective on Human rights for Contemporary China," in: Bauer J R and Bell D A, (eds.), *The East Asian Challenge for Human Rights*, 1999.; L Miles and S H Goo, "Corporate Governance in Asian Countries: Has Confucianism Anything to Offer?," in: *Business and Society Rev*, 118, 2013.

[20] See Dowell-Jones, *supra* note 17, passim.

[21] Ibid., at 401–407.

[22] B M Castelo, "Banks and CSR," in: Idowu S E, (ed), *Encyclopedia of Corporate Social Responsibility*, 2013, at 141–148 and 142.

require a comprehensive approach to identifying and managing potential adverse human rights impacts and related risks to the financial institution and rights holders.[23] Financial markets professionals and human rights experts are aware of the difficulty of this endeavor.[24]

There is a common public perception that financial institutions have strong influence, or leverage over their clients' behavior and can, and should, seek to influence client actions to promote good practice. In practice, the degree of leverage is often a great deal less than popularly believed – and the degree to which it is feasible for financial institutions to exert influence on their clients' behavior is a matter of complexity.[25]

It has, however, been argued that financial institutions frequently try to hide behind this so-called "veil of complexity."[26] Arguably, financial transactions have reached a level of complexity today that makes it difficult even for experts to fully comprehend the multilayered structures behind profits and loss in the financial industry. Nevertheless, with regard to the financial and social consequences of the crisis of 2007/08, the banking sector can no longer rely on using complexity as an excuse as there is now no alternative to taking human rights seriously in the financial sector.[27]

National governments are, as the Guiding Principles restate, the primary duty bearers of human rights. Commercial organizations, comprising financial institutions, cannot be expected to become human rights "regulators" as a substitute for government action. Nevertheless, they may find themselves linked to human rights violations committed by their clients, and accordingly have an interest and a responsibility to ensure that their actions and decisions do not harm human rights.[28]

A financial institution may apply international human rights standards wherever possible but if doing so means that its employees in a particular jurisdiction are acting in breach of local law and may be subject to legal revenge, then it may decide to comply with local law and seek alternative means of compliance with acknowledged principles. Avoiding operations in all countries that do not apply international human rights standards would not necessarily be helpful to the advancement of human rights, as engagement and positive example by companies seeking to apply best practice has the potential to encourage change.[29] Nevertheless, a serious approach to human rights issues in the financial industry will should

---

[23] Discussion Paper, *supra* note 10, at 5.
[24] Dowell-Jones, *supra* note 17, at 434 and 441.
[25] Discussion Paper, *supra* note 10, at 5.
[26] Dowell-Jones, *supra* note 17, at 440.
[27] See also P Koslowski, *The Ethics of Banking, Conclusions from the Financial Crisis*, 2012, 8–11.
[28] Discussion Paper, *supra* note 10, at 5.
[29] Ibid.

allow for the possibility of not entering into a financial relationship with a potentially profitable client.[30]

Implementation of a Human Rights Framework

As outlined, financial institutions need to scrutinize (i) how the UN Guiding
Principles can best be applied across all types of products and services provided
to customers; and (ii) what the range and depth of their human rights responsibilities and due diligence requirements should be. This task also encompasses the
assessment of what can reasonably be achieved in terms of their leverage over
clients. Financial institutions should consider assessing the human rights impacts
inherent in a business opportunity and to what extent it is possible to eliminate or
diminish adverse effects.[31]

Awareness Raising and Information Provision

First, there is a need to identify significant internal stakeholders and to understand
the external relations the financial institution maintains that may provide sector
specific information and precedent on human rights issues and practice. These
efforts could include the EP Association, the United Nations Environment
Program (UNEP) Finance Initiative, International Finance Corporation, OECD
Guidelines, independent consultants, and industry trade associations such as the
International Council for Mining and Metals. Other sources may be other banks,
development banks, export credit associations, legal advisors and customers who
may be familiar with dealing with human rights issues.[32] All these participants in
financial markets could fruitfully assist each other in this endeavor by exchanging
information and best practice.

Secondly, from an internal perspective, it is useful to identify and build relationships with departments and managers who may contribute usefully to the management of human rights issues. These may include teams with responsibility for:
credit risk policy, transaction level risk assessment, project finance, investment
banking client relationships, compliance, legal, public policy, corporate responsibility, internal and external communications, among others with similar goals.[33]

It is usually difficult to connect a financial institution's internal processes directly
with human rights abuses. Furthermore, human rights lawyers and activists frequently lack the necessary knowledge of financial services to be able to identify the
relevant mechanism.[34] Accordingly, internal initiatives of financial market actors

---

[30] See also Dowell-Jones, *supra* note 17, at 426 and 442.
[31] Discussion Paper, *supra* note 10, at 5.
[32] Ibid., at 6.
[33] Ibid.
[34] Dowell-Jones, *supra* note 17, at 404.

are a vital part of any possible progress in the area of human rights and financial institutions. It is perhaps easier to train a securities trader in human rights law than a human rights specialist in systemic risks and market dynamics, as well as all possible financial products. Generally, teams have to be established within financial institutions that not only have the necessary knowledge to manage human rights issues, but also have the power to prevent a financial transaction or relationship that has a negative impact on human rights, rather than being limited to intervening in the aftermath of an existing investment that potentially impacts human rights.[35]

Risk Management Model

In implementing a human rights framework, consideration should be given to developing a risk management model that goes beyond traditional parameters in addressing (i.e., identifying, managing and mitigating) human rights risks to external stakeholders. The objective of this model would be to identify and assess potential adverse impacts on rights holders as well as risks to the financial institution itself. Awareness of human rights issues and responsibilities within a financial institution at all levels and across all aspects of operations should be captured within this framework.[36]

As part of this framework, a statement of policy and governance framework must be developed that aims to do the following:[37]

- Express the financial institution's public commitment to respect human rights.[38]
- Generate awareness and understanding throughout the organization of the importance and relevance of human rights issues to business decisions, including the focus on "doing no harm" and the impact on the business and stakeholders of getting it wrong.
- Apply to all parts of the business, including client and other business relationships, transactions, projects, products, operational decisions, strategy and planning.
- Assist the identification of negative human rights impacts.
- Signpost tools and guidance to assist personnel in dealing with issues in their part of the financial institution; these should assist in identifying and assessing human rights-relevant aspects, and include links to any existing policies that already have a human rights dimension.

---

[35] Ibid., at 443.
[36] See Discussion Paper, *supra* note 10, at 5 and 6 for further details.
[37] See Ibid. at 6 for further details.
[38] Which should already be in place in most financial institutions.

- Be embedded in established procedures and proactively communicated through dialogue with employees, clients, business partners, investors, suppliers, and other external stakeholders.
- Establish clear accountabilities and allocation of responsibility, monitoring and reporting requirements and an escalation procedure for evaluating risks or dilemmas as they arise.
- Be subject to regular review, audit and consultation, and sign off via a high-level governance process.

Due Diligence Principles

All financial institutions conduct due diligence and risk assessments on customer relationships, transactions and operational decisions. Furthermore, they usually have processes in place to ensure compliance with the law (including human rights laws), international sanctions, financial crime prevention measures, and other internal and external requirements. The due diligence outlined in the UN Guiding Principles, however, has additional parameters covering potential adverse effects and related risks that may occur in the context of the financial institution's own activities or through the providing of financial products and services to clients. This due diligence is a constant process, not something to be completed once and not reexamined.[39]

A "one size fits all" approach to due diligence will not be feasible across the many relationships, transactions, and operations of a multinational financial institution. Greater due diligence should be conducted whenever significant potential impacts are identified, for example, when considering financing a project in a conflict region, when providing financial services to a sector with strong human rights sensitivities, or when developing financial products associated with exposed client segments.[40] Furthermore, a targeted approach is needed when establishing the composition and sphere of influence of a compliance team. A larger enterprise needs a bigger team, whereas a small or medium-sized financial institution might be able to address all human rights issues with just a small number of people.[41] In general, the size of financial institutions today will necessitate a considerable amount of human rights knowledge paired with financial skills.[42]

The due diligence outlined in the Guiding Principles requires that businesses, including financial institutions, take a wide view of their possible impacts beyond

---

[39] Discussion Paper, *supra* note 10, at 9.
[40] Ibid.
[41] R Bretschger, *Unternehmen und Menschenrechte: Elemente und Potenzial eines informellen Menschenrechtsschutzes*, 2010, at 169.
[42] Dowell-Jones, *supra* note 17, at 442 and 443; J G Ruggie, "Current Developments: Business and Human Rights: The Evolving International Agenda," *American Journal of Int'l Law* 101, 2007, at 839 and 840.

their own commercial or reputational risks. This means looking at transactions, relationships, products, and operational decisions differently to ensure that potential adverse human rights effects on third parties, which may not necessarily have been reviewed previously, are evaluated.[43] This evaluation should be approached from a practical and sensible perspective, considering the significance of the impact and the degree of linkage to the business operation. It will, however, not be possible to evaluate every impact of every business decision regardless of proximity.[44]

Financial institutions do business with many types of clients: from individuals via retail and private banking, to commercial businesses via corporate and investment banking, to investors via asset management activities, combined with a variety of products and services offered to clients. Each category of client and product range has its own risk profile and needs tailored human rights risk management approaches. Human rights due diligence undertaken should be commensurate with the human rights impacts and risks present and should be part of the overall due diligence performed on clients and/or products.[45]

Different transactions and client relationships result in different amounts of information being shared with the financial institution. Accordingly, the relevant information that a financial institution has can vary. Generally, if the financial institution has access to high levels of information from the customer, it will be possible to conduct more comprehensive due diligence. These relationships tend to be those where there is the most leverage and engagement with the customer. If the transaction type requires little information to be shared with the financial institution, there is less scope for leverage; moreover, when a transaction involves little leverage and no ongoing relationship, the ability for engagement with the customer is likely to be very restricted. Leverage is therefore a substantial factor in considering the potential for human rights influence and risk mitigation.[46] Further thought should, however, be given to the idea, that the potential human rights impacts of an investment or transaction could be a deciding factor in whether to engage in a transaction with a client in the first place.

Financial institutions can prioritize the assessment of their potential negative impacts on human rights and related risks by using two criteria: first, the impact on rights holders themselves (severity and number of affected people); and second, the financial institution's degree of connection to these negative impacts. Dedicated attention needs to be paid to groups who are particularly vulnerable to human rights violations in a specific context, even though the financial institution's connection to these violations may be remote. Since decisions need to be taken in real time, a risk-based and prioritized approach to due diligence is vital to ensure

---

[43] See also Ruggie, *supra* note 42, at 839 and 840.
[44] Ibid.
[45] Ibid.
[46] Ibid.

that financial institutions can exert sufficient leverage prior to deal approval. Within these limitations, financial institutions will need to guarantee that any human rights due diligence conducted is effective, efficient, and appropriate to the business in question.[47]

As mentioned, "The issue of leverage is an important aspect in the consideration of human rights impacts."[48] Given the vast number of stakeholders involved in financial business processes, combined with the multitude of suppliers who may contribute to that activity, effectively addressing potential human rights impacts throughout their business activities is indeed complex for financial institutions. For example, in a competitive mass market, the provision of many products and services offers limited opportunity to apply influence on nonfinancial issues. The decision of the institution may in practice be limited to whether or not it should conduct the business. Furthermore, it is not only the institution itself that decides on which investment will be made, but also the owners, that is, shareholders, also have a say in these decisions.[49] The potential capacity to proactively address potential adverse impacts on human rights through client relationships therefore varies, and in practice depends on a number of factors.[50] In addition, though, the possibility to influence the human rights situation is accompanied by the necessity for an institution to comply with requirements of shareholders and customers. The scope of doing this is particularly problematic to communicate when the company concerned is involved in human rights infringements. Financial institutions should, therefore, assess the human rights impacts inherent in a business opportunity and to what extent it is possible to eliminate or reduce adverse effects.[51]

Human Rights Compliance in Specific Fields of Activities

In their Discussion Paper the Thun Group banks issued a possible approach to human rights for financial institutions in different fields of financial activities. Specifically: The Discussion Paper looks at retail and private banking, corporate and investment banking, and asset management. It is the first suggestion for possible forms of implementing a human rights framework in financial institutions of its kind. The following discussion is largely based on that Discussion Paper.

Retail and Private Banking

Retail banking includes consumer credit, leasing and mortgage products for individuals, and cash management and commercial banking services for small

---

[47] Ibid.; see also Kaufmann, *supra* note 1, at 512 and 513.
[48] Discussion Paper, *supra* note 10, at 5.
[49] Discussion Paper, *supra* note 10, at 5.
[50] Kaufmann, *supra* note 1, at 515 and 516.
[51] Kaufmann, *supra* note 1, at 516.

businesses and corporate clients. Private banking includes the provisions of similar services to high net worth individuals. Retail and private banking may raise possible adverse impacts on human rights and connected risks to the financial institution in several ways.

Adverse impacts can arise from a business relationship with a client who is connected to human rights violations or controversies due to a political or governmental function he or she may hold or may have held. These influences may vary in significance depending on (i) the diversity of countries in which retail branches and private banking offices are operated and the quality of their governance infrastructure and (ii) the array of customer segments served.[52]

However, it should be remembered that retail and private banking policies and practices in certain fields, particularly financial inclusion and microfinance, potentially contribute to the realization of human rights, in addition to mitigating risk.

Potential human rights risks in a retail and private banking business may therefore cover a range of issues:[53]

- Association with politically sensitive clients associated with human rights infringements;
- Association with clients who are the owners of companies involved in human rights controversies, or who hold influential directorships in such companies;
- Association with products and/or services that may be associated with human rights controversies;
- Financial institution's own conduct that may have an impact on the human rights of clients (for example, discrimination/exclusion/inappropriate marketing, treatment of vulnerable clients);
- Country-specific risk (operating retail networks in countries where national laws/practices conflict with internationally accepted standards and specific bank policies).

According to the Thun Group in "retail and private banking, human rights due diligence should be based on existing policies and practices covering Anti-Money Laundering (AML) and Politically Exposed Persons (PEP). If the client has been identified as a PEP, a thorough assessment is required into any involvement of the individual in human rights infringements conducted by the political entity for which the client holds or held office. This could range from civil unrest and armed conflict to forced displacement of communities and discrimination against ethnic groups."[54] The Discussion Paper states that policies and practices may already

---

[52] See Discussion Paper, *supra* note 10, at 12.
[53] Ibid., at 12.
[54] Ibid.

address human rights issues or be adapted to include a human rights component, for example, most multinational financial institutions will have[55]

- AML policies and procedures to establish the identity of clients and beneficial owners prior to engaging in business relationships with such persons;
- PEP policies requiring enhanced due diligence in relevant circumstances;
- Antidiscrimination policies;
- New product approval processes (which may be extended to cover human rights implications);
- Financial inclusion policies and activity (basic bank account service/ partnerships with service providers who may reach excluded groups/ microfinance);
- Country risk policies and procedures (which may be extended to cover human rights issues);
- Strategy and planning policies.

Corporate and Investment Banking

Corporate and investment banking offers a wide-ranging choice of products and services to customers, such as corporate loans, merger or acquisition advice, or raising equity or debt capital among investors or through the stock exchange. Correspondingly, different products and offers carry different levels of risk, entail various degrees of leverage, and come with varying levels of information available to the financial institution. When handling corporate and investment banking, financial institutions can encounter human rights issues in a number of ways. For example, by providing financial products and services to companies (private or state-owned) with a challenging human rights track record or that are involved with countries with a similarly questionable human rights situation.[56]

Based on these issues as well as on the type of businesses and operations the financial institution is engaged in, a mapping of the potential adverse impacts on human rights would need to be undertaken to identify the relevant risks. Firstly, the human rights that are at stake have to be identified, and it must be established which of these are most significant. Secondly, it is important to assess in which areas of operations human rights risks are most likely to occur, that is, in which states or for what type of customers or which financial products and services. Thirdly, the significance of these risks has to be established, that is the scope and severity. Lastly, the financial institution has to identify the extent of its leverage

---

[55] Ibid.
[56] Ibid., at 14 for further details.

associated with each of the human rights risks/financial products to facilitate its evaluation of possible mitigation actions and remediation processes.[57]

Based on the results of the human rights risks mapping, financial institutions could evaluate existing procedures and identify potential gaps in addressing identified human rights risks. In a further step, appropriate measures to remedy such gaps would have to be found. The mitigation measures that a financial institution can apply will depend on the type of financial products or services concerned as well as on the extent of the business relationship with the customer.[58]

With regards to country risk, the necessary level of due diligence could be influenced by the location of the assets being financed and by the location of the customer's operations. Furthermore, past and present conflicts in the respective country should be taken into account, as well as the human rights track record of the customer and the relevant jurisdiction. The country risk will be determined by the political structure of the government, the level of government control over the state's security forces, and by levels of poverty and corruption.[59]

With regard to sector-specific risk, the level of due diligence could be influenced by the following factors[60]:

- Human rights risk inherent in particular industries or products;
- Standards and practices predominant in particular industry sectors;
- The application of best practice standards and voluntary codes.

Sector risk will be determined by the potential for products or services to be connected to human rights abuses, the prevailing working environment in the industry, as well as the potential for customer operations to impact on the health, safety, livelihoods or cultural heritage sites of affected communities.[61]

Additionally, the ability of a customer to manage risk is a crucial factor in the risk assessment process. Firstly, it will be important to assess whether the customer can show conformity with the UN Guiding Principles, for example, by the publication of a human rights policy.[62] Secondly, it has to be examined, whether the customer is capable of managing human rights risks. Factors to consider in ensuring a client's capability include the presence of established human rights policies and governance processes, experience in operating in the sector and a solid performance track record.[63]

---

[57] Ibid.
[58] Ibid.
[59] See ibid. for further details.
[60] See ibid., at 14 and 15.
[61] Ibid., at 15.
[62] As for example: include adherence to relevant national and international voluntary standards (such as Voluntary Principles on Security and Human Rights, Kimberley Process, Roundtable on Responsible Palm Oil, Extractive Industry Transparency Initiative); see ibid., at 15, for further details.
[63] See ibid., for further details.

When funding or advising corporate customers it is important to determine the use that the proceeds of a financial product or service will be put to, that is, whether the funds are intended for general corporate purposes or whether they will be used for a particular project. If the customer plans to use the funds for a defined purpose, for example, to buy another company or to develop a specific project such as a new coal mine, the potential human rights impact of these specific investments should be assessed in addition to the company's general management of human rights.[64]

In order to evaluate the effectiveness of the customer's systems and procedures in managing human rights risks, financial institutions may base their analysis both on public disclosures made by the customer, and on a review of external commentary on the company by stakeholders such as regulators, environmental, social and governance (ESG) rating agencies, NGOs, or trade unions. Stakeholder opinion can help the financial institution to identify areas where its customer has been facing problems in managing human rights issues. This will help the financial institution to target its intervention if difficulties with the customer arise concerning human rights.[65]

To ensure that human rights risks are managed effectively, the financial institution should include reference to human rights impacts in its risk assessment policies and processes for related financial products. When considering project finance and advisory roles, policies on social risk, covering human rights, may already be in place – especially if the institution has adopted the Equator Principles. If the financial institution's due diligence identifies significant human rights risks in the project, actions should be agreed with the customer and implemented to manage and mitigate their impact. The scope for this depends, as has been stated previously, on the restrictions of the customer relationship and the leverage and influence the specific product or service involves. In certain circumstances where the risk is significant and cannot, in the financial institution's judgment, be mitigated sufficiently, it may opt not to pursue the business opportunity.[66]

During the life of a project, unforeseen developments may occur that can change the human rights risk profile of the business relation. These developments may be entirely outside of the control of the customer, such as a regime change in one of its countries of operations, or they might be partly or fully controllable, as, for example, when the customer decides to buy another company or is being taken over by another enterprise. The financial institution should ensure that it can be in a position to observe these developments and their impact on the client. Unforeseen events may require a rapid update of impact assessments and action planning, and actions may have to be taken on a case-by-case basis. Accordingly, due diligence should be carried out at the stage of client onboarding as well as on

---

[64] Ibid.
[65] Ibid., at 15 and 16.
[66] Ibid.

a transactional basis. The periodical assessment of corporate client relationships, projects or loans provides a further opportunity to review any human rights issues and associations that may change the risk profile of the relationship.[67]

Asset Management

Asset management refers to all business activities related to the creation and management of investment funds, property or credit portfolios, investments managed on behalf of a customer, as well as other assets held on a financial institution's own account. Ownership rights for these funds lie with the asset management client who often set out strict investment guidelines.[68] However, investment decisions may be taken for the customer by the asset management business within the scope of specific instructions or general portfolio management constraints.[69]

Asset managers may be confronted with human rights issues in several ways, such as[70]

- Investing in businesses (shares, bonds) with a difficult human rights track record or investing in countries with a challenging human rights situation, on behalf of customers
- Establishing and managing funds of companies or states with a difficult human rights track record or a challenging human rights situation
- Establishing and managing funds concerning a topic that could be viewed critically from a human rights perspective (for example, a defense industry fund, a fund focusing on the topic of security)

As part of their investments evaluation and due diligence processes, asset managers should consider including suitable structures, policies, and processes to mitigate the potential human rights risks associated with relevant customers or products. However, the scope to influence a customer might be constrained by the type of investment and by customer or mandate restrictions. Nevertheless, there can be situations where a financial institution may decide not to engage in an investment activity due to an identification of perceived legal or ESG risks.[71]

---

[67] Ibid.

[68] See also J Sandberg, "(Re-)Interpreting Fiduciary Duty to Justify Socially Responsible Investment for Pension funds?" in: *Corporate Governance: An Int'l Rev*, 2013, at 440 and 441.

[69] See Discussion Paper, *supra* note 10, at 17.

[70] Ibid.

[71] See ibid., at 17, for further details. Since 2004 Norway has a so-called Council of Ethics that advises on the ethics of investments as follows: "The role of the Council on Ethics for the Government Pension Fund Global is to provide evaluation on whether or not investment in specified companies is inconsistent with the established ethical guidelines. The Ministry of Finance makes decisions on the exclusion of companies from the Fund's investment universe based on the Council's recommendations." See www.regjeringen.no/en/sub/styrer-rad-utvalg/ethics_council.html?id=434879.

Policies and ownership practices that address ESG issues may already be in place, especially if the financial institution (or its asset management business) is a signatory of the UN Principles for Responsible Investment (UNPRI). Nonetheless, financial institutions should review their policies and ownership practices, including the following[72]:

- Capacity to identify human rights risks in existing due diligence procedures through prudent management of ESG issues both in product development and investment decision processes;
- Consideration of human rights among other ESG issues when exercising ownership rights and actively engaging with management of investee or potential investee entities.

In order to avoid or mitigate association with potential human rights violations, due diligence in asset management procedures should also contain "know your customer (KYC)," country, industry and company/asset factors. The level of due diligence depends on the related circumstances.[73]

To foster implementation of the UN Guiding Principles in its due diligence, an asset management business should[74]:

- Include consideration of ESG research, including human rights aspects;
- Establish specialized teams dedicated to the analysis of ESG concerns;
- Integrate ESG research into sustainable and socially responsible (SRI) and mainstream investment procedures;
- Provide guidance on how to actively engage with companies/assets and on proxy voting;
- Offer guidance for the (potential) exclusion of assets (from investment vehicles);
- Within the scope of its fiduciary duty, draw the customer's attention to potentially material human rights impacts if and when it is asked about investing in companies known for a challenging human rights track record;
- Add considerations on human rights into the KYC process before beginning a business relationship with a customer.

Similar to corporate finance and investment banking, during the life of an investment or a customer relationship the human rights profile or related issues may change. Financial institutions should accordingly develop efficient ways of monitoring such changes. Investments need to be assessed in their entirety including, among other aspects, human rights concerns.[75]

---

[72] Ibid., at 17 and 18.
[73] Ibid.
[74] Ibid.
[75] Ibid., at 18.

Ongoing Monitoring and Surveillance

Senior management support for a human rights implementation project is vital from the outset.[76] "Tone from the top" is important in gaining backing from other parts of the firm, especially when making explicit reference to human rights in a range of policies and integrating a human rights perspective in decisions and processes. Lack of confidence or experience among staff in interpreting the policy can be mitigated by support from senior managers in considering the issues.[77] A competent human rights surveillance team that is equipped with the necessary capacity, could be the key ingredient in enabling other employees to make the desired progress on human rights issues.

Furthermore, as human rights, similar to ethics or business conduct, are a subject that is relevant to all business activities, it is not sufficient to ring-fence a human rights policy in solely one part of the company. To be comprehensive there should be a human rights dimension to every decision making process so that ownership and responsibility is widely spread and awareness may be maintained across the business. Thinking about the issues can then become a part of the culture of a company. The challenge is to establish a consistent awareness of human rights and to build knowledge, experience and confidence among the managers of an institution that fosters the effective implementation of the policy. Training, seminars, and other methods of internal communication are helpful, as well as the sharing of practical experience and precedent that reinforces the learning. Ongoing exchange on human rights issues is important and will help generate feedback that enhances familiarity with the language of human rights.[78]

From an external perspective, a financial institution should aim to establish an appropriate level of transparency on human rights policies, processes, and procedures that it has implemented. The most obvious option for formal human rights reporting is an annual report, a sustainability report or a website. In reporting on human rights the financial institution may use other well-known reporting channels (for example, the Global Reporting Initiative or the UN Global Compact's Communication on Progress). Using such frameworks also helps to ensure that human rights data and information are communicated in a clear, structured manner.[79]

A particular focus of a financial institution's human rights reporting should be its own actions and processes for considering impacts as well as risks associated with the provision of services to its customers. This is certainly a challenge since it is often difficult to report on outcomes that concern the impacts of third party activities because customer-related data belongs to the customer and is subject to

---

[76] Bretschger, *supra* note 41, at 169.
[77] Discussion Paper, *supra* note 10, at 7.
[78] Ibid.
[79] Ibid., at 19.

the usual rules of confidentiality. A financial institution could, therefore, choose to encourage customers to reveal their relevant human rights-related issues in their own reporting processes.[80]

In addition to its annual reporting a financial institution should also make use of other communication channels to ensure a flow of relevant human rights-related information to stakeholders. In contrast to reporting, which is usually a "one-way" communication, conducting a dialogue with stakeholder groups on the topic of human rights will allow the financial institution to draw directly upon their feedback on relevant issues. Interacting with its employees is also important to maintaining awareness and commitment to applying consistent standards of human rights due diligence.[81]

OUTLOOK

The Thun Group has recognized that the current development of CSR implies that businesses from all industries, including financial institutions, are liable for their implementation of human rights.[82] Its guidance focuses on the consequences for banks of UN Guiding Principles 16–21, which cover the corporate responsibility to respect human rights in the areas of policy development and commitment, due diligence in terms of scope, accountability and implementation, as well as tracking and reporting. These principles are regarded as those that are most relevant to financial institutions' potential adverse impacts on human rights and that tend to be challenging in their implementation. However, in doing so the Thun Group Discussion Paper openly admits that it does not focus on the general effects the banking industry has on society.[83] It is obvious therefore that the Group is aware of the still unresolved problems within the tense relationship between financial institutions and human rights.

Need for More Standardization or Even Harmonization

To make further progress in the area of financial institutions and human rights, it is important that an initiative like the Thun Group of Banks is complimented by other work. The question, however, arises as to whether enforceable law should be introduced to ensure an international development toward the inclusion of human rights in financial institutions.

The Thun Group's Discussion Paper is, undoubtedly, a new approach chosen by financial institutions to promote the implementation of human rights.

---

[80] Ibid.
[81] Th Müller, *Compliance-Management, Dargestellt am Beispiel der Versicherungswirtschaft,* 2007, at 84.
[82] For further details see Kaufmann, *supra* note 1, at 517–523.
[83] Discussion Paper, *supra* note 10, at 3.

Nevertheless, it is questionable what the compilation of well-intended lists of sectoral guidance alone will achieve from a long-term perspective.

The main goal should be to ensure the observance of commonly acknowledged standards.[84] The achievement of this is encouraged through building on existing informal control mechanisms such as reputational, governmental and private incentive structures, self-regulation, soft law initiatives, and occasional binding obligation at the national level.[85] Through the processes of standardization and harmonization of industry practice, the strength of these instruments could be enhanced.

Nonetheless, such informal standards as such do not have a status a source of law in the traditional sense as they are of a nonbinding, recommendatory nature. Most standards will qualify as so-called soft law, lacking a legitimate authority for adoption and enforcement but nevertheless providing a concrete benchmark for the behavior of market participants. However, if incorporated into binding law, such standards can gain legal force[86]. Even in the form of soft law, though, international financial standards can have a substantial influence on the behavior of financial intermediaries, for example, if noncompliance with a specific standard can lead to liability.[87]

Standardization of international financial services constitutes an important element in the process of regulating international financial markets. Since standards efficiently remove market access barriers, they are also open to harmonization procedures and are often introduced in the course of the liberalization of financial services in order to prevent forum shopping and to better review financial activities.[88] With the increasing globalization of markets, international standardization is important not only to provide a level playing field for national and foreign financial services firms but also to ensure that important financial services meet internationally recognized levels of performance and safety[89].

Harmonization, which is different to the process of standardization, implies the process of unification of law, which often follows a previous approach of standardization. Harmonization should not therefore be seen as contrasted with

---

[84] Bretschger, *supra* note 41, at 184.

[85] Ibid., at 185–190 for more details; see also R H Weber, *Mapping and Structuring International Financial Regulation – A Theoretical Approach*, EBLR, 2009, at 657. (cited as: Mapping and Structuring)

[86] R H Weber, "Corporate Social Responsibility as Gap-Filling Instrument?," in: Newell A P, (ed.), *Corporate Social Responsibility, Challenges, Benefits and Impact on Business Performance*, 2014, at 90.

[87] See R H Weber, "Overcoming the Hard Law/Soft Law Dichotomy in Times of (Financial) Crises," in: *Journal of Governance and Regulation*, 2012, 8–14, for further details.

[88] Weber, *Mapping and Structuring*, *supra* note 85, at 661.

[89] See ISO/IEC, "About Standardization and Conformity Assessment – International Standardization," available at: www.standardsinfo.net/info/livelink/fetch/2000/148478/6301438/aboutstd .html.

standardization but rather as a further step in the direction of legal convergence.[90] An advantage of harmonization is that it does not necessarily mandate the type of national law being harmonized, for example, the resolution of a conflict of interest through contract law or corporate law, or through the application of supervisory or criminal law. The choice must be made on the basis of a cost-benefit analysis of the different forms of regulations in order to determine which regulatory technique is best suited for which type of financial service, and which type of domestic regulation will be the most effective for large-scale application. From the perspective of consumers and investors, harmonized international rules in the financial sector are usually preferred to diverging national laws as they foster legal certainty and may reduce transaction costs for international investments.[91] For the time being it might be premature to harmonize ethical standards in banking, however, this objective should be kept in mind in the medium term.

Need for Clear Timelines

In the context of standardization and harmonization it is therefore important to note that while globalization may have many drawbacks, it also facilitates a gradual process of international expansion of informal human rights protection. Nevertheless, the road ahead is still long. Accordingly, it would be unfortunate if the opportunity presented by the UN Guiding Principles on Business and Human Rights, as well as the Thun Group of Banks Discussion Paper would be lost "because the current acquis may become synonymous with compliance with"[92] human rights principles in the financial sector.

Looking at the development of the implementation of human rights standards in economic conduct from the 1970s until the 2000s, it is evident that several attempts within the UN to draft binding human rights obligations for transnational corporations failed to gain the necessary endorsement. In 2011, however, as outlined earlier, after a long process within the UN, in the final phase of his mandate, Professor Ruggie proposed a set of Guiding Principles on Business and Human Rights offering high level guidance on implementing the Principles' 'Protect, Respect and Remedy' Framework. These were endorsed by the Human Rights Council and received widespread support from governments, business and civil society.[93]

Since then, a Working Group on the issue of human rights and transnational corporations and other business enterprises has been appointed by the UN to maintain oversight of the implementation of the Principles. This comprises five

---

[90] Weber, *Mapping and Structuring, supra* note 85, at 658 and 659.
[91] See generally, E Carbonara and F Parisi, "The Paradox of Legal Harmonization," *Pub. Choice* 132, 2007, at 367.
[92] Dowell-Jones, *supra* note 17, at 433.
[93] Discussion Paper, *supra* note 10, at 21.

independent experts from different geographies for a three-year term. They will oversee an annual two-day forum on business and human rights. In January 2012 the Working Group held its first session to determine its key priorities, establish a program of activities, and review suggestions submitted by interested parties. Since December 2012, the Working Group has held an annual Forum on Business and Human Rights at the United Nations in Geneva where stakeholders discuss progress and challenges in the implementation of the Guiding Principles.[94]

The work on this new human rights framework is in full play. International developments and standardization take time and are of necessity complex processes. Nevertheless, there is no real doubt that after the crisis there has to be significant international movement toward a broader understanding of human rights in the financial sector; and toward a more general application of newly founded processes within banks and other financial institutions that are deemed useful to promote the protection of human rights issues concerning people's savings, pensions, houses and other essentials.[95] A general perception among financial sector participants that there is still a lot of work to be done is, therefore, vital.

---

[94] Ibid.
[95] See also Dowell-Jones, *supra* note 17, at 411–414, 428 and 429, 431–434.

21

Reconceptualizing the Role of Standards in Supporting Financial Regulation

William Blair

The backdrop of this discussion is well known, and it unnecessary to add anything about the causes of the global financial crisis. Attention has tended to focus on events in New York in September 2008, but is worth recollecting the simultaneous events in London. In October 2008, the UK Government effectively nationalized three of the country's biggest banks, including Royal Bank of Scotland, one of the world's largest at the time, which otherwise would have failed.

Not surprisingly, there has been a profound debate on how this could have happened in a country with a long financial tradition. A particular focus in the United Kingdom has been on standards in the industry. A Parliamentary Commission on Banking Standards was established in July 2012 in the wake of the problems with London Interbank Offered Rate (LIBOR) to conduct an inquiry into professional standards and culture in the UK banking sector. It issued its final report in June 2013[1] making recommendations (to quote the Government response of July 2013[2]) "around sanctions, standards and remuneration in order to strengthen accountability and incentives for bankers to behave ethically and in a way that supports the long term sustainability of banks."

This paper is a revised version of a paper given at International legal symposium in the honor of the 50th anniversary of The Marianne and Marcus Wallenberg Foundation, which was published in the Stockholm Centre for Commercial Law publication, number 22 "Functional or dysfunctional – the law as a cure? Risks and liability in the financial markets." The author thanks the organizers and publishers for their permission to include in the current volume.

[1] Banking Commission Publishes Report on Changing Banking for Good, Report of the Parliamentary Commission on Banking Standards, 19 June 2013, UK Parliament, www.parliament.uk/business/committees/committees-a-z/joint-select/professional-standards-in-the-banking-industry/news/changing-banking-for-good-report.

[2] HM Treasury and Department for Business, Innovation and Skills, "The Government's Response to the Parliamentary Commission on Banking Standards," July 2013, www.gov.uk/government/uploads/system/uploads/attachment_data/file/211047/gov_response_to_the_parliamentary_commission_on_banking_standards.pdf.

Following the report, the UK banking industry set up the Banking Standards Review chaired by Sir Richard Lambert, which reported in May 2014.[3] This recommended the establishment of a Banking Standards Review Council setting standards of good practice in the industry. Later that month this received the backing of the Bank of England, in a speech by the Governor explicitly endorsing the role of ethics in finance, and saying that through a range of measures (including codes that are "seeking to re-establish finance as a true profession, with broader societal obligations") "finance can help to deliver a more trustworthy, inclusive capitalism – one which embeds a sense of the systemic and in which individual virtue and collective prosperity can flourish."[4]

This is a new way of speaking about finance, and these issues remain subject to debate, and differing views are held. But there is a growing acceptance that standards of a nonlegally binding nature have an important part to play, and that the culture of a financial business is something in which society has a legitimate interest. This in turn has sparked debate on the relationship between law (principally but not solely in the form of financial regulation) and broader ethical principles. These issues are international in nature, since in most if not all parts of the world, finance plays a significant role, and financial systems are axiomatically interconnected.

It is not just, of course, in the United Kingdom that there is serious concern about how standards in the banking industry operated in the run up to the crisis. Whether such concern is justified, and the extent to which it was a cause of the crisis, is not an issue which is discussed further. The question is how best to address the standards issue. It is well worth exploring alternatives to traditional methods of financial regulation that may be capable of achieving international consensus.

There is an initial question to be answered. Is it not enough to obey the law? If standards need changing, the law can be changed. Why should financial institutions aspire to meet some further indefinite moral standards? In a well-known passage in his book *Capitalism and Freedom*, Milton Friedman called the doctrine of social responsibility "fundamentally subversive" in a free society, and said that in such a society, "there is one and only one social responsibility of business – to use its resources and engage in activities designed to increase its profits so long as it stays within the rules of the game, which is to say, engages in open and free competition without deception or fraud."[5]

However, so far as this implied that "staying within the rules of the game" excluded any wider ethical responsibility, that view was controversial at the time,

---

[3] Richard Lambert, "Banking Standards Review," 19 May 2014, *Banking Standards Review*, www.bankingstandardsreview.org.uk/assets/docs/may2014report.pdf.

[4] Mark Carney, *Inclusive Capitalism: Creating a Sense of the Systemic*, Bank of England, Speech given at the Conference on Inclusive Capitalism, London, 27 May 2014, page 10, available at www.bankofengland.co.uk/publications/Documents/speeches/2014/speech731.pdf.

[5] Milton Friedman, *Capitalism and Freedom* (University of Chicago Press, 1962, p.133).

and has not won the day. Further, it is no longer the case (if it ever was) that the law requires directors to act narrowly in maximizing shareholder value by increasing corporate profits. For example, the UK Companies Act 2006 now explicitly includes in the director's statutory duty an obligation to promote the success of the company and a duty to have regard to "the impact of the company's operations on the community and the environment" (s.172(1)(d)). Such formulations are sometimes called "enlightened shareholder value."[6]

What is significant in the present context is that senior management of financial institutions internationally are themselves arguing for higher standards. A sound business case can be made out for encouraging what may be called an ethical approach to the conduct of banking business. The term "ethics" is now widely used by financial institutions and their leaders, and it is suggested rightly so. As used in the context of culture, it connotes shared standards of appropriate behavior that are not in the form of legal rules.

On the other hand, there is an important question as to how effective these statements of intent really are. That is not to call into question their sincerity. But in the highly competitive business of finance, particularly perhaps international finance, an avowed commitment to higher standards may mean little in itself without something to back it up.

For example, many financial institutions have for some time had codes of conduct that attempt to enshrine these standards. This is a development to be welcomed. On the other hand, these codes are not universal, their effectiveness is as yet unproven, and ethical principles are not easy to calibrate in a competitive market context. There is also a fundamental issue: are these codes to be treated as purely exhortatory in nature, or do they require something else to give them traction?

THE LAW AS A CURE?

The response to the financial crisis has principally been to address perceived shortcomings in financial regulation with a view to avoiding the kind of systemic risk which necessitated public intervention in 2008. In other words, the law in the form of financial regulations is seen as the principal means to avoid recurrence. One view is that this is a sufficient response, and that codes of ethics and the like belong in the realm of the purely voluntary.

The law is clearly central. Law has always played a role in regulating financial activity. But whilst its principal purpose has been to prescribe the enforcement of financial transactions, it has also traditionally sought to alleviate the effect of such transactions. This can be traced right back: the laws of Babylon recognized loans and pledges, but also recognized that relief for the debtor was needed

---

[6]   Kershaw, *Company Law in Context*, 2nd ed, OUP, 2012, p. 382.

in some cases.[7] Thereafter, a vast corpus of such rules developed, enforcing the loan contract between debtor and creditor, but also alleviating its effects, in the case of usury for example, and abusive practices by creditors of various kinds. Some remain significant in finance to this day, including doctrines such as relief against forfeiture, which apply in commercial transactions as well as in personal transactions in which they were first devised.[8]

Such rules developed over long periods of time, and primarily have to do with protecting individual debtors. A feature of contemporary financial regulation, which is much more recent in origin,[9] is that it has to do with promoting the interests of society in general.

Noone argues that the changes that are in train in relation to financial regulation can be expected to avoid financial crises arising in the future,[10] but the reform process is nevertheless essential. At a time of globalization and complexity in finance, the system is being made more robust in important ways.

Equally, it has to be recognized that there are limits as to what further regulation can achieve. Two examples will be given from prudential regulation and conduct of business respectively.

As regards capital adequacy, the reform of the Basel rules has been a necessary adjunct to strengthening financial institutions. But defining let alone measuring capital is a complex and inexact exercise, a point made by Andrew Haldane of the Bank of England.[11] As the European Banking Authority, whose objective is to provide a single set of harmonized prudential rules for financial institutions throughout the EU, puts it, "significant implementation challenges remain ahead."[12]

Further, it must not be forgotten that the global financial crisis affected different parts of the world in different ways, leading to concerns about the regional effects of the new rules. It has been said that

---

[7] For example, §48 of Hammurabi's Code excused a debtor of the obligation to pay interest for a year in which his fields were flooded by storms: see G.R. Driver and John C. Miles, *The Babylonian Laws*, Oxford, Clarendon Press, vols I and II, 1952 and 1955.

[8] Such as that in *Cukurova Finance International Ltd v Alfa Telecom Turkey Ltd* [2013] UKPC 20, concerning the enforcement of a pledge of shares in a mobile phone company with a view to the lender gaining control of the company rather than repayment of the loan.

[9] The United Kingdom did not have a formal statutory regime governing banking until 1979, when the Banking Act was enacted to implement the First Banking Directive of what was then the European Economic Community. It may be noted that the primary objective of European legislation at that time was to encourage a single market in banking services.

[10] In *Manias, Panics, and Crashes: A History of Financial Crises*, Palgrave Macmillan, 5th edition (with Robert Aliber), Charles Kindleberger writing in 2005 lists his "top ten" financial bubbles, beginning with the unlikely Dutch tulip bubble of 1636–7. The crisis of 2007–8 would certainly make it into any list of the top ten, probably right at the top.

[11] Andrew G Haldane, "The Dog and the Frisbee," (presented at Federal Reserve Bank of Kansas City's 6th Economic Policy Symposium: *The Changing Policy Landscape*, Wyoming), 31 August 2012, p. 10.

[12] *Risk Assessment of the European Banking System*, European Banking Authority, July 2013, p. 4.

Asian economies were largely unaffected by the direct financial impacts of the crisis, since they held relatively little in the way of toxic financial assets, generally had less "sophisticated" financial systems and stricter regulation, and had strong balance sheets, in no little part in response to the trials of the Asian financial crisis a decade earlier. Also, supervision and regulation were more interventionist in those economies. . . .There have been persistent concerns that the G20-sponsored new financial regulations could have potentially negative impacts on the growth prospects of emerging economies, including those in Asia.[13]

What is true of systemic regulation is also true of conduct of business rules. Taking the example of disclosure,[14] whilst disclosure may be necessary, it is often not sufficient. This is due to the complexity of modern financial markets. It has been said that accurately valuing even a single collateralized debt obligation (CDO), for example, demands a multifaceted analysis of an enormous volume of legal and financial data. The information costs associated with valuing a portfolio of these instruments are orders of magnitude higher. Viewed from this perspective, what matters is not just the *availability* of information in a strictly technical sense, but also the amount and complexity of this information and, consequently, the human capital and other endowments necessary to *process* it in any meaningful way.[15]

Finally, there is the problem of complexity in financial regulation itself. This problem has been recognized for a long time, and was an early driver of attempts to move toward principle-based regulation. It is difficult to deal with, and with the torrent of rule-making since the crash, has become more so.[16] In Philip Wood's phrase, "The law has power. But the law can also be another bubble."[17] There will come a time when the volume of financial regulation becomes counterproductive. In any case, apart from inevitable issues as to interpretation and application, regulatory perimeters will always be susceptible to arbitrage.

Private law is open to the same limitations. The courts of London and New York tend to take a caveat emptor attitude to the sale of complex derivatives products. In particular, standard terms disadvantageous to the user may be given full effect.

---

[13] Asian Development Bank Institute, Working Paper Series, *An Asian Perspective on Global Financial Reforms*, Peter J. Morgan and Victor Pontines, No. 433, August 2013, p.3.

[14] For a good discussion in the context of derivatives, see *Federal Register*, Vol. 77, No. 33, February 17, 2012, Commodity Futures Trading Commission, Business Conduct Standards for Swap Dealers and Major Swap Participants.

[15] Dan Awrey, William Blair, and David Kershaw, *Between Law and Markets: Is There a Role for Culture and Ethics in Financial Regulation?* 38 DEL. J. CORP. L, 191 (2013), at 200–201. We say there that ultimately it is the asymmetrical distribution of these endowments which renders disclosure, in and of itself, a relatively ineffective strategy for addressing opportunism within the context of bilateral counterparty relationships.

[16] The effects are tangible. Barclays Bank had approximately 1,500 compliance staff in 2012, up from 600 in 2008 ("An Independent Review of Barclays' Business Practices," *Salz Review*, April 2013, para 3.13).

[17] Phillip Wood, "Can the law prevent another financial crisis?," Allen and Overy, 17 December 2008, www.allenovery.com/publications/en-gb/Pages/Can-the-law-prevent-another-financial-crisis-.aspx.

Where there is no real parity between seller and buyer the result may be that lawful selling is seen as inequitable in a wider sense, with an attendant loss of trust.

THE IMPORTANCE OF AN ETHICAL CULTURE

These well-understood limits of the law mean that it is important to encourage an appropriate corporate culture to support the legal framework. This has been long recognized by regulators. As Richard Breeden, a former SEC chairman put it in a remark that has often been quoted, "It is not an adequate ethical standard to aspire to get through the day without being indicted."[18]

The importance of values has also been advocated at the top of the banking industry,[19] and the financial crisis has made it manifest. There is a growing literature on the subject of ethics specifically in the context of financial services.

Governor Subbarao of the Reserve Bank of India outlined the dilemma that arises when compliance with the law leads to results which are unacceptable in a broader ethical sense:

> At one level, it is possible to argue that nobody in the entire chain did anything legally wrong. But that is too simplistic an argument. We do not govern our behaviour simply by what is allowed by law or regulation. Our code of conduct should be held to a stricter test. Was the behaviour of actors across the chain of the financial sector fair, ethical and moral or was it swayed by the opportunity of making quick profits afforded by information asymmetries? Were sub-prime borrowers adequately warned that there is a good chance that asset prices would fall? Did investment advisers tell their clients of the risk they were taking in buying MBAs and CDOs? Did credit rating agencies not compromise their standards and cut corners? In sum, were professionals in the financial sector legally right, but only legally right and morally wrong?[20]

Financial institutions have had to react to these sentiments, and this has been very pronounced in the United Kingdom. The case of Barclays Bank (whose Chairman and Chief Executive resigned following the bank's LIBOR settlement with regulators) may show what went wrong, but it also shows the efforts that have been made at redress. In January 2013, the new CEO announced five values that the bank will seek to embed throughout the bank. These are respect, integrity, service,

---

[18] K V Salwen, "SEC Chief's Criticism of Ex-Managers of Salomon Suggests Civil Action is Likely," *Wall Street Journal*, Nov 20, A10.

[19] See for example, Stephen Green (former Group Chairman of HSBC) in *Good Value: Reflections on Money, Morality and an Uncertain World* (Allen Lane, London, 2009): "Everyone knows about the importance of truth and honesty for a sustainable business."

[20] Address at a Conference on "Ethics and the World of Finance" organized by Sri Sathya Sai University, Andhra Pradesh, on August 28, 2009. MBA in this quotation stands for "mortgaged backed-asset."

excellence, and stewardship. By "integrity" is meant that the bank should "act fairly, ethically and openly in all we do."[21]

It would be shortsighted to dismiss this kind of action as window dressing forced on the institution by scandal. These changes are seen as essential to the future of a business that is among the top twenty world banks.[22] This approach, it is suggested, is to be encouraged, because it is good for banking as a business, and good for society as a whole.

Barclays also commissioned an independent review of its business practices and culture, which reported in April 2013. The review made a number of recommendations as to the bank's culture and business model.[23] It is a theme of the review that legal rules need to be supplemented by a clear set of values that are understood through discussion and application, and that develop into a culture that tends to ensure good rather than bad behaviors.[24]

This cultural change is seen not only as part of proper business practice, but as an essential aspect of effective regulation:

> Regulators need healthy bank cultures to enable them to do their work effectively. They can never have sufficient resources to monitor every bit of the banks' work, so culture is the crux to ensuring that organisations comply not just with the law but with the spirit too. Markets rely on rules and laws, but those rules and laws in turn depend on truth and trust. Better cultures should require less regulation, fewer laws and fewer regulators.[25]

PRINCIPLES AND CODES

So we need more than just regulation. But what do we need? How can better standards be defined? Can they ever be underpinned by some form of sanction, other than reputational? These are not new questions. There have been various statements of principle, before and after the crisis. In 2004, the respected central banker Eddie George drafted succinct Principles for Good Business Conduct of international financial services providers. These principles say that compliance with rules must be "underpinned by behaviour that is rooted in trust, honesty and integrity."[26]

---

[21] Barclays Strategic Review, *Barclays PLC: Becoming the Go-To Bank*, Barclays, (12 February 2013), www.barclays.com/content/dam/barclayspublic/docs/InvestorRelations/IRNewsPresen tations/2012News/antony-jenkins-presentation-to-investors-12-february-2012.pdf.

[22] As ranked by The Banker in 2013.

[23] Led by Sir Anthony Salz, Executive Vice-Chairman of Rothschild, and former senior partner of Freshfields Bruckhaus Deringer, "An Independent Review of Barclays' Business Practices," *Salz Review*, April 2013, http://online.wsj.com/public/resources/documents/SalzRe view04032013.pdf.

[24] Ibid at 3.14.

[25] Ibid, Appendix B.

[26] John Thirwell, *The Worshipful Company of International Bankers*, p. 19, http://international bankers.org.uk/wp-content/uploads/2014/07/company-history.pdf.

In the wake of the crisis, the *Principles for Enhancing Corporate Governance* set out by the Basel Committee on Banking Supervision (BCBS *Principles*) in 2010 stated that a demonstrated corporate culture that supports and provides appropriate norms and incentives for professional and responsible behavior is an essential foundation of good governance.[27]

The BCBS *Principles* also make clear that a bank is expected to have in place a code of conduct, or comparable policy document. Such code or policy should "articulate acceptable and unacceptable behaviours." It "...should also discourage the taking of excessive risks as defined by internal corporate policy."[28]

What is the evidence that these principles have been acted on? In November 2012, the Financial Stability Board published an updated list of twenty-eight global systemically important banks (G-SIBs), using a methodology developed by the BCBS. Preliminary research suggests ethics have assumed greater visibility since 2008. The approach differs from country to country, with U.S. banks in particular having codes of ethics linked to codes of conduct. In other countries, ethical issues appear to be dealt with in the context of employee conduct and/or corporate responsibility.

Taken from their websites, the position as regards the top ten banks in The Banker's Top 1000 World Banks ranking published on 1 July 2013 can be expressed in tabular form[29]:

On the face of it, this table shows compliance particularly by U.S. banks, but a considerable lacuna as regards banks in China. However that may not present the full picture for China. It is thought that the introduction of a wide corporate social responsibility (CSR) provision into China's *Companies Law 2006* has had a significant impact in relation to professional ethical standards in the financial services industry. Article 5 provides that "[w]hen undertaking business operations, a company shall comply with the laws and administrative regulations, social morality and business morality. It shall act in good faith, accept the supervision of the government and the general public, and bear social responsibilities..."[30]

In general, it seems that ethical requirements of the kind under discussion have been built into professional conduct rules in three tiers.[31] The first is at

---

[27] Basel Committee on Banking Supervision, *Principles for Enhancing Corporate Governance*, Bank for International Settlements, October 2010, p. 8, www.bis.org/publ/bcbs176.pdf.

[28] At [26–27], and at [92]: "Sound corporate governance is evidenced, among other things, by a culture where senior management and staff are expected and encouraged to identify risk issues as opposed to relying on the internal audit or risk management functions to identify them. This expectation is conveyed not only through bank policies and procedures, but also through the 'tone at the top' established by the board and senior management."

[29] I am indebted to Roland Susman of the Financial Markets Law Committee and Juan Pablo Puerto Reyes of the Centre for Commercial Law Studies for undertaking this research.

[30] See further William Blair, *CSR in Finance: the Development of International Norms*, published in *Studies on Corporate Social Responsibility*, ed Jianbo Lou, Peking University Press, Beijing 2009, pp. 559–566.

[31] I am indebted to Dr. Bo Xie of Dundee University and Zhao Yang of White and Case for these observations.

BANK	COUNTRY	ETHICAL CODE/CODE OF CONDUCT
1. *Industrial and Commercial Bank of China (ICBC)*	China	Annual CSR report: Chairman's 2012 statement mentions building a Code of Ethics
2. *JP Morgan Chase & Co.*	U.S.A.	Code of Ethics supplements the Code of Conduct (latest version June 2013)
3. *Bank of America*	U.S.A.	Code of Ethics has 11 key themes (including "We act ethically"): the Code was amended 25 April 2013
4. *HSBC Holdings*	United Kingdom	Among other Codes, Business Principles and Values, there is a Code of Ethics applying to Senior Financial Officers
5. *China Construction Bank Corporation*	China	Annual CSR report
6. *Citigroup*	U.S.A.	Code of Ethics for financial professionals April 2012 supplements 2011 Code of Conduct
7. *Mitsubishi UFJ Financial Group*	Japan	Principles of Ethics and Conduct
8. *Wells Fargo & Co*	U.S.A.	2012 Code of Ethics and Business Conduct
9. *Bank of China*	China	Annual CSR report
10. *Agricultural Bank of China*	China	Annual CSR report (core values underlying integrity, sound operations)

the watchdog level through the China Banking Regulatory Commission. The Commission issued *Guidance on Professional Conduct for Staff of Banking and Financial Institutions* in 2009. The second is at the industry association level, in that the China Banking Association issued *Guidance on Professional Conduct for Staff of Banking and Financial Institutions* in 2007. The third is at the institutional level, in that the major banks have produced their own sets of employee codes of professional conduct, codes of compliance requirements, etc. It seems that the principles and rules set out in these documents are similar to those in other international banks.

There are two other points. The first is that CSR of the kind now embraced by major financial institutions covers wider ground than what is usually regarded as ethics in business, but it can be seen as part of the same picture.[32] The other is that a good business culture is not only about client service. As Governor Carney put it, "... new codes are seeking to re-establish finance as a true profession, with broader societal obligations."

HOW TO GIVE EFFECT TO THESE VALUES?

The advantage of a voluntary approach as set out in codes of this kind is that it has the potential of encouraging good business practices without the disadvantage of

[32] Shuguang Wang, *Financial Ethics* (Peking University Press) 2011

further regulation, and without detracting from necessary competition and innovation. On the debit side, since it is voluntary, it may become a paper exercise. A fair criticism of the approach advocated in this paper is that without sanctions, there is no substance.

What can we do therefore to make these standards and values real? The standards themselves are vital as a first step but they are not good enough as an end point. One answer is demonstrated by the general opprobrium heaped on some financial institutions in the wake of the crisis, which already been mentioned. There is a price to pay for behavior perceived as unethical in reputation terms. Reputational sanctions may be real.

On the other hand, as the crisis recedes, and finance revives, there can be no guarantee that this will continue. One reason that precrisis behavioral lapses were not treated with the attention they deserved was that overall, the financial system was seen as working well, with markets such as the derivative markets seen as distributing risk. So it is important to find a solid basis for implementation. Emerging from current practice there are a number of concrete means to provide support for a more ethical culture.

There are practical steps that can be taken within institutions, some of which are already in place. U.S. banks typically have ethics "hot-lines" that can give the caller anonymity.

The Salz Review commissioned by Barclays Bank (see previous section) makes a number of recommendations. These include learning programmes for staff, targets against which to assess progress on embedding the values necessary to build a strong ethical culture, regular updates to the code, and annual attestation by employees as to their compliance with the code. The review recommends that in all recruiting, but particularly for senior managers, the bank should look beyond a candidate's financial performance and include an assessment of their fit with its values and culture.

There may also be merit in having a board-level ethics committee, perhaps with a broader CSR remit, as is already in place in a number of institutions.

As regards remuneration, the UK FSA's Remuneration Code requires that "nonfinancial performance metrics form a significant part of the performance assessment process."[33] The identified nonfinancial risk metrics include "risk management and compliance with the regulatory system."[34] Some financial institutions have voluntarily gone further than this. Morgan Stanley, for example, has recently altered the provisions in senior banker remuneration to enable claw-backs where, inter alia, there are violations of the firm's ethical standards.[35]

Another approach is to involve regulators by focusing on the two areas of behavior within the banking industry that have come in for particular adverse comment since the crisis. One has to do with the unfair treatment of counterparties

---

[33] Remuneration Code, SYSC 19A.3.37.
[34] Ibid.
[35] Morgan Stanley, Schedule 14A: Proxy Statement Pursuant to Section 14(a) of the Securities Exchange Act of 1934, at 28–29 (Apr. 5, 2012).

in financial transactions, whether based on information asymmetries, or otherwise; and the other has to do with socially excessive risk taking.

In these respects at least, there is a case for financial regulators to engage with banks' internal systems and processes, not with a view to prescribing the content of codes of ethics, and certainly not adding a further layer of rules and regulations, but with a view to monitoring how ethical considerations are carried forward within organizations.[36] This approach would allow bodies to develop their own solutions, the regulator concerning itself with broad objectives and the adequacy of the processes in place to achieve them. Such an approach was suggested by the present author and others in a recent article.[37]

In financial transactions, such objectives could include a commitment to treat counterparties fairly, and as sophisticated as well as retail customers. This would involve fair disclosure of relevant information about products and refraining from marketing products that even sophisticated market participants would be unlikely to understand and price accurately. Such nonbinding objectives go well beyond what is required by the law.

As regards risk taking, the emphasis would be on taking externalities seriously, that is, paying regard to the adverse effects of particular activities on particular institutions and more generally on society. The objective would be to foster a culture in which systemic risk taking is identified and avoided, and better understanding the consequences.

Further proposals were published in May 2014 as regards setting up a UK Banking Standards Review Council (BSRC).[38] Its objective will be to contribute to a continuous improvement in the behavior and competence of all banks (and building societies) doing business in the United Kingdom. It will do this by the following:

- Requiring participating banks to commit to a programme of improvement under the headings of culture, competence, and customer outcomes.
- Setting standards of good practice, for example, whistleblowing protocols, the approach to retail sales incentives, processes for handling small businesses in distress, and the management of high-frequency trading.
- Publishing an annual report.
- Meeting annually with nonexecutive directors to discuss the institution's progress relative to the previous year and to its peers.
- Working with the industry and its stakeholders to develop a single principles-based code of practice in alignment with the high-level principles now being considered by the regulators.

---

[36] In a different context see Julia Black, *Rules and Regulators* (Clarendon Press, 1997).
[37] Awrey et al., *supra* note 15.
[38] Richard Lambert, Banking Standards Review, (19 May 2014), www.bankingstandardsreview
.org.uk/assets/docs/may2014report.pdf.

- Identifying and encouraging good practice in learning, development and leadership, with a particular focus on behavior and ethics.
- Helping banks to meet the obligations being placed on them by new legislation, such as the Certified Persons regime.
- Working with the professional bodies already active in the banking industry to increase the value placed on professional qualifications.

The BSRC will not act as a lobbyist for the banks and the building societies. It will not absolve the leadership of banks and building societies from their prime role in raising banking standards, and it will not attempt to do the work of the regulators. Also, it will not handle customer complaints.

TENTATIVE CONCLUSIONS

The issues raised in this paper are current issues, not theoretical ones. A number of tentative conclusions can be expressed.

(1) The idea that ethics, and in particular an ethical culture, has a place in finance, is widespread. It is seen to be an essential adjunct to the law as it applies in the form of financial regulation.

(2) Financial institutions, if not necessarily embracing the idea, seem increasingly comfortable with it. Whether this is an involuntary response to public pressure, or is the result of corporate social responsibility principles mandated by the law, or is simply a reflection of a good business case, does not really matter, because the potential for improved standards is there.

(3) It is recognized that promoting ethical behavior within an institution is a matter of culture. This cannot be legislated for, and comes through adoption by example, particularly from a bank's leadership. The importance of values and leadership implies real, not perfunctory, values leadership.

(4) One means by which banks have sought to do this is through "codes of ethics" or documents having similar effect. The significance of these documents is that they represent an attempt by institutions to articulate their own view of what is meant by "ethical conduct." This is important, because what conduct is ethical is not always easy to pin down in the highly competitive commercial environment of international finance.

(5) These codes should not be treated in the same way as legal obligations, or seen as quasibinding as is the case with formal guidance issued by regulators. The reasons for this are twofold. First, the duties are necessarily expressed at a high level. Second, they are properly treated as aspirational in nature, in that they implicitly acknowledge that standards aimed for are not necessarily achieved.

(6) Further analysis of the codes could usefully be done to identify what is common ground, and where the differences are. Common themes appear to revolve around the fair treatment of customers and the avoidance of socially excessive risk taking.

(7) There are reputational incentives for institutions to seek to implement the values expressed in such codes. There are also practical steps that can be taken within institutions to promote an ethical culture. Some of these have been envisaged for the United Kingdom's new Banking Standards Review Council.

(8) There is a case for financial regulators to engage with banks' internal systems and processes, not with a view to prescribing the content of codes of ethics, and certainly not adding a further layer of rules and regulations, but with a view to monitoring how ethical considerations are carried forward within the organization.

According to the CFA Institute/Edelman *Investor Trust Study 2013*,[39] investors cited compliance with a voluntary code of ethics and maintaining independence and objectivity as actions that matter most. The President of the CFA Institute commented on the "... significant opportunity for investment professionals and firms to actively build a culture where ethical practices are valued as highly as investment performance."[40] Public support for higher standards, along with the stated commitment of financial leaders, has created an opportunity to promote the ethical culture that they want to achieve. It is in the interests of their businesses, as well as society as a whole.

---

[39] CFA Institute and Edelman, *Investor Trust Study 2013*, www.cfainstitute.org/learning/future/getinvolved/Documents/cfa_institute_edelman_investor_trust_study.pdf.

[40] *CFA Institute/Edelman Study: Only Half of Investors Trust Investment Firms to Do What is Right*, Edelman, Press Release, 14 August 2013, www.edelman.com/news/cfa-instituteedelman-study-only-half-of-investors-trust-investment-firms-to-do-what-is-right.

Conclusion

22

Conclusion

Emilios Avgouleas, Douglas W. Arner and Ross P. Buckley

To paraphrase the famous remark of Justice O. W. Holmes[1] the life of finance proved to be experience rather than stylized theories and elegant mathematical models that ultimately could either not survive beyond the financial laboratory or serve society properly. The same applies to the policy ideas and technical schemes employed to regulate global finance. In our experience financial systems have proved not only fragile but also prone to generate catastrophic externalities. Similarly financial markets and banks had served up to the late 1990s as the engine of progress and growth in most acceptable economic growth models as well as in practice. An enormous amount of effort has been expended to restore global finance to health since 2008. New restraints on institutions' and individuals' risk- and rent-seeking and new legal and technical infrastructure for the conduct of transactions have been introduced. Tailor-made regimes for the regulation of different aspects of financial markets and resolution of financial institutions have also been erected. While this gigantic reform effort has tackled the causes of the post-2008 crisis, loopholes and dysfunctions remain.

In its distinctively global approach the present volume provides an extensive and complex wealth of analysis of post-2008 reform efforts (Singh and Hodges, Arner and Taylor, Alexander and Schwarcz, Hui Huang, Yingmao Tang) and their likelihood of success. But authors writing in this volume do not stop here, they also discuss the loopholes of the *ancien* regime in global finance, be it cultural changes (Buckley) and "rotten" ethics (Blair) that proved catastrophic, leading to series of scandals (Brian Tang), shaky assumptions in the science of finance (Gelpern and Gerding), or inherently risky forms of organization of financial intermediation (Avgouleas). In particular, they highlight the self-serving and rent-seeking nature of recent financial innovations (Donald, Gelpern and Gerding, Avgouleas, Buckley).

---

[1] "The life of the law has not been logic: it has been experience." O. W. Holmes, *Common Law* (Little, Brown & Co., 1882), Lecture 1, p. 5.

The authors of the essays included in this volume also map the contours of the current regulatory landscape as regards regulatory architecture, the relationship of dual causality between the financial system and the real economy and the matter of regulatory perimeter exploring also new thinking in the respective areas. In this context, they explore (a) the dynamics developed around the configuration of regulatory competence, with central banks recovering their key role in financial regulation and financial policy (Masciandaro), (b) conceptual and architectural tensions surrounding macroprudential regulation (Alexander and Schwarcz), and (c) the thorny and multifaceted challenge of regulating shadow banking (Hui Huang, Yingmao Tang). They also identify continuums between the *ancien* regime and the new reality of the markets, such as the continued survival of the fractional reserve banking system (Avgouleas) and of "safe" assets (Gelpern and Gerding), based on the post-2008 experience about the causes of the Global Financial Crisis ("too-big-to-fail," the "run on the repo" markets[2]), and ensuing regulatory reform.

Characteristically this volume highlights the global nature of regulation of international finance (Baxter, Zaring, Arner and Taylor, Shinar). It does so in a nuanced way, as it also offers analysis of the incentives and considerations of market actors that drive the growth of global capital markets (Licht). It also expands the net of analysis to cover new thinking about the workings, culture, and motivations of global finance and novel approaches that may be employed to fix a broken system. These novel approaches encapsulate the current debate on the role that ethics could play in augmenting the quality and safety of finance (Blair), the distributive role that financial markets ought to play in order to safeguard legitimacy (Donald, Avgouleas), and the role of finance in championing the wider global agenda in the realm of human rights (Weber).

The question of how to regulate global finance remains one of the most important challenges facing the post-2008 world (Arner and Taylor, Zaring, Baxter). Pertinent to answering this question is the identification of the global as well as domestic consensus that underpins the implementation of international financial standards, especially at the national level. There is normally a host of political economy considerations surrounding such implementation and they often relate to the role and regulatory preferences of very powerful domestic interests, such as, for example, the influence of the largest Chinese banks (Chao Xi). Moreover, there are clearly no easy answers (Zetzsche) in the dilemma between further harmonization (Singh and Hodges) and equivalence (Zetzsche). While regulatory competition ought to be at the center of an efficient global market that affords suppliers and users of capital and financials services in general much room for choice, same competition has also been at the heart of much damaging

---

[2] G. B. Gorton, A. Metrick, "Securitized Banking and the Run on Repo," NBER Working Paper No. 15223, August 2009.

regulatory arbitrage. Thus, coordination issues will remain for the foreseeable future, at least outside of the European Union, notwithstanding the oversight role of the G20 and the strengthening of FSB functions and powers (Arner and Taylor).

In many ways the development of financial markets and global finance has been driven by private sector actors in search of rents (Donald) and of new markets and, in some cases, of more advantageous legal infrastructure environments (Licht). These bind together global markets in a multitude of visible and invisible ways (Licht, Chao Xi). Normally, regulators play a catch up game and in this sense the flexibility of transnational regulatory networks may be a helpful aspect of the contemporary global soft law-based regulatory edifice (Baxter). Yet not only the edges of the soft law regime are hardening by the aforementioned strengthening of FSB's monitoring role (Arner and Taylor), but also the operations of many of the lesser known networks have been much tighter and more influential than previously thought (Zaring). Arguably, Zaring's essay on how regulation emerges, sometimes in uncoordinated ways, in all corners of global finance adds fuel to the debate on how global financial regulation ought to be configured. Moreover, the studied approach taken by China to internationalize its currency, using mostly the Hong Kong gateway (Shen Wei), and the role that trade surpluses (widely implicated in the past crisis as well)[3] can play in the process, underscore the multiplicity of interests dominating global finance, which, are by all means not confined to private sector actors.

Chinese government's efforts to internationalize the use of the Renminbi are of course only one illustration of the relationship between government policies and development of global markets. Another illustration is sovereign debt finance whose importance is sometimes underestimated, although the preference for use of sovereign debt instruments as collateral (in their guise as "safe" assets) is one of the essential mechanisms underpinning the workings of global finance (Gelpern and Gerding).

Given the role of technology as facilitator and propeller of global finance, it is worth exploring whether this is a welfare enhancing or a rent-seeking process. David Donald's and Yingmao Tang's chapters show that it can be both. In this context, they explain why regulatory conceptualizations of the impact of technology on markets matter. For example, the traditional approach to the regulation of securities markets and of their infrastructure that seeks to enshrine the principle of efficiency above all other goals can lead to rent-seeking and social waste (Donald). Similarly regulation may confuse the boundaries of what is useful, for example, Internet payments, thus, giving rise to efficiencies, and what is risky, for example, ponzi-like shadow banking schemes (Yingmao Tang).

---

[3] M. Obstfeld and K. Rogoff, "Global Imbalances and the Financial Crisis," Paper prepared for the Federal Reserve Bank of San Francisco Asia Economic Policy Conference, Santa Barbara, CA, October 18–20, 2009.

In a sense the present volume mirrors the wealth of thinking that has developed around global finance and its regulation since 2008 and plausibly so, since, at least, in part, the 2008 catastrophe was based on a long list of intellectual flaws.[4] Several of these problems persist. For example, Schwarcz and Alexander explain why fundamental issues about the reach and focus of macroprudential regulation as well as in respect of its coordination with other strands of regulatory and general risk prevention policies are the key to its success. Similarly, Avgouleas explains that the too-big-to-fail threat has not entirely disappeared, inspite major breakthroughs in the guise of structural reform and new bank resolution regulations, including worldwide introduction of bail-in regimes. Gelpern and Gerding elucidate the trade-offs regulators face in the treatment of unsafe assets as "safe" in order not to disrupt the role that these play in augmenting the expansion of transactionalisation in global finance, which, in turn, has major costs and benefits.

Ultimately human societies may have to admit that endogenous shocks emanating from global finance and certain macroeconomic developments are as unpredictable as extreme weather and what we really need is some radical rethinking of what finance does and the modalities and goals of financial markets. In this respect, Justice William Blair's essay has vividly explained the role that ethics could play in the governance of finance. Clearly a new model of finance professional is required (Buckley, Brian Tang). In addition, from a complementary and equally critical viewpoint, Donald's and Avgouleas' chapters highlight the need to shift toward notions of capital and banking markets' effectiveness that encompass social utility and impact on long-term growth. The pursuit of these goals ought not to inhibit welfare enhancing innovation as rightly argued by Yingmao Tang.

Finally, none of the aforementioned reforms and forthcoming regulatory initiatives may fully succeed, if we do not heed, in the words of Justice Blair, the need "to promote the ethical culture [in the financial sector] ... in the interests of ...[business] as well as society as a whole."[5]

---

[4] See further Emilios Avgouleas, *Governance of Global Financial Markets: The Law, the Economics, the Politics* (Cambridge University Press, 2012), chapters 2 and 3.

[5] This volume, Chapter 21.

Index

g Source UK Ltd.
ynes UK
939240519
UK00009B/100/P